THE PAPAL ENCYCLICALS

Catholic Church. Pope.

THE PAPAL ENCYCLICALS 1740-1878

[v. 1]

CLAUDIA CARLEN IHM

A CONSORTIUM BOOK
McGRATH PUBLISHING COMPANY

Nihil Obstat: James E. McSweeney, V.G.

Imprimatur: ✠ F. Joseph Gossman
Bishop of Raleigh

Raleigh, October 30, 1981

Printed and bound in the United States of America

Library of Congress Catalog Card Number: 81-84885

ISBN: 0-8434-0765-4 (complete set)
ISBN: 0-8434-0760-3 (this volume)

This book was composed in Goudy Oldstyle. Typography was designed by Robert W. Frizzell, and composed by Linda Stanfield and Patricia Paterson. Production was by Barbara Ellis. The Papal Coats of Arms were drawn especially for this edition by Robert W. Frizzell.

This edition was printed on Booknatural acid free paper and bound in Roxite C linen cloth by Edwards Brothers Incorporated. Case design was by Stephanie D. West, West and Wohler Associates Inc.

Acknowledgements and Sources

The following encyclicals appear here in original translation and are copyright © 1981 by McGrath Publishing Company. They are included in this publication by permission of the copyright owner.

Ubi primum, December 3, 1740; *Quanta cura*, June 30, 1741; *Nimiam licentiam*, May 18, 1743; *Vix pervenit*, November 1, 1745; *Magnae Nobis*, June 29, 1748; *Peregrinantes*, May 5, 1749; *Apostolica Constitutio*, June 26, 1749; *A quo primum*, June 14, 1751; *Cum Religiosi*, June 26, 1754; *Quod Provinciale*, August 1, 1754; *Allatae sunt*, July 26, 1755; *Ex quo primum*, March 1, 1756; *Ex omnibus*, October 16, 1756; *A quo die*, September 13, 1758; *Cum primum*, September 17, 1759; *Appetente Sacro*, December 20, 1759; *In Dominico agro*, June 14, 1761; *Christianae reipublicae*, November 25, 1766; *Summa quae*, January 6, 1768; *Decet quam maxime*, September 21, 1769; *Inscrutabili divinae sapientiae*, December 12, 1769; *Cum summi*, December 12,

1769; *Salutis nostrae*, April 30, 1774; *Inscrutabile*, December 25, 1775; *Charitas*, April 13, 1791; *Diu satis*, May 15, 1800; *Ubi primum*, May 5, 1824; *Quod hoc ineunte*, May 24, 1824; *Charitate Christi*, December 25, 1825; *Traditi humilitati*, May 24, 1829; *Summo iugiter studio*, May 27, 1832; *Cum primum*, June 9, 1832; *Mirari vos*, August 15, 1832; *Quo graviora*, October 4, 1833; *Singulari Nos*, June 25, 1834; *Commissum divinitus*, May 17, 1835; *Probe nostis*, September 18, 1840; *Quas vestro*, April 30, 1841; *Inter praecipuas*, May 8, 1844; *Qui pluribus*, November 9, 1846; *Praedecessores Nostros*, March 25, 1847; *Ubi primum*, June 17, 1847; *Nostis et Nobiscum*, December 8, 1849; *Exultavit cor Nostrum*, November 21, 1851; *Nemo certe ignorat*, March 25, 1852; *Probe noscitis Venerabiles*, May 17, 1852; *Inter multiplices*, March 21, 1853; *Neminem vestrum*, February 2, 1854; *Optime noscitis*, March 20, 1854; *Apostolicae Nostrae caritatis*, August 1, 1854; *Optime noscitis*, November 5, 1855; *Singulari quidem*, March 17, 1856; *Cum nuper*, January 20, 1858; *Amantissimi Redemptoris*, May 3, 1858; *Cum sancta mater Ecclesia*, April 27, 1859; *Qui nuper*, June 18, 1859; *Nullis certe verbis*, January 19, 1860; *Amantissimus*, April 8, 1862; *Quanto conficiamur moerore*, August 10, 1863; *Incredibili*, September 17, 1863; *Maximae quidem*, August 18, 1864; *Meridionali Americae*, September 30, 1865; *Levate*, October 27, 1867; *Respicientes*, November 1, 1870; *Ubi Nos*, May 15, 1871; *Beneficia Dei*, June 4, 1871; *Saepe Venerabiles Fratres*, August 5, 1871; *Quae in patriarchatu*, November 16, 1872; *Quartus supra*, January 6, 1873; *Etsi multa*, November 21, 1873; *Vix dum a Nobis*, March 7, 1874; *Omnem sollicitudinem*, May 13, 1874; *Gravibus Ecclesiae*, December 24, 1874; *Quod nunquam*, February 5, 1875; *Graves ac diuturnae*, March 23, 1875; *Grande munus*, September 30, 1880; *Iampridem*, January 6, 1886; *Quod multum*, August 22, 1886; *Pergrata*, September 14, 1886; *Etsi cunctas*, December 21, 1888; *Magni Nobis*, March 7, 1889; *Catholicae Ecclesiae*, November 20, 1890; *In ipso*, March 3, 1891; *Pastoralis officii*, September 12, 1891; *Inimica vis*, December 8, 1892; *Custodi di quella fede*, December 8, 1892; *Ad extremas*, June 24, 1893; *Constanti Hungarorum*, September 2, 1893; *Non mediocri*, October 25, 1893; *Caritatis*, March 19, 1894; *Inter graves*, May 1, 1894; *Litteras a vobis*, July 2, 1894; *Christi nomen*, December 24, 1894; *Permoti Nos*, July 10, 1895; *Insignes*, May 1, 1896; *Militantis Ecclesiae*, August 1, 1897; *Quam religiosa*, August 16, 1898; *Quum diuturnum*, December 25, 1898; *Paternae*, September 18, 1899; *Omnibus compertum*, July 21, 1900; *Gravissimas*, May 16, 1901; *Reputantibus*, August 20, 1901; *Urbanitatis veteris*, November 20, 1901; *Quod votis*, April 30, 1902; *Quae ad Nos*, November 22, 1902; *Dum multa*, December 24, 1902; *In hac tanta*, May 14, 1919; *Principi Apostolorum Petro*, October 5, 1920; *Saeculo exeunte octavo*, June 13, 1940; *Communium interpretes dolorum*, April 15, 1945.

The publisher gratefully acknowledges permission to include the specified encyclicals from the following sources.

AMERICA PRESS—From *On the Sacred Liturgy*, edited by Gerald Ellard, © 1954: *Mediator Dei*, November 20, 1947. From *The Catholic Mind: Humani generis Redemptionem*, June 15, 1917 (Volume 15, Pages 393-408, © September 8, 1917); *Sacra propediem*, January 6, 1921 (Volume 19, Pages 101-109, © March 22, 1921); *Fausto appetente die*, June 29, 1921 (Volume 19, Pages 301-306, © August 22, 1921); *Quinquagesimo ante*, December 23, 1929 (Volume 28, Pages 93-107, © March 8, 1930); *Ad salutem*, April 30, 1930 (Volume 28, Pages 333-364, © September 8, 1930); *Dilectissima Nobis*, June 3, 1933 (Volume 31, Pages 241-251, © July 8, 1933); *Ad catholici sacerdotii*, December 20, 1935 (Volume 34, Pages 41-79, © February 8, 1936); *Mit brennender Sorge*, March 14, 1937 (Volume 35, Pages 185-204, © May 8, 1937); *Nos es muy conocida*, March 28, 1937 (Volume 35, Pages 213-226, © May 22, 1937); *Ingravescentibus malis*, September 29, 1937 (Volume 35, Pages 433-440, © November 8, 1937); *Summi Pontificatus*, October 20, 1939 (Volume 37, Pages 890-918, © November 8, 1939); *Quemadmodum*, January 6, 1946 (Volume 44, Pages 129-133, © March 1946); *Optatissima pax*, December 18, 1947 (Volume 46, Pages 65-67, © February 1948); *Auspicia quaedam*, May 1, 1948 (Volume 46, Pages 417-420, © July 1948); *Summi maeroris*, July 19, 1950 (Volume 48, Pages 628-630, © October 1950); *Mirabile illud*, December 6, 1950 (Volume

49, Pages 135-137, © February 1951); *Orientales Ecclesias*, December 15, 1952 (Volume 51, Pages 244-250, © April 1953).

AMERICAN CATHOLIC HISTORICAL ASSOCIATION—From *Catholic Historical Review: Quanta cura*, December 8, 1864 (Volume 13, Pages 247-253, © July 1927).

AMERICAN CATHOLIC QUARTERLY REVIEW—*Annum Sacrum*, May 25, 1899 (Volume 24, Pages 774-779, July 1899); *Depuis le jour*, September 8, 1899 (Volume 25, Pages 56-71, January 1900); *Fin dal principio*, December 8, 1902 (Volume 28, Pages 380-386, April 1903); *Une fois encore*, January 6, 1907 (Volume 32, Pages 138-144, January 1907).

BENZIGER BROTHERS—From *The Great Encyclical Letters of Pope Leo XIII*, edited by John J. Wynne, 1903: *Au milieu des sollicitudes*, February 16, 1892; *Longinqua*, January 6, 1895; *In amplissimo*, April 15, 1902.

BRUCE PUBLISHING COMPANY—From *Papal Documents on Mary*, edited by William C. Doheny and Joseph P. Kelly © 1954: *Magnae Dei Matris*, September 8, 1892, and *Adiutricem*, September 5, 1895.

CATHOLIC BIBLICAL ASSOCIATION OF AMERICA—From *Catholic Biblical Quarterly: In multiplicibus curis*, October 24, 1948 (Volume 11, Pages 89-90, © January 1949); *Redemptoris nostri cruciatus*, April 15, 1949 (Volume 11, Pages 325-327, © July 1949).

DAUGHTERS OF ST. PAUL—From *Papal Teachings: Our Lady*, © 1961: *Deiparae Virginis Mariae*, May 1, 1946.

DOUBLEDAY AND CO., INC.—From *The Church Speaks to the Modern World*, edited by Etienne Gilson, Image Books, © 1954 (Note: Gilson states that the translations in this book were provided variously by The Catholic Truth Society, London; Paulist Press; *The* (London) *Tablet*; The Catholic World; and Benziger Brothers. He does not specify the source of any of the translations.): *Inscrutabili Dei consilio*, April 21, 1878; *Quod Apostolici muneris*, December 28, 1878; *Aeterni Patris*, August 4, 1879; *Arcanum*, February 10, 1880; *Diuturnum*, June 29, 1881; *Humanum genus*, April 20, 1884; *Immortale Dei*, November 1, 1885; *In plurimis*, May 5, 1888; *Libertas*, June 20, 1888; *Sapientiae christianae*, January 10, 1890; *Rerum novarum*, May 15, 1891; *Graves de communi re*, January 18, 1901.

DUBLIN REVIEW—*Licet multa*, August 3, 1881 (Volume 89, Pages 465-467, © October 1881).

EASTERN CHURCHES QUARTERLY—*Orientales omnes Ecclesias*, December 23, 1945 (Volume 6, Pages 290-314, © April-June 1946); *Sempiternus Rex Christus*, September 8, 1951 (Volume 9, Pages 229-244, © Spring 1952).

B. HERDER BOOK CO.—From *The Encyclicals of Pius XI*, translated by James H. Ryan, © 1927: *Ubi arcano Dei consilio*, December 23, 1922; *Rerum omnium perturbationem*, January 26, 1923; *Ecclesiam Dei*, November 12, 1923; *Maximam gravissimamque*, January 18, 1924; *Rerum Ecclesiae*, February 28, 1926; *Rite expiatis*, April 30, 1926; *Iniquis afflictisque*, November 18, 1926.

INCORPORATED CATHOLIC TRUTH SOCIETY—From *Selected Letters and Addresses of Pius XII*, 1949: *Orientalis Ecclesiae*, April 9, 1944.

OUR SUNDAY VISITOR—From *The Pope Speaks: Fulgens corona*, September 8, 1953 (Volume 1, Pages 43-53, © First Quarter, 1954); *Sacra virginitas*, March 25, 1954 (Volume 1, Pages 101-123, © Second Quarter, 1954); *Ecclesiae fastos*, June 5, 1954 (Volume 1, Pages 171-185, © Second Quarter, 1954); *Ad Sinarum gentem*, October 7, 1954 (Volume 1, Pages 397-403, © Fourth Quarter, 1954); *Ad Caeli Reginam*, October 11, 1954 (Volume 1, Pages 323-335, © Fourth Quarter, 1954); *Musicae sacrae*, December 25, 1955 (Volume 3, Pages 7-23, © Spring/Summer 1956); *Haurietis aquas*, May 15, 1956 (Volume 3, Pages 115-149, © Autumn 1956); *Luctuosissimi eventus*, October 28, 1956 (Volume 3, Pages 347-349, © Spring 1957); *Laetamur admodum*, November 1, 1956 (Volume 3, Pages 350-352, © Spring 1957); *Datis nuperrime*, November 5, 1956 (Volume 3, Pages 353-354, © Spring 1957); *Fidei donum*, April 21, 1957 (Volume 4, Pages 295-312, © Winter 1957/1958); *Invicti athletae*, May 16, 1957 (Volume 4, Pages 213-220, © Autumn 1957); *Le pèlerinage de Lourdes*, July 2, 1957 (Volume 4, Pages 107-117, © Autumn 1957); *Miranda prorsus*, September 8, 1957 (Volume 4, Pages 319-346, © Winter 1957/1958); *Ad Apostolorum Principis*, June 29, 1958 (Volume 5, Pages 189-199, © Spring 1959); *Meminisse iuvat*, July 14, 1958 (Volume 5, Pages 29-37, © Summer 1958); *Ad Petri Cathedram*, June 29, 1959 (Volume 5, Pages 359-383, © Autumn 1959); *Sacerdotii Nostri primordia*, August 1, 1959 (Volume 6, Pages 7-33,

© Winter 1959/1960); *Grata recordatio*, September 26, 1959 (Volume 6, Pages 68-72, © Winter 1959/1960); *Princeps Pastorum*, November 28, 1959 (Volume 6, Pages 123-145, © Spring 1960); *Mater et Magistra*, May 15, 1961 (Volume 7, Pages 295-343, © April 1962); *Aeterna Dei sapientia*, November 11, 1961 (Volume 8, Pages 7-22, © July 1962); *Paenitentiam agere*, July 1, 1962 (Volume 8, Pages 111-119, © October 1962); *Pacem in terris*, April 11, 1963 (Volume 9, Pages 13-48, © July 1963); *Ecclesiam suam*, August 6, 1964 (Volume 10, Pages 253-292, © Summer 1965); *Mense maio*, April 29, 1965 (Volume 10, Pages 220-224, © Spring 1965); *Mysterium Fidei*, September 3, 1965 (Volume 10, Pages 309-328, © Fall 1965); *Christi Matri*, September 15, 1966 (Volume 11, Pages 221-225, © Summer 1966); *Populorum progressio*, May 26, 1967 (Volume 12, Pages 144-172, © Spring 1967); *Sacerdotalis caelibatus*, June 24, 1967 (Volume 12, Pages 291-319, © Summer 1967); *Humanae vitae*, July 25, 1968 (Volume 13, Pages 329-346, © Fall 1969).

PAULIST PRESS—From *All Things in Christ*, edited by Vincent A. Yzermans, © 1954: *Acerbo nimis*, April 15, 1905; *Il fermo proposito*, June 11, 1905; *Pieni l'animo*, July 28, 1906; *Editae saepe*, May 26, 1910; *Singulari quadam*, September 24, 1912.

PONTIFICAL COURT CLUB OF LONDON—From *Catholic Documents: Doctor Mellifluus*, May 24, 1953 (Number 13, Pages 7-18, November 1953).

ST. MEINRAD ARCHABBEY—From *Rome and the Study of Scripture*, © 1958 (published by Abbey Press): *Spiritus Paraclitus*, September 15, 1920, and *Divino afflante Spiritu*, September 30, 1943.

SHEED AND WARD, NEW YORK—From *The Angelic Doctor* by Jacques Maritain, 1931: *Studiorem Ducem*, June 29, 1923.

THE TABLET, LONDON—*Sancta Dei civitas*, December 3, 1880 (Volume 56, Pages 820-821, © December 25, 1880); *Etsi Nos*, February 15, 1882 (Volume 59, Pages 284-286, © February 25, 1882); *Auspicato concessum*, September 17, 1882 (Volume 60, Pages 527-529, © September 30, 1882); *Cum multa*, December 8, 1882 (Volume 61, Pages 9-10, © January 6, 1883); *Supremi Apostolatus officio*, September 1, 1883 (Volume 62, Pages 401-402, © September 15, 1883); *Nobilissima Gallorum gens*, February 8, 1884 (Volume 63, Pages 241-242, © February 16, 1884); *Superiore anno*, August 30, 1884 (Volume 64, Page 361, © September 6, 1884); *Spectata fides*, November 27, 1885 (Volume 66, Page 989, © December 19, 1885); *Quod auctoritate*, December 22, 1885 (Volume 67, Pages 5-6, © January 2, 1886); *Vi è ben noto*, September 20, 1887 (Volume 70, Page 521, © October 1, 1887); *Officio sanctissimo*, December 22, 1887 (Volume 71, Pages 93-95/133-135, © January 21/28, 1888); *Quod anniversarius*, April 1, 1888 (Volume 71, Page 593, © April 14, 1888); *Saepe Nos*, June 24, 1888 (Volume 72, Page 81, © July 21, 1888); *Paterna caritas*, July 25, 1888 (Volume 72, Pages 321-322, © September 1, 1888); *Quam aerumnosa*, December 10, 1888 (Volume 72, Page 972, © December 22, 1888); *Exeunte iam anno*, December 25, 1888 (Volume 73, Pages 73-76, © January 12, 1889); *Quamquam pluries*, August 15, 1889 (Volume 74, Pages 281-282, August 24, 1889); *Dall'alto dell'Apostolico seggio*, October 15, 1890 (Volume 76, Pages 673-676, © October 25, 1890); *Pastoralis*, June 25, 1891 (Volume 78, Pages 245-246, © August 15, 1891); *Octobri mense*, September 22, 1891 (Volume 78, Pages 573-575, © October 10, 1891); *Quarto abeunte saeculo*, July 16, 1892 (Volume 80, Pages 167-168, © July 30, 1892); *Laetitiae sanctae*, September 8, 1893 (Volume 82, Pages 633-635, © October 14, 1893); *Providentissimus Deus*, November 18, 1893 (Volume 83, Pages 5-11, © January 6, 1894); *Iucunda semper expectatione*, September 8, 1894 (Volume 84, Pages 497-498, © September 29, 1894); *Satis cognitum*, June 29, 1896 (Volume 88, Pages 5-14, © July 4, 1898); *Fidentem piumque animum*, September 20, 1896 (Volume 88, Pages 633-634, © October 17, 1896); *Divinum illud munus*, May 9, 1897 (Volume 89, Pages 909-912, © June 5, 1897); *Augustissimae Virginis Mariae*, September 12, 1897 (Volume 90, Pages 549-551, © October 2, 1897); *Affari vos*, December 8, 1897 (Volume 91, Pages 24-25, © January 1, 1898); *Caritatis studium*, July 25, 1898 (Volume 92, Pages 229-231, © August 6, 1898); *Spesse volte*, August 5, 1898 (Volume 92, Pages 245-247, © August 13, 1898); *Diuturni temporis*, September 5, 1898 (Volume 92, Pages 549-550, © October 1, 1898); *Tametsi futura prospicientibus*, November 1, 1900 (Volume 96, Pages 869-872, © December 1, 1900); *Mirae caritatis*, May 28, 1902 (Volume 100, Pages 5-9, © July 5, 1902); *E supremi*, October 4, 1903 (Volume 102, Pages 589-592, © October 10, 1903); *Ad diem illum laetissimum*, February 2, 1904 (Volume 103, Pages 281-284, © February 20,

1904); *Iucunda sane*, March 12, 1904 (Volume 103, Pages 549-554, © April 2, 1904); *Vehementer Nos*, February 11, 1906 (Volume 107, Pages 281-284, © February 24, 1906); *Tribus circiter*, April 5, 1906 (Volume 107, Pages 897-898, © June 9, 1906); *Gravissimo officii munere*, August 10, 1906 (Volume 108, Pages 242-243, © August 18, 1906); *Pascendi dominici gregis*, September 8, 1907 (Volume 110, Pages 501-515, © September 28, 1907); *Communium rerum*, April 21, 1909 (Volume 113, Pages 789-793/829-832, © May 15/22, 1909); *Iamdudum*, May 24, 1911 (Volume 117, Pages 882-883, © June 10, 1911); *Lacrimabili statu*, June 7, 1912 (Volume 120, Pages 204-205, © August 10, 1912); *Ad beatissimi Apostolorum*, November 1, 1914 (Volume 124, Pages 787-790, © December 12, 1914); *Quod iam diu*, December 1, 1918 (Volume 132, Page 679, © December 14, 1918); *Paterno iam diu*, November 24, 1919 (Volume 134, Page 741, © December 6, 1919); *Pacem, Dei munus pulcherrimum*, May 23, 1920 (Volume 136, Pages 787-789, © June 12, 1920); *Annus iam plenus*, December 1, 1920 (Volume 137, Page 872, © December 25, 1920); *In praeclara summorum*, April 30, 1921 (Volume 138, Pages 624-626, © May 14, 1921); *Quas primas*, December 11, 1925 (Volume 147, Pages 72-75, © January 16, 1926); *Mortalium animos*, January 6, 1928 (Volume 151, Pages 71-74, © January 21, 1928); *Miserentissimus Redemptor*, May 8, 1928 (Volume 151, Pages 728-732, © June 2, 1928); *Rerum Orientalium*, September 8, 1928 (Volume 152, Pages 368-370, © September 22, 1928); *Mens Nostra*, December 20, 1929 (Volume 155, Pages 7-10, © January 4, 1930); *Non abbiamo bisogno*, June 29, 1931 (Volume 158, Pages 52-59, © July 11, 1931); *Nova impendet*, October 2, 1931 (Volume 158, Pages 474-475, © October 10, 1931); *Lux veritatis*, December 25, 1931 (Volume 159, Pages 108-110/140-144, © January 23/30, 1932); *Caritate Christi compulsi*, May 3, 1932 (Volume 159, Pages 696-698/728-730, © May 28/June 4, 1932); *Acerba animi*, September 29, 1932 (Volume 160, Pages 504-507, © October 15, 1932); *Vigilanti cura*, June 29, 1936 (Volume 168, Pages 49-52, © July 11, 1936); *Anni Sacri*, March 12, 1950 (Volume 195, Page 209, © March 18, 1950).

UNITED STATES CATHOLIC CONFERENCE, PUBLICATIONS OFFICE—*The Christian Education of Youth*, 1936 (*Rappresentanti in terra*, December 31, 1929); *Christian Marriage*, © 1931, Reprinted 1969 (*Casti connubii*, December 31, 1930); *On Reconstructing the Social Order*, © 1931, reprinted 1942 (*Quadragesimo anno*, May 15, 1931); *Atheistic Communism*, © 1937 (*Divini Redemptoris*, March 19, 1937); *To the Church in the United States*, © 1939 (*Sertum laetitiae*, November 1, 1939); *Mystical Body of Christ*, © 1943 (*Mystici Corporis Christi*, June 29, 1943); *On Reciting the Rosary*, 1951 (*Ingruentium malorum*, September 15, 1951); *Redeemer of Man*, 1979 (*Redemptor hominis*, March 4, 1979).

VATICAN POLYGLOT PRESS—*Fulgens radiatur*, March 21, 1947; *Humani generis*, August 12, 1950; *Evangelii praecones*, June 2, 1951; from pamphlets issued by the National Catholic Welfare Conference. *Dives in misericordia*, November 30, 1980, as published in *Origins*, Volume 10, Pages 402-416, © December 11, 1980. *Laborem exercens*, September 14, 1981, as published in *Origins*, Volume 11, Pages 226-244, © September 24, 1981.

THE TASK OF THE CHURCH IN SOCIETY
IS TO STAND AS A SIGN AND SAFEGUARD
OF THE TRANSCENDENT DIGNITY OF MAN.

GAUDIUM ET SPES

FOREWORD

Catholics sometimes give the impression that there are only two categories of papal teaching: infallible doctrine and mere opinion. The truth of the matter is that most papal teaching ranges somewhere between those two extremes. Infallibility is rarely exercised, and "mere opinion" when expressed by a pope is seldom mere opinion.

The pastoral leadership of the Holy Father is exercised most of the time through homilies, speeches, and written statements that carry less authority than an infallible definition, but much more authority than mere opinion.

An awareness of the teachings in this middle area is critical for those who preach or teach or do theological research or even attempt to form important decisions of conscience. It is not necessary for such people to consult or take seriously anything ever written or spoken on a particular topic. It is necessary, however, to take seriously the authoritative teaching of the Holy Father. While this teaching may not always call for the kind of assent required of infallible teaching, it always calls for very serious attention, and all Church teaching must be done in its light.

The encyclicals of the popes occupy a very special place in this category. They are an essential part of what the great theologian Karl Rahner would call the "pastoral magisterium" of the Church. You cannot do theology, you cannot preach, you cannot teach, without taking these into account. You can miss a lot of other articles and statements by theologians and bishops around the world, but these you cannot miss. They are essential.

The bishops of the United States, in their initial response to the encyclical *Humanae vitae*, put it best and most succinctly when they said through their president Cardinal Dearden:

> Recognizing [the Holy Father's] unique role in the universal Church, we the bishops of the Church of the United States, unite with him in calling upon our priests and people to receive with sincerity what he has taught, to study it carefully, and to form their consciences in its light.

Sister Claudia Carlen has done all preachers, teachers, and theologians a great service through this publication. She has drawn together, categorized, and made readily available one of the basic resources of Church teaching. No one else has ever done this, and her work will become an indispensable tool for future generations.

I would like to add a personal note. We are indebted to Sister Claudia Carlen not only for her hard work and skill in putting this publication together. We are also indebted to her as a Church person. May God bless her for giving us this publication, and more importantly, for giving us herself as a scholar, a religious, a woman, and a Catholic who truly loves and lives the Church.

✠ Kenneth E. Untener
Bishop of Saginaw
April 26, 1981

CONTENTS

PIUS IX (1846-1878) 275

INTRODUCTION

What is an encyclical? This is a frequently asked question and one that has had a variety of answers. Perhaps the most recent answer was given by Pope Paul VI when he announced the imminent publication of his first encyclical letter. The Latin text, he pointed out, "would begin with the words that would serve to identify it: *Ecclesiam Suam*." Although he had issued other letters, he called this his "first" since it "had the precise character of an official *Lettera Enciclica*." An encyclical letter, he went on to say, "is a document in the form of a letter sent by the Pope to the bishops of the entire world: *encyclical* means circular. It is a very ancient form of ecclesiastical correspondence that characteristically denotes the communion of faith and charity that exists among the various 'churches,' that is, among the various communities that make up the Church."[1]

As indicated by Pope Paul, these letters are striking examples of that vast epistolary correspondence that helped to unify the Church in the early days of Christianity. "In earliest times the heads of the main communities used to send circular letters to their brother bishops and to all the faithful too; hence, these letters were also called *catholicae*, that is, directed to the whole Christian people."[2] The Christians learned to write as they learned to love; the Apostles began it; the Basils and Gregorys, the Jeromes, Augustines, and Chrysostoms developed it; and the successive pontiffs have carried it on to the present time. In the early days such letters were eagerly sought for; neither labor nor expense was considered in obtaining them; scribes painstakingly copied and multiplied them, for whatever happened in Christendom was recorded directly or indirectly in a letter from Rome.[3]

Although the encyclical form has been used from an early date, it was not commonly adopted by the popes before the eighteenth century. Benedict XIV was the first "to revive the ancient custom" of using the encyclical form as a means of insuring unity within the Church, as he himself points out in his preface to the *Bullarium*.[4] Having revived the practice, Benedict used it freely for many pontifical documents, even for those of a purely disciplinary nature. His successors on the other hand, from Clement XIII through Gregory XVI, employed it more sparingly. During this entire period the terms *encyclical letter* and *encyclical epistle* seemed to be used interchangeably, and there is no clear set of criteria for defining them.

Since the latter part of the nineteenth century the encyclical letter and the encyclical epistle have come into favor as instruments of the ordinary teaching of the pope,[5] and have been used extensively to treat not only dogmatic questions but also problems that are primarily social and ethical in scope.[6] Pius XI, however, was the first to make a clear distinction in the use of the terms; this distinction has been maintained by his successors.[7] Today the *encyclical letter* is used almost exclusively to indicate a circular letter addressed to all the bishops on matters affecting the Church at large, while the *encyclical epistle* is reserved for letters in the nature of exhortations concerning a particular need or for those addressed primarily to the bishops of a particular country or to a specific group of the hierarchy.[8]

Throughout the pronouncements of the popes one finds a reiteration of the same bond of faith and charity. Linked with this essential unity, however, there is a gradual clarification, development, and growth as theological and moral principles are applied to ever new and ever more complicated issues. As someone has said, the encyclicals are "writings of circumstance" and the sense and full impact of the texts cannot be understood without placing them against the historical background of their times and in the context of contemporary theological writings and other papal pronouncemnets.

Karl Rahner has developed the thesis that today "in the situation of pluralism and secularism the Church leaves society to develop along its own lines. Now precisely because it is incapable of shaping the course of society in its concrete decisions in an integralist, doctrinal, or juridical sense, the Church itself has a quite new task in relation to this society, a task that might perhaps be characterized as 'prophetic.' "[9]

In commenting on some of the recent papal encyclicals, Rahner points out that "while they rightly and necessarily contain much that is fundamental and of permanent validity in the way of 'doctrine,' the true focal point of their significance, that in them that is so striking, and that actually 'shocks' those who expect them to remain at the purely theoretical level, consists in their underlying purpose, which following the language of the Second Vatican Council we can characterize as primarily 'pastoral.' "[10] He quickly goes on to explain, however, that we must not understand this pastoral element as merely the practical consequences that can be drawn from the universal principles. "The climactic significance of these documents plainly lies in certain 'imperatives,' in certain assignments of emphasis, in the unfolding of an historical programme that summons the world to certain decisions." And in view of the nature of the Church, the discovery of these imperatives directed toward society can only be characterized as 'prophetic.'"[11]

Much is still to be done in the Church if this task is to be fulfilled effectively. Among other things a "mental attitude would have to be developed in believers in which they no longer confronted the official Church with the dilemma, either to make pronoucements that are doctrinally binding or else to be uninteresting." Rahner calls for a new attitude that would be ready to respond seriously to these "prophetic" impulses and to share in the formation not only of opinions but of resolves also.[12]

But all this presupposes a knowledge of and ready access to the texts of the documents of the popes. Throughout the years there have been countless requests for a collection of the texts of the encyclicals in English.

The Papal Encyclicals (1740-1981), a collection of the encyclicals in English from Benedict XIV to John Paul II, is an attempt to fill this need. The purpose of the work is to provide a collection to which students and scholars can turn when they are searching for a specific text or attempting to study the entire corpus of papal teaching. Collections in the past have been limited in extent. An Italian edition, Momigliano's *Tutte le encicliche*[13]—despite its title—omits many of the essential texts. A Spanish collection, well-edited and accompanied by an excellent index, is limited to the period 1832-1965.[14] Mention should also be made of the many fine but also limited French editions,[15] e.g., the La Bonne Presse series of *Actes*; *Les enseignements pontificaux*, by the monks of Solesmes; *La communauté humaine*, by Emile Marmy; *Aux sources de la vie spirituelle*, by Cattin-Conus; and the invaluable French translations of the Utz and Groner German collections published by the Paulusverlag in Fribourg (Switzerland).[16] These volumes are all comprehensive, well indexed, and accompanied by helpful chronological lists and summary outlines, but they are still partial or selective compilations.

In the present edition, the classification of the texts to be included from 1840 to 1981 is based on the categories given in the *Acta Pii IX*, *Acta Leonis XIII*, *Acta Pii X*, *Acta Sanctae Sedis* (official from 1904-1909), the *Acta Apostolicae Sedis* (1909 to date). For the earlier popes the task was more difficult. Many years ago Father Robert Leiber,

S.J., then private secretary of Pius XII, advised the editor that there was no official classification of documents prior to the publication of the various semi-official and official Acta. He suggested that a principle of classification be established for the selection of documents as encyclicals. His specific recommendation was that such criteria could be based on the statement that "an encyclical is a pontifical document a) directed to all the bishops of the world or at least to all of a particular region, b) intended to be made known to the faithful, and c) treating of matters of faith and morals."[17] With these criteria in mind the editor made a careful search through reference works and collections of papal documents to identify texts as encyclicals. Documents frequently referred to in reference sources (and even in papal pronouncements) as encyclicals but not meeting the criteria of this publication have been listed at the end of this introduction with reference to the *Bullarium* and *Acta* in which they may be found.

Where English translations were already available, as for example, in *The* (London) *Tablet, The Catholic Mind, The Pope Speaks, Origins*, USCC publications, and various other periodicals and books, these have been used. For those texts for which translations were not located or were not available, original translations were provided by a group of translators commissioned by the publisher.

This work could never have been carried through to completion without the generous and encouraging assistance of the many who have personally and by correspondence aided in its compilation. Some names, however, should be singled out for special mention. Grateful acknowledgement is made to His Eminence John Cardinal Dearden for the inspiration of his continual example of love for the Church, to the translators for the difficult task of working with eighteenth- and nineteenth-century Latin; to the copy editors for their care with the many details; and finally to the librarians of the Vatican Library, The Catholic University of America, Marygrove College, and the faculty and staff of St. John's Seminary for helpful assistance at all times.

Claudia Carlen, IHM
St. John's Seminary
Plymouth, Michigan
September 15, 1981

†

REFERENCES:

1. Address, *Questa udienza settimanale* (August 5, 1964), *Insegnamenti*, 4 (1965), 472; cf. *The Pope Speaks*, 10 (1965), 249.
2. Ibid.
3. C. Carlen, *Guide to the Encyclicals*, 1878-1937 (New York: H. W. Wilson Co., 1939), p. 6; see also Francisco D. Bencini, *De literis encyclicis* (Turin: Mairisse, 1728-1730), 2 v.
4. *Bullarium*, 1 (1845), viii-ix.
5. For a discussion of the authority of the encyclicals see Paul Nau, *Une source doctrinale: les encycliques* (Paris: Les Editions de Cèdre, 1952), 87 p.; Arthur Peiffer, *Die Enzykliken und ihr formaler Wert für die dogmatische Methode* (Freiburg, Schweiz: Universitätsverlag, 1968), 221 p.; and Gustave Weigel, S.J., "The Significance of Papal Pronouncements," in *The Papal Encyclicals in Their Historical Context*, by Anne Fremantle (New York: The New American Library, 1956), p. 1-20.
6. Hermann Tüchle, "Päpstliche Rundschreiben im Laufe der Jahrhunderte," *Das Wort der Päpste*, hrsg. von Wilhelm Sandfuchs (Wurzburg: Echter-Verlag, 1965), p. 14-17.
7. John Paul II, however, has issued only three encyclical letters to date (September, 1981).
8. In his address of August 5, 1964, Paul VI also used the terms *litterae* to indicate "encyclicals addressed to a group of bishops of a particular region," and *epistulae* for those addressed "to all bishops in communion with Rome." This use of the terms *litterae* and *epistulae* does not seem to apply to his encyclical letter *Ecclesiam Suam* issued one week later and addressed to all bishops. It could reflect the definition given by Raoul Naz in his article "Encyclique" (*Dictionnaire de droit canonique*, 4 (1948), col. 338-39). Paul Nau (*Une source doctrinale*, p. 14) calls attention to the contradiction in Naz and points out that the placement of encyclical letters before encyclical epistles in the *Acta Apostolicae Sedis* also seems to indicate the former's greater importance.
9. "Theological Reflections on the Problem of Secularisation," *Theological Investigations*, tr. by David Bourke (New York: Herder and Herder, 1973), 10:330.
10. Ibid., p. 333.
11. Ibid., p. 334.
12. Ibid., p. 336.
13. *Tutte le encicliche dei Sommi Pontefici*; raccolte e annotate da Eucardio Momigliano, 4. ed. (Milano: dall'Oglio, 1964), 1678 p.
14. *Colección completa; encíclicas pontificias*, 1832-1965; 4^{a} éd., corr. y aum., por el P. Federico Hoyos, SVD (Buenos Aires: Editorial Guadalupe, 1966), 2 v.
15. *Les enseignements pontificaux*; présentation et tables par les moines de Solesmes (Tournai: Desclée, 1952-1967), 13 v.; *La communauté humaine selon l'esprit chrétien: documents* [éd. par] E. Marmy; nouv. éd. (Fribourg, Editions St.-Paul, 1949); *Aux sources de la vie spirituelle: documents* [éd. par] Paul Cattin et Humbert Conus (Fribourg: Editons St.-Paul, 1951).
16. E.g., *La doctrine sociale de l'Eglise à travers les siècles; documents pontificaux du xveme au xxème siècle* [éd. par] A. F. Utz et M. Boeglin (Paris: Beauchesne, 1973), 4 v.
17. Robert Leiber, S.J., to the editor (March 27, 1957): "Notae specificae esse possunt: documentum pontificium

a) directum ad omnes Episcopos totius mundi vel saltem ad omnes alicuius regionis; b) destinatum, ut omnibus fidelibus notum fiat; c) agens de rebus fidei et morum."

SOURCES OF THE ORIGINAL TEXTS OF THE ENCYCLICALS:

Acta Apostolicae Sedis; commentarium officiale. Città del Vaticano, Typis Polyglottis Vaticanis, 1909 - to date.

Acta Gregorii Papae XVI; edidit A. M. Bernasconi. Romae, Ex Typographia Polyglotta S. C. de Propaganda Fide, 1901-1904. 4 v.

Acta Sanctae Sedis. Romae, Ex Typographia Polyglotta S. C. de Propaganda Fide, 1865-1908. 41 v.

Bullarium Benedicti XIV [et] *Bularii Romani continuatio*. Prati, In Typographia Aldina, 1845-1856. 9 v. in 14.

Codicis Iuris Canonici Fontes; edidit Petrus Cardinal Gasparri. Romae, Typis Polyglottis Vaticanis, 1923-38. 8 v.

Leonis XIII Pontificis Maximi Acta. Romae, Ex Typographia Vaticana, 1881-1905. 23 v.

Magnum Bullarium Romanum; ed. H. Mainardi et C. Coquelius. Romae, 1733-62. 18 v.

Pii IX Pontificis Maximi Acta. Romae, Typographia Vaticana, 1854-1878. 9 v.

Pii X Pontificis Maximi Acta. Romae, Ex Typographia Vaticana, 1905-1914. 5 v.

Discorsi e Radiomessaggi di Sua Santità Pio XI. Romae, Tipografia Poliglotta Vaticana, 1963. 3 v.

Discorsi e Radiomessaggi di Sua Santità Pio XII. Romae, Tipografia Poliglotta Vaticana, 1940-1966. 21 v.

Discorsi, Messaggi, Colloqui del Santo Padre Giovanni XXIII. Romae, Tipografia Vaticana, 1960-67. 6 v.

Insegnamenti di Paolo VI. Romae, Tipografia Poliglotta Vaticana, 1963-1979. 16 v.

Insegnamenti di Giovanni Paolo I. Città del Vaticano, Libreria Editrice Vaticana, 1979. 116 p.

Insegnamenti di Giovanni Paolo II. Romae, Tipografia Poliglotta Vaticana, 1979-1980. 3 v.

Leges Ecclesiae post Codicem Iuris Canonici; editae, collegit digessit notisque orbavit Xaverius Ochoa Sanz. Romae, Commentarium pro Religiosis, 1966-1974. 4 v.

DOCUMENTS NOT INCLUDED IN *THE PAPAL ENCYCLICALS*: (The following documents have been sometimes referred to as encyclicals but do not meet the criteria of this editor.)

January 11, 1741, *Matrimonii perpetuum*, *Benedict XIV Bull.*, 1: 57-58.

May 4, 1741, *Non ambigimus*, *Benedict XIV Bull.*, 1:63-65

June 1, 1741, *Cum Sacrarum*, *Benedict XIV Bull.*, 1: 69-70

August 15, 1741, *Grave et permolestum*, *Benedict XIV Bull.*, 1: 86-88

August 22, 1741, *In suprema*, *Benedict XIV Bull.*, 1: 91-92

August 26, 1741, *Quamvis Paternae*, *Benedict XIV Bull.*, 1: 94-96

November 27, 1741, *Satis Vobis*, *Benedict XIV Bull.*, 1: 113-16

December 20, 1741, *Immensa*, *Benedict XIV Bull.*, 1: 123-25

February 7, 1742, *Etsi minime*, *Benedict XIV Bull.*, 1: 136-40

May 22, 1742, *Acerbi plene doloris*, *Benedict XIV Bull.*, 1: 195-97

August 12, 1742, *Nihil profecto*, *Benedict XIV Bull.*, 1: 233-34

November 13, 1742, *Certiores effecti*, *Benedict XIV Bull.*, 1: 239-40

November 17, 1742, *Satis Vobis*, *Benedict XIV Bull.*, 1: 240-45

November 27, 1742, *Etsi dubitare*, *Benedict XIV Bull.*, 1: 247-49

December 14, 1742, *Cum illud*, *Benedict XIV Bull.*, 1: 250-56

March 16, 1743, *Magna non minus*, *Benedict XIV Bull.*, 1: 288-90

March 23, 1743, *Quemadmodum preces*, *Benedict XIV Bull.*, 1: 292-93

July 31, 1793, *Ad Nostras manus*, *Bull. Rom. Cont.*, 6^3: 2642-43

August 13, 1799, *Quoties animo*, *Bull. Rom. Cont.*, 6^3: 3112-14

August 15, 1801, *Tam multa*, *Bull. Rom. Cont.*, 7^1: 165-68

August 15, 1801, *Ecclesia Christi*, *Bull. Rom. Cont.*, 7^1: 184-88

February 17, 1809, *Vix nova a Nobis*, Migne, V. P. ed., *Theologiae cursus completus* (Paris, Barriere d'Enfer, 1841), 25: 707-

June 12, 1817, *Vineam quam*, *Bull. Rom. Cont.*, 7^2: 1471

August 25, 1819, *Dominici gregis*, *Bull. Rom. Cont.*, 7^2: 1970-71

May 16, 1820, *Praeclara quam*, *Bull. Rom. Cont.*, 7^2: 2117

September 13, 1821, *Ecclesiam a Jesu Christo*, *Bull. Rom. Cont.* 7^2: 2180-82

October 4, 1822, *Apostolicae Sedis*, *Bull. Rom. Cont.*, 7^2: 2293-95

January 25, 1825, *Ad plurimas easque*, *Bull. Rom. Cont.*, 8: 278-80

June 18, 1829, *In supremi apostolatus*, *Bull. Rom. Cont.*, 9: 28-30

February 9, 1831, *Chiamati dalla*, *Acta Greg. XVI*, 1: 1-2

April 5, 1831, *Quel Dio*, *Acta Greg. XVI*, 1: 11-13

July 12, 1831, *Le armi valorose*, *Acta Greg. XVI*, 1: 31-32

February 3, 1832, *Inter gravissimas*, *Acta Greg. XVI*, 1: 107-09

October 3, 1832, *E principio certo*, *Acta Greg. XVI*, 1: 193-95

December 2, 1832, *Plura post susceptam*, *Acta Greg. XVI*, 1: 200-02

April 23, 1835, *Perlatae dudum*, *Acta Greg. XVI*, 2: 27-28

June 3, 1835, *Melchitarum catholicorum*, *Acta Greg. XVI*, 2: 48-49

September 26, 1835, *Dum acerbissimas*, *Acta Greg. XVI*, 2: 85-87

May 2, 1836, *Studium paternae*, *Acta Greg. XVI*, 2: 107-08

December 12, 1840, *Augustissimam*, *Acta Greg. XVI*, 3: 95-97

April 1, 1842, *Inter ea*, *Acta Greg. XVI*, 3: 208-09

February 27, 1846, *Inter gravissimas*, *Acta Greg. XVI*, 3: 466-67

September 13, 1896, *Apostolocae curae*, *Acta Leonis*, 16: 258-75

January 22, 1899, *Testem benevolentiae*, *Acta Leonis*, 19: 5-20

January 18, 1952, *Cupimus imprimis*, *Acta Apost. Sedis*, 44 (1952), 153-58

December 24, 1743, *Demandatam*, *Benedict XIV Bull.*, 1: 328-34

February 2, 1744, *Inter omnigenas*, *Benedict XIV Bull.*, 1: 338-43

August 19, 1744, *Cum semper*, *Benedict XIV Bull.*, 1: 394-400

November 20, 1744, *In suprema*, *Benedict XIV Bull.*, 1: 457-59

February 18, 1745, *Cum multorum*, *Benedict XIV Bull.*, 1: 507-08

June 10, 1745, *Libentissimae*, *Benedict XIV Bull.*, 1: 526-32

July 7, 1745, *Suprema omnium*, *Benedict XIV Bull.*, 1: 535-38

November 5, 1745, *Ab eo tempore*, *Benedict XIV Bull.*, 1: 594-601

July 16, 1746, *Accepimus*, *Benedict XIV Bull.*, 2: 111-15

December 16, 1746, *Quemadmodum*, *Benedict XIV Bull.*, 2: 150-51

November 30, 1747, *Praeclara*, *Benedict XIV Bull.*, 2: 318-19

January 1, 1748, *Inter cetera*, *Benedict XIV Bull.*, 2: 319-22

September 30, 1748, *Alias*, *Benedict XIV Bull.*, 2: 450-51

December 12, 1748, *Cum sicut*, *Benedict XIV Bull.*, 2: 460-62

February 19, 1749, *Annus qui*, *Benedict XIV Bull.*, 3^1: 16-28

October 31, 1749, *Gravissimo*, *Benedict XIV Bull.*, 3^1: 85-86

December 3, 1749, *Inter praeteritos, Benedict XIV Bull.*, 3^1: 160-92

June 19, 1750, *Anno vertente, Benedict XIV Bull.*, 3^1: 212-15

December 25, 1750, *Benedictus Deus, Benedict XIV Bull.*, 3^1: 201-05

January 1, 1751, *Celebrationem, Benedict XIV Bull.*, 3^1: 231-39

January 1, 1751, *Prodiit jamdudum, Benedict XIV Bull.*, 3^1: 248-51

February 20, 1751, *Elapso proxime Anno, Benedict XIV Bull.*, 3^1: 255-57

May 18, 1751, *Providas, Benedict XIV Bull.*, 3^1: 283

June 2, 1751, *Magno cum animi, Benedict XIV Bull.*, 3^1: 286-96

May 30, 1753, *Apostolicum, Benedict XIV Bull.*, 3^2: 93-103

August 8, 1755, *Quam ex sublimi, Benedict XIV Bull.*, 3^2: 285-87

August 2, 1757, *Quam grave, Benedict XIV Bull.*, 3^2: 425-29

January 23, 1759, *Quam in cunctis, Bull. Rom. Cont.*, 4^1: 96

March 21, 1759, *Pastoralis officii, Bull. Rom. Cont.*, 4^1: 116-18

June 9, 1762, *Quanto in dolore, Bull. Rom. Cont.*, 4^1: 643-45

January 14, 1764, *Ubi primum accepimus, Bull. Rom. Cont.*, 4^1: 845

May 8, 1765, *Quanta auxilii vestri, Bull. Rom. Cont.*, 4^2: 952-54

June 25, 1766, *Quam graviter animo, Bull. Rom. Cont.*, 4^2: 1088-89

September 11, 1758, *Venimus in altitudinem, Bull. Rom. Cont.*, 4^1: 27-30

June 25, 1768, *Accedamus cum fiducia, Bull. Rom. Cont.*, 4^2: 1433-35

September 21, 1769, *Inter multiplices, Bull. Rom. Cont.*, 5: 42-46

September 11, 1769, *Inscrutabili divinae, Bull. Rom. Cont.*, 5: 40-42

March 16, 1771, *Magna atque, Bull. Rom. Cont.*, 5: 290-92

December 25, 1775, *Summa Dei in Nos, Bull. Rom. Cont.*, 6^1 186-90

March 6, 1779, *Nuper pro parte, Bull. Rom. Cont.*, 6^1: 559

April 23, 1791, *Adeo nota, Bull. Rom. Cont.*, 6^3: 2333-41

March 19, 1791, *In gravissimis, Bull. Rom. Cont.*, 6^3: 2476-79

June 13, 1792, *Ubi Lutetiam, Bull. Rom. Cont.*, 6^3: 2529-33

October 10, 1792, *Satis nota, Acta Pii VI*, I: 343-45

November 21, 1792, *Ignotae nemini, Bull. Rom. Cont.*, 6^3: 2559-61

November 24, 1792, *Quae causa Nos, Bull. Rom. Cont.*, 6^3: 2562-65

January 23, 1793, *Ex iis quae, Acta Pii VI*, 2: 1-9

July 31, 1793, *Ad Nostras manus, Bull. Rom. Cont.*, 6^3: 2642-43

August 13, 1799, *Quoties animo, Bull. Rom. Cont.*, 6^3: 3112-14

August 15, 1801, *Tam multa, Bull. Rom. Cont.*, 7^1: 165-68

August 15, 1801, *Ecclesia Christi, Bull. Rom. Cont.*, 7^1: 184-88

February 17, 1809, *Vix nova a Nobis*, Migne, V. P. ed., *Theologiae cursus completus* (Paris, Barrière d'Enfer, 1841), 25: 707-

June 12, 1817, *Vineam quam, Bull. Rom. Cont.*, 7^2: 1471

August 25, 1819, *Dominici gregis, Bull. Rom. Cont.*, 7^2: 1970-71

May 16, 1820, *Praeclara quam, Bull. Rom. Cont.*, 7^2: 2117

September 13, 1821, *Ecclesiam a Jesu Christo, Bull. Rom. Cont.* 7^2: 2180-82

October 4, 1822, *Apostolicae Sedis, Bull. Rom. Cont.*, 7^2: 2293-95

January 25, 1825, *Ad plurimas easque, Bull. Rom. Cont.*, 8: 278-80

June 18, 1829, *In supremi apostolatus, Bull. Rom. Cont.*, 9: 28-30

February 9, 1831, *Chiamati dalla, Acta Greg. XVI*, 1: 1-2

April 5, 1831, *Quel Dio, Acta Greg. XVI*, 1: 11-13

July 12, 1831, *Le armi valorose, Acta Greg. XVI*, 1: 31-32

February 3, 1832, *Inter gravissimas, Acta Greg. XVI*, 1: 107-09

October 3, 1832, *E principio certo, Acta Greg. XVI*, 1: 193-95

December 2, 1832, *Plura post susceptam, Acta Greg. XVI*, 1: 200-02

April 23, 1835, *Perlatae dudum, Acta Greg. XVI*, 2: 27-28

June 3, 1835, *Melchitarum catholicorum, Acta Greg. XVI*, 2: 48-49

September 26, 1835, *Dum acerbissimas, Acta Greg. XVI*, 2: 85-87

May 2, 1836, *Studium paternae, Acta Greg. XVI*, 2: 107-08

December 12, 1840, *Augustissimam, Acta Greg. XVI*, 3: 95-97

April 1, 1842, *Inter ea, Acta Greg. XVI*, 3: 208-09

February 27, 1846, *Inter gravissimas, Acta Greg. XVI*, 3: 466-67

September 13, 1896, *Apostolocae curae, Acta Leonis*, 16: 258-75

January 22, 1899, *Testem benevolentiae, Acta Leonis*, 19: 5-20

January 18, 1952, *Cupimus imprimis, Acta Apost. Sedis*, 44 (1952), 153-58

CHRONOLOGICAL LIST OF ENCYCLICALS

BENEDICT XIV (PROSPERO LAMBERTINI): POPE, 1740-1758

1740	December 3	1. UBI PRIMUM: On the duties of bishops. 2,150 words.
1741	June 30	2. QUANTA CURA: Forbidding traffic in alms. 900 words.
1743	May 18	3. NIMIAM LICENTIAM: To bishops of Poland: on validity of marriages. 3,350 words.
1745	November 1	4. VIX PERVENIT: To the bishops of Italy: on usury and other dishonest profit. 1,980 words.
1748	June 29	5. MAGNAE NOBIS: To the bishops of Poland: on marriage impediments and dispensations. 2,675 words.
1749	May 5	6. PEREGRINANTES: To all the faithful: proclaiming a Holy Year for 1750. 2,850 words.
1749	June 26	7. APOSTOLICA CONSTITUTIO: On preparation for the Holy Year. 10,400 words.
1751	June 14	8. A QUO PRIMUM: To the bishops of Poland: on Jews and Christians living in the same place. 2,400 words.
1754	June 26	9. CUM RELIGIOSI: To the bishops of the States of the Church: on catechesis. 1,400 words.
1754	August 1	10. QUOD PROVINCIALE: To the bishops of Albania: on Christians using Mohammedan names. 1,075 words.
1755	July 26	11. ALLATAE SUNT: To missionaries of the Orient: on the observance of Oriental rites. 17,275 words.
1756	March 1	12. EX QUO PRIMUM: To bishops of the Greek rite: on the Euchologion. 21,475 words.
1756	October 16	13. EX OMNIBUS: To the bishops of France: on the apostolic constitution, *Unigenitus*. 1,950 words.

CLEMENT XIII (CARLO REZZONICO): POPE, 1758-1769

1758 September 13 — 14. A QUO DIE: Unity among Christians. 4,850 words.

1759 September 17 — 15. CUM PRIMUM: On observing canonical sanctions. 3,750 words.

1759 December 20 — 16. APPETENTE SACRO: On the spiritual advantages of fasting. 990 words.

1761 June 14 — 17. IN DOMINICO AGRO: On instruction in the faith. 1,850 words.

1766 November 25 — 18. CHRISTIANAE REIPUBLICAE: To bishops of Austria: on the dangers of anti-Christian writings. 1,190 words.

1768 January 6 — 19. SUMMA QUAE: To the bishops of Poland: on the Church in Poland. 975 words.

CLEMENT XIV (GIOVANNI GANGANELLI): POPE, 1769-1774

1769 September 21 — 20. DECET QUAM MAXIME: To the bishops of Sardinia: on abuses in taxes and benefices. 9,800 words.

1769 December 12 — 21. INSCRUTABILI DIVINAE SAPIENTIAE: To all Christians: proclaiming a universal jubilee. 875 words.

1769 December 12 — 22. CUM SUMMI: Proclaiming a universal jubilee. 2,550 words.

1774 April 30 — 23. SALUTIS NOSTRAE: To all Christians: proclaiming a universal jubilee. 1,900 words.

PIUS VI (GIOVANNI ANGELO BRACCHI): POPE, 1775-1799

1775 December 25 — 24. INSCRUTABILE: On the problems of the pontificate. 3,335 words.

1791 April 13 — 25. CHARITAS: To the bishops of France: on the civil oath in France. 5,825 words.

PIUS VII (BARNABA CHIARMONTI): POPE, 1800-1823

1800 May 15 — 26. DIU SATIS: To the bishops of France: on a return to Gospel principles. 3,200 words.

LEO XII (ANNIBALE DELLA GENGA): POPE, 1823-1829

1824 May 5 — 27. UBI PRIMUM: To all bishops: on Leo XII's assuming the pontificate. 3,100 words.

1824 May 24 — 28. QUOD HOC INEUNTE: Proclaiming a universal jubilee. 2,800 words.

1825 December 25 — 29. CHARITATE CHRISTI: Extending jubilee to the entire church. 4,700 words.

PIUS VIII (FRANCESCO SAVERIO CASTIGLIONI): POPE, 1829-1830

1829 May 24 — 30. TRADITI HUMILITATI: On Pius VIII's program for the pontificate. 2,690 words.

GREGORY XVI (MAURO CAPPELLARI): POPE, 1831-1846

1832 May 27 — 31. SUMMO IUGITER STUDIO: To the bishops of Bavaria: on mixed marriages. 1,600 words.

1832 June 9 — 32. CUM PRIMUM: To the bishops of Poland: on civil obedience. 900 words.

1832	August 15	33. MIRARI VOS: On liberalism and religious indifferentism. 3,600 words.
1833	October 4	34. QUO GRAVIORA: To the bishops of the Rhineland: on the "pragmatic Constitution." 2,450 words.
1834	June 25	35. SINGULARI NOS: On the errors of Lammenais. 1,210 words.
1835	May 17	36. COMMISSUM DIVINITUS: To clergy of Switzerland: on Church and State. 2,750 words.
1840	September 18	37. PROBE NOSTIS: On the Propagation of the Faith. 1,795 words.
1841	April 30	38. QUAS VESTRO: To the bishops of Hungary: on mixed marriages. 1,490 words.
1844	May 8	39. INTER PRAECIPUAS: On biblical societies. 3,000 words.

PIUS IX (GIOVANNI MARIA MASTAI-FERRETTI): POPE, 1846-1878

1846	November 9	40. QUI PLURIBUS: On faith and religion. 1,827 words.
1847	March 25	41. PRAEDECESSORES NOSTROS: On aid for Ireland. 1,025 words.
1847	June 17	42. UBI PRIMUM: To religious superiors: on discipline for religious. 1,640 words.
1849	February 2	43. UBI PRIMUM: On the Immaculate Conception. 882 words.
1849	December 8	44. NOSTIS ET NOBISCUM: To the bishops of Italy: on the Church in the Pontifical States. 5,125 words.
1851	November 21	45. EXULTAVIT COR NOSTRUM: On the effects of jubilee. 1,025 words.
1852	March 25	46. NEMO CERTE IGNORAT: To the bishops of Ireland: on the discipline for clergy. 1,435 words.
1852	May 17	47. PROBE NOSCITIS VENERABILES: To the bishops of Spain: on the discipline for clergy. 900 words.
1853	March 21	48. INTER MULTIPLICES: To the bishops of France: pleading for unity of spirit. 1,845 words.
1854	February 2	49. NEMINEM VESTRUM: To clergy and faithful of Constantinople: on the persecution of Armenians. 3,800 words.
1854	March 20	50. OPTIME NOSCITIS: To the bishops of Ireland: on the proposed Catholic university for Ireland. 1,330 words.
1854	August 1	51. APOSTOLICAE NOSTRAE CARITATIS: Urging prayers for peace.. 1,380 words.
1855	November 5	52. OPTIME NOSCITIS: To the bishops of Austria: on episcopal meetings. 1,230 words.
1856	March 17	53. SINGULARI QUIDEM: To the bishops of Austria: on the Church in Austria. 4,200 words.
1858	January 20	54. CUM NUPER: To the bishops of Sicily: on care for clerics. 1,710 words.
1858	May 3	55. AMANTISSIMI REDEMPTORIS: On priests and the care of souls. 2,080 words.
1859	April 27	56. CUM SANCTA MATER ECCLESIA: Pleading for public prayer. 580 words.
1859	June 18	57. QUI NUPER: On Pontifical States. 380 words.

1860	January 19	58. NULLIS CERTE VERBIS: On the need for civil sovereignty. 1,535 words.
1862	April 8	59. AMANTISSIMUS: To bishops of the Oriental rite: on the care of the churches. 2,665 words.
1863	August 10	60. QUANTO CONFICIAMUR MOERORE: To the bishops of Italy: on promotion of false doctrines. 2,410 words.
1863	September 17	61. INCREDIBILI: To the bishops of Bogotá: on persecution in New Granada. 1,230 words.
1864	August 18	62. MAXIMAE QUIDEM: To the bishops of Bavaria: on the Church in Bavaria. 1,000 words.
1864	December 8	63. QUANTA CURA: Condemning current errors. 2,565 words.
1865	September 30	64. MERIDIONALI AMERICAE: To bishops of South America: on the seminary for native clergy. 295 words.
1867	October 27	65. LEVATE: On the afflictions of the Church. 1,475 words.
1870	November 1	66. RESPICIENTES: Protesting the taking of the Pontifical states. 2,870 words.
1871	May 15	67. UBI NOS: To all bishops: on Pontifical States. 2,050 words.
1871	June 4	68. BENEFICIA DEI: On the twenty-fifth anniversary of his pontificate. 1,230 words.
1871	August 5	69. SAEPE VENERABILES FRATRES: On thanksgiving for twenty-five years of pontificate. 820 words.
1872	November 16	70. QUAE IN PATRIARCHATU: To bishops and people of Chaldea: on the Church in Chaldea. 2,590 words.
1873	January 6	71. QUARTUS SUPRA: To bishops and people of the Armenian rite: on the Church in Armenia. 8,200 words.
1873	November 21	72. ETSI MULTA: On the Church in Italy, Germany, and Switzerland. 4,100 words.
1874	March 7	73. VIX DUM A NOBIS: To the bishops of Austria: on the Church in Austria. 2,050 words.
1874	May 13	74. OMNEM SOLLICITUDINEM: To bishops of the Ruthenian rite: on the Greek-Ruthenian rite. 1,435 words.
1874	December 24	75. GRAVIBUS ECCLESIAE: To all bishops and faithful: proclaiming a jubilee for 1875. 2,680 words.
1875	February 5	76. QUOD NUNQUAM: To the bishops of Prussia: on the Church in Prussia. 1,410 words.
1875	March 23	77. GRAVES AC DIUTURNAE: To the bishops of Switzerland: on the Church in Switzerland. 1,130 words.

LEO XIII (GIOACCHINO VINCENZO PECCI): POPE, 1878-1903

1878	April 21	78. INSCRUTABILI DEI CONSILIO: On the evils of society. 2,750 words.
1878	December 28	79. QUOD APOSTOLICI MUNERIS: On socialism. 2,900 words.
1879	August 4	80. AETERNI PATRIS: On the restoration of Christian philosophy. 6,750 words.

1880	February 10	81.	ARCANUM: On Christian marriage. 6,375 words.
1880	September 30	82.	GRANDE MUNUS: On SS. Cyril and Methodius. 3,180 words.
1880	December 3	83.	SANCTA DEI CIVITAS: On mission societies. 2,625 words.
1881	June 29	84.	DIUTURNUM: On the origin of civil power. 4,125 words.
1881	August 3	85.	LICET MULTA: To the bishops of Belgium: on Catholics in Belgium. 1,125 words.
1882	February 15	86.	ETSI NOS: To the bishops of Italy: on conditions in Italy. 3,175 words.
1882	September 17	87.	AUSPICATO CONCESSUM: On St. Francis of Assisi. 3,000 words.
1882	December 8	88.	CUM MULTA: To the bishops of Spain: on conditions in Spain. 2,250 words.
1883	September 1	89.	SUPREMI APOSTOLATUS OFFICIO: On devotion to the rosary. 1,925 words.
1884	February 8	90.	NOBILISSIMA GALLORUM GENS: To the bishops of France: on the religious question. 2,675 words.
1884	April 20	91.	HUMANUM GENUS: On Freemasonry. 6,000 words.
1884	August 30	92.	SUPERIORE ANNO: On the recitation of the rosary. 1,100 words.
1885	November 1	93.	IMMORTALE DEI: On the Christian constitution of states. 6,175 words.
1885	November 27	94.	SPECTATA FIDES: To the bishops of England: on Christian education. 750 words.
1885	December 22	95.	QUOD AUCTORITATE: Proclaiming an extraordinary Jubilee. 2,050 words.
1886	January 6	96.	IAMPRIDEM: To the bishops of Prussia: on Catholicism in Germany. 2,900 words.
1886	August 22	97.	QUOD MULTUM: To the bishops of Hungary: on the liberty of the Church. 3,400 words.
1886	September 14	98.	PERGRATA: To the bishops of Portugal: on the Church in Portugal. 2,375 words.
1887	September 20	99.	VI E BEN NOTO: To the bishops of Italy: on the rosary and public life. 1,250 words.
1887	December 22	100.	OFFICIO SANCTISSIMO: To the bishops of Bavaria: on the Church in Bavaria. 6,400 words.
1888	April 1	101.	QUOD ANNIVERSARIUS: On his sacerdotal jubilee. 1,125 words.
1888	May 5	102.	IN PLURIMIS: To the bishops of Brazil: on the abolition of slavery. 5,250 words.
1888	June 20	103.	LIBERTAS: On the nature of human liberty. 7,850 words.
1888	June 24	104.	SAEPE NOS: To the bishops of Ireland: on boycotting in Ireland. 950 words.
1888	July 25	105.	PATERNA CARITAS: To the Patriarch of Cilicia and the archbishops and bishops of the Armenian people: on reunion with Rome. 1,875 words.
1888	December 10	106.	QUAM AERUMNOSA: To the bishops of America: on Italian immigrants. 1,125 words.

1888	December 21	107. ETSI CUNCTAS: To the bishops of Ireland: on the Church in Ireland. 380 words.
1888	December 25	108. EXEUNTE IAM ANNO: On the right ordering of Christian life. 4,100 words.
1889	March 7	109. MAGNI NOBIS: To the bishops of the United States: on the Catholic University of America. 750 words.
1889	August 15	110. QUAMQUAM PLURIES: On devotion to St. Joseph. 1,675 words.
1890	January 10	111. SAPIENTIAE CHRISTIANAE: On Christians as citizens. 7,375 words.
1890	October 15	112. DALL'ALTO DELL'APOSTOLICO SEGGIO: To the bishops and people of Italy: on Freemasonry in Italy. 4,875 words.
1890	November 20	113. CATHOLICAE ECCLESIAE: On slavery in the missions. 1,475 words.
1891	March 3	114. IN IPSO: To the bishops of Austria: on episcopal reunions in Austria. 1,575 words.
1891	May 15	115. RERUM NOVARUM: On capital and labor. 11,250 words.
1891	June 25	116. PASTORALIS: To the bishops of Portugal: on religious union. 1,975 words.
1891	September 12	117. PASTORALIS OFFICII: To the bishops of Germany and Austria: on the morality of dueling. 1,475 words.
1891	September 22	118. OCTOBRI MENSE: On the rosary. 3,950 words.
1892	February 16	119. AU MILIEU DES SOLLICITUDES: To the bishops, clergy, and faithful of France: on the Church and State in France. 3,950 words.
1892	July 16	120. QUARTO ABEUNTE ESAECULO: To the bishops of Spain, Italy, and the two Americas: on the Columbus quadricentennial. 1,875 words.
1892	September 8	121. MAGNAE DEI MATRIS: On the rosary. 3,575 words.
1892	December 8	122. INIMICA VIS: To the bishops of Italy: on Freemasonry. 1,325 words.
1892	December 8	123. CUSTODI DI QUELLA FEDE: To the Italian people: on Freemasonry. 3,000 words.
1893	June 24	124. AD EXTREMAS: On seminaries for native clergy. 1,625 words.
1893	September 2	125. CONSTANTI HUNGARORUM: To the bishops of Hungary: on the Church in Hungary. 2,750 words.
1893	September 8	126. LAETITIAE SANCTAE: Commending devotion to the rosary. 2,500 words.
1893	October 25	127. NON MEDIOCRI: To the bishops of Spain: on the Spanish College in Rome. 1,350 words.
1893	November 18	128. PROVIDENTISSIMUS DEUS: On the study of Holy Scripture. 8,875 words.
1894	March 19	129. CARITATIS: To the bishops of Poland: on the Church in Poland. 3,725 words.
1894	May 1	130. INTER GRAVES: To the bishops of Peru: on the Church in Peru. 1,850 words.
1894	July 2	131. LITTERAS A VOBIS: To the bishops of Brazil: on the clergy in Brazil. 1,650 words.

1894	September 8	132. IUCUNDA SEMPER EXPECTATIONE: On the rosary. 2,625 words.
1894	December 24	133. CHRISTI NOMEN: On the propagation of the Faith and churches. 1,025 words.
1895	January 6	134. LONGINQUA: To the bishops of the United States: on Catholicism in the United States. 4,400 words.
1895	July 10	135. PERMOTI NOS: To the bishops of Belgium: on social conditions in Belgium. 1,500 words.
1895	September 5	136. ADIUTRICEM: On the rosary. 3,000 words.
1896	May 1	137. INSIGNES: To the bishops of Hungary: on the Hungarian millenium. 2,800 words.
1896	June 29	138. SATIS COGNITUM: On the unity of the Church. 12,100 words.
1896	September 20	139. FIDENTEM PIUMQUE ANIMUM: On the rosary. 2,150 words.
1897	May 9	140. DIVINUM ILLUD MUNUS: On the Holy Spirit. 5,625 words.
1897	August 1	141. MILITANTIS ECCLESIAE: To the bishops of Austria, Germany, and Switzerland: on St. Peter Canisius. 2,625 words.
1897	September 12	142. AUGUSTISSIMAE VIRGINIS MARIAE: On the Confraternity of the Holy Rosary. 2,425 words.
1897	December 8	143. AFFARI VOS: To the bishops of Canada: on the Manitoba school question. 2,200 words.
1898	July 25	144. CARITATIS STUDIUM: To the bishops of Scotland: on the Church in Scotland. 3,000 words.
1898	August 5	145. SPESSE VOLTE: To the bishops, priests, and people of Italy: on the suppression of Catholic institutions. 3,050 words.
1898	August 16	146. QUAM RELIGIOSA: To the bishops of Peru: on civil marriage law. 860 words.
1898	September 5	147. DIUTURNI TEMPORIS: On the rosary. 925 words.
1898	December 25	148. QUUM DIUTURNUM: To the bishops of Latin America: on Latin American bishops' plenary council. 475 words.
1899	May 25	149. ANNUM SACRUM: On consecration to the Sacred Heart. 1,975 words.
1899	September 8	150. DEPUIS LE JOUR: To the archbishops, bishops, and clergy of France: on the education of the clergy. 7,800 words.
1899	September 18	151. PATERNAE: To the bishops of Brazil: on the education of the clergy. 1,475 words.
1900	July 21	152. OMNIBUS COMPERTUM: To the Patriarch and bishops of the Greek-Melchite rite: on unity among the Greek Melchites. 925 words.
1900	November 1	153. TAMETSI FUTURA PROSPICIENTIBUS: On Jesus Christ the Redeemer. 4,700 words.
1901	January 18	154. GRAVES DE COMMUNI RE: On Christian democracy. 4,125 words.
1901	May 16	155. GRAVISSIMAS: To the bishops of Portugal: on religious orders in Portugal. 464 words.
1901	August 20	156. REPUTANTIBUS:To the bishops of Bohemia and Moravia: on the language question in Bohemia. 1,075 words.

1901 November 20 — 157. URBANITATIS VETERIS: To the bishops of the Latin church in Greece: on the foundation of a seminary in Athens. 1,200 words.

1902 April 15 — 158. IN AMPLISSIMO: To the bishops of the United States: on the Church in the United States. 775 words.

1902 April 30 — 159. QUOD VOTIS: To the bishops of Austria: on the proposed Catholic University. 248 words.

1902 May 28 — 160. MIRAE CARITATIS: On the Holy Eucharist. 5,100 words.

1902 November 22 — 161. QUAE AD NOS: To the bishops of Bohemia and Moravia: on the church in Bohemia and Moravia. 272 words.

1902 December 8 — 162. FIN DAL PRINCIPIO: To the bishops of Italy: on the education of the clergy. 3,170 words.

1902 December 24 — 163. DUM MULTA: To the bishops of Ecuador: on marriage legislation. 600 words.

PIUS X (GIUSEPPE SARTO): POPE, 1903-1914

1903 October 4 — 164. E SUPREMI: On the restoration of all things in Christ. 4,000 words.

1904 February 2 — 165. AD DIEM ILLUM LAETISSIMUM: On the Immaculate Conception. 5,150 words.

1904 March 12 — 166. IUCUNDA SANE: On Pope Gregory the Great. 6,200 words.

1905 April 15 — 167. ACERBO NIMIS: On teaching Christian doctrine. 4,500 words.

1905 June 11 — 168. IL FERMO PROPOSITO: To the bishops of Italy: on Catholic action in Italy. 5,500 words.

1906 February 11 — 169. VEHEMENTER NOS: To the bishops, clergy, and people of France: on the French Law of Separation. 4,875 words.

1906 April 5 — 170. TRIBUS CIRCITER: On the Mariavites or Mystic Priests of Poland. 2,000 words.

1906 July 28 — 171. PIENI L'ANIMO: To the bishops of Italy: on the clergy in Italy. 2,800 words.

1906 August 10 — 172. GRAVISSIMO OFFICII MUNERE: To the bishops of France: on French associations of worship. 1,500 words.

1907 January 6 — 173. UNE FOIS ENCORE: To the bishops, clergy, and people of France: on the separation of Church and State. 2,400 words.

1907 September 8 — 174. PASCENDI DOMINICI GREGIS: On the doctrines of the Modernists. 21,375 words.

1909 April 21 — 175. COMMUNIUM RERUM: On St. Anselm of Aosta. 8,100 words.

1910 May 26 — 176. EDITAE SAEPE: On St. Charles Borromeo. 7,200 words.

1911 May 24 — 177. IAMDUDUM: On the Law of Separation in Portugal. 1,950 words.

1912 June 7 — 178. LACRIMABILI STATU: To the bishops of Latin America: on the Indians of South America. 1,250 words.

1912 September 24 — 179. SINGULARI QUADAM: To the bishops of Germany: on labor organizations. 1,550 words.

BENEDICT XV (GIACOMO DELLA CHIESA): POPE, 1914-1922

1914	November 1	180. AD BEATISSIMI APOSTOLORUM: Appealing for peace. 4,000 words.
1917	June 15	181. HUMANI GENERIS REDEMPTIONEM: On preaching the Word of God. 3,000 words.
1918	December 1	182. QUOD IAM DIU: On the future peace conference. 350 words.
1919	May 14	183. IN HAC TANTA: To the bishops of Germany: on St. Boniface, 3,600 words.
1919	November 24	184. PATERNO IAM DIU: On children of central Europe. 625 words.
1920	May 23	185. PACEM, DEI MUNUS PULCHERRIMUM: On peace and Christian reconciliation. 2,700 words.
1920	September 15	186. SPIRITUS PARACLITUS: On St. Jerome. 10,000 words.
1920	October 5	187. PRINCIPI APOSTOLORUM PETRO: On St. Ephrem, the Syrian. 4,175 words.
1920	December 1	188. ANNUS IAM PLENUS: On children of central Europe. 1,050 words.
1921	January 6	189. SACRA PROPEDIEM: On the Third Order of St. Francis. 2,400 words.
1921	April 30	190. IN PRAECLARA SUMMORUM: To professors and students of fine arts in Catholic institutions of learning: on Dante. 2,400 words.
1921	June 29	191. FAUSTO APPETENTE DIE: On St. Dominic. 2,425 words.

PIUS XI (ACHILLE RATTI): POPE, 1922-1939

1922	December 23	192. UBI ARCANO DEI CONSILIO: On the peace of Christ in the Kingdom of Christ. 8,000 words.
1923	January 26	193. RERUM OMNIUM PERTURBATIONEM: On St. Francis de Sales. 4,100 words.
1923	June 29	194. STUDIORUM DUCEM: On St. Thomas Aquinas. 5,100 words.
1923	November 12	195. ECCLESIAM DEI: On St. Josophat. 2,700 words.
1924	January 18	196. MAXIMAM GRAVISSIMAMQUE: To the bishops, clergy, and people of France: on French diocesan associations. 1,500 words.
1925	December 11	197. QUAS PRIMAS: On the feast of Christ the King. 5,100 words.
1926	February 28	198. RERUM ECCLESIAE: On Catholic missions. 5,300 words.
1926	April 30	199. RITE EXPIATIS: On St. Francis of Assisi. 6,400 words.
1926	November 18	200. INIQUIS AFFLICTISQUE: On the persecution of the Church in Mexico. 3,600 words.
1928	January 6	201. MORTALIUM ANIMOS: On religious unity. 3,300 words.
1928	May 8	202. MISERENTISSIMUS REDEMPTOR: On reparation to the Sacred Heart. 3,900 words.
1928	September 8	203. RERUM ORIENTALIUM: On the promotion of Oriental studies. 3,400 words.
1929	December 20	204. MENS NOSTRA: On the promotion of the Spiritual Exercises. 5,100 words.

1929	December 23	205. QUINQUAGESIMO ANTE: On his sacerdotal jubilee. 4,700 words.
1929	December 31	206. RAPPRESENTANTI IN TERRA: On Christian education. 11,700 words.
1930	April 30	207. AD SALUTEM: On St. Augustine. 9,900 words.
1930	December 31	208. CASTI CONNUBII: On Christian marriage. 15,800 words.
1931	May 15	209. QUADRAGESIMO ANNO: Commemorating the fortieth anniversary of Leo XIII's *Rerum novarum*: on reconstruction of the social order. 14,000 words.
1931	June 29	210. NON ABBIAMO BISOGNO: On Catholic Action in Italy. 8,100 words.
1931	October 2	211. NOVA IMPENDET: On the economic crisis. 1,200 words.
1931	December 25	212. LUX VERITATIS: On the Council of Ephesus. 7,100 words.
1932	May 3	213. CARITATE CHRISTI COMPULSI: On the Sacred Heart. 4,900 words.
1932	September 29	214. ACERBA ANIMI: To the bishops of Mexico: on persecution of the Church in Mexico. 3,250 words.
1933	June 3	215. DILECTISSIMA NOBIS: To the bishops, clergy, and people of Spain: on oppression of the Church in Spain. 3,800 words.
1935	December 20	216. AD CATHOLICI SACERDOTII: On the Catholic priesthood. 12,000 words.
1936	June 29	217. VIGILANTI CURA: To the bishops of the United States: on motion pictures. 4,200 words.
1937	March 14	218. MIT BRENNENDER SORGE: To the bishops of Germany: on the Church and the German Reich. 6,600 words.
1937	March 19	219. DIVINI REDEMPTORIS: On atheistic communism. 6,300 words.
1937	March 28	220. NOS ES MUY CONOCIDA: To the bishops of Mexico: on the religious situation in Mexico. 4,000 words.
1937	September 29	221. INGRAVESCENTIBUS MALIS: On the rosary. 2,000 words.

PIUS XII (EUGENIO PACELLI): POPE, 1939-1958

1939	October 20	222. SUMMI PONTIFICATUS: On the unity of human society. 10,500 words.
1939	November 1	223. SERTUM LAETITIAE: To the bishops of the United States: on the one hundred and fiftieth anniversary of the establishment of the hierarchy in the United States. 3,600 words.
1940	June 13	224. SAECULO EXEUNTE OCTAVO: To the bishops of Portugal and its colonies: on the eighth centenary of the independence of Portugal. 4,100 words.
1943	June 29	225. MYSTICI CORPORIS CHRISTI: On the Mystical Body of Christ. 14,500 words.
1943	September 30	226. DIVINO AFFLANTE SPIRITU: On promoting biblical studies, commemorating the fiftieth anniversary of *Providentissimus Deus*. 7,600 words.
1944	April 9	227. ORIENTALIS ECCLESIAE: On St. Cyril, Patriarch of Alexandria. 3,750 words.
1945	April 15	228. COMMUNIUM INTERPRETES DOLORUM: To the bishops of the world: appealing for prayers for peace during May. 750 words.

1945	December 23	229. ORIENTALES OMNES ECCLESIAS: On the three hundred and fiftieth anniversary of the reunion of the Ruthenian Church with the Apostolic See. 8,000 words.
1946	January 6	230. QUEMADMODUM: Pleading for the care of the world's destitute children. 1,350 words.
1946	May 1	231. DEIPARAE VIRGINIS MARIAE: To all bishops: on the possibility of defining the Assumption of the Blessed Virgin Mary as a dogma of faith. 375 words.
1947	March 21	232. FULGENS RADIATUR: On St. Benedict. 4,500 words.
1947	November 20	233. MEDIATOR DEI: On the sacred liturgy. 21,000 words.
1947	December 18	234. OPTATISSIMA PAX: Prescribing public prayers for social and world peace. 750 words.
1948	May 1	235. AUSPICIA QUAEDAM: On public prayers for world peace and solution of the problem of Palestine. 1,000 words.
1948	October 24	236. IN MULTIPLICIBUS CURIS: On prayers for peace in Palestine. 900 words.
1949	April 15	237. REDEMPTORIS NOSTRI CRUCIATUS: On the holy places in Palestine. 850 words.
1950	March 12	238. ANNI SACRI: On the program for combatting atheistic propaganda throughout the world. 1,100 words.
1950	July 19	239. SUMMI MAERORIS: On public prayers for peace. 900 words.
1950	August 12	240. HUMANI GENERIS: Concerning some false opinions threatening to undermine the foundations of Catholic doctrine. 4,250 words.
1950	December 6	241. MIRABILE ILLUD: On the crusade of prayer for peace. 800 words.
1951	June 2	242. EVANGELII PRAECONES: On the promotion of Catholic missions. 7,800 words.
1951	September 8	243. SEMPITERNUS REX CHRISTUS: On the Council of Chalcedon. 4,650 words.
1951	September 15	244. INGRUENTIUM MALORUM: On reciting the rosary. 1,300 words.
1952	December 15	245. ORIENTALES ECCLESIAS: On the persecuted Eastern Church. 2,400 words.
1953	May 24	246. DOCTOR MELLIFLUUS: On St. Bernard of Clairvaux, the last of the fathers. 3,750 words.
1953	September 8	247. FULGENS CORONA: Proclaiming a Marian Year to commemorate the centenary of the definition of the dogma of the Immaculate Conception. 3,700 words.
1954	March 25	248. SACRA VIRGINITAS: On consecrated virginity. 7,500 words.
1954	June 5	249. ECCLESIAE FASTOS: To the bishops of Great Britain, Germany, Austria, France, Belgium, and Holland: on St. Boniface. 4,800 words.
1954	October 7	250. AD SINARUM GENTEM: To the bishops, clergy, and people of China: on the supranationality of the Church. 2,200 words.
1954	October 11	251. AD CAELI REGINAM: Proclaiming the Queenship of Mary. 2,250 words.

1955 December 25 — 252. MUSICAE SACRAE: On sacred music. 7,400 words.

1956 May 15 — 253. HAURIETIS AQUAS: On devotion to the Sacred Heart. 11,000 words.

1956 October 28 — 254. LUCTUOSISSIMI EVENTUS: Urging public prayers for peace and freedom for the people of Hungary. 500 words.

1956 November 1 — 255. LAETAMUR ADMODUM: Renewing exhortation for prayers for peace for Poland, Hungary, and especially for the Middle East. 600 words.

1956 November 5 — 256. DATIS NUPERRIME: Lamenting the sorrowful events in Hungary and condemning the ruthless use of force. 350 words.

1957 April 21 — 257. FIDEI DONUM: On the present condition of the Catholic missions, especially in Africa. 6,000 words.

1957 May 16 — 258. INVICTI ATHLETAE: On St. Andrew Bobola. 2,300 words.

1957 July 2 — 259. LE PELERINAGE DE LOURDES: Warning against materialism on the centenary of the apparitions at Lourdes. 3,500 words.

1957 September 8 — 260. MIRANDA PRORSUS: On the communications field: motion picture, radio, television. 10,000 words.

1958 June 29 — 261. AD APOSTOLORUM PRINCIPIS: To the bishops of China: on Communism and the Church in China. 3,375 words.

1958 July 14 — 262. MEMINISSE IUVAT: On prayers for persecuted Church. 2,500 words.

JOHN XXIII (ANGELO GIUSEPPE RONCALLI): POPE, 1958-1963

1959 June 29 — 263. AD PETRI CATHEDRAM: On truth, unity, and peace, in a spirit of charity. 8,550 words.

1959 August 1 — 264. SACERDOTII NOSTRI PRIMORDIA: On St. John Vianney. 8,574 words.

1959 September 26 — 265. GRATA RECORDATIO: On the rosary: prayer for the Church, missions, international and social problems. 1,250 words.

1959 November 28 — 266. PRINCEPS PASTORUM: On the missions, native clergy, lay participation. 7,800 words.

1961 May 15 — 267. MATER ET MAGISTRA: On Christianity and social progress. 15,300 words.

1961 November 11 — 268. AETERNA DEI SAPIENTIA: On the fifteenth centennial of the death of Pope St. Leo I: the See of Peter as the center of Christian unity. 4,450 words.

1962 July 1 — 269. PAENITENTIAM AGERE: On the need for the practice of interior and exterior penance. 2,580 words.

1963 April 11 — 270. PACEM IN TERRIS: On establishing universal peace in truth, justice, charity, and liberty. 15,800 words.

PAUL VI (GIOVANNI BATTISTA MONTINI): POPE, 1963-1978

1964 August 6 — 271. ECCLESIAM SUAM: On the Church. 13,400 words.

1965 April 29 — 272. MENSE MAIO: On prayers during May for the preservation of peace. 1,234 words.

1965	September 3	273. MYSTERIUM FIDEI: On the Holy Eucharist. 5,250 words.
1966	September 15	274. CHRISTI MATRI: On prayers for peace during October. 1,090 words.
1967	May 26	275. POPULORUM PROGRESSIO: On the development of peoples. 10,500 words.
1967	June 24	276. SACERDOTALIS CAELIBATUS: On the celibacy of the priest. 9,950 words.
1968	July 25	277. HUMANAE VITAE: On the regulation of birth. 5,500 words.

JOHN PAUL I (ALBINO LUCIANI): POPE, 1978

JOHN PAUL II (KAROL WOJTYLA): POPE, 1978-

1979	March 4	278. REDEMPTOR HOMINIS: On redemption and the dignity of the human race. 16,844.
1980	November 30	279. DIVES IN MISERICORDIA: On the mercy of God. 16,372 words.
1981	September 14	280. LABOREM EXERCENS: On human work. 17,000 (est.) words.

POPE BENEDICT XIV
1740-1758

On August 17, 1740 in the midst of the intense heat of the Roman summer, the longest conclave of the century on its 255th ballot elected Prospero Lambertini pope. Significantly, as Ludwig von Pastor points out in his *History of the Popes from the Close of the Middle Ages*, Lambertini himself departing from the tradition of the conclave gave his vote "not to the Cardinal Deacon, but to the candidate, Aldrovandi, who had been the centre of so much contention." Lambertini took the name of Benedict XIV, in honor of the pope to whom he owed his promotion, and began a pontificate of eighteen years, the most illustrious of the century.

Prospero Lorenzo Lambertini was born in Bologna on March 31, 1675 of a noble Bolognese family. He received his early education from private tutors but at the age of thirteen (1688) was sent to the Collegium Clementinum in Rome. Here he studied for four years concentrating on law and theology but also making himself thoroughly familiar with the Fathers of the Church, the decrees of the Councils, and the pronouncements of the popes. In 1694 he received a doctorate in law and theology from the University of Rome.

He began his public career as an assistant to an auditor of the Rota, held the office of consistorial advocate (1701), *promotor fidei* (1708), and assessor at the Congregation of Rites (1712). In 1718 he became secretary of the Congregation of the Council. Named titular bishop of Theodosia in 1725, he was appointed to the archbishopric of Ancona in 1727. Created a cardinal in 1728 (reserved *in petto* from December 9, 1726), he was transferred to the see of Bologna (1731) and elected to the papacy in 1740.

Benedict XIV's previous experience had admirably prepared him for the task he now assumed. He was a man of broad theological, legal, and medical learning, experienced in church government and administration, endowed with an irresistible sense of humor but with it all a man of decisive action primarily concerned with the truth. Not satisfied with mere condemnation of error he began in the first years of his pontificate to issue encyclical letters in order to apply the doctrine of the Church to the problems of his age, fully aware of the need to integrate the divergent cultures of scientific and religious thought.

Although referred to as a "scholar's pope" he evidenced his deep pastoral concerns by his example and many instructions. Shortly after assuming office he established a congregation to select worthy bishops, reminded ordinaries of their duties, emphasized the importance of the formation of priests, improved living conditions in the papal States, and restored major and minor churches. He was beloved by many although some historians have judged that he adapted himself too much to the spirit of the age. It is a fact that in matters unconcerned with dogma he was extremely conciliatory. This is evident in his handling of the negotiations with the monarchs of Europe, the crisis between the French bishops and the Parlement, the difficult question of mixed marriages, and the legislation relating to the *Index*.

His *De servorum Dei beatificatione et beatorum canonizatione* (1734-38) grew out of his practical experience as promoter of the faith and is still the classic reference on beatifications and canonizations. His extensive work on diocesan synods, *De synodo dioecesana*, was based on his experience in Ancona and Bologna. He carried on a correspondence with scholars throughout the world. His letters, of which more than 760 are extant, reveal a remarkable man: brilliant and devout, courageous and forthright, a man who had concern for "hearts as well as heads."

To encourage historical studies he founded a number of academies in Rome, enlarged the Vatican Library, and initiated the compilation of a detailed catalogue of its manuscripts. He gave his wholehearted approval for the appointment of two women as professors at the University of Bologna, and established chairs of chemistry, mathematics, and experimental physics at the Sapienza.

A few weeks before his death (May 3, 1758) he appointed Cardinal Saldanha to investigate the charges made against the Jesuits in Portugal. Saldanha did not receive the brief until after Benedict's death. Nevertheless, exceeding the powers conveyed to him, he pronounced judgment on the Jesuits before the elevation of Benedict's successor thus leaving a major problem for the latter.

UBI PRIMUM

ENCYCLICAL OF POPE BENEDICT XIV
ON THE DUTIES OF BISHOPS
DECEMBER 3, 1740

1

To Our Venerable Brothers, the Patriarchs, the Primates, the Archbishops, and the Bishops.

Venerable Brothers, Greetings and Apostolic Benediction.

When it first pleased God to raise Us to the supreme See of Saint Peter, He entrusted to Us the power of the Vicar of Christ as governor of His universal Church. We heard the divine voice: "Feed my lambs; feed my sheep." The care of both the lambs of the Lord's flock (who are the people scattered through the entire world) and of the sheep, (the bishops who act as tender parents of the lambs) is entrusted to the pope. Therefore, brothers, receive the words of your shepherd through this letter. You are called to share in Our concerns. Understand from Our warnings and exhortations how much the desire to fulfill Our duties presses upon Us. Keep in mind also the strength of Our love for you, which leads Us to earnestly desire the eternal joy of the shepherds which comes from the progress of the flock.

Importance of Clergy

Above all, see to it that the clergy excel in character and in zeal for divine worship and that ecclesiastical discipline is kept in good condition or restored where it has suffered. The example of dedicated clerics is the best inspiration for the faithful. Therefore, direct the keenness of your mind so that those men are chosen for the clergy from whom it can reasonably be expected that their lives will command respect from all who walk in the law of the Lord and who go from virtue to virtue. Their work will bring spiritual benefit to your churches. It is better to have a few ministers who are upright and effective, than many who labor in vain to build up the Church. You are aware of how much caution the holy canons require the bishops to exercise in this matter. Do not allow yourselves to be led away from this rule, which should be observed in its entirety, by any human consideration or by the requests of patrons. Observe the precept of the Apostle not to conduct the laying on of hands too hastily—especially when it concerns the promotion to the sacred mysteries and Holy Orders. Attaining the age which the holy laws of the Church have prescribed for each order is not sufficient. Neither should everyone who is now in lower orders be indiscriminately promoted to a higher order, as if it is his right. You should diligently investigate whether the way of life of those in lower orders and their progress in sacred learning are such that it may be said to them: "Rise to a higher place." It is more expedient for some to remain in an inferior position, rather than be promoted to a higher one, which would bring danger to them and scandal to others.

Seminaries

2. Because this matter concerns those who are called to the Lord's portion, you should take care to educate them to piety, integrity of life, and to the canonical discipline from an early age. Where there are still no seminaries, they should be established as soon as possible. Where seminaries exist already, they should be enlarged if it is necessary due to the increased number of students. The bishops have already been instructed in the means to use to that end. We shall add other things to these instructions if We learn of their necessity from you. You should cherish these colleges with special concern by visiting them often, by studying the life, talent, and progress in studies of each of the young men, and by appointing suitable teachers and men endowed with an ecclesiastical spirit. Honor their literary exercises and their ecclesiastical functions with your presence occasionally. Finally, confer some benefice on those who are outstanding examples of virtue or who win the greatest honors. It should not grieve you to water these tender shoots in this manner as they mature. Your work will then bring you a happy harvest in an abundance of good laborers. Bishops usually complain that the harvest is indeed great, but the laborers are few. Perhaps it also ought to be lamented that the bishops did not expend the necessary efforts in order to prepare enough good laborers for the harvest. Good and strong laborers are not born, but made. But the making of them is a matter for the work and the skill of the bishops.

Selecting Clerics

3. It is of the utmost importance that you entrust the care of souls to exemplary men who are conspicuous for their doctrine, piety, purity, and good works. They should truly be and should be considered the light and the salt of the people. These men are your principal aides in forming the flock entrusted to your care, governing it, purifying it, leading it in the path of salvation, and rousing it to Christian virtue. You should choose as parish priests men who may be judged suited to the fruitful governing of people. Concentrate on this matter above everything else, so that all those who exercise the care of souls may nourish the people entrusted to them with salutary words at least on Sundays and other feast days. They should teach those things which the faithful must know for their salvation and explain the main principles of divine law and Catholic dogma. They should also teach the children the basics of that same faith once they have completely removed any wicked habits contrary to it. How can the people hear if there is no one to preach to them? How can they know the faith and lead holy lives if the men who have the care of their souls are sluggish, idle, or remiss? It is impossible to overstate the tremendous threat to the Christian community which arises when those who have care of men's souls neglect the training of the young, especially their catechetical instruction. Those who exercise this office and others who hear confessions would benefit greatly if you could see to it that they have a few days rest each year for spiritual exercise. They will be spiritually renewed by such a retreat and strengthened from on high. They will return to their tasks quickened and eager to work for the glory of God and the salvation of souls.

Necessity of Residency

4. You know, brothers, that the divine precept commands all pastors to know their sheep and to nourish them by preaching, by the administration of the sacraments, and by the example of every good work. Those priests are by no means able to fulfill these or the other duties of the pastoral office who neither look after their flock nor assiduously guard the Lord's vineyard, over which they have been placed as watchmen. Therefore, you should remain at your post and maintain your personal residence in the church or diocese to which you have been bound by the duty of your office. The many decrees of the general councils and the constitutions of Our predecessors clearly commanded this.

Do not consider it appropriate for a bishop to be absent from his diocese for any reason for a period of three months each year. For this to be permitted to bishops, it is necessary that there be a compelling reason requiring such an absence. At the same time, it should be determined that no harm would come to the flock in the interim. Remember that He who sees and knows everything will be your judge. Therefore, see to it that your reason is truly one which can be judged worthy by the Prince of the shepherds who will demand an account of the sheep entrusted to you. Certainly a shepherd would try in vain to protect himself in that judgment with the excuse that the wolf captured and devoured the sheep while he was away and unaware. If we consider the matter carefully, it is apparent that the evil which besets a diocese abandoned by its bishop can be attributed to him whose duty it is to recall his subjects who stray from the right path with warnings, to entice them with examples, to strengthen them by word, and to keep them together by his authority and love. In addition, everyone understands that it is much better for others to take care of business elsewhere than for the bishop himself, tarrying outside his diocese, to do so. The bishop, and not administrators, should take care of the protecting and the governing of the flock. As suitable and upright as the priests may be, nevertheless the sheep are not accustomed to hearing the voice of the priests as the voice of the true shepherd. Nor can their vicarious work substitute for the vigilance and the work of the bishop, to whom the special grace of the Holy Spirit gives assistance for this matter, as experience clearly shows.

Visitation

5. As in every domestic matter, there is nothing more beneficial than for the head of the family to examine everything frequently and nourish the labor and diligence of his family with his own vigilance. We therefore enjoin upon you the obligation of visiting your churches and dioceses yourselves (unless a serious matter arises which requires you to entrust this duty to others) in order to acquaint yourselves with your sheep and with the appearence of your flock. That sentence which we recalled above is full of fear and terror: namely that no excuse is allowed to the shepherd if the wolf devours the sheep and the shepherd does not know it. The bishop will be unaware of many things and many things will be hidden from him if he does not visit every part of his diocese himself and if he does not look, listen, and examine everywhere for which evils a remedy may be prepared. He should probe the causes of those evils and then take preventive measures lest they come to life again. The condition of human weakness is such that thorn bushes, prickles, and weeds grow gradually in the Lord's field, the cultivation of which is entrusted to the bishop. If the gardener does not return frequently to pluck them out, his seedlings will wither with the passage of time.

But neither is it sufficient that you examine your dioceses and that there is provision for the administration of the dioceses by your precepts. It remains that you put into effect those things which were decided during your visitations. For even the best laws are worthless unless that which is sanctioned in words is actually executed by those to whom this task falls. Therefore, after you have prepared remedies to cast out or prevent diseases of the soul, do not relax your concern. Rather, promote with all your strength the execution of the precepts you decreed. You can achieve this best through repeated visitations.

Exhortation

6. Finally, to cover many matters in a few words, it is fitting that you yourselves be the promoters, the leaders, and the teachers in every sacred and ecclesiastical function and in every exercise of divine worship and of piety. Thus, both the clergy and the whole flock may be enlightened, as if by the brightness of your holiness and may be warmed by the fire of your love. Therefore, be an example for your flock in the frequent celebration of the Mass, in devout offering, in solemn celebration of Masses, in administering the sacraments, in reciting the breviary, in respect for and in the splendor of the churches in the discipline of your household and of your spiritual family, in love for the poor and in helping them, in looking after the sick and supporting them, in welcoming pilgrims with hospitality, and finally in every good work of Christian virtue. Thus, all may be imitators of you just as you are imitators of Christ as is fitting for bishops whom the Holy Spirit placed in charge of the Church of God which Jesus redeemed by His blood. Look back often on the apostles to whose place you have succeeded. Follow in their footsteps in works, in vigilance, in bearing hardship, in keeping the wolves away from your sheep, in removing the roots of vices, in teaching the evangelical law, and in leading back to salutary penance those who have strayed.

The omnipotent and merciful God will surely be with you. In that comforter, we can do everything. We trust that religious princes will give you their help. In addition, this Holy See will assist you whenever you think Our Apostolic authority will be helpful. May all of you whom

We love in Christ Jesus come to Us with confidence as Our brothers, Our helpers, and Our crown of glory. Come to the Holy Roman Church, your mother and the head and teacher of all the churches. The source of religion comes from her. The rock of faith and the fount of priestly unity resides here, as well as the teaching of uncorrupted truth. We desire nothing more and find nothing more pleasant than to serve the glory of God with you and to work for the protection and the propagation of the Catholic faith. We want to save souls for whom We would willingly offer Our lives if necessary. Finally, may the great reward which waits for you rouse you and spur you on. When the Prince of Shepherds appears, you will receive an unfading crown of glory and a crown of justice which is reserved for those faithful dispensers of the mysteries of God and for those energetic and vigilant observers of the house of Israel, the Holy Church of God. Though unworthy, We take the place of God on earth; accordingly, We bless your brotherhood lovingly. We impart Our apostolic blessing to your clergy and faithful people with paternal affection.

Given in Rome, at St. Mary Major, on the third day of December, 1740, the first year of Our pontificate.

†

LATIN TEXT: *Bened. XIV Bull.*, 1: 3-6, omits #5-7 in numbering of paragraphs; *Magnum Bull.*, 16:3-5.

ENGLISH TRANSLATION: Norman Desmarais.

QUANTA CURA

ENCYCLICAL OF POPE BENEDICT XIV
FORBIDDING TRAFFIC IN ALMS
JUNE 30, 1741
2

To the Venerable Brothers, the Primates, the Metropolitans, the Archbishops, and all the Bishops who are in Communion with the Holy See.

Venerable Brothers, Greetings and Apostolic Benediction.

There is no Catholic who does not know the care required to ensure that the Holy Sacrifice of the Mass is not only celebrated with due reverence and veneration, but also that all semblance of payment of any kind is removed from the dignity of such a sacrifice: both the base demand—rather than request—for alms and other similar practices which are not far removed from the sin of simony or at least from dishonest profit.

It is true that the avarice—which is the bondage of idolatry—of many clerics and laymen has already progressed to the point that they collect alms or stipends for the celebration of the Mass. These have been prescribed by local customs or sanctions of the diocesan synods for the maintenance of the priests. They then take this money and have the Mass celebrated elsewhere, where the alms or stipends given for each Mass are lower than would be given there where the fee was received.

2. Everyone clearly understands how foreign this is to the expressed or silent desire of those who give alms piously. Nor is it to be judged otherwise. Everyone desires that the Masses be celebrated in the church upon which he bestowed alms or in which he is buried, rather than in another church, which may be unfamiliar to him. Such frustration of the intentions of the faithful is motivated by the desire for base profit, just as is the case in the conduct of trade. Accordingly, it is not immune to the suspicion of avarice and vice, even of theft, whence it may be subject to restitution. Thus many good people, gravely offended by the news of such business, abstain from offering more alms for the celebration of Masses.

3. The Roman Pontiffs, Our predecessors, detested this lethal abuse which gradually insinuated itself. For this reason they wanted a decree both from the Congregation of the Cardinals of the Universal Inquisition of the Holy Roman Church and from the Congregation of the Cardinals Interpreters of the Council of Trent against the heretical depravity. This decree stated that if a priest received a stipend or alms of a certain value for the celebration of the Mass, a lesser fee must not be paid to another priest for celebrating such a Mass. This holds even if the first priest were to inform the second that he had received a stipend or alms of greater value, and

the second priest were willing to accept the lower fee.

4. For this reason, Venerable Brothers, We ask and exhort you who share Our concerns and are associated with Us in the apostolic ministry to keep watch over your flocks. Exert yourselves so that this disease may spread no further, but rather may be entirely eradicated. Avarice is the root of all evil. Some people who chased after it have strayed from the faith and have brought upon themselves many sorrows. There is no greater pestilence than avarice, which corrupts the opinion of priestly dignity and perfection and casts it out. Avarice, which teaches people to esteem God less than riches and to serve Mammon, causes the greedy to lose their inheritance in the kingdom of Christ and of God. If this can hardly be tolerated among laymen and should be restrained by law, what about churchmen who have sent forth this message in earthly matters, who have been called to share the work of the Lord, and who have delivered themselves up to the Lord? What about those who, with contempt for holy laws and with disdain for the priestly character, are led astray into avarice, not through worldly profits, but through the ministry of the altar? Strive therefore, Venerable Brothers, to whom the care of Christ's flock is entrusted, not only to shine forth in word and example so that you may be an ambassador of Christ in every place and the people may follow in your footsteps, but also to teach both the clergy and the laity to shun pastures poisoned with vice and to run to the heavenly fold.

5. Since by the fear of present punishment there may be readier compliance with salutary warnings, make the following pronouncement known in all your dioceses. If anyone collects alms or stipends for the celebration of the Mass at the level which the customs of the place or synodical statutes demand and keeps part of this fee for himself, causing the Mass to be celebrated either there or elsewhere where lower fees are paid for celebrating Masses, he will be punished. A lay person who does this will automatically incur the penalty of excommunication in addition to the other penalties which you might invoke according to your decision. The cleric will automatically incur the penalty of suspension, from which no one can absolve except Ourselves or the Roman Pontiff ruling at the time, unless there is danger of death. We trust in the Lord that each one, mindful of his condition, will not belittle such salutary laws and ecclesiastical censures. Meanwhile, We lovingly impart Our apostolic blessing on your brotherhood and on the people entrusted to your care.

6. We also wish that the same confidence be placed in copies of this letter—even printed ones—which are signed by a notary public and guaranteed by the seal of an ecclesiastical official, as would be placed in the original letter if it were displayed or shown.

Given in Rome at St. Mary Major under the ring of the fisherman on the thirtieth day of June in the year 1741, the first year of Our pontificate.

†

LATIN TEXT: *Bened. XIV Bull.*, 1: 77-78; *Magnum Bull.*, 16: 35-36.

ENGLISH TRANSLATION: Norman Desmarais.

NIMIAM LICENTIAM

ENCYCLICAL OF POPE BENEDICT XIV ON
VALIDITY OF MARRIAGES
MAY 18, 1743
3

To the Venerable Brothers, Archbishops and Bishops of the Kingdom of Poland.

Venerable Brothers, Greetings and Apostolic Blessing.

We deplore the abuse by which Christian marriages, even long-stable ones, are now dissolved in the Ecclesiastical Courts of Poland. This abuse involves dissolution without due cause or in violation of canon law, and threatens grave injury to the faithful. We warned about this in Our Brief of April 11, 1741, and We exhorted you in the name of the Lord to watch over the flock entrusted to your care. We also warned that We were considering measures of redress and a suitable opportunity to pursue this matter.

Hidden Marriages

Meanwhile We had learned that an evil custom of hidden marriages, more popularly known as marriages of joint knowledge, has spread throughout much of the Christian world. Among the resulting irregularities is that hidden marriages of this sort were themselves being dissolved where other marriages were publicly celebrated. In another encyclical letter to the Venerable Brothers, Patriarchs, Primates, and all Bishops on August 26 of the same year, We prescribed that the aforementioned evil custom must be abrogated and the provisions of the sacred canons and the decrees of the Council of Trent must be accurately observed.

Rules for Valid Marriages

2. Besides all this, in Our well-known letter of November 3, 1741, We enjoined laws and rules concerning the validity and nullity of marriages. Therefore ecclesiastical judges, carried away neither by fault or dishonesty nor by inexperience or ignorance, can safely pass sentence on the validity or nullity of marriages, using justice rather than their own inclinations.

Selection of Good Judges

3. Moreover it was alleged and objected that this sort of evil arose because such cases were handled by unqualified judges. In another encyclical addressed to all the bishops, We therefore enjoined and commanded that each one, together with the council of the Cathedral church, make a list of suitable judges and send it to the Apostolic See. Also Our letter of November 3, 1741 took pains to add that in appropriate circumstances attention should be turned to the authority of nearby bishops; if it should happen that this is not possible, only then

should another proficient and suitable judge be selected.

New Abuses

4. We were thus confident that these abuses and all irregularities everywhere would with God's blessing be completely abolished; however, We learned with sorrow that new deceptions and subterfuges had been found there by which these saving ordinances could be eluded. The soul shudders to repeat the agreements which the litigants now reached. For instance one of them, after the ecclesiastical judge had nullified the marriage, dared to appeal and was held for the payment of a sum of money to the other (who acquiesced in the opinion). The soul also shudders because the judge instructed the appellant to make all kinds of payment.

Improper Customs in Poland

5. Having thoroughly investigated these matters, We have concluded that the irregularity and confusion in Poland arise for the most part from the manner and custom by which marriages are conducted there. Very often indeed the proper pastor is not even present for the marriage ceremony because the duty to witness the marriage has been delegated to a randomly-selected priest, even without the knowledge of the proper pastor. The banns announcing a couple's intent to marry must appear on three feast days during a solemn mass in the parish church of both. But these are often dispensed with, even though there is no legitimate and urgent reason to do so.

6. Therefore all avenues are closed by which one could determine whether a marriage is contracted with the necessary liberty and consent; when any such impediment exists between the contracting parties, the marriage must be dissolved and declared void. So the conditions are set for annulling marriages, even those consecrated in the Church. At times it is argued that the marriage was entered upon by force or by fear, in either case without the free consent of one or the other of the contracting parties; at other times a legitimate and canonical impediment is alleged, which could have been known before the marriage was contracted if it had not been purposefully concealed; also at times, and this happens more frequently, a marriage is annulled because it was contracted before another priest, even with the consent of the parish priest or of the ordinary bishop but without the necessary and usual formalities. Certainly it is clear that these dissolutions of marriages in Poland are a source of evil and an open door to crime. Furthermore the canonical benefit of appeal, which one of the spouses can enjoy after the case is decided in favor of the other, is impeded by these frauds and subterfuges. Finally these frequent marriage dissolutions are not without the gravest offense and scandal to the upright.

Annulment and Excommunication

7. To remedy this pernicious evil, We, with certain knowledge and after mature deliberation, declare all pacts between spouses for the dissolution of marriages to be null, invalid, and ineffectual, both now and for the future. We also annul those pacts which interfere with the appeals process, even if the pacts were approved by oath, and even if they were agreed upon before the publication of our most recent letter. So that no such pact may ever be considered valid and obligatory, We inflict the penalty of excommunication on anyone entering into a pact, from which no one can obtain absolution except through Us and Our successors, except at the hour of death. Besides We declare that any judge who may have dared to announce and further the pacts We mentioned before also incurs or will incur the same penalty of excommunication. We again confirm whatever is contained in the aforementioned last letter or in our Constitution, and especially all that concerns the procedure and order of the appeals from the unsuccessful defender of the marriage, and the sentence of the judge against the annulment. We bid your Brotherhood again to publish and disseminate the same letter and command that this be done as though it had been expressly inserted word for word in the present letter, just as We desire its tenor to be expressed and inserted in this present letter.

Advice to Clergy

8. What We have said on the subject of matrimony up to this point sufficiently informs the faithful of the sanctity of marriage. They may now approach this great sacrament with that reverence and piety which is fitting, and regard it as indissoluble. Nevertheless We feel that We must also set forth to you the distinguished and

salutary rules of other well-organized dioceses where lawsuits concerning marriages and their annulment are rare.

9. The pastor is obliged to witness in person the marriages celebrated in his parish unless a legitimate and grave reason prevents him.

Nuptial Banns

10. Before the publication of the banns, the pastor himself must take care to question both groom and bride separately to determine whether they consent voluntarily and freely to marry. He must also strive to determine whether there is any impediment and, if so, what the nature of the impediment is; whether one of the contracting parties has been engaged and given a solemn promise to another, and whether the sons and daughters contract with the consent of the parents. After the pastors have diligently explored these and other relevant matters, if they find anything in these questionings either lacking or potentially harmful, they must suspend the banns and refer the possible obstacles to their own bishop, who will judge the matter.

11. Now if the parish priests find nothing to prevent the banns from being announced publicly and according to custom, then the banns are published on three successive feast days during the mass. This follows the prescriptions of the Lateran Council under Pope Innocent III and those of the Council of Trent, so that any impediment heretofore unknown may be revealed by those who hear the banns.

Pastor as Witness

12. Bishops watching vigilantly over their sheep know that matrimony is valid before any priest, not just the parish priest, if the proper pastor or the ordinary of the place has granted the necessary permission. The bishops can also dispense with the banns, or permit only one instead of three, or even none, to be read, if an urgent and legitimate reason exists. Nevertheless they should take diligent care that they do not use this authority indiscriminately, both in dispensing with the banns and in permitting any priest rather than the proper pastor to witness the marriage. Should necessity demand, they are not to grant this authority at once, but only after they are convinced that there is no impediment between the contracting parties.

Dispensations from the Banns

13. Concerning dispensations from the banns, the bishops clearly understand that theirs is not at all an unbridled and immoderate authority over this matter, but an authority for reasons of prudence to deal with legitimate occasions that may arise. This authority is to be used cautiously, so that in all cases they recall the words of the Council of Trent: "But if at times there is a proable suspicion that a matrimony might be wrongfully impeded if so many as three banns preceded, than let only one be made, or at least let the matrimony be celebrated before the presence of the pastor and two or three witnesses. Then before the marriage is consummated, let the banns be published in the church so that if there are any impediments, they may more easily be uncovered."

14. This kind of episcopal concern and diligence regarding matrimony removes almost all dissolutions of marriages; let us therefore follow this path. Direct your steps on to the age-old, well-trodden way, commended by the Council of Trent and established for all the bishops to follow. See to it that parish priests and other spiritual leaders, called in part to share your labors, expend similar diligence and integrity in exercising their ministry. Do not let an easy goodwill remove the juridical presence of the proper pastor, necessary for contracting marriage; likewise, do not grant another priest permission to witness a marriage for some trifling reason. The canonical laws concerning nuptial banns are to be scrupulously kept, since they can hardly be passed by without offending and scandalizing many. Keep them yourselves, and see to it that they are observed by other interested parties.

15. Do not abuse the easy dispensation of the banns without due cause. It has inflamed lawsuits and loathing, and cannot serve as a model for further action. A pernicious custom does not establish a norm for action, but serves as a reproach of evil deeds.

16. It is asserted that the hasty and extensive granting of these commissions and dispensations was due to the example and encouragement of the Ordinary of the Apostolic See in Poland, at the time Nuncio, who was excessively indulgent in this area. Whether truly or not, in virtue of the authority given him, he can grant these and other dispensation, We have restrained the authority of the present Polish Nuncio in this matter, so that your Brotherhood, with the example and encouragement abolished, may for the future abstain from these commissions and dispensations.

Remedies

17. Therefore, We want you to know that We intend to apply our authority to more efficacious and stringent remedies for curing these evils. Even after so many exhortations and prescriptions of Apostolic providence and authority, We did not succeed in abolishing the former litigation concerning marriage and separation. You certainly understand that We could justly and reasonably reserve the trials of matrimonial cases even in the first process. But We leave to the bishops the first and to the metropolitan the second process. We then decree that in Polish matrimonial trials the sentence concerning the nullity of a marriage, both in the first process by the bishops and in the second by the metropolitan, may not be executed unless both judgments with their arguments are first examined and approved by the Cardinals, who are the interpreters of the Council of Trent. Moreover any marriage contracted after both judgments have been delivered in your courts, whether or not the Cardinals are considering the matter, We declare to be null and void, both now and for the future.

18. This present letter and whatever it contains is to stand firm, valid and efficacious, and to obtain its plenary and full effect, is to be observed inviolate by all whom it concerns now and will concern.

19. Finally We desire that all the copies and imprints signed by the hand of any public notary and bearing the seal of a person of an ecclesiastical dignity, are to be given the same faith in the courts and outside of them which would be given to the present letter if it were presented or displayed.

20. For the rest, We beseech and exhort you to choose individual ministers and officials for your curias who are outstanding in all the Christian virtues, and commended by long experience. Vigorously enjoin on them that each one has many tasks to perform in his ministry. And you yourselves must maintain your vigilance. Remember the account to be rendered to the Prince of pastors Jesus Christ for the flock entrusted to your care, and remember the eternal reward in heaven promised to those who have fought lawfully. Meanwhile as a sign of your success, and of a richly deserved abundance of heavenly grace, We lovingly impart the Apostolic Blessing to your Brotherhood.

Given at Rome, at St. Mary Major, under the Ring of the Fisherman, on May 18, 1743, in the third year of our Pontificate.

†

LATIN TEXT: *Bened. XIV Bull.*, 1: 301-06; *Magnum Bull.*, 16: 160-63.

ENGLISH TRANSLATION: Bernard A. Hausmann, S. J.

VIX PERVENIT

ENCYCLICAL OF POPE BENEDICT XIV
ON USURY AND OTHER
DISHONEST PROFIT
NOVEMBER 1, 1745

4

To the Venerable Brothers, Patriarchs, Archbishops, Bishops and Ordinary Clergy of Italy.

Venerable Brothers, Greetings and Apostolic Benediction.

Hardly had the new controversy (namely, whether certain contracts should be held valid) come to our attention, when several opinions began spreading in Italy that hardly seemed to agree with sound doctrine; We decided that We must remedy this. If We did not do so immediately, such an evil might acquire new force by delay and silence. If we neglected our duty, it might even spread further, shaking those cities of Italy so far not affected.

Therefore We decided to consult with a number of the Cardinals of the Holy Roman Church, who are renowned for their knowledge and competence in theology and canon law. We also called upon many from the regular clergy who were outstanding in both the faculty of theology and that of canon law. We chose some monks, some mendicants, and finally some from the regular clergy. As presiding officer, We appointed one with degrees in both canon and civil law, who had lengthy court experience. We chose the past July 4 for the meeting at which We explained the nature of the whole business. We learned that all had known and considered it already.

2. We then ordered them to consider carefully all aspects of the matter, meanwhile searching for a solution; after this consideration, they were to write out their conclusions. We did not ask them to pass judgment on the contract which gave rise to the controversy since the many documents they would need were not available. Rather We asked that they establish a fixed teaching on usury, since the opinions recently spread abroad seemed to contradict the Church's doctrine. All complied with these orders. They gave their opinions publicly in two convocations, the first of which was held in our presence last July 18, the other last August 1; then they submitted their opinions in writing to the secretary of the convocation.

3. Indeed they proved to be of one mind in their opinions.

I. The nature of the sin called usury has its proper place and origin in a loan contract. This financial contract between consenting parties demands, by its very nature, that one return to another only as much as he has received. The sin rests on the fact that sometimes the creditor desires more than he has given. Therefore he contends some gain is owed him beyond that which he loaned, but any gain which exceeds the amount he gave is illicit and usurious.

II. One cannot condone the sin of usury by arguing that the gain is not great or excessive, but rather moderate or small; neither can it be condoned by arguing that the borrower is rich; nor even by arguing that the money borrowed is not left idle, but is spent usefully, either to increase one's fortune, to purchase new estates, or to engage in business transactions. The law governing loans consists necessarily in the equality of what is given and returned; once the equality has been established, whoever demands more than that violates the terms of the loan. Therefore if one receives interest, he must make restitution according to the commutative bond of justice; its function in human contracts is to assure equality for each one. This law is to be observed in a holy manner. If not observed exactly, reparation must be made.

III. By these remarks, however, We do not deny that at times together with the loan contract certain other titles—which are not at all intrinsic to the contract—may run parallel with it. From these other titles, entirely just and legitimate reasons arise to demand something over and above the amount due on the contract. Nor is it denied that it is very often possible for someone, by means of contracts differing entirely from loans, to spend and invest money legitimately either to provide oneself with an annual income or to engage in legitimate trade and business. From these types of contracts honest gain may be made.

IV. There are many different contracts of this kind. In these contracts, if equality is not maintained, whatever is received over and above what is fair is a real injustice. Even though it may not fall under the precise rubric of usury (since all reciprocity, both open and hidden, is absent), restitution is obligated. Thus if everything is done correctly and weighed in the scales of justice, these same legitimate contracts suffice to provide a standard and a principle for engaging in commerce and fruitful business for the common good. Christian minds should not think that gainful commerce can flourish by usuries or other similar injustices. On the contrary We learn from divine Revelation that *justice raises up nations; sin, however, makes nations miserable.*

V. But you must diligently consider this, that some will falsely and rashly persuade themselves—and such people can be found anywhere—that together with loan contracts there are other legitimate titles or, excepting loan contracts, they might convince themselves that other just contracts exist, for which it is permissible to receive a moderate amount of interest. Should any one think like this, he will oppose not only the judgment of the Catholic Church on usury, but also common human sense and natural reason. Everyone knows that man is obliged in many instances to help his fellows with a simple, plain loan. Christ Himself teaches this: "Do not refuse to lend to him who asks you." In many circumstances, no other true and just contract may be possible except for a loan. Whoever therefore wishes to follow his conscience must first diligently inquire if, along with the loan, another category exists by means of which the gain he seeks may be lawfully attained.

4. This is how the Cardinals and theologians and the men most conversant with the canons, whose advice We had asked for in this most serious business, explained their opinions. Also We devoted our private study to this matter before the congregations were convened, while they were in session, and again after they had been held; for We read the opinions of these outstanding men most diligently. Because of this, We approve and confirm whatever is contained in the opinions above, since the professors of Canon Law and Theology, scriptural evidence, the decrees of previous popes, and the authority of Church councils and the Fathers all seem to enjoin it. Besides, We certainly know the authors who hold the opposite opinions and also those who either support and defend those authors or at least who seem to give them consideration. We are also aware that the theologians of regions neighboring those in which the controversy had its origin undertook the defense of the truth with wisdom and seriousness.

5. Therefore We address these encyclical letters to all Italian Archbishops, Bishops, and priests to make all of you aware of these matters. Whenever Synods are held or sermons preached or instructions on sacred doctrine given, the above opinions must be adhered to strictly. Take great care that no one in your dioceses dares to write or preach the contrary; however if any one should refuse to obey, he should be subjected to the penalties imposed by the sacred canons on those who violate Apostolic mandates.

6. Concerning the specific contract which

caused these new controversies, We decide nothing for the present; We also shall not decide now about the other contracts in which the theologians and canonists lack agreement. Rekindle your zeal for piety and your conscientiousness so that you may execute what We have given.

7. First of all, show your people with persuasive words that the sin and vice of usury is most emphatically condemned in the Sacred Scriptures; that it assumes various forms and appearances in order that the faithful, restored to liberty and grace by the blood of Christ, may again be driven headlong into ruin. Therefore, if they desire to invest their money, let them exercise diligent care lest they be snatched by cupidity, the source of all evil; to this end, let them be guided by those who excel in doctrine and the glory of virtue.

8. In the second place, some trust in their own strength and knowledge to such an extent that they do not hesitate to give answers to those questions which demand considerable knowledge of sacred theology and of the canons. But it is essential for these people, also, to avoid extremes, which are always evil. For instance, there are some who judge these matters with such severity that they hold any profit derived from money to be illegal and usurious; in contrast to them, there are some so indulgent and so remiss that they hold any gain whatsoever to be free of usury. Let them not adhere too much to their private opinions. Before they give their answer, let them consult a number of eminent writers; then let them accept those views which they understand to be confirmed by knowledge and authority. And if a dispute should arise, when some contract is discussed, let no insults be hurled at those who hold the contrary opinion; nor let it be asserted that it must be severely censured, particularly if it does not lack the support of reason and of men of reputation. Indeed clamorous outcries and accusations break the chain of Christian love and give offense and scandal to the people.

9. In the third place, those who desire to keep themselves free and untouched by the contamination of usury and to give their money to another in such a manner that they may receive only legitimate gain should be admonished to make a contract beforehand. In the contract they should explain the conditions and what gain they expect from their money. This will not only greatly help to avoid concern and anxiety, but will also confirm the contract in the realm of public business. This approach also closes the door on controversies—which have arisen more than once—since it clarifies whether the money, which has been loaned without apparent interest, may actually contain concealed usury.

10. In the fourth place We exhort you not to listen to those who say that today the issue of usury is present in name only, since gain is almost always obtained from money given to another. How false is this opinion and how far removed from the truth! We can easily understand this if we consider that the nature of one contract differs from the nature of another. By the same token, the things which result from these contracts will differ in accordance with the varying nature of the contracts. Truly an obvious difference exists between gain which arises from money legally, and therefore can be upheld in the courts of both civil and canon law, and gain which is illicitly obtained, and must therefore be returned according to the judgments of both courts. Thus, it is clearly invalid to suggest, on the grounds that some gain is usually received from money lent out, that the issue of usury is irrelevant in our times.

11. These are the chief things We wanted to say to you. We hope that you may command your faithful to observe what these letters prescribe; and that you may undertake effective remedies if disturbances should be stirred up among your people because of this new controversy over usury or if the simplicity and purity of doctrine should become corrupted in Italy. Finally, to you and to the flock committed to your care, We impart the Apostolic Benediction.

Given in Rome at St. Mary Major, November 1, 1745, the sixth year of Our Pontificate.

†

LATIN TEXT: *Bened. XIV Bull.*, 1:591-94; *Magnum Bull.*, 16:328-29.

ENGLISH TRANSLATION: Bernard A. Hausmann, S. J.

COMMENTARIES:

Cafarra, C. "Ermeneutica della *Vix pervenit* di Benedetto XIV." *Atti del III Congresso Nazionale dei Moralisti [Padova, 1970]*, (Bologna, Ed. Dehoniane, 1970), p. 257-69.

Passage, Henri du. "Commentaire." *Actes Pontificaux*, no. 1 (Montréal, L'École Sociale Populaire, 1946), 9-10.

MAGNAE NOBIS

ENCYCLICAL OF POPE BENEDICT XIV ON MARRIAGE IMPEDIMENTS AND DISPENSATIONS

JUNE 29, 1748

5

To the Kingdom of Poland, to the Primate, Archbishops and Bishops.

Venerable Brothers, Greetings and Apostolic Benediction.

It was a painful surprise to learn from trustworthy reports and letters that a certain false opinion had spread in Poland. It is said that some matrimonial dispensations had been granted and sent out, indeed, that they are customarily granted and sent out, by this Apostolic See, in which the canonical impediments for a legitimate and valid marriage are removed, even though one or both of the contracting parties openly profess a heretical sect. Since this could only be disseminated by injustice and intolerable calumny, We would be lacking in our Apostolic ministry if We did not clarify the constant rule of action in this matter. At the same time, We earnestly admonish and beseech all of you and your subordinates in Poland, a kingdom renowned for its faith and religion, to read and weigh the letters of matrimonial dispensation which are sent out by the Apostolic See for the people of that kingdom. We are certain that if there ever was any sin in this matter, it was not the fault of this Apostolic See or of its officials; truly it must be attributed entirely to the Ordinaries of places or to their ministers, who did not take care either to read or to weigh sufficiently the letters of dispensation which they received.

Condemnation of Marriages with Heretics

2. Nor is it necessary for us to prove in full the antiquity of the discipline by which the Apostolic See always condemned the marriage of Catholics with heretics. But it will be sufficient to bring forward only some evidence with which We may show that the same discipline and rule which has been diligently preserved down to our own time flourishes now, by Us no less religiously preserved. This is what our predecessor Pope Urban VIII testifies to concerning his own times in his Apostolic Letters dated December 30, 1624; these may be read in the book of Cardinal Albitius entitled *De inconstantia in Fide*, chap. 37, no. 127, where he writes: "Granted that We hold that the marriages of Catholics with heretics are all-together to be avoided, and, as far as it depends on us, We aim to keep them far from the Catholic Church." Also our predecessor Pope Clement XI, in the letters dated June 25, 1706, and found in the collection of his briefs and letters published in Rome in 1724, expresses himself no less clearly. On page 321 we read: "We consider it most important not to transgress the rules

of the Church of God, of the Apostolic See, of our predecessors and of the holy people, all of whom shrink from the marriage of Catholics with heretics, unless the good of the entire Christian community should demand it." And in other letters dated July 23, 1707, in the same collection, page 391: "Indeed the Church shrinks from such marriages which present so many proofs of deformities and spiritual danger."

3. Our judgment in this matter is sufficiently clear in the Decretal Rescript published by our authority November 4, 1741, and printed in volume I of *Bullarii nostri*, no. 34, sect. 3, as follows: "In the first place his Holiness grieves very much that some Catholics today are demented in their base love. They no longer shrink from these destestable marriages which the Church has always condemned and forbidden. He praises those bishops who strive to restrain Catholics from marrying heretics by imposing more severe penalties. Also "He seriously admonishes all bishops and Vicars Apostolic, parish priests, missionaries, and other faithful ministers in Holland and Belgium to frighten away Catholics of both sexes from entering upon such marriages to the destruction of their souls, and to impede these same marriages by every good means, and to strive effectively to prevent them." Further along, concerning a marriage already contracted by a Catholic party with a heretical partner, we read: "The Catholic spouse, whether a man or a woman, ought to resolve to do penance for the grave crime committed, to beg God for pardon, and to strive to bring back to the Catholic Church the spouse wandering from the true faith and so to win his soul; this could obtain remission for the crime committed because, as has already been said, he will be forever bound by the chain of that marriage."

Heresy Must Be Abjured

4. When a dispensation is requested to allow a Catholic to marry a heretic or to remove some canonical impediment which exists between the contracting parties, neither the permission nor the dispensation is granted except with the addition of this expressed law or condition, namely that *the heresy must first be abjured*. Pope Innocent X was on his guard and ordered that such dispensations should not be granted at all unless there was proof, supported by authentic documents, that the heretical fault of the heterodox contracting party had been rejected under oath; this testimony was left us by Cardinal Albitius, at that time Assessor of the Congregation of the Universal Inquisition, in the tractate mentioned above, *De Inconstantia in Fide*, chap. 18, no. 44. Clement XI, in the Congregation of the Holy Office held in his presence on June 16, 1710, ordered the Archbishop of Malines to give no permission or dispensation for marriages to be celebrated between a contracting Catholic and a heretic unless the abjuration of heresy had indeed preceded; he ordered that the theologians who had opinions contrary to this practice be sharply admonished. Vicenzo Cardinal Petra recorded this in his Commentary on the Constitution XII in Suo C of John XXII, *Operum*, vol. 4, p. 76, no. 14.

5. Some examples are found of Roman Pontiffs who either gave permission to contract marriages or gave dispensations concerning some impediment, without the condition of first abjuring heresy. We say first of all that these concessions were very rare and most of them were granted for marriages to be contracted among the highest princes, and not without an urgent and grave cause, a cause which concerned the public welfare. Besides, opportune safeguards were always added, lest the Catholic spouse might be perverted by the heretical one; the former would know that he must strive for the conversion of the latter. In addition, children of both sexes born of the union must be educated in the sanctity of the Catholic religion. It is easy then to realize that in such concessions no opportunity for error was open to the executors unless they wished knowingly and deliberately to fail in their duty. Finally, from what We have said so far, it is obvious that the Apostolic See has always both disapproved and condemned such marriages unless the abjuration of the heresy preceded; it still abominates and detests them.

Justification for Dispensation

6. Sometimes the justifications for dispensations are not openly mentioned in the petitions; the ministers and officials of the Holy See cannot divine this. Therefore, to silence accusers and calumniators, it is sufficient to point out that every dispensation is given to a specified executor, who is to determine the truth of everything in the deposition. Since he knows that the marriage of Catholic with heretics is condemned by the Apostolic See, he can also understand that the

evil of heresy, which affects one of the contracting parties and which is not mentioned in the letters of dispensation, was concealed from the Apostolic See. It is his duty to suspend the execution of such letters and to notify the Roman Pontiff and his officials of the reason for the suspension, as Pope Alexander III prescribed in his letter to the Archbishop of Ravenna. This was entered in the Codex of Decretals to insure its perpetual effect, in the chapter *Si quando, de Rescriptis*, where we read: "Diligently consider the nature of this business and either comply with Our orders or by your letter explain the reasonable cause which prevents you; for if you do not, We will maintain what was suggested to Us by an evil report."

Presumption that Both Parties are Catholic

7. In truth the circumspection of the Apostolic See and its officials does not stop here. Sometimes when a dispensation to remove some canonical impediment for a reasonable cause is requested it comes from a region in which Catholics live together with heretics. When it is not certain from other sources whether both of the petitioners or only one of them is Catholic, the above Pontifical officials always presume both to be Catholics. Therefore they set forth their wishes in a little book (called *Supplicationum*) to which the Papal signature is applied: "The afore-said petitioners, who are truly members of the orthodox faith and live under obedience to the Holy Roman Catholic Church, and intend so to live and die, etc." These words agree with others which are added in provisional and conditional form, namely: "Provided the petitioners mentioned are truly worshipers of the orthodox faith, and live in obedience to the Holy Roman Church and intend so to live and die."

8. Considering the above, We ask: when letters of matrimonial dispensation are conceived in such words and sent in that way, if later it is learned that the contracting parties are heretics, or one of them is Catholic and the other heretic, and nevertheless the dispensation is executed, whose fault is it and who can be accused of issuing an improper dispensation? Is it he who in good faith has granted it after applying opportune safeguards and adding legitimate conditions; or is it not rather he who, without regard for such conditions and with no previous examination of the contracting parties, executes the dispensation and permits it to have an undue effect contrary to the will of the one granting it?

Magnae Nobis
5

Girls Less Than Twelve Years Old

9. But some one may object that not all dispensations sent out for execution were armed with such clauses; for in the kindgom of Poland itself, not many years ago, a certain dispensation was sent from Rome which did not display any conditions of this kind. The dispensation concerned age in favor of a girl who was six months short of 12 years, which is the legal age for girls to enter matrimony. In the concession it was explained that "craft complemented age so that legally she could contract marriage." Hence it should be considered a declaratory document rather than a dispensation, since the faculty of contracting marriage before the time prescribed, as often as craft supplies for age, comes from the very provisions of the law and canons. Indeed the bishops themselves and the ordinaries of places may decide on this question, which is one of fact: whether indeed craft, as is stated, has supplied for age. Consequently they have the authority to give permission to contract marriage. It is not necessary to appeal to the Apostolic See, except for greater solemnity of the act or "lest there might arise some question of the validity of such a marriage on the score of insufficient age," as the formula which is customarily used in declaratory letters concerning insufficient age states. Indeed canonists teach that there is an extraneous right of the Apostolic See and of ordinary judges to decide in this matter, whether indeed craft, as is asserted, may supply for age. But only the Holy See has the right of granting a dispensation to contract marriage to a minor, who is not yet mature for conjugal union, but has attained that use of reason sufficient to understand its purpose and nature. Indeed for the validity of matrimony, just as natural and divine law requires the use of reason, so positive canon law requires the natural power of conjugal union. The Roman Pontiff is above canon law, but any bishop is inferior to that law and consequently cannot modify it.

10. But let us pass over the question of whether permission to contract a marriage before the legal age, when craft supplies for age, is properly called a dispensation or rather has the force of a declaration, and therefore whether it ought to be classified as an act of grace or of justice. When one of the contracting parties or both are

infected with heresy, and this is not mentioned in the application and could not be known in any other way, the apostolic letters granted in this matter lack those words and conditions which are customarily added to other dispensations. Let us see nevertheless whether others of equal force are present by which the executor of such letters should abstain from executing them. There can be no doubt about this, however, if we refer to what was required of the executor in such letters, "that he inform himself diligently about the premises" and see "whether it is really and legitimately obvious in such a minor that craft does supply for the defect in age." The same executor is commissioned to permit the applicant to marry "provided there is no other canonical impediment to contracting matrimony with a person legally free to marry, or with a person to whom an Apostolic dispensation has been granted, according to the norms of the Council of Trent." These words surely indicate that he should be no means permit a minor to enjoy such a dispensation or declaration if he learns that the minor was planning to marry a heretic.

11. But our discussion has been longer than We intended at the beginning of our letters. We do not at all regret this. We are concerned that the truth about facts and events be known and that false rumors spread against the sacred Chair of Peter do not find credence. If anything is done anywhere against the sacred canons, may the fault not be ascribed to the innocent.

12. But that the end of Our letters may return to where they began; to you, venerable brothers, and to the other ordinary bishops of that kingdom, We again earnestly command that you and your respective officials study the Apostolic Letters of dispensation which are sent to you for execution; certainly, if you find anything in them abnormal and of a new kind, you should look into its truth or falsity. There is much malice among men on earth, nor is it given us to know to what lengths the audacity of deceitful men can go. Indeed it has come to our ears that someone, disregarding the impediment of grade, married a heretical man to a Catholic woman; afterwards when he learned that his deed was open to criticism, he did not hesitate to assert that he was justified in this matter by an Apostolic dispensation which he had received from Rome. When, however, he was called upon to produce such letters of dispensation, he was never able to do so, since, in fact, he had never received them.

13. Truly We believe that such a detestable crime as this could not have been committed in the midst of the renowned nation of the Polish people, which We embrace with paternal love. Nor could the bishops of that kingdom, all of whom together and individually We hold in great honor, have participated in this. To you, however, venerable brothers, and to the flock committed to you, We bestow the Apostolic Benediction from the depths of our soul.

Given at Rome at St. Peter's, June 29, 1748, in the eighth year of Our Pontificate.

†

LATIN TEXT: *Bened. XIV Bull.*, 2:347-51; *Magnum Bull.*, 17:230-32.

ENGLISH TRANSLATION: Bernard A. Hausmann, S. J.

PEREGRINANTES

ENCYCLICAL OF POPE BENEDICT XIV PROCLAIMING A HOLY YEAR FOR 1750

MAY 5, 1749

6

To all the faithful of Christ, Greetings and Apostolic Benediction.

That we are pilgrims from the Lord and seekers after our future homeland, that we all have sinned and have frequently abandoned the way of God's commandments and like foolish sheep have wandered astray, is well established. If we should say that we have not sinned, we deceive ourselves. Our conscience bears witness to our many transgressions, which cause us to fear death and the approaching judgment of God. If we should say that we have not sinned, we make God a liar. But of course His judgments are true and just, and we must endure His scourges because we have sinned against Him, have acted unjustly, and have committed iniquity. For this reason He does not cease to punish and castigate us so that we may return to Him before Judgment Day.

Care for Sinners

The Church continually looks after its members so that it may recall sinners to the path of salvation and obtain pardon for their sins. The Church offers mercy to the guilty; but few listen to the salutary warnings of the Church. Many are entangled with evil affections or bound by the cares and pleasures of life. They fly from the spirit of penitence and the discipline of improving their character; they despise God's goodness, patience, and forebearance. The Church generously offers indulgences at all times, but some neglect them ruinously and others make no effort to acquire them properly and deserve them. Meanwhile our days are running out, and we shall be poured out like water on the earth. But when the just Judge has appeared, we may learn too late that our hard and impenitent hearts have stored up wrath for us and that whatever we have not done penance for remains to be punished by the divine Judge.

Holy Year

2. Therefore, Our predecessors chose certain times during the course of the centuries to remind all the faithful of the approaching end of the world, and to instill in them a greater zeal for correcting their sins, thus obtaining the salvation of their souls. This was done of old each hundredth year. Later, considering the length of a generation, they decided to enact a holy year every twenty-five years. In this way, almost everyone—at least once in his lifetime—could experience these general means for obtaining propitiation and indulgence. The Church would also

prescribe an appropriate list of penitential exercises. This holy year, a year of renovation, penance, reconciliation, and grace, will begin on the next winter solstice. We beseech all who answer to the name of Catholic to observe it.

3. The kingdom of heaven is at hand; heed Our preaching and do penance. Little children, it is the last hour; return to the Lord and be reconciled with God. The world and its concupiscences will pass; but eternal life is promised only to those who have done the will of God. What is the will of God but your salvation? To fulfill this will, the Church calls you. She devotes the entire coming year to public exercises of religion and piety; she desires that all her children who have been nourished with the milk of Catholic doctrine, may merit the mercy and grace of God, both for themselves individually as well as for the whole brotherhood. She opens the doors of the churches and her charitable heart to the arriving multitudes. To all who ask sincerely, she promises forgiveness.

4. One can have an unshakeable confidence in this promise for a number of reasons. First of all is the supreme power of binding and loosing, given by the Redeemer to Peter and his successors, and Peter's inestimable merits. The treasury of satisfaction, composed of the merits, sufferings, and virtues of Christ, His Virgin Mother, and all the saints and entrusted to Us for dispensation also inspires confidence. The blood of the Apostles and martyrs of old, poured out on the earth like water to build up the Church, cries to the Lord for pardon and peace for the faithful. In addition, Church discipline has been conformed both to the rigor of the ecclesiastical rule by assigning works of penance and to the spirit of Christian clemency by granting indulgences. Finally, the holiness of the proposed goal, the profit of the Christian people, and the example of those who have gone before us in the faith provide still more reasons for confidence in this promise.

5. Therefore, what time and the custom of Our predecessors recommend, We shall accomplish. We proclaim and promulgate a great and universal Jubilee in this Our City for next year, 1750. It is to begin with the first vespers of the vigil of the Nativity and is to continue for the entire year. It will glorify God Himself, exalt the Catholic Church, and sanctify all the Christian people.

Requirements for the Indulgence

6. During this year We mercifully grant complete indulgence, remission, and pardon of all their sins to all the faithful of Christ, both men and women, who are truly penitent and who fulfill the following spiritual exercises. They must have confessed and communed. If they are residents of Rome or of Vatican City they must have piously visited the basilicas of the Blessed Peter and Paul, of St. John Lateran, and of St. Mary Major at least once a day for thirty successive or interrupted days. These days may be computed by the natural rhythm of the sun or by the ecclesiastical rhythm of the daily divine service. In the latter case a day is to be counted from first vespers of one day until the end of twilight of the following day. If they are pilgrims or foreigners, they must visit these churches for at least fifteen such days. Both Romans and non-Romans must have piously prayed for the exaltation of the Holy Church, for the extermination of heresies, for concord among Catholic princes, and for the salvation and tranquility of the Christian people.

Some Unable to Fulfill all Conditions

7. Some who set out to fulfill these requirements may be physically unable to complete their visitations to the churches. If they are truly penitent, have confessed, and received holy communion, We want them to share in the indulgence and remission mentioned above just as if they had actually fulfilled all the conditions.

8. Rouse your enthusiasm at the announcement of so great a gift offered you. Undertake the task that can save your souls with great eagerness and fervor. Let not the comforts of home hold you back; let not the labor of the journey frighten you. Weigh the spiritual gift by the standards of the Christian faith and do not permit the eagerness of worldly men for earthly treasure to surpass the desire of the faithful for heavenly treasures.

The New Rome

9. The great reward of your journey will be spiritual renewal. What can delight a Christian more than to behold the glory of the cross of Christ where it shines supreme on earth and to see with one's own eyes the monuments of victory by which our faith has conquered the world? It will even be possible to see the summit of the ages bowed in reverence to religion. This one-time Babylon no longer extends the threats of arms and war for the destruction of nations and the subjugation of kingdoms. Rather, it recommends proper discipline for the education and salvation of the peoples. Once the memory of old superstitions had been buried in oblivion, sincere worship of the true God and the majesty of sacred rites shone everywhere like a jewel. When the shrines of false deities had been overturned by true religion, then churches were consecrated to the supreme God. In addition, the impious games and mad spectacles of the circus were obliterated from the minds of men; the cemeteries of the martyrs were visited; the monuments of tyrants were overthrown; tombs of the Apostles were built by the emperors themselves; the precious ornaments of Roman pride were transformed into places of worship; and the more eminent shrines to the provincial gods were converted from pagan temples into Christian churches. Finally, the sight of the countless multitudes converging on the City this year from everywhere will fill your heart with joy. When each one recognizes so many other Catholics of different nations and languages and rejoices with them all in brotherly love in the presence of their common Mother, the Roman Church, he will perceive the dew of heavenly benedictions, as if it descends from the top of Hermon near at hand and is poured out on him and on the inhabitants of the Holy City.

Those Who Have Left the Church

10. Our great hope is that those who long ago, deceived by lies of the devil, left the Church might now return to the unity of the Catholic faith. Do they not hear her voice calling them most lovingly to her embrace? Do they not understand that when they left the faith they began to direct their course by human conventions and they handed themselves over to be taught by others who willfully led them astray with various foreign doctrines? But alas! How many there are among them who are not ignorant of these things! And indeed they do not deny that the foundations of each individual sect are weak and, if shaken a little, collapse easily. But what is more to be deplored is their evil lack of interest in the things of God. Because of this they despise the light of truth and the voice of their conscience. As enemies both of the Catholic Church and of their own souls, they refuse to understand what they ought to do. Nor do they wish to examine the straight way of the Lord which is the only way back to the portals of salvation. May they at least be awakened by the example of your faith and devotion to consider that they will have no excuse on the Judgment Day if they continue to spurn the reasons which have been offered to them for recognizing the truth. May your obvious agreement in the worship of God, in the discipline of Christian life, and in reverence toward the Pope, spiritual Father of every Catholic, all serve as an incentive for emulation and an occasion for shame among those who have left the Church. Our whole desire is that the earth be filled with the knowledge of the Lord, the honor of God, and the purity of the Christian faith, and that holiness of character flourish and increase among all nations. We ask this as though drawing up a line of battle. We hope to obtain this through the intercession of your prayers. The most clement Lord says that He is moved by your intercessions. At the same time We shall pray for peace for the Catholic Church, for the happiness of Christian princes, and the safety of all the faithful.

Wage a New Kind of War

11. But you, Venerable Brothers, leaders of the Catholic religion, Patricians, Primates, Archbishops, and Bishops who serve as ambassadors among the Christian people, call a meeting, gather the people, announce to them the holy year. Endeavor to see that our plan is effective, both for the glory of God and the benefit of the whole Church. God has granted His people peace after the calamities of a long war; may this gift which God gave for the temporal tranquility of His people lead also to the improvement and, finally, to the eternal salvation of this same people. A new kind of war against the enemies of our salvation must now be waged. The license of thinking and acting must be curbed. The luxury and the pride of life must be restrained and cupidity for gain must be kept in check. All impurity must be purged and all enmity eliminated. All hatreds must be abolished.

12. To action, therefore, you priests, ministers of God. Sound the trumpets and declare a spiritual war against the enemies of the cross of Christ. Strengthen the languid hands of your soldiers and straighten their bent knees. In the first place, make straight the path for those who have decided to come to this citadel of religion, this impregnable stronghold. Let them hear from you that they are not called here for leisurely roaming nor to view strange sights; but they are summoned to carry arms in a Christian militia and to undertake the labors of fighting and war. What are the arms that Satan fears if not the vigils of the pious, their prayers, fastings, almsgivings, their works of Christian humility and of mercy? By these the tyrannical domination of human cupidity is overcome, and the kingdom of love is strengthened and extended.

13. While going forth into this pious war, it is fitting that those protected by the cross of Christ and those gathered together in the armor of God advance so that no occasion of doing harm is given to the attacking enemy. Let these peaceful, harmonious, modest, and religious soldiers proceed on their journey. While they ask the guidance, mercy, and assistance of God (whose banner they profess to follow), may His discipline prove them worthy so that they may deserve to obtain the promised crown of victory. But you, Venerable Brothers, while you strive to inspire them with these goals, bear in mind that the office of exhortation and persuasion is easy. Example, however, is stronger than words; it is more effective to teach by doing than by talking. Therefore, let the splendor of your holy actions shine before them, so that seeing your good works they may conform their lives and habits to the standard of yours. Do not forget hospitality, service, and sharing. While the Church shows a more abundant mildness for the spiritual needs of the faithful, let the temporal necessities of the poor also be relieved with greater mercy.

Advice to Secular Leaders

14. Our most dear sons in Christ, the Emperor elect, the kings, and all Catholic princes, have received blessing upon blessing from Him by whom kings rule. We beg that they may be ardently inflamed with pious zeal to promote the glory of God. Above all, may they aid the zeal and vigilance of Our Venerable Brothers, the bishops and higher leaders, and order their magistrates and ministers to help them, so that the license of evildoers may be restrained and the zeal of the good supported by kingly aid and favor. Especially let them show generosity toward pilgrims. Let them see to it that they travel safely without being harrassed by wicked men. Rather, let them be received lovingly in hospitals, homes, and public inns and, after being refreshed with food and necessities, let them proceed happily on their journey returning with joy to their fatherland. In this way kings and princes may incline God favorably toward themselves, so that they may live long and happily on earth. Then in the end, they may be received into the eternal tabernacles by these same poor people toward whom they showed mercy and in whom Christ is fed and nourished.

15. Now in order that the knowledge of this letter may more easily reach all the faithful, We desire that copies of it, printed and signed by a public notary and marked with the seal of an ecclesiastical dignitary, have the same authority which the present letter would have if shown and displayed.

16. No one may weaken or oppose this document of Our indiction, promulgation, concession, exhortation, petition, and will. But if any one does presume to do so, may he know that he will incur the indignation of the omnipotent God and of His apostles, Peter and Paul.

Given in Rome, at St. Mary Major, in the year of the Incarnation of our Lord 1749, May 5, the ninth year of our Pontificate.

†

LATIN TEXT: *Bened. XIV Bull.*, 3^1: 108-12; *Magnum Bull.*, 18: 70-76, Latin and Italian in parallel columns.

ENGLISH TRANSLATION: Bernard A. Hausmann, S. J.

APOSTOLICA CONSTITUTIO

ENCYCLICAL OF POPE BENEDICT XIV ON PREPARATION FOR THE HOLY YEAR

JUNE 26, 1749

7

To all Patriarchs, Archbishops and Bishops.

Venerable Brothers:

Pilgrimages

The Apostolic Constitution which We have recently promulgated announces to Christ's faithful the celebration of a Holy Year. It summons them to undertake holy pilgrimages, thus performing a work highly recommended in the Old Testament, which records the numerous journeys to the holy places of Jerusalem in the first centuries of the Church. This continuous custom has brought even emperors and kings to visit the sacred monuments of this fair City, especially the blessed tomb of the holy apostles Peter and Paul. Although heretics despise pilgrimages, Our writers have defended them convincingly. For if such pilgrimages are organized in a fitting and orderly manner by those who direct the churches, they unite the strivings of piety and religion; those who question pilgrimages seriously will understand this.

History of Pilgrimages

2. In the old law God commanded all sons of the Israelites to approach the Tabernacle or the Temple of the Lord with devotion three times each year. "On three occasions throughout the year all your males will appear in the sight of the Lord your God in the place which He has chosen at the festivals of Azymes, of Weeks and of Tabernacles" (Dt 16). Elcana and his wife Anna carefully obeyed this command (1 Kgs 1). And Our most beloved Redeemer, accompanied by His mother the Blessed Virgin and His foster-father St. Joseph, came to the Temple at the appointed times (Lk 2). So in order that even the Gentiles should come in great numbers to the Temple built by Solomon, Solomon himself besought God in his kindness to grant the requests of foreign peoples who visited the Temple after lengthy journeys even if they were not reckoned among the Israelites: "In addition when the foreigner who is not of Your people Israel comes from a far land for the sake of Your name (for Your great name will be heard and Your strong hand and Your arm outstretched everywhere) . . . You will hear in heaven and in the firmament of Your habitation and You will do all that the foreigner asks of You." (3 Kgs 8).

3. Eusebius supplies a shining testimony when he records the arrival of St. Alexander, bishop of Cappadocia, in Jerusalem to gaze on those holy places and reverence them, saying: "Alexander was urged on by a divine oracle when

he set out for Jerusalem from Cappadocia, where he had previously been ordained bishop, both to pray and to visit the places" (Hist Eccl, bk 6, chap. 11). But a much more eloquent witness to this practice is given by St. Jerome in epistle 46 (35) in the following words: "It would be a lengthy undertaking now to review the bishops, martyrs, and Christian teachers who have visited Jerusalem from the ascension of the Lord down to the present day. They felt that they had less devotion, less knowledge, and had not achieved the pinnacle, so to speak, of the virtues until they had worshipped Christ in those places where the Gospel first shone from the Cross."

4. It is not Our purpose here to append a long disquisition on the numerous visits of kings, bishops, prelates, and faithful on continual pilgrimages to the tombs of the Apostles, particularly since several famous scholars have previously treated this whole subject. We refer of course to Onuphrius Pavinus in his treatise *On the Eminence of the Basilica of the Vatican*, which We read often before its publication as it rested safely in the archives of the basilica. At the time, We were still among the lesser clergy, that is, appointed to the canons of the Vatican basilica and acting as Prefect of the Archives of this basilica; We refer also to Jacobus Gretserus, *de sacris Peregrinationibus* in tome 4, bk. 2, chap. 12ff, of the new edition of his works; Coccius, *Thes. Catholic.*, bk. 5, chap. 17; Stanislaus Hosius, *cap. de Caeremoniis*; Rutilius Benzonius, *de anno Sancti Jubilaei*, bk. 6, chap. 1f; Drexellius, tome 13, part 1, chap. 7, pp. 126ff of the Monachian edition; and quite recently Trombelli, *de Cultu Sanctor*, tome 1, pt. 2, chap. 46f. But the formula of the monk Marculf who lived in the seventh century is never mentioned by the above writers. His formula describes the way letters of recommendation, written for those setting out on pilgrimages, should be composed. These letters are addressed to the supreme pontiff and to bishops. This formula is to be found in bk. 2, chap. 49, and reads as follows: "The bearer of this, considering hard and toilsome journeys of little account, not because of idleness (others read: for the sake of wandering) but in the name of the Lord, and desirous of approaching the tombs of the blessed apostles of the Lord, Peter and Paul, to gain the benefits of their prayers, has asked me in my littleness to recommend him to your kindness." St. John Chrysostom writes thus on this subject: "in the royal city of Rome emperors, consuls, and military commanders hasten without their retinue to the tombs of the fisherman and the tentmaker" (*Quod Christus sit Deus*, tome 1, p. 570, no. 9, Paris, 1718). Eginhard testifies that the emperor Charlemagne in the course of forty-seven years, under the spur of devotion, came to Rome four times, saying: "Charlemagne, within a span of forty-seven years, travelled to Rome to pray and accomplish what he had vowed." And We must mention the fine testimony of Nicholas I, who flourished in the ninth century, which records the very numerous pilgrimages to this city in honor of the blessed remains of the Apostle Peter. "So many thousands of men hastening from every region of the earth betake themselves daily to the protection and intercession of blessed Peter the prince of the Apostles, and purpose to remain near his tomb to the very end of their lives. By analogy with the incident recorded in *Acts* when the vessel was let down from heaven in which all kinds of living things were shown to this same Blessed Peter who is their guide, the Catholic Church is signified by the City of Rome alone, in which the bodily presence of this Apostle is carefully reverenced, and which contains as in a vessel all nations of all animals (whose spiritual significance is men)" (Epistle 8 to Emperor Michael).

Defense of Pilgrimages

5. However, Our writers have excellently defended the practice of pilgrimages against the falsehoods of the heretics, and the Church's prelates have ensured that these pilgrimages are properly conducted and free from all scandal. Without wishing to compose a dissertation or treatise, We merely indicate what Jonas, bishop of Orléans, a writer of the ninth century, wrote against Claudius of Turin who was opposed to holy images and so to holy pilgrimages as well. We also indicate what Aegidius Carlerius, Dean of the church of Cameraca, said in his famous sermon at Basel against the errors of Nicholas the Taborite, in which he clearly demolished by learned arguments whatever objections his opponent raised to pilgrimages, as is obvious to the reader of this sermon in Harduin, *Collectionis Conciliorum*, tome 8, pp. 1896ff. Likewise to be borne in mind are the decrees of the second coun-

cil of Cabilone in the year 813 (chap. 45) and the fuller expression of the council of Bourges in the year 1584 (Harduin, tome 10, pp. 1466ff), for it will be clear that some canons were formed to remove certain nonsense which had managed to infect holy pilgrimages. And the information which Laurentius Bochelli carefully assembled on this subject in *in Decretis Ecclesiae Gallicanae*, bk. 4, 14, *de Peregrinationibus*, should not be passed over in silence.

6. We also know well the two little works of St. Gregory of Nyssa, one *de iis, qui adeunt Jerosolymam* and the other *ad Eustatiam, Ambrosiam, et Basilissam (Operum*, tome 3, pp. 651ff, Paris, 1638), which the heterodox often misuse to deride and condemn the journeys of the faithful to holy places. We realize too that a serious dispute has arisen among scholars as to the authenticity of these works. Lippomano, Baronius, Natalis, Alexander, Tillemont, and Ceillerus believe them to be genuine. On the other hand, Cardinal Bellarmine considers them of doubtful authenticity. Gretserus even condemns them as forgeries and apocryphal and attempts to prove this by many arguments in his precise annotations on p. 71ff in tome 3 of the above edition. But let us leave the dispute to one side; grant the works to be genuine and grant that St. Gregory inveighed against the abuses which had infected pilgrimages to the holy places of Jerusalem. Let us condemn the ridiculous opinion of those who say that these pilgrimages are altogether necessary for the attainment of eternal salvation. All of this does not weaken or destroy the truth We put forward at the start. For We do not insist on the necessity of sacred journeys, but simply recommend them as beneficial. We do not defend the nonsense which sometimes develops in the course of long journeys, but as will later be clear, We prevent scandals from arising by applying timely remedies. Even if the over-zealous holy Doctor at times uses a vehement style to attack the holy pilgrimages to Jerusalem, either some harsh opinions are to be believed about the inferior morals of pilgrims or about the general sense and custom of the Church. It considers the holy journeys of Christians to be pious and devout works, provided that they are organized with proper modesty and discipline. The Church's judgment is preferable even to that of a Doctor renowned for his holiness and teaching.

Responsibilities of Those Going on Pilgrimages

7. We especially recommend pilgrimage to the bishops, provided that their physical health is good and that no loss will befall their flock from the absence of the shepherd. Indeed they should remember that many of their predecessors—at least those who lived reasonably close—came to the holy city every year to join the Roman Pontiff in celebrating the feast days of the most holy Apostles Peter and Paul; this is well known from Letters 13 and 16 of St. Paulinus. We exhort also the priests and the rest of the clergy to come, provided that they bring dimissorial letters from their bishops, as is proper. For this law originated in the earliest centuries of the Church, as is clear from Canons 41 and 42 of the Council of Laodicea in the year 372 (Harduin, tome 1, pp. 789-790). We exhort the Regular clergy also to come, provided that they obtain the appropriate approval of their superiors. With equal zeal We exhort the laity to come, provided that they learn properly what they should do from their parish priest or confessor before they undertake the journey. However, to prevent the priests or confessors from being easily misled, they should put the questions to the laity very carefully according to the theologians, especially Theophilus Raynardus in his treatise *Heteroclita spiritualia* (*Operum*, tome 15, p. 217, no. 13). "A pilgrimage," says Raynardus, "is a work of supererogation and belongs to voluntary devotion. Its performance is not of equal worth with acts of virtue which are an obligation. Thus a husband who is bound to cleave to his wife by the tie of marriage will do evil if he undertakes a long pilgrimage against the will of his wife and leaves her at home, etc. Indeed, even if his wife consents, a long pilgrimage by the husband could constitute an aberration, if the absence might result in the loss of virtue by either of the spouses. Similarly, it would be unusual for the father of a family to go on a pilgrimage, since he is needed at home to support his family. The same judgment must be made on an impoverished man who chooses to visit the holy places when the only way he can repay his debts is by staying in some one place and working."

Everyone knows of the plenary indulgence for sins by Urban II at the Council of Clermont bestowed on those who enlisted in the holy army for the recovery of the holy places in Jerusalem and wore the emblem of the Cross. "Whosoever journeys to Jerusalem to free the Church of God solely from devotion, and not for the sake of acquiring honor or money—let that journey be considered a full repentance"—these are the words of the above-mentioned council which was held in 1095 and are contained in Labbe's edition, tome 10. To the question of "Whether a man can take the Cross if there are fears for his continence?" St. Thomas answers, in accordance with the teaching which We have set out above, that "it necessarily devolves on a husband to carry his wife's cross since the husband is the head of his wife. But to take the Cross and go over the seas lies in the sphere of his own will. Therefore if his wife cannot go with him because of some impediment and her continence is questioned, he must not be advised to take the Cross and leave his wife. The case is different, however, if the wife willingly proposes continence or wishes and is able to go with her husband" (quodlibet. 4, art. 11). But We do not discourage even women from coming to Rome at the time of the year of Jubilee, if it is for their good and they are not bound by laws of enclosure. For there are many examples at hand which recommend holy journeys by women. St. Ambrose describes the haste of St. Helena in going to the holy places. Socrates records the pilgrimages to Jerusalem of Eudoxia, who married Theodosius. St. Jerome shows the Roman matron Paula anxious to visit the places in the Holy Land. With the same great zeal St. Bridget journeyed to Compostella and Rome to kiss the tomb of the holy Apostles. During the long period We have spent in this city as a servant of the Holy See, We have witnessed the repeated arrival of women of all ages and classes. However, to prevent the enemy sowing weeds where the cautious father of the family sows wheat, We beseech those who are entrusted with the protection of discipline and morals to guard carefully against the sins which easily arise from young women when they encounter those of different character, disposition, and sex. But if married women undertake a journey, their brothers should act as guardians in the absence of their husbands; or at least they should be entrusted to men whose kinship both frees them from suspicion and makes them concerned about the preservation of chastity.

Tomb of Peter and Paul

8. It now remains for Us to reveal at last the purpose of Our exhortation. But We cannot explain this well without first setting out some noteworthy facts from the holy Fathers and the records of Church history. St. John Chrysostom asserts that the city of Rome is worthy of praise because its size, antiquity, beauty, huge population, riches, and her war-time victories elicit great wonder. But this is not the chief reason for his commendation. For he saw another object in Rome which not only elicited praises but in addition, inspired the greatest love and longing—the sacred remains of the holy Apostles Peter and Paul, which greatly increase the noble glory and dignity of Rome. "Therefore," says the holy Doctor, "although I could praise Rome for other reasons, for its size, its antiquity, its beauty, its huge population, its power, its riches, and its fine martial feats, I pass over all these reasons and proclaim Rome blessed for the single reason that Paul in his lifetime wrote to the Romans and loved them and spoke to them in person and ended his life there. For this reason then, rather than all the others, Rome is more famous, and like a great strong body the city has two shining eyes, the bodies of these saints. The sky is not so shining when the sun sends forth its rays as the city of the Romans in its possession of those two lanterns which send forth light over the whole world" (Homily 32, *in Epistolam ad Romanos*, tome 9, p. 757, of the edition mentioned earlier). He reverenced the bodies of the blessed Apostles from afar since he could not gaze on them in person and impatiently desired to visit Rome. "Who will now give me the power," he continues, "to embrace the body of Paul, to cleave to his tomb, to see the dust of that body which brought to completion the work of Christ, which bore His stigmata and spread abroad in every place His preaching?" and a little later: "Oh! to see the tomb where lie the arms of righteousness, the arms of light, and the limbs which now live, since they were dead in his lifetime while Christ lived in them all, the members which were crucified to the world, the members of Christ, which put on Christ, the temple of the Spirit, the holy building, the limbs which were bound together by the Spirit, which were transfixed by the fear of God and carried the stigmata of Christ. This body,

more than any towers and walls, protects Rome as if with walls and the body of Peter accompanies it. For Paul honored him in his lifetime: 'I went up to see Peter.'"

History of Idolatry

9. So We can safely follow St. John Chrysostom in saying that Our city with its spacious buildings and its wonderful adornments may justly attract and please its beholders. However Our prayers and exhortation to the faithful do not rest on this foundation. The chief glory of Rome is that the head of the Catholic religion and the center of its unity established residence here. Because idolatry prevailed in the city for so long, it is wonderful to see how completely it has been destroyed. Scholars are acquainted with the opinion of Petrus Angelus Bargaeus in his well-known letter, *de privatorum publicorumque aedificiorum Urbis Romae eversoribus*, in which he tries to prove that the magnificent theatres, temples, and baths as well as the many images of idols were not destroyed by the Goths, Vandals, and other savage nations. He contends that they were demolished by the Roman Pontiffs, especially St. Gregory the Great, and others so as to remove completely from their presence all remembrance of idolatrous worship and the provocation of superstition. But whether or not this is true, he certainly succeeded in completing a laborious treatise on the profane and superstitious remains of the pagans interred in the churches. He has also named and counted the churches which were built upon the foundations of profane pagan temples; these can still be seen in Rome. So We recommend sacred pilgrimages in order that the faithful may visit these holy places with the same spirit of piety which strongly inspired St. John Chrysostom even though he never was able to visit Rome.

Origin of the Indulgence

10. But We have not yet set out all the reasons for Our present exhortation. What is said to have occurred in 1300 in the time of Boniface VIII is well known. At that time a rumor spread that in the first year of every century a plenary indulgence for sins was granted to all who approached the tombs of the holy apostles. The originator of this rumor, which was rife not only in Rome but also in many other parts of the world, despite a long and careful search, was never found. Thereupon Boniface VIII at the very turn of the century published his famous constitution *Antiquorum habet fida relatio* in which he granted the fullest forgiveness of sins to all who confessed with true repentance and visited the basilicas of the Holy Apostles Peter and Paul fifteen times if they were strangers and thirty times if they were Romans. And furthermore he conferred forever on the first year in future centuries the same benefit of most ample indulgences obtainable on the same conditions. The whole progress of this affair was recorded by the trustworthy pen of Jacobus Cajetan Cardinal Deacon of St. George in Velabra, the nephew of this Pontiff, and is printed in *Bibliothecae Maximae Patrum*, tome 25, p. 937f, of the Lyons edition. Similarly the period of a hundred years prescribed by Boniface VIII was reduced to fifty years by Clement VI, to thirty-three years by Urban VI, and finally to twenty-five years by Paul II. Clement VI added a visitation of the Lateran basilica and Urban VI, of the Liberian basilica. In Our recently published Constitution, We have made no changes in the customary practice of the Church, either regarding the churches to be visited or the number of visits or works prescribed for obtaining indulgences, except for adding the reception of the Holy Eucharist.

Exhortation

Finally, Our aim is to ensure that the pious works undertaken on these pilgrimages are accomplished with the proper humility and devotion. For the performance of these works is mandatory, not just advisable. Now We address all the faithful with the words with which Augustinus Valerius, the watchful bishop of the church of Verona (soon to be an excellent Cardinal of the holy Roman Church), exhorted the beloved people of his city and diocese in his *in Pastorali epistola* in 1574. This was published on the occasion of the Jubilee Gregory XIII solemnized in the following year. The citation from the epistle is translated from Italian into Latin: "Brothers, the grace of the Holy Spirit summons you to Rome in the coming year of Jubilee; likewise the great treasure which is offered to you invites you. I exhort you all equally for your part to don the vestment of joy which is the permanent companion of a good conscience. For so it will come about that on receiving the grace of sanctification in this year of Jubilee, you will return from the holy pilgrimage more ready than before to serve God."

St. Charles Borromeo

11. We would similarly like to make Our own, the words used by St. Charles Borromeo, the famous Archbishop of the church of Milan, in two letters to the flock entrusted to him, written in Italian in order to be understood by all. The first letter was written on September 10, 1574, that is, in the year preceding the Jubilee proclaimed by Gregory XIII, the second in the year 1576 when the time of Jubilee was over. We are glad to reproduce a portion from each letter in a Latin translation. In the earlier letter he writes: "The opportunity which brings these great advantages for your souls, dearest sons, is not to be despised. Do not, we beseech you, reject this great benefit because you fear the journey will tire you temporarily. Reflect on how diligently you pursue earthly benefits and advantages. For their sake you readily undertake long dangerous journeys, without being deterred by toil, pain, or discomfort. Shame on you then if you are more concerned with your body than your soul. For if it is a matter of gaining freedom from a temporal burden, some of you do not hesitate to undertake very difficult journeys, but this holy pilgrimage obtains freedom from many serious sins which encumber the soul. Because it is so advantageous for the soul, you ought to be inspired to undertake this holy journey. The traditional devotion of the faithful and the ancient example of peoples and princes summon you." St. Charles wrote the second letter when the year of Jubilee had ended. The Pope at St. Charles' request had transferred the plenary indulgence of the Jubilee to Milan for the benefit of those who had not gone to Rome in the preceding year. This is what St. Charles said: "You know how we prayed last year that all of you should make a pilgrimage to Rome and not let any business or hindrance deter you. We encouraged everyone to hasten to gain spiritual riches for himself and to reverence the Church by going to Rome. By so doing, one could obtain in person the Apostolic blessings, revere the holy bodies of blessed Peter and Paul and the relics of the other saints, and see the ancient, venerable churches and other places which the blood of martyrs has stained and consecrated. For that City was singled out when God established there forever the See of St. Peter, the infallible truth of the Catholic Faith and the magisterium of discipline and morals. The earth, walls, altars, churches, martyrs' tombs, and every view of the city presents some holy object to the mind; those who visit those holy retreats in a properly prepared state feel and know this. Hence We many times exhorted you by voice and urged you on by letter and advised you by the example of our own pilgrimage, since we felt we should lead you in this situation."

Importance of Instruction

12. We thought We could end Our encyclical letter now, but contrary to Our preconceived expectation, many points still remain to be dealt with. The fathers of the second synod of Cabilona in 813 in Canon 45 mention several foolish practices which were common in their time on the occasion of pilgrimages and which perhaps could occur even in our day. "For some make a serious mistake," says the canon, "and travel to Rome, Tours, and other places without instruction, under the pretext of prayer. Some priests, deacons, and other clerics who live carelessly think that they will be cleansed from sins and fulfill their ministry if they arrive at the aforesaid places. Likewise some lay peole think they are safe from the penalties of past or present sins by thronging to these places. They are so senseless as to think that the mere visitation of holy places cleanses them of their sins" (Harduin, tome 4, p. 1039). The abbot Albert von Staden in his *Chronico* similarly records other foolish notions of succeeding times which render the pilgrimages of the faithful ineffectual. "I have never or hardly ever seen anyone who came back improved from lands over sea or the tombs of the saints." To meet those abuses the fathers of Cabilona prescribed the following remedies: "Those who have confessed their sins and have been advised by their priests to do penance, show praiseworthy devotion in wishing to visit the tombs of the Apostles or other saints while praying urgently, giving alms, correcting their way of life, and putting their morals in order." The abbot of Staden also does not conceal the remedies, saying: "I think this results when they neither leave nor come back with proper devotion: for they should set out with the attitude that they are about to depart this life." Therefore We should concentrate on obviating all these evils and on explaining the necessary preconditions for receiving indulgences.

13. As everyone knows, several months intervene between the issue at Rome of the Bull proclaiming the year of Jubilee and the actual start of this Holy Year. Continuing the ancient practice of the Church, the holy door is opened on the next vigil of the Birth of the Lord; then the Year of Jubilee begins. We use these intervening months to hold missions in different districts of Rome. We highly recommended their usefulness in Our pastoral Edicts when We were Archbishop of Bologna. These appeared in print and were soon translated into Latin. We impress upon the evangelical laborers in missions to instruct the people in order to explain the Catholic doctrine of indulgences and of the universal Jubilee, rather than in purely academic questions of Apologetic and Moral Theology. The faithful must be fully aware that sin and its eternal punishment are remitted by the Sacrament of Penance if one makes proper use of it; however the entire temporal punishment is very seldom taken away. This must be removed either by satisfactory works in this life or by the fire of Purgatory after death. The holy Council of Trent in session 6, chap. 4, and canon 30 of the same session teaches this under the heading *de Justificatione*. Inform the Christian people of the unfailing treasury in the Church which was constituted by the immeasurable abundance of the merits of Christ and increased by the merits of His saints. Distribution from this treasury has been entrusted by Christ the Lord to His vicar on earth, the Roman Pontiff; consequently the Pontiff prudently decides when these merits can be applied, either by way of absolution for the living or by way of prayer for the dead, provided that the living have destroyed their sin and its eternal punishment by Penance, and that the dead have departed this life united with God in charity. This distribution of merits is in the form of indulgences. When one obtains one, he is freed from the temporal punishment due to sins to the extent granted and defined by the lawful distributor. This we read in the constitutions of the Supreme Pontiffs and especially in the famous Decretal of Our Predecessor Leo X to Cardinal Tommaso de Vio, otherwise known as Cajetan, when he was serving as Apostolic Legate in Germany. The result is that the practice of indulgences is most beneficial to Christians; hence the evil idea which either denies the benefit of indulgences or deprives the Church of the power of conferring them is to be condemned. This was decided by the Council of Trent, session 25, in the decree on Indulgences. Finally, the Christian people must be advised that the Indulgence of the Jubilee year is a plenary one, but is distinguished from other plenary indulgences also distributed on the occasion of the Jubilee by the fact that in a holy year of Jubilee, confessors designated for this purpose receive a wider power both of absolving from sins and of dispensing from certain bonds and impediments which often ensnare the consciences of penitents.

Constitution of Leo X

14. We feel it is appropriate to reproduce here the constitution which Leo X promulgated: "We indicate to you by the present document that the Roman Pontiff can forgive sin and can remove the punishment due to actual sins—sin by means of the sacrament of Penance, and the temporal punishment by means of ecclesiastical indulgence. He can for reasonable causes grant indulgences to the faithful who are members of Christ, be they in this life or in Purgatory. The Church can, by Apostolic authority, grant an indulgence both for the living and the dead. It is accustomed both to confer the indulgence itself by way of absolution and to transfer it by way of prayer; accordingly all, both living and dead, who have obtained these indulgences are freed from as much temporal punishment due to their actual sins as corresponds to the indulgence which was granted and acquired. We decree etc. by Our Apostolic authority etc. that this doctrine must be held and preached by all."

Instruction of the Faithful

15. This will sufficiently inform the people on the subject of indulgences. But since special pains must be taken to ensure that the faithful do seek indulgences, the clergy should provide further instruction. With Apostolic zeal they should attack in their preaching the vices of the age which flourish everywhere, remembering the words of Isaiah 58: "Cry out; do not stop. Raise up your voice as a trumpet and announce their crimes to My people, their sins to the house of Jacob." Let them proclaim the need for penance and insist on the inevitable loss of the soul unless sins are destroyed by means of repentance, as is conveyed in the saying of Christ the Lord, Luke 13: "Unless you do penance, you will all likewise perish." In addition, let them extol the riches of God's mercy which are poured out for those who completely cast off their former evil ways and provide themselves with a new heart and a new spirit. All the while they should be aware of the Lord's words in Ezekiel 18: "Be converted and do penance for all your iniquities, and you shall not be destroyed by iniquity. Cast from you all your prevarications and make yourselves a new heart and a new spirit. . . . For I do not wish for the death of the one who is dying, says the Lord God, turn again and live." And in chapter 33: "As I live, says the Lord God, I do not wish for the death of the sinner, but rather that the sinner be converted from his way and live."

Benefits of Confession

16. When they have dwelt on the virtue of penance, they should then preach on the sacrament of Penance redoubling their exhortations and advice to the faithful to enter on the year of Jubilee with the proper dispositions, fortified by this most wholesome sacrament. Then they should teach the people how to make a beneficial confession and explain the absolute necessity for repeating former void confessions. Furthermore they should encourage even those who do not consider themselves obliged to do so, to confess again their past sins in the sacrament of Penance and to make a general confession of their sins. "Although it is not necessary to confess the same sins twice, still We consider it salutary to do so on account of the shame felt, which is so large a part of repentance," as Our predecessor Benedict XI wrote in his decretal *Inter cunctas de Privilegiis,* to be found among his general Occasional Decretals. St. Charles Borromeo writes in agreement with this view in his *ad Confessarios Monitis*, a work which Our predecessor Innocent XII had reprinted in Rome to be an example and pattern for those who hear confessions. "Confessors," says St. Charles, "should encourage their penitents to make a general confession, having regard to the nature of each person and the suitability of time and place. This way, in reviewing their past, they may return to the Lord with greater eagerness, making good any mistakes from previous confessions."

17. St. Francis de Sales, in many of his writings, recommends the benefit to be derived from general confessions. We cite here in Latin translation the gentle words he wrote in a letter to a woman who had been widowed: "I have received a letter from your father requesting me to reveal to him some measure which would assist him in saving his soul. I gladly, and perhaps more readily than I should, accede to his desire. The advice I am giving him can be summed up in two points: one is the careful and comprehensive examination of his previous life followed by a general confession and corresponding repentance. For no good man avoids this before death. The second point consists in aiming at a gradual detachment of the mind from the attractions of the world." The text of this letter can be found in tome I of his *Operum*, p. 914, no. 6, Paris, 1669. Benefits from general confessions during holy missions are referred to in the Italian biography of St. Vincent de Paul, founder of the Congregation of the Mission. Hence the Rules of this Congregation, approved by the Holy See, state that one of their ministries is: "to encourage and hear general confessions of a penitent's entire earlier life." The words of Urban VIII contained in the bull *Salvatoris nostri*, confirming the establishment of this Congregation, have the same tenor, for he recommends the beneficial practice of general confession as follows: "From the abundant success of these (i.e. of the works and ministries proper and peculiar to the institution of the Congregation), it seems manifest that this pious institute is most acceptable to God, of great benefit to men, and altogether necessary: for by means of it the practice of sacramental confession and of general confession and of the most holy Eucharist has become frequent, although previously it was rare."

Hence Our predecessor Innocent XII, reflecting on the serious losses which can result from the making of past invalid confessions, exhorts each pilgrim before his departure to make a general confession. This exhortation is in the Instruction which he published after the proclamation of the year of Jubilee. Here is Our Latin translation of his words: "The one who is on the point of leaving (on a pilgrimage) should first make a valid general confession; he should be advised of this in order to cure any possible defects of his previous confessions." Assuredly directors of conscience agree unanimously that general confession is beneficial. The entire account of one's life is reviewed and this results in fear and humility; a greater horror of sin develops; one's strength is increased to meet and rout any temptation to evil; a most pleasant peace and quiet enters the mind and the defects of previous confessions are repaired.

Advice to Confessors

18. We know well that sacramental confessions—whether made to remove everyday faults, to rectify invalid confessions, or to gather together all the sins of one's life—will only produce the desired results if they are heard by ministers of Penance who are upright, learned, and properly educated in the sound doctrine of the Church. When We were in charge of the Archbishopric of Bologna, We appointed as ministers of Penance only those whom We personally or others in Our presence approved after an examination in which they had to give substantial proof of morals and doctrine. We did not give anyone unlimited authority to hear confessions. Rather, We granted a limited authority for a short period of time in order that, once proven, they might be examined a second time either by Ourselves or by others in Our presence. Although this was a great bother to confessors, it was of great benefit to penitents. Currently, however, We are so engaged in governing the universal Church, a task practically beyond Our strength, that We have left the examination of confessors for the city of Rome to the judgment of other trustworthy men. Only when Lent approaches do We indicate to Preachers and Parish Priests whom We have convened all matters which are beneficial to their position and to the salvation of souls. But a much more important reason impels Us to address all confessors on the occasion of the coming year of Jubilee, and accordingly to offer them the following advice and exhortations in the strongest possible words and with vehemence of spirit.

19. In the first place We remind them that they are guilty of serious sin if, while sitting in the holy tribunal of Penance, they hear their penitents carelessly without advising or questioning them, but immediately pronouncing the form of absolution when the penitent has completed the list of sins. Such a procedure is, of course, far different from that of a skilful doctor who pours oil and wine on the wound. Yet every minister of the sacrament of Penance does a doctor's work. So they should examine carefully not only the circumstances of the sins but also the character and disposition of the one who has committed the sins; then the minister can prescribe the appropriate remedies to enable him to obtain the salvation of his soul. "But the priest should be discerning and prudent, so that as an experienced doctor does, he likewise may pour oil and wine on the wounds of the afflicted person by carefully investigating the circumstances both of the sinner and of the sin. Thus he may discover the proper advice to offer and the proper remedy to apply by taking different measures for the cure of the sick man." These are the words of Our famous predecessor Innocent III at the General Council of the Lateran, chapter *Omnis utriusque sexus, de Poenitentiis et remissionibus*. The Roman Ritual approved by Paul V, likewise Our predecessor, in an Apostolic Constitution, agrees with this doctrine, where it states under the heading *de Sacramento Poenitentiae*: "If the penitent does not mention the number, kind, and circumstances of sins, the priest should prudently question him." But if the confessor knows that the penitent has not confessed certain sins, whether from forgetfulness or ignorance, the confessor must circumspectly and prudently remind him of his omissions since otherwise the confession would lack completeness. He must warn and correct him that by proper preparation, he may obtain the fruit of the sacrament of Penance. This is the opinion of St. Bernardine of Siena, who answers in the affirmative the question whether the confessor is obliged to investigate and examine the conscience of the sinner carefully. He says that "this is to be done not only regarding omissions through carelessness or shame but also regarding his ignorant silence, because sinners do not know the things of God. So, if the confessor hears anything from the penitent or knows of anything through a probable conjecture, he should remind him of it. Otherwise, it may be feared that the penitent is crassly ignorant, which according to William does not excuse him. Perhaps though he does not know that such an act is a sin, for according to Isidore the ignorant man sins every day and does not know it" (tome 2, serm. 27, art. 2, chap. 3, p. 167).

20. The theologians give clear direction in these cases, even those not known as strict disciplinarians. For We are not here discussing so-called invincible ignorance of positive law, when the penitent has fallen into some sin known only to the confessor, which could occasion greater evil if the penitent was made aware of it. We are speaking of vincible ignorance, when the penitent either does not know certain actions to be sins, although he should know it, or he is surrounded by circumstances of action which confirm the sinner in evildoing if the confessor passes them by without comment. This would then scandalize others, who could infer that certain acts are permissible from seeing them done without penalty by persons who regularly receive the Church's sacraments. In these cases the opinion of the theologians is unanimous that a confessor must assist the penitent by advice and questioning, even when he sees that this will make the penitent sorrowful. But if at the time the result does not correspond to the advice of the confessor, there is still hope that it will be of benefit later on, since God is helping. Among theologians of the Order of Preachers or of those who accept the teaching of St. Thomas, reference may be made to Solo, *in 4. Sententiar.*, dist. 18, quest. 2, sect. 4, and Silvius, *in 3. par. D. Thomae*, vol. 4, quest. 9, arts. 2 to 7. Among the students of the Franciscan family and the other disciples of Scotus, Cardinal de Laureaea, *in 4. Sentent.*, vol. 2, *de Sacrament. Poeniten.*, disp. 21, art. 3, n. 64ff. Among the writers of the Society of Jesus: Suarez, *in 3. part. D. Thomae*, vol. 4, disp. 32, sects. 3 and 4; Theophilus Reynaudus, vol. 16, *Heteroclit. spiritual.*, pt. 9, n. 4; Cardinal Antonius, *tract. de Poenitent.*, art. 3, quest. 3; and Cardinal de Lugo, *de Sacram. Poenitent.*, disp. 22, sect. 2, where in his burning zeal for the salvation of souls he attacks the lazy confessors of bishops, prelates, princes, and governors who, though they hear no self-accusation for sins which are public knowledge, stay silent, and with no exhortation dispense the grace of absolution after a hasty decision.

"In the second place," he says, "I consider what must be said of the obligation of confessors of prelates, princes, governors and suchlike when they see or know that their penitents do not really fulfill their duty in conferring benefits, selecting ministers or in governing their subjects, in giving alms from the excess of the church revenues or the like. In these cases it should be noted that ignorance is seldom invincible and without fault. Also their ignorance is seldom not a scandal to their subjects, who readily believe that what they observe their prelates and princes doing is permissible, or at least not very harmful. Therefore the confessor is obliged to advise all penitents of their obligations. He does not fulfill his function by absolving the sins which the penitent tells him; if he does only this, then he is responsible for what his penitent overlooked. Then as a blind man leading the blind, they both will fall into the eternal pit. So if he trembles in the presence of the powerful, let him not take on himself the office of shepherd, but modestly excuse himself as one less fit to bear that burden." This salutary opinion of Cardinal de Lugo refers not only to those who hear the confessions of bishops and princes. It also binds equally all confessors who hear the confessions of penitents whose morals and example are a proximate occasion of sin, if not of externally sinful actions at least of evil desires and morose delectations, and who in spite of this customarily accommodate themselves to the penitent unaffected by any concern for manifesting the miserable state of a sinful life.

21. Another warning for confessors is this, that if it should happen (and it tends to happen rather often) that the minister of confession hears something from his penitents which deserves to be specially investigated, he should beware of responding by intuition, but should devote suitable time and thought to the matter before settling it. It would certainly be desirable that every confessor should be endowed with what is called "eminent" knowledge, but since this is given to few men, it is wholly necessary that each be provided with at least competent knowledge. More cannot be expected: since moral theology deals with so many important questions which depend on a knowledge of the sacred canons and the apostolic constitutions, it is obviously a hard task for anyone to know all these well and immediately to solve every question as those men often do who excel in eminent knowledge. It will then be sufficient if confessors of lesser mark duly settle the more difficult questions by consulting books. Our predecessor Innocent IV wisely observes: "We consider a knowledge eminent if it can discuss and define subtle problems and quickly find their solutions. But that man has an average knowledge who can investigate matters in a certain manner; although he cannot answer all questions, he can search out the truth in books and so does not arrive at all his solutions quickly" (*in Commentariis ad Cap.*, *Cum in cunctis*, no. 2, under the heading *de electione, et electi potestate*. So when a more difficult question or a new kind of deed is reported to the confessor and he must consequently consult books, he must do so carefully and selectively. For it is well known that among so many writings there are some whose opinions and assertions do not well agree with the simplicity of the Gospel and the teaching of the holy Fathers. "Many opinions advocate a relaxation of Christian discipline and bring ruin to souls, some being old opinions revived, others newly invented, and the great license of rank minds grows daily more extravagant. By this means, a way of thinking completely at variance with the simplicity of the Gospel and the teaching of the holy Fathers has crept in concerning matters of conscience. If the faithful should adopt it as correct, a mighty corruption of the Christian life would ensue," to quote Our predecessor Alexander VII (decree published September 7, 1665). On this subject We do not want to use plainer speech; We do not want to touch on the disputed questions of the trustworthiness of authors and the soundness of their doctrine. It will be enough to advise confessors not to rely on their own opinion in a doubtful matter. Before judging the case they should refer to as many books as possible, especially those with more substantial doctrine, and then support the opinion which reason suggests and authority confirms. This is exactly what We taught in Our encyclical on usury where We wrote: "They should not cleave excessively to their own private opinions, but before giving an answer they should examine many authors who are especially commended and then take the side which they see is upheld both by reason and authority" (*Bullarii nostri*, tome 1, ord. 143, sect. 8). We repeat this advice now. For Our statement is not limited to matters of usury, but refers also to all matters which can in any way contribute to the sacramental forum or the proper direction of consciences.

22. In the third place We advise confessors to consider the celebrated saying of venerable Cardinal Bellarmine: "there would not be such ready sinning if there were not such ready absolution." We also advise them to recall the propositions Our predecessors anathematized, especially propositions 60-63, condemned by Innocent XI on March 2, 1679, and so to learn the cases in which absolution is to be granted, denied, or deferred. "The diligent priest should understand when and to whom absolution should be granted, denied, or deferred. He should not absolve those who give no signs of sorrow or are unwilling to lay aside hate and enmity, to make restitution to others if they are able, to leave the proximate occasion of sin or to abandon sins in other ways and to change their life for the better. Nor should he absolve those who have given public scandal, unless they make public satisfaction and remove the scandal." These are the words not of a theologian of the stricter school, but of the Roman Ritual. This also commands confessors, in cases where they deny or defer absolution, to explain to their penitents in a mild spirit and gentle words the reasons for their doing so, and show them that it is necessary to do so for the salvation of their souls. Then they should encourage them to return as soon as possible and inspire them to perform properly everything which they are commanded before their return; then when they return to the sacramental court, they may receive absolution. But when they grant absolution, especially to those who seldom approach the sacrament of Penance or only when burdened with many sins, they should exhort them continually. They should emphasize to them the wretched life they have lived under the yoke of sin and explain the vileness of their sins in order, of course, that they may be heartily sorry and seriously resolve to abandon sin in the future. For it is considered that strong serious exhortations by confessors delivered in the forum of Penance are much more effective than the holy sermons of preachers in separating a penitent from his sins. For the hearers of sermons tend to refer the criticism they hear to others rather than to themselves. This, however, cannot occur in the case of a private warning from one's confessor which strikes one individual penitent and is brandished before his eyes unalloyed with any palliation of or excuse for his sins. Confessors should not reply that this is impossible when the large number of penitents encourages brevity, for the golden statement of St. Francis Xavier resolves this difficulty: "He considered that penitents should be helped carefully, not hurriedly, advising that confessors should prefer to hear a few confessions properly than many at a rash speed" (Tursellini *in ejus Vita* [S. Francisci Xaverii], bk. 6, chap. 17).

23. Our fourth point concerns satisfaction, the final part of the sacrament of Penance and necessary for its completeness. Our loving mother the Church, in sympathy for human weakness, has softened in some ways primitive severity and abandoned the practice of the Penitential canons. "In the weakness of our times when not only men's merits but their bodies are weak, that ancient strict censure is not allowed to remain for all offenses" (*in Can. Fraternitatis*, dist. 34). Therefore it is not right for confessors to rashly impose a sacramental satisfaction as a whim, but in so doing they should unite the laws of justice, prudence, and fairness. "In ordaining a penalty for satisfaction, the priests will consider that nothing is to be imposed from their own judgment, but all is to be guided by justice, prudence, and piety. This is laid down in the Roman catechism for the use of priests, which was composed at the command of the Council of Trent and published by Our predecessor St. Pius V under the heading *de Poenitentia.* The Council of Trent ordained these matters when it laid down this salutary doctrine: "Therefore the priests of the Lord should impose salutary and fitting satisfaction as their spirit and their prudence suggest, in accordance with the kind of sins and the means of the penitents. In this way, they can avoid sharing in the sins of others by perhaps overlooking their sins and dealing too leniently with penitents in imposing very light works for the gravest faults. But they should be conscious that the satisfaction is not only a guardian of their new life and a medicine against weakness, but also a punishment and chastisement for their past sins. For, as the ancient Fathers believe and teach, the keys of the priests were given not for loosing alone but also for binding" (chap. 8, session 14, *de poenitentia*). However, a knowledge of the penitential canons will assist the confessor in getting sinners to readily accept the suitable satisfaction imposed on them. For although he should not resume the practice of those Canons, he can still use them to explain the measure of the penalties formerly laid down for these sins. The penitent as a result will both recognize the great malice of sin and gladly accept the satisfaction imposed on him, although otherwise it might have seemed too severe to him. He will do so, of course, after comparing his punishment with what he would have suffered for the same sins if he had approached a confessor in the far-off days when the penitential canons were in force, before the kind discipline of the Church softened the severity of the old Canons. This is the conclusion too of many authors outstanding for piety and doctrine. We recorded their names in *in nostro Tractatu de Synodo*, bk. 7, chap. 62, and think it ineffective to repeat them here. We do add, however, that the life and morals of the faithful who come to the sacrament of confession in Our day are far different from the kind of life which once won praise for glorious Agnes, renowned for her imperial rank and her pursuit of piety. For when she came to Rome to do reverence at the tombs of the Apostles, she revealed all the stains of her former life in the sacramental forum to Blessed Peter Damian, an excellent Cardinal of the Holy Roman Church, and left the confessional without any satisfaction being imposed on her by a confessor so famous for his goodness and doctrine.

24. Blessed Peter Damian speaks of this event in *Opusculo*, 56, chap. 5 in tome 3, p. 432, of his *Operum* (Paris edition) and treats it as an example for others. "So that those who converge on the tombs of the Apostles may imitate your holy devotion even in the secret confessional, I will affirm that you made me sit before the holy altar, and through sorrowful groans and bitter sighs you gave a faithful account of every slight and minute affection of the depths of your humanity and of every vanity in your thoughts and every superfluity in your speech. You covered your life from age five to now. In turn I decided to impose no penance beyond repeating the praise of the divine mission: 'Do what you are doing, continue the work you are engaged in' and the message of the Angel to those in Theatyra: 'I will not send another burden on you, only keep what you have' (Ap 2). For, as God is witness, I did not impose even a day's fasting or other punishment, but I commanded you only to persevere in the holy works you had begun."

25. But in our day, on the other hand, there are many sinners (among whom We Ourselves are reckoned as no doubt were others in Blessed Peter Damian's time) who not only in the general confession of their sins, but also in the many confessions they make each year are burdened with serious sins. So in the sacred forum of Penance they are liable to make the satisfaction which corresponds to the seriousness of the sins in accordance with the canons of the Council of Trent. This is especially important since they produce few, if any, good works if they remain in their accustomed manner of life, and do not, as they should, equably bear the pains which sometimes afflict them. Consequently they lose the richer fruit which the prayers of the Church request from God for penitents in these words: "That whatever good you do, or whatever ill you patiently endure, may be for you a remission of sins, an increase of grace, and the reward of eternal life."

26. Here then, venerable brothers, We have presented the entire list of what We have done or decreed to be done, so that all the inhabitants of Our City may receive the spiritual fruits of the Holy Year. We wish you to take the same measures so that your people who, in the coming year will undertake holy pilgrimages to this City, may obtain equal benefit and the same abundance of heavenly blessings. What We have hitherto said on the subject of pilgrims making a sacramental confession before their departure had already been decreed by the Council of Bourges in 1584: "Whosoever makes a pilgrimage to the holy places should be fortified by the due and complete confession of their sins and by the sacrament of the Eucharist before they set out" (canon 2 in Harduin, tome 10, pp. 1466f). Our predecessor Innocent XII echoes this teaching in his proclamation of the year of Jubilee in 1700; in his proclamation, he especially insists on a salutary expiation of sins, saying: "Be sanctified, therefore, most beloved sons, and prepare your hearts for the Lord. Be washed, be pure, remove your evil thoughts from God's sight and, renewed in the spirit of your mind, be urgent in prayers, fast often, and give alms." To prevent the conclusion that he addressed these words only to Romans, he wisely added words to include others. "Adorned furthermore with these ornaments of the Christian life, fortified with the aid of the virtues, come with confidence, impetuously and with a holy speed of spirit, to this holy city of God on earth as to the throne of grace, that you may obtain mercy."

27. We are perfectly confident that on your way to this city (provided that the ministry of your pastoral office permits it), whether on your journey or while you dwell in Rome, you will want to emulate the mode of living which St. Charles Borromeo decided to embrace on his pilgrimage to Rome for the year of Jubilee in 1575. This holy pilgrimage of the excellent prelate is described by Charles of St. Peter's basilica, bishop of Novaria, in the third book of the History he composed on the life and deeds of St. Charles. We hope that in the course of the journey and its various stopovers, the pilgrims will not trouble the bishops there who must take watchful precautions against the development of the scandals that in times past occasioned some to speak ill of holy pilgrimages. When they arrive in Rome, We shall zealously see to it that they lead an upright and moral life, perform the prescribed works properly, visit the basilicas, and practice various acts of Christian penance. We devote great zeal and effort to ensure that all pilgrims return home, permanently improved by the example of holy living which flourishes in Rome, firm in the faith, fervent in virtue, and confirmed in their obedience to the Holy See. We share the desire of Our predecessor and fellow citizen Gregory XII as he solemnized the year of Jubilee which recurred in his time, as is clear from the annals of his reign, bk. 3, chap. 24. Now that these matters have been decided in this way, We have a firm hope that with the Lord's help, to whom We recommend this entire affair with Our most humble prayers, the pilgrims will return to their own land undeserving of the censure with which St. Jerome insults some who had made holy pilgrimages to the city of Jerusalem. "It is not praiseworthy merely to have been in Jerusalem, but to have led a good life at Jerusalem" (*in epist. 58, ad Paulinum, Operum*, tome 1, p. 318, Verona edition).

28. For the whole year of Jubilee, penitentiary priests and others designated to hear confessions will be available in Rome. They will be given the appropriate powers to hear penitents and grant deserved absolution and dispensation, both for those who live in Rome and those who come there from other places, to enable them to obtain the spiritual riches of the Holy Year. In this period of time preachers of the word of God will be plentiful. We shall speak Ourselves and designate others to speak also, but in so doing We shall not enter on theological controversies which involve merely the disputes of the different schools. Both We Ourselves and those who speak in Our name will be concerned with explaining clearly the force and significance of the phrasing of that section of Our Bull which refers "to the faithful who are truly repentant, have confessed their sins, and been refreshed by holy communion." We shall likewise show by fact and examples how worthless and vain is the opinion of those exiles from the Catholic communion

who falsely assert that repentance is lessened or even destroyed by the use of indulgences. Furthermore, to forestall the suspicion that We or those who preach by Our authority will adopt the stricter opinion, We will employ the same method which the renowned Father Bourdaloue of the Society of Jesus recommended and employed in his Sermon delivered just before the year of Jubilee (*Sermonum*, tome 2, p. 517ff, Paris 1709, 2nd edition).

In the time that We spent in Bologna, We repeatedly issued Our instructions to the people. These were first collected in several tomes and soon were gathered in one folio volume in a Latin translation. In one Instruction (tome 3, 12 of the Italian edition, no. 53 of the Latin), passing by the disputes of the theologians, We exhorted the entire people of Our diocese on the occasion of the Plenary Indulgence proclaimed by Our predecessor Clement XII, to add other works of piety to the works prescribed and to produce fruits worthy of repentance. We cited for them the golden statement of venerable Cardinal Bellarmine (*Controversiarum in tractatu de Indulgentiis*, tome 2, bk. 1, chap. 12, sect. 3): "Wise Christians receive Papal indulgences in their zeal to produce fruits worthy of repentance, and at the same time to make satisfaction to God for their sins." But We also added the remark of Cardinal Pallavicinus in his *in Historia Concilii Tridentini* bk. 24, chap. 12, no. 6, that those are wrong who think that by using indulgences, Christians become lazy and distracted from making proper satisfaction to God who punishes our sins. Indeed since men are wholly uncertain that they have in reality obtained the fruit of indulgences, this is an added incitement for many to strengthen their hopes by renewing their practice of salutary works. Moreover the works prescribed for obtaining indulgences increase piety when they are put into practice, and as is daily experienced they introduce a new habit which enables its possessor to perform more readily the other works of virtue. Boniface VIII prescribed visits to the basilicas—fifteen times for visitors and thirty times for Romans—and made the obtaining of indulgences dependent on this work. But he did not for this reason pass over in silence the other works of virtue; rather in his occasional decretal *Antiquorum, de poenitentiis, et remissionibus*, which is found among his general occasional decretals, he expressly adds: "Each person, however, will merit more and will more effectively obtain an Indulgence the oftener and the more devoutly he visits the basilicas." These words agree closely with those which We emphasized above. Those advised the faithful to practice other relevant works apart from the prescribed ones. The words of the traditional formula for a solemn blessing used by Our predecessors and Ourselves express the same meaning. For when the ceremony of blessing is completed, a Plenary indulgence is granted. Then humble prayers are also made to God to confer on the people present not only "perseverance in good works, but also a continually repentant heart," that is, a heart duly prepared for new works of repentance to atone for past sins, even though hopefully the fault of past sins and their punishment has been remitted in the sacrament of penance, and the temporal punishment which remains has been washed away by the previously granted Indulgence.

29. We read in the lives of Our Predecessors Zacharias and Paschal, by the renowned Anastasius, that several guest houses were built near the church on the Vatican, to welcome and refresh pilgrims who had come to visit the tombs of the Apostles. These buildings, either in the passage of time or by human harm have long been destroyed. But the Romans have built others in different parts of the city which are always open to pilgrims who arrive in this city to reverence the tombs of the blessed apostles and obtain the treasures of indulgences especially in a holy year of Jubilee, to supply in full measure the necessities both for bodily nourishment and spiritual refreshment with the aid of upright priests. These are the matters We judged We should indicate to you. And with the full benevolence of Our spirit We confer on you and on your whole flock the Apostolic Blessing.

Given at Castelgandolfo on the 26th of June 1749 in the ninth year of Our Pontificate.

†

LATIN TEXT: *Bened. XIV Bull.*, 3^1: 118-32; *Magnum Bull.*, 18: 78-97, Latin and Italian in parallel columns.

ENGLISH TRANSLATION: Padraig M. O'Cleirigh.

A QUO PRIMUM

ENCYCLICAL OF POPE BENEDICT XIV ON
JEWS AND CHRISTIANS LIVING
IN THE SAME PLACE
JUNE 14, 1751
8

To the Primate, Archbishops and Bishops, of the Kingdom of Poland.

Venerable Brothers, We give you Greeting and Our Apostolic Blessing.

God in his goodness allowed Catholicism to take root in Poland at the end of the tenth century during the reign of Our predecessor Leo VIII. At the time, the efforts of King Mieszko and his Christian consort Dobrava (Dlugosz, *Annalium vestrorum Scriptorum*, 2, 94) encouraged the spread of Christianity. Since then pious and devout Poles have continued the faithful practice of their new religion. During this time various sects have attempted to establish themselves in Poland and to spread the seeds of their errors, heresies, and evil opinions. But the faithful Polish people have strongly withstood their efforts.

We esteem the glorious memory of Polish martyrs, confessors, virgins and holy men; their exemplary lives are recorded in the holy annals of the Church. We also recall the many successful councils and synods which gloriously defeated the Lutherans who tried tenaciously, using a variety of methods, to establish a foothold and welcome in this kingdom. At that time indeed the great council of Piotrków met under Our great predecessor and fellow citizen Gregory XIII, with prelate Lippomano, bishop of Verona and Apostolic nuncio, as its president. To the great glory of God it prohibited the principle of freedom of conscience; adherents of this principle were seeking to introduce and establish it in Poland. Another threat to Christians has been the influence of Jewish faithlessness; this influence was strong because Christians and Jews were living in the same cities and towns. However their influence was minimized because the Polish bishops did all they could to aid the Poles in their resistance to the Jews. What the bishops did is recorded in the large tome which contains the constitutions of the synods of the province of Gniezno. These facts establish most clearly and plainly the great glory which the Polish nation has won for its zeal in preserving the holy religion embraced by its ancestors so many ages before.

2. In regard to the matter of the Jews We must express our concern, which causes Us to cry aloud: "the best color has been changed." Our credible experts in Polish affairs and the citizens of Poland itself who communicated with Us have informed Us that the number of Jews in that country has greatly increased. In fact, some cities and towns which had been predominantly Christian are now practically devoid of Christians.

The Jews have so replaced the Christians that

some parishes are about to lose their ministers because their revenue has dwindled so drastically. Because the Jews control businesses selling liquor and even wine, they are therefore allowed to supervise the collection of public revenues. They have also gained control of inns, bankrupt estates, villages and public land by means of which they have subjugated poor Christian farmers. The Jews are cruel taskmasters, not only working the farmers harshly and forcing them to carry excessive loads, but also whipping them for punishment. So it has come about that those poor farmers are the subjects of the Jews, submissive to their will and power. Furthermore, although the power to punish lies with the Christian official, he must comply with the commands of the Jews and inflict the punishments they desire. If he doesn't, he would lose his post. Therefore the tyrannical orders of the Jews have to be carried out.

3. In addition to the harm done to Christians in these regards, other unreasonable matters can result in even greater loss and danger. The most serious is that some households of the great have employed a Jew as "Superintendent-of-the-Household"; in this capacity, they not only administer domestic and economic matters, but they also ceaselessly exhibit and flaunt authority over the Christians they are living with. It is now even commonplace for Christians and Jews to intermingle anywhere. But what is even less comprehensible is that Jews fearlessly keep Christians of both sexes in their houses as their domestics, bound to their service. Furthermore, by means of their particular practice of commerce, they amass a great store of money and then by an exorbitant rate of interest utterly destroy the wealth and inheritance of Christians. Even if they borrow money from Christians at heavy and undue interest with their synagogues as surety, it is obvious to anyone who thinks about it that they do so to employ the money borrowed from Christians in their commercial dealings; this enables them to make enough profit to pay the agreed interest and simultaneously increase their own store. At the same time, they gain as many defenders of their synagogues and themselves as they have creditors.

4. The famous monk, Radulph, inspired long ago by an excess of zeal, was so inflamed against the Jews that he traversed Germany and France in the twelfth century and, by preaching against the Jews as the enemies of our holy religion, incited Christians to destroy them. This resulted in the deaths of a very large number of Jews. What must we think his deeds or thoughts would be if he were now alive and saw what was happening in Poland? But the great St. Bernard opposed this immoderate and maddened zeal of Radulph, and wrote to the clergy and people of eastern France: "The Jews are not to be persecuted: they are not to be slaughtered: they are not even to be driven out. Examine the divine writings concerning them. We read in the psalm a new kind of prophecy concerning the Jews: God has shown me, says the Church, on the subject of my enemies, not to slay them in case they should ever forget my people. Alive, however, they are eminent reminders for us of the Lord's suffering. On this account they are scattered through all lands in order that they may be witnesses to Our redemption while they pay the just penalties for so great a crime" (epistle 363). And he writes this to Henry, Archbishop of Mainz: "Doesn't the Church every day triumph more fully over the Jews in convicting or converting them than if once and for all she destroyed them with the edge of the sword: Surely it is not in vain that the Church has established the universal prayer which is offered up for the faithless Jews from the rising of the sun to its setting, that the Lord God may remove the veil from their hearts, that they may be rescued from their darkness into the light of truth. For unless it hoped that those who do not believe would believe, it would obviously be futile and empty to pray for them." (epistle 365).

5. Peter, abbot of Cluny, likewise wrote against Radulph to King Louis of France, and urged him not to allow the destruction of the Jews. But at the same time he encouraged him to punish their excesses and to strip them of the property they had taken from Christians or had acquired by usury; he should then devote the value of this to the use and benefit of holy religion, as may be seen in the Annals of Venerable Cardinal Baronius (1146). In this matter, as in all others, We adopt the same norm of action as did the Roman Pontiffs who were Our venerable predecessors. Alexander III forbade Christians under heavy penalties to accept permanent domestic service under Jews. "Let them not continually devote themselves to the service of Jews for a wage." He sets out the reason for this in the decretal *Ad haec, de Judaeis.* "Because Jewish ways do not harmonize in any way with ours and they could easily turn the minds of the simple to their own superstitions and faithlessness through continual intercourse and unceasing acquaintance." Innocent III, after saying that Jews were being received by Christians into their cities, warns that the method and condition of this reception should guard against their repaying the benefit with evildoing. "They on being admitted to our acquaintance in a spirit of mercy, repay us, the popular proverb says, as the mouse in the wallet, the snake in the lap and fire in the bosom usually repay their host." The same Pope stated that it was fitting for Jews to serve Christians rather than vice versa and added: "Let not the sons of the free woman be servants of the sons of the handmaid; but as servants rejected by their lord for whose death they evilly conspired, let them realize that the result of this deed is to make them servants of those whom Christ's death made free," as we read in his decretal *Etsi Judaeos.* Likewise in the decretal *Cum sit nimis* under the same heading *de Judaeis, et Saracenis,* he forbids the promotion of Jews to public office: "forbidding Jews to be promoted to public offices since in such circumstances they may be very dangerous to Christians." Innocent IV, also, in writing to St. Louis, King of France, who intended to drive the Jews beyond the boundaries of his kingdom, approves of this plan since the Jews gave very little heed to the regulations made by the Apostolic See in their regard: "Since We strive with all Our heart for the salvation of souls, We grant you full power by the authority of this letter to expel the Jews, particularly since We have learned that they do not obey the said statutes issued by this See against them" (Raynaldus, Annals, A.D. 1253, no. 34).

6. But if it is asked what matters the Apostolic See forbids to Jews living in the same cities as Christians, We will say that all those activities which are now allowed in Poland are forbidden; these We recounted above. There is no need of much reading to understand that this is the clear truth of the matter. It is enough to peruse decretals with the heading *de Judaeis, et Saracenis*; the constitutions of Our predecessors, the Roman Poniffs Nicholas IV, Paul IV, St. Pius V, Gregory XIII and Clement VIII are readily available in the Roman Bullarium. To understand these matters most clearly, Venerable Brothers, you do not even need to read those. You will recall the statutes and prescripts of the synods of your predecessors; they always entered in their constitutions every measure concerning the Jews which was sanctioned and ordained by the Roman Pontiffs.

7. The essence of the difficulty, however, is that either the sanctions of the synods are forgotten or they are not put into effect. To you then, Venerable Brothers, passes the task of renewing those sanctions. The nature of your office requires that you carefully encourage their implementation. In this matter begin with the clergy, as is fair and reasonable. These will have to show others the right way to act, and light the way for the rest by their example. For in God's mercy, We hope that the good example of the clergy will lead the straying laity back to the straight path. You will be able to give these orders and commands easily and confidently, in that neither your property nor your privileges are hired to Jews; furthermore you do no business with them and you neither lend them money nor borrow from them. Thus, you will be free from and unaffected by all dealings with them.

8. The sacred canons, prescribe that in the most important cases, such as the present, censures should be imposed upon the recalcitrant; and that those cases which bode danger and ruin to religion should be reckoned as reserved cases in which only the bishop can give absolution. The Council of Trent considered your jurisdiction when it affirmed your right to reserve cases. It did not restrict such cases to public crimes only, but extended them to include more notorious and serious cases, provided they were not purely internal. But we have often said that some cases should be considered more notorious and serious. These are cases, to which men are more prone, which are a danger both to ecclesiastical discipline and to the salvation of the souls which have been entrusted to your episcopal care. We have discussed these at length in Our treatise *On the diocesan synod*, Book 5, 5.

9. In this matter We will help as much as possible. If you have to proceed against ecclesiastics exempt from your jurisdiction, you will doubtless encounter additional difficulties. Therefore We are giving Our Venerable Brother Archbishop Nicaenus, Our Nuncio there, a mandate

appropriate for this business, in order that he may supply for you the necessary means from the powers entrusted to him. At the same time We promise you that when the situation arises, We will cooperate energeticaly and effectively with those whose combined authority and power are appropriate to remove this stain of shame from Poland. But first Venerable Brothers, ask aid from God, the source of all things. From Him beg help for Us and this Apostolic See. And while We embrace you in the fullness of charity, We lovingly impart to you, Our brothers, and to the flocks entrusted to your care, Our Apostolic Blessing.

Given at Castelgandolfo on the 14th of June 1751 in the eleventh year of Our Pontificate.

†

LATIN TEXT: *Bened. XIV Bull.*, 3^1: 297-300; *Magnum Bull.*, 18: 222-24.

ENGLISH TRANSLATION: Padraig M. O'Cleirigh

CUM RELIGIOSI

ENCYCLICAL OF POPE BENEDICT XIV
ON CATECHESIS
JUNE 26, 1754
9

To *the Patriarchs, Archbishops, and Bishops of Italy.*

Venerable Brothers, We give you Greeting and the Apostolic Blessing.

Removal of Impediments to Marriage

Religious men, devoted to the improvement of divine worship, have informed Us that it would be best to appoint special ministers in Our patriarchal basilicas, St. John Lateran, St. Peter's on the Vatican, and St. Mary Major's; their purpose would be to instruct those sent to these basilicas by the Apostolic Chancery to perform there the required servile works. These works are required before they are granted the object of their journey to Rome, which is the removal of an impediment to marriage. The aim of this instruction is to enable these people to be duly and beneficially cleansed by the Sacrament of Penance and to partake of the Sacrament of the Altar in a worthy manner. The Chancery demands that they receive both of these sacraments in addition to making the sacred pilgrimage to the seven churches and to ascending the holy stairway. We have issued timely orders on this subject before, as may be seen from Our encyclical letter of last January 16th to the Cardinals who are archpriests of the said basilicas. We have subsequently been reliably informed of the great zeal shown in this important work by some of the canons and other clergy of the said basilicas; they constantly and eagerly press on with the careful carrying out of Our commands. Because of these reports, We have experienced a specially deep joy, and with all Our heart, have rendered due thanks to the Most High God Who is the source of all good things.

Many Ignorant of the Mysteries of the Faith

We could not rejoice, however, when it was subsequently reported to Us that in the course of religious instruction preparatory to Confession and Holy Communion, it was very often found that these people were ignorant of the mysteries of the faith, even of those matters which must be known by *necessity of means*; consequently, they were ineligible to partake of the Sacraments. Although the ministers mentioned continue unceasing instruction to eradicate this great evil, yet this evil greatly distresses the people requesting and waiting for their dispensation. For oppressed by poverty and begging for their food with their own hands, they wish to leave the city as quickly as possible, to return to their homelands and marry; this is the purpose of their

journey, and they are undeterred by the discomforts of public and heavy penance.

Bishops Not at Fault

2. At the start of Our pontificate, We wrote an encyclical letter to increase the zeal of Our Venerable Brothers to ensure that in every diocese the elements and precepts of Christian doctrine be explained and learned. We have read both the old and new reports of their diocesan synods; We know they are filled with instructions and exhortations, and that they include everything helpful for transmitting Christian doctrine. Therefore We heartily assert Our conviction that in this matter none of the bishops can be found lacking in the Apostolic office entrusted to him; the fact that some members of their dioceses are ignorant is not due to their fault or negligence. It must clearly be attributed either to the obstinacy of their subjects who, despite the commands of their superiors, have avoided instruction in their Christian doctrine; they have, in fact, seldom if ever gathered to hear the word of God explained in preaching. Or it could be attributed to the slowness of some for learning what is taught. Or perhaps it is because that although they learned the elements of Christian teaching in their earliest years, when they were older, they ceased learning and building upon the foundation of their youth. Because of this, they are gradually reduced to a state like that of people who were not taught in their early years or who never received instruction in Christian doctrine. Although these setbacks have continued in spite of every measure taken by Our Venerable Brothers, We must nonetheless stir up their zeal again by this encyclical letter. And they are obligated anew to take every step and care possible in this matter on which the eternal salvation of the souls entrusted to them depends.

Work of St. Charles Borromeo

3. Each one of you, Venerable Brothers, has thoroughly understood the measures taken by St. Charles Borromeo, both in his own large diocese of Milan and in the entire province of which he was Metropolitan. He took these measures in order to establish a fruitful method of transmitting Christian doctrine, and he labored greatly in order to strongly sustain this religious education. And when he observed that his toil had not borne the fruit he desired, he did not despair, but instead increased his cares and concerns as is seen in the fifth synod of Milan: "We have hitherto shown great care in looking after the instruction of individual Christians in the fundamental doctrines in the Christian faith; but since we realize that we have profited little so far, we are led by the importance of the matter to make these additional decisions." For it was enough for that holy prelate to see that the need still existed, and thus to address himself to the work a second time; in this endeavor, he added cares to cares and minimized the many measures he had employed up till then. In like manner, it was enough for the Assyrian king to be informed that the nations did not know the commands of God: "and it was announced to the king of the Assyrians, and said: the nation which you transferred and sent to dwell in the cities of Samaria do not know the laws of God's land." He at once sent a priest to teach those nations the commands of God: "And the King of the Assyrians gave commands, saying: bring there one of the priests which you led off as prisoners and let him go and dwell with them and teach them the laws of God's land" (4 Kings 17).

Teach the Fundamentals of the Faith

4. Therefore with the example of St. Charles Borromeo before Us, We encourage you and implore you by the mercy of Jesus Christ not to despair in this important work of handing on the fundamentals of the Christian faith, even if hitherto you have devoted all your zeal and care to it. See to it that every minister performs carefully the measures laid down by the holy Council of Trent and by the statutes of your synods: that on fixed days school-masters and mistresses should teach Christian doctrine; that confessors should perform this part of their duty whenever anyone stands at their tribunal who does not know what he must by *necessity of means* know to be saved; that priests should also provide this instruction before uniting spouses in marriage; that fathers of families and lords of houses should be gravely advised of the duty imposed on them of being themselves instructed and of seeing to the instruction in the commandments of Christian doctrine of their sons and of the members of their household; that the practice of reciting aloud properly-composed acts of Faith, Hope and Charity by the priest and people before or after the parish mass should be preserved in

the dioceses in which it is customary and be carefully introduced where it is not. Parish priests should not avoid their duty of at least on feast days, explaining the Gospel to the people from the altar when there is no sermon. In addition, they are obliged to teach them the chief mysteries of our holy religion, the commandments of God and the Church, and everything which is necessary for their worthy partaking of the Sacraments. Preachers should also follow this path, recalling the salutary advice that they should join instruction to exhortation whenever their hearers stand in need of both. Finally, the best method for instructing ignorant men in Christian doctrine is indicated by St. Augustine who says (*de Cath. Rud.*, 10) that the most fruitful procedure is to ask questions in a friendly fashion after the explanation; from this questioning one can learn whether each one understood what he heard or whether the explanation needs repeating. In order that the learner grasp the matter, "we must ascertain by questioning whether the one being catechised has understood, and in accordance with his response, we must either explain more clearly and fully or not dwell further on what is known to them, etc. But if a man is very slow, he must be mercifully helped and the most necessary doctrines especially should be briefly imparted to him." We are assured that you yourselves will pursue many more paths than We point out to you in this encyclical letter. In the meantime, Venerable Brothers, We lovingly impart to you and to the flock entrusted to your care Our Apostolic Blessing.

Given at Castelgandolfo on the 26th of June 1754 in the fourteenth year of Our Pontificate.

†

LATIN TEXT: *Bened. XIV Bull.*, 3^2: 196-98, first use of *Encyclicae literae* in superscription; *Magnum Bull.*, 19: 108-10. Latin and Italian in parallel columns.

ENGLISH TRANSLATION: Padraig M. O'Cleirigh

QUOD PROVINCIALE

ENCYCLICAL OF POPE BENEDICT XIV ON CHRISTIANS USING MOHAMMEDAN NAMES

AUGUST 1, 1754

10

To Our Venerable Brothers the Archbishops and Bishops as well as Our Beloved Sons, the Parish Priests and Missionaries of the Province of Albania.

Venerable Brothers and Beloved Sons, We give you Greeting and Our Apostolic Blessing.

Forbidding Use of Mohammedan Names

The Provincial Council of your province of Albania, Venerable Brothers and Beloved Sons, was held in the year 1703 during the pontificate of Our predecessor Pope Clement XI. It decreed most solemnly in its third canon, among other matters, as you know, that Turkish or Mohammedan names should not be given either to children or adults in baptism. It also decreed that the faithful of Christ should not allow themselves to be called by Turkish or Mohammedan names which they had never received, for the purpose of either exemption or immunity from taxes, or the advantage of free trading, or avoiding penalties. We have confirmed and commanded the observance of this decree in Our encyclical letter *Inter omnigenas*, addressed to the kingdom of Serbia and its neighbouring regions. This encyclical letter, covering many subjects of religion and discipline, was published on the 2nd of February 1744 in the fourth year of Our pontificate. This prudent and saving statute was established by your predecessors with great wisdom and devotion as a shining example of your Catholic faith and sincere Christian piety; in our 1744 encyclical, We strictly ordered it to be imitated and fully observed by other churches. Just as adhering to it clearly results in the greater fame and reputation of your province and in greater benefits for securing the eternal salvation of souls, so if it should be neglected, it would greatly dishonor your province and openly endanger these souls.

In Our letter mentioned above, We designated that abuse as a cowardly concealment of the Christian profession, approaching infidelity. Since then, We have learned with great mental anguish that many people in that province continue to take Turkish or Mohammedan names despite the consideration of their eternal salvation. They do so not only in order to be immune and free from those taxes and burdens which have often been and continue to be imposed on the faithful of Christ, but also in order that neither they themselves nor their parents may be thought to have abandoned the Mohammedan sect, thereby avoiding the requisite penalties. For all this cannot take place without a pretense of the errors of Mohammed, even if the faith of Christ is adhered to in the heart, and this is at

variance with Christian sincerity. It involves a lie in a most serious matter and includes a virtual denial of the Faith, most insulting to God and scandalous to their neighbors. It even gives the Turks themselves a suitable opportunity to rate all Christ's faithful as hypocrites and deceivers, and accordingly to persecute them justly and deservedly.

2. Our sorrow and anguish is further increased by the fact that some of you yourselves, venerable brothers, and of you also, beloved sons, parish priests and missionaries, take no measures against so vile and hateful a pretense. In fact, some of you even connive at it; by being impressed by empty motives to find excuses for sins, you do not hesitate to allow those who take common Turkish or Mohammedan names and desire to be addressed by them, to partake of the Sacraments with no pang of conscience at all, to the public offense of the obedient faithful.

3. We who are entrusted with the care of all the churches and the supreme administration of the sacred Apostolate; in this capacity, We are obliged to lead all Christians back to the way of salvation and to present them to God pure and sincere, walking in the spirit and in truth without stain. We have heard Our Venerable Brothers, the Cardinals of the Holy Roman Church, who are general Inquisitors for evil heresy on this subject. In accordance with their advice, We first renew and confirm by Our Apostolic authority in this letter the praiseworthy canon of the council of your province of Albania, and We command that it be strictly observed. Also We extend the decrees of Our church by the same authority and uniformity to include your province; We equally strictly prohibit any of Christ's faithful from daring to take Turkish or Mohammedan names in order to be considered Mohammedans, in any case, under any pretext, or in any conceivable circumstances.

4. Furthermore, venerable brothers and beloved sons, We ask and urge you in the Lord to think seriously about your ministry and the strict account you will have to give to the Eternal Judge Jesus Christ, the Supreme Prince of Pastors, for the sheep entrusted to each one of you; to this end, We urge you to take personal care by your good works that your election will be assured. Since it would be very careless and negligent on your part not to, do not fail to patiently convince, implore, and exhort the faithful of Christ in your Province to lead a good life among the nations. Urge them in all affairs to conduct themselves so as to be an example of good works in order that those who oppose them may be chagrined since they have nothing evil to say of them, and they cannot accuse them of being evildoers who for the sake of base gain profess one thing with their lips while believing differently in their hearts. But if they do not accept your warnings and Our commands, they must be compelled by the rod to follow the norm of Apostolic discipline. The sanctions and penalties provided for by your Albanian council and by Our letter mentioned above must be fully applied in their case: that is, they must be declared unfit to receive the Sacraments in their lifetime, and if they die unrepentant, to benefit from prayers after death. Insofar as it is necessary, We renew and reapply these penalties; We enjoin you to ensure their due execution. This should not be hard for any one of you, venerable brothers and beloved sons, for none of the schismatics and heretics has been rash enough to take a Mohammedan name, and unless your justice abounds more than theirs, you shall not enter the kingdom of Heaven.

5. Finally, gravely advise those who have converted from Mohammedanism or the children of such converts, if they lack confidence in their constancy in the Faith, fearing punishment by their rulers if they abandon their Turkish names, to emigrate secretly from those territories and come for refuge to Christian lands. There they shall in no way lack the help of God who gives food to all flesh, or the charity of the faithful, especially if their Bishops provide them with letters of recommendation. In the meantime, We lovingly grant you Our Apostolic Blessing, venerable brothers and beloved sons, and We desire each Venerable Brother Bishop to extend it in Our name to all the orthodox faithful of Christ in his own diocese.

Given at Rome in St. Mary Major on the first day of August, 1754, in the fourteenth year of Our Pontificate.

†

LATIN TEXT: *Bened. XIV Bull.*, 3^2: 199-201; *Magnum Bull.*, 19: 111-12.

ENGLISH TRANSLATION: Padraig M. O'Cleirigh

ALLATAE SUNT

ENCYCLICAL OF POPE BENEDICT XIV ON
THE OBSERVANCE OF ORIENTAL RITES
JULY 26, 1755
11

To *Missionaries Assigned to the Orient.*

Beloved Sons, We give You Greeting and Our Apostolic Blessing.

There has been brought to the Cardinals, who are in charge of the Propagation of the Faith, the letter of a certain priest who was assigned to conduct holy missions in the city of Balsera. This city, commonly called *Bassora*, is about fifteen days' journey from Babylon, a city well-known for the dealings of merchants. In his letter, he informed the Cardinals that many Catholics of the Oriental rite, Armenians or Syrians, live in that city. Because they have no temple of their own, they come to the church of the Latin missionaries where their priests offer masses and perform other sacred ceremonies in accordance with their own rite. But lay people attend these ceremonies and receive the sacraments from the priests. So he inquired whether these Armenians and Syrians should observe their own Catholic rite or whether, to avoid different practices in a church which Latins also attend, it would be more appropriate that the Armenians and Syrians should abandon their ancient calendar and accept the new one to establish the dates of Easter and movable feastdays. He further inquired whether if the observance of the new calendar were decreed for the Armenians and Syrians of Balsera, it should also be imposed on other orientals who, because their own church is small, generally come to the church of the Latins for their sacred functions.

Abstinence from Fish

2. Furthermore, this missionary also reported that although abstinence from fish is prescribed on fast days for Armenians and Syrian Catholics, many of them do not observe this regulation. This is not from any contempt, but in part from natural weakness and in part from seeing that Latin Catholics have a different custom. Accordingly, he suggested that it would be appropriate to give missionaries the power of allowing particular individuals to eat fish in a season of fasting, provided that this gives rise to no scandal and that they are obliged to perform some other work of piety in place of abstaining from fish.

Decree Forbidding Dispensations

3. These questions were, as We have said, submitted by this missionary to the Congregation for the Propagation of the Faith. As is customary, it sent them to the Congregation of General Inquisition. This Congregation met in Our presence on March 13. The Cardinals Inquisitor

unanimously answered that "no innovations were to be made." We confirmed this decision in conformity with a former decree of the Congregation for the Propagation of the Faith published on January 31, 1702; it has subsequently been renewed and confirmed several times. That decree reads as follows: "At the instance of its Secretary, R.P.D. Carolus Augustinus Fabronus, the Sacred Congregation has commanded that it be ordered, and by the present decree it is so ordered, that each and every missionary and prefect of Apostolic missions should not dare in future, in any circumstance or under any pretext, to give a dispensation to Catholics of any oriental nation in matters of fasts, prayers, ceremonies, and suchlike from the prescriptions of their own national rite which are approved by the Holy and Apostolic See. Moreover, the Sacred Congregation has decided that it neither has been nor is permitted for those Catholics to abandon in any respect the custom and observance of their own rite which has likewise been approved by the Holy Roman Church. The complete and straightforward observance of this decree, renewed and confirmed by each and every prefect and missionary, has been commanded by these most eminent fathers." This decree, indeed, applies to Catholics of the Oriental Church and to their rites which have been approved by the Apostolic See. As everyone knows, the Oriental Church is composed of four rites—Greek, Armenian, Syriac, and Coptic; all these rites are referred to by the single name of the Greek or Oriental Church, just as the name of the Latin or Roman Church signifies the Roman, Ambrosian, and Mozarabic rites, as well as the special rites of different Regular Orders.

4. The meaning of the decree is too clear to require any commentary. So the purpose of this encyclical letter is to ensure that this law is known and understood by everyone and is thereupon carried out with care. For it can be justly suspected that the missionary of Balsera submitted his questions with no knowledge of the decrees which had already been issued. We gather from many other indications that Latin missionaries devote thought and care to destroying or at least weakening the Oriental rite in the course of converting Orientals from the error of schism to the unity of the Holy Catholic Religion; they induce Oriental Catholics to embrace the Latin rite with the sole motivation of zealously spreading religion and performing a good work pleasing to God. We have thought it fitting for this reason (since We have set Our mind on writing) to treat as briefly as possible in this encyclical letter the proper procedure in all cases when Orientals are converted to the Catholic Religion. This procedure is to be observed in the case of Oriental Catholics who live both in places where there are no Latins and where Latin Catholics dwell together with Oriental Catholics.

Oriental Church United With Roman Church

5. Certainly, that man would have to be declared utterly inexperienced in ecclesiastical history who did not know of the mighty efforts of the Roman Pontiffs to bring the Orientals into unity since the fatal schism of Photius; he laid hold of the See of Constantinople when the lawful Patriarch St. Ignatius was forcefully ejected in the time of Pope St. Nicholas I. Our Predecessor St. Leo IX sent his legates to Constantinople to put an end to this schism, which, after almost two centuries' respite, had been renewed by Michael Cerularius; but their efforts came to nothing. Subsequently Urban II summoned the Greeks to the council of Bari. They accomplished very little though, even though St. Anselm, Archbishop of Canterbury, was fully engaged in working for unity between them and the Roman Church and in revealing to them the errors of their ways by the light of his teaching. At the Council of Lyons which Blessed Gregory X convened, the emperor Michael Palaeologus and the Greek bishops accepted unity with the Roman Church, but then changed their minds and abandoned it again. The Council of Florence, in the pontificate of Eugenius IV, which was attended by John Palaeologus and Joseph, Patriarch of Constantinople, together with the other Oriental bishops, decreed union; everyone present accepted it. At the same Council the churches of the Armenians and the Jacobites returned to obedience to the Apostolic See. When Pope Eugenius left Florence for Rome, he received an embassy from the king of the Ethiopians and restored the Syrians, Chaldaeans, and Maronites to obedience to the Roman See. But as it is written in St. Matthew's Gospel, chap. 13, the seed which fell on a rock produced no fruit

since it had no place to put down roots: "These are those who at once receive the word of God with joy but do not have roots in themselves; when tribulation and persecution come on account of the word, they stumble at once." Thus, scarcely had Mark, Archbishop of Ephesus, like a new Photius, tried to destroy the union by raising his voice against it, than all the desired fruit immediately vanished.

6. That man too would betray his ignorance of ecclesiastical history who did not know that the union with the Orientals confirmed that they would accept the dogma of the procession of the Holy Spirit from the Father and the Son, and add to the Creed the word *Filioque* ("and from the Son"); that they would admit that both leavened and unleavened bread was matter for the Sacrament of the Eucharist; that they would accept the dogma of purgatory, of the beatific vision and of the primacy of the Roman Pontiff; in a word, that every care was taken to overthrow all errors opposed to the Catholic faith. But there was never any question of causing harm to the venerable Oriental rite. That man would be utterly ignorant also of the present discipline of the Church who had not discovered that the Roman Pontiffs, undeterred by past fruitless attempts, have always intended to restore the Greeks to union and have always followed and still follow the path We have explained just above. This can be clearly gathered both from their words and from their deeds.

Leo IX Supported Greek Church in 11th Century

7. In the eleventh century, several Latin churches observing the Latin rite thrived in Constantinople, Alexandria, and the Patriarchate of Jerusalem; just as in Rome, Greek churches performed sacred ceremonies in the Greek rite. Michael Cerularius, the impious restorer of the schism, commanded the closing of the Latin Churches. St. Leo IX, however, did not respond in kind although he could readily have done so; rather than closing the Greek churches in Rome, he desired them to remain open. And so when he complained of the insult done to the Latins, he added: "See how much more restrained, moderate, and kindly towards you the Roman church is here! Although there are many Greek monasteries or churches, both inside and outside Rome, none of these has yet been disturbed or forbidden to follow the tradition of its fathers or its own custom; rather all of them are advised and urged to observe it." (I Ep 9)

Thirteenth Century Support for Greek Churches

8. At the start of the thirteenth century the Latins gained control of Constantinople. Innocent III then decided to establish a Latin Patriarch in that city with jurisdiction over Greeks as well as Latins; but he still was careful to state openly that he did not want any harm done to the Greek rites, excepting only those traditional customs which endangered souls or were at variance with the honor of the Church. The decretal of this pope, issued at the Fourth Lateran Council, is to be found both in Harduin's *Collectionis Conciliorum*, vol. 7, p. 22, and in the chapter *Licet, de Baptismo*. "Although the Greeks have returned to obedience to the Apostolic See in Our day, We desire them as greatly as We can in the Lord to cherish and hold in honor their custom and rites, except for those customs which give rise to danger for souls and detract from the honor of the Church, for in these cases We neither should nor do We want to respect them." Later Honorius III, the immediate successor of Innocent, used the same words in a letter to the king of Cyprus who wanted two bishops in some cities in his kingdom, a Latin bishop for the Latin inhabitants and a Greek bishop for the Greeks living in the same district. This letter of Honorius is printed in the *Annals* of Raynaldus, 1222, a. 5.

9. There are many documents of this kind from the thirteenth century. For instance the letter of Innocent IV to Daniel, King of Russia, praises the particular devotion of the king to the Catholic Church and allows to be preserved in his kingdom rites which are not at variance with the faith of the Catholic Church. He writes: "Therefore, dearest son in Christ, We are moved by your prayer and grant by the authority of this letter to the bishops and other priests of Russia permission to consecrate leavened bread in accordance with their custom and to observe their other rites which are not opposed to the Catholic faith held by the Church of Rome." (Raynaldus, 1247, no. 29.) Such is the tenor, too, of the same Pope's letter to Cardinal Otho of Tusculum, Legate of the Holy See on the Island of

Cyprus, whom he had entrusted with the authority to settle some disputes which had arisen between Greeks and Latins: "But since some of the Greeks are at last returning to their devotion to the Apostolic See, and obey it with reverence and respect, We may and should tolerate and preserve their customs and rites as far as God and their obedience to the Roman Church permits. However, We ought not—nor do We wish to—yield to them in the slightest matter which could produce danger for souls or lessen the honor of the Church" (*in veteri Bullario*, vol. 1, no. 14, constitution *Sub Catholicae*). But in the same letter after he laid down what the Greeks had to do, he listed the practices which he thought they should be allowed to observe and ends with the following words: "But on Our authority, order the aforesaid Archbishop of Nicosia together with his Latin suffragans not to disturb or harass the Greeks contrary to Our decision in these matters." The same Pope Innocent IV appointed his confessor Laurentius Minorita as Apostolic Legate and gave him full authority over all the Greeks who lived in the kingdom of Cyprus and the patriarchates of Antioch and Jerusalem, as well as over the Jacobites, Maronites and Nestorians. He commanded him especially to protect by his authority all the Greeks from harassment from the Latins: "As regards the Greeks of those regions, whatever their affiliation, We command you to protect them by apostolic authority, and to prevent their being disturbed by acts of violence or any harassment by fully correcting all wrongs and offenses done by Latins and by strictly commanding the Latins to give up such acts for the future" (Raynaldus, 1546, no. 30).

10. Alexander IV, the immediate successor of Pope Innocent, observed that the desire of his predecessor had not been achieved and that disorderly dissensions between Greek and Latin bishops continued to break out in the kingdom of Cyprus. Accordingly he commanded the Latin bishops to summon Greek clerics to their synods. But when he declared that they were subject to the decrees of the synods, he added the following condition: "(that they are) to accept and observe the statutes of the Synods, provided that these statutes do not conflict with the Greek rites which are not opposed to the Catholic faith and are tolerated by the Church of Rome." Elias, Archbishop of Nicosia, followed this praiseworthy precedent in 1340 when he included this declaration in the decrees of his synod: "We do not purpose by this decree to prevent Greek bishops and their subjects from observing their own rites which are consonant with the Catholic faith, in accordance with the arrangement proposed by Pope Alexander, and accepted by both Greeks and Latins in the kingdom of Cyprus" (Labbe, *Collectione*, vol. 14, p. 279, and vol. 15, p. 775, Venice edition).

11. The end of the thirteenth century is marked by the Union of Greeks and Latins decreed at the General Council of Lyons in the pontificate of Blessed Gregory X. Gregory sent to Michael Palaeologus the confession of faith and the decree of union confirmed by the Council which the eastern legates had sworn to, in order that the emperor himself and the other Greek bishops should accept them. The emperor and the Orientals performed all that was required, but they added the condition: "But we ask of Your Greatness etc. to be allowed to preserve the rites which we used before the schism since these rites are not opposed to the Faith or to the divine commandments" (Harduin, *Collectionis*, vol. 8, p. 698). Although the reply of Pope Gregory to this letter of the Orientals has not survived, it may rightly be taken that he approved this condition since he believed that they had firmly accepted the union. And of course Nicholas III, the successor of Gregory, through the legates he sent to Constantinople, revealed his mind in the following words: "As to the other Greek rites, however, the Roman Church gladly proposes that the Greeks observe them to the full extent that God allows, and permits them to continue in those rites which in the decision of the Apostolic See do not injure the integrity of the Catholic faith or detract from the holy decrees of the Canons" (Raynaldus, 1278).

Fifteenth Century

12. For the fifteenth century, we will mention only the union decreed at the council of Florence. Pope Eugenius approved it and John Palaeologus accepted it with the proviso "that no changes should be made in the Rites of our Church" (Harduin, *Collectionis*, vol. 9, p. 345). But since We do not intend to review in particular detail the actions of the Roman pontiffs in subsequent centuries, We shall touch on several main incidents which suggest clearly that while they tried zealously to correct the misconceptions of the Orientals, at the same time they indicated that they desired to preserve entire those rites used before the schism with the approval of the Apostolic See. They never demanded that Orientals who wished to be Catholic should embrace the Latin Rite.

Further Support

13. The Greek Manual, published at Benevento, contains two Constitutions of Popes Leo X and Clement VII which vigorously criticize Latins who abuse the Greeks for practices which the Council of Florence permitted them: in particular that they may offer the Sacrifice of the Mass with leavened bread, that they may take a wife before receiving Holy Orders and keep their wife after Ordination, and that they may offer the Eucharist under both species even to children. When Pius IV decreed that Greeks living in the Dioceses of Latins should be subject to the Latin bishops, he added that "by this decree, however, We do not purpose that the Greeks themselves should be drawn away from their Greek rite, or that they should be hindered in any way in other places by the local Ordinaries or others" (*veteris Bullarii*, vol. 2, const. no. 75, *Romanus Pontifex*).

14. The annals of Gregory XIII, written by Fr. Maffei and printed at Rome in 1742, relate several deeds of this pope which aimed at restoring the Copts and Armenians to the Catholic faith, though quite unsuccessfully. But of especial interest are his words concerning the foundation of three colleges in Rome which he had established for the education of Greek, Maronite, and Armenian students, in which he provided that they should continue in their oriental rites (*in novo Bullario*, vol. 4, pt. 3, const. 63, and pt. 4, const. 157 and 173).

A solemn union of the Ruthenians with the Apostolic See was enacted in the time of Pope Clement VIII. The decree prepared by the Ruthenian archbishops and bishops for establishing union contains the following condition: "However, the ceremonies and rites of the divine liturgy and holy sacraments shall be preserved and fully observed in accordance with the custom of the oriental church; only those points shall be corrected which are a hindrance to union; everything shall be done in the ancient manner as they were long ago when the union was in existence."

Shortly afterwards a disturbance was caused by a widespread rumor that the union had put an end to all the old rites which the Ruthenians followed in the divine psalmody, the sacrifice of the Mass, the administration of the sacraments, and other holy ceremonies. Paul V in an apostolic brief written in 1615 and printed in the Greek Manual, solemnly declared his will in the following words: "Provided that they are not opposed to truth and the teaching of the Catholic faith, and they do not prevent communion with the Roman church, it was not and it is not the intention, understanding, or will of the Roman church to remove or destroy them by means of this union; and this could not and cannot be said or thought; instead these rites have been allowed and granted to the Ruthenian bishops and clergy by Apostolic kindness."

Allatae sunt 11

15. It is proper here to remember the churches which in later times different popes entrusted to Greeks, Maronites, Armenians, Copts, and Melchites in Rome. These still exist, with each group performing the holy ceremonies in accordance with its own rite. It can also be recalled that Clement VIII (in his constitution 34, sect. 7 of *Veteris Bullarii*) established a Greek bishop in Rome to ordain, according to the Greek rite, Italo-Greeks who lived in Latin dioceses. Another Greek bishop was established in the Diocese of Bisiniana by Our immediate predecessor Clement XII, and his constitution *Pastoralis*, to ordain Italo-Greeks and spare those who lived far from Rome the long journey to obtain ordination at the hands of the Greek Bishop of Rome. Catholic bishops of the Maronites, Copts, and Melchites who from time to time live in Rome are not denied the faculty of ordaining men of their own nation according to their own rite, provided suitable candidates are found. Whenever a dispute arises about the practice of the Orientals or the Italo-Greeks, the Apostolic See makes every effort to ensure that they correct what clearly needs correction, but states at once that it desires the Oriental rite to remain untouched and unshaken in all other respects. It also proclaims that laws affecting Italo-Greeks who live among us and are subject to the jurisdiction of Latin bishops should be understood to affect only these and should not in any way be extended to the Oriental Greeks who live far from us and are subject to their own Greek Catholic bishops.

16. This is learned from the confirmation of the provincial synod of the Ruthenians which met at Zamoscia in 1720. At that time Benedict XIII appointed Us to examine this matter as secretary of the Congregation of the Council. He thought the suggestions of the fathers of this synod should be approved, although they restrained or removed by their decrees some Greek rites which were in practice. He confirmed the synod in his apostolic brief in 1724, but added the following statement: "However Our confirmation of this synod should not be thought to derogate in the least from the constitutions of the popes who preceded Us or from the decrees of the General Councils on the subject of Greek Rites. Notwithstanding this confirmation, these rites should always remain strong."

The same message is gathered from many of Our own constitutions which can be found in Our *Bullarium* under the general headings of the rites of the Copts, Melchites, Maronites, Ruthenians, and Italo-Greeks and also specifically on the rites of the clergy of the collegiate church of Messana called St. Mary's de Grafeo, and finally on the Greek rite observed in the Order of St. Basil. In constitution 87 (*Bullarii*, vol. 1) on the rites of the Greek Melchites the following passage occurs: "So on the rites and customs of the Greek Church We have decided to command firstly and in general that no one has been or is permitted on any pretext or authority or rank even of a patriarch or a bishop to make any changes or introduce anything to detract from their full precise observance."

In the earlier constitution 57, *Etsi Pastoralis*, sect. 9, no. 1, the following measures are taken in regard to Italo-Greeks: "Since the rites of the Oriental Church, which derive mainly from the holy Fathers and tradition, have so impressed themselves on the minds of the Greeks and of other men, the Roman pontiffs, Our pred ecessors, have wisely preferred to approve and allow these rites, in so far as they are not at variance with the Catholic faith, dangerous to souls, or disreputable for the Church, rather than to reduce them to the form of the Roman ceremonies etc." And sect. 9, no. 24: "Furthermore everything which We have earlier granted, commanded, or forbidden to Italo-Greeks is not intended to prejudice any rights of the Oriental Greeks under their own Catholic bishops, archbishops, or patriarchs, or any of the rites of other Christian peoples which have been approved or allowed by the Holy See. These include all rights whether of law or custom or other legal grounds either from apostolic constitutions or the decrees passed by General or Special Councils or of the Congregations of the Cardinals on the subject of the rites of the Greeks or other Orientals."

Profession of Faith by Orientals

17. Passing by these questions, We will declare freely that the Roman pontiffs have carefully and tirelessly attempted to overcome the heresies which gave rise to the schism between the western and the eastern church, and that consequently they have commanded orientals who want to return to the unity of the Church to reject these errors, to find out if they really belong in union with the Apostolic See.

There are two forms of this profession of faith. The first was prescribed for Greeks by Pope Gregory XIII (*veteris Bullarii*, vol. 2, 33) while the second was demanded of Orientals by Pope Urban VIII. Both were published at the Congregation for the Propagation of the Faith, the first in 1623 and the second in 1642. Subsequently, in 1665, the Patriarch of Antioch, Syriacus of Hierapolis, and the Archbishop of the Syrians in Hierapolis sent their profession of faith to Rome. Father Lorenzo de Lauraea of the Order of Conventuals Minor of St. Francis, then a consultor of the holy office and later a Cardinal, was asked to examine the question and on April 28th he produced his written verdict. It was subsequently approved by the Congregation, which concludes as follows: "All should be received, but those whom it concerns should be informed that they should not hereafter use a profession of faith different from that prescribed for Orientals by Urban VIII of happy memory, since this profession contains a rejection of many heresies and other matters needful for those districts."

Correction of the Greek Euchologion

18. Since the enemy, in order to sow weeds among the wheat, has driven some men so deeply into wickedness that they have inserted errors in Missals, Breviaries, and Rituals to mislead the clergy, the popes with timely wisdom have had new editions of the missals of the Copts, Maronites, Illyrians, etc., published by the Congregation for the Propagation of the Faith after a careful examination of each of them. And We must mention the care which was devoted to the correction of the Greek Euchologion published in recent months by the press of the same Congregation.

The examination of this work was begun zealously under Pope Urban VIII, but it was interrupted after a short time. It was taken up again under Clement XII, but God reserved for Us the joy of beholding the completion of this very important work. During Our pontificate Cardinals, Prelates, theologians, and men trained in the languages of the east devoted long hours to work and discussion. We Ourselves read the discussions and weighed every matter which called for examination.

The work was revised scrupulously to avoid the slightest injury to the Greek rite and to ensure that this rite remained unimpaired and entire. This course was followed, even though previously, in their utter ignorance of the Oriental liturgies and rites which existed in the eastern church before the time of the schism, some of our theologians whose expert knowledge was confined to the western rite, used to condemn every detail which differed from this rite. In short, the chief concern of the popes in securing the return of Greeks and Oriental schismatics to the Catholic religion has ever been to pluck completely from their minds the errors of Arius, Macedonius, Nestorius, Eutyches, Dioscuros, the Monothelites, and others, into which they had wretchedly fallen. But the rites which they observed and professed before the schism and the practice which depends on these ancient liturgies and rituals have always been left unchanged. Indeed the popes have never asked those returning to the Catholic faith to give up their own rite and assume the Latin rite. For this would involve the complete extermination of the eastern church and of the Greek and other Eastern rites, an objective which this Holy See has certainly never planned or striven for.

19. Many inferences can be made from Our present exposition. First, the missionary who is attempting with God's help to bring back Greek and eastern schismatics to unity should devote all his effort to the single objective of delivering them from doctrines at variance with the Catholic faith. Their forefathers accepted these errors as some sort of pretext for leaving the unity of the Church and for refusing the pope the respect and obedience which is his due as head of the Church.

A missionary should make use of the following proofs. Since the Orientals are greatly devoted to their own Church Fathers, Leo Allatius and other notable theologians have studied the question carefully and have shown clearly that the more notable Fathers of the Greek and Latin Church fully agree on all points of doctrine; they specifically reject the errors which fetter the east now. Consequently the study of those books will be beneficial.

Allatae sunt 11

In the last century the Lutherans tried to draw Greeks and Orientals into their own errors. The Calvinists, who bitterly attack the Real Presence of Christ in the Sacrament of the Eucharist and the transubstantiation of bread and wine into His Body and Blood, made the same attempt; it is reported that they won over the Patriarch Cyril to their view. However the Greeks, schismatic as they are, realized that the new errors were at variance with the teaching of their Fathers, especially SS. Cyril, John Chrysostom, Gregory of Nyssa, and John Damascene; with firm proofs drawn from their own liturgies which affirm the Real Presence and Transubstantiation, they rejected the deceptions and refused to abandon any aspect of the Catholic truth (see Schelestratus *De perpetua consensione Orientalis Ecclesiae contra Lutheranos*, the chapter *De transubstantiatione*, p. 717, vol. 2, of *Actorum Ecclesiae Orientalis*). In two synods they unanimously condemned Patriarch Cyril and the Calvinist doctrines published under his name (see Christian Lupus, *ad Concilia Generalia, et Provincialia*, part 5, and particularly his treatise *De quibusdam locis*, chap. 9, at end).

In the first place this gives substantial hope that when they are confronted with the teaching of the Fathers, which strongly supports our Catholic doctrine and attacks their own more recent errors, they will be inspired to a genuine conversion and find it very easy to return. Secondly, it can be seen that there is no need to harm or destroy their rites in recalling them to the way of unity since the Apostolic See has always opposed this procedure. This See has been able to separate the weeds from the wheat in these holy rites as often as the need arose. Moreover the attempt to destroy their rites will only jeopardize the desired union, as Thomas of Jesus rightly reflects: "It must also be shown that the Roman church approves and favors each Church maintaining its own rites and ceremonies, since of course the schismatics are very attached to their own rites. A timely effort must be made to persuade them that they will be confirmed in the observance of their own ceremonies in order to prevent any false suspicion developing that these rites would be abolished and any consequent turning away from the Roman church, which has no such objective" (*De conversione omnium gentium procuranda*, bk. 7, chap. 2).

Thirdly and finally, from what has already been said it can be inferred that a missionary who wants to convert an eastern schismatic should not attempt to make him accept the Latin rite. For the only work entrusted to the missionary is that of recalling the Oriental to the Catholic faith, not that of making him accept the Latin rite.

Transferring from Latin to Greek Rite Forbidden

20. When Union was effected at the Council of Florence, some Latin Catholics living in Greece thought that it was lawful for them to go over to the Greek rite. They may have been attracted by the freedom retained by the Greeks for priests to keep wives after Ordination if they were married before being ordained. But Pope Nicholas V carefully applied a timely remedy to this abuse: "It has come to Our attention that many Catholics in districts with a Greek Catholic bishop are shamelessly going over to the Greek rites under pretext of the Union. We are greatly astonished, since We do not know what inspired them to leave the practice and rites in which they were born and reared for foreign rites. Even though the rites of the oriental church are praiseworthy, it is not permitted to confuse the rites of the churches. The holy council of Florence never allowed this" (constitution in *Bullarii recenter Romae editi*, vol. 3, part 3, p. 64).

Since the Latin rite is the rite of the holy Roman church and this church is mother and teacher of the other churches, the Latin rite should be preferred to all other rites. It follows that it is not lawful to transfer from the Latin to the Greek rite. Nor may those who have come over to the Latin rite from the Greek or Oriental rite return again to the Greek Rite, unless particular circumstances occasion the giving of a dispensation (constitution *Etsi Pastoralis* 57, sect. 2, no. 13, in Our *Bullarii*, vol. 1). Such dispensations have sometimes been given in times past, and are still given in the Roman College of the Maronites. When a priest there enters the Society of Jesus, he is given a dispensation to transfer to the Latin rite, and sometimes he receives an additional dispensation to say Mass and perform his Divine Office in the church of this College in the Syrian and Chaldaean rite in order to teach this rite to the students there. This is quite clear from many Decrees of the Congregation of the Holy Office, e.g. the Decrees of December 30, 1716; December 14, 1740; and the more recent Decree of August 19, 1752.

Transferring from Greek to Latin Rite

21. We have dealt with transferring from the Latin to the Greek rite. Transferrals in the opposite direction are not forbidden as strictly as the former. Still, a missionary who hopes for the return of a Greek or Oriental to the unity of the Catholic Church may not make him give up his own rite. This can cause great harm.

Melchite Catholics used to transfer willingly from the Greek to the Latin rite, but they have been forbidden to do so. Missionaries have been warned not to urge them to transfer. Permission to do so has been reserved to the private decision of the Apostolic See. This is clear from Our constitution *Demandatam*, 85, sect. 35 (*Bullarium*, vol. 1): "Moreover We expressly forbid henceforth all Melchite Catholics who observe the Greek rite to transfer to the Latin rite. We give strict orders to all missionaries not to encourage anyone rashly to transfer to the Latin from the Greek rite, nor even to allow them to do so if they want to without the permission of the Apostolic See, under the penalties which will be set out below and other penalties to be decided on by Us."

The same teaching is conveyed in the Decrees of Urban VIII in reference to the Greco-Ruthenian rite, issued at the Congregation for the Propagation of the Faith in his presence on February 7 and July 6, 1624. While it might seem fair to allow Italo-Greeks to transfer freely from the Greek to the Latin rite, since they live among us and are subject to a Latin bishop, it has nevertheless been laid down that the consent of the Apostolic See is necessary in the case of the transference of secular or regular clergy. If lay people want to transfer, the permission of their bishop is sufficient. He may give this permission with restraint to certain specified individuals, but never to a whole group. In the latter case the consent of the Apostolic See is required (see constitution *Etsi Pastoralis* 17, sect. 2, no. 14, *Bullarium*, vol. 1).

22. It is not difficult to respond to the claim that Orientals and other Greeks who reject their heresy and return to unity can be lawfully exhorted to abandon their own rite and accept the Latin rite on the grounds that approval has been given in the past and still continues for Orientals and Greeks to practice individual Latin rites.

First Category—Some Greeks Insist that Latins Follow Their Rites

There are two classes, as it were, of Greeks and Orientals. The first class consists of men who are not satisfied with the concessions made to them by the Apostolic See in order to preserve the Union. They are carried shamelessly beyond the bounds of decency; they claim that all their own practices are correct and that the Latins are mistaken not to follow the same practices.

Unleavened Bread

Take the example of unleavened bread. Greeks and Orientals must admit as Catholics that unleavened as well as leavened bread is suitable matter for the Sacrament of the Eucharist, and that each person should follow the rite of his own church. Consequently any condemnation of the rite of the Latin church which uses unleavened bread in consecrating the Eucharist falls into error.

The monk Hilarion, in his Dialectical Oration, says: "I have written this to you, beloved Greeks, without attacking your bread, which I respect and reverence as much as I do our own unleavened bread. But I have explained that your conduct is neither correct nor Christian when you insult and injure in word and deed the unleavened bread of the Latins. In both cases, as has been said, Christ is truly present" (Latin translation of the Greek by Leo Allatius in *Graeciae Orthodoxae*, vol. 1, p. 762, 1652).

Married Clergy

Another example is the freedom enjoyed by priests of the Oriental and Greek church to remain married to their wives after their ordination (see can. *Aliter*, dist. 31 and chap. *Cum olim, de Clericis Conjugatis*). Considering that this practice was at variance neither with divine nor natural law, but only with Church discipline, the popes judged it right to tolerate this custom, which flourished among Greeks and Orientals, rather than to forbid it by their apostolic authority, to avoid giving them a pretext to abandon unity. So does Arcudius assess the matter (*Concordia*, bk. 7, chap. 33).

Nevertheless, incredible though it sounds, some Greeks and Orientals still accuse the Latin church of rejecting marriage simply because it requires celibacy of its subdeacons, deacons, and priests in imitation of the Apostles (see Hincmar of Rheims, *Operum*, vol. 2, letter 51).

Confirmation Following Baptism

A third and final example is provided by some of the Copts, whose rite prescribes that Confirmation should be conferred immediately after Baptism. The western church does not observe this practice, but generally requires that candidates for Confirmation be old enough to be able to distinguish between good and evil. The Roman Church does not oppose the ancient practice of the Copts. However—again this is incredible—some of them reject Baptism conferred by Latins because the Sacrament of Confirmation was not conferred after this Baptism.

For this reason they are rightly convicted and condemned in Our constitution 129 (*Eo quamvis tempore* in Our *Bullarium* vol. 1): "Just as it befits the gentleness and patience of the Apostolic See to allow the Copts to continue in their long-established practice which has been tolerated by this See, so it is intolerable that they bitterly reject Baptism conferred in the Latin rite separately from Confirmation."

The Second Category—Greeks Who Follow Some Latin Rites

23. In the second category are those Orientals and Greeks who in the main observe their own rites, but out of respect follow some of the rites of the Latins and the Western Churches. This has been their practice from ancient times, and their bishops have examined and approved it. It has also been confirmed either expressly or tacitly by the Apostolic See. To this category belong the Armenians and Maronites who have abandoned the use of leavened bread in celebrating the Eucharist. Like the Latins they use unleavened bread (Abraham Echellensis, *Eutychio vindicato*, p. 477). Some of the Armenians attribute this practice to St. Gregory the Illuminator, their first bishop. At the start of the fourth century in the time of King Tiridates, he won the martyr's crown. Others claim that Pope St. Sylvester or St. Gregory the Great approved the practice in meetings with the Armenian people. Pope Gregory IX refers to these in his letter to the king of Armenia (Raynaldus, 1139), no. 82). Gregory, Patriarch of Sis, certainly states that this practice was given to the Armenians by the Roman Church in his letter to Haytonis the cenobite, father of King Leo of Armenia: "So we hve recently received from the Holy Roman Church the practice of mixing water (with the wine in the chalice) just as we formerly received the use of unleavened bread, the episcopal mitre, and the method of making the sign of the Cross (Clement Galanus, *Conciliatione Ecclesiae Armenae cum Romana*, vol. 1, p. 449).

Using Unleavened Bread

The practice of using unleavened bread dates from antiquity among the Maronites. This is clear from Morinus, *Praefatione ad Maronitarum Ordinationes*, and from the *Bibliotheca Orientali Assemani senioris*, vol. 1, p. 410. It was also affirmed at the national synod held at Mt. Libanus in 1736 and confirmed by Us in Our constitution no. 31, *Singularis* (*Bullarium*, vol. 1). We wrote there that: "This custom has been followed both in our church and among the Armenians in the east since time out of mind, and we can produce genuine proofs that this is so" (chap. 12, *de Sacramento Eucharistiae*, in the section on unleavened bread).

In emulation of this practice of the Armenians and Maronites, Cardinal Bessarion, first Commendatory Abbot of Grottaferrata in the diocese of Tusculum, brought it about that Greek monks in the abbey should consecrate unleavened bread (constitution 33, *Inter multa*, sect. *Ut autem*, Our *Bullarium*, vol. 2). This practice is still observed in the Collegiate Church of St. Mary de Grafeo in the diocese of Messana, even though this church's clergy follow the Greek rite (constitution 81, *Romana Ecclesia*, sect. 1, Our *Bullarium*, vol. 1).

Generally speaking, Italian Greek priests in Italy and the nearby islands observe their own practice of consecrating the Eucharist with leavened bread. Priests of both the Latin and Greek rite should be warned to be careful to consecrate and distribute the Eucharist in accordance with their own rite, as We have stated in Our constitution, *Etsi Pastoralis*, 57, sect. 1, no. 2, and sect. 6, no. 10f (Our *Bullarium*, vol. 1).

The Sacrament of the Eucharist Immediately Following Baptism

24. For several centuries the practice prevailed in the Church of giving children the Eucharist after the sacrament of baptism. This practice flourished as a simple rite and custom; it involved no belief that it was necessary for the eternal salvation of the children, as the fathers of Trent wisely remarked (session 21, chap. 4). Among the errors of the Armenians which Pope Benedict XII condemned, the fifty-eighth was their declaration that the Eucharist as well as Confirmation must be given to children at baptism to ensure the validity of their baptism and their eternal salvation (Raynaldus, 1341, sect. 66).

For the last four centuries, the Western church has not given the Eucharist to children after baptism. But it must be admitted that the Rituals of the Oriental churches contain a rite of Communion for children after baptism. Assemanus the Younger (*Codicis Liturgici)*, bk. 2, p. 149) gives the ceremony of conferring baptism among the Melchites. On page 309, he quotes the Syrians' baptismal ceremony as it was published by Philoxenus, the Monophysite Bishop of Mabbug, and on p. 306, the ceremony from the ancient Ritual of Severus, Patriarch of Antioch and leader of the Monophysites. He gives also the ceremonies of baptism observed by the Armenians and Copts (bk. 3, p. 95 and 130). All of these ceremonies command that the Eucharist should be given to children after baptism.

St. Thomas says that this practice was still observed by some Greeks in his time (*Summa Th.* 3, qu. 70, art. to the third). But Arcudius writes that this is the practice of the Greeks although some of them gradually abandoned it on account of the difficulties which arose repeatedly from offering the Eucharist to children at baptism (*de Sacramento Eucharistiae*, bk. 3, ch. 11.). Canon 7 of the Maronite Synod gathered at Mt. Lebanon on 18 September 1596 under Sergius Patriarch of Antioch and presided over by Fr. Jerome Dandin S.J., Nuncio of Pope Clement VIII, reads as follows: "Since Christ's Holy Communion can hardly be given to children with propriety and due respect for the holy sacrament, all priests should in the future beware of allowing anyone to receive before he attains the use of reason." The fathers of the synod of Zamoscia in 1720 agree with this view (sect. 3, *de Eucharistia*). And the Synod of Lebanon confirmed it in 1736: "In our old Rituals as well as in the old Roman ordo and in the Greek Euchologies, the minister of Baptism is clearly told to give the sacrament of the Eucharist to infants as soon as they are baptized and confirmed. Still, both from due respect for this most august sacrament and since this is not necessary for the salvation of children and infants, we command that the Eucharist should not be offered to infants when they are baptized, not even under the appearance of wine" (chap. 12, *Sanctissimo Eucharistiae Sacramento*, no. 13). We made the same provision in Our constitution for Italian Greeks *Etsi Pastoralis* (Our *Bullarium*, vol. 1, sect. 2, no. 7).

Distributing Communion Under Both Species

25. The Oriental and Greek practice of distributing the Eucharist under both species even to lay people has been discussed at length by Arcudius in *in Concordia Occidentali, et Orientali in Sacramentorum administratione*, bk. 3, chap. 4, and by Leo Allatius in his first note in *de Ecclesiae Occidentalis, atque Orientalis consensione*, p. 1614f. In the Greek College built in Rome by Gregory XIII, observance of the Greek rite is obligatory. Leo Allatius affirms this in his treatise on *de aetate, et Interstitiis*, p. 21. In accordance with the Constitution of the College confirmed by Pope Urban VIII, the students must make a confession every week and receive the holy Eucharist every fortnight as well as on solemn feast days and every Sunday in Advent and Lent, following the Latin rite, But on the greater feasts, at Easter, Pentecost, and Christmas, they are obliged to receive the Eucharist under both species in the Greek rite with leavened bread and unmixed wine. The wine is given to them by means of a small spoon. All other Greeks who come to Mass on those days, or who ask to receive the Eucharist according to the Greek rite on other days of the year, are given communion in the same way.

However, Our constitution 57 *Etsi Pastoralis*, sect. 6, no. 15, forbids the reception of Communion under both species by Italian Greeks except in places where this rite has been strongly upheld. Some Greeks and Orientals have gradually abandoned the practice of receiving communion under both species, even though it is the established custom of the whole Oriental church.

The famous Lucas Holstenius, writing to Bertoldus Nimissius, relates that he gave the Eucharist in the Vatican Basilica to an Abyssinian priest who came with others to communicate at the altar. When he had given him communion under the appearance of bread alone, he inquired of him as well as of other Ethiopians whether they in their own rite usually received the Eucharist under the appearance of bread alone, both on feast days and ordinary days and as viaticum for the dying. He declares that they answered that they always received communion under the appearance of bread alone, and that this ancient custom prevailed in the Ethiopian church (*in Opusculis Graecis, ac Latinis* of Leo Allatius, p. 436).

Allatae sunt 11

Among the statements requested by Pope Gregory XIII from the Patriarch of the Maronites is the following: "We celebrate Mass only with unleavened bread, but our laity communicate under both species." The Pope replied: "If they wish to consecrate unleavened bread, it is obvious that they should not be prevented, but the laity should be slowly discouraged from communicating under both species. For all Christ is present under one species, and there is great danger of spilling if the chalice is used" (Thomas of Jesus, *de Conversione omnium gentium*, p. 486f).

The fathers at the Synod of Lebanon, 1736, passed a similar decree: "Next, following the practices of the Holy Roman Church, we order and strictly command that laity and minor clerics are not to receive Communion under both species, but under one species only, that of bread" (part 2, chap. 12, no. 21). They allowed only deacons to receive the Eucharist under both species at a high Mass, first under the appearance of bread, then of wine, without the use of a spoon as We mentioned above: "But we allow deacons, especially at High mass, to receive from the priest the host dipped in the Blood. A spoon however should not be used. We decree that the use of spoons at Communion should be absolutely abolished."

Pouring Water into the Chalice

26. Our final point on the Sacrament of the Eucharist concerns the other Oriental and Greek rite in which the priest pours a little warm water into the chalice, after consecration but before

communion. Matthaeus Blastares mentions this rite and explains its meaning in his *Syntagmate Alphabetico*, chap. 8 (*Synodicon Graecorum*, vol. 2, p. 153), Euthymius, Archbishop of Tyre and Sidon, made some inquiries of Pope Clement XI in 1716. He asked whether the Melchites of Syria and Palestine should be forbidden to add warm water to the Divine Blood after the Consecration. The reply he received contained a clear, careful instruction which the Pope approved and ordered sent to the superiors of missions in the Holy Land, Damascus, Tyre, and Sidon. He ordered the Archbishop not to forbid this practice, since it was an ancient rite which the Apostolic See had examined and allowed to Greek priests even in Rome. The warm water signified the warmth of faith which should burst out in great flames in the face of so mighty a mystery. Pope Benedict XIII gave a similar answer on March 31, 1729, to Cyril, Greek Patriarch of Antioch. This rite is allowed to Italian Greeeks in Our constitution 57, *Etsi Pastoralis*, sect. 6, no. 2.

Subsequently, in the Congregations formed for the careful revision of the books of the Eastern Church, when a long dispute arose as to whether the rite of pouring warm water into the chalice after the consecration should be prohibited, the answer was given on May 1, 1746, that "no changes should be made." It is true that Cardinal Humbertus of Silva Candida had vigorously attacked this rite in earlier times, but it was discovered that his arguments against the rite lacked substance. Still the fathers of the Synod of Zamoscia in 1720 forbade Ruthenian priests to pour warm water into the chalice after the Consecration. "For a serious reason, the synod forbids and abolishes the rite which is tolerated in the Eastern Church of pouring warm water into the chalice after the Consecration before communion" (sect. 4 on the celebration of Mass).

27. Such occurrences—and many could be recalled—are invoked by those who favor transference from the Oriental and Greek rite to the Latin rite. They think they act rightly in their eager attempts to bring Oriental converts to abandon, without Our prior consent, the rite they used to observe, even though this has been firmly maintained from ancient times by all other Orientals and Greeks.

But the events mentioned above and those which could be mentioned do not in the least support their opinion. For in the first place, transferring from an Oriental rite to the Latin rite removes all the prescriptions of the Oriental rite which are at variance with Our rite. But this is not what happened in the events We have mentioned; although a specific Greek ritual was abolished, the Greek rite itself and all its other prescriptions were preserved unchanged. In addition, to remove even a part of the rite is not within the power of any individual, but requires the intervention of the public authority of the supreme head of the universal Church, the Roman Pontiff.

For the Apostolic See possesses the preeminent right to decide what rituals are to be taken over from the Oriental church by the Latin church. As often as this Apostolic See has noticed that a dangerous or unfitting rite has made its way into the Oriental Church, it has condemned, criticized, and forbidden its use in the Latin Church. Lastly, whenever the Apostolic See sees Orientals or Greeks eager to take up a Latin ritual, particularly when this ritual is ancient, widely established, and either expressly or implicitly approved by the bishops, it has confirmed this practice by toleration and approval.

The Creed

28. The Creed is said in both the Latin and Greek liturgy. The practice of saying the Creed during the sacrifice of the Mass was first established in the Greek Church and then introduced in the Latin Church. This is evident from Canon Two of the third Council of Toledo in 589: "That the creed of the faith be said in all churches of Spain or Galicia in accordance with the form of the Oriental churches and of the council of Constantinople at which 150 bishops were present; that it be sung with clear voice by the people before the Lord's prayer is said" (Labbe, *Collectionis*, vol. 5, p. 1009).

Since the fathers at Toledo appealed to the rite of the Oriental churches in establsihing the practice of saying the Creed during Mass, it is quite evident that this practice was first established in the east and spread from there to the west. This is the opinion both of Cardinal Bona, *Rerum Lyturgic*, bk. 2, chap. 8, no. 2, and of Georgius, *de lyturgia Romani Pontificis*, vol. 2, chap. 20, no. 2, p. 176.

Adoration of the Cross

Continuing with Our topic, Amalarius in his *de Divinis Officiis*, chap. 14 (relying on the authority of St. Paulinus' *Epistola ad Severum*) relates that the Cross on which Christ hung was exposed for the adoration of the faithful in the church at Jerusalem on Good Friday of Holy Week only. He declares that the ceremony of the adoration of the Holy Cross which forms part of the Good Friday service in every Latin church until the present day derived from this practice of the Greeks.

Trisagion

The *trisagion*: "Holy God, Holy Strong One, Holy Immortal, have mercy on us" is a pious and oft-repeated prayer in the Greek liturgy; Goarius correctly observes this in his *in notis ad Euchologium*, p. 109, in reference to the Mass of St. John Chrysostom. This prayer originated in a miracle which occured in Constantinople in the middle of the fifth century. Emperor Theodosius, Patriarch Proclus, and all the people were beseeching God on open ground for deliverance from the destruction which threatened them from violent earthquakes. They suddenly saw a boy snatched up to heaven; when he was returned to earth, he reported that he had heard the angels singing the *trisagion*. At the bidding of the Patriarch Proclus, the whole people sang it with devotion and the terrifying earthquakes ceased, as is related by Nicephorus, bk. 14, chap. 46, and mentioned by Pope Felix III in his third letter to Peter the Fuller (Labbe, *Collectionis*, vol. 4). This same *trisagion* is sung in the western church in Greek and Latin on Friday of Holy Week, as Cardinal Bona remarks (*Rerum Lyturgicar.*, bk. 2, chap. 10, no. 5).

Blessing of Water at Epiphany

The blessing of water on the eve of the Epiphany derives from the rite of the Greek Church, as Goarius shows at length in the case of the Euchology or Ritual of the Greeks. At the present time, on the same day, this ceremony is performed in Rome in the Church of the Greeks, as We recalled in constitution 57, sect. 5, no. 13, and the faithful are permitted to be sprinkled with this holy water.

On the transmission of this rite from the Oriental Church to some western churches two authorities may be consulted: Martene, vol. 4, *de antiqua Ecclesiae disciplina in Divinis celebrandis Officiis*, chap. 4, no. 2, and Fr. Sebastianus Paulus of the Congregation of the Mother of God, *De ritu Ecclesiae Neritinae exorcizandi aquam in Epiphania*, Naples, 1719. The latter writer (part. 3, pp. 177ff) gives bishops an appropriate admonition not to give cause for rioting by attempting to abolish certain ceremonies which have at a great distance in time made their way into their dioceses from the Greek church. To attack these ceremonies, he says, would give the appearance of criticizing the way the Apostolic See has acted in regard to these rites. Although this See was well aware that these ceremonies had come from the Greek church it permitted them to be observed and attended. On p. 203 he quotes the letter of Cardinal Sanctorius of Sancta Severina written in 1580 to Fornarius, Bishop of Nerita, on this topic of the blessing of water at Epiphany which was performed in his diocese.

Stripping and Washing the Altar

The ceremony of stripping and washing the altar on Holy Thursday is also Greek. A reference to this ceremony is found in the fifth century. St. Sabas mentions it in his *Typico*, the Order of saying the Divine Office throughout the year. According to Leo Allatius, he died in 451 (*de Libris Ecclesiae Graecae*, dissert. I, p. 9). If it could be asserted with certainty that the Roman order published by Hittorpius was composed at the command of Pope St. Gelasius, the ceremony of washing the altars on Holy Thursday would be almost as ancient in the Latin Church as it is in the Greek Church, since Gelasius died in 496. But the antiquity of this Order is disputed and, apart from it, St. Isidore, Bishop of Hispala, is the first of the Latins to mention this ceremony. He died in 646. So probably this ceremony came to the west from the east and is observed to this day in some Latin churches with papal approval. In particular it is performed each year on Holy Thursday with great solemnity in the Vatican Basilica.

Suarez, Bishop of Vasionum and Vicar of this Basilica, and John Chrysostom Battellus, Archbishop of Amaseno, who were recently appointed Beneficiates of this Basilica, have each published a thoughtful treatise elucidating this ceremony. Therefore, it is evident from these examples that the Apostolic See, for good reasons, has adopted for the whole Latin Church ceremonies which belong to the Greek Church and has allowed some Latin churches to observe particular ceremonies.

Trisagion

29. We have mentioned above the miraculous way in which the *trisagion* entered the liturgies of the Greek Church. Peter the Fuller, surnamed Gnaphaeus, a promoter of the heresy of the Apollinarists who are called Theopaschites, attempted to add to the *trisagion* the words: "You who were crucified for us" (Theodorus Lector, *Collectanear*, bk. 1). And some eastern bishops, especially Syrians and Armenians, at the instigation of one James the Syrian, accepted this addition (Nicephorus, bk. 18, chap. 52). When this happened, the Roman popes with their usual watchful concern opposed this error from the start and prohibited the addition. They did not accept the interpretation which claimed that the *trisagion* referred to the person of the Son alone, not to the three divine persons, and so avoided all suspicion of error. For a danger of associating with heretical teaching still remained, and the human mind for all its rashness could not plausibly refer to Christ alone a hymn sung by the angels in honor of the Holy Trinity, as Lupus rightly observes (Notes *ad Trullanum*, canon 81). After relating that the addition to the *trisagion* had been condemned by Pope Felix III and a Roman synod, Lupus continues: "They declare firmly that the hymn eternally sung to the Trinity alone by the holy angels and transmitted to the Church by God Himself and the holy angels by means of the miraculous boy was confirmed by the cessation of the earthquakes which were threatening Constantinople. They were approved in this sense by the whole Council of Chalcedon (he refers both to the bishops who attended the Council and to those others who rejected the addition to the *trisagion*). Therefore the words of the hymn cannot be daringly twisted to signify Christ alone."

St. Gregory VII, with similar zeal, condemned the addition in his letter to the Archbishop of Patriarch of the Armenians (bk. 8, 1). Gregory XIII acted in like manner in his Brief of February 14, 1577, to the Patriarch of the Maronites. In the Congregation for the Propagation of the Faith which met on January 30, 1635, the liturgy of the Armenians was examined. Among the matters which were carefully discussed was whether the addition to the *trisagion* could be tolerated on the grounds that it could be understood to refer to the person of the Son alone. The answer given was that it should not be allowed and that the addition should be utterly deleted.

Women Assisting at Mass

Pope Gelasius in his ninth letter (chap. 26) to the bishops of Lucania condemned the evil practice which had been introduced of women serving the priest at the celebration of Mass. Since this abuse had spread to the Greeks, Innocent IV strictly forbade it in his letter to the bishop of Tusculum: "Women should not dare to serve at the altar; they should be altogether refused this ministry." We too have forbidden this practice in the same words in Our oft-repeated constitution *Etsi Pastoralis*, sect. 6, no. 21.

Eucharist for Viaticum

On Thursday of Holy Week, in memory of the Lord's Supper, there is peformed the ceremony of consecrating the bread which is kept for a full year as viaticum for the mortally ill who request Holy Communion. Sometimes too a little of the consecrated wine is added to this consecrated bread. Leo Allatius describes this ceremony in his treatise, *de Communione Orientalium sub specie unica num*, no. 7. Pope Innocent IV in his letter to the bishop of Tusculum forbade the Greeks to perform this ceremony. "They should not reserve for a year the Eucharist which has been consecrated on Holy Thursday on the pretext that the sick may receive communion from this." He added that they should always have the Eucharist ready for the sick, but that they should replace it every fortnight.

Arcudius, *de Concordia Ecclesiae Occidentalis, et Orientalis*, bk. 5, chap. 55 and 56, points out the extremes to which this ceremony leads and beseeches the popes to abolish it entirely. Clement VIII did this in an Instruction, as did We in Our constitution 57, *Etsi Pastoralis*, sect. 6, no. 3f. It was decreed at the Synod of Zamoscia, which was studied by the Congregation of the Council as well as by the Congregation for the Propagation of the Faith, that the ceremony of consecrating the Eucharist on Holy Thursday, pouring on it a drop of the Blood and keeping it for a full year for the sick should for the future be discontinued wherever it was still in practice. Parish priests should keep the Eucharist for the sick but replace it every week or fortnight (sect. 3, *de Eucharistia*). The fathers of the synod of Lebanon, which We confirmed, acted in the same way (chap. 12, *de Sacramento Eucharistiae*, no. 24).

These examples show clearly that the Apostolic See has always forbidden ceremonies to the Greeks, even if they already were prevalent among them, whenever it saw that these ceremonies were already or were in danger of becoming evil and destructive.

Procession of the Holy Spirit from the Father and the Son

30. Whenever the union of the Greek and Latin Church has been discussed, the chief matter of contention has been the procession of the Holy Spirit from the Father and the Son. Examination of this point involves a triple aspect, and so is dealt with here under three headings. The first question is whether the procession of the Holy Spirit from the Father and the Son is a dogma of the Faith. This question has always been firmly answered that there is no room for doubting that this procession is a dogma of the Faith and that every true Catholic accepts and professes this.

Granting that this is so, the second question is whether it is permissible to add the phrase "and from the Son" to the Creed in the Mass even though this phrase was not used at the Council of Nicea or the Council of Constantinople. The difficulty is increased in that the Ecumenical Council of Ephesus decreed that no additions should be made to the Nicene Creed: "The holy Council decrees that it is lawful for no one to produce or compose a Faith other than that defined by the holy fathers who assembled at Nicea together with the Holy Spirit." It has been asserted in answer to this question that it is indeed lawful and very appropriate to make this addition to the Nicene Creed. The Council of Ephesus forbade only additions which are contrary to the Faith, presumptuous, and at variance with general practice, but not those additions which are orthodox and express more plainly some point of faith implied in that Creed.

On the assumption that the first two answers are accepted, the third and final question is whether Orientals and Greeks can be allowed to say the Creed in the way they used to before the Schism, that is to say, without the phrase "and from the Son." On this final point, the practice of the Apostolic See has varied. Sometimes it allowed the Orientals and Greeks to say the Creed without this addition. This allowance was made when it was certain that they accepted the first two points, and it realized that insistence on the addition would block the way to union. At other times this See has insisted on Greeks and Orientals using the addition. It has done this when it had grounds to suspect that they were unwilling to include the addition in the Creed because they shared the false view that the Holy Spirit does not proceed from the Father and the Son or that the Church had no power to add the phrase "and from the Son."

Allate sunt 11

The former approach was used by two popes—Blessed Gregory X at the Council of Lyons and Eugenius IV at the Council of Florence—for the reasons already mentioned (Harduin, *Collectionis Conciliorum*, vol. 7, p. 698D, and vol. 9, p. 305D). The latter position was taken by Pope Nicholas III when he realized that Emperor Michael was not acting in good faith and was not abiding by the promises he had made in establishing union with his predecessor Pope Gregory X. The evidence for this comes from the Vatican Archives and is printed in Raynaldus, 1278, sect. 7. Martin IV and Nicholas IV acted in the same manner. Although the sources are contradictory about the attitude of these popes to this affair, Pachymeres, who was then writing the history of Constantinople, openly declares that they did not imitate the fair judgment of their predecessors. Rather they required that Orientals and Greeks add "and from the Son" to the Creed, in order to remove doubts about their orthodoxy, "to make a definite trial of the faith and opinion of the Greeks; the suitable pledge of this would be for them to say the same Creed as the Latins."

Pope Eugenius IV at the Council of Florence allowed the Orientals to say the Creed without the addition. But when he later received the Armenians into union he obliged them to include it (Harduin, vol. 9, p. 435B) perhaps because he had learned that the Armenians were less averse to the addition then were the Greeks.

Similarly, Pope Callistus III, when he sent Brother Simon of the Order of Preachers to Crete in the capacity of Inquisitor, commanded him to watch carefully that the Greeks said "and from the Son" in the Creed, since in Crete there were many Greek refugees from Constantinople which had fallen to the Turks two years earlier (Gregory of Trebizond, *epistola ad Cretans*, in his *Graeciae Orthodoxae*, quoted by Allatius, p. 537, and confirmed by Echardus, *Scriptorum Ordinis Sancti Dominici*, vol. 1, p. 762). It may be that the Pope suspected that the Greeks from Constantinople were weak in this dogma of the faith.

There is nothing at variance with the decrees of the Council of Florence in either of the two forms of the Profession of Faith which, as We have mentioned, were required of the Greeks by Gregory XIII and of the Orientals by Urban VIII. Constitution 34, sect. 6, of Clement VIII (*veteris Romani Bullarii*, vol. 3) and Our constitution *Etsi Pastoralis*, sect. 1, are both addressed to Latin bishops with Greeks and Albanians who observe the Greek rite living in their dioceses. These people should not be ordered to say the Creed with the addition of the phrase "and from the Son," provided that they confess that the Holy Spirit proceeds from the Father and the Son and that they recognize the Church's power of making this addition. They should be obliged to say the additional phrase, however, it its ommission would cause scandal, if this particular custom of reciting the Creed with its addition prevailed in their locality, or it were thought necessary to obtain unambiguous proof of the correctness of their faith. However, both the fathers of the synod of Zamoscia (heading I, *de Fide Catholica* and the fathers of the synod of Lebanon (pt. I, no. 12) were right to prudently decree, in order to remove every doubt, that all priests subject to them should use the Creed with its additional phrase in accordance with the custom of the Roman Church.

31. The obvious conclusion from the foregoing remarks is that in this matter the Apostolic See has sometimes agreed in certain circumstances and in consideration of the character of individual people to make specific concessions which it has refused to others in different circumstances among different peoples. So to complete the task which We have begun, We have only to show that this Apostolic See has kindly allowed an Oriental or Greek people to use a Latin ceremony to which they were devoted, particularly if they adopted this ceremony in ancient times and if the bishops did not oppose it at any time, but approved it either expressly or implicitly.

Latin Rite Adopted by Oriental Church

We referred to evident examples of this occurrence above, in mentioning the category of Orientals and Greeks who respect equally the Latin and Greek rites. In the main they observe their own ceremonies, but are attached to some of Ours. Therefore, We will refrain from useless repetition, merely recalling here what was fully presented earlier in this letter. We shall add just two examples from the Maronites. For several centuries the episcopal and priestly vestments of the Maronites have resembled exactly the vestments prescribed in the Latin rite (Synod of Lebanon 1736, chap. 12, on the sacrament of the Eucharist, no. 7). Pope Innocent III in his letter *Quia Divinae Sapientiae bonitas* to Patriarch Jeremiah in 1215 exhorted them to imitate the episcopal vestments of the Latin Church. In consequence this pope and his successors sent them gifts of holy vestments, chalices, and patens (Patriarch Peter in two letters to Leo X in Labbe, *Collectionis Conciliorum*, vol. 14, p. 346f). Recently at the synod of Lebanon (chap. 13), unanimously and with Our approval, the Maronites adopted the Latin rite in regard to the Mass of the Presanctified. They celebrate it only on Good Friday, since they have abandoned for just reasons the practice of the Greeks who offer only the Mass of the Presanctified on the days of the Lenten fast, except on Saturdays, Sundays, and the feast of the Annunciation when it occurs in Lent, as is laid down in Trullan Canon 52. On these days the priest divides the consecrated bread into as many pieces as will suffice for celebrating the Mass of the Presanctified on the following days. On these days he consumes and distributes to the congregation these pieces, which he had reserved in the ciborium (Leo Allatius in his prolegomena to Gabriel Naud, *de Missa Praesanctificatorum*, p. 1531, n. 1).

32. One might think that this letter could end at this point. It has answered the questions raised by the missionary priest at Balsera by stating that "no changes should be made." Also it has mentioned the stringent rules to be followed by missionaries engaged in recalling Orientals from schism and error to the unity of the holy Catholic faith. The Canons and Apostolic Constitutions prohibit those who convert Orientals from attempting to destroy the Oriental and Greek rite in matters which the Apostolic See allows and prohibits trying to make converts abandon the rite they previously observed and embrace the Latin rite. Nevertheless, before ending, We may fittingly touch on some additional points which are quite relevant to the questions raised by the missionary who has been told that "no changes should be made."

Additional Points

33. Now it is true that in the city of Balsera, Armenian and Syrian Catholics of the Oriental rite who have no church of their own assemble at the church of the Latin missionaries. Their priests celebrate Mass and other ceremonies there according to their own rite in the presence of the laity, who also receive the Sacraments. Still, it is not difficult to uphold the decision that "no changes should be made"; therefore the prevailing practice should continue, that is, that the priests and laity should continue celebrating in the Latin church the rites they have celebrated until now.

Canon Law decrees that the Oriental and Greek rite should not be mixed with the Latin rite. See the entire Decretal of Celestine III in Gonzales, chap. *Cum secundum: de temporibus Ordinationum*; in the decretal of Innocent III, see chap. *Quanto: de consuetudine*; chap. *Quoniam: de Officio Judic. Ordinar.*; and the Decretal of Honorius III, chap. *Literas: de celebrat. Missar.* But there are no good grounds for declaring that this mixing of rite forbidden by Apostolic Constitution is being practiced in the simple case of an Armenian, Maronite, or Greek celebrating Mass or other ceremonies with their own laity according to their own rite in a Latin church. Nor are there grounds in the opposite case of a Latin doing likewise in an Oriental church, especially when there is a just cause for doing so. Clearly such a cause exists in the present case, since the Orientals in the city of Balsera have no church of their own. If they were deprived of the Latin church, they would have nowhere to offer the sacrifice of the Mass and perform the essential ceremonies with the laity of their rite which maintain and nourish them in holy unity.

34. An example of the forbidden mixing of rite would be a Latin consecrating leavened bread and giving communion from it to Latins. It would be the same if Orientals who do not consecrate unleavened bread were to do so and to distribute it to their people for holy communion. Latin Ordinaries who have Italian Greeks subject to them should show a careful concern "that Latins receive communion from unleavened bread and Greeks from leavened bread where they have their own parish" (Our constitution *Etsi Pastoralis*, sect. 6, no. 14).

Another example of forbidden mixing of rites would be a priest celebrating Mass at one time according to the Latin rite and at another time according to the Greek rite. St. Pius V forbids this in his constitution 21, *Providentia* (*Bull. novi*, vol. 4, pt. 2, Rome). He revokes absolutely all faculties of so doing which had previously been granted to some priests. Our constitution 57, sect. 7, no. 10, agrees with this constitution of Pius V. Even though priests in charge of colleges of Orientals in Rome who became Jesuits and transferred from the Greek to the Latin rite have received a dispensation to sometimes offer the sacrifice of the Mass in the Greek and Oriental rite, as already mentioned, this has been approved in order that their students may learn how to celebrate Mass in their own rite since they are bound to profess the Greek and Maronite rite and conduct divine services in accordance with it thoughout their lives. The particular circumstances of this obviously unique case show clearly enough that it cannot be used as an exemplary argument for gaining similar dispensations.

Cardinal Kollonitz advised Pope Clement XI that allowing Latin missionaries in Hungary to celebrate in the Greek rite whenever this appeared necessary, while remaining at liberty to return to the Latin rite, would be beneficial to the Church. The Pope rejected the Cardinal's advice because he felt that each one should remain in his own rite in accordance with the provisions of the Canons and that a priest should not be permitted to change the rite in which he celebrated Mass. This is clear from his Brief to the Cardinal on May 9, 1705 (*Epistolar. et Brev. selectior, ejusdem Pontificis typis editor*, p. 205).

35. These among many other examples refer to the mixing of rite, which is forbidden by the Church's laws. But there is no forbidden mixing of rites involved if, for a lawful cause, priests of the Oriental rite are allowed to celebrate Mass and other services in a Latin church and administer the sacraments to their own people. We see this happening openly in Rome where our churches are available to Armenian, Coptic, Melchite, and Greek priests for the celebration of

Mass to satisfy their piety, even though they have their own churches where they could offer the sacrifice of the Mass. They have only to bring with them the vestments and other necessities for celebrating Mass according to their rite, as well as a server from their own people; they must also take appropriate steps with guards and prefects of the sanctuary to prevent riotous tumults among the bystanders on account of the novelty of the event. These matters are fully discussed in the edict promulgated at Our command on February 13, 1743, by Our Vicar General in the City and its district, Giovanni Antonio Guadagni, who then was titular priest of Sts. Sylvester and Martin on the Mountains and is now Bishop of Tusculum and Cardinal.

Important for this topic is the following event: about the middle of the fifteenth century, as is well known, Mahomet II began to attack Constantinople. Some of the Greeks who had rejected the errors of the Schismatics and preserved union with the Latin Church retreated to Venice and remained there. When the Greek Cardinal Isidore came there, he informed the Senate of the Pope's wishes to have a church assigned to these people of the Greek rite for their services. The piety of the Senate was aroused, and they gave the refugees the Church of St. Blasius. In one chapel of this church for many years the Greeks performed the divine services in the Greek rite, while in the other chapels, the Latins worshipped in the Latin rite. This is attested by the renowned Flaminius Cornelius Scriptor, *Venetarum Ecclesiarum*, Decad. 14, p. 359: "So the services of both rites were celebrated for several years in different chapels of the same church." This practice continued until the Greeks' numbers rose and another church in addition to the Church of St. Blasius was allotted to them for their own private use.

36. This incident concerns Greeks who were allowed to celebrate their services in Latin Churches. But to show more clearly that this does not entail the mixing of rites forbidden by the Church, it will be appropriate to mention also Latins who for a just reason were permitted to offer the sacrifice of the Mass and perform divine services in Greek churches. This will not only confirm the opinion We have presented, but will help much to show the necessity of unanimity and benevolence among Catholics of different rites.

In White Russia, Ruthenian Catholics, who are known as United, have many churches while the Latins have few; these are far distant from the districts of the Latins who live among the Ruthenians. Sometimes the Latins are deprived of Mass for a long period because their business prevents them from travelling as far as the nearest Latin church. Latin priests could not easily travel to the few Latin churches there to celebrate Mass since those churches were so far from their own place of residence. So to avoid depriving the Latins for long periods of Mass celebrated in the Latin rite, there was only one solution: for Latin priests to celebrate the Mass in the Latin rite for the welfare of the Latins in the Ruthenian churches. At this point a difficulty was recognized in that Greek altars have no holy stone, since they offer Mass on the *antimensia*, that is, linens consecrated by the bishop with relics of the saints at the corners. For this reason Latin priests were obliged to bring the holy stone with them at great inconvenience, and risk breaking it in the course of the journey. But at last a timely remedy was discovered and applied to all these inconveniences by God's help. With the agreement of the Ruthenians, Latin priests were allowed to celebrate Mass in the Latin rite in the Ruthenian churches, and on the *antimensia*. This was approved more readily because Ruthenian priests who sometimes came to say Mass in Latin churches consecrated the sacrifice on our altar stones. This matter is treated in full in Our constitution 43, *Imposito nobis* (*Bullarii nostri*, vol. 3).

37. The following fact is also important. Learned men are divided as to whether the ancient practice of the western church was to have one or more altars in basilicas. Schelestratus declares that there was only one altar (*Actor. Ecclesiae Orientalis*, pt. 1, chap. 2 *de Missa Privata in Ecclesia Latina*). On the other hand Cardinal Bona, on the authority of Walfrid, chap. 4, shows that there were many altars in the Roman basilica of St. Peter (*Rerum Lyturgicar*, bk. I, chap. 14, no. 3). But if one considers the Oriental and Greek churches and basilicas, it seems evident that there was only one altar in them, and even today this is generally the case. This can be seen from the drawings of these churches in Du Cange, *Constantinopoli Christiana*; Beveregius, *ad Pandectas Canonum*; and Goarius *in Euchologium Graecorum*. Since in the Greek Church of St.

Athanasius in Rome there are many altars, Leo Allatius in his letter to Joannes Marinus *de Templis Graecorum recentiorum*, no. 2 states with certainty that this church has no Greek form except the *Bema* or enclosure which separates the main altar from the rest of the church.

At this altar, only one Mass may be celebrated each day. This practice of the Greeks is mentioned by Dionysius Barsalibaeus, the Jacobite bishop of Amida, *in Explanatione Missae*, and by Cyriacus, Patriarch of the Jacobites, as the Jacobite Gregorius Barhebraeus says in his *Directorio*. Assemanus quotes these writers in his *Biblioth. Oriental.*, vol. 2, p. 184, and vol. 3, part 1, p. 248. Cardinal Bona writes on this practice as follows: "They have a single altar in their churches, and they consider it wrong to repeat the Sacrifice in the sanctuary on the same day" (*op. cit.* chap. 14, no. 3).

Euthymius, Archbishop of Tyre and Sidon, and Cyril, Greek Patriarch of Antioch, several times during the pontificates of Clement XI, Benedict XIII, and Clement XII inquired whether they should allow this practice to continue which forbade the offering of a second Mass at the same altar on the same day. They always received the response that no changes were to be made and the ancient rite was to be preserved entire. The people came to believe mistakenly that the reason for not offering a second Mass at the same altar on the same day was that the second priest to celebrate Mass in the same vestments as the first was infringing a period of fasting. So in Our encyclical letter to the Greek Melchite Patriarch of Antioch and the Catholic bishops subject to him, We commanded them to inform the people that this was an error. They were to do this, however, without changing the practice of one priest only offering Mass on the same day at the same altar (constitution 87, *Demandatam, Bullarii Nostri*, vol. 1).

38. Finally, it was custom in both the western and the eastern church for the priests to offer Mass together with the bishop. The evidence is collected by Christianus Lupus in the Appendix on the Council of Chalcedon in his *ad Concilia Generalia, et Provincialia*, vol. 1, p. 994, of the first edition, where he interprets the words of Bassianus: "He used to celebrate Masses with me and to communicate with me"; and by Georgius, *Lyturgiae Pontificiae*, vol. 2, p. 1f, and vol. 3, p. 1f. The rite of concelebration is now out of fashion in the western church, except at priestly ordinations performed by the bishop and at episcopal consecrations where two bishops assist the consecrating bishop. But this rite continues to thrive in the Oriental Church, and priests often concelebrate with the bishop or with the priest as chief celebrant. This practice is derived from the *Apostolic Constitutions*, bk. 8, and the eighth Apostolic Canon. And wherever this custom is practiced among Greeks and Orientals, it is approved and to be preserved as We command in Our constitution *Demandatam*, sect. 9.

Allatae sunt 11

39. Some have used this Greek and Oriental rite of concelebration as an argument for questioning whether there is any place in their church for private Masses said by an individual priest, since there is only a single altar in Greek churches and only one Mass is offered at it and priests concelebrate with the bishop or a chief celebrant. The Lutherans were careful to send the Augsburg Confession, which abolished private Masses, to Jeremiah, Patriarch of Constantinople, for his approval and acceptance. But since the traditional practice of private Mass in the Oriental Church is derived from Trullan Canon 31, and defended by this canon and the commentary on it written by Theodore Balsamon, both the rite of frequent concelebration and the practice of private Masses have remained unharmed in the Oriental Church. So the efforts of the Lutherans came to nothing. They were told that the East as well as the West condemned the evil practice of men who approached the altar with a wicked desire of obtaining offerings, but not the actions of men who with religious piety celebrated private Masses in order to offer to God an acceptable sacrifice. This is evident from Schelestratus, *ex Actis Ecclesiae Orientalis contra Lutheranos*, chap. 1: on private Masses in the Greek Church, towards the end. For the convenience of priests who want to offer a private Mass, while preserving the custom of offering only one Mass at the one altar in the church, the Greeks began to set up *Paracclesias*. These are mentioned by Leo Allatius in his letter to Joannes Morinus. Paracclesiae are oratories beside the church in which there is an altar for the celebration of Masses which cannot be said in the church because Mass has already been said there on that day.

40. Some have with reason feared that this practice would permanently prevent Latin priests from offering Mass in Greek Churches, since these have only one altar which cannot be used twice on the same day for the celebration of Mass. In that case, Latin priests could not use the oratories for saying Mass since these were built for Greeks only. But to dispel this fear, it can be seen that today Greek churches generally have a second altar at which Latin priests can celebrate Mass. Goarius describes three kinds of Greek churches in his *Euchologium Graecorum*. The third kind has a second altar built, as Goarius thinks, for Latin priests, and Schelestratus follows him in this view (p. 887).

In the Maronite and Greek churches in Rome, besides the main altar, there are other altars at which Latin priests say Mass. In Our constitution *Etsi Pastoralis*, sect. 6, no, 8-9, We deal with the best way of treating Italian Greeks, and in this passage We forbid Latin priests ever to celebrate Mass at the main altar in Greek churches except in a case of absolute necessity and then only with the consent of the Greek parish priest. We also allow the Greeks to build altars in their churches apart from the main altar and at these, Latin priests may, if they wish, celebrate Mass.

41. The previous statements show clearly that the Catholic Armenians and Syrians who live among the Latins in Balsera and have no church of their own should be allowed to continue meeting in the Latin church as they have been doing, in order to hold the holy services in accordance with their rite. This permission is given not only because their action does not constitute a mixture of rite which is forbidden in the Apostolic Constitutions, but also because the situation calls for kindness, or rather compliance with the law of equity. This demands that a place should be gladly given to those who have no place in which to perform what they are required by law to perform. Therefore it only remains to command that the binding laws of love be observed and that a chapel or part of a church be assigned to the Orientals for holding their services. All care should be taken to hold the Latin and the Greek services at different times. Otherwise more disputes which so plagued Our two predecessors Leo X and Clement VII might be caused.

At that time, contrary to the argument made at the Council of Florence under Eugenius IV that the Greeks should not be hindered in the observance of their rites, these popes learned that certain Latins were going to Greek churches and celebrating Mass in the Latin rite at their altar with the design of preventing Greek priests from offering the Sacrifice in their own rite. On several occasions Greeks were deprived of the Sacrifice of the Mass even on feast days. "Under a strange inspiration, they (the Latin priests) sometimes take possession of the altars of parish churches and there, against the will of the Greeks, they celebrate Mass and other services. The result is that the Greeks often remain without Mass to their great annoyance on feast days and other days when they usually attend Mass." These complaints of the Pope are contained in the document beginning *Provisionis nostrae* and can be found on page 86 of the Greek Manual published at Beneventum in 1717. We have no reason to join in their complaints. But if We ever hear that Our Latins are preventing the Orientals at Balsera from holding their services in the Latin churches, Our severe complaints will be accompanied by appropriate remedies.

42. A second question in regard to these Armenians and Syrians is whether they may use the old calendar in fixing the date of Easter and of the other moveable feasts, or whether they should follow the revised calendar when they hold services in the Latin churches. It is also asked to what extent the use of the old calendar is lawful for them and whether this decision also binds those Orientals who, because they have only a small church which cannot hold them all, are forced to come in great numbers to Latin churches.

43. Everyone knows the provisions of Popes St. Pius and St. Victor and of the Council of Nicea concerning the proper celebration of Easter. All likewise are aware that the Council of Trent reserved to the Pope the question of revising the calendar, and that finally the matter was resolved in all its details in the time of Pope Gregory XIII. For this reason Bucherius writes in the preface to his *Commentario de doctrina temporum*: "At the bidding of Pope Gregory XIII, Clavius has fully seen to the definite reckoning of Easter in future years." Clavius was a Jesuit priest with scientific talents who contributed greatly to the correction of the calendar. The Pope also studied the calculations of Aloysius Lilius, which had taken years to complete. Finally, after weighing all aspects of the difficulty during many meetings and after consulting with many experts, he published in 1582 his constitution *Inter gravissimas* which established the regular calendar (*in veteri Bullario*, vol. 1, cons. 74).

44. This papal constitution revoked the old calendar and ordered Patriarchs, primates, archbishops, bishops, and abbots to use the newly revised calendar. This can be seen both in the constitution itself and in the Annals of Gregory XIII, vol. 2, p. 271. Rome 1742. But since there is no mention of Orientals in the constitution, the question arises as to whether it applies to Orientals. This question has been raised not only by learned men such as Azorius, *Instit. Moral.*, vol. 1, bk. 5, chap. 11, qu. 7; and Baldellus, *Theologia Morali*, vol. 1, bk. 5, disp. 41, but it was also discussed by the famous gentlemen who met in the palace of Cardinal Pamphilius, later Pope Innocent X, on July 4, 1631. These men concluded that "the subjects of the four eastern patriarchates should not be bound by new papal constitutions except in three cases: first, on the subject of teachings of the faith; second, if the Pope mentions them expressly in his Constitution and makes arrangements; third, it they are implicitly included in the arrangements of the Constitution as in cases of invitation to a future council." This resolution is reported by Verricellus, *de Apostolicis Missionibus*, bk. 3, chap. 38, no. 4, and by Us in Our work on *de Canonizatione Sanct.*, bk. 2, chap. 38, no. 15.

45. We pass this question by since there is no pressing need to discuss it at present. It is sufficient for Us to point out how the Apostolic See has acted in this affair. On the evidence of this See in earlier actions, the wisest answer it has made to the question is that "no changes are to be made."

The Apostolic See has ordered Italian Greeks who live among us, subject to the authority of the Latin bishops in whose dioceses they reside, to adopt the new calendar (*Etsi Pastoralis*, 57, sect. 9, no. 3f). The clergy of the Collegiate Church of St. Mary *de Graphaeo* in Messana who observe the Greek rite, follow the new calendar most carefully (constitution 81, *Romana Ecclesia*, sect. 1, Our *Bullarii*, vol. 1). Still its adoption is not so stringently insisted on that no room is left for fairness when serious reasons demand it. The Armenian Catholics living in Lebanon refused to accept the Gregorian calendar and were dispensed from using it by Pope Innocent XII.

At the Congregation of the Holy Office on Wednesday, June 20, 1674, this decree was issued: "There has again been mention of the letter of the Apostolic Nuncio at Florence sent on April 10 concerning the petitions made to him by Armenians for permission to pray for the Armenian patriarch during Mass, to celebrate Easter and the other feasts according to their own rite, that is, according to the old computation which was in force before the revision of the calendar etc. . . . Reference was also made to the answer of the Congregation for the Propagation of the Faith on the matter of praying for the Armenian Patriarch during Mass: "Let the nuncio be answered that in this matter the Sacred Congregation abides by the decrees issued on June 7, 1673; that is, it cannot be done and should be absolutely forbidden. As regards the celebration of Easter and the other feasts they similarly abide by the decrees that the Armenians in Liburnum should observe the Gregorian Calendar." So when these Armenians refused to obey this decree, investigation of the matter was entrusted to a special congregation of learned Cardinals. Among these were Cardinal Joannes Franciscus Albanus, who was later elected Pope, and Cardinal Henricus Norisius, who was famous in learned circles.

Allatae sunt 11

This congregation issued the following decree on September 23, 1699, and the Pope confirmed it on the same day: "After prolonged consideration of the subject and its many details, they decided in accordance with the original proposals that the Armenian Catholics living in Liburnum who have their own church could be allowed the use of the old calendar until they are disposed to accept the full observance of the Gregorian Calendar. This would be allowed at the good pleasure of the Apostolic See with the further condition that they should refrain from servile works and be required to hear Mass on the feast days of obligation in the Gregorian calendar."

46. The Oriental Greeks were asked to use the newly revised calendar, but this request was in vain. The articles and conditions presented to the Ruthenians in the time of Clement VIII when a union was effected mentioned accepting the calendar. They replied that "we will accept the new calendar if it can be made to accord with the old" (Thomas of Jesus, *Operum*, p. 329). Although there was some ambiguity in this reply, We learn of no further steps taken in this matter, nor did the theologian appointed to investigate the case pass any judgment on this article (*op. cit.*, p. 335f).

Sometimes, however, Orientals have of their

own accord adopted the new calendar, as can be seen from the statement of the provincial synod of the Maronites in 1736 to which We have often referred. "We command that the Roman calendar revised by Pope Gregory XIII, the eminent benefactor of Our people, be strictly observed in all our churches in reckoning both fast days and feast days, whether movable or immovable. And We order that the method of use of this calendar be taught to the boys in every church by their teachers in addition to Church music."

But whenever the Orientals did not accept it and there was good reason to fear riotous protests if the use of the new calendar was imposed on them, the Apostolic See has tolerated the observance of the ancient practice of the Orientals and Greeks in distant places. It has done this by allowing them to follow the old calendar until a more favorable opportunity developed for introducing the use of the newly revised calendar. The decrees of the Congregation for the Propagation of the Faith of August 22, 1625, and April 30, 1631, and the Holy Inquisition of July 18, 1613, and December 14, 1616, are in harmony with this procedure. Sometimes, indeed, missionaries have even been allowed to follow the old calendar while living in districts where only the old calendar was in use (Decrees of the Congregation for the Propagation of the Faith, April 16, 1703, and December 16, 1704).

47. It remains to discuss the final enquiry about fasting. Syrian and Armenian Catholics abstain from fish on fast days in accordance with their rite. But when they see the Latins eating fish, it is claimed that it is impossible or at least very hard for them to refrain from fish. So the seemingly reasonable suggestion is made that missionaries should be empowered to give them a dispensation with circumspection and without risk of scandal, and to substitute another pious work for abstinence from fish.

This would be an ideal place to deal with the antiquity of fasting in the east and of how its obligations have always been strictly observed despite their severity. To avoid excessive length, however, We confine Ourselves to saying that the Apostolic See has always opposed the Patriarchs whenever they wanted to relax the ancient harshness of the fast imposed on their subjects. Peter the Maronite Patriarch permitted the archbishops and bishops subject to him to eat meat as the laity did although the ancient practice had them abstain from meat. He allowed his entire people to eat fish and drink wine in Lent although this had been forbidden to them. But Pope Paul V wrote a Brief to the Patriarch who succeeded Peter on March 9, 1610, commanding him to restore the earlier state of affairs by revoking the concessions of Patriarch Peter.

During Our own pontificate the excessive good-natured laxity of Euthymius, Archbishop of Tyre and Sidon, and of Cyril Patriarch of Antioch, towards the Greek Melchites was investigated and condemned (constitution 87, *Demandatam*, sect. 6). "Judging that this innovation and relaxation of rigorous abstinence tends to the excessive harm of the ancient practice of the Greek churches, even though these measures have no force without the authority of the Apostolic See, We expressly revoke them by Our authority. We command that they should have no effect for the future nor be implemented in any way, but that everything should be restored to its former condition. Moreover, We order that the praiseworthy custom of your fathers of abstaining from fish every Wednesday and Friday throughout the year be observed in all the Patriarchate of Antioch, just as it is practiced among the neighboring peoples of the Greek rite."

It is nonsensical to affirm that a dispensation, or rather a general faculty of dispensing, should be granted on the grounds that Orientals are easily tempted to eat fish themselves by the sight of Latins eating fish on a fast day, yielding to the weakness of their nature and not from contempt. For if this argument were at all persuasive it would lead to an absolute mixture of rites. A further result would be that Latins at the sight of Greeks living in ways which are forbidden to Latins could seek a dispensation to allow them to do what they see the Greeks doing. They would claim that they accepted the Latin rite, but that from the weakness of their nature they could no longer observe it.

48. We thought We should explain these matters in this encyclical letter to reveal the bases of the answers given to the missionary who raised the questions mentioned at the beginning. But We also wanted to make clear to all the good will which the Apostolic See feels for Oriental Catholics in commanding them to observe fully their ancient rites which are not at variance with

the Catholic religion or with propriety. The Church does not require schismatics to abandon their rites when they return to Catholic unity, but only that they forswear and detest heresy. Its great desire is for the preservation, not the destruction, of different peoples—in short, that all may be Catholic rather than all become Latin.

We end Our letter at last, imparting to its every reader the Apostolic Blessing.

Given at St. Mary Major, July 26, 1755, in the fifteenth year of Our pontificate.

†

LATIN TEXT: *Bened. XIV Bull.*, 3^{2}: 249-72; *Magnum Bull.*, 19: 151-66.

ENGLISH TRANSLATION: Padraig M. O'Cleirigh.

EX QUO PRIMUM

ENCYCLICAL OF POPE BENEDICT XIV
ON THE EUCHOLOGION
MARCH 1, 1756

12

To the Archbishops, Bishops and Other Clerics, Secular and Regular, of the Greek Rite Who Enjoy Favor and Communion with the Apostolic See.

Venerable Brothers and Beloved Sons, We Give You Greeting and Our Apostolic Blessing.

Ever since We first became Pope, We have proven Our fatherly love in embracing in Christ Our beloved eastern clergy and people, the *Uniates* as they are called, who are in agreement with Us and are free from the stain of schism. We have made every attempt to induce the schismatics to abandon their errors and join Us in Catholic unity. We do not intend to recall here all the measures We took for this purpose since the records of the Congregation for the Propagation of the Faith are filled with Our decrees on this subject and everyone can refer to Our apostolic letters and constitutions on eastern affairs in the volumes of Our *Bullarium*. Our present purpose is to inform you that the work of correcting the Greek Euchologion is now completed. It has already been printed by the press of the Congregation for the Propagation of the Faith following a lengthy scrutiny of every detail and most careful correction.

Consequently We exhort you to set aside previous editions which have been found to contain too many different errors, and to use this edition in sacred rites. The errors of former editions, however, are not to be wonderered at, for errors are readily made whenever the same work goes through many editions and the editors do not exert the strictest care. Such care is necessary to prevent the repeated insertion or addition of matters which are not found in the earliest and most faithful editions, whether through deceit or ignorance. Then since these errors have to be excised or somehow restrained, corrections and new editions more faithful to the original eventually are necessary. This has obviously occurred in the Western Church too, even though it is not as subject to these errors as the Eastern Church. Accordingly the Roman Pontiffs have often had to see to it that Missals, Rituals, Breviaries, and Martyrologies were newly issued in improved editions after appropriate corrections.

In regard to the corrections of your Euchologion (which, as you well know, is no more than the collection of prayers and blessings of the Church and so with Goarius We can appropriately term it the Ritual, Manual, Sacerdotal, or Pontifical of your Church), We propose to address two subjects in particular in this letter: namely, to set down first, the history of the new corrected edition which has just been completed, and then to expound in greater detail certain admonitions which have been suitably placed at the beginning of the Euchologion. We have postponed making known to you several other matters relating to the Euchologion itself. These could not properly be included in the present letter since they would make it immoderately long and would impose excessive toil on Us quite unsuited to Our age and not easily included with the other important concerns which particularly engage Us at present in Our Apostolic ministry and cannot now be laid aside.

Correction of the Euchologion

2. Philip IV, Catholic King of the Spains, towards the beginnng of 1631, had recourse to the Apostolic See. He revealed that he had been informed by Greek Uniate inhabitants of this realm that a Euchologion containing many errors had been published by the Greek schismatics; he asked at that time for the application of appropriate remedies to this source of foolish confusion. At once Urban VIII formed a special Congregation for the correction of the Euchologion and personally appointed to it certain Cardinals, Prelates of the Roman Curia, and renowned theologians. At that time, he summoned to Rome others with a worldwide reputation for ecclesiastical learning, intending to appoint them also to this Congregation. Among those summoned was Dionysius Petavius, a priest of the Society of Jesus living in France; however, he understandably excused himself from so long a journey because of his advanced age. Jean Morin, a priest of the Gallican oratory, was also called to Rome; he attended many sessions and made many noteworthy proposals which aided the organization and direction of the undertaking. These We will discuss in another place.

3. The members of this Congregation conscientiously undertook the work entrusted to them; their careful work was approved by Leo Allatius who wrote in a discussion of the Greek Euchologion: "I could relate and investigate many matters about the book, but since it is submitted to the censure and judgment of keen scholars, I wait for a true statement and an infallible verdict concerning it." They met indeed for eighty-two sessions, as was long ago affirmed by Cardinal Franciscus Barberinus the elder at the meeting of the Congregation for the Propagation of the Faith. Pope Innocent X attended this meeting on January 23, 1645, shortly after the death of his predecessor Urban, the uncle of this cardinal. Yet the correction of the Euchologion was not finished, and the new edition could not be brought to completion.

New Congregation on the Euchologion

4. With succeeding popes, although the work was never completely abandoned, it proceeded slowly while, as often happens, its final conclusion was held up by the emergence of new and later business. But when God raised Us to the supreme pontificate, among Our first concerns was the correction of the books of the Oriental Church, particularly of the Euchologion of the Greeks. So We soon gave the following orders and were careful to have them carried out so that We might finally reach Our desired goal. First, the transactions of the Congregations which met in the reign of Urban VIII and his successors were collected and put in order to ascertain the form of those resolutions which had been adopted but not reinforced by papal confirmation: for apparently the popes had not condemned these resolutions but had deferred their consideration, possibly for good reasons, to more suitable times. Next, after the deaths of all who served on the Congregation, We assigned other Cardinals and Consultors to press on with the important task. Among the Cardinals who died were Antonio Xaverio Gentili, Philippo Monti, Gioachimo Besozzi, and Aloysio Lucini, in that order. As Prefect of the Congregation, We established the presbyter cardinal Fortunato Tamburini, who is still living. As Consultors We designated Brother Giuseppi Agustino Orsi of the Order of Preachers, the master of Our Apostolic palace; Leonardus Siderer, a priest of the Society of Jesus; Domenico Vitali, a monk of the Order of St. Basil; Thomas Sergius, a priest of the Pious Workers; and Domenico Teoli, a Roman priest. Some of these are still living. Finally We appointed as Secretary of this Congregation Master Niccolo Antonelli, Our domestic prelate. All of these men were obliged to deal with the matters submitted to their judgment. This they did diligently for an entire ten years.

At the start a dispute arose as to the method to be followed in the investigating—some judging that the forms of the Sacraments should be examined first, while others urged that matters relating to the duty of simple priests should be dealt with separately from those pertaining to bishops. We removed this problem by commanding that the revision and correction of the Euchologion should proceed in stages from the first page to the following pages in the order in which the Euchologion itself is arranged and printed. Finally We required the Secretary of the Congregation to produce an agenda before every session, for timely delivery not only to each of the Cardinals and Consultors who were to meet but also to Us, since We wanted to know of every matter to be discussed in the Congregation. In this agenda he was to list the headings of the questions to be brought forward, and to add notes on the considerations adduced and conclusions arrived at on these matters in the Congregations of previous popes insofar as they had been dealt with in former Congregations, followed by opinions on these questions from theological authors and ecclesiastical records.

Secretary of the Congregation

5. It was unnecessary, as one would expect, to advise the Secretary on the subject of examining and comparing old Euchologia. He is expert in the Greek language, outstanding in sacred learning and teaching, and ready to undertake any great labor in obedience to and for the benefit of the Apostolic See; he has often shown this on other occasions when affairs demanded it, and also by zealously publishing books.

Everyone is aware that Father Jacobus Goarius of the Order of Preachers, a Frenchman by race, spent eight years in eastern parts examining all matters closely, and then came to Rome about 1640. There he conferred at length with outstanding scholars and experts in Greek affairs; with Leo Allatius, a Prelate of the Roman Curia; Basilio Falasca, Procurator General of the Order of St. Basil; Giorgio Coresio; and Pantaleone Ligaridio. Fr. Echardus records this in *De scriptoribus Ordinis Praedicatorum* (vol. 2, p. 574). Finally he returned to France and published the Greek Euchologion together with a Latin translation. The excellence of this work is enhanced by the careful learning with which the author examined and evaluated many manuscript codices and printed books, and criticized them in his Preface to the Reader. He added variant readings everywhere and occasionally inserted appropriate and learned notes. He first published that work at Paris in the year of the Lord 1647. It was reprinted at Venice in 1739.

Importance of Extant Manuscripts of Old

6. Men of learning are also aware that several manuscript examples of the Greek Euchologion are preserved in the Vatican library, and that the Library of the Barberini has the famous *Euchologium Barberinum S. Marci*, so called because it was brought there long ago from the monastery of St. Mark at Florence. They know that this is more than ten centuries old, since Leo Allatius testified that already in his day it was considered to be more than nine hundred years old by the greatest experts of his time: "The Barberini codex surpasses all the others in point of antiquity. It is a most accurate copy in square letters on parchment and was written more than nine hundred years ago in the opinion of those who are considered foremost in judging these matters." Learned men must also know of the precious codex preserved in the archive of the monastery of *Grottaferrata* which is called the *Euchologium Patriarchale*. It was left to the monks of that abbey by the will of the great Cardinal Bessarion, who was the first Commendatory Abbot of that monastery. He always regarded it very highly since he had received it as a gift from Cardinal Giuliano Cesarino, who had in turn been given it at the Council of Florence by the Cretan priest Georgius Varj, as Arcudius testifies. All these copies of the Euchologion have been examined and critically compared as a guide to accuracy and soundness in the new edition of the Euchologion. This work was done both by the prelate who is Secretary and by other members of the Congregation who are skilled in Greek usage. Moreover there was no need for Us to advise this measure, since they themselves of their own accord undertook this trouble and performed it with great care.

7. Likewise We did not need to remind the learned Cardinals and Consultors in the Congregation of those wise remarks of the renowned Joannes Morinus in the preface to his work *De Sacris Ordinibus*, of Lukas Holstein in his *in Dissertatione I, de Sacramento Confirmationis*, and finally of the author of the *Vindiciarum P. le Brun* where he writes on the form of the Sacrament of the

Eucharist. These remarks should be certainly kept in mind if one desires to judge the Greek rites correctly. For it would of course be unjust, mistaken, and opposed to the peace and unity of the Church to make judgments concerning the Greek Rites solely on the basis of a knowledge of the Latin Rituals and what is reported by some of our writers. Even though they are expert in our practices, they are uninstructed in Greek customs, and do not know how the Apostolic See has always regarded them. So they unhesitatingly condemn everything in the sacred Greek rites which they discover to be dissimilar and not in agreement with the Latin rite.

As We say, there was no need to remind the Cardinals and Consultors selected for the correction of the Euchologion of these matters, since they had already themselves decided on this method of action and judgment and had thoroughly followed it. We acknowledge that this was also done by the cardinals and prelates who gave their opinion in the Congregations which met on this subject under Urban VIII. All the measures which We insisted on, as mentioned above, were fully implemented and the unceasing care and effort expended by all the members of the Congregation in completing the work cannot be sufficiently emphasized. Not only did the Secretary show Us the agenda before each of their sessions, but also after each session he carefully reported to Us the statements and resolutions of the Congregation. We read them all attentively and after due consideration approved and confirmed them insofar as it seemed expedient to do so. By keeping to this method the correction of the Euchologion was completed and the new edition of it was printed in 1754, at the press of the Congregation for the Propagation of the Faith. We were desirous of bringing these matters to your attention to acquaint you with the great zeal, toil, and care which were devoted to the publication of the corrected edition of your Euchologion.

Four Admonitions

8. At the beginning of this most recent edition four admonitions are to be found. We want to explain briefly to you in this letter the reasons for the presence of these remarks.

First Admonition—Commemoration of Pontiff in the Mass

9. The first admonition is thus expressed: "It must be known that the priests who will use the Euchologion should be acquainted with the ecclesiastical canons of the holy Fathers and the Constitutions of the Catholic Church in order that they may avoid obvious mistakes in administering the divine Sacraments and performing their other duties. Therefore where commemorations are customarily made in the sacred liturgy, the Roman Pontiff should be first commemorated, then one's own bishop and patriarch, provided they are Catholic. But if either or both of them are schismatic or heretic they should by no means be commemorated." Certainly this is in full agreement with the decrees passed at the meeting of the Congregation on May 1, 1746, which We approved and confirmed. The following question was raised at that meeting: "whether the name of the supreme pontiff should be put into the prayers said by priest and deacon at the Offertory as well as in the other prayers, that is, For the supreme pontiff N." This response was given to that question: "In the instruction which is to be added at the start of the Euchologion, Greek priests should be advised to make a commemoration of the supreme pontiff and of their bishop or archbishop if he is in union with the Roman Catholic Church, and moreover a rubric should be put in the margin of the Liturgy referring them to the instruction." For it seemed best to add in this manner such matter as was missed in the text of the Euchologion itself.

This Practice is Long-Standing

10. We have Ourselves dealt with the commemoration of the Roman pontiff in the sacrifice of the Mass, and with the antiquity of this practice in Our treatise *De Sacrificio Missae*, sect. I, n. 219. But since the publication of this book, the same subject has been treated with many extraordinary observations by Dominicus Georgius (who in his lifetime was Our dear sacristan) in his *De Liturgia Romani Pontificis*, vol. 3, chap. 3, no. 14, where he writes: "It has ever been customary in the Catholic Church to recite the name of the Roman pontiff during the sacred mysteries." In no. 22 he adds: "All the ancient testimonies and the oldest copies of the sacred canon agree concerning the name of the supreme pontiff." Indeed, that such a commemoration had been made in the Mass is shown by the Ambrosian Liturgy, the Mozarabic Mass, and the Latin Mass which the Lutheran Flaccus Illyricus copied from one ancient manuscript and published. So also does

the most ancient Liturgy which is found in the old manuscript on the Sacraments of the Roman Church which was published by Venerable Cardinal Thomasius. Finally, this is also shown in all the sacred canons of the Mass, whether printed or written by hand, as the prelate Niccolo Antonelli amply shows in the long and learned dissertation which he wrote as a necessary part of his duty as Secretary of the Congregation for the Correction of the Euchologion; he had it printed when a dispute on this subject arose among the Cardinals and Consultors. A reprint of this can also be found in the Appendix to the old Lateran Monastic Missal in the *Collectio Liturgica*, vol. 1, made by Fr. Emanuele de Azevedo.

11. So far the testimonies mentioned relate to the Latin Church. As regards the Greek Church, Cardinal Bona says that it is not known whether in the early centuries it recalled the Roman pontiff in the sacrifice of the Mass: "But whether in the first centuries Orthodox Greece commemorated the Roman pontiff is unclear" (*Rer. Liturgicar*, bk. 2, chap. 11, no. 3). Moreover Isaac Habertus admits that among the records of the early age, he has found none to establish that it was customary in the Oriental Church to commemorate the Roman pontiff during the celebration of Mass: "I could wish it was done and if it had been done I would approve of it, but even so I do not read that it was done." But he says that the name of the Roman Pontiff had been added to that of the Patriarch in the time of Pope Nicholas I, that is about 858, since the following words are found in several ancient copies of the Holy Liturgy of John Chrysostom: "Long be the days of most holy Nicholas the universal pope" (*Observationes ad Pontificale Graecorum*, pt. 8, observ. 12).

But Antonelli, whom We have praised, argues in his dissertation that it was customary in the Greek Church to commemorate the Roman Pontiff during Mass long before the period assigned by Habertus. He proves his point especially by the fact reported by Nicephorus in his *in Historia Ecclesiast.*, bk. 16, chap. 17, where he depends on the testimony of a more ancient and serious historian, Basilius Cilix. Acacius, bishop of Constantinople, a supporter of the Eutychian heresy, prevailed on the emperor Zeno to publish his ill-fated edict, the *Henoticon*, which rendered void the definition of the holy Council of Chalcedon which opposed the heresy of Eutyches. When Pope Felix III could not ignore this and therefore deprived Acacius of communion, he had the audacity in the year of the Lord 484 to erase the name of the Roman pontiff Felix from the sacred diptychs in a new and hitherto unheard-of excess of rashness. For this reason the memory of Acacius was then condemned. The Greek church accepted this condemnation in the time of Pope Hormisdas and Emperor Justin, although the two predecessors of Hormisdas, Anastasius II and Symmachus, had failed to win this acceptance. So in the great church of Constantinople (whose example was doubtless followed by the other lesser churches of the east) the name of the Roman pontiff *was* in the sacred diptychs; therefore it must be asserted that he was prayed for by name during the celebration of Masses. Acacius is described as the first to erase this name and his deed was on this account particularly punished since, without any precedent, he committed a new sort of outrage till then unheard of, even though in former times there had been no lack of offense and disagreements between the Roman pontiffs and the bishops of the imperial city. It is thus abundantly proved that long before the time of Acacius and so in the early centuries, the name of the Roman pontiff was written in the sacred diptychs of the Greeks and thus it was customary to pray for him during the celebration of Mass.

But however it may be with this disputed point of ecclesiastical learning, it suffices Us to be able to state that a commemoration of the supreme pontiff and prayers offered for him during the sacrifice of the Mass is considered, and really is, an affirmative indication which recognizes him as the head of the Church, the vicar of Christ, and the successor of blessed Peter, and is the profession of a mind and will which firmly espouses Catholic unity. This was rightly noticed by Christianus Lupus in his work on the Councils: "This commemoration is the chief and most glorious form of communion" (tome 4, p. 422, Brussels edition). This view is not merely approved by the authority of Ivo of Flaviniaca who writes: "Whosoever does not pronounce the name of the Apostolic one in the canon for whatever reason should realize that he is separated from the communion of the whole world" (Chronicle, p. 228); or by the authority of the famous Alcuin: "It is generally agreed that those who do not for any reason recall the memory of the Apostolic pontiff in the course of the sacred mysteries according to custom are, as the blessed Pelagius teaches, separated from the communion of the entire world" (*de Divinis Officiis*, bk. 1, chap. 12).

Pope Pelagius II who held the Apostolic See in the sixth century of the Church gives this weightier statement on Our present subject in his letter: "I am greatly astonished at your separation from the rest of the Church and I cannot equably endure it. For Augustine, mindful that the Lord established the foundation of the Church on the Apostolic sees, says that whosoever removes himself from the authority and communion of the prelates of those sees is in schism. He states plainly that there is no church apart from one which is firmly established on the pontifical bases of the Apostolic sees. Thus how can you believe that you are not separated from the communion of the whole world if you do not commemorate my name during the sacred mysteries, according to custom? For you see that the strength of the Apostolic See resides in me, despite my unworthiness, through episcopal succession at the present time" (Labbe, *Conciliorum Collectione*, vol. 5, col. 794f and 810). This letter of Pelagius has also been used by St. Agobard, the great archbishop of Lyons, in his treatise *De comparatione utriusque regiminis*. This is printed in the *in Magna Bibliotheca Patrum* (vol. 14, p. 315, no. 21, Lyons) and was reissued by Balutius with other writings of this saint (col. 2, p. 49).

13. Moreover it suffices Us to be able to affirm without peril that at whatever time the practice of praying by name for the Roman pontiff at Mass was finally accepted by the Greek Church, this practice was definitely in force in Greek churches many centuries before schism broke out, and was only broken off after the fatal separation. A letter dated 1053 of Peter, patriarch of Antioch, to Michael Cerularius, the well-known reviver of the Photian schism, survives. This letter is published in Greek and Latin by Joannes Baptista Cotelerius in the second volume of his *Monument. Eccles. Graec.* Michael had said that he was surprised that Peter of Antioch himself as well as the bishops of Alexandria and Jerusalem mentioned the Roman pontiff in the sacred diptychs (p. 140 of the abovementioned volume). But Peter most sharply rebuked the rashness of the maddened man in showing that both at Antioch and at Constantinople, the commemoration of the Roman pontiff had never been omitted up to his time: "Of these matters I too am an unexceptionable witness, as are the many others who with me hold high office in the Church, that in the time of Lord John (patriarch of Antioch), the Pope at Rome, also called John, was included in the sacred diptychs. Furthermore, when I came to Constantinople forty-five years ago I found that under Patriarch Sergius the Pope was mentioned at holy Mass along with the other Patriarchs."

It is said in addition that no discussions on restoring unity were ever begun without the acceptance of the prior condition that the commemoration of the Roman pontiff should be included in the sacred liturgy, nor was a union which had been agreed on regarded as complete until the previous condition had actually been put into effect. The clear result of all this is that the Latin and Greek churches agree in recognizing and affirming that the commemoration implies a profession of due subjection to the Roman pontiff as head of the Church, and of a willingness to remain in the unity of the Church. On the other hand the omission of this commemoration signifies the intention of steadfastly espousing schism.

14. When Michael Palaeologus, Emperor of Constantinople, in 1263 and thereafter, affirmed his desire to return in company with his Greek subjects to unity and concord with the Roman Church, Urban IV aptly proposed the condition "that in sacred ceremonies from the diptychs, the name of the Pope should be commemorated together with the four patriarchs" (Nicetas, bk. 5, chap. 2). And when thereafter the negotiation of this union was again undertaken by Emperor Michael and Patriarch Giovanni Vecco and was seriously debated at the General Council of Lyons held in the year of the Lord 1274, the Pope, Blessed Gregory X, with the agreement of the assembled council fathers, first proposed several indispensable conditions for the effective negotiation of union. The first of these was "that the Pope be included in the diptych with the other four patriarchs and commemorated during the holy services" (Nicetas, as above). And Pachymeres (bk. 5, chap. 22) testifies that this condition was accepted by the Greeks and carried out in practice: "There were two immediate results of this arrival of the ambassadors who brought back word that peace had been made on the strength of the previous agreements: the deposition of the Patriarch and the public commemoration of the Pope in holy services."

15. His son Andronicus succeeded Michael

Palaeologus as emperor, and was so extreme a supporter of the schism which had been condemned that he allowed his father's body to be buried beyond the sacred precinct because he had attempted to establish a union of the Greek Church with the Latin. Because the emperor could hardly hope for success in his intended revival of the schism while the Catholic patriarch, Giovanni Vecco, was leader of the church at Constantinople, he imposed as patriarch a certain Joseph who was tainted with the stain of heresy. As a result affairs began to deteriorate and a sincere reconciliation of the churches was no longer possible. Finally, at the meeting of the General Council of Ferrara, later transferred to Florence, in the year 1434, after proper deliberations of the issues by the Greek and Latin fathers, the wall of division was cast down which had for so long kept the one church apart from the other. To attest to everyone the reality of the enacted union John Palaeologus, emperor of the Greeks, gave orders that the name of the Pope be replaced in the sacred diptychs, as is testified even by the schismatic author Sylvester Sguropolus in his *Historia Concilii Flor.*, sess. 10. chap. 2. Afterwards when the decree of established union had been brought to Philotheus, patriarch of Alexandria, he was careful to state in his answer to Pope Eugenius IV that he had also decided that the commemoration of the Roman pontiff in the sacrifice of the Mass should be placed before that of the other patriarchs: "Hence in company with our Egyptian bishops and other clergy, we decided that everywhere in all of Christ's churches during the sacrifice of the Mass, we should commemorate Your Blessedness before the other Patriarchs, as is provided for in the sacred canons." This passage may be found in the collection of the transactions of the Council of Florence made by Cardinal Justinianus (pt. 2, collect. 22, p. 323).

16. Constantine was the Greek emperor after John Palaeologus. When he sent ambassadors to Nicholas V to beseech help for his faltering fortunes, he was careful to profess that he would make every effort to implement as fully as could be desired the harmony which was agreed on at Florence, and that consequently he would see to it that the name of the Roman pontiff was restored to the sacred diptychs. This is attested by Ducas in his *Historia Byzantina*: The emperor had already sent to Rome to request reinforcements with the additional purpose of strengthening the harmony achieved at Florence and of having the Pope's name proclaimed from the sacred diptychs during the liturgies of the great church." The Pope showed himself ready to give him as much aid as he could and continued at the same time to exhort him to promulgate the decree of the union which had been agreed on at the Council of Florence. He urged him to see to it that the name of the Roman pontiff "was proclaimed in the diptychs and that the whole Greek church prayed for him expressly and by name, as was the former practice of men who were pleasing to God, both patriarchs of Constantinople and emperors" (Raynaldus, *Annales*, 1451 A.D., no. 2).

Ex quo primum
12

17. This is all We want to say on the first part of the first Admonition which deals with the obligation of celebrants to pray for the pope in the sacrifice of the Mass. Nothing further is to be added except that even before this Admonition, Catholic Greek Oriental bishops were careful to decree this very measure in their synods. We Ourselves did not neglect the publication of such suitable decrees for Italian Greeks. In 1720, a provincial synod was held at Zamoscia on the order of Pope Clement XI, under the presidency of Hieronymus Grimaldus. He was then the archbishop of Edessa and nuncio of the Apostolic See in the kingdom of Poland; later, he was raised to the honor of the Cardinalate by Pope Clement XII. In the decrees of this synod, which were confirmed after proper investigation by Pope Benedict XIII, the following words are found under the heading *de fide Catholica*: "For the same reason"—that is, to remove all suspicion of schism—"and to show a sincere union of the members with their head, it has decided and commanded under penalties to be applied at the judgment of the Ordinary that wherever a Roman pontiff is to be commemorated, especially at the Offertory of the Mass, it should be made in clear and definite words which can signify none other than the universal Bishop of Rome."

In agreement with this view are the fathers of the Synod of Lebanon which occurred in 1736 under the presidency of Joseph Simonius Assemanus, a prelate of the Roman curia and an Apostolic envoy. In the decrees of this council too, under the heading *de Symbolo Fidei, ejusque professione*, no. 12, these words are found: "Let us not neglect to repeat the commemoration of the most holy Roman pontiff, both in Masses and in the divine services, before the name of the most reverend lord patriarch, as has hitherto been our custom." After the strictest investigation, We confirmed this council with Apostolic authority, as may be seen in Our constitution *Singularis* (Bullarium, vol. I, no. 31). Peter Arcudius in his work *de Concordia Ecclesiae Occidentalis et Orientalis*, bk. 2, chap. 39, offers an admonition for Latin bishops with Greeks living in their dioceses to zealously impel them to commemorate the Roman pontiff in the Mass, to banish the last shade of suspicion of any inclination to schism: "The Latin bishops should see to it that the Greek priests subject to them are in Catholic unity and recognize the Supreme Pastor, and according to the ancient custom solemnly pray for him" in the sacrifice of the Mass—the subject under discussion in this passage. In agreement with this most just admonition, the following provision was made in Our constitution issued for the Italian Greeks, *Etsi Pastoralis* (*Bullarium*, vol. 1, 57, sect. 9, no. 4): "Next a commemoration should be made of the Supreme Roman Pontiff and of the Local Ordinary in Masses and divine services."

First Admonition—Commemoration of Bishop and Patriarch

18. Now follows the second part of this first admonition which, as was mentioned above, obliges the Greek priest during Mass, after praying for the Roman pontiff, to pray for his own bishop and his patriarch if they are Catholic. For if either is or both are schismatic or heretic, a commemoration should not be made.

19. In the Latin Church there is usually no difficulty in commemorating the bishop in whose diocese the priest celebrates Mass. We Ourselves have dealt with this subject in Our work *de Sacrificio Missae* (sect. 1, no. 220 in the Latin edition) and have shown that the priest who celebrates Mass in any diocese should commemorate the bishop of that diocese rather than the bishop in whose diocese he was ordained or the one to whose Ordinary jurisdiction he is subject. We added that it was not permissible for regular clergy to commemorate their Superior General or for other priests to commemorate during Mass any lesser prelate of a separate territory to whom they are subject. For this honor is to be conferred only on the superior or prelate who possesses the episcopal authority and order. In that work We adduced the writings of the men who transmit to us all these matters and establish them by their testimony. So at this point We will add no more except to quote the remarks of the above-mentioned Dominicus Georgius in his treatise *De Liturgia Romani Pontificis* in which he studied many ancient manuscripts, which has appeared since the publication of Our work: "Nearly all the most ancient copies of the sacred canon of the Mass note the name of the bishop after the Roman Pontiff as is attested by Florus and the more ancient writers on the Mass whom We give in an appendix" (*Op. cit.*, vol. 3, chap. 3, no. 23, p. 52).

20. Still in reference to the Latin practice, We will also note that when a bishop is celebrating Mass, he prays for himself as an "unworthy servant." This practice is in harmony with the words of the apostolic constitutions where the celebrant, after praying for others, prays for himself in these words: "We now beseech you for a man of no worth, for myself who am offering to You" etc. (*Ap. Const.*, bk. 8, in Cotelerius, *Opera Patrum Apostolicorum*, vol. 1, p. 407). Moreover it should be known that in Rome commemoration is made only of the Roman Pontiff since he is not only Supreme Pontiff, but also the bishop of the city of Rome in particular. When the Pope himself says Mass, he prays for himself in precisely the same way as any bishop prays for himself during Mass. In reply to the bishop of Orense who enquired how the Pope commemorated himself during the celebration of Mass, Innocent III, in a letter not yet published but preserved in the Vatican archives (bk. 9, no. 33) replied as follows: "You have also asked to be instructed as to the words used by the Roman Pontiff at the place in the canon of the Mass where a priest of lower rank says 'together with our Pope,' since the Pope is then obviously praying for himself and is subordinate to no bishop. Our reply to your devotedness is this: at that place We say 'together with me your unworthy servant.'"

Finally it must be remarked that Latin priests make no commemoration of an archbishop such as a metropolitan in the canon. This point is also rightly made by P. Merati in his *Commentaria ad Gavantum* (pt. 2, head. 8, no. 5) and the case is the same even if the episcopal see is vacant: "But if the bishop, who is Ordinary of the place in which Mass is being celebrated, has departed this life, the aforesaid words are omitted"—that is, a commemoration is not made—"but it is to be noticed that the Vicar Capitular cannot be named instead of the bishop, since although while the see is vacant he is Ordinary of that place, he is still not the bishop of that diocese. Moreover, the archbishop or the patriarch of the province which includes the diocese of the dead bishop cannot be named, even though he has a certain jurisdiction over it, since an archbishop or a patriarch is not said to be Ordinary in the dioceses of his suffragans."

21. Turning now to the Greeks, We consider first the Italian Greeks. These are entirely subject to the jurisdiction of the Latin bishop in whose diocese they live, in accordance with constitution 74, *Romanus Pontifex*, of Our predecessor, Pope Pius IV. This is to be found in volume two of the *Bullar. Rom.* and We have discussed it at length in Our treatise *De Synodo Dioecesana*, bk. 2, chap. 12, of the most recent Roman edition. Therefore these Italian Greek priests, in offering the sacrifice of the Mass, are required to follow the Latin practice and commemorate the Roman Pontiff and the local bishop. They should never commemorate eastern bishops or patriarchs even if they are Catholic, since these possess no jurisdiction in Italy and the adjacent islands, as has been discussed in Our constitution *Etsi Pastoralis* (*Bullarium*, vol. 1, const. 57, sect. 9 no. 4).

Of course in the *Dictatus* of Pope St. Gregory VII (can. 10) we find the dictum: "That the name of the Pope alone be pronounced in the church." This *Dictatus* is included in the collections of the councils (Royal Parisian, vol. 26; Labbe, vol. 6, pt. 1). Still We are well aware that there is a vigorous debate among scholars as to whether this is an authentic work of the holy pontiff or rather a forgery. Indeed Fr. Mabillon in his treatise *De Studiis Monasticis* has ranked this among the more difficult questions which professors of Church history can engage in solving. But laying aside this problem also—as to whether the *Dictatus Papae* is an authentic work of St. Gregory VII—the real and pertinent meaning of the Canon quoted is not that in the Latin Church the name of the diocesan bishop be removed from the Canon of the Mass, but that the name of Oriental Patriarchs should not be included there.

The Patriarchs indeed professed their agreement with the condition, that the name of the Roman Pontiff should be replaced in the Liturgy and that prayers should be offered for him in all the churches of the east, if in turn the Pope would consent to their names being pronounced in the Canon of the Mass by Latin priests of the Roman Church and of the other churches in the Patriarchate of Rome. Lupus wisely notes: "Purposing to abandon his schism, Michael (Cerularius, Patriarch of Constantinople) tried to have his name inscribed on the Roman tablets and he promised to restore the name of the Pope to the tablets of all of his churches. But Leo (Pope Leo IX) would not consent: for the reciprocal pronouncement of the names of Patriarchs was practiced only among the equal sister sees of the eastern patriarchs, but never by the Roman see. For this see is not only sister but also mother and head of the eastern sees and so has never pronounced any other name than the bishops" (*ad Concilia*, pt. 4, p. 437, Brussels edition). He continues in this way on the following page: "The names of the eastern patriarchs have never been pronounced by the Roman church nor for that matter by any Latin church."

22. The foregoing discussion relates to the Italian Greeks. But as regards the rest of the Greeks and Orientals, the admonition in the preface of the Euchologion, which We are now considering, by no means prevents them from commemorating their metropolitans and patriarchs during the Mass, but merely forbids this if they should be schismatic or heretic. It is beyond dispute that the commemoration of patriarchs in the prayers of the Mass is an ancient custom in the Greek church. Theodorus Balsamon in his *de Patriarcharum juribus* has written: "It is established that in every church of God, whether on the Euphrates or on the edge of the Ocean, the names of the patriarchs are mentioned together." Goarius cites this as the established practice that in the Greek liturgy the priest prays for all the bishops and for the metropolitan (*in Notis ad Rituale Graecorum*, p. 63). Meratus, after establishing the fact that We mentioned earlier, that in the Latin church a commemoration of the archbishop is not made in the Mass even during a vacancy in a suffragan church, adds that: "This however is not the practice of the Greeks and other Orientals. These name the patriarch and the metropolitan" (*in notis ad Gavantum*, vol. 1, p. 539, Roman edition).

This practice is not absolutely forbidden to them in the admonition in question, but only in the cases when the metropolitan or patriarch is schismatic or heretic. This is in accordance with rules which were established and accepted before the correction of the Euchologion was undertaken. When this practice was dealt with in the Congregation of the Holy Office in 1673, the following decree was published: "At the General Congregation of the Holy Office on June 7, 1673, the question was posed whether a priest in the town of Lebanon during Mass might name the patriarch of the Armenians, who is schismatic, with the purpose of praying for him. The petition for this concession was made with great urgency in order by this means to attract that people to a greater friendship for the Latins. The Sacred Congregation responded that it could not be done and should be utterly forbidden. In the same Congregation on June 20, 1674, there was read a letter of the nuncio at Florence written on April 10, 1674, sent to the Sacred Congregation for the Propagation of the Faith and forwarded by this Congregation to the Sacred Congregation of the Holy Office. It was decided that a reply should be sent to the nuncio informing him that on the subject of prayer in the liturgy for the patriarch of the Armenians, the Sacred Congregation abided by its decrees published in 1673, that is, that it could not be done and should be utterly forbidden."

23. In harmony with this decision is another very similar decree of the Congregation on the corrected edition of the Coptic Missal made in 1732. Among other disputed questions the following was proposed: "Whether, and in what way, the words in which the priest commemorates the patriarch, bishop, etc. are to be corrected." This was the answer which was given: "A rubric should be placed at the beginning of the missal to advise and inform the priest on points relating to the celebration of Mass. Here should be placed a special rubric on the commemoration of the Roman pontiff as well as of the patriarch and bishop, provided that they are in union with the Roman Church. This rubric should be consulted in its own place." Moreover heretics and schismatics are subject to the censure of major excommunication by the law of Can. *de Ligur.* 23, quest. 5, and Can. *Nulli*, 5, dist. 19. But the sacred canons of the Church forbid public prayer for the excommunicated as can be seen in chap. *A nobis*, 2, and chap. *Sacris* on the sentence of excommunication. Though this does not forbid prayer for their conversion, still such prayer must not take the form of proclaiming their names in the solemn prayer during the sacrifice of the Mass. This fully accords with the ancient practice, as may be seen in Estius *in 4. Sententiar.*, dist. 12, sec. 15. For that purpose it is sufficient to beseech to lead back the wanderers to the way of salvation and to the bosom of holy Mother Church, as is expounded by Sylvius, *in 3. part. D. Thomae*, vol. 4, quest. 83, art. 1, qu. 9.

Here is the teaching of St. Thomas himself *in 4. Sent.*, dist. 18, quest. 2, art. 1, in answer to the first difficulty: "Prayer can be offered for the excommunicated, although this should be done apart from prayers which are offered for members of the Church." This does not necessarily involve a confusion of the Church's laws which exclude from the roster of its faithful followers the names of those who have cut themselves off from it. In forbidding public prayers to be offered for them, the Church definitely rules out commemorating them in the celebration of Mass. Very relevant is the view of Ven. Card. Bellarmine: "Someone will ask whether at the present time it it permissible to offer the sacrifice of the Mass for the conversion of heretics or the infidels. The reason for doubt is that the entire liturgy of the Latin church, as it is now performed, relates to the faithful, as is clear from the prayers of the offertory both before and during the canon. I answer that I consider it permissible, provided that no addition is made to the Mass, but the sacrifice is applied to the conversion of the infidels or heretics only by the intention of the priest. For this is the practice of pious and learned men, with whom we cannot disagree, and it is not forbidden by the Church" (*Controversarium*, vol. 3, bk. 6, *de Missae*, chap. 6).

Should the King be Commemorated?

24. In this first admonition, however, there is no mention at all of commemorating or saying a prayer for an emperor or king and his whole palace and army. But since this matter is very closely connected with the other matters mentioned in the first admonition, We judge it appropriate to append the following remarks.

25. All the euchologies, whether manuscript or printed, which are earlier than the revision of Leontius, included prayers for the emperor, the king, his palace, and army. In the May 1, 1746, session of the Congregation for the Correction of the Euchologion, it was disputed whether these prayers should be removed. It was decided, with

Our subsequent approval, that "they should be left in the canon or the liturgy." But since the Greeks of old used to offer these prayers at the prothesis as well, but later removed them, it was added that "they are not to be said during the prothesis or preparation." For it seemed pointless to say such prayers at the prothesis when they were already being said in the canon, or liturgy." The newly corrected edition of the Euchologion has treated the matter in just this way.

26. We Ourselves in Our treatise *de Sacrificio Missae*, sect. 1, no. 221, have already discussed the commemoration in the canon of the emperor or king, as is customary in some districts belonging to their temporal realm. Cardinal Bona provides evidence that in many Latin churches the name of the king is commemorated in the canon (*Rer. Liturgicar.* bk. 2, chap. 11, no. 4). Furthermore Martène in his work *de antiquis Ecclesiae Ritibus*, bk. 1, chap. 4, art. 8, no. 9, after adducing the appropriate evidence, comes to the following conclusion: "From the unchanging tradition of the Church as it was received from the Apostles, it is certain that prayers for kings and princes have always been offered during the sacred mysteries." It is quite evident that the writer is here relying on the words of the Apostle (1 Tm 2) commanding that prayers and petitions be made for kings and all who are in high places, as well as on the text of the apostolic constitutions: "We also beseech You, Lord, for the king and for those who are in high places and for all the army that our affairs may prosper" and "Let us pray for kings and those of exalted power that our affairs may enjoy peace" (Cotelerius, *Patrum Apostolicorum*, col. 1, bk. 8, chap. 12 and 13). On this point Gregorius too may be consulted (*de Liturgia Rom. Pont.*, bk. 4, chap. 3, no. 4). However it may be with the dispute conducted between Balutius and Lupus, on the date when the emperor's name was replaced by that of the king in the lands subject to the sway of kings (a question treated at great length by Lupus (can. 10, *Dictatus S. Greg. VII*), it is sufficiently established that in the Latin church a commemoration of the king is made in those districts in which it has long been an accepted custom or where a concession of the Apostolic See has allowed it, as Meratus remarks (*ad Gavantum*, vol. 1, pt. 1, p. 539, no. 6 of the Roman edition).

27. But among the Oriental peoples this practice of commemorating the king in the sacred liturgy is common, as may be seen in the Liturgies of the Armenians, Copts, Ethiopians and Syrians. But if it should be asked how it can be endured where it is certain that the kings for whom they pray and whom they commemorate in the liturgy are infidels, Ven. Card. Bellarmine would reply (as in fact he replied in the chapter quoted above) that it is by no means forbidden *by the nature of the object*, as theologians say, to pray during Mass even for infidels since the sacrifice of the Cross has been offered for all men. And of course St. Thomas teaches that although St. Augustine wrote in his work *de origine Animae* that the sacrifice is offered only for those who are members of Christ, his statement must be understood to include both those who are already members of Christ and those who are able to become such (*in 4. Sentent.*, dist. 12, quest. 2, art. 2, quest. 2, to the fourth). Therefore, the Cardinal adds that the whole question should be assessed in terms of what the Church has forbidden: "It is certain from the nature of the object that if the Church has not prohibited it, it is permissible to offer prayers for those men (i.e., the infidels)." Although there is such a prohibition against the excommunicated and so against heretics and schismatics, there is none against infidels and these are not bound by excommunication. This is enough, he says, to allow commemoration of them during Mass and even the offering of the sacrifice for them in accordance with the evident tradition in this matter and with the apostolic constitution. "But someone may ask whether it is permissible if the king is an infidel as in Greece, where the Turk is ruler, and as in India, Japan and China where pagans rule, for priests there to offer prayers expressly for the king. I answer that I consider it permissible provided that the king is not excommunicated as are heretic kings, but is a pagan. For this tradition, this constitution, is apostolic, as I showed just above. To my knowledge there is no clear prohibition of this by the Church." A useful addition to the present discussion is the text of Tertullian: "We offer sacrifice for the health of the Emperor but we offer it to our God and his in the prayerful way commanded by God. For God the Creator of the whole world has no need of honor or of anyone's blood" (*ad Scapulam*, chap. 2).

28. However, We may leave aside these statements without further inquiry, since they are unnecessary for justifying the retention of the

commemoration of emperors or kings in the text of the Greek Euchologion. But it is worth remarking that when Greek Catholics were asked if, in making these commemorations they intended to offer prayers for the Turks to whose temporal sovereignty they have been subject since they were deprived of their own leaders, they answered that their intention at all times was to pray for Orthodox kings and Christian princes. This is asserted by Goarius in his *in notis ad Euchologium*, p. 38, where he says that when he asked Greek Catholics whether they intended to include Turks in their prayers, they invariably replied that they meant only our Christian kings, and that they proclaimed in the churches as lords in faith and religion those whom they wanted as rulers. For those alone they unfailingly desired to pray even when the published books suppressed the prayers."

Second Admonition

29. The second of the admonitions in the preface of the new edition of the Greek Euchologion is expressed as follows: "In addition the priest in the sacred liturgy approaches the gifts while singing the glory of God; raising these in a fitting religious manner above his head, he carries them to the altar in a procession around and up through the church. Meanwhile the people devoutly bow the head and kneel as they pray that they may be remembered in this procession of the gifts. But some of the faithful who kneel think these gifts are the Body and Blood of Christ and adore them as such, perhaps because they confuse them with the entry of the presanctified, that is when previously consecrated bread is carried, and do not understand the difference between the two carryings. The priest therefore should carefully teach and inform all the faithful of the difference between these two processions of the gifts, since in one case they have been changed and sanctified by the word of God. These gifts should be worshipped and adored most religiously since under the appearance and symbols of bread and wine, they contain the Body and Blood of Christ. But the case is different before they are consecrated and consummated."

The Greater Entrance

30. You already know well that your liturgy has two entrances, called the smaller and the greater. The smaller entrance is when the book of the holy Gospel is brought in, but the greater entrance is when the unconsecrated gifts of bread and wine are carried to the holy altar from the small altar or table known as the prothesis on which they were prepared. Accordingly the second sentence of this admonition deals with the greater, not with the smaller entrance. At the greater entrance, the practice of this Rite is for either the deacon or the priest to carry over his head the bread on a paten covered with a veil. The deacon carries the bread when a solemn Mass is celebrated with a deacon as assistant and minister. On such an occasion, he holds the paten with the bread above his head with his left hand and with his right he incenses the priest who is carrying the chalice with wine. When the priest celebrates without a deacon, he is incensed by the lector while he holds the paten with the bread over his head with his left hand and with his right he carries the sacred chalice on a level with his breast. It is at this greater entrance, then, that the people bow, or, in accordance with the different customs of different districts, prostrate themselves, and strike the ground with their foreheads just as if the Body and Blood of Christ the Lord were contained under the appearances of the bread and wine even before consecration. "The people everywhere address and adore the King of Heaven as if He were present in this offering; in Greece they bow very low but avoid bending the knee so as not to appear to imitate the Latins even on weekdays; while in Russia they prostrate themselves and strike the ground with their foreheads" (Peter Arcudius, *De Concordia Eccles. Occid. et Orient.*, bk. 3, chap. 19).

31. The rite of the greater entrance when a patriarch or a metropolitan celebrates Mass is described by Christianus Lupus, *Operum super Conciliis*, pt. 3, p. 760 of the Brussels edition. In his *Vocabulario Ecclesiastico* under the word *Prothesis*, Magri describes in detail the actions performed by the Emperor while standing at the sacred assembly on the day of his coronation as emperor. Goarius explains most carefully the complete ceremony of the greater entrance in his *in notis ad Liturgiam Sancti Joannis Chrysostomi*, no. 110, as does Cardinal Bona in *Rer. Liturgic.*, bk. 2, chap. 9, no. 4. Everything done by the Greeks on this occasion is likewise done by the Armenians, Copts, Ethiopians, and Syrian Jacobites, as can be seen in Le Brun, *Explanatione*

Missae, vol. 3; in Chardon, *Historia Sacramentorum*, vol. 2, chap. 2; and in Renaudot, vol. I, on *in notis ad Liturgiam Cophtorum*. Why, even in the city of Rome, on the feast of St. Athanasius, the Greeks may be seen in their own church performing all the ceremonies We have reviewed above. "And in this way even today the Greeks perform the liturgy on the feast of St. Athanasius in his basilica in Rome" (Lupus, *loc. cit.*).

Adoration of Consecrated Hosts

32. You understand also that in accordance with your Rite during the days of the Lenten fast, only the Mass of the Presanctified is celebrated among you, except on Saturdays and Sundays and on the feast of the Annunciation of the Blessed Virgin Mary if it occurs in the Lenten period as is specified in the Trullan Canon 52. "On all days of the holy Lenten fast except on Saturday, Sunday, and the holy day of the Annunciation, the sacred ministry of the Presanctified should take place." As you already know, the priest who celebrates Mass in Lent on the days when he is permitted to do so, that is on Saturday and Sunday, consecrates and consumes one host but reserves another consecrated host. He divides this into as many pieces as will suffice for the number of Masses of the Presanctified which are to be celebrated on the following days, at which he will give communion to himself and to the other communicants, if there are any, from the Eucharistic bread which was consecrated on the preceding days. This is how Leo Allatius rightly describes the entire ceremony in the prolegomena to Gabriel Naud's *de Missa Praesanctificatorum*, p. 1531, no. 1: "Each priest counts on his fingers the days of the coming week on which he is going to celebrate, then breaks off at the offertory as many pieces of bread as will suffice for the Masses he is going to say. He consecrates these as well as the piece he will consume on the same day and preserves in the pyx the consecrated pieces after dipping them in the Lord's Blood, as is customary. He removes a piece from the pyx at an appropriate time later, when he is about to celebrate (leaving the others there for future use), places it on the paten and, after bringing it to the greater altar, he consumes it."

33. On this occasion likewise a solemn procession through the church is made. The deacon carries above his head the sacred pyx in which is contained the sacrament under the appearance of bread, while the priest carries in his hands a chalice containing wine mixed with water which has been blessed but not consecrated. If the priest celebrates alone—since he does not always have the assistance of a deacon in saying Mass—he carries the pyx in his left hand over his head and holds the chalice in his right, proceeding in this way from the small to the larger altar. This is stated by Arcudius in the work already mentioned, bk. 3, chap. 58: "The Greeks have the custom in liturgies of the Presanctified of placing the Sacrament on a paten on a small altar of offering, and of pouring wine into a chalice without prayers before the ceremony begins. Then about the middle of the Mass, the priest, if he is celebrating alone, holds the paten above his head, takes the chalice in his right hand, and brings them to the larger altar, etc. But if the priest is celebrating this kind of Mass with the assistance of a deacon, it is customary for him to give the paten with the Sacrament to the deacon who carries it above his head, while he himself takes the chalice and follows after the deacon." At that point the people bend the knee, beat the breast, and adore the consecrated Bread carried by the priest or by the deacon, as We have mentioned above.

It is claimed that this is why people offer the same reverence during the greater entrance, when the bread and wine which are not yet consecrated are carried through the church in a rite of supplication. This is indeed the problem, and it is on the basis of this that criticisms have been leveled against the greater entrance. Nicolas Cabasilas writes: "If, however, there are some who prostrate themselves on the ground when the priest enters with the gifts, and adore and address these gifts as if they were the Body and Blood of Christ, these people have been confused by the entrance of the presanctified gifts and do not understand the difference between the two kinds of sacrifice; for in the first kind the gifts are not sanctified and not yet perfected at the entrance, while in the second kind they are perfected and sanctified and are the Body and Blood of Christ" (*in Expositione Liturgiae*, chap. 24). Later Arcudius gives this account: "Therefore the people through not understanding the difference between the two kinds of liturgy behave in the same way at ordinary and presanctified liturgies. And so they make a serious mistake, since of course when the priest carries the true Body of Christ on the paten at liturgies of the Presanctified, it is right that they prostrate themselves on the ground and adore it. But at sacrifices of the other kind, they should behave with more restraint since the offertory in these cases is made before the consecration" (*Op. cit*, bk. 3, chap. 19). In later chapters of this book, Arcudius refutes Gabriel, Archbishop of Philadelphia, a voluminous defender of this rite. Even Goarius, in the passage quoted above, considered it necessary to adduce some appropriate arguments in defense of this rite.

The following passage occurs in the latest edition of a work called *Perpetuitas Fidei Catholicae de Sacramento Eucharistiae, adversus Claudium vindicata*, p. 68: that "the Greeks, far from not adoring the sacrament of the Eucharist, are rather obliged to cleanse themselves, thereby demonstrating that they do not pass beyond the limits of what is right and do not honor still unconsecrated bread and wine with the same acts of adoration as they use to reverence them after consecration." Le Brun asserted without hesitation that the nature of the rite called for some measure of reformation. In relating that he observed with his own eyes the performance of this ceremony among the Armenians, Tournefort (vol. 3, pp. 411f) expresses a certain indignation. Chardon in the passage noted above cites from the writings of Tournefort and Fr. Le Brun, but then leaves the point of the question undecided. So the fathers of the council held at Zamość in 1720, in their decree *de celebratione Missarum*, sect. 4, unhesitatingly prohibited any genuflection or bowing of the head while still unconsecrated bread and wine were being brought from the small altar to the main altar. "The synod forbids all genuflection and bowing of the head while the bread of oblation is being brought for consecration from the smaller altar to the main altar during the period of the offertory. It commands the parish priests to admonish the people on this matter, to prevent their exposure to the danger of idolatry." In making this decree, the fathers may have had in mind the incident related in 2 Kings 18 of Ezechiah, King of Judah, who broke the bronze snake made by Moses because the children of Israel burned incense for it even up to his time.

34. We were able to gather the preceding passages from the books which have treated of this rite. Now We will add the opinions and decisions regarding this rite which emerged both in the Congregations convened under Urban VIII and in those which were held in Our days, whose decrees We Ourselves subsequently approved.

35. It was first prudently observed that to abolish the ceremony of the greater entrance (a course which incidentally would have put the blade to the root, as the saying is) would be extremely odious to the Greek church. It would also be inconsistent with the established practice of the Latin church which had always tried to preserve as much as possible the Greek rite in the Greek church. Such a course would be all the more unacceptable because the ceremony is ancient. It is usually said in explanation of this rite that it preserves an ancient custom in reference to the triumphal entrance of Christ when He came from Bethany to Jerusalem. Germanus, Patriarch of Constantinople, wrote on this very subject: "For at that time on the human level a great crowd and the children of the Hebrews sang a hymn as for a king and the conqueror of death, but on the spiritual plane the angels with the cherubim rendered the hymn, Thrice Holy." He then added that the smaller entrance signifies the humble coming of the Son of God into this world.

36. In the second place, attention was directed to the difference between the words sung during the transference of the presanctified and those sung by the clergy during the procession of the greater entrance. In the latter case the words are, "As men who are about to welcome the king of all things," and these point not to a king who is present, but to one who is to come hereafter. In the former case they omit the hymn of the cherubim and repeat the following words: "Behold the mystical and consummated sacrifice." So great is the difference that everyone, even men of the slightest intelligence, can distinguish between the two ceremonies. For in the transference of the Presanctified, Jesus Christ is shown as present under the appearances of bread, while in the ceremony of the greater entrance the same Lord is referred to, not as present under the appearances of bread and wine, but as very soon to be present after the words of consecration have been pronounced by the priest.

External Acts of Adoration

37. Thirdly, it was considered that the Greeks who are learned in religious matters understand fully that the Body and Blood of the Lord are not yet present under the appearances of

Ex quo primum
12

bread and wine during the greater entrance. If they also know, as they surely must, that acts of worship (*latria*) are due to God alone, no one can justly suspect that they intend to offer worship to still unconsecrated species by the external actions of veneration which they practice at the entrance of the offerings. These same signs of external reverence are usually offered at different times to the Creator and to created things. Thus the holy Scriptures say that Abraham adored the angels, that Jacob more than once prostrated himself before his brother Esau, and that the prophet Nathan did likewise in the presence of David. The condemnation of this Greek rite is unnecessary also because worship (*latria*) is not constituted by external acts alone, but particularly by the inner disposition of the mind which determines the external actions. Moreover if the Greeks at the Mass of the Presanctified show reverence by the same acts of external adoration to the bread which is consecrated and at the same time to the wine contained in the chalice which is admittedly not consecrated, they are not for this reason accused of adoring with an equal act of worship the bread which has been consecrated and the wine which has only been blessed in the Mass of the Presanctified. This accusation is not made, of course, because external actions are guided by the mind. Therefore in accordance with different intentions, one and the same act can convey at one time the adoration of worship, at another the implication of a lesser reverence.

This point sufficiently establishes that even if during the greater entrance, in the presence of the still unconsecrated bread and wine, the Greeks perform the same external acts of adoration as they are accustomed to offer to the Eucharistic bread and consecrated chalice, it cannot be asserted that they worship ordinary bread and unconsecrated wine. For every action should be measured by the intent, which can direct the same external actions after the consecration to express an adoration of worship towards the Eucharistic Bread and Wine. It can also exclude the act of worship from the performance of the same actions before the consecration at the solemn entrance of the offerings. So the following passage of Leo Allatius is relevant: "This service is not called worship, which is due to God alone, but it is such as is demanded by the veneration of creatures. For a gesture of external reverence such as uncovering the head, kissing the hands, joining them in an attitude of supplication, stretching them out, raising them on high and the like, as well as kneeling and prostrating oneself on the ground, is offered not only in adoration of God but of creatures too. No wrong is done in such cases provided that we mentally distinguish God the Creator from the creation, and a more excellent creature from a less excellent one. So through external gestures of the body, service rendered to God in adoration is considered worship not on account of the nature of these actions, but on account of the intention which determines them, since otherwise in their mere nature they are indifferent. For the inner will and intention of pleasing the divine honor through these external actions makes these acts suitable for the service of God, and allows the external adoration of God to be exercised through them" (*Tractat. de Missa Praesanctificatorum*, no. 8).

St. Thomas teaches as follows: "Adoration chiefly consists in an inner reverence of God, but in a secondary way in certain bodily signs of humility, just as we bend the knee to show how weak we are in comparison with God and we prostrate ourselves to proclaim that, of ourselves, we are nothing" (*Summa Theol.* 2.2, quest. 84, art. 82, answer to the second). In explaining this teaching, Sylvius adds these words: "It is fitting that adoration chiefly consist in an interior reverence for God, but secondarily in certain bodily signs. This is true, although there is hardly any bodily sign of reverence or service which cannot be offered in homage to a creature as well as to God. Consequently external acts of homage must be distinguished on the basis of the intention of the offerer. For if he intends by an external mark of reverence to offer an honor appropriate only to God and to honor Him as supreme, then such a service will pertain to divine worship; but if it is intended to offer reverence to an outstanding creature pleasing to God, it will be an instance of the service of *Dulia* or *Hyperdulia*. I said "hardly" since no doubt there is an external sacrifice which can be offered only to God." Thus Sylvius states that the one outer sign which necessarily implies a service of *Latria* is an external sacrifice which is most definitely offered to God alone, as is shown at length by St. Thomas too (*Summa Theol.* 2.2, quest. 85, art. 2). So we read in the Acts of the Apostles that when the Laodiceans thought that Paul and Barnabas were gods, they at once considered the need of offering sacrifice to them.

Suárez hands on precisely the same doctrine: "External acts are not of their own nature fixed to the extent that they cannot be performed both to reverence God and to honor a creature, etc. Therefore, in these external acts, the distinction of the Latria due to God alone from the reverence of a creature depends chiefly on the inner intention" (*in 3. part. Divi Thomae*, vol. 1, quest. 25, art. 2, disput. 61, sect. 4). The same writer, it is true, adds a little later that it is not only the agent's inner will which confers on an external act the nature of divine reverence; the act can become such and be so considered if such a meaning is assigned to it by one who has the requisite authority: "Apart from inner intention a public imposition must be considered. For if these signs are imposed by sufficient authority and power to signify God and His service, they can only be used for the service of God. Then if such service is imparted to creatures, it will be at least external idolatry even if it does not proceed from the intention or arises from a mistaken judgment." But this teaching can have no application to Our present subject for there exists nowhere a decree of public authority that the external acts described above as performed by the Greeks at the procession through the church at the greater entrance must be considered as acts and signs of a service of Latria.

38. Fourthly and finally, the Congregation for the Correction of the Euchologion at its meeting on September 5, 1745, discussed the question of whether the rite of the greater entrance which We have been describing should be abolished or corrected. After full discussion, it decided that no innovations should be made; we subsequently confirmed this decision. No different, of course, were the opinions of the Congregations which examined this very question in the time of Urban VIII. However they advised that Bishops and others who have the care of souls should be sure to teach the uninstructed laity that the Body and Blood of Our Lord Jesus Christ are not present under the appearances of the sacred gifts while these are being carried in solemn rite from the prothesis to the main altar, since they have not yet been consecrated. Therefore, the external acts of reverence displayed towards the still unconsecrated gifts are not performed to offer the service of Latria, which is due to God alone, but to render a lesser service directed to the approaching transubstantiation of those gifts into the Body and Blood of the Lord.

A similar measure was employed by the fathers of the Council of Trent when they discussed the veneration and service of sacred images. They decided, that while no change should be made in the ancient practice of the Church in this matter, it was incumbent on the bishops and on others who teach to instruct the Christian people on the relevant points (session 25, *Decreto de invocatione, et veneratione, et Reliquiis Sanctorum, et Sacris Immaginibus*). With more immediate relevance to Our subject, Goarius in the passage mentioned earlier likewise advised that the rite of the greater entrance should not be abrogated, but that the people should be taught with appropriate proofs: "Certainly the faith of that simple people should be instructed, but their devotion should never be quenched nor their external cult wholly abolished." So too, Philipus de Carboneano in his *Appendix ad Tract. P. Antoine de Eucharistia*, sect. 3, concludes that "there are no grounds for blame in this case, but the simple people should be taught not to reverence those gifts as the Body and Blood of Christ."

But if you take this measure, as We are confident you shall, you will wholly escape the accusation levelled by Arcudius at the Greek bishops of his day. He stated that while the people then lived in the darkest ignorance, the bishops could easily have cured their blindness by means of appropriate teaching, if they had not refrained from undertaking this task through fear of worldly censure. "The Greek bishops could and should carefully advise the people, and if they worked together they could achieve much. But perhaps they themselves are afflicted with the same disease and live in the same error on account of their ignorance. Or if some of them indeed understand, these few fear the majority because they fear to lose earthly glory and human regard and they dread that their name will be trodden underfoot by the mob like the heretics'. And so they give an excellent imitation of the others' error, at least outwardly, and they ignore these matters in deep silence, pretending they do not exist. So the blind lead the blind and they all fall into the ditch" (*de Concordia*, bk. 3, chap. 19).

39. Furthermore, before the celebrant carries the sacred gifts from the small table to the main altar, he approaches the prothesis clad in the sacred vestments and divides the bread for consecration into many pieces. The large piece is offered to show due service to God who is best and greatest, in remembrance of Our Savior Jesus Christ. The other smaller pieces, called *merides*, are likewise offered to Almighty God, but of these one is offered in honor of the glorious Virgin Mary, Mother of God; another in honor of St. John the Baptist, the holy Apostles, and the other saints whom the priest names; another for the salvation of the living whose names are mentioned by the priest; another for the dead who are likewise commemorated by name; another in honor of the saint whose feast day is being celebrated. The priest may still offer the Sacrifice especially for the person or persons of his choice. That this rite of dividing the Bread into pieces is long established is proved by Montfaucon's edition of the *Typico* of the Empress Irene (*Analect. Graecor.* vol. 1, chap. 34). But if a bishop or the priest who takes the part of the main celebrant concelebrates with other priests, and deacons also assist as ministers in the service, not only each priest but each deacon as well offers one larger host together with the smaller *merides*. If at the end any of the smaller pieces have not been consumed by the celebrant or celebrants, they are distributed to those present who wish to receive holy communion. All these matters are related in careful detail by Cardinal Bona, *Rer. Liturgicar*, bk. 2, chap. 1, no. 7; Arcudius *de Concordia*, bk. 2, chap. 9; and Goarius, *ad Rituale Graecorum, in notis ad Liturgiam S. Joannis Chrys.*, p. 98f.

40. There is no dispute among Catholics about the rite of the large and smaller hosts, called *merides*. For when this rite was examined at the ecumenical council of Florence, it was noted in the Proceedings that the Archbishop of Mitylene fully answered the questions which were raised. Although the content of his answers is not given, it must be assumed that he could satisfy his questioners only by demonstrating the antiquity of this rite. It has been observed throughout many centuries in the Oriental church to indicate the various ends for which the sacrifice is being offered. "He will have said he considered it to be an ancient custom of the Oriental Church which was used to state different ends of the sacrifice" (Arcudius, *op. cit.*, bk. 3, chap. 9). Moreover, We have said that no dispute over this rite has arisen among Catholics. But among the schismatics it is generally accepted that Simeon, Archbishop of Thessalonica, betrayed certain doubts about the consecration of the particles in his treatise *de Sacramentis*. But everyone can easily see how unreasonable his doubting was. The priest at the sacred altar pronounces the form of consecration over the smaller particles no less than over the larger piece. Since his intention is equally aimed at consecrating all of them, and the matter of all of them is suitable for sacramental transformation, the smaller particles must certainly be consecrated too if the larger piece receives consecration.

41. Catholics, however, have disputed whether the oblation can be performed by the deacons, as We mentioned above. Arcudius shows that this is wholly unlawful for them according to the Sacred Canons (bk. 3, chap. 17). Goarius states that oblation by the deacon was not an accepted usage in the great church of Constantinople (*ad Euchologium*, p. 72). Many feel that the words relating to the oblation by the deacon should be struck from the Euchologion on the grounds that they had been added by the schismatics. On the other side of the question, Cardinal Bona knows of no canon opposed to this rite. While the sacred canons exclude the deacon from rashly making the oblation at the holy altar, they do not forbid the oblation which he performs at the prothesis. Indeed this is nothing but the preparation for the other oblation which the priest will perform at the holy altar (*Rer. Liturgic.* bk. 2, chap. 1, no. 7). He also shows that the rite of oblation by the deacon is ancient and has been practiced for many centuries in the Greek Church. In fact, when it was questioned at the council of Florence, the fathers assembled there were satisfied by the answers of the Archbishop of Mitylene. Likewise Berlendis recognizes the oblation at the prothesis as an office of deacons even though the right of making oblation at the altar is forbidden to them as belonging only to priests. "The office of making oblation given to the deacon means the first oblation of the particles while they are still on the table, called the prothesis, but not the other two oblations which are performed by the priest during the liturgy" (*Tractatu de Oblationibus*, sect. 5, p. 143, Venice, 1743).

42. St. Ambrose extolled the virtue of St. Lawrence, who as a deacon desired to be led to martyrdom together with Pope St. Sixtus. He imagines him speaking as follows: "Test me, and see if you have appointed a suitable minister to be entrusted with the distribution of the Lord's

Blood!" We know, of course, that some copies read "consecration" for "distribution," but here "consecration" merely means the ministry of assistance given to the consecrating priest. Peter of Blois says: "to us deacons the consecration of the saving Host is entrusted, not so that we may consecrate it but that we may humbly help those who do" (epistle 123). Similar is the explanation of Peter Cantor given in Menard, *in notis et observationibus ad librum Sacramentorum S. Gregorii*, p. 287. It has always been forbidden to subdeacons to administer the Eucharist to the people either under the appearance of bread or under the appearance of wine, according to canon 25 of Laodicea (see the notes on this canon by Balsamon, Zonaras and Aristenus in Beveregius, vol. 1, p. 464). But this was not the case with deacons, who of old were particularly entrusted with the sole distribution of the Lord's Blood. Later this privilege was taken from them on account of certain abuses which had developed (Cotelerius, *Constitutionum, quae Apostolicae dicuntur*, vol. 1, on bk. 8, chap. 13).

43. Now the Congregations which met under Urban VIII, as well as those during Our pontificate, carefully examined the question of whether the oblation by the deacons at the prothesis should be abolished. The Congregation held on January 3, 1745, issued a directive that "no innovations should be made," and We gave this directive Our approval. For the reasons in favor of this rite adduced by Cardinal Bona seemed stronger and weightier than those assembled by Arcudius for its abolition. So in the new edition of the Euchologion, the rite of oblation by the deacon remains unchanged. Although this rite is not mentioned in the statement of the second admonition which We have hitherto discussed, We still thought it proper to enter a little on the subject here. For not only is it one of the sacred actions which are performed at the prothesis to which We have directed the foregoing remarks, but We also avail Ourselves of every occasion to assure you that the Roman church is not at all hostile to your rites. Rather it makes every effort to preserve them unchanged when they contain no error or disgrace.

Third Admonition—Sacrament of Extreme Unction

44. We come now to the third admonition which consists of two parts and is expressed as follows: "The priests should remember that the sacrament of holy oil, called *euchelaeon*, was instituted by Christ as a heavenly medicine for the health of the body as well as that of the soul. Accordingly it is to be given only to the sick at the time they desire it and while they are still in possession of their faculties. So coming with faith and a devout will to be anointed with the holy oil, they will receive additional grace from the sacrament. Likewise it must be understood that although bishops of the Oriental Church customarily use many spices in preparing the sacred chrism, only oil and balm are required. Then with these, in accordance with the ancient custom of the Oriental Church, other spices may rightly be mixed if they are available. But if some are lacking, since they are not required, the holy chrism may duly be prepared with only oil and balm."

45. This sacrament is called "extreme unction" by both the Latins and the Greeks. At the second general council of Lyons convened by the leaders of east and west in 1274, Latins and Greeks approved and signed a statement of faith (Harduin, *Collect.*, vol. 7, p. 695). The Greeks also call this sacrament the oil consecrated and sanctified by the prayers of priests, and the perfecting or fulfillment of the sacrament of penance. It is named *euchelaeon* in the Euchologion of Goarius, p. 346, no. 42 and p. 349, no. 1. The same name is used by writers of the next generation as can be seen in Georgius Pachymeres, *Hist. Palaeol.*, bk. 6, chap. 32, and Possinus uses the same name in Bk. 1 *Glos.*, p. 386 in Gabriel Philadelphius *De Sacramento Euchelaei* and *Acta Ecclesiae Orientalis*, vol. 1, p. 338. Moreover, the Greeks sometimes call this sacrament *Heptapapadum*. At the synod in Constantinople which met under Patriarch Giovanni Veccos in 1277, the Patriarch accepted the confession of faith agreed upon at the Council of Lyons. He wrote to the Roman Pontiff John XX (XXI) that: "We also accept extreme unction as we accept the other sacraments. It is named *heptapapadum* from our way of conferring it," that is, the service of seven priests, since the Greeks administer the sacrament in this way.

46. We shall not speak in this letter of the institution of this sacrament by Christ or of its effect. Nor shall We deal with the rules to be observed in administering it, namely that it should be conferred not on those who are in good health but only on the faithful who are seriously ill while they are still fully conscious. We shall not treat, either, of certain rites of the Greek church, such as the blessing of the oil of the sick by a priest and not only by a bishop as is the Latin practice, or the administering of the sacrament of extreme unction by many priests rather than by one only. For We have given a detailed account of all these matters in Our treatise *de Synodo Diocesana*, bk. 8, chaps. 1-8 of the latest edition. But simply to cast light on the first part of the third admonition, We will add that both in the time of Urban VIII and in the earlier years of Our pontificate, a lengthy dispute took place concerning whether words should be struck from the Greek Euchologion which apparently suggested that it was permissible to confer this sacrament even on those in good health. In the assembly on September 3, 1747, the Congregation decided that no changes should be made in the text, but that necessary points of observance should be mentioned in an admonition placed at the start of the Euchologion. We then approved this decision. This has been done in the words quoted above which warn Greek priests not to confer the sacrament of extreme unction on those in good health, but only on those who are seriously ill. There was clearly no need to alter the text of the Euchologion at this point, since the words could be interpreted correctly. For it does not state that the sacrament may be conferred on those in good health, but that persons who come to the church may also be anointed. This can be easily understood of those who, though grievously ill, are still able either to walk to the church or to be brought there by the assistance of others to ask for the sacrament of extreme unction. Examples of this kind can be found even in the western church as can be seen in Martene, *de antiquis Ecclesiae Ritibus*, bk. 2, chaps. 7, art. 2, no. 7-8, and in Mabillon's preface to the first century in *Acta Sanctorum Ordinis Benedictini*, sec. 9, no. 101.

47. The two following points are to be noticed in connection with the first part of the third admonition. First, even though the Greeks have been clearly forbidden to confer the sacrament of extreme unction on any but the seriously ill, they have not been prohibited from anointing sick or possessed people with the oil of the lamp, which is kept in the church, as well as others who ask for it either out of devotion or for deliverance from some affliction. For the oil which is kept in the lamp was not consecrated by the bishop or priest for use in administering extreme unction. We are well aware that the request has previously been made for permission for the Greeks to be anointed with the oil of extreme unction in cases other than serious illness without the sacramental form being spoken by the priest. They of course reasoned that the sacrament is conferred not by the mere application of the matter, but necessarily requires that the form be pronounced at the same time. But this request was not acceptable since We can never permit a sacrament established by Christ to be converted into any whimsical ceremony even if it is a pious one. This is rightly observed by Fr. de Carboneano in his *Appendix ad Tractatum P. Antoine de Extrema Unctione*, sect. 4, p. 661. Despite the affirmation of Quintaduenas that parish clergy may send the holy oil of the sick upon request to the ill and others in order that they may anoint themselves in their sickness (Treatise 5, *de Extreme Unctione*, sing. 11), anyone who attempts to do this is punished with heavy penalties by the ecclesiastical tribunal, either for misuse of a sacrament of the church or being under suspicion of unorthodox belief concerning the sacrament, as Clericatus aptly remarks (*de Sacramento Extremae Unctionis*, sect. 70, no. 32).

48. Furthermore, since it is forbidden to administer the sacrament of extreme unction except in a case of serious illness, a penitent may no means be obliged to receive anointing with oil of extreme unction as penance or satisfaction for his sins. As Pope Eugene IV established in his *Decretum pro Instructione Armenorum*, satisfaction for sins or penance imposed by confessors on their penitents should consist chiefly in prayers, fasting, and almsgiving. In times past such anointing was introduced among eastern Christians. That it was purely ceremonial may be gathered from canon 74 or the Council of Nicaea (from the Arabic translation, Harduin, *Collect.* vol. 1, p. 492). There it is decreed that if one of the faithful shall live impurely with an unbeliever, he may be reconciled to the Church after extended penance "through holy water and the oil of the sick." This was the source of a further abuse. According to Joannes Nathanael, *de Moribus Graecorum*, and François Richard, *de Expeditione Sacra*, rich penitents were often obliged to receive this anointing as penance for their sins; thus this practice was quite profitable for the clergy.

Pope Innocent IV opposed this serious error

in his letter to the Bishop of Tusculum: "Confessors may not impose on anyone any mere anointing in satisfaction for their sins" (sect. 6). The synod of Nicosia passed a similar decree (Harduin, *Collect*. vol. 7, p. 1714) and We renewed this precept in Our constitution, *Etsi Pastoralis*, sect. 5 (*Bullarium*, vol. 1, no. 57). Thiers, *de Superstit*., bk. 8, chap. 6, should also be consulted. Arcudius, moreover, refers to Greek priests who impose this on their penitents; he states that they usually employ the sacramental words in performing the anointing. He criticizes them severely for this (*de Concordia*, bk. 5, chap. 4, sect. *Ego praesentem*). However, Goarius asserts that the Greeks did not intend to confer the sacrament in performing this anointing: "They do not consider that the infirmities of the soul are removed automatically by the anointing and prayers, but only that the devotion of the penitent or the prayerful charity of the minister, that is, the intention of the agent, may possibly have this effect" (*in notis ad Euchologium*, p. 350). Still, even he criticizes this custom since, as he says, the Greeks should be careful to act in this affair in accordance with the teaching of the holy Roman Church. Many serious errors stem from this practice of anointing: either the sacrament of extreme unction is conferred on one in good health and so incapable of receiving this sacrament, or the matter and form of the sacrament is used without the intention of conferring the sacrament itself.

49. The second part of the third admonition concerns the holy chrism. The Greeks make this not only from oil and balm, but with additional spices. This section indicates that the addition of spices is not forbidden, but that the chrism must consist of oil and balm. So even if some of those spices are absent, sacred chrism may still be prepared.

50. The imposition of hands while conferring this sacrament is not prescribed for the Greeks. In his treatise *de Confirmatione*, chap. 4, Morinus writes: "The Latins have always joined the imposition of hands to anointing, but the Greeks have always kept these rites separate and have used only anointing in conferring this sacrament. Neither old nor new euchologies mention the imposition of hands." The same point is made by Goarius, *in Euchologio*, p. 299, no. 28. Renaudot in his *Opus de Perpetuitate*, vol. 5, bk. 2, chap. 12, affirms that for many centuries in the Greek church no evidence is to be found of an imposition of hands in conferring the sacrament of Confirmation. As authorities for this statement he cites the modern Greek theologians, Simeon of Thessalonica, Gabriel of Philadelphia, Sirinus, and others. Recently Chardon, *in Historia Sacramentorum*, bk. 1, chap. 1, *De Confirmatione*, argues that in earlier centuries the Greek church did include the imposition of hands in the rite of Confirmation, but he does grant that for many centuries since then, there is no evidence for this. Finally Guiseppe Agostino Orsi O. P., at present the master of Our apostolic palace, proves by marshalling much learned evidence in his historical theological dissertation, *de Chrismate Confirmatorio*, that among the Greeks the matter of the sacrament of Confirmation is the holy oil, not the imposition of hands. This gives no grounds for asserting, as some have rashly done, that the sacrament of Confirmation does not exist in the Greek church because it does not include the imposition of hands. For no one can believe that the sacrament of Confirmation did not exist for many centuries in so large a portion of the Christian world especially in a church renowned for its learning and its sanctity. Goarius (*loc. cit.*) gives an apt expression to Our opinion: "Few men in my judgment will attempt to assert that so large a portion of the Christian world, which is learned and loyal to apostolic and ecclesiastical rules, either rejected, neglected or remained in ignorance of this perfect sacrament."

51. The main issue of this unfair and untimely disagreement between the Latin and Greek churches derives from the controversies in which our theologians habitually engage. Some dispute whether the Apostles conferred the sacrament of Confirmation by laying on of hands or by using holy oil, and as usual some assert what others deny. They also dispute whether the imposition of hands alone is the matter of this sacrament. Some hold that this is the case, while others consider the holy oil to be the remote matter of the sacrament; in this case the application of this oil in the sign of the Cross to the forehead of the confirmand is considered the proximate matter. These last argue from the text of the decree for the Instruction of the Armenians published by Pope Eugenius IV: "The second sacrament is Confirmation whose matter is chrism. Chrism is made from oil and balm which has been blessed by the bishop. The oil signifies a good conscience and the balm, good reputation." In speaking of the imposition of hands which the Apostles used in conferring this sacrament, Pope Eugenius adds: "In place of that imposition of hands, however, Confirmation is given in the Church." Finally, others join together the imposition of hands and the chrism, stating that both are equally the matter of the sacrament of Confirmation, but that either is insufficient by itself. Only when these two are joined together do they comprise the full matter of the sacrament.

As regards the imposition of hands, some think it consists in the stretching out of the hands of the bishop towards the confirmands at the start of the ceremony while he is saying the opening prayers. Others understand it to consist in the very act of anointing of the forehead of the confirmand by the bishop, since it is impossible to anoint the forehead without laying a hand on it. These are controversies which engage our theologians, and everyone may embrace the interpretation he finds most persuasive. But it is wrong for anyone to assert that the sacrament of Confirmation does not exist in the Greek Church. For this opinion is contradicted by ancient eastern practice as found in the Greek Rituals which make no reference to the imposition of hands as matter either sufficient or insufficient of the sacrament of Confirmation. And this practice has never been condemned or criticized by the Apostolic See although it was well-known. So to esscape the labyrinth of this difficulty, a different line must be followed, a line which is open to the careful seeker. This line avoids a condemnation of a view which has many supporters among the orthodox, on the basis of an uncertain and undefined proposition.

52. What is beyond dispute should be stated: that in the Latin church, the sacrament of confirmation is conferred by the priest pronouncing the words of the sacramental form while he makes the sign of the Cross on the forehead of the candidate with holy chrism, that is olive oil mixed with balm and blessed by the bishop. In those areas where genuine balm is not be to found, the popes have readily allowed the use of a sweet-smelling juice or liquid, generally taken for real balm, in preparing chrism. This is clear from constitution 180 of St. Pius V which grants this privilege to the bishops of the Indies, and from constitution 97 of Sixtus V (*in Bullario nova*, vol. 4, pt. 3, Roman edition). Pope Sixtus explains that real balm is scarce chiefly because the Turks completely destroyed its main source, the trees which once flourished in Palestine and particularly in the Jericho valley. He accordingly gives permission to the Archbishops and Bishops of Portugal to use balm from Brazil and other areas of the New World in preparing holy chrism. In so doing the Pope asserts that he is following the example of his predecessors Pius IV and Gregory XIII. The prudence of these popes has been praised by Morinus in his posthumous work *de Sacramento Confirmationis*, p. 35.

Ex quo primum
12

Likewise in the Greek church the sacrament of confirmation is conferred by means of holy oil. This is made from olive oil and balm, but in addition twenty-three kinds of other herbs are used as well as a little wine. These herbs are carefully listed by Habert, *in librum Pontificalem Ecclesiae Graecae*, observation 5, on the rite of chrism; and by Berti, *Theologia*, vol. 7, bk. 32, chap. 5. The latter, however, thinks it practically impossible for the Greeks to add all the herbs mentioned by Habert since some of them are so unknown that they receive scant mention in dictionaries and specialized writings on plants and herbs. Whatever the truth of this question, the rite has been left unchanged in the admonition under discussion, since the practice of adding these herbs is an ancient one. The Greeks are merely advised that they should not consider these herbs essential for the matter of the sacrament; they should recognize the sacrament as valid when it is performed only with oil and balm blessed by the bishop, even though some of the herbs which they usually add in accordance with their rite are lacking. Wisely and with good cause did the fathers at the Synod of Zamoscia in 1720 affirm that whatever herbs were added to the balm, care should be taken "that the largest part of the chrism should always be oil mixed with balm" (sect. 2, *de Confirmatione*).

53. Now that the second part of the third admonition has been completed, We shall add here in the form of an appendix some comments well-suited to Our present purpose, since they are related both to the doctrine of the sacrament of confirmation and to the revision of the Euchologion.

54. The form of the sacrament of confirmation in the Greek church, according to the generally received opinion, consists in the words: "the sign of the gift of the Holy Spirit" uttered by the minister while making the sign of the Cross

with the holy oil on the forehead of the candidate. This is clear from canon 7 of the First Council of Constantinople (Harduin, *Collect.* vol. I, p. 811) as Cardinal Bessarion correctly understands the words of that canon (*in Opuscolo de Eucharistia*, printed in the Library of the Fathers, vol. 26, p. 765, Lyons edition): "The Second Ecumenical Council gives the words of consecration for holy chrism in the seventh canon as follows: 'While signing them, that is while anointing them with the most holy chrism, we say: the sign of the gift of the Holy Spirit.' According to them these words confer the sacrament of confirmation." But although this statement of the Cardinal has been contested by Lupus, *in notis ad Canonem 95. Concilii Trullani*, he is not likely to win much support for his opinion since his antagonist is Cardinal Bessarion. Arcudius draws attention to this point when he cites Bessarion's statement and continues: "Bessarion speaks thus and certainly no one could excel him in knowledge of the practices of the eastern church in administering the sacraments" (bk. 2, chap. 7). Goarius shares this opinion (*in notis ad Euchologium*, p. 302, no. 31). So too does Habert (*in suis notis ad Pontificale Graecorum*, observ. 4, n. 2). It would be easy to assemble many other testimonies, but it will suffice to state what the Synod of Zamoscia said when treating the sacrament of confirmation: "The form of the sacrament which is recommended by the approved Euchologia which are more ancient than the schism itself, is this: 'The sign of the gift of the Holy Spirit, amen' and this should be said once only while the anointing is conferred."

55. The decree of St. Methodius, Patriarch of Constantinople, is well-known in the Greek church. Methodius was Patriarch about the middle of the ninth century and tirelessly strove to call the wanderers back home to holy unity. His decree lays down the method of restoring to the Church those who have left it and subsequently returned: "At the end of the prayer he takes the holy oil in accordance with the custom of the baptized, and anoints him, making the sign of the Cross on his forehead, eyes, nostrils, mouth, both ears, hands, breast, and shoulders while he says: 'the sign of the gift of the Holy Spirit.'"

This passage certainly gives rise to a great difficulty, for apparently it must be admitted either that the words "the sign of the gift of the Holy Spirit" are not the form of the sacrament of confirmation in the Greek church or that this sacrament is conferred a second time on those who have already received it validly once, if after the sin of apostasy they desire to return to the Church. The latter view is of course contrary to the established opinion that sacraments, which impress a character on the soul, can never be conferred again on those who have received them validly once. This was defined by the Council of Trent, session 7, on the sacraments in general, canon 9. There is no use in appealing to canon 7 of the Council of Constantinople, which was mentioned above. This canon lays down that Arians, Macedonians, Novatians, and Apollinarians who turn from their heresy and come to the Church are to be received with holy chrism. This ruling refers only to these heretics, since they confer the sacrament of confirmation invalidly, if at all; the decree of St. Methodius though is general and applies to all who wish to return after leaving the Church. Moreover, since provisions similar to those of the decree of Methodius are made in some euchologies in the section on the reconciliation of penitents, the same difficulty arises in these cases.

56. The subtlety of scholars has been fully deployed to solve this problem. Some assert that the decree in question was not issued by St. Methodius, Patriarch of Constantinople in 842, but by a different Methodius, the schismatic Patriarch of Constantinople, in 1240. But Goarius states that he saw several documents anterior to the latter Methodius which assign the decree to St. Methodius the Patriarch (*in notis ad ipsum Decretum* in his elucidation of the Euchologion, p. 698). That is enough to deprive this solution of its weight.

Others grant that the words "the sign of the gift of the Holy Spirit" are the form of the sacrament of confirmation, and recognize that the same words are to be said during the anointing of repentant apostates who are being received back into the Church in accordance with the decree of St. Methodius. They think, however, that this does not give grounds for saying that the sacrament of confirmation has been conferred on men who have already received it, since the intention of the minister is necessary for the conferring of the sacraments. In this case it is quite clear that the intention of the minister is not to confer the sacrament but to reconcile a returned apostate to the Church. This solution is embraced by the following writers: Du Hamel, *Theologiae*, vol. 6, p. 383, Paris 1605; Goarius, *in notis ad Euchologi.*, p. 598; Tournely, *in Tractatu de Confirmatione*, p. 612f; and Assemanus the Younger, Codex Liturgicus, bk. 3, *De Confirmatione*, p. 63.

However, many others are dissatisfied with this solution. Juveninus, in particular, raises two objections. In the first place he notices that there is no Greek evidence to suggest that it is not the minister's intention to confer the sacrament of confirmation when he reconciles an apostate by anointing him with holy oil and using words which contain the form of the sacrament. He suggests secondly that if a minister applies the matter and form of a sacrament to one who is not capable of receiving it, his act is wrong and sinful, even if his intention is not to confer the sacrament.

Finally, others point out that evidence from the early centuries establishes that apostates in the Western church were sometimes reconciled by an imposition of hands. They admit that it is now forbidden to confer the sacrament of confirmation a second time on those who have already validly received it, but they claim that it was not so in the early days of the Church. Hence, they conclude that it should not seem so strange that the decree of St. Methodius, which relates to the Eastern church, requires returned apostates to be confirmed a second time despite their first valid confirmation.

But this argument is fragile. For some of the early evidence states plainly that apostates were received back by the imposition of hands *alone*. If this is to be understood as the conferring of confirmation, it will have to be shown that this sacrament was then conferred by the imposition of hands alone without any anointing. If it is said, and there is some evidence to this effect, that holy oil as well as the imposition of hands was used in reconciling this type of penitent, it will still have to be shown what form of words if any was used by the minister who imposed hands and anointed with chrism in order to establish that the sacrament was repeated. Marcus Rehmensis describes many types of imposition of hands in his treatise on *in Tractatu de variis Capitibus Ecclesiae*, chap. 18. The author of the Gloss on the *Can. Manus impositio*, 1, quest. 1, also gives a careful account of this matter. Sirmondus and Morinus, both illustrious, consider that the imposition of hands, which is now in question, imparted Confirmation (Sirm., *in suo Antirbetico secundo*, chap. 5; *Mor. de Sacram. Confir.*, chap. 12, p. 56 and *in Tract. de Poenitentia*, bk. 9, chap. 9-10). But Peter Aurelius argues that the imposition of hands given when receiving heretics back was purely ceremonial and did not confer the sacrament. This opinion is shared by Lupus *in Can. 7. Constanti nopolitanum*, vol. 2, p. 46f; Arcudius, bk. 2, chap. 18; Suarez, *in 3. part. Divi Thomae*, vol. 3, quest. 72, disp. 34, sect. 1, resp. 3, and disp. 36, art. 11, sect. 3. Accordingly Witasse, after reviewing all the evidence for both views, finally judges both possible and leaves the matter there (*Tract. de Sacram. Confirmat.*, esp. p. 63). The author of the additions to Estius *in bk. 4. Sentent.*, dist. 5, sect. 16, lit. B, p. 87, behaves with similar caution.

Ex quo primum 12

57. So a different way must be found to solve the difficulty under discussion. First of all, as regards the decree of St. Methodius, the text We gave above is quite different from that found in the much-used *Annals* of Cardinal Baronius for 842 A.D. The text given by Baronius does not prescribe the use of the words "the sign of the gift of the Holy Spirit" in receiving back an apostate, although it requires that he be anointed with holy oil. The text reads: "Let them be anointed with chrism as those who are baptized are usually anointed." Even admitting that these words are authentic rather than a later addition as there is some reason to believe, their obvious sense will always be that when an apostate is received back, the same parts of the body should be anointed as are anointed when Confirmation is administered after Baptism. And since no mention is made of saying the words: "The sign of the gift of the Holy Spirit," the whole force of the problem is dispersed.

There is the additional consideration that the legates sent by Pope Nicholas I to Bulgaria conferred the sacrament of confirmation on those who had already received it from Greek priests. Their main reason for so doing was that the Greek ministers had not received the faculty for administering this sacrament from the Apostolic See. Photius launched a bitter attack against them in his encyclical letters, accusing them of conferring the sacrament of chrism on people who had been confirmed already. "Who ever heard of such madness as was unwaveringly engaged in by those fools? They have confirmed a second time people already anointed with chrism, making trivial mockery of exalted mysteries." This proves clearly that St. Methodius did not intend to prescribe that penitent apostates on returning to the church should be given the sacrament of chrism a second time if they had already been confirmed. For Photius, who was Patriarch about forty years after St. Methodius, despite his perverse mind, enjoyed a constant reputation for learning and circumspection. He would never have accused the apostolic legates so bitterly for repeating the sacrament of chrism if St. Methodius had previously decreed or intended that apostates should receive the same sacrament a second time upon returning to the Church. For he would have foreseen that the legates would answer that they had only followed the custom of the eastern church in receiving the wanderers back to unity in accordance with the decree of St. Methodius.

58. The occurrence in some of the euchologies of the words, "the sign of the gift of the Holy Spirit," in conjunction with anointing when reconciling the repentant is to be attributed to the interpolation of schismatics. Theodore Balsamon convinced them that any Latin who seceded to the Greeks should be confirmed again. This is stated by Gregory Protosyncellus in his *Apologia* against Marcus of Ephesus (Harduin, *Collect.*, vol. 9, p. 640). But the use of the words in question is not prescribed in the many manuscript copies of the Euchologion examined and compared by Joannes Matthaeus Cariophylus Cydonius, a trustworthy witness, according to Arcudius, *de Reformat.*, bk. 2, chap. 18. Neither are they found in the famous Euchologion of Grottaferrata, a point of great importance. Therefore the Congregations for the Correction of the Euchologion which met in the time of Urban VII and in Our day decreed with Our approval that the rite of reconciling penitents should be printed in the revised Euchologion exactly as it is described in the Euchologion of Grottaferrata; this has been done. At the meeting of the Congregation on January 7, 1748, the question was raised as to whether the rite of receiving back apostates on their return to the Church should be made to conform to the decree of St. Methodius. It was pointed out that this anointing was to be performed in the way that those who are baptized are anointed, but that the requirement of saying at the same time the words, "the sign of the gift of the Holy Spirit," was to be found only in a few modern euchologies. Therefore the Congregation of February 18, decreed that "the euchology should be revised to conform to the patriarchal euchology of Cardinal Bassarion, now of Grottaferrata." On receiving this report, We examined the matter and gave Our approval to the decree.

Fourth Admonition — Removing Impurities

59. Next We must deal with the fourth admonition, which concerns the removal of certain impurities by blessings and prayers which are included in the Euchologion. The words of the admonition are: "Finally, it should be known that if anything unclean or defiled chances to fall in a well or other receptacle of liquid, or if an unclean thing is touched or eaten, or if an impure animal is born or dies in a church, the priests of the eastern church in accordance with the custom of their Church use the prayers and blessings contained in the Euchologion. However they are not attempting to observe the precepts of the old Law which as everybody knows have been revoked by the coming of Christ."

60. In the revised Euchologion, just as in the Euchologion of Grottaferrata, once Cardinal Bessarion's, and in the most ancient manuscripts, there is a prayer which mentions the distinction made in the old Law between clean and unclean foods as well as the uncleanness in the eyes of the Law of anyone who ate unclean food. The prayer goes on to say that the one who has eaten unclean foods cannot receive the precious Body and Blood of Christ without sin. The contents and expressions of this prayer and others like it occasioned a discussion of whether one might well suspect that the observance of the legal ceremonies of the old Law was being added to or retained alongside the new law and the Gospel. To understand whether there are any grounds for this suspicion, We will touch briefly on the following considerations. They will throw light on all aspects of the question and the reason for each detail will be plain.

61. The first consideration is that the ceremonies of the Mosaic Law were abrogated by the coming of Christ and that they can no longer be observed without sin after the promulgation of the Gospel. Since, then, the distinction made by the old Law between clean and unclean foods belongs to the ceremonial precepts, it may justly be affirmed that such a distinction no longer

exists and ought not be insisted on. It is true that the holy Apostles forbade the faithful to eat blood or the flesh of animals which had been strangled. This view was expressed by James at the Council of Jerusalem: "Therefore I judge that those of the Gentiles who turn to God should not be disturbed, but that we should write to them to abstain from what has been sacrificed to idols, from unchastity, from the meat of strangled animals, and from blood" (Acts 15). But it is clear that this was ordained to remove all occasion of disagreement between Jewish and Gentile converts to Christ. Since this reason has long since vanished, its consequence should also be said to have vanished. "Similarly, we profess that the legalities of the Old Testament, the ceremonies of the Mosaic Law, the rites, sacrifices, and sacraments have ceased at the coming of Our Lord Jesus Christ; they cannot be observed without sin after the promulgation of the Gospel. The distinction of clean and unclean foods found in the old Law pertains to the ceremonies which have passed away with the rise of the Gospel. The Apostles' prohibition on food offered to idols, blood, and the meat of strangled animals was suitable at that time to remove cause for disagreement between Jews and Gentiles; but since the reason for this prohibition has ceased to be, the prohibition too has come to an end."

62. The preceding words are from the Profession of Orthodox Faith which Pope Urban VIII required of Orientals, as published in 1642 by the Congregation for the Propagation of the Faith. They are in harmony with the teaching of St. Thomas (*Summa* 1, 2, quest. 103, art. 4, to 3rd). Moreover this teaching is confirmed by ancient documents. St. Gregory II in his capitular letter (chap. 7) appointing Bishop Marinianus and the priest George as legates to Bavaria, writes: "No food should be considered unclean to eat, except what was sacrificed to idols since, as we learn from the apostolic teaching, every creation of God is good and whatever is taken with thanks is not to be rejected." Likewise St. Nicholas I in his answer to the 43rd decree of the Bulgarians regarding clean and unclean animals, said: "God showed clearly, in my opinion, what animals or birds may be eaten when, after the flood, he gave all animals to Noah and his sons to eat. . . . Therefore, every animal may be eaten whose flesh is definitely not harmful to the body and is regarded as food by human society." So the Decree for the Jacobites of the Council of Florence reads: "The holy Roman Church firmly believes, professes, and preaches that every creature of God is good and not to be rejected if it is taken with thanks. According to the Lord's word, a man is not defiled by what enters his mouth. The Church affirms that the distinction made by the Mosaic Law between clean and unclean foods belongs to the ceremonial laws which have passed away with the coming of the Gospel. . . . So it declares that no kind of food is to be condemned which human society regards as food, and no distinction is to be made between animals on the basis of gender or the manner of their death. However many things which are not forbidden may and should be given up for the health of the body, the practice of virtue, and regular Church discipline. As the Apostle says: 'All things are permitted, but not all are expedient.'"

Ex quo primum 12

63. The second consideration is that although the ceremonial precepts of the old Law have come to an end with the promulgation of the Gospel, and the new Law does not contain any precept which distinguishes between clean and unclean foods, nevertheless the Church of Christ has the power of renewing the obligation to observe some of the old precepts for just and serious reasons, despite their abrogation by the new Law. However, precepts whose main function was to foreshadow the coming Messiah should not be restored, for example, circumcision and the sacrifice of animals, as Vasquez aptly remarks *in 1, 2, Divi Thomae*, vol. 2, disp. 182, chap. 9, sect. *ex quibus omnibus*. Precepts regarding external discipline and cleanliness of body, the kind which contain the precepts on clean and unclean foods, may be restored. The Western as well as the Eastern Church assumed this practice; this is documented from the earliest centuries.

64. The Gentiles invented the calumny about the early Christians eating the flesh of infants and drinking human blood. Such calumny was occasioned by the prevailing practice of religious secrecy. The faithful kept secret the Real Presence of Christ's Body in the Eucharistic meal which they ate, but the Gentiles got some vague rumor of this Mystery and used this as a basis for inventing and spreading this falsehood against the Christians. This is shown by Schelestratus in his *Dissertat. de Disciplina Arcani*, artic. unic., chap. 4, sect. 17.

Equally renowned is the answer the ancient Apologists gave to the Gentiles on behalf of the Christians without disclosing the secret. They asserted that it was quite impossible that the disciples of Christ should eat human flesh and drink human blood since, as was well known, they even abstained from the blood of animals and from the flesh of strangled animals. Tertullian uses this proof in his *Apologetici*, chap. 9. This answer, however, proves clearly that in the first centuries Christians distinguished between foods for some reason and abstained from blood and the meat of strangled animals. This is wisely noted by both Nicholas le Nourry, vol. 2, *Apparatus in Biblioth. Patr.*, diss. 4 on Tertullian, chap. 12, art. 2, and by Pamelius, *in dictum cap. 9 Tertulliani*, no. 138.

Those Christians did not think that the Mosaic Law was still binding in this matter. They knew that the apostolic prohibition regarding abstinence from blood and the meat of strangled animals had been removed. They did not consider these foods prohibited in any way, yet they abstained from them on the grounds that it was fitting to observe the custom handed down by the fathers. Natalis Alexander writes that "the custom of abstaining from blood and the meat of strangled animals was so religiously observed in those churches because they had received this custom from their fathers, not because they considered that these foods were absolutely prohibited" (*Hist. Ecclesiast. Saecul.* 1, diss. 10).

65. In his *Comment.* on the words "from strangled animals and blood" (Acts 15), Calmet states that some Latin churches distinguished between clean and unclean foods and abstained from blood and strangled meat as late as the tenth and eleventh century. He does not at this point offer any proof for his statement but its truth is quite evident to anyone who has the slightest acquaintance with Christian writing. For Canisius published an old Roman penitential from the end of the eighth or the start of the ninth century; under the heading "On strangled meat," it prescribes a penance for eating the meat of a strangled animal, and under the heading "On mangled flesh," it prescribes penances and fasts for eating fish which died in the pool or for drinking water from a well in which a mouse or a hen died before thoroughly cleansing the well.

Humbertus, Cardinal of Silva Candida, as Legate of Pope St. Leo IX at Constantinople, argued violently with the Greeks, but he openly admitted during the disputations that on this subject Latins and Greeks did not disagree since this practice was still observed in some Latin and Greek churches. "Maintaining the ancient custom or tradition of our fathers, we too hold these things in abomination; apart from the great danger to life, a heavy penance is imposed on those among us who eat blood or corpses or polluted waters or animals which died by accident." And elsewhere he says, "So even though the Lord and the Apostles give us permission to eat everything which does not harm our own health nor that of our brother, the custom of some areas and the precepts of our fathers make us abstain from some foods. We do this not because they are bad or unclean, but either because at times they are not expedient, or they revolt us now that long-lasting habit has become nature for us."

66. There is no trace of this abstinence left in the Latin churches, if we may believe Cornelius à Lapide (*in Commentar. in Actus Apost.*, chap. 15, "and from blood"). But it is still strong in the Greek church which considers it praiseworthy to maintain the apostolic precept on abstinence from blood and strangled meat. So say Calmet and à Lapide. Christianus Lupus says further that "the Greeks too have for a long time afterwards observed unchanged this apostolic law" (Notes on Canon 67 of the Trullan Synod). This Trullan Canon 67 says, "The divine scripture has commanded us to abstain from blood, strangled meat, and fornication. We fittingly punish those who for the pleasure of the belly skillfully season, serve, and eat the blood of an animal. So if anyone henceforth eats the blood of an animal in any way, he should be deposed if a cleric and separated if a layman."

The Armenians alone, to Our knowledge, have publicly abandoned this custom of the Greeks upon entering into union with the Roman Church. For the schismatic Vartanes had persuaded them to abstain from certain foods which the Mosaic Law called unclean with the sole exception of pork; this he claimed had been allowed by St. Gregory the Illuminator, their first patriarch. He also instructed them to destroy vessels of oil and wine if a fly or suchlike drowned therein. Nevertheless the conferences which effected the union of the Armenians with the Roman Church decreed that "the Armenian fathers at both the synods of Sis and Adana in uniting their church with the Church of Rome have approved the Dogmatic Letter of Gregory, Patriarch of Armenia, to King Haytones, which rejects the Jewish distinction of foods by the words, "We command that all impure foods be considered purified, as St. Paul says, especially in the case of the poor. The lord Nierses, that is, Ghelajensis, also a Doctor and Patriarch of Armenia, taught that such foods should be blessed with prayers" (Galanus, vol. 2 *De conciliatione Ecclesiae Armenae cum Romana*).

67. The third and final point suggested by the text of the fourth admonition is that Greek priests are not forbidden to use any of the prayers or blessings which are in their Euchologion by reason of references to matters which were subject to the ceremonial precepts of the Old Law. They should, however, do everything with the intention not of obeying the precepts of the old Law, which has now been abrogated, but of respecting the new Law of the Church or canonical custom made strong by long and unbroken observance.

In dealing with the Greek custom of abstaining from blood and strangled flesh, Lorinus notes that "if the Greeks today abstain from blood on the grounds that they are bound by this law, they are superstitious. This law now binds nobody and its observance savors of the ceremonies of the old Law. But they should not be blamed if they reject this food from a natural revulsion or other good reason" (*in cit. Actuum Apos.* 15.20). Goarius, in writing *in variantibus lectionibus* in the Greek Euchologion, considers the prayer "for those who have eaten forbidden and unclean things." He notes that "the Orientals avoid partaking of unclean foods through zeal for the Church, rather than for the Mosaic Law, etc. Consequently, despite the babbling calumny of Catumsyritus, they are far from observing Jewish ritual since they are observing the traditions of the Church." Catumsyritus would have some basis for his daring statement if the Greeks acted as they do not for these reasons, but from wrongly thinking that they are bound by the Apostolic precept on abstinence from blood and strangled meat. William Beveregius unfortunately attempts to defend this opinion in his *Codex Canonum Ecclesiae primitivae*, vol. 2, chap. 7, no. 5.

Certain schismatics have tried to calumniate the Latin church by saying that it judaizes by consecrating unleavened bread, observing the Sabbath, and retaining the anointing of kings among the sacred rites. But Leo Allatius counters their rash claim in his splendid work *de perpetua consensione Ecclesiae Occidentalis et Orientalis*, bk. 3, chap. 4. He refutes them particularly by arguing as follows: "Since Jews observe Sabbaths, a man who observes Sabbaths acts in Jewish fashion: therefore the man who does not eat the flesh of strangled animals acts in Jewish fashion since the Jews are forbidden by the Law to eat such food: but the Greeks do not eat such food: therefore, the Greek judaize" (*loc. cit.* n. 4). Then to Our purpose he concludes (n. 9) that it cannot be absolutely asserted that that man judaizes who does something in the Church which corresponds to the ceremonies of the old Law. "If a man should perform acts for a different end and purpose (even with the intention of worship and as religious ceremonies), not in the spirit of that Law nor on the basis of it, but either from personal decision, from human custom, or on the instruction of the Church, he would not sin, nor could he be said to judaize. So when a man does something in the Church which resembles the ceremonies of the old Law, he must not always be said to judaize."

68. Since We have added an appendix to Our treatment of each of the first three admonitions, before ending Our encyclical We now want to add to this fourth admonition an appendix relevant both to the subject of the admonition and to the publication of the revised Euchologion.

69. In the Book of Leviticus, chap. 12, it is decreed that a woman who has borne a boy is unclean for seven days and remains for a further thirty-three days in "the blood of her purification." If she has been delivered of a girl, she is unclean for two weeks and remains for sixty-six days "in the blood of her purification." She may not enter the sanctuary before this time has elapsed. When she first enters the temple, she is to bring a prescribed offering.

70. It cannot be denied that this prohibition continued for some time in the Church. In the Penitential Canons of Theodorus, quoted by Ivo in his decree and mentioned by Cardinal Baronius under 266 A.D., it is said that "a woman who enters the church before her blood is clean after birth must do penance for thirty-three days if she brought forth a boy and for fifty-six days if she bore a girl. If any woman rashly enters the church before the prescribed time, she must do penance on bread and water for as many days

as she should have stayed away from the church."

But it also cannot be denied that this prohibition was removed in the Latin Church in the course of time. "If at the same hour as she has brought forth, a woman enters the church to give thanks, she does not commit any sin," said Pope Gregory, and his words are quoted in the Decree of Gratian, can. 2, dist. 5. In his decretal *Volens, De purificatione post partum*, Innocent III cites the text, "The law was given through Moses: grace and truth came through Jesus Christ." He adds that a woman who wishes not to enter the church for a time after childbirth is not forbidden to do so, but that a woman who comes to church does not sin. "So they commit no sin and are not to be forbidden to enter the churches. To forbid them would obviously imply that their punishment was a sin. Still if they want to stay away for some time out of a feeling of reverence, We do not believe that their devotion should be condemned."

The Blessed Virgin Mary willingly subjected herself to the law of Leviticus, although this law did not apply to her, when she presented herself and her divine Son in the Temple at the proper time after childbirth. In memory of this remarkable event, the rite which is found in the Roman Ritual published by order of Pope Paul V was established. After childbirth a woman goes to the church and is met at the door by a priest. He prays over her and sprinkles her with holy water. Then holding the hem of the priest's stole, she goes up to the altar, genuflects before it, and offers thanks to God for the benefits she has received. In the Latin church, however, this blessing of the woman after childbirth is not obligatory and there is no sin involved if it is omitted, although to omit it from contempt would be a sin as Quartus warns in his work *de Benedictionibus*, tit. 3, sect. 12, diff. 1).

71. In the Greek Church, however, the law regarding childbirth is observed religiously as if a commandment, and a woman who has given birth is not allowed to come to the church before the appointed time. Indeed in earlier centuries the practice of the Greeks was so strict that women during menstruation were prevented from sharing the Eucharist, even when critically ill. For this practice they were severely criticized by Cardinal Humbertus of Silva Candida (Baronius, 1054 A.D.). This strictness was later modified to the extent that women during menstruation who were in danger of death were allowed to receive the Eucharist. This is seen both from the Canonical Letter of Dionysius of Alexandria and from Novella 13 of Emperor Leo the Wise. The remark of Cardinal Baronius (266 A.D., no. 11) should be recalled here. He notes that Dionysius in this letter merely expressed his own opinion and submitted it to the judgment of Basilides and others. "I have written this not as a teacher, but to make my opinion public with all appropriate simplicity. After repeated examination, write and tell me the conclusion you have come to and whether this is the best view of the matter." On the other hand the reasoning of St. Gregory the Great is clearly true: "The excess of nature cannot be counted as a sin, and it is not just to prevent a woman from entering the church because of what she endures against her will" (cited by Gratian, can. 4, dist. 5).

As regards partaking of the Eucharist, the holy Doctor openly declares that he does not condemn a woman for communicating even at this time, although he does not disapprove if she abstains from doing so from reverence. "She should be praised if she does not presume to receive the sacrament from a feeling of great reverence, but if she does receive she is not to be condemned. For it is characteristic of good people to see sins in some measure in actions of their own which involve no sin."

Therefore Theophilus Raynaudus criticizes the practice of the Greeks in this matter (*Operum*, vol. 16, *Heteroclita Spiritualia*, p. 33, no. 28, Lyons). And even Goarius, who is otherwise so constant a promoter and defender of Greek rites, frankly admits that the law which forbids communion to women during menstruation is too severe and contrary to all order. "Still women who are defiled should be treated more mildly, despite all the arguments and subterfuges of the Greeks, etc. The weakness is one of nature which relieves itself automatically" (*in notis ad Euchologium*, p. 270). He then invokes the authority of St. Gregory by quoting the passage from his letter which is given above.

72. Whatever be the case with women during menstruation entering the church and being allowed to receive the Lord's body, We turn back now to women after childbirth. As has been said, in the Latin Church observance of a period following birth is simply advised but not prescribed, while the Greek Church obliges women not to enter the church for a specified number of days. As Goarius says (p. 269): "The Greeks demand this behavior as a duty, the Latins only as a demonstration of reverence." But the Euchologion contains prayers to be said by the priest on this occasion as part of the whole ritual of the ceremony surrounding childbirth.

73. Accordingly this matter was carefully examined and discussed in the Congregations which met for the revision of the Euchologion both under Urban VIII and during Our pontificate. No one proposed the entire elimination from the Euchologion of the rites surrounding childbirth, but the suggestion was made that the prescribed period of forty days should be changed, and that different prayers should be substituted for the prayer in the Euchology which seemed to refer excessively to the legal uncleanness which caused the Jews to prevent their wives from doing any business for forty days after birth and from entering the temple. It seemed especially unfitting to beseech God to "cleanse etc. the defilement of her body from all the defilement of sin and wash away the stains of the soul in the course of forty days."

74. But others remarked wisely that some, surely, of the ceremonial rites of the old Law could be observed under the new Law if only they were not done as obligations of the old Law, which was abrogated, but as a custom, or lawful tradition, or as a new precept issued by one enjoying the recognized and competent authority to make laws and to enforce them, as Vasquez observes (vol. 3, in the 3rd part of the *Summa*, disp. 210, quest. 80, art. 7). It was decided that there was no real ground for surprise that the observance of a period after childbirth should be simply a counsel for Latin women, but obligatory law for the Greeks. Moreover, since the Greeks perform the rite in a different way than the Jews of old in not making an offering to the priest in the Jewish way, and since they sanctify the rite with suitable prayers, beseeching God to forgive any sins the woman has committed, and since the patronage of the Virgin Mother of God is invoked for this very purpose, it was decided on January 8, 1747, by those whom We had placed in charge of the revision of the Euchologion, to make no changes in this section. We subsequently approved their decision.

For it is easy to arrive at a correct understanding of the words quoted from the Greek prayer, by saying that God is thereby asked both to cleanse the woman's soul from every sin and to free her body from all uncleanness, natural not legal, insofar as it indicates a spiritual uncleanness. For cleanliness of body also is part of the service and reverence due to the churches and holy things. Therefore in the early centuries the faithful used to enter the churches only after carefully washing themselves, as St. John Chrysostom says, and in private they always washed their hands before touching the volume of the Gospels.

75. We thought We should explain these matters to you in this encyclical letter, venerable brothers and beloved sons, to inform you of the reasons why the Apostolic See has for a long time felt that the laborious task of revising your Euchologion should be undertaken, and to make known to you the care, zeal and cautious reasoning with which the work was undertaken and brought to completion. No changes were made in the oldest and most authoritative euchologies; only what seemed to have been included in some more recent editions by the credulity or wickedness of some men was eliminated or emended. Everything was kept which could possibly be kept, and some benevolent interpretation was employed to save your Rite from any appearance of attack.

We do not doubt that all of this speaks of Our real love for you and of the love of the Apostolic See. We are also certain that you will understand how great Our zeal and concern is that you persevere firmly in holy union and that the wanderers be recalled one day by God's grace to the same union and the way of salvation. It is up to you to use this revised edition of the Euchologion and to see to it carefully that any new edition of it conforms in every point to this edition, which has been published in 1754 at the press of the Congregation for the Propagation of the Faith. This will ensure that all the errors and nonsense which formerly found their way into and spoiled other editions will be kept out.

Finally We ask you to assist Us by your prayers in Our difficult task of governing the universal Church and We lovingly impart to you Our Apostolic blessing.

Given at Rome in St. Mary Major's on the lst of March 1756 in the sixteenth year of Our Pontificate.

†

LATIN TEXT: *Bened. XIV Bull.*, 3^2: 299-329; *Magnum Bull.*, 19: 192-211.

ENGLISH TRANSLATION: Padraig M. O'Cleirigh.

EX OMNIBUS

ENCYCLICAL OF POPE BENEDICT XIV
ON THE APOSTOLIC CONSTITUTION
UNIGENITUS
OCTOBER 16, 1756

To Our Venerable Brothers, Cardinal of the Holy Roman Church, and Archbishops and Bishops of France.

Greetings and Apostolic Blessing.

From all the regions of the Christian world to which our pastoral care extends, many things have made us concerned for the state of each and every church. But We have been especially troubled by the controversies and dissensions afflicting the flourishing Catholic nation of France some years ago. We did not cease, during the whole time of your disturbance, to ask the God of peace to restore a true and solid tranquillity to your disturbed church. Often too by Apostolic letters We sought the help of Louis, the Christian King of France, for the protection and defense of ecclesiastical peace. We have declared Ourselves ready to sacrifice the remainder of Our life for the peace of the French church, which We embrace with a sincere and constant love. We have also supported proposals for redress that were apt and suitable to cure the malady, if they were likely to succeed and if they seemed to approach the intended end.

Support from France

2. The letters which the French Assembly sent Us on October 31 of last year relieved some of Our concern. Indeed, reading them, We learned of your unanimous constancy in preserving true and salutary doctrine, and in retaining your age-old veneration of the Apostolic See of Blessed Peter, the center of Catholic unity. Nor did we find any dissension among you regarding canonical rules and principles; the only differences concern the choice of means for applying the common principles in practice. Although this is a most undesirable state of affairs, it should not be a cause of wonder for those who know that dissension in serious matters has arisen among other bishops renowned for their learning and holiness. We have been further consoled by the exceptional piety of the king, a piety joined with his hereditary submission to this Apostolic See. This is clear not only from his recent letter dated December 19 of last year (which included the aforementioned letter of the clergy), but also in all his other writings. We have always understood the French king, whose thinking greatly becomes an orthodox Prince endowed with true reverence for God and the Roman See. We firmly approve his desire to restore and preserve peace in his kingdom.

Denial of Viaticum

3. The authority of the apostolic constitution which begins with the word *Unigenitus* is

certainly so great and lays claim everywhere to such sincere veneration and obedience that no one can withdraw the submission due it or oppose it without risking the loss of eternal salvation. Now, a controversy has risen concerning whether viaticum must be denied to those who oppose the constitution. The answer must be given without any hesitation that as long as they are opposed publicly and notoriously, viaticum must be denied them; this follows for the universal law which prohibits a known public sinner to be admitted to Eucharistic communion, whether he asks for it in public or in private.

4. Now public and notorious objectors in the matter under discussion are those who have been so declared by the sentence of a competent judge (because they have contumaciously refused the reverence and obedience due the constitution *Unigenitus*) and who have admitted their guilt in court. There are others, also objectors, who, although they have not been condemned by a judge and have not admitted the crime in court, nevertheless, at the time when they are about to receive the sacred viaticum, voluntarily confess their stubborn resistance to the constitution. Still others are known to have done something manifestly opposed to the veneration and obedience due to this constitution, and to have continued in that state; this is so commonly known that the public scandal arising from it has not yet subsided. In these latter cases, We are as confident of Our judgment as when a sentence has been passed in court.

Two Kinds of Notoriety

5. In this matter, however, a difference must be maintained between the notoriety in which a certain fact is apprehended and guilt consists in the external action itself, such as the notoriety of the usurer or of the person living in concubinage, and another kind of notoriety in which the external fact is noted but the guilt depends very much on the disposition of the mind. It is this latter kind of notoriety which We shall discuss. The former must certainly be established with grave proofs; the latter must be proven with more certain and more serious evidence.

6. The required certainty is not present when the crime is supported by mere conjecture, presumption, and rumor, which generally originate in hostility, prejudice, or partisan interest. When we lend credence to these things, experience shows how many ways men can err and be led into hostility.

7. But some pastors and ministers, renowned for piety and zeal, are influenced by such conjectures and presumptions; they are perplexed when called to administer viaticum to certain men and fear that it may not be possible for them to administer the sacrament without danger to their own conscience. We append a certain rule of action which they may follow.

Rule of Action on Viaticum

8. They ought first to consider whether the person who is asking for viaticum has been to holy communion previously, especially during the Easter season, and has received holy communion from the pastor of the place where he was living; if indeed it was not denied him in life, this will be an argument that the man is free of all blame, or at least that he was not considered a truly public sinner. From this it will follow that it is not possible to deny him when he publicly asks for viaticum at the end of his life, unless perhaps in the meantime he has done something to incur the stigma of a public and notorious sinner with reference to the aforesaid issue.

9. Sometimes, however, no certain conclusions can be reached, but from other sources valid presumptions and grave indications against the sick man are present, so that these zealous pastors cannot rid themselves of the scruple that has arisen. In these circumstances they should, delaying any decisions, address the sick person with all gentleness and mildness, not like one who disputes and is anxious to convince. They should show him the reasons why the conduct of his life is suspect and implore him to come to his senses. Then they should convince him that although they are prepared to administer the Body of Christ, and actually may even administer it, this will not itself make him safe before the tribunal of Christ. If indeed he had not repented, it will make him guilty of a new and horrible crime, eating and drinking judgment on himself. In addition they will administer the sacrament of the Body of Christ to him for no other reason than to obey the Church, which strives to avoid public scandal, and to prevent infamy for the sick person himself. Although she considers him to be a sinner in the sight of God, she does not recognize him as a public and notorious sinner in her tribunal.

10. You must now propose this norm of judging and acting which We approve to all who legitimately administer the sacraments. Indeed, this decision is supported by ecclesiastical regulations, by the decrees of councils held in France, and by the opinions of serious theologians in your own country. Following the example of your predecessors, you sent Us your controversies and the doubts that they occasioned and asked Us for guidance in reestablishing and preserving peace for your churches. Now it is your duty to enforce this rule wherever it pertains. We expect that you will do so, since We feel that We have omitted no diligence or study either in weighing and discussing the articles which the bishops proposed in assembly (though not unanimously); or in taking into account their differences of opinion to better understand the whole matter and to reach a right judgment; or in reading and weighing the written opinions of the Cardinals, whose advice We had requested on this matter; or in carrying out all other things to merit the aid of the divine illumination for which We have prayed

11. Nor do We doubt that your illustrious king, who approved your council and wrote to Us concerning the matter, will in his piety for God and the Church, offer his strong aid to your Fraternity. Accordingly both you and the lower ministers of the Church may be free to regulate the administration of the sacred mysteries according to the norm described above. Because of this confidence, We did not consider it necessary to address your other articles concerning episcopal regulation over participation in the same sacraments and the various controversies that have arisen concerning these matters. Rather We decided to communicate with the king so that he may protect the sacred rights of the episcopate by his own magnanimity and virtue. And We are confident that he will do this according to his own custom and that of his ancestors, so that the nobel churches of France may rejoice to have retained their former glory and may soon regain the tranquillity which was disturbed for a time. As an auspice of this desired event, We lovingly give to your Fraternity and the people entrusted to your care the Apostolic Benediction.

Given in Rome at St. Mary Major, October 16, 1756, in the seventeenth year of Our Pontificate.

†

LATIN TEXT: *Bened. XIV Bull.*, 3^2: 384-86; *Magnum Bull.*, 19: 251-52

ENGLISH TRANSLATION: Bernard A. Hausmann, S.J.

POPE CLEMENT XIII
1758-1769

"You French must always contradict the Holy Spirit" was the comment made by Cardinal Guadagni when Cavalchini was excluded as a papal candidate by the French veto, the last public exclusion of the eighteenth century and the only one ever exercised by the French. The deadlock of the electoral contest was broken when the mild and gentle Cardinal Rezzonico was proposed as a compromise candidate and elected pope on July 6, 1758, taking the name of Clement XIII.[1]

Carlo della Torre Rezzonico, a native of Venice, was born on March 7, 1693. His family originated in Como but had migrated to Genoa and thence to Venice (1646) where the family name was enrolled in the book of nobles. Carlo studied humanities and philosophy with the Jesuits at Bologna and received a doctorate in theology and law at the University of Padua. In 1714, anticipating a career in the diplomatic service, he entered the Accademia dei Nobili Ecclesiastici in Rome. Ordained two years later, he served as a prothonotary, was appointed governor of Rieti and of Fano successively, but was called to Rome in 1725 as a member of the Consulta. Four years later he was selected as an auditor of the Rota for Venice. Created a cardinal in 1737, he succeeded Pietro Ottoboni as bishop of Padua in 1743. The conscientious discharge of his duties here is reflected in his three-volume *Decisiones S. Rota Romanae coram R. P. D. Carlo Rezzonico*. His lavish almsgiving endeared him to the people wherever he went, although his administration of justice was judged to be too lenient.

Elected to the papacy in 1758, he continued to show benevolence and a pastoral care for his people. In the droughts of 1763 and 1764 he set up granaries, bought oil for the people, built shelters for those who poured into Rome, and attempted to drain the Pontine marshes. He was a patron of the arts and learning and completed the Fontana de Trevi (1762) and the Villa Albani (1763). He offered his patronage to the painter Raphael Mengs and the engraver Giovanni Battista Piranesi although these artists along with many others deplored the clothing of the "indecent" statues in the Villa and the painting over of the nudes in the Sistine Chapel's "Last Judgment," both ordered by an overly conscientious pope. He enlarged the Vatican Labrary but, in order to remedy irregularities in the administration of the library, set up unfortunate regulations which prevented scholars from using the collections. These ill-advised regulations were not completely withdrawn until the time of Leo XIII.

Clement's pontificate had to cope with the campaign of the French Encyclopedists under the leadership of Voltaire. Influential in all the Bourbon courts of Europe this group was determined to work against the Society of Jesus as a first step in its attack on Christianity. One of Clement's first official acts was to annul Saldanha's commission to investigate the state of the Society in Portugal, but it was too late to stem the tide. The Bourbon courts throughout Europe were bent on destroying the Jesuits who were at a high point of influence. This struggle became the preoccupation of the remainder of Clement's reign.

Portugal and the Holy See severed relations in 1760 after the Jesuits were expelled; France followed Portugal's example in 1761. In 1764 French Jesuits were forced to go into exile and Louis XIV abolished the Society by law in his kingdom. To this action the pope replied by an official letter of protest, *Apostolicum pascendi munus* (January 7, 1765) but the document was ignored. In 1767 the Jesuits were expelled from Spain and soon after from Parma and Naples. The ambassadors of Spain, Naples, and France demanded complete and irrevocable destruction of the Society and the secularization of its members throughout the world. In order to delay action Clement called for a special consistory to decide the fate of the Jesuits, but he died of a stroke the day before the meeting was to take place (February 3, 1769).

†

REFERENCE:
1. Pastor, *The history of the popes*, 36:153.

A QUO DIE

ENCYCLICAL OF POPE CLEMENT XIII
ON UNITY AMONG CHRISTIANS
SEPTEMBER 13, 1758
14

Venerable Brothers, Greetings and Apostolic Blessing.

Cooperation of the Bishops and the Papacy

Since that day when the unbelievable and unexpected happened, when God took Our unworthiness and placed it in the Holy See of St. Peter, the summit of all the churches, We have been troubled by a bitter and constant concern. A much heavier burden of sorrow has been placed on Us than We are able to bear. We would certainly have given Ourselves over to weeping if something had not deterred Us from this excessive sadness—something similar to what happened to the most holy prophet, the dynamic leader of Israel. Moses exclaimed to the Lord: "Why do you treat your servant so badly? And why have you placed the weight of all this people on me? I am not able to carry this nation by myself; the weight is too much for me."[1] In order that Moses might not fail in spirit and that he might bear the burden he had assumed, God commanded him to gather seventy men from the elders of Israel. He granted the spirit of Moses to them so that they could be teachers of the people and share the burden with Moses. That same consolation alone sustains Us now, Venerable Brothers. God himself chose you much sooner from among the multitude of the faithful to care for souls. He gave you to Us as Our helpers and assistants. When you were ordained to the episcopacy, He abundantly filled you with His own spirit so that We might beconfident in the aid and excellence of God and supported by your singular wisdom. You are on fire to fulfill your duties, and We conclude that much of Our sorrow and concern has been removed. Therefore, in order to find encouragement in our mutual faith[2] and to arouse your sincere mind to remembrance,[3] We write this letter to you. We know that you are ardent and upright against the foul enemy of the human race and have organized yourselves as in a battle line. Nevertheless We exhort you to meet the enemy more quickly and courageously, to wage the war well. Standing in battle, may you fight for the house of Israel.[4]

Call to Unity and Love

2. In so many and such dangerous battles, the hope of victory is that much better and that much more certain if we preserve unity in the close bond of peace.[5] Therefore, Venerable Brothers, may your love in all its strength remove from the hearts of the faithful the seeds of any kind of dissension. It is your responsibility that

everybody seeks peace,[6] that everybody searches for the elements of peace.[7] The Lord Jesus, a short time before He gave himself up to die, said to His apostles, "Peace I give you; my own peace I give you."[8] He does not leave the inheritance of peace only to the apostles, but also to us. He says "Not only for these but for those also who through their words will believe in me. May they all be one, Father, may they be one in us as you are in me and I am in you."[9] Venerable Brothers, see to it that by eliminating spiritual dissensions, we constantly and continually preserve so great and so precious an inheritance which the Lord Jesus transmitted to us. The apostle says that the Holy Spirit is a pledge of this inheritance. When we place ourselves before Him and beseech Him to make holy the sacrifice of the Church, we ask nothing more than that the bond of love be preserved unbroken in the Church by spiritual grace. It is good for us all to remember that when the Lord asked "who do men say the Son of Man is" and whom the disciples believed He was, they answered that there were various opinions about Him. But St. Peter confessed that He was the son of the living God, not revealed by flesh and blood but by the Father.[10]

3. From this, you can easily see that there is a difference between the sons of light and the sons of the world. The latter disagree among themselves with various and diverse opinions, while the former, initiated into the mysteries of unity, profess the one faith of all by the mouth of one, through the head of all. Therefore, concentrate all your attention on increasing peace among the faithful. Uproars, contentions, rivalries, animosities, and dissensions should be silenced.[11] In this way those who go by the name of Catholic can all be perfect in the same sense, in the same opinion,[12] saying the same thing together,[13] knowing the same thing and understanding it thoroughly. They should understand that if they want to be members of Christ, they cannot have concord with the head if they want to be in disagreement with the members. Nor can those who have not lived in fraternal love be counted as brothers by the Almighty Father.

4. The apostle shows us remarkable signs of love and reliable pointers, so that nobody strays in a matter which contains the salvation of the human race. He says: "Love is patient and kind; it is never jealous; love is never boastful or conceited; it is never rude or selfish; it does not take offense and is not resentful."[14] From this, we should clearly understand that where love is absent, there reigns that malice which we men have brought about from the beginning of the human race. Arrogance and proud contempt, stubbornness and avarice, intolerance and ambition, envy and the inordinate desire for glory—these and other depravities of the spirit flare up from this like the torches of our soul. All of these things are produced by the corruption of lust in the world.[15]

5. Let swelling of the spirit and stubborn customs depart from episcopal government. We who say we dwell in Christ should walk just as He walked.[16] We should not seek an example anywhere else than from the Lord Jesus, whom we should imitate. For when the disagreement among the disciples arose about who should be reckoned the greatest, He said: "Among pagans it is the kings who lord it over them. This must not happen with you. No; the greatest among you must behave as the least; the leader as if he were the one who serves. Here I am among you as one who serves."[17] Therefore, just as the Lord Jesus Christ forbade the apostles to rule, we believe that we have come not to rule the Church but to serve it. May we concentrate all our thoughts, labors, and counsels to that purpose, so that we might preserve safe and sound in the Church those sheep entrusted to us by the Lord. We should desire nothing more than their welfare.

6. Therefore, elders, We speak to you in the words of the prince of the apostles: "I am an elder myself and a witness to the sufferings of Christ, and with you I have a share in the glory that is to be revealed. Be shepherds of the flock of God."[18] Watch over the sheep, not like the hired hand who sees the wolf coming, abandons them, and runs away,[19] but gladly, because God wants it.[20] Be like the shepherd who gives his life for his sheep,[21] not for sordid money but freely.[22] Do not lord over the clergy, but become examples for the flock. There is no more offensive or dangerous poison than the desire to rule. If a bishop is corrupted by this, it is inevitable that the church entrusted to him will be shaken, if not destroyed. Therefore, a bishop should not want to be powerful, but rather to be useful. Having made himself an example for the flock, he should like a torch radiate blameless conduct, moral integrity, piety, and religion. When the people see this, they will walk happily and quickly in the way of the Lord,

for they will see that they have been given a leader and not a master.

7. It is especially characteristic of love to be lifted up with joy when someone in the Church of God flourishes in piety and learning, someone who longs to save souls and fulfills his priestly duty with industry, labor and diligence. We have often thought that such a man is exposed to the envy of his neighbor.[23]. Every sane man sees that he is being destroyed by the disparagement of the envious, and it is not fitting that this happen. When Eldad and Medad were prophesying in the camp,[24] Joshua, son of Nun, warned Moses that he should prohibit them. Moses responded that he very much wanted everybody to prophesy. He said: "are you jealous on my account? If only the whole people would prophesy and the Lord gave his Spirit to them all!"[25] The love of the bishop considers it a crime to burn with anger. It does not consider the man led astray by harmful desires as an enemy but rather lays hold of him as a brother, coaxing him, encouraging him, and warning him.[26] It calls him back from error and leads him back to the path of righteousness. If something should happen which requires a more serious verbal castigation, beware lest the words cut too harshly. Let severity abstain from every affront.

Desire for Glory

8. We cannot be silent concerning the useless desire for glory which a certain bishop correctly called hidden destruction. Once it has shown itself, there is perhaps nothing more hostile to love. Servility creeps up on whatever bishop this deadly plague gets hold of and infects; it attacks his most noble part, the soul. It captures him with its poisonous flatteries and constantly besieges him. It drives the wretch to the point that he no longer seeks the glory of God but only his own, increasing enormously that distorted and excessive self-esteem by which each of us is greatly deceived. Even the Lord Jesus denied that He sought this.[27] Detraction and lying follow flattery as destructive attendants and ministers, so that nothing is left safe and sound for the eminent and virtuous men in the company of the bishop. For this reason, Solomon in his wisdom warns that it is better to be seized by wisdom than deceived by the flattery of fools.[28] He also says: "Turn your back on the mouth that misleads; keep your distance from lips that deceive."[29] Bishops should always keep this in mind: "When a ruler listens to false reports, all his ministers will be scoundrels."[30] We must stop being envious of glory.[31] Thus, glory will be the downfall of those who think earthly things are important.[32] Let us look higher—let us look upon that heavenly home of eternal glory. Let us not think that our true, solid, and serious glory comes from the lips of men.[33] We have all sinned, and we all need the glory of God. Having died to our sins,[34] we should not glory in ourselves. The Father should be glorified in the Son,[35] so that we might be filled with the fruit of justice through Jesus Christ for the glory of God,[36] to whom alone belong all glory, majesty, authority, and power.[37]

A quo die 14

Mercy to the Poor

9. Among the fruits of justice, mercy to the poor should certainly be considered the most important. That justice which comes from faith belongs to Jesus Christ.[38] It is true that "if one of the brothers or one of the sisters is in need of clothes and has not enough food to live on, and one of you says to them, 'I wish you well; keep yourself warm and eat plenty' without giving them these bare necessities of life, then what good is that?"[39] Thus, the apostle James questions all Christians. Every faithful person, especially everyone who is a little more wealthy than the others, should out of mercy come to the assistance of the poor. They require our generosity as their principal right, for we hold the goods of the Church, which are the prayers of the faithful, the price of sins, and the inheritance of the poor, not as our own but as if in trust. It is not justifiable to use it for ourselves in such a way that nothing remains for those who could rightfully cry out, "What you spend is ours!" Where does such a great abundance of things come to us from, if not from the gifts of the Church? Like a bride, we should be content[40] with the good things we receive, that is, food and shelter,[41] considering piety with sufficiency as a great profit. It is certainly a special gift when it replenishes more abundantly those things which we need to protect, nourish, and embellish the bride. It is certainly everybody's great gain, because we obtain grace from God by almsgiving. Our blind mind is illuminated by it and we who are broken and fallen with a natural weakness are raised up and supported. When we pour forth our souls in desire and replenish our afflicted spirit, our light

will rise in the darkness and our shadows will become like noon, for the Lord will fill our souls with his splendors.[42]

Prayer and Eucharist

10. Actually to obtain light for the mind from God and to obtain the grace and devotion without which the episcopal duties would languish, almsgiving has great power. But it is no more efficacious than prayer and the most holy sacrifice of the Mass. The apostle orders us to pray without interruption and to give thanks to God in everything because it is the will of God that we not extinguish the spirit of faith and love.[43] This spirit helps us in our weakness and expresses our plea through groans that could never be put into words.[44] If a certain bishop needs wisdom, he should ask God for it and God will give it to him.[45] Let him not hesitate to seek anything in faith. He should ask that God arouse in his soul as great a faith as Moses had when he saw the invisible God.[46] It is necessary to have humility to attain that faith. David cried: "I am poor and needy. God help me."[47] These words of the Lord show us how great is the power of perseverance and persistence in prayer: "It is necessary to pray always without ceasing."[48] In that constancy and perseverance, let us wait for the majesty of God if there is a delay: it will appear and will not deceive us because it comes gradually.[49] We should not be concerned only about our weaknesses, but we should also consider that the problems of others afflict us and are on the same level as our own. Our prayers should be addressed more ardently and more perseveringly to God. It is through this prayer that we obtain from the Lord, as a decisive intermediary of the Church's faithful, the faith, hope, and love of all—virtues which are necessary for each and every one of us and for all the faithful in the world. The holy sacrifice of the Eucharist will build the road for us to beseech God and will open the way to obtain anything we want. For this reason, entangled in the great preoccupations of our office, we shall not refuse to offer the holy body and blood of Jesus Christ frequently to God. We do not think that we have been given any greater task than to offer repeatedly a sacrifice of appeasement to God the Father for our sins and those of the faithful.

Teach the People

11. As We are in a certain manner intermediaries between God and mankind, We offer to God the prayers of the people, and in the same way We communicate the will of God to them. This is the will of God: Our sanctification.[50] Thus it is Our duty to proclaim and reveal the mystery of Christ,[51] just as it is fitting for Us to speak. It is necessary, first of all to teach this to the people: The body of Christ was similar to ours, with the exception of sin. It is not only but also sanctifying, capable of suffering, exposed to death, and able to stand in the stead of all of us. Christ offered his body, and us at the same time, to satisfy divine justice.[52] He handed himself—and us at the same time—to all the torments which our crimes merited. He was condemned to the sorrows of death and suffered the curse given to sinners by the law: death under the harshest tortures. He satisfied the law, for the death and burial of Jesus Christ abolished all sin. The Lord Jesus rose from the grave with the same flesh but it was stripped of its mortality and adorned with glory of eternity. In order that they may be justified, it is necessary for sinners to die with Christ, who died in their place and in their name. Then they must enter the grave with Christ, in order to leave behind the flesh defiled by sin. They must hand over the old man to the wrath of God and to the death of the sinner, so that by baptism a new man might return to life in us and live again with Christ in immortality and eternal glory. Therefore all Christians should think about that eternal life and not this brief one. They should remove from their hearts the desire for pleasures and riches which are the instruments of pleasure. Cast off pride, in which all harmful desires are contained. The world is passing away, as well as what it craves for; however, he who keeps the will of God will endure forever.[53]

12. You can easily see, Venerable Brothers, how important it is for you yourselves to teach the people these and all other things which pertain to God's mysteries. Therefore, you should carefully consider that those whom you choose to exercise the priestly ministry and to teach the people the fundamentals of Christianity should possess great purity of life, moral integrity, chastity, justice, piety, and devotion. How serious it would be if something bad, if something vicious, if something perverse were to infect their character with bad habits. Cautiously and prudently remove this danger from the pastors. Help and instruct each of your neighbors with salutary advice. Give the soul of the faithful wings with which to fly from the earth to contemplate heavenly matters; once it is snatched away from the world, give that soul to God and recall the divine image in it to its original purity. On the other hand, it should not be said that pastors who ask to give an account of their lives cannot themselves bear this scrutiny. Nor should they reproach the character of another, so that they themselves must be contradicted. The learning which is perceived as worthy of a clergyman should attain pure and holy habits. They should have a knowledge of the Scriptures: "All Scripture is inspired by God and can profitably be used for teaching, for refuting error, for guiding people's lives and teaching them to be holy that the man of God may be complete, equipped for every good work."[54] They should go to both testaments of the Bible, to the traditions of the Church, and to the writings of the holy fathers, as if they were going to springs from which pours forth a pure and undefiled teaching of faith and character. They should read often and reflect upon the Roman Catechism, the summation of Catholic teaching, which provides holy sermons to give to the faithful.

Suitability for the Priesthood

13. In considering someone's suitability for the ministry, do not rely only on individual enthusiasm or on someone's recommendation. You should consider as best suited to be a faithful minister and to receive a part of the Lord's flock the man whose timid virtue shirks the ministry. "Do not be too quick to lay hands on any man"[55] which happens if we do not consider and test the men over and over again. Lest we pay the price to God for imprudent rashness and share in another's sin,[56] let him be tested carefully and accurately and judged severely. It should not weary you if We dwell a little longer on this matter which requires great attention. In whatever manner the priests behave, the majority of the people will behave in the same way. Everyone looks upon them—especially if they are parish priests—as if in a mirror. For this reason, nobody deserves anything more destructive from the Church than evil priests, who infect the people with their vices and so corrupt the Church that they seem to harm it more by their example than by their sin.

A quo die
14

Priestly Duties

14. Associate with distinguished men in the sacred ministry, not because we consider ourselves inadequate in the duty of preaching the gospel, but rather so that we might seem to leave in the hands of others the nets which the Lord gave to us to become fishers of men.[57] The principal duty of the bishop is to preach the word of God, for the apostle cried: "Woe to me if I do not preach the gospel. It is a duty which has been laid on me." [58] The Lord Jesus Christ did not send him primarily to baptize—even though this is a holy action—but especially to preach the gospel.[59] We know that the ministry of the word held first place in the minds of the apostles and that these holy men did not neglect this duty.[60] For this reason they thought it fitting to entrust to deacons the rest of the charitable works toward their neighbors. St. Paul writes to Timothy: "Make use of the time until I arrive by reading to the people, preaching, and teaching."[61] If someone feels that he lacks the ability to preach or says that his talents do not measure up to the responsibility, do not allow him to neglect his duty in other matters which pertain to the word of God. Therefore, if the bishop commands the priests to teach the basics of Christian doctrine to the children, he should also give his assistance in that work. He should join himself as an assistant to the pastors in teaching the faithful, so that his duty of preaching the word might be preserved on all sides. This should make everybody hasten to fulfill his duty. Thus, he should not feel it burdensome to administer the sacraments to the faithful occasionally with his brother priests, to enter the choir in the meantime and sing the psalms with the canons, and to preside over the meetings which he has convened. From this the priests will receive a great share in the spirit of his holy ministry, just as the seventy men received the Spirit in the time of Moses. The people who witness this will be filled with the greatest esteem for divine worship, and the tainted men will be frightened away from the sacred ministry by the same venerable spectacle, so that they will not dare in the least to aspire to it.

The Bishop's Duties

15. Because the bishop cannot manage the Church and supervise his flock if he is away, you should not be absent from your churches for any length of time. This was solemnly ratified by natural law and by the holy canons, especially by the decrees of the Council of Trent. The bishop should visit all the places in his diocese to protect the power of their laws when they begin to fail, either through the laziness of the ministers or through the stubbornness of the faithful. If there is a serious and necessary reason for you to leave your diocese and if it is necessary to be absent for any length of time, We ask you not to allow the Church to be weakened by the desire of her pastor. Whenever you are absent, this danger is present.

16. In addition, example should accompany words. We should show ourselves in all things as an example of good works[62] so that our opponents will respect us and not have anything bad to say about us.[63] Deeds should not be silent without words, nor should the lack of deeds shame the words. In addition, we believe in our heart that the perfect leader of the Church has been furnished with the perfect goods of the greatest virtue, so that his life might be adorned by what he says and his teaching by what he lives. The home of modesty should be our own, as well as the teacher of modesty. The ecclesiastical discipline which we follow should be full of dignity and harmony. If we are not committed to anybody's will and pleasure, we will not indulge in the softness and weakness of our spirit and we will not single out anyone for special treatment. This often creates great turmoil in the administration of the Church and gives serious offense, providing contempt and envy for the bishop.

17. As for what concerns Us, We have already taken care[64] that We establish as bishops in the various countries those who bring to the episcopacy a sound doctrine, a life beyond reproach, and a mind prepared for all things for the sake of Jesus Christ. We believe that the responsibility should go to him who presides over it; let him not swell up with the greatness of the honor but diminish in humility. In scrutinizing and testing men whom We want to place over such a great responsibility, We shall use you as witnesses and authorities, trusting in the holy devotion of your testimony and in your faith. We do not doubt in the least that you will not use any human rationale, but only thoughts for Him who has called you to the work of the ministry for building up the body of Christ.[65]

Encouragement to the Clergy

18. It remains, Venerable Brothers, that We advise you concerning the fortitude and strength of spirit needed to oppose those things which are against the orthodox faith, which harm piety or which damage the integrity of moral living. Let us be strong in the spirit of the Lord, in good judgment, and in courage.[66] We should not be like dumb watchdogs unable to bark,[67] allowing our flocks to fall prey to looting and our sheep to be devoured by every wild animal in the field.[68] Nor should anything deter us from throwing ourselves into battle for the glory of God and for the salvation of souls: "Think of the way he endured such opposition from sinners."[69] If we are afraid of the audacity of worthless men, it affects the strength of the episcopacy and its sublime and divine power to govern the Church. Nor can we Christians endure or exist any longer—if it has come to that—if we become overly frightened by the snares or threats of the damned. Therefore, trusting not in ourselves but in the God who raises the dead to life,[70] we despise human affairs and cry out to the Lord: You are my hope in the day of disaster.[71] Let us never be exhausted in body or in spirit, for we are fellow workers with God.[72] The Lord Jesus is with us always even to the end of time.[73] Therefore let us not be weakened by scandal or persecution, lest we seem ungrateful for God's favor, since his assistance is as strong as His promises are true.

19. In the Last Judgment We shall be called to give account on behalf of everybody and before everybody who is reckoned in the name of Christ. Therefore We beseech you that if some scandal or disagreement arises which you are unable to put down, to refer it to this See of the blessed Prince of the apostles. As from the head and apex of the episcopacy, that very episcopacy and every authority which bears the same name comes from here. All waters flow from here as if from their very source, and they flow uncorrupted from a pure head through the various regions of the whole world. From here all the churches take what the water worthy of clean bodies avoids teaching and the people whom, as though fouled in unpurged filth, the water avoids washing. We trust first of all in the strength of God, then in the protection of St. Peter, whose care holds all present. We shall help you with advice, resources, and authority, for We are ready to be very near you, [74] to keep the churches and the brothers safe and sound. As for the rest, We trust in God under the weight of this burden we have received;[75] since He is the originator of this burden, He will also help us. In order that human weakness does not falter under the greatness of His grace, He who gave the dignity will also give the strength. Meanwhile in humble entreaty, beseech God in His merciful goodness to subdue now those who fight against Us, to strengthen your faith, and to increase devotion and peace. May He produce in Us, His humble servant, whom He wanted to oversee the government of His Church and to show the riches of His grace, enough strength in such a labor. May He make Us useful for your protection, and may He strive to extend to Our Papacy what was given to the age, for the profit of devotion. The grace of our Lord Jesus Christ be with you; We bless you and We greet you with a holy kiss. We lovingly impart to all of you, brother priests, and to all the faithful of your churches Our apostolic blessing. Given in Rome at St. Mary Major on September 14, in the year 1758 in the first year of Our pontificate.

†

LATIN TEXT: *Bull. Rom. Cont.*, 4^1: 30-37.

ENGLISH TRANSLATION: Norman Desmarais

REFERENCES:

1. Nm 11.11,14.
2. Rom 1.12.
3. 2 Pt 3.11.
4. Ez 13.5.
5. Eph 4.3.
6. 1 Pt 3.11.
7. Rom 14.19.
8. Jn 14.27.
9. Jn 17. 20,21.
10. Mt 16.14f.
11. 2 Cor 12.20.
12. 1 Cor 1.10.
13. 2 Cor 13.11.
14. 1 Cor 13.4,5.
15. 2 Pt 1.4.
16. 1 Jn 2.6.
17. Lk 22.25.
18. 1 Pt 5.1-2.
19. Jn 10.12.
20. 1 Pt 5.1-2.
21. Jn 10.11.
22. 1 Pt 5.1-2.
23. Eccl. 4.4.
24. Nm 11.27.
25. Nm 11.29.
26. 2 Thes 3.15.
27. Jn 8.50.
28. Wis 7.6.
29. Prv 4.24.
30. Prov 29.12.
31. Gal 5.26.
32. Phil 3.19.
33. Rom 3.23.
34. 1 Pt 2.24.
35. Jn 14.13.
36. Phil 1.11.
37. Jude 1.25.
38. Phil 3.9.
39. Jas 2.15.
40. 1 Tm 6.6.
41. 1 Tm 6.8.
42. Is 58.10,11.
43. 1 Thes 5.17-18.
44. Rom 8. 26.
45. Jas 1.5.
46. Heb 11.27.
47. Ps 70.6.
48. Lk 18.1
49. Hab 2.3.
50. 1 Thes 4.3.
51. Col 4.3.
52. 1 Pt 3.18.
53. 1 Jn 2.17.
54. 2 Tm 3.16-17.
55. 1 Tm 5.22.
56. 1 Tm 5.22.
57. Mt 4.19.
58. 1 Cor 9.16.
59. 1 Cor 1.17.
60. Acts 6.2,4.
61. 1 Tm 4.13.
62. Ti 2.7.
63. Ti 2.8.
64. Ps 76.5.
65. Ept 4.12.
66. Mi 3.8.
67. Is 56.10.
68. Ez 34.8.
69. Heb 12.3.
70. 2 Cor 1.9.
71. Jer 17.17.
72. 1 Cor 3.9.
73. Mt 28.20.
74. 2 Cor 12.15.
75. 1 Thes 2.2.

CUM PRIMUM

ENCYCLICAL OF POPE CLEMENT XIII ON
OBSERVING CANONICAL SANCTIONS
SEPTEMBER 17, 1759
15

To Our Venerable Brothers, all the Patriarchs, Primates, Archbishops, and Bishops who Enjoy Grace and Communion with the Apostolic See.

Venerable Brothers, Greetings and Apostolic Blessing.

Ever since We first accepted the care of the Lord's flock, through the incomprehensible wisdom of the eternal shepherd presiding over the See of St. Peter, We have received reports from many fervent and zealous churchmen. Many of them were from pastors and preachers of the word of God, who travel through the cities and provinces preaching penance and correction of character to the people. Their unanimous complaint was that among the abuses and corruptions which they observed and strove to reform in the exercise of their ministry, they frequently encountered an avarice and greed on the part of certain clergymen that cried out for correction. As the Holy Spirit called this the root of all evil, it is no wonder that it draws into more heinous crimes all those whose soul it fills. It renders them apathetic in the fulfillment of their duties and in their worship of God. Once avarice converts them to worldly desires, they become devoted to worldly cares and preoccupations. They publicly disavow these while they profess that among the mysteries of the holy initiation, they recognize only God as the portion of their inheritance. Thus they necessarily become contentious and ready to throw everything into confusion, so as not to lose some vile profit which they either hope for or have already received. They are not ashamed to lower themselves to any lowly duty or service, to the disgrace of their order and status. As a result many laymen despise not only those who do such things, but often even the whole priestly company. Rather, let them be bitter and scornful toward the kind of person whose lawsuits and contentions they must endure in worldly affairs, or through whom honest means of providing for their own welfare and that of their loved ones seems to be forestalled.

2. We believe that these accounts are more than adequately supported by the facts. Indeed, even some monks allow themselves on occasion to be taken beyond the bounds of ecclesiastical moderation, away from the concern they imposed on themselves regarding the temporal gains of their communities. We are thus aroused to satisfactorily remove from our midst such a corruption, which brings scandal to the faithful and damaging effects to others.

Some Clergy Seek Temporal Wealth

3. It is true that from the very beginning of the Church right up to our own times, there was

nothing more plainly or more attentively legislated either by the decrees of the councils or by the constitutions of the popes who preceded Us. Nothing seemed to be stressed more frequently or more eagerly by the holy fathers and the pastors of the churches than that the ministers of the church, both clergy and monks, abstain from the desire for temporal wealth and that they should remove themselves from worldly concerns. Not only spiritual censures but also very serious temporal punishments were decreed for those who presumed to infringe or violate the canonical rules in this matter. Having carefully considered everything, We think that there is nothing left for Us to do, Venerable Brothers, other than to exhort you to cling to the intention of Our predecessors and the spirit of the church in all things. We exhort you to be zealous in obtaining the observance due these holy laws by all churchmen—both those subject to your ordinary jurisdiction as well as those subject to your delegated jurisdiction—according to the example of the sacred canons and the decrees of the Holy See and the synodical statutes of each diocese.

Penalties for Transgressions

4. In order to clarify this matter, We devote Our constant attention and that of the Holy See to the religious observance of the aforementioned laws. At the same time, We approve, confirm, and renew through this letter each and every canon and constitution of Our predecessors against those clerics who act as businessmen and who involve themselves in worldly matters. We mention especially those decrees published and proclaimed by Pius IV, Urban VIII, and Clement IX, including the most recent one which Our predecessor Popes Benedict XIV promulgated on February 25, 1741, the first year of his pontificate, along with each and every penalty and the censures respectively ordained by them. Similarly, the decrees contained in the above-mentioned laws as well as their punishments and sanctions should be inserted word for word in Our present letter. At the same time let all efficacy be removed from every opposing custom and practice—which ought rather to be called by their proper names, corruptions and abuses—by which certain churchmen strive to cover up their criminal dabbling in worldly matters. We declare and decree that all clergymen—both from the secular clergy and from the regular clergy of whatever order, congregation, society, or institute, are subject to and should be subject to all the aforementioned laws and penalties. We should also mention specifically those favored with special and extensive indults, privileges, and exemptions. Thus, whoever transgresses these laws incurs the penalties prescribed in them as well as those applicable according to the differences of circumstances and the method of procedure prescribed by the Council of Trent or by the Holy See. They should be punished notwithstanding any custom or practice to the contrary, even very old ones which can be considered indigenous to some places, dioceses, or regions. We condemn, proscribe, and nullify this practice, considering it a damnable abuse and an intolerable corruption in the present state of affairs.

5. We exhort all of you, then, to watch over the integrity of ecclesiastical discipline and the salvation of the souls of all the clergy subject to you, both by ordinary and by delegated law. Inquire diligently into their course of action; if you discover that some of them are infected with the stain of this greed and that they sin against the canons and apostolic constitutions, do not neglect to proceed against them dutifully and stringently, according to the example of the same canons and constitutions.

6. There are two things which you should especially beware of in this matter. First of all, do not allow your vigilance to be foiled by the crafty arts of the evildoers. It often happens that those who know the decrees of the laws fraudulently arrange their affairs so that even if their crime should be brought to court, they can be on guard against admitting any violation of those laws. Sometimes they will use an intermediary to serve their greed, or else conduct business matters under a different name, which they record in the tables and account books while they firmly maintain that they are not in the least concerned in the matter under investigation. Sometimes they are aware that the more restrictive judgment of the laws is constrained within certain limits; they strive to behave so that they have a defense if they are accused of financial aspirations by their superiors. They can maintain that they were not primarily led by base greed to seek profit, but that they worked solely at avoiding evil through cautious planning and that they obtained an undesired profit through the fortuitous goodness of time. Sometimes it is not their own property

which is involved in the business matters but that of their relatives or those joined to them by some other bond of need. They will say that they obtain their support out of the duty of love or under the title of management.

7. We are sufficiently aware, through Our own experience in exercising the episcopal office, of how difficult it is to make a judgment in certain cases in which the good or bad intention of the one who is accused of unlawful business is of paramount importance. However, you should not think for that reason that your diligence will be ineffectual when the clergy at least understands that you will not ignore such a serious violation of church discipline. You will derive great benefit from that very thing because you will more often call to witness your mind and that of the Church, which shrinks from the shadier collusions even of these men. Given the opportunity, you will announce to them that the God who scrutinizes the innermost recesses of man will not be mocked. Before His supreme tribunal, those sometime-sophistries, which now deceive the bishop and escape the legally-appointed penalties, will be of no avail. Besides, it will not be impossible to recognize for the most part the hidden truth of the matter and subdue the secret crime, if the character of the men involved, which reveals itself in the total conduct of their lives, and the accompanying circumstances, which render the proffered excuses more or less admissible, are weighed with the appropriate skill and care. We could easily illustrate this with examples, if We did not trust in the Lord concerning the wisdom of your brotherhood and in your experience.

Interpretations of Canon Law

8. The other thing, which you should equally beware of, is that you not allow to flourish among you wrong interpretations of canon laws, which diminish the strength of those laws and give excessive scope to indulgence. These interpretations arise from private reflection, outside the mind and spirit of the Church and without the agreement of a legitimate superior. They are adapted to any circumstances at will. This problem may arise when the affairs of both the secular and regular clergy are appealed to you for judgment. If there is any question concerning the nature of the contract which clergymen customarily enter into in certain dioceses, whether such a thing is permissible or should be forbidden, it will hardly be fair to rule on the basis of either the frequency of those acts whose nature is in question or the ideas of the contracting parties. But to remove every doubt and to restrain the excesses and audacity of those who await a decision, the most expeditious recourse is to this Apostolic See, which has defined many similar questions through the Congregation of the Cardinals, the interpreters of the Council of Trent. Thus, it will be possible in the future to see what was decided in given cases, and what were the suitable responses which can provide precedents for acting and judging.

Money Changing

9. A clear decision has been requested from Us and the Holy See on the matter of whether it is permissible for clergymen to change money. Even though we think that it is difficult to find another matter less subject to doubt, We nevertheless declare and define in this letter, so as to remove all doubt, that money changing is by its very nature a true and proper act of business. Therefore, it should be considered forbidden to all clergymen, both to contract in their own name or through an intermediary. Any cleric, either secular or regular, who changes money will be considered liable to all the penalties and censures which have been established for clergymen who engage in business.

10. A clergyman may try to excuse his involvement in worldly business by pleading indigence. This plea is not valid since the canonical title of ordination should at least be a sufficient and adequate inheritance for each and every clergyman to sustain himself. If there are needy clerics, each should look after his own needs through more proper means which are in agreement with his vows. The indigence will rather be that of his parents or sisters or some other person whom he is dutifully bound to help. First of all, We decree that the ecclesiastical superior should never allow such an excuse. We cannot permit that cleric not to be punished in proportion to his guilt according to the prescriptions of canon law, unless he shows that he has already expressed the aforementioned needs to the Apostolic See, if he lives in Italy or the adjacent islands. If he lives in more remote regions, he should at least have explained matters to the Ordinary of the place. He should also have sought a suitable dispensation after the consideration of those matters. Finally he should have requested the Holy See or the Ordinary for authorization to help the aforementioned person through his labors.

11. Next, as for what concerns the Curia in this matter, We clarify our thoughts and desires. Such dispensations and authorizations should never be granted unless the alleged causes of the situation are based on fact and unless it is clear that the aforementioned needs cannot be alleviated in any other way. In the same case, let it never be permitted for churchmen to assume any kind of business dealings whose administration is not befitting their clerical status and character. Rather, in those rescripts or letters of indult, let more suitable ways to bring assistance to his poor relatives be indicated and prescribed for the cleric, in accordance with just moderation and the measure of true need. The Ordinaries to whom this pertains should similarly comply with everything in the granting of such dispensations and authorizations. Either they or the Holy See have sometimes permitted certain indults to certain clerics for special reasons, with just causes accompanying. Perchance these indults have come into wider use—for example hiring church-owned farmland for cultivation at a fixed annual rate. See to it particularly that other clerics do not usurp these things as if they were conceded generally to everybody without just cause and without a special indult.

12. As for the rest, We resolve that those very authorizations—even those obtained in the above-mentioned manner—should always be considered harmful right up to the time they are revoked. Thus, they should be considered null and void and revoked in their own right as soon as the alleged needs of the relatives cease or another legitimate reason opportunely provides for them. We desire to burden the vigilance and the conscience of the local Ordinary with the execution and observance of all these matters.

Other Abuses

13. It is true that the current depression of ecclesiastical dignity is not to be attributed solely to business dealings. There are other abuses which do not clearly oppose the letter of the sacred canons and constitutions published by the Holy See. Yet, clergymen decide to use them and thereby cast aside ever more frequently and more certainly the proper dignity of the cleric and the reputation of their whole order. They are confident that they will not be subject to the censures and the penalties established by those canons and constitutions. We know that many clergymen are prominent in their unseemly activities: in the administration and care for their own goods; in selling the fruits, animals, and other things which grow and are fed on their own farms or those of the Church; and in preparing things which they need for their own use or for setting in order the aforementioned farms. Thus they show themselves completely given over to the cares and concerns of this world, these clerics who covet worldly gain. Those who have risen above the lot of the human condition through the eminence of Holy Orders in this way lower themselves below men of the lowest status. Those who should be and appear to be the sons of light seem to outdo the sons of this generation in their concern for worldly greed. Our reports relate that they attend all the markets and sales with almost the same splendor and elegance as laymen, and they find anything preferable to the appearance of clerical moderation and modesty or of the seriousness and honor of the Church.

14. We proclaim openly that We will not forbid them anything which was judged permissible, in regard to the very nature of the business, for the correct and prudent administration of the Church's patrimony or which the holy fathers and the writers of Church laws entrusted to their care. For there are many things which clerics are not forbidden in regard to the substance of the matter, things which they are permitted to use under certain limitations; but the holy canons will inflict both temporal punishments and spiritual censures on those who go beyond the prescribed limitations or who violate the established rule of ecclesiastical discipline. The general rules of canon law and the individual statutes of the various dioceses contain many examples of this, examples which prescribe many things to observe or avoid in regard to the life, honesty, habit, or tonsure of the clerics. Thus, Venerable Brothers, you should watch over the motives of all the clergymen living in your dioceses in regard to the things We have just mentioned. If they approach you frequently to allow something which might not be in conformity with their clerical status, you should teach them through suitable instructions that they should comtemplate the eminence of the dignity they have chosen for themselves. They should not think that they are allowed to debase it with indecent acts or to wipe away from the souls of the laity the esteem and reverence due the ecclesiastical order, an esteem which greatly benefits the spiritual well-being of the faithful. Mindful that they were called to share in the Lord's portion, they should seek for and be concerned about the things which concern Jesus Christ and not themselves. In addition, you know that it is necessary to meet such turpitude and greed on the part of the clergy with suitable decrees strictly established, and you know that you must restrain and punish the faults of the evildoers. Given the choice of a greater or lesser scandal, first of all denounce the evil. Then correct it with salutary penitence; finally, restrain and punish it with the unsheathed sword of penalties and censures as an example for others.

15. Another kind of corruption infects many clergymen and, We understand, draws them from church service to worldly concerns. This demands as much or even more concern and constancy from your pastoral zeal. There are some who give over in object service to the laity all the labor and effort which they should expend in divine worship and in aiding their neighbors according to the law of love. Sometimes they even hire out their services to administer the business affairs of laymen for vile, temporal pay. In this matter it is difficult to judge whether the blindness of those who trample upon the dignity of their own order is to be regretted more, or the presumption of the laity. This laity takes so lightly the holy ministers from whom they should seek examples of Christian life and aids to eternal salvation that they do not hesitate to use them in servile ministries.

16. This certainly disturbs Us more, that an evil of this kind should come from an abuse which is just as detestable. Whenever someone rashly aspires to the clerical state, it sometimes happens that he deceives his Ordinary with false or forged documents, and he is promoted to holy orders by a false estate which either bears no fruit or which does not belong to him, without sufficient revenue to maintain an upright living. For this reason, none of you should be surprised, Venerable Brothers, if We take this opportunity to strongly exhort and warn each and every one of you to be more careful and more vigilant in this matter. Thus, no one subject to you should be given an opportunity to steal up to holy ordination if he does not receive a certain amount of annual income from an ecclesiastical benefice or ecclesiastical pension or from an estate created for him, in cases permitted by law. All fraud and collusion should be eliminated—if, that is, he does not receive that amount of annual return which was decreed either in the statutes of the diocesan synods or by legitimate custom.

17. Take care to recall to the precepts of ecclesiastical life and to the duties of the clerical soldier those clergymen and priests who devote themselves in the homes of the laity to these kinds of services which do not befit their class and profession. These duties lead them away from God's service from concern for their own spiritual progress to worldly business dealings and servile occupations, even though they sometimes strive to conceal their activities with the appearance of fine titles. Do not allow them to soil themselves peacefully in their shame or to glory with obstinate impunity in their defection from the camp of the Church. To these ends use every zeal and as much pastoral concern as necessary; use all the authority of ordinary and delegated jurisdiction, and all the while observe those things which must be observed.

18. Venerable Brothers, these are the things We wanted to suggest and strongly commend to your care, out of the duty of Our apostolic ministry in order to protect and vindicate the honor and the dignity of holy orders. In this matter, which greatly depends on individual circumstances, it is necessary that you who are present in your respective territories have the major roles. You are better able to recognize and more certainly judge the deeds of those subject to you, the accompanying circumstances, the needs of the regions, the customs of the people, and whatever might appear decent or indecent among prudent and upright men. In order that you might be free to correct and reform whatever might be wrong in these matters, We rely on your prudent judgment to regulate any indult of dispensation or authorization granted by any office of the Roman Curia up to now concerning these matters. We do not want to grant anything further until We have heard the reports of your brotherhood, as well as the desires and the accompanying formula and conditions of the indult, by which you have the entire authority to know about its execution and effect. Thus, no clergyman should be allowed to conduct any business dealings under any pretext or to assume a less upright ministry contrary to your prohibition or to retain it and prolong it once it has been granted. Meanwhile, We take pleasure in your pastoral zeal, and We lovingly grant to your brotherhood the apostolic blessing. Given in Rome at St. Mary Major on the 17th day of September, 1759, in the second year of Our pontificate.

†

LATIN TEXT: *Bull. Rom. Cont.*, 4^{1}: 248-53.

ENGLISH TRANSLATION: Norman Desmarais

APPETENTE SACRO

ENCYCLICAL OF POPE CLEMENT XIII ON THE SPIRITUAL ADVANTAGES OF FASTING

DECEMBER 20, 1759

16

To the Venerable Brothers the Patriarchs, Primates, Archbishops, and Bishops.

Venerable Brothers, Greetings and Apostolic Blessing.

Desirability of Fasting

The holy season of Lent approaches, which is full of mysteries but not without mystery. It precedes that great celebration of Easter, by which alone the dignity of all other religious occasions is consecrated. Venerable Brothers, you should see that the faithful religiously observe this holy fast, which was recommended by the testimony of the laws and the prophets, consecrated by the Lord Jesus Christ, and handed on by the apostles. The Catholic Church has always preserved it so that by the mortification of the flesh and the humiliation of the spirit, we might be better prepared to approach the mysteries of the Lord's passion and the paschal sacraments. Likewise through fasting we might rise again in the resurrection of Him whose passion and death we joined after we put off the old man. Our predecessor Benedict XIV aroused you with two earlier briefs, that you might zealously preserve such a holy and salutary institution. Your work and zeal should recall the discipline of the Lenten fast, now weakened by many corruptions, to its original observance. For this reason, Pope Benedict XIV removed from your midst many quibblings which impaired fasting. However, as there are many persistent threats to the Lord's flock from the foul and dangerous enemy of the human race, we should be wary lest the sly old fox add new calculations and perverse customs to the minds of the weaker faithful. These things will weaken the strength of the fast and make it sink back to that point from which it was recently recalled. We think it is necessary to send you this letter to show your brotherhood how fearful We are that the old corruption might remain, or that a new stain might come upon ecclesiastic discipline in this matter, with the resulting destruction of the souls of the faithful.

Consumption of Milk Products

2. We understand that it is just as necessary to lessen this fear of Ours as it is to increase your pastoral vigilance by it. After Our predecessor's letters, it perhaps remains for you to eradicate with God's help anything pertaining to the old or new corruption for breaking the laws of the fast, or the fabrications of opinions, or the customs which shy away from the true power and nature of the fast. Among these We number that abuse which rumor has brought to Us: while many

people were permitted by dispensation to eat meat for just and legitimate reasons, they thought it was also permitted to consume drinks mixed with milk, contrary to what Our predecessor thought was right. He was of the opinion that those who were permitted by dispensation to have meat, as well as those who were fasting in any way, with one mixture excepted, were comparable to those who had no dispensation. Accordingly they can have meat, or whatever originates from meat, in only one mixture.

Penance

3. You will begin most appropriately, and with hope of the greatest profit, to recall men to the observance of the holy law of fasting, if you teach the people this: penance for the Christian man is not satisfied by withdrawing from sin, by detesting a past life badly lived, or by the sacramental confession of these same sins. Rather, penance also demands that we satisfy divine justice with fasting, almsgiving, prayer, and other works of the spiritual life. Every wrongdoing—be it large or small—is fittingly punished, either by the penitent or by a vengeful God. Therefore we cannot avoid God's punishment in any other way than by punishing ourselves. If this teaching is constantly implanted in the minds of the faithful, and if they drink deeply of it, there will be very little cause to fear that those who have discarded their degraded habits and washed their sins clean through sacramental confession would not want to expiate the same sins through fasting, to eliminate the concupiscence of the flesh. Besides, consider the man who is convinced that he repents of his sins more firmly when he does not allow himself to go unpunished. That man, already consumed with the love of penance, will rejoice during the season of Lent and on certain other days, when the Church declares that the faithful should fast and gives them the opportunity to bring forth worthy fruits of penance. After all, it is always necessary to subdue concupiscence, for it is written, "Do not follow behind your desires, and do not turn away from your will." Let the faithful easily turn their attention during this most holy time of year to lessening the intemperance of the body by fasting. In this way the soul might understand how it should prepare itself to recall the holy mysteries of the passion, death, and resurrection of Jesus Christ. Therefore, those who are spurred on by penance do not seek the delicacies of the table, which seem indistinguishable from forbidden foods, even with abstinence. However, one can rightfully say that whoever sets them on his table does not so much put aside his customary delicacies as give his appetites over to unusual enticements. Finally, those spurred on by penance do not seek escapes by which they might withdraw from fasting, nor do they seek various subtleties to break ecclesiastical law.

4. It is your duty, Venerable Brothers, to inspire enthusiasm and love of penance in the faithful by word and example. Thus, they will approach the fast more quickly, observe it according to the laws prescribed by the Catholic Church, and sanctify it through almsgiving and prayer. Finally—and this matter greatly concerns the Church—they should understand that they have died and been buried with Christ. They have been called to the new life of the new man in the paschal feast so that they can come to the risen Lord Jesus Christ in full confidence. The grace of our Lord Jesus Christ be with all of you, to whom We most lovingly impart the apostolic blessing as a pledge of Our love and good will toward you. Given in Rome, at St. Mary Major, on the 20th day of December in the year 1759, in the second year of Our pontificate.

†

LATIN TEXT: *Bull. Rom. Cont.*, 4^1: 294-96; *Bull. Rom. Cont.*, 4^2: 1024-26, included in apost. const. *Universalis Ecclesiae*, 9-21-1765.

ENGLISH TRANSLATION: Norman Desmarais.

IN DOMINICO AGRO

ENCYCLICAL OF POPE CLEMENT XIII ON
INSTRUCTION IN THE FAITH
JUNE 14, 1761
17

To the Venerable Brothers, the Patriarchs, Primates, Archbishops and Bishops.

Venerable Brothers, Greetings and Apostolic Benediction.

In the Lord's field, for the tending of which Divine Providence placed Us as overseer, there is nothing which demands as much vigilant care and unremitting labor in its cultivation than guarding the good seed of Catholic teaching which the Apostles received from Jesus Christ and handed on to Us. If in laziness this is neglected, the enemy of the human race will sow weeds while the workers sleep. Then weeds will be found which should be committed to the flames rather than good grain to store in the barns. However, St. Paul strongly encourages Us to protect the faith that the saints handed on to Us.[1] He told Timothy to preserve the sacred trust[2] because dangerous times were coming[3] when evil and deceitful men would exist in the Church of God.[4] The insidious tempters would use their work to try to infect unwary minds with errors which are hostile to evangelical truth.

Difficulty of Making Doctrinal Statements

2. It often happens that certain unworthy ideas come forth in the Church of God which, although they directly contradict each other, plot together to undermine the purity of the Catholic faith in some way. It is very difficult to cautiously balance our speech between both enemies in such a way that We seem to turn Our backs on none of them, but to shun and condemn both enemies of Christ equally. Meanwhile the matter is such that diabolical error, when it has artfully colored its lies, easily clothes itself in the likeness of truth while very brief additions or changes corrupt the meaning of expressions; and confession, which usually works salvation, sometimes, with a slight change, inches toward death.

Limits of Instruction

3. The faithful—especially those who are simple or uncultivated—should be kept away from dangerous and narrow paths upon which they can hardly set foot without faltering. The sheep should not be led to pasture through trackless places. Nor should peculiar ideas—even those of Catholic scholars—be proposed to them. Rather, only those ideas should be communicated which are definitely marked as Catholic truth by their universality, ambiguity, and harmony. Besides, since the crowd cannot go up to the mountain[5] upon which the glory of the Lord came down,

and if whoever crosses the boundaries to see will die, the teachers of the people should establish boundaries around them so that no word strays beyond that which is necessary or useful for salvation. The faithful should obey the apostolic advice not to know more than is necessary, but to know in moderation.[6]

4. The popes clearly understood this. They devoted all their efforts not only to cut short with the sword of anathema the poisonous buds of growing error, but also to cut away certain developing ideas which either could prevent the Christian people unnecessarily from bearing a greater fruit of faith or could harm the minds of the faithful by their proximity to error. So the Council of Trent condemned those heresies which tried at that time to dim the light of the Church and which led Catholic truth into a clearer light as if the cloud of errors had been dispersed. As our predecessors understood that that holy meeting of the universal Church was so prudent in judgment and so moderate that it abstained from condemning ideas which authorities among Church scholars supported, they wanted another work prepared with the agreement of that holy council which would cover the entire teaching which the faithful should know and which would be far removed from any error. They printed and distributed this book under the title of *The Roman Catechism.*

Excellence of the Roman Catechism

There are aspects of their action worthy of special praise. In it they compiled the teaching which is common to the whole Church and which is far removed from every danger of error, and they proposed to transmit it openly to the faithful in very eloquent words according to the precept of Christ the Lord who told the apostles to proclaim in the light what He had said in the dark and to proclaim from the rooftops what they heard in secret.[7] They have obeyed His bride, the Church, whose words are, "Show me where you recline at midday."[8] For where it is not midday and the light is not so bright that truth can be clearly known, error can easily be mistaken for truth because of its appearance of truth and can be distinguished from truth only with difficulty in the darkness. They knew that there were before and would again be people who attract those who seek food by the promise of more abundant pastures of wisdom and knowledge and that many people would come to those pastures because stolen waters are sweeter and hidden bread more delightful.[9] Therefore, in case the Church should be deceived and wander after the flocks of the companions who are themselves wanderers and unsettled with no certainty of truth, who are always learning[10] but never arriving at the knowledge of truth, they proposed that only what is necessary and very useful for salvation be clearly and plainly explained in the Roman Catechism and communicated to the faithful.

5. But even though this book, composed with remarkable work and effort, was universally approved and welcomed with the highest praises, at that time, the love of novelty almost wrested it from the priests' hands by inspiring the production of more and more catechisms which could compare in no way with the Roman Catechism. Thus two evils arose. Agreement on a method of teaching was almost destroyed, and the weak members of the faithful were scandalized at finding that they were no longer united by the same language and topics. On the other hand, contentions arose from different ways of transmitting Catholic truth and disunity of spirit and great disagreements from rivalry while one declared he was a follower of Apollo, another of Cephas, and another of Paul. We think that nothing can be more fatal to God's greater glory than the bitterness of those disagreements. Nothing can eliminate more disastrously the fruits which the faithful should gain from Christian discipline.

Reissue of the Roman Catechism

Thus, in order to remove the double evil from the Church, We must return to that method from which some, setting themselves up in the Church as wiser, have insolently and imprudently led the faithful away for some time. We think that the Roman Catechism should be offered to the priests again so that just as it once strengthened the Catholic faith and strengthened the minds of the faithful in the Church's teaching which is the pillar of truth,[12] it may now turn them away from new ideas which neither antiquity nor unanimity recommend. To make the book more easily accessible and to correct the errors which have occurred in course of production, We have ensured that the copy published by Our predecessor St. Pius V in accordance with the decree of the Council of Trent is reprinted in Rome with all care. The vernacular translation of it which was made and published by order of the same St. Pius will be reprinted very soon by Our order and will finally be published.

6. So since Our care and diligence are providing a very suitable aid to remove the deceptions of wicked ideas at this very difficult time for the Church and to spread and establish true and sound teaching, it is your duty to see to it that the faithful accept it. Because the popes wanted this book set before pastors almost as the norm of Catholic faith and Christian discipline in order that unanimity might exist also in the method of transmitting doctrine, We now strongly recommend it to you, venerable brothers. We strongly encourage you to order that everybody who has the care of souls should use it in instructing the faithful in the Catholic truth in order to preserve unity of learning, charity, and harmony of spirits. For it is your duty to be attentive to everybody's serenity. Finally, it is the bishop's duty to watch carefully that nobody breaks the bond of unity and creates schisms by proudly acting in his own interests.

Qualities of the Good Teacher

7. If those who ought to present and explain these books to the faithful are unsuitable teachers, they will prove useless or almost useless. Therefore, it is of the utmost importance that you choose for the office of communicating Christian teaching to the faithful not only men endowed with theological knowledge, but more importantly, men who manifest humility, enthusiasm for sanctifying souls, and charity. The totality of Christian practice does not consist in abundance of words nor in skill of debating nor in the search from praise and glory but in true and voluntary humility. There are those whom a greater wisdom raises up but also separates from the society of other people. The more they know, the more they dislike the virtue of harmony. Wisdom itself warns them with the word of God: "Have salt in yourselves and be at peace among us."[13] Thus it is necessary to have the salt of wisdom to preserve the love of neighbor and to offset weaknesses. If they turn from zeal for wisdom and from concern for their neighbor to disagreement, they have salt without peace—not a gift of virtue but a cause for condemnation. The more they know, the worse they fail. The Apostle James condemns them with these words: "If you are jealous and have contentions in your hearts, do not boast and be liars against the truth. This wisdom did not come down from on high. Rather, it is earthly, animal, diabolical. Inconstancy and every wicked deed accompany jealousy and contention. The wisdom which comes from on high is first of all pure. Then it is peaceful, modest, persuasive, agreeable to good things, full of mercy and good fruits. It does not judge and is without rivalry."[14]

8. Therefore, while We pray to God in affliction of spirit and in humility of heart to bestow his indulgence and mercy on our efforts to prevent disagreement disturbing the faithful, and to ensure that in the bond of peace and in charity of spirit, we all know, praise, and glorify the one God and our Lord Jesus Christ, We greet you with a holy kiss and We lovingly impart Our apostolic blessing to all of you and to all the faithful of your churches.

Given at Castel Gandolfo on the 14th day of June, 1761, the third year of Our Pontificate.

†

LATIN TEXT: *Bull. Rom. Cont.* 4^1: 522-25.

ENGLISH TRANSLATION: Norman Desmarais.

REFERENCES:

1. Heb 3.
2. 2 Tm 1.14.
3. Ibid., 3.1.
4. Ibid., 3.13.
5. Ex 19.12.
6. Rom 12.3.
7. Mt 10.27.
8. Ct 1.7.
9. Prv 9.17.
10. 2 Tm 3.7.
11. Gn 11.1.
12. 1 Tm 3.15.
13. Mk 9.49.
14. Jas 4.

CHRISTIANAE REIPUBLICAE

ENCYCLICAL OF POPE CLEMENT XIII ON THE DANGERS OF ANTI-CHRISTIAN WRITINGS

NOVEMBER 25, 1766

18

To Our Venerable Brothers, all Patriarchs, Primates, Metropolitans, Archbishops, and Bishops Who Enjoy Grace and Communion with the Apostolic See.

Venerable Brothers, Greetings and Apostolic Blessing.

The well-being of the Christian community which has been entrusted to Us by the Prince of shepherds and the Guardian of souls requires Us to see to it that the unaccustomed and offensive licentiousness of books which has emerged from hiding to cause ruin and desolation does not become more destructive as it triumphantly spreads abroad. The distortion of this hateful error and the boldness of the enemy has so increased, especially at this time, in sowing weeds among the wheat either in word or in writing that unless We lay the scythe to the root and bind up the bad plants in bundles to burn, it will not be long before the growing thorns of evil attempt to choke the seedlings of the Lord Sabaoth. For accursed men who have given themselves over to myths and who do not uphold the stronghold of Sion from all sides vomit the poison of serpents from their hearts for the ruin of the Christian people by the contagious plague of books which almost overwhelms us. They pollute the pure waters of belief and destroy the foundations of religion.

Contents of Bad Books

They are abominable in their activity. Secretly sitting in ambush, they draw arrows out of the quiver which they shoot at the righteous in the dark. They have not restrained their impious minds from anything divine, holy, and consecrated by the oldest religion of all time; rather in their attack they have sharpened their tongues like a sword. They have run first of all against God in their pride. Armed with a thick neck, they have strengthened themselves against the Almighty. They raise again from the ashes the absurdities of the impious which have been destroyed so often. They deny God even though He makes Himself known everywhere and comes before their eyes daily, not because of the dullness of their mind, but only on the urging of their depraved will. Or else they represent God Himself as lazy and indolent. They do not respect His providence nor do they fear His justice. They preach with a detestable and insane freedom of thought that the origin and nature of our soul is mortal although it was created in the image of the supreme creator little lower than the angels. Whether they think matter has been created or foolishly imagine that it is eternal and independent of the causes, they consider that nothing else exists in this universe. Or else if they are forced to admit that spirit exists with matter, they exclude the soul from the spirit's heavenly nature. They are unwilling to understand that in this very weakness of which we are formed something spititual and incorruptible abides in us. By its power we know, act, will, look to the future, attend to the present, and remember the past.

Presumptuous Theologians

On the other hand, there are others who, even if they judge correctly that the fog of earthly reasonings should be dispelled and the smoke of worldly wisdom should be driven from the eye of enlightened faith, still dare to examine with human measures the hidden mysteries of faith which surpass all understanding. Having become investigators of greatness, they are not afraid of being overwhelmed by its glory. They ridicule the faith of simple people. They lay open the mysteries of God. They rashly discourse on questions concerning the highest matters. The bold mind of the enquirer takes everything for itself, examines everything, reserves nothing for faith, and deprives faith of merit by seeking proof for it in human reason.

Immoral Literature

Should we not also be angry with those who use the most wicked indecency of word and example to corrupt pure and strict morals by mortal sin, who recommend to the minds of the unwary an accursed license of living, and who cause an extreme loss of faith? Then consider how they sprinkle their writings with a certain refined splendor, a seductive pleasantness of speech and allurement so as to penetrate more easily into the readers' minds and infect them more deeply with the poison of their error. Thus they will give the snake's poison in the cup of Babylon to the unwary who are seduced and blinded by their smooth speech and so do not recognize the poison that kills them. Finally, who can avoid deep sadness when he sees the bitter enemy exceed the bounds of modesty and due respect and attack with the publication of outrageous books now in open battle, now in dissimulated combat the very See of Peter which the strong redeemer of Jacob has placed as an iron column and as a bronze wall against the leaders of darkness. Perhaps they are led on by the desperate thought that if they shatter the head of the Church, they will be able more freely to tear to pieces its members.

Bishops' Duty to Destroy Bad Books

2. Therefore since the Holy Spirit has made you bishops to govern the Church of God and has taught you concerning the unique sacrament of human salvation, We cannot neglect our duty in the face of these evil books. We must arouse the enthusiasm of your devotion so that you, who are called to share in Our pastoral concern join together to oppose this evil with all energy possible. It is necessary to fight bitterly, as the situation requires, and to eradicate with all our strength the deadly destruction caused by such books. The substance of the error will never be removed unless the criminal elements of wickedness burn in the fire and perish. Since you have been constituted stewards of the mysteries of God and armed with His strength to destroy their defenses, exert yourselves to keep the sheep entrusted to you and redeemed by the blood of Christ at a safe distance from these poisoned pastures. For if it is necessary to avoid the company of evildoers because their words encourage impiety and their speech acts like a cancer, what desolation the plague of their books can cause! Well and cunningly written these books are always with us and forever within our reach. They travel with us, stay at home with us, and enter bedrooms which would be shut to their evil and deception.

Aid for Catholic Rulers

Since you have been constituted ministers of Christ for the nations, in order to make holy his Gospel, exert yourselves and do everything in your power both by word and example to cut down the shoots of falsehood. Block up the corrupt springs of vice. Sound the trumpet in case as their leader you have to account for the souls who are lost. Act according to the position you hold, according to the rank with which you are vested, and according to the authority which you have received from the Lord. In addition, as nobody could or should avoid sharing in this sadness and insofar as there is one common reason for everyone to grieve and to help in this great crisis of faith and religion, call to your aid when it is necessary the time-honored piety of Catholic leaders. Explain the cause of the Church's sorrow and arouse its beloved sons who have always served it well on many occasions to bring their help. Since they do not carry the sword without cause, urge them with the united authority of state and of priesthood, to vigorously rout those accursed men who fight against the armies of Israel.

It is principally your duty to stand as a wall so that no foundation can be laid other than the one that is already laid. Watch over the most holy deposit of faith to whose protection you committed yourselves on oath at your solemn consecration. Reveal to the faithful the wolves which are demolishing the Lord's vineyard. They should be warned not to allow themselves to be ensnared by the splendid writing of certain authors in order to halt the diffusion of error by cunning and wicked men. In a word, they should detest books which contain elements shocking to the reader; which are contrary to faith, religion, and good morals; and which lack an atmosphere of Christian virtue. We manifest to you Our great happiness in this matter that most of you, following the apostolic customs and energetically defending the laws of the Church, have shown yourselves zealous and watchful in order to avert this pestilence and have not allowed the simple people to sleep soundly with serpents.

Certainly We who are distressed and distracted by Our concern for all the churches and for the salvation of the Christian people, are unsparing of Our efforts, and We promise you assistance too in your own grave danger. Meanwhile, We will not cease to ask God with deep humility to grant you help from His holy place to deflect the cunning of the insidious enemy and to entirely fulfill the duties of your ministry. As a pledge of the desired outcome, we lovingly impart Our apostolic blessing to you and your flock.

Given in Rome in St. Mary Major's on the 25th day of November in the year 1766, the ninth year of Our pontificate.

†

LATIN TEXT: *Bull. Rom. Cont.* 4^2: 1119-21.

ENGLISH TRANSLATION: Norman Desmarais.

SUMMA QUAE

ENCYCLICAL OF POPE CLEMENT XIII ON
THE CHURCH IN POLAND
JANUARY 6, 1768
19

To Our Venerable Brothers, the Archbishops, and Bishops of the Kingdom of Poland.

Venerable Brothers, Greeting and the Apostolic Blessing.

We are greatly concerned with the protection of the entire Christian flock and with the needs of Our brothers who tend it; we feel we must either instruct or exhort and admonish them. Indeed, We have often done this with you, Venerable Brothers, especially after We foresaw the storms arising which sought to undermine religion in your country. The well-being of religion in Poland is the result of the outstanding defense of your people on behalf of it.

2. However, the calamity which We feared is now upon us and has weighed more heavily on Our mind than usual; therefore, We are moved with a more intense zeal for your nation. Our concern for your will-being requires fuller and more vehement expression in order to rekindle the heavenly grace with which you were endowed from on high at your episcopal consecration. This is particularly important since God now seeks and even demands from you the due and necessary fruits of His gifts.

3. With extreme distress We have learned that impious compacts have been entered into in your country. This is because truth is put together with falsehood, and the splendor of light with squalor and darkness. Because of this, your faithful people might be easily drawn to destruction by the conjunction of dissimilar things. The abomination of desolation might even be brought into the holy place. Truly Our spiritual anguish would significantly increase if in so great a disturbance of affairs, the voices of the bishops were to be silent, and if We were to see none of them distinguish himself in calling back from contagion the minds of the people and confirming them in the doctrinal truth. All the more so, if anyone, acting out of fear or a base desire to please men more than God, should pervert and thus suppress the dignity and authority given to each of you for the defense and embellishment of the Church.

4. We cannot believe that lips once consecrated to preaching the divine word would lack the force and ability to put the lie to flight when it dares to demand for itself a place of victory in the very temple of God; that hands ennobled by handling the body of Christ would be employed in writing for the propagation of the rashness and license of error; that ears accustomed only to the most sweet voice of the Church would harken to the delusions and snares of the devil. Nevertheless, We have seen the machinations of the

enemy of human nature progress so far that practically everything must be feared.

5. We hope that no one would allow himself to be so carried away by error and fraud that, because he recognizes himself to be incapable of warding off overwhelming attacks, he would thereby believe himself also freed from the laws of his pastoral office; that having abandoned the role imposed on him by the Church, while retaining that other given by the state and public authority, he would willingly consent to the losses inflicted on him. That would indicate that these twin features of his function could be separated and disjoined, and that he should not constantly reckon the former preferable to the latter.

6. Wherefore, in the name of almighty God, whose vicarious authority We, however unworthy, bear, We declare to you that he who allows himself to be drawn into this deceit and error is totally blind and permits himself to be led by the blind. Furthermore he cannot be excused by any of the pretexts he employs. By neglecting his episcopal office, he has been condemned by God in the words of the prophet Hosea (4.6-10): "Because you have rejected knowledge, I reject you from being a priest to me, and since you have forgotten the law of your God, I will also forget your children." Wherefore, Venerable Brothers, do not let ignorance, error, fear, or human considerations prevent you from zealously carrying out your episcopal duties. The powers and forces of this world may gather violently for the destruction of the Church; nevertheless, the actions and plans of holy pastors must conform to the gospel, tradition and ecclesiastical discipline.

7. Let them realize that the first role of their ministry is to act as a firm wall of defense for the house of Israel against all hostile attacks. Let them consider themselves as deserters of their flocks, the Church and God if they aid the wiles of the enemy or in any way consent to their deceits by connivance or forbearance. Great calamities may threaten; exile and the loss of goods, fortune, and even life itself may ensue. Let them bear all this with equanimity as long as they do not soil their priestly hands by consenting to another's crime. Nor should their actions in any way weaken the integrity of religion and contaminate the sanctuary itself. Surely he will be considered most blessed who because of the constancy of his resolve is able to exchange the brief and fleeting condition of this life for an infinite and eternal reward. He would then be found worthy to receive that incorruptible crown which we believe is prepared by that best of Shepherds for those who have laid down their lives for the sheep entrusted to them.

8. These, Venerable Brothers, are Our words of warning for you in a most serious matter that is most necessary for your own salvation and that of your flock. May Our Lord Jesus Christ, by the assistance of His grace, confirm and strengthen in you those sentiments which are consonant with your vocation. May He likewise grant to you the eager willingness and fortitude to live up to it. In imploring the richness of these divine gifts for you, We grant you most lovingly the apostolic blessing as a presage of the same.

Given in Rome, at St. Mary Major under the Fisherman's ring, 6 January 1768, in the 10th year of Our pontificate.

†

LATIN TEXT: *Bull. Rom. Cont.*, 4^2: 1391-93.

ENGLISH TRANSLATION: Robert F. Healey, S.J.

POPE CLEMENT XIV
1769-1774

Giovanni Vincenzo Antonio Ganganelli, son of a surgeon, was born on October 31, 1705 at Sant'Arcangelo near Rimini. He studied with the Jesuits at Rimini and the Piarists at Urbino, but in 1723 entered the novitiate of the Conventual Franciscans at Mondaino taking Lorenzo as his religious name. Solemnly professed in 1724, he completed his studies at the College of St. Bonaventure in Rome and received a doctorate in theology in 1731. After several years of teaching philosophy and theology at convents in Ascoli, Milan, and Bologna he was appointed rector at St. Bonaventure's (1740).

His theological defense, published in Milan in 1743, was dedicated to St. Ignatius Loyola and included a foreword of praise for the Society of Jesus. Named a consultor of the Holy Office in 1746, he was created a cardinal in 1759. Ten years later he was elected pope after a turbulent conclave strongly influenced by the Bourbon courts who refused to recognize any pope who was not prepared to suppress the Jesuits.

Like the conclave that had elected him, his entire pontificate was dominated by the question of the suppression of the Society of Jesus. The chief aim of his pontificate seemed to be to preserve peace with the Catholic powers of Europe in order to gain support for the Church. Clement tried to conciliate the courts of Europe by taking specific measures against the Jesuits, but the Bourbon pact was relentless in settling for nothing less than total suppression. Finally persuaded that the Society would prove to be a hindrance rather than an advantage to the progress of the Church, Clement yielded to the pressure and signed the brief of suppression on June 9, 1773. The brief, *Dominus ac Redemptor*, dated July 21, was promulgated on August 16, 1773 at the Gesu in Rome disappointing the anti-Jesuitical factions that it was not a more formal bull.

The consequences of the *suppressio et extinctio Societatis Jesu* were not what Clement had hoped for. Frederick II of Prussia and Catherine II of Russia prevented the brief from being promulgated in their territories. The secular authorities continued to interfere with ecclesiastical affairs, and hostilities arose in many quarters. The advocates of Gallicanism, Jansenism, Febronianism, and Rationalism still struggled against papal authority. Clement himself found little favor with the Roman patricians or the College of Cardinals because of his treatment of them. He was criticized by the citizens for spending so much money on the museums.

He did, however, suspend the annual promulgation of the bull *In coena Domini* which contained the censures reserved to the Holy See although he did not, as he had hoped, revise or adapt it to contemporary needs. He received the Patriarch of the Nestorians and six of his bishops into reunion with Rome (1771), and brought new hope for Catholic emancipation in England. He patronized the arts by commissioning Raphael Mengs to decorate the Vatican Museum, acquired antiquities for the Museo Clementino, increased the papal coin collection, and decorated the fourteen-year old prodigy Mozart with the order of the Golden Spur (1770).

In the end Clement lost the cooperation of those who surrounded him by his desire to do everything on his own and as secretly as possible. His lack of will power and his timidity made him more and more unpredictable. Weighed down by worry and the realization that the people of Rome were hopelessly alienated, he spent the last fourteen months of his life depressed, fearful, and in seclusion. He died on September 22, 1774.

DECET QUAM MAXIME

ENCYCLICAL OF POPE CLEMENT XIV ON ABUSES
IN TAXES AND BENEFICES
SEPTEMBER 21, 1769
20

To the Bishops of Sardinia.

Venerable Brethren, Greetings and Apostolic Blessing.

It is altogether befitting for the ministers of the Church and the dispensers of divine mysteries to be exempt from any suspicion, however light, of avarice; then they can be free to exercise their sacred ministry in such a way that they can justly glory that their hands have acted free of any reward. In fact Christ ordered this when He sent His disciples to preach the gospel with the words,"Freely give what you have freely received" (Mt 18.8). Paul also stated (1 Tm 3.8; Ti 1.7) that this should be required of those chosen for the ministry of the altar. This, finally, Peter inculcated in those in charge of the care of souls, saying, "Be shepherds of the flock of God entrusted to you, watching over it not for sordid gain, but freely" (1 Pt 5.2).

Pastors of the Church, who ought to be an example to the faithful, must diligently observe this divine command and thus show themselves irreprehensible; they must also be vigilant so as not to permit the lower ministers over whom they have charge to perpetrate anything to the contrary. They should always remember that noble sentiment of Ambrose (Commentary on Lk 4.52), "Nevertheless, it is not sufficient if you yourselves do not seek profit: the hands of your household must also be restrained. Therefore instruct your household, exhort and watch over it: and if your servant deceive you, let him be repudiated, if apprehended, as scripture instructs."

Accordingly, both the holy councils and previous Roman Pontiffs have repeatedly advocated that every possible avenue be closed so that such evil abuses never creep into the Church of God, or if, by chance, they had already done so, they be totally eradicated from its midst. It is lamentable that these sanctions have either lacked effect in some dioceses or been insufficiently strong or valid enough to root out totally all contrary usages. And We know that this has come about because those whose duty it was to carry them out most strictly have put forward various excuses, such as ancient and inveterate custom or the need of bestowing some reward on the ministers of ecclesiastical curias or the necessity of making up for the lack of the means of support required for a proper and decent manner of living in keeping with one's state.

Because he understood all this properly, Innocent XI, desiring to invalidate any excuses whatsoever, in 1678 ordered that everything pertinent to the matter be collected from the sacred

canons, the Council of Trent, the interpretations given by the congregations of this Council, and proposals from consultations with bishops. Furthermore he ordered that an explicit determination and mention by name be made of all ecclesiastical affairs for which the reception of any payment on the part of ecclesiastical courts and episcopal curias was forbidden. The sole exception concerned what ought to go to the Chancellor alone as a proper remuneration or as a necessary payment. The same document also provided that in these matters the same procedure and uniform discipline be observed in all ecclesiastical curias; any custom to the contrary should be completely repudiated. Innocent XI approved and confirmed this on October first of the same year and ordered its promulgation and observance.

Nevertheless, not even this was enough to restore the univeral collapse of ecclesiastical discipline or to curb depraved customs rooted in various dioceses. One objection was that the aforesaid did not impose a law to be observed in ecclesiastical curias outside of Italy as well. Nonetheless the decrees contained in it were taken from sacred canons and principally from the Council of Trent, which all ecclesiastical curias must obey.

2. Accordingly, with sorrow We have learned that many abuses in the exercise of spiritual power (which not only totally destroy ecclesiastical discipline, but also enfeeble and bring the greatest shame upon your dignity and power) still exist in your ecclesiastical curias. To be sure your piety, your holy mode of life, your solicitude for your churches is more than sufficiently known to Us. We also know that these abuses have been introduced in the past, first from some secondary ministry or other, and have been gradually spread from diocese to diocese, perhaps without the knowledge of bishops. In certain places the greater dignity of a particular church has even led to the increase of such abuses. Some ministers, whose successors in office or ministry paid little attention and incautiously followed the footsteps of their own predecessors, deemed these long standing and customary abuses worthy of being proposed for approval by synodal constitutions. Accordingly, you can in no way be blamed; rather you are worthy of commendation because, as We have learned, you are grieved by these abuses and wish to extirpate them.

We, however, perceiving how much you will be detested for this and how great the obstacles will be unless the Apostolic Authority assists you in this enterprise, accordingly make this intervention. We do this especially because of the diversity of the fees and the varying practices in different dioceses. As a result of Our intervention, We anticipate conformity among all dioceses. Wherefore We are confident that you will faithfully carry out Our decrees which were requested by Charles Emmanuel, the illustrious king of Sardinia. We are also confident that you will see to it that they are diligently observed by all to whom they pertain.

Remuneration for Ordinations

3. First, as far as concerns holy orders, you can hardly be ignorant of the practically innumerable laws of the Church which forbid bishops and others ordaining or any officials to receive anything from conferring orders. This was most clearly forbidden by the Ecumenical Council of Chalcedon in 451 (canon 2), by the Roman Synod held under St. Gregory the great in 600 or 604 (canon 5) and elsewhere in his *Epistles* (bk. 4, epistle 44, indictment 13), by the Second Ecumenical Council of Nicaea in 787 (canon 5), by that of Pavia in 1022 (canon 3), by the Fourth Lateran Council under Innocent III in 1215, as well as by the councils of Tours, Braga and Barcelona, among others (collected by Christian Wolf in *dissert. 2 proem. de simonia*, chap. 9, tome 4 and by Gonzales in chapter *Antequam* I *de simonia*, no. 9), and, most recently, by the Council of Trent (session 21, chap. 1 on reform) which emended the ancient canons allowing a spontaneous offering to be accepted and restored ecclesiastical discipline concerning ordination to its pristine and ancient purity.

Decree of Council of Trent

The decree of the Council is as follows: "Since all suspicion of avarice must be absent from ecclesiastical ordinations, the bishops or other conferrers of orders or their ministers may not accept anything for the conferring of any order whatsoever, even ecclesiastical tonsure, or for dimissorial letters and testimonials, or for the seal or anything else, even if spontaneously offered, under any pretext whatever. Where the commendable custom of not accepting anything is not prevalent, notaries may receive one tenth of an aureus for dimissorial or testimonial letters, but only when no salary is provided for their office. The bishop, however, may not receive, directly or indirectly, any remuneration from that given to the notary for these letters. Ordaining bishops and their ministers are to offer their services freely. All contrary decrees and customs, which are rightly called abuses and simoniacal corruptions, are rendered null and void. Those acting to the contrary, both those giving and those receiving shall *ipso facto* incur, in addition to divine retribution, the punishments inflicted by law."

4. Therefore We instruct and order you not to accept anything, even when offered spontaneously, for the bestowing of any orders whatsoever, even for clerical tonsure, for dimissorial or testimonial letters, for the seal, or for any other reason. The single exception is the offering of a wax candle, which is the custom of the Roman pontifical. The quality of the candle and its weight must be left completely up to the judgment and free will of those who are being ordained. Likewise your vicar generals will observe the same sanction as well as vicars forane, chancellors, other ministers, associates, and members of your retinue whom the Council of Trent forbids to receive or demand under any title any emolument, reward, or gift on the occasion of sacred ordinations.

5. However, in those dioceses where no stipend or salary is provided for the chancellor or notary of the ecclesiastical curia for the carrying out of their office, We grant them permission, in the case of an order already conferred, to be able to exact for each dimissorial letter the tenth part only of a single aureus or ten obols of Roman coinage. They may receive the same in cases of clerical tonsure, its dimissorial letters, and ordinations to be received from a bishop who comes from outside the diocese. They may not receive remuneration from an order priest bound by vows of strict poverty and not having the use of money. When the above-mentioned testimonial or dimissorial letters refer to several orders already conferred or to be conferred by an outside bishop, the same scale of remuneration must be observed: it is by no means permitted to increase or multiply the stipend of ten obols in proportion to the number of individual orders contained in the same letters. By this, however, it is not Our mind to oblige the chancellor or notary to be required to describe simultaneously different orders conferred at different times and at different ordinations in the same testimonial letters; this We order to take place only when it is a question of those orders, viz. minor orders, which were conferred at one and the same ordination. As for dimissorial letters which are given for several orders to be received from an outside bishop, We forbid that their texts be multiplied or anything else be demanded for requesting the conferral of the orders or for access to the place of ordination or under any other title of gift or reward.

Decet quam maxime *20*

6. Moreover, regarding the order of the subdiaconate, there may be greater labor on the part of the chancellor or the notaries to establish the veracity and propriety of the titles of patrimony or benefice under which each one wishes to be promoted. For this labor as well as for the other acts which must precede the conferring of the said order, We grant them the right to receive some remuneration congruent with their labor. This is to be estimated by the bishop according to his judgment and conscience, which is to be weighty, provided that the stipend for the inscription, seal and all other things does not exceed one aureus or sixteen and a half julios. Those who are to be promoted to orders, or their parents, to be free to use any notary legitimately approved for the composing of such decrees without being compelled to appear before the aforesaid curias together with the necessary witnesses for the establishment and stipulation of the patrimony and for the other required acts. The notary of the curia to whom the decree is given, may accept remuneration from the bishop as described above or the sum of one aureus or sixteen and one-half julios, either for registering it or for any other labor. However, he under no pretext can ask for or receive anything for the publication of the decree or for letters of publication. This is explicitly stated in the decree of the Council of Trent cited above; it is clearly affirmed by the Sacred Congregation of the Council in the case of the diocese of Vicenza, 7 February 1602 and by the sacred Synod of bishops in the case of the diocese of Gerona, 25 October 1588 (to be found in Fagnani in his chapter on ordination and simony, number 32ff.).

7. There are always two conditions to be observed when notaries and the chancellor receive remuneration: first, they must not be receiving a stipend or salary for exercising their office; secondly, no part of the remuneration may go to the bishop, to any other conferrer of orders, or to any official or minister, as has been declared by the same Council of Trent.

8. In some curias there is the custom whereby the bishop or the vicar general demands money before permission is granted for recently ordained priests to celebrate their first Mass. Money is also requested from priests, coming from another diocese with commendatory letters from their respective bishops, before they are allowed to carry out divine services. We can hardly conceive of such base practices as being free from the suspicion of shameful profit and avarice. This custom, although introduced and preserved under the title of a stipend or remuneration given to the one who examines the priests regarding their knowledge of sacred rites and ceremonies, must, nevertheless, be totally eliminated. It is alien to the sacred canons and has been frequently repudiated.

9. What We have said up to this point concerning holy ordinations can be equally applied to the conferral or provision of ecclesiastical benefices. This is evident if you read the canons of the Church which have been drawn up to eradicate completely abuses springing up in this matter at various times (cf. chapter *si quis* q. 3, chapter *non satis* 8, chapter *cum in ecclesia* 9, chapter Jacobus 44 *de simonia* and elsewhere in Christian Wolf in his cited dissertation *de simonia* chapter 10). And although nothing was specifically decreed by the Council of Trent, nevertheless the Sacred Congregation of the Council, with the approval of the Supreme Pontiff Gregory XIII, declared that the decree (chapter 1, session 21 *de ref.*) had force also in the conferring of benefices, especially those having the care of souls. It also declared that nothing could be accepted for the seal, notwithstanding any time-honored custom to the contrary (Garz. *de benef.* part. 8 chapter 1, numbers 76ff., Fagnan. chapter *In ordinando de simonia*, number 31, Gallemart. in chapter 1, session 21 *de reform.*). Hence this same Sacred Congregation, with the approval of the Supreme Pontiff, declared in a letter to the bishop of Molfetta, that bestowers of benefices, no matter what dignity they might possess, could neither accept nor demand anything for conferring or disposing of benefices. They are not allowed to accept or demand, whether directly or indirectly or under any title including that of annate, any portion of the fruits of such benefices, even from those offering or giving spontaneously. The notaries of those granting benefices and any other officials who receive a fixed salary from other sources should exactly observe the same norms. Those giving and receiving benefices who fail to follow these norms are considered bound by the penalties against simony given in the sacred canons and as having incurred these penalties *ipso facto*; notaries and other officials are suspended from their offices (Garz. *loc. cit.*).

10. We have called these matters to your attention, venerable brothers, so that you might know how greatly abhorrent to ecclesiastical discipline are the customs which exist here and there in your dioceses concerning the conferral of benefices and with what care you must strive to remove them totally. When you confer ecclesiastical benefices—those involving the care of souls, those which are residential, those which have no obligations, and those which are called revocable chaplaincies, establish and observe the rule that you neither demand nor receive anything under any pretext or title, even that of a gift, reward or voluntary offering, especially when approving or selecting the most worthy candidates for parochial churches or the possession of benefices. The same canonical sanctions apply to any other bestowers, vicars general, chancellors, relatives, friends and members of your households, all of whom are forbidden to receive anything.

11. From this general regulation are exempted only chancellors or notaries who, as We have indicated elsewhere in this letter, receive no stipend or salary for the exercise of their office. In this case the chancellor, if it is a question of benefices involving the care of souls, can exact ten obols for the edict or letter which publicly announces the availability of the benefice, five obols for each copy thereof, and five obols for posting them. If the announcement must be posted outside the city, he may receive a daily remuneration, determined by each diocese, for the expenses of the journey and its necessary arrangements. When a chancellor sends a letter bestowing a benefice which either involves the care of souls or entails no obligations, he may receive a suitable recompense for his labor according to the judgment of the bishop. This, however, may not exceed one aureus or ten julios of Roman coinage for the writing, the seal and other details, as has been frequently declared by the Sacred Congregation of the Council, especially on 15 January 1594 (Gallemart. *loc. cit.*) and in a letter to the bishop of Vicenze, 8 March 1602 (Fagnan.

loc. cit. n. 32) and by the Sacred Congregation of Bishops of 25 October 1588 (Fagnan. ibid. n. 25). And, finally, for inscribing the requisite documents for taking possession of these benefices, he may receive three julios if they are within the city, four julios if in the suburbs, and what each diocese determines for his daily expenses if they are elsewhere. If the benefice is located in a place where there is a chancellor or notary of the vicar forane, the person receiving the benefice may, without any constraint, choose to summon the chancellor of the episcopal curia for the act of taking possession. A notary may as a recompense accept only two julios from persons who, having been examined as applicants for a benefice, receive testimonial letters of approval and use them as proof of their suitability.

12. We are well aware that the chancellor or notary labors greatly in the selection of candidates for parish churches: he accepts testimony as to the qualities, merits, and good works of the applicants on behalf of the Church; he places in the record of the selection process the requirements to be exhibited by the applicants; he summarizes these requirements and makes several copies of the same for the bishop or the vicar general taking his place; he delivers to the individual examiners the material acquired so that they may make a judgment regarding the knowledge of the applicants, their way of life, and the other gifts necessary for them to administer a church. Moreover he draws up the moral questions proposed by the same examiners, counts their votes, proposes the act of selection, watches over the applicants for two and at times three days, and presides in person over the examination of the above-mentioned moral questions, etc. That some account should be taken of this labor We grant by way of indulgence, leaving it to the judgment and conscience of the bishop to determine a remuneration appropriate only to the labor involved.

13. There are certain benefices reserved to and conferred by the Holy See. There are also benefices involving the care of souls for which testimonial letters of approval are given to the Apostolic Dataria as well as notice of the selection of the candidates held according to the form of the Council of Trent. Finally there are those benefices without the care of souls, especially residential benefices, for which testimonial letters concerning the manner of life, morals and suitability of the applicants are likewise customarily offered to the same Apostolic Dataria. In all these cases let chancellors beware not to ask for any remuneration, reward or anything else, even if spontaneously offered, for these letters except two julios for the actual writing, the paper and the seal on the letter of suitability. They may also accept two julios for testimonial letters about the manner of life and moral qualities of the applicants.

Decet quam maxime 20

14. For the execution of the apostolic letters, when these are to be sent in the form which is called *gratiosa*, let neither the bishops nor other officials presume to claim for themselves the office of executors. It depends on the judgment and choice of those who have been given the benefices to elect an executor or notary for the act of taking possession of the benefice. There are two instances, however, when the chancellor might receive remuneration: when the chancellor is selected as the official for a person provided with a benefice; and when the apostolic letters, sent in the forum called *dignum*, are directed to the ordinary, his officialis or vicar, and are to be carried out by them. In both cases, if there is no one who legitimately contests the appointment so that there is only an executor, the chancellor may receive remuneration for copying the same apostolic letters, placing them in the record, and for carrying out properly the other customary duties. This payment, not to exceed a gold scutum or sixteen and a half julios, is to be determined in proportion to the task by the judgment and conscience of the bishop. The bishop or any other prelate, his vicar, officialis, friends, and household members, however, are absolutely forbidden to receive any remuneration, gift, or other offering. However, if someone contests the appointment so that a judicial process must be inaugurated, it is left to the serious judgment and conscience of the bishop to determine a recompense that conforms to the work undertaken by the notary or chancellor. In no case is any part of this payment to be given, either directly or indirectly, to the bishop or others mentioned above. Moreover, for the act of taking possession of the benefice, let the same provisions mentioned above be observed.

15. As for benefices which are given by way of patronage, if the fiscal promoter or the one receiving the benefice contests that it is not given by way of patronage but is freely conferred, everything is to be observed as determined above concerning benefices freely given when someone contests the appointment. Thus the chancellor may receive two julios for the edict against the contestor or contestors, ten obols for each copy of the edict, and one aureus or sixteen and a half julios for the letter of institution. For posting the same edict he may receive what was decreed in the case of benefices involving the care of souls. Should a dispute arise among the co-patrons or their representatives concerning not the right of patronage but its applicability, then let the case be considered as profane, and the emoluments may be exacted which correspond to the customary rates of each curia.

16. Likewise, We generally prohibit bishops, other prelates, their vicars and officiales from presuming to exact anything in the following cases: from removable chaplaincies; from establishing or erecting chaplaincy benefices, sodalities, and congregations; from establishing, blessing, consecrating, visiting, and approving churches or oratories in accord with apostolic or ordinary authority. The chancellor alone may receive a recompense befitting his labor as decided by the bishop, provided that it does not exceed sixteen and a half julios.

17. As for matrimony or espousals, We propose that you observe what the sacred canons (chapter *cum in ecclesia* 9, chapter *suam nobis* 29, *de simonia*), St. Gregory the Great (epistle to Januarius the bishop of Cagliari (book 4, indict. 12, epistle 27) and others to be found in the praiseworthy work of Christian Wolf (*in dissertat.* chapter 7) and most recently the Council of Trent (session 22, chapter 5, *de reformat. Matrimon.*) have decreed. Bishops, their vicars, and officials, members of their households, and ministers should freely offer their services in these matters. They shall not presume to exact any reward or compensation, even if freely offered, for any of the following: decrees concerning marriage dispensations received from the Holy See; their labor in examining witnesses for such dispensations; the reception of other testimony; the writing of testimonial letters as to a person's canonical or other freedom to marry; dispensing from the banns, required by the Council of Trent, to be announced during Mass on three consecutive feast days by the pastors of those to contract a marriage, granting permission to marry at home or elsewhere; allowing marriages to take place during inappropriate or forbidden times or before a priest other than the pastor. The same is true for any other act which must be performed. All this has been declared by the Sacred Congregation of the Council with the approval of the Supreme Pontiff, any contrary custom however ancient notwithstanding (Garz. *de benefic.* part. 8, chapter 1, number 102 and ff. and Fagnan, chapter *quoniam, ne praelati vices suas*, number 30).

18. The same is especially true where bishops are accustomed to grant pastors permission to proclaim banns of marriage in the church on three successive feast days or to be present at the celebration of the marriages when these pastors know there is no impediment. Such permission should be obtained gratis. Care should also be taken that any indiscriminate requirement that this permission be obtained before the celebration of marriage not render the contract of marriage more difficult and afford an occasion for great hardships. The Sacred Congregation of Bishops in its reply to the bishop of Gerona on 25 October 1585 took care to remedy both these evils (cf. Fagnan chapter *In ordinando de simonia*, n. 41). The canons and chapter of Gerona had inquired regarding a decree of the bishop wherein he forbade pastors to join spouses in marriage, even though the solemnities required by the Council of Trent had been fulfilled, unless these pastors had permission in writing, which was not to be given without the payment of one half julio. The same Congregation replied as follows: "If for some reasonable cause pastors are required, even when the solemnities of the same Council have been fulfilled, to have previous permission from the bishop before joining spouses in matrimony, this results from no law prescribed for the bishop. It is left to his conscience and authority, provided that the substance decreed by the same Council is observed regarding the solemnities. Likewise, although it is sometimes proper to require this of pastors in certain villages or cities, it should only be done for some urgent reason. For just as bishops should see to it that marriages take place with all the prescribed solemnities, so also they should take care that the contract of marriage not be rendered more difficult by adding new requirements without grave cause. If, however, permission is required, nothing whatsoever can be exacted for it even by the notary. If by chance ancient custom prescribes that something be offered gratis to the bishop as a sign of happiness, this does not seem entirely reprehensible."

19. Where the chancellor receives no set salary for exercising his office, he may receive as recompense for his labor and as a necessary stipend for his support some remuneration for the execution of apostolic letters for matrimonial dispensations. When the chancellor himself examines witnesses to establish the truth of what is contained in the petition, he may receive something proportionate to the number of witnesses and the gravity of his labor, but this should not exceed five julios. If, however, the testimony of the witnesses is examined by another, the chancellor may receive only two julios for the letter of delegation; he may receive absolutely nothing for the decree, seal or anything else. The chancellor may also receive two julios for testimonial letters regarding freedom to marry: this would recompense him for their writing, the paper and seal and everything else. He may also receive ten obols for each of the witnesses he examines regarding a person's freedom to marry and the lack of any canonical impediment. Ten obols may be given when he acknowledges testimonial letters of freedom to marry on behalf of those residing elsewhere, unless there is need to examine another witness to remove all possible doubt. The chancellor may also receive ten obols for any necessary examination in the disposition of witnesses.

20. To exact money or anything else in the dispensation of the sacraments has always seemed equally detestable. It is a practice proceeding from avarice and greed. Therefore the sacred canons have frequently denounced it as infected with simony and have taken care to repress it with proper punishments and ecclesiastical censures, as is clear from chapter 9 *cum in ecclesiae corpore*, chapter 42 *ad apostolicam, de simonia* and from several decrees of councils (cf. Christian Wolf *loc. cit.* chapters 7 and 8). Adhering faithfully to these principles the Sacred Congregation of the Council has at no time allowed the exacting of anything in the administration of the sacraments. For instance, when a doubt was proposed whether the pastor could receive the dish used for the administration of extreme unction, the same Congregation, in a letter to the bishop of Alba, 20 February 1723, replied: "Its reception is not to be permitted" (*Thes. resolut.* tome 2, page 280). Likewise, when the bishop of Vaison during the synod held in 1729 drew up an assessment to be observed in his diocese in which, among other things, the following directions concerning baptism were instituted: "The godfather or godmother shall supply at least one candle and a white cloth for the baptismal ceremony, unless they prefer to give five bronze coins for these and the recording of the act in the public baptismal record," the question was proposed: "Should the tax prescribed in the said synod be observed?" The congregation replied in a letter to the bishop of Vaison on 6 February 1734: "Emphatically no" (*Thes. resol.* tome 6, page 209).

Decet quam maxime 20

21. Among other things which are more frequently and bitterly denounced by the sacred canons and councils is the custom which once prevailed here and there of demanding money for the reception of chrism and holy oil. Bishops have vainly tried to excuse this practice under various names, e.g., a cathedraticum, an Easter offering, or an episcopal custom (chapter 8 *non satis*, chapter 16 *ea quae*, chapter 36 *in tantum, de simonia* and elsewhere in Christian Wolf, *loc. cit.*, chapter 7 *secundum sacramentum*). Accordingly, when the Patriarch of the Maronites at Antioch had been accustomed to receive a monetary offering during the distribution of the holy oils, although it was clear that the money was not given or received as payment for the oil but as an alms for the patriarch and as a support for the tasks incumbent on the patriarchal office and dignity, nevertheless to remove any suspicion of simony the aforesaid custom was rejected by the particular congregation to which the affairs of the Maronites belong, and Benedict XIV confirmed its decree (*constit. apostolica* 43, *Bullar.* tome 1).

22. We think that this is more than enough, venerable brethren, for you to understand your duty in the administration of the sacraments, for carrying it out perfectly, and for totally eradicating the improper practices prevailing in some dioceses whereby money is demanded by the bishop or the prefect of the sacristy in the distribution of holy oils. This practice has been frequently reprobated by the Sacred Congregation of the Council especially in a reply to the diocese of Amalfi, 18 July 1699, confirmed on 6 February 1700, to doubt 12, "Is the archbishop required tc demand that the holy oils be given gratis to the pastors of churches?" to which the Congregation replied "affirmatively." And the Sacred Congregation of Bishops held in Acerenza, 18 March 1706, prescribed the same

(Petras *Comment. ad constitut.* 5 *Innocentii IV* number 38).

23. As to the offering of a candle to the bishop administering confirmation, which We have heard takes place in some of your dioceses, it is evident that the pontifical ritual books do not mention this practice. Moreover, the sacred function of ministry compels all ministers to observe moderation in the reception of offerings and in their way of proceeding so that their ministry not be censured by giving the impression of avarice or greed for money with the result that the reverence due to so great a sacrament becomes thereby cheapened. Consequently great care must be taken lest there arise a suspicion that the candle is not freely offered but demanded. In the latter case the faithful, especially the poor, would refrain from receiving the sacrament or delay its reception longer than is proper. Therefore it is most desirable that this custom be totally removed or, at least, that it be observed in such a way that it depend completely on the free will of those making the offering.

24. The same laws, moreover, prescribe that bishops, their chancellors, and notaries ought to exercise their ministry gratis when, after previous examination and approbation, faculties are given to anyone for hearing sacramental confessions, for administering the sacraments, and for exercising ecclesiastical ministries. The same is true when they appoint suitable vicars whether permanent or removable, economic officials, and coadjutors. This is stated in *cap. ad nostrum de simonia* and is declared by the frequently cited reply to the diocese of Vicenza of 7 February and 8 March 1602 and by the reply to the diocese of Gerona, 25 October 1588, question 7, which repudiate any pretext otherwise, even that of recompense for drawing up letters permitting the exercise of these ministerial offices.

25. We judge that none of you can be ignorant of how it has been frequently and severely forbidden to demand money for funeral and burial services (cf. Christian Wolf, *loc. cit.* chapter 12 and Van-Espen. in *jus eccles. univ.* chapter 4, paragraph 2, title 38). Let it suffice to indicate what St. Gregory the Great wrote in his letter to Januarius, the bishop of Cagliari (book 9, indict. 2, epistle 3 and also book 7, indict. 2, epistle 56): "A most famous woman, Nereida, has complained to Us that your fraternity has not blushed to ask of her a hundred solidis for the burial of her daughter . . . If this is true, it is a very serious matter; it is far from the office of a priest to ask a price for ground allotted for decomposition and to desire profit from another's grief. We have forbidden this improper custom in Our church and We have never allowed this evil custom to take over . . . Wherefore, I reprove this vice of avarice; may no one presume to practice it elsewhere." Nevertheless, these laws have never condemned the laudable and pious custom, observed from the earliest days of the Church, of making an offering for the dead at funerals; nor have the clergy ever been forbidden to receive them. Accordingly, Gregory (*loc. cit.*) immediately adds: "If, indeed, parents, relatives or heirs of such a one wish to spontaneously offer something for the lighting of candles, We do not forbid it being accepted. But to demand or ask for something We totally prohibit." Likewise, Innocent III made the same decision at the Lateran Council (chapter *ad Apostolicam* 42 *de simonia*).

26. To be sure, in the absence of personal tithes and with a decline in bequests of property or mixed goods to monasteries and chapters of canons, it was sometimes necessary to compel, as it were, the laity to offer pious oblations, which are now customary, so as to provide for the necessities of pastors and parish churches. Nevertheless, the sanctity of ecclesiastical discipline has always been considered, and caution has been taken lest there be aberrations with regard to these laudable customs on the part of clerics through excess or the laity by defect. Therefore, among other things, it was forbidden that funeral services and burials of citizens or foreigners be impeded or delayed for the sake of demanding emoluments introduced by pious custom. It was also forbidden that anything be demanded for permission to transfer the corpse or to bury it in one place rather than another.

27. Except for the traditional offering bestowed with a view to pious offices offered for the benefit of soul and body, nothing else is to be tolerated in your dioceses. The pastor may not receive anything, whether occasionally or habitually, with respect of the circumstances and various dignity of persons or in consideration of the prestige of the place of burial, whether in the church or in a more imposing place belonging to the church. It is also abhorent to the sacred canons that the bishop demand or receive any money for burying either an adult or a child in any diocesan church, even that of religious communities, as the Sacred Congregation of the Council declared against the bishop of Vicenza and as the holy synod of bishops maintained against the bishop of Gerona (Fagnan. in the chapter *In ordinando, de simonia* 10, numbers 32 ff.), notwithstanding any custom, however ancient, or any pretext, title, or claim to the contrary.

28. In the visitation of your dioceses do not even allow yourselves to be suspected of avarice or base gain. It should be obvious that you seek not your own good but that of Jesus Christ's when you carefully observe what the fathers of the Council of Trent enjoin in this regard: "Let (visitors) not be troublesome by useless or burdensome expenses. Neither they nor any of their staff are to accept any money or gift under any title even from bequests for pious purposes unless this is due by law, despite any custom to the contrary, no matter how long standing. They may receive only a frugal or modest sustenance for only necessities during the time of visitation. However, those being visited may decide whether to give what they were formerly accustomed to pay, that is a certain sum of money, or to provide the aforesaid sustenance" (session 24, chapter 3, *de ref.*).

29. The Sacred Congregation of the Council has issued various declarations and edicts on this decree. Some may be mentioned here. First, it has often been disputed whether the bishop can exact what are called "provisions" for visiting the cathedral or the clergy residing within the city or any other place where he usually resides. Some have observed that the statutes enacted by the Council of Trent applied only to the visitation of the diocese without any mention of the city. And sustenance, some argued, was to be given "for only necessities during the time of visitation," and such necessity surely does not seem to be present when the bishop visits places in which he is bound to reside or is accustomed to live at least some part of the year. The Sacred Congregation, however, decided that any traditional canons or customs to the contrary were abolished by the aforementioned decree of the Council of Trent. The same Congregation constantly replied negatively in the case of Castro on 17 November 1685, in the case of Amalfi on 18 July 1705, in the case of Policastro on 1 June 1737 and, most recently, in the case of Torre San Gennaro on 30 January 1768. The same was the opinion of the sacred synod of bishops, as is clear from the letter sent to the Patriarch of Venice on 26 May 1592.

30. The aforementioned decree of the Council of Trent, also agreeing with what is found in the chapter *Si episcopus de off. Ordinarii*, 6, expressly states that neither bishops nor any of their staff are to accept any money or gift under any title. They may receive only sustenance or, if those being visited prefer, money corresponding to this sustenance. And yet there were some who argued that they could receive sustenance in addition to money, or along with sustenance transportation by horse for themselves and their ministers, or something else under some title or pretext of a civic nature. These, however, have always lost their case in the Sacred Congregation of the Council which has constantly disapproved their manner of action as alien to the Council of Trent. In the case of the visitation of St. Mark the following two questions, among others, were asked: V. "Must the clergy pay anything to the ministers and other officials for the visitation of the bishop?" VI. "Must the same clergy pay for transportation by horse for a visiting bishop?" On 7 July 1708, the following prescript was sent: "Earlier decrees must be followed: as to Proposition V that issued to the bishop of Amalfi, 18 July 1699 (to Proposition III, *Decret.*, book 49, page 252); as to Proposition VI that issued to the bishop of Abruzzo, December 1784 (*Decret.*, book 4, page 10)." Consequently the response of the Congregation, according to the decrees it indicated, was: "To Proposition V, sustenance is owed only as determined by the Council; to Proposition VI, negative." In another case concerning St. Mark, the Congregation on 16 January 1723 replied to various questions. Question III: "Should the accustomed sum of money, reckoned according to the practice of the place to be visited, be paid for supplying provisions, and for providing three meals to the bishop and his retinue, and for providing transportation, habitation and other necessities?" Question IV: "Are food and other necessities to be provided for the bishop and his retinue throughout the whole visitation?" Replying to Question III, the Congregation stated: "It is the option of those being visited to provide either sustenance or money, but if money is paid the three meals are excluded; and as for transportation by horse, follow the decree of 7 July 1708 in the case of St. Mark, Proposition

Decet quam maxime
20

VI. Regarding Question IV, the answer is provided in III." Likewise, in the case of Policastro the same topic came up in question II: "Can the bishop demand from the archpriest and clerics XV ducats in money in addition to food and transportation on horseback for himself and his retinue?" The Congregation's response on 1 June 1737 was "No."

31. It was also disputed whether the bishop and his officials could demand for themselves some remuneration if in the course of the visitation they examine wills and legacies on behalf of pious causes and hand them over for execution. On this matter the Sacred Congregation of the Council declared in the case of the bishop of Mallorca, 7 August 1638, that the bishop and his officials may not receive a salary for decrees or decisions of execution of pious legacies in the course of the visitation, despite any longstanding customs to the contrary. A similar question arose in 1645 between the bishop of Vicenza and royal officials of the city of Manresa. This was brought to the same Congregation which responded on 18 March 1645: "The Congregation decided that bishops and their officials receive nothing in their visitation for decrees or judgments concerning the execution of wills or legacies, but that must all be done gratis, notwithstanding any ancient custom. Likewise outside the visitation by the bishop and his officials nothing can be received for such decrees and judgments, but a moderate sum may be paid to the notary for his writing and labor." The same response was given to Question VIII in the case of La Muga on 28 March 1648. It is not out of place to add here what was decreed by the fifth provincial council of Milan: "The notary or the chancellor may not exact anything during the visitation from those being visited nor accept any gift, however small or however offered. The same holds true for proclaiming decrees and orders during the visitation, for their writing and for making copies of them, whether for individuals, churches, clerics, or others who are visited after the decree of visitation has been published. He may, however, be recompensed, according to the assessment that has or will be determined by the episcopal curia, for the labor expended in making copies of such decrees and orders when later requested by an interested third party.

32. The same is to be observed when inspecting records of pious legacies and their satisfaction and when requisitioning accounts pertaining to the administration of churches, confraternities, pious monetary institutions and similar places. The bishop and all his officials are to carry out these tasks freely. This is clear from what has been said above and from the responses of the Sacred Congregation of the Council. On 27 June 1637 the Council declared in the case of the bishop of Vicenza: "Neither the bishop nor his officials can receive anything for examining accounts of the administration of pious works or for the execution of will or pious intentions but should carry out these tasks gratis, notwithstanding any custom to the contrary." In the case of the confraternity of Lanciano, the following question was proposed: "Should the archbishop for the revision of accounts employ syndics or accountants chosen by the confraternity or can he employ someone else who seems good to him?" On 20 September 1710 the Congregation replied: "No to the first part, yes to the second, but gratis" (*Thes. res.* tome 6, page 164). Although the bishop certainly ought to take care that these types of records be reviewed gratis and that an account be demanded by his own notary, the financial official of his household, or someone else in his service, it can sometimes happen that for a grave or urgent reason he ought to depute for the task some outsider who is in no way connected with the matter. As often as this happens, the bishop will conscientiously assign some remuneration, proportionate to the labor alone, for the reduction, as the Sacred Congregation stated in the case of the bishop of Veroli, 30 January 1682 (decret. f., book 35, page 283), in the case of Benevento, 7 June 1683, and in the case of Pisa, 11 December 1683.

33. Since the declarations of the Sacred Congregation are firmly based on the sacred canons, it is difficult to reconcile with the decrees of the Council of Trent the following rather corrupt customs of bishops and their officials: receiving during the visitation a remuneration for inspecting certain wills or for reviewing the accounts required from administrators of churches and pious places; receiving transportation on horseback or at least their provisions for the entire time of the visitation; or claiming as their own lamps or candles placed on the main and other altars of the church. Being contrary to the sacred canons, these and similar practices are to be completely eliminated.

34. Although the 18 March 1645 decree of

the Sacred Congregation of the Council in the case of Vicenza states that the bishop and his officials may never receive anything for decrees and judgments relative to the execution of wills and legacies, he may, nevertheless, during the visitation receive the portion due him from pious legacies and offerings and other things which come to the church on the occasion of a funeral. This is customarily called the fourth canonical part, and its acceptance was allowed by the same Congregation in responding to Question VIII in the case of the bishop of Urgel on 25 January 1676 and 14 February 1693. The bishop has this right from the sacred canons (chapter 14 *officii, et requisiti* 5, *de testamentis*). That the Council of Trent wished this right to remain in force is clear insofar as the Council severely prohibits bishops from receiving anything for the visitation even from testaments for pious uses "except that which is owed to them from pious bequests by law" (session 24, chapter 3, *de ref.*). In exacting this portion or canonical fourth, bishops must observe the correct limits as determined by the same holy canons (chapter *finali de testamentis*), which state: "The canonical portion. . . .ought not be deducted from what is bestowed to churches or other pious places for building, decoration, candles, anniversaries on the seventh, twentieth, or thirtieth days, or for perpetuating divine worship. Practically the same is found *in cap. ex parte de verb. signif.* Moreover nothing is deducted from a legacy providing a marriage dowry for girls, as the Sacred Congregation of Bishops responded in the case of Nocera, on 14 September 1592. Nor is anything taken from legacies for the celebration of Masses. The Sacred Congregation of the Council on 13 January 1714 in the case of Nocera declared this to be so (*quartae canonicae, decret.*, book 64) even though from time immemorial the same fourth was granted to bishops from all legacies.

35. As for convents of nuns or houses of pious women who live apart from the world in the manner of nuns, the apostolic constitutions and the Congregations both of Bishops and of Religious have decreed, with the approval of the Supreme Pontiffs, that bishops, prelates, vicar generals, special delegates, officials, as well as relatives and members of their households may not demand or receive remuneration of any kind for the following: admitting girls to the religious life; approving their dowries; examining their motive for entering an institute of religious life; receiving their profession; allowing girls to receive their education within a convent; assisting at their renunciation of goods before they are admitted to profession; presiding at the election of an abbess or other superior; granting permission for doctors, surgeons and other professional men to enter the convent; granting a person permission to address nuns or others living in the cloister; delegating confessors, chaplains, financial officials, administrators of temporal goods, and other ministers; and, in general, for any act necessary for nuns to pursue their way of life.

Decet quam maxime
20

36. An exception to this general rule is made for the sustenance required by the bishop or prelate on the occasion of some of these actions. And yet this may be provided only by way of recompense or donation, and it is not to exceed an amount sufficient for three days. The chancellor, however, may be recompensed for his labor in drawing up the documents of renunciation and in depositing the dowry, but this should never exceed ten julios.

37. In addition to the above, there are many more acts that should be utterly free from any remuneration. These pertain either to the exercise of spiritual power or to those episcopal functions for which the bishop, although permitted to receive his sustenance, may neither directly nor indirectly accept any remuneration under any pretext or title, even that of a gift or a spontaneous offering. The same applies to their vicars, officials, and household members. We shall specifically enumerate at least the most important of these. Drawn from the sacred canons, apostolic constitutions, and decrees of the sacred congregations, they are frequently mentioned by eminent authorities and are rather commonly known.

38. For granting letters patent, as they are called, or permission to preach in Lent and Advent and any other time and in any place (Council of Trent, session 5, chapter 2, *de reform.*).

For granting permission to perform servile works on feast days for a grave cause (Urban VIII in his constitution, *Universa*) several decrees of the sacred congregations of the council and the bishops (Ferrar. *verba festa*, numbers 31 ff.), although the money which is received from using this permission is to be converted to pious uses.

For reviewing administrative accounts of churches and pious places, and for the revision of these accounts whether done by the bishop, some general delegate or a delegate specifically chosen by the bishop, with the exception, however, indicated above.

For recognizing, approving, and promulgating relics, indulgences, and privileged altars.

For granting permission to seek alms or anything else, even if granted to those from outside the diocese.

For appointing church custodians and sacristans.

For granting testimonial letters of poverty or another state of life. The chancellor, however, may receive ten obols.

For granting testimonial letters which state that someone has not entered any order or received clerical tonsure. The chancellor may be offered ten obols only.

For the act of renunciation of the clerical state and its admission as well as for letters of attestation as to its renunciation. For these documents the chancellor can require ten obols.

For searching the episcopal archives to find parochial books listing baptisms, confirmations, weddings, and deaths. For each book the chancellor can require only twenty obols. The same may be asked for a letter attesting a particular record. It is, however, allowable to accept a larger remuneration depending on the dignity of the person requesting or whether the testimonial letters are to be used outside the diocese or kingdom.

It might happen, however, that the parochial records are unclear regarding the matter for which testimony is sought, and consequently it is necessary to obtain proof from witnesses. In this case the chancellor may not only receive the prescribed assessment for examining witnesses and for recording their testimony, but also another fifteen obols for writing the testimonial letters. The vicar general may receive thirty obols for the decrees ordering information to be sought and for ordering the letters testifying as to the information he received and evaluated.

For granting permission to relinquish churches or benefices (Council of Trent, session 23, chapter 1, *de ref.*). Likewise for commendatory letters required by priests, clerics or others moving to other dioceses.

For writing letters of warning of excommunication in cases where hidden matters have been made public, whether these letters are issued by the episcopal curia or by the ordinary of the place, or whether they come from the Holy See. The chancellor may receive ten obols for his labor in writing them. Likewise he alone will be given another sum, reckoned according to the conscience of the bishop, for making copies of these letters and for procuring the previous decree of the vicar.

For writing warnings, sentences, or declarations of censures received for striking a cleric or any other cause; also for the sentence of absolution and for the absolution itself from censures (chapter *ad aures de simonia*). The chancellor may exact twenty obols as recompense for their writing, provided that it is not a question of carrying out letters of the Sacred Apostolic Penitentiary; in this case the chancellor may not be recompensed. Twenty obols can also be paid to the chancellor for the list of censures commonly called a schedule and for the list of those censures which are customarily imposed. The same is observed when absolving from an oath but in the following manner: if the absolution is granted in the ecclesiastic curia, the chancellor may be paid twenty obols only for its attestation; when done outside the curia, he may receive the same fee only for the letters of delegation.

For granting permission to exercise pontifical rights.

For executing apostolic letters that impart blessings or absolutions, and for writing letters by which pastors or others are granted the faculty contained in the same apostolic letters, the chancellor may receive only thirty obols for both.

For executing apostolic letters or faculties granted by a congregation pertaining to the purchase, sale, or exchange of churches and pious places, or pertaining to a census, the chancellor may be remunerated according to his labor, but this is not to exceed ten julios. If the Holy See has requested the bishop to inquire into the truth of what is contained in the libellus of supplication, then the chancellor may receive ten obols for each witness examined. He may also receive something for drawing up edicts, for examining witnesses as to the usefulness of any sale, and for anything else in this matter. The sum, granted in accord with his labor, is to be determined by the conscientious judgment of the bishop.

For writing the decree of sale which by force of chapter 12, *terrulas*, question 2, only takes place with the authority of the ordinary.

39. Fines or monetary punishments, when imposed in proportion to the crime or the nature of the wrongdoer, must be expended only for pious purposes and the exactment of justice so that nothing can in any way accrue for the private gain of the bishop, his vicar, or any other official. So that all doubt or suspicion of improper use be removed, it may be well or even necessary that the sentences themselves designate the pious uses or the churches benefitting from aforementioned pecuniary punishments, although those most in need and the domicile of the offenders should always be kept in mind.

40. We must now add other things pertaining to the forum of settling disputes, so that ecclesiastical discipline in these matters too be restored to its pristine splendor and dignity. Deliberations must be characterized by a more mature judgment, and We are to be fully informed of the customs existing in dioceses. There is one thing, meanwhile, which We must impress upon you, namely, that ecclesiastics who pass sentence in spiritual matters should fulfill their task with such sanctity and piety that nothing obscures the candor of ecclesiastical purity. Therefore your ecclesiastical judges shall not demand or accept any remuneration, even for delivering sentences in spiritual cases and in those especially which have to do with religion, such as those against people suspected of heresy and found guilty of superstition, or which concern espousal, matrimony, censures and other such matters. In the words of Innocent III to the prelates and clerics of Lombardy (chapter *cum ab omni de vita et honestate clericorum*), "Realizing that there are revenues deputed for you and for other clerics so that you might live properly, you should not reach out to base gain or look for evil rewards. Your light should shine as an example to the laity and, unlike seculars, you should not seize the occasion of the law for evil commerce. Just as you abstain from these exactions in other respects and are eager to grant the force of the law to litigants, even when they are deceitful, so the same is demanded from those passing judgments, since not even judges are allowed to sell a just judgment and even secular laws reject sentences that can be bought."

41. In keeping with Our apostolic office and its obligations, We propose these things to you. If you rightly carry them out, they will aid the splendor of ecclesiastical discipline, the tranquillity of your consciences, and the best guidance of your flocks. We do not think that they will be burdensome and harmful to you, although they will somewhat reduce your customary emoluments. Even the least suspicion about you is absent in view of your exemplary piety, proven religious sentiments, and your zeal for preserving ecclesiastical discipline whereby what till now was gain for you will in the future be considered a loss for Christ. You will place your true gain in this alone, that the worship of God be ever increased, that the people committed to you be more easily and felicitously fed by your word and example.

Moreover, those versed in the ecclesiastical affairs of your island and especially those representing the king have informed Us that your accustomed revenues, except for those few which you are now forbidden to demand or receive, can provide for your episcopal dignity and will suffice for the necessities of your churches. So that you do not think that you have any support for these customs, even most ancient, upon which you have relied till now, you must be mindful of what Alexander III (chapter *cum in ecclesis, de simonia*) wrote as He upbraided those who unduly clung to their customs, "Many think that they may have permission since they believe that the law concerning the dead has force by reason of its age. Blinded by cupidity, they are not sufficiently aware that crimes are the more heinous the longer they shackle the spirit." We declare and teach that these customs, even though most ancient or supported by synodal constitutions and any other authority, even apostolic, are to be considered as abuses and corruptions. That you will in no way be wanting in zeal, diligence and industry on behalf of Our concern for your churches, is Our certain and most firm hope. Meanwhile, as a pledge of Our paternal love and benevolence for you, We grant you the apostolic blessing.

Given in Rome, at St. Mary Major, 21 September 1769, in the first year of Our Pontificate.

†

LATIN TEXT: *Bull. Rom. Cont.*, 5:46-60.

ENGLISH TRANSLATION: Robert F. Healey, S.J.

INSCRUTABILI DIVINAE SAPIENTIAE

ENCYCLICAL OF POPE CLEMENT XIV PROCLAIMING A UNIVERSAL JUBILEE

DECEMBER 12, 1769

21

To all the Faithful who read this Letter, Greetings and Apostolic Blessing.

Since We have been elevated to the Papacy by the inscrutable counsel of divine wisdom and goodness and by no merits of Our own, while acknowledging the gift of God, We also fear His judgment. And so, as often as We seriously contemplate the task entrusted to Us, We are frightened by its gravity. Our awareness of the weakness of Our own resources deeply disturbs Us. If We were not confident of His help, We could lose courage altogether. Therefore, We implore the help of all Christians in invoking God to strengthen Us, to fill Us with the knowledge of His will, and to pour into Us the spirit of wisdom and understanding, the spirit of knowledge and holiness, and the spirit of counsel and fortitude. Then in the midst of so many difficulties, We may come to know what must be done, and with Our eyes ever directed to Him, We may carry out profitably what is right. Let us beseech Him to watch over the chosen vineyard which He has planted and to foster with the gifts of His grace His people walking in the ways of His commandments in this earthly pilgrimage and happily bring them to the promised rewards of eternal life.

Plenary Indulgence

2. To achieve these goals, following the ancient custom of Our predecessors, We have decided to draw from the treasury of divine grace, whose disposal is entrusted to Our keeping, for the felicitous inauguration of Our Pontificate. Therefore, We grant and concede to each and all of the faithful of both sexes, wherever they may reside, a plenary indulgence if they fulfill the usual requirements. They must visit at least once churches designated by the Ordinaries of the places or their Vicars or Officiales or by their authority, or, where these are lacking, by those who exercise care of souls, after this Encyclical has come to their notice, or any church of such nature, which has been made the object of such visits. This must be done within the space of fifteen continuous days or two weeks after the publication of this designation by the Ordinaries or their Vicars or Officiales or others, as declared above, (which weeks, We greatly hope, may fall in the favorable time of Lent in the case of those to whom this Encyclical has arrived in time, and there shall have devoutly prayed to God for some period of time. They shall have fasted on Wednesday, Friday, and Saturday of either week and

shall have confessed their sins and reverently received Holy Communion on the Sunday immediately following or any day of the same week in either of the two weeks. Finally, they shall have given to the poor some alms, as each one's devotion suggests. Upon completion of these requirements, they receive a plenary indulgence and remission of all their sins, as is customarily conceded to those who visit certain churches within and without the city of Rome in Jubilee Years. Moreover, those making journeys by sea or by land may receive the same indulgence when they have returned to their homes after having performed the above mentioned actions and having visited the cathedral or principal or parish church of their domicile.

3. In the case of religious men and women, even those living in perpetual cloister, and others both laity and clergy whether in prison or restrained by some bodily infirmity or some other impediment, who cannot perform any or all of the above conditions, We grant that a confessor approved before or after the publication of this Encyclical may commute or postpone for a relative period of time their works of piety and enjoin other works as their penitents can perform.

4. Moreover, We grant to each and all of the faithful of both sexes both laity and clergy, whether secular or religious of any order, congregation or institute, the permission and authority to select for this purpose any priest as confessor, whether secular or regular of any order or institute, from those approved before or after the publication of this encyclical. This time only and in the forum of conscience he may absolve and free them from excommunication, interdict suspension and any other ecclesiastical sentence, censure and penalty either inflicted by law or personally imposed for whatever occasion or cause. Under the same conditions, He may also absolve them from all sins, excesses, crimes, and delicts, however grave or enormous, even those reserved in any way to the ordinary of the place or to Us and the Apostolic See or otherwise reserved through Our own or former papal constitutions, whose tenor We wish to be considered expressly. He may also commute any vows (except those having to do with religious life and chastity) to other pious and salutary works, having enjoined, however, in all the above cases, a salutary penance and other acts according to the decision of the same confessor.

5. In keeping with the intention of Our predecessors in proclaiming a Jubilee, however, We do not intend to dispense from any public or hidden irregularity, infamy, defect or incapacity or unsuitability, however contracted, or to grant the faculty of dispensing, making competent or restoring one to a former state, even in the forum of conscience. Nor do We intend that this encyclical be used in any way on behalf of those who have been excommunicated, suspended or interdicted by Us or any other prelate or ecclesiastical court, unless within the time of the Jubilee they have made satisfaction and been reconciled with the parties involved.

6. Notwithstanding anything to the contrary, on this particular occasion and for the purpose given above We repeal all things contrary to Our decree, even when special, specific, expressed, and individual mention is made explicitly and not merely through general clauses having the same meaning or where some other expression is used for this purpose, with the understanding that We have sufficiently understood their tenor and preserved their form. So may the holy apostles, Peter and Paul in whose power and authority We trust intercede for you all with the Lord.

7. Meanwhile may the almighty and merciful Lord grant you indulgence, absolution, and remission of all your sins, time for a true and fruitful repentance and emendation of life, the grace and consolation of the Holy Spirit, and final perseverance in good works. Trusting in His kindness and mercy We lovingly grant you Our apostolic blessing. We wish, moreover, that printed copies of this encyclical, signed by notary publics and attested by the seal of a person of ecclesiastical dignity in all places and nations, have the same authority as the encyclical letter itself.

Given in Rome at St. Mary Major under the fisherman's ring, 12 December 1769, in the 1st year of Our Pontificate.

†

LATIN TEXT: *Bull. Rom. Cont.*, 5:68-70.

ENGLISH TRANSLATION: Rober F. Healey, S.J.

CUM SUMMI

ENCYCLICAL OF POPE CLEMENT XIV PROCLAIMING A UNIVERSAL JUBILEE

DECEMBER 12, 1769

22

To Bishops, Archbishops, Patriarchs and Primates Concerning the Universal Jubilee.

Venerable Brothers, Greetings and Apostolic Blessing.

When We contemplate Our position and consider the gravity of its burden, We are deeply disturbed both because of the magnitude of the task itself and the weakness of Our resources. We seem to have been called into the depths of the sea from the peace of a quiet life as if from a most safe harbor to rule the bark of blessed Peter, to be shaken by great floods and to be all but submerged by the force of the tempest. Truly this is the Lord's doing, and it is marvelous in our eyes. It was not because of human counsel but rather by His inscrutable judgment that such a care had been unexpectedly laid upon Us. Therefore, we are buoyed up by a certain hope that He who has chosen Us will Himself remove Our fear and infirmity and will hear Us in the depths of the storm. The memory of Peter trembling in the sea and of the Lord reproving his little faith will confirm Us in the same trust. Surely He wishes Us to put aside all doubt about obtaining His help and to act with the hope of His grace, rather than from fear of Our weakness. Therefore, We obey His will, and We hand Ourselves over to His faithfulness and power. For if He has decided to aid Our labors in the present circumstances for the safety of His Church, everyone will surely perceive Him alone as its author and source; hence they will realize that the honor and glory must be given to Him alone. Therefore, We proceed eagerly to undertake this great burden, and We will strive to trust in His powerful help. We will consider no care too great in carrying out our task.

2. When We ponder the nature of Our administration and look to all regions of the Christian world, We behold you in your exalted posts. We are refreshed by your presence; We recognize that you are Our helpers, the custodians of the Lord's flock and laborers in the evangelical vineyard. Therefore at the beginning of Our apostolate, We wish to address you. If We seem in any way to exhort and reprove you, attribute it to Our fear for Ourselves or consider that it comes for Our confidence in your virtue and devotion to Us.

Joint Effort

3. First of all, We beseech you never to cease imploring God to strengthen Us. Return Our love for you, and thus join the mutual aid of your prayers with Us so that we may sustain each

other. By doing this, you will confirm your unity with Us. For, to be sure, the edifice of the whole church is one, whose foundation was placed by blessed Peter in this See. Many stones are joined for its construction, but all rest on one rock. One is the body of the church, whose head is Christ, and all cohere in it. We vicariously administer His power and preside over others by His will. You and We are the more prominent members of the same body. For, what can happen to individual members which does not affect all or pervade each? Accordingly, whatever concerns you concerns Us, and vice versa. Therefore, together we must all labor for the health and safety of the church, so that, without blemish or strain, it may flourish. With God's help we can accomplish this if each of you is enkindled by as strong a zeal for his flock as possible and if your one concern be to remove from his flock all contagion of evil and pitfalls of error and to strengthen it diligently with all the aids of sound doctrine and holiness.

Repel Attacks on Religion

4. If ever those in charge of the Lord's vineyard should be concerned about the salvation of souls, they must be so in this age especially. For many ideas aimed at weakening religion arise almost daily. When men are enticed by novelty and led on by an eagerness for alien knowledge, they come together more eagerly for this very purpose and more willingly embrace it. Wherefore, We lament that the destruction of souls is propagated more widely each day. Accordingly you must work all the harder and exercise diligence and authority to repel this audacity and insanity which stalks even divine and most holy matters. Be confident that you will accomplish this by simplicity of sound doctrine and by the word of God which penetrates more than any two-edged sword. You will easily be able to contain the attack of enemies and blunt their weapons when in all your sermons you preach and present Jesus Christ crucified. By His own laws and institutions He founded and reenforced this holy city which is His Church. To it he entrusted, as it were, the deposit of faith in Him to be preserved piously and without contamination. He wished it to be the bukwark of His teaching and truth against which the gates of hell would never prevail. We, therefore, the overseers and guardians of this holy city, must preserve the magnificent heritage of Our laws and faith which has been passed down intact to Us; We must transmit it pure and sound to our successors. If We direct all our actions to this norm found in sacred scripture and moreover cling to the footsteps of our ancestors, We will be best equipped to avoid whatever could weaken and destroy the faith of the Christian people and loosen in any way the unity of the Church.

Scriptures and Tradition

5. Whatever pertains to religious worship, to moral training, to right living can be found in the two-fold instrument of scriptures and tradition. From this source we learn the depth of mysteries and the duties of piety, honesty, justice, and humanity. We learn, thus, what we owe to God, to the Church, to our country, our fellow citizens, and all other men. From no other source than these laws of true religion do we recognize more clearly the established rights of citizens and society. Accordingly, no one has ever attacked the divine sanctions of Christ without likewise disturbing public tranquillity, without lessening obedience owed to rulers, and without rendering everything unsafe and uncertain. For there is a strong bond between divine and human rights; therefore those who realize that rulers are protected by the authority of the Christian law, obey them, venerate their authority, and protect and cherish their dignity.

Civil Rulers

6. Therefore, We exhort that after God and the Church, you concern yourselves with instilling in people obedience and deference to rulers. For they protect public safety and enforce the equity of law. They are ministers of God and not without reason do they carry the sword as vindicators in wrath on him who does wrong; moreover they are beloved sons and patrons of the Church, whose part it is to cherish it like a parent and protect its interest and rights. Let your followers learn from the cradle itself to maintain their loyalty to rulers, to obey authority, and to venerate the law not only because of fear, but also because of conscience. This will benefit both the tranquillity of civic life and also the profit of the church, for these cannot be separated. To this end, add to the daily prayers for your people certain special petitions for the rulers, that they may be kept safe and that they may rule in equity, peace, and justice, so that recognizing God himself ruling in the kingdom of men, they may

protect and advance His cause. Thus, you will satisfy your episcopal task no less than the well-being of all.

Clergy Set an Example

7. As for the rest, we consider it superfluous to review with you the other aspects of your pastoral office in any detail. For why should We pursue details and exhort you in matters you clearly know and of which, moreover, you have the added advantage of day-to-day experience and a spiritual outlook fully consonant with your function? One thing only We will mention: try to follow the example of our Leader and the Chief of the apostles in all things, and to exemplify in yourselves that model of holiness, charity, and humility. For if Christ, assuming the weakness of our flesh, wished that men reclaimed by His humility and love become adoptive sons of God and His coheirs, then what can be better than for Us to preserve this union of men with Christ, and to ourselves as an example to all? For what other reason is there for him who preaches the gospel for Sion to climb a high mountain? If once you are inflamed with this desire, then this same ardor will spread among all your people. Indeed the force and authority of the pastor for moving the spirits of his flock is truly marvellous. For when they recognize that all his thoughts and actions are conformed to this model of true virtue, when they see in him nothing harsh, nothing arrogant, and nothing exalted, but rather charity, meekness, and humility, then truly they will feel themselves drawn most keenly to imitate these qualities. Moreover, when they see him paying no attention to private gain, instead serving the advantage of everyone else, coming to the aid of the needy with his resources, of the afflicted with his consolation, of the ignorant with his teaching, of all men with his service, advice and piety, even preferring their salvation to his life, they will listen to his voice as he teaches, exhorts, implores, and even blames and reproves in a most loving manner. For if pastors are hampered by private interests and prefer worldly things to heavenly, how can they rouse others to love of God and mutual kindness? If they seek after wealth, pleasure, honors, how can they rouse others to the contempt of human things? If they are puffed up with pride and arrogance, how can they rouse others to meekness and humility? Therefore, since you have taken upon yourselves the office of instructing souls in the knowledge of Jesus Christ, you must adhere to his holiness, innocence, and gentleness. Consider, too, that your proper business, is to instruct the people in this fashion, and that by carrying out this task correctly will come all your praise and good fortune, from neglecting it, your calamity and turpitude. Therefore, seek only those riches that come from gaining souls for Christ. Seek only that glory which comes from promoting divine worship, from adding to the beauty of the house of God, and from extirpating vice and promoting virtue.

8. Not even when you have been long and much tried in these labors should you think that there will ever be a limit to practicing virtue. To be sure, it is the condition of your office, the nature of the episcopal life, never to be free from cares or to attain leisure. But the expectation of the immortal and infinite reward awaiting you will lighten all troubles. Moreover, in addition to this hope of immortality, you will experience abundant joy even in sustaining the labors of the pastoral life, when you behold your people joined with the mutual bonds of charity, honesty, and piety and when you behold all the other outstanding fruits of your vigilance and toils gained for the Church. Would that We might see that splendid felicity of religion of ancient days returned to the Church in this time of Our apostolate as a result of the unanimous accord of all our wills and labors.

9. At the same time as We send this Encyclical to you, Venerable Brothers, We also send another to all the faithful announcing the customary Jubilee for imploring divine aid for a salutary governance of the holy Catholic Church at the beginning of Our pontificate. Direct your people to properly perform these prayers in faith, piety, and humility and inspire them to care for their salvation as well as the general welfare of the Christian people.

10. As a pledge of Our love We impart the apostolic blessing to you, Venerable Brothers, and the faithful of your churches.

Given in Rome at St. Mary Major, 12 December 1769, in the 1st year of Our pontificate.

†

LATIN TEXT: *Bull. Rom. Cont.*, 5:70-73.

ENGLISH TRANSLATION: Robert F. Healey, S.J.

SALUTIS NOSTRAE

ENCYCLICAL OF POPE CLEMENT XIV PROCLAIMING A UNIVERSAL JUBILEE

APRIL 30, 1774

23

Clement, Bishop and Servant of the Servants of God.

Our Greetings and Apostolic Blessing to all the Faithful who read this Letter.

Our salvation was accomplished when Our Lord Jesus Christ by His passion and death rescued men from their ancient slavery to sin and gave them life and freedom as sons of God, coheirs of His own glory. As an additional benefit He has given them a means of expiating sin when by the weakness of their nature and their own wickedness they wretchedly abandon their excellent state as heirs of God. By giving to the Prince of the Apostles the power of forgiving sins together with the keys of the heavenly kingdom, He made it possible for sinners to be restored to their former righteousness and to receive the fruits of redemption.

Announcement of Holy Year for 1775

2. Since this is the only way for sinners to recover divine grace and salvation, the successors of St. Peter have made it their chief concern to summon all men to this fountain of mercy. They have done this by offering the promise of forgiveness to the repentant and by encouraging sinners by every means to seek remission. Although this has been a constant concern of their Apostolic ministry, they also wanted to establish some especially suitable times for summoning sinners to repentance. In this way, they could make available to all the treasure of indulgence entrusted to their keeping. Accordingly, so as not to deprive any generation of the great benefit of propitiation, they decided to celebrate every twenty-five years a holy year of jubilee, a year of forgiveness and grace. They established this merciful refuge in this holy city. We follow this salutary custom in announcing that the year which is now approaching will be a Holy Year. We urge you to effect salvation for your souls by utilizing the aids which are available for your sanctification. We shall unlock all the riches of mercy proceeding from the blood of Christ which have been entrusted to Our dispensing. Moreover We shall open for you the rich store of satisfaction formed by the merits of the most holy mother of God and the apostles, by the blood of the martyrs and by the virtuous actions of all good men; this will render peace and forgiveness more accessible. For assuredly, as we are gathered together in the one body of the Church which is the Body of Christ, we are joined with the illustrious society and communion of the saints. All of us are cleansed and made alive by the blood of Christ,

and we can benefit each other. For Christ has desired that His great love and mercy and the infinite force of His passion and merits should be made more resplendent by the addition of the other parts of His mystical body. In this way men should be helped both by reciprocal action among themselves and by the sharing of benefits flowing from that source of grace. Then God would be moved to show clemency to us for the sake of His Son's goodness and the infinite value of His blood, as well as by the merits of the saints and by prayerful petition.

So We summon you to share in this richness of indulgence, in these treasures of the Church. In accordance with traditional practice, and in agreement with the cardinals, by the authority of Almighty God, of the blessed apostles Peter and Paul, and of Ourselves, for the glory of God, the exaltation of the Catholic Church and the sanctification of the entire Christian people, We proclaim and promulgate that the great universal jubilee of the Holy Year is to be celebrated in Rome next year, 1775, beginning at first Vespers on this Christmas Eve and lasting a full year.

Requirements for Obtaining Indulgence

3. During this year of jubilee We grant and impart in the Lord a full indulgence, remission, and forgiveness of all their sins to all the faithful of either sex who confess their sins with true repentance, receive Holy Communion, and devoutly visit the city basilicas of Sts. Peter and Paul, St. John Lateran, and St. Mary Major; in addition, they must pray to God for the exaltation of Holy Church, the destruction of heresies, peace among Catholic rulers, and the safety and quiet of the Christian people. Romans and residents of Rome must make their visits on thirty different days. These can be in broken or unbroken sequence and can be reckoned in natural or ecclesiastical days, that is, a day measured from the first vespers of one day to the end of vespers the next evening. Pilgrims or other non-residents should make at least fifteen such visits.

Hindrances to Obtaining Goal

4. Some of those who set out for Rome with this purpose may not be able to fulfill the condition of visiting the basilicas for the requisite number of days either because they die on the way or are prevented by illness or some other lawful reason. We therefore decree that they share in the same indulgence and remission when they have confessed their sins and received Holy Communion as if they had actually visited the basilicas on the prescribed days. Although hindered by the necessities mentioned, they still obtain their desired goal.

Advantages of Pilgrimages

5. Do not let these days of salvation pass by without using the great opportunity to appease divine justice and obtain grace. For it is not fitting that you should be less eager in obtaining the abundance of heavenly grace and in visiting the courts of the Lord than men greedy for profit or zealous for travel. Yet these allow no inconveniences or hindrances to detain them. The very labors, if they are undertaken with the proper intentions, can be of great assistance in gathering the rich fruits of penance. It was for this reason that the Church has always regarded the ancient custom of making pilgrimages as very beneficial. The troubles and weariness incurred in the course of pilgrimage make reparation for past sins and strengthen the desire of repentance. Even if ardent resolution and love for God remove or lighten your experience of such troubles, this eagerness of spirit is very powerful in obtaining forgiveness and is accounted part of the satisfaction due for sins since much is forgiven the one who loves much.

Therefore, go up to the city of Sion and be filled with the riches of the Lord's house. The sight of this city of faith and home of piety, the tombs of the apostles, and the reminders of the martyrs will move you to repentance which appeases God. When you gaze on the earth which was stained by their blood and on the traces of their holiness which are everywhere to be seen, you will inevitably repent of your poor imitation of the practices and laws which they followed and which you profess to follow. The majesty of the churches and the dignity of their divine service will remind you that you are the temple of the living God; they will increase your zeal to adorn with the gifts of divine grace this temple which you were formerly inclined to defile, grieving the Holy Spirit. You will also be inspired to piety and repentance by the tears of others who bewail their sins and by the groans of men beseeching forgiveness from God. But in your sadness and grief, the very crowd of peoples and races assembled for the works of penance and justice will cause you joy. For this will be the most delightful and beautiful sight, foreshadowing in public view the triumph of the Cross and religion. Our own joy at this universal assembly of the Church's children will be especially great. We consider that your striving in love and piety promises great aid and assistance to Ourselves. For We trust that you will remember your most loving father in your prayers to God. We also trust that when you join Us in prayer for the safety of the Catholic faith, for the return of all peoples who have strayed from its unity, for the peace of the Church, and for the happiness of Christian princes, you will assist Us to support the weight of Our office.

Encourage the Faithful

6. Venerable brothers, patriarchs, primates, archbishops, and bishops, assist Us in these concerns and proclaim this time of repentance and reconciliation to the peoples entrusted to your care. By means of diligence and influence, see to it that this opportunity of obtaining forgiveness, which making available to all, occasions the greatest benefit for the salvation of souls. Let them know what works of Christian humility and mercy they should perform to prepare themselves for gathering this great harvest of heavenly grace. Let them understand by your words and your example that they should fast, pray, and give alms. All of you who will add this task to your pastoral cares should bring a section of your flock to this citadel of religion and source of mercy, to Our fatherly welcome and embrace. Your visit will add luster to Our celebration and you will, of course, obtain great stores of divine mercy from so fine and laborious an undertaking. You will carry home those stores like rich cargo and joyfully share them with the rest of your people.

7. We are perfectly sure that Our beloved sons in Christ, the emperor-elect and all Catholic kings and princes, will use their authority to assist Us in ensuring that Our plans for the salvation of souls will enjoy the great success which We desire. So We strongly urge and beseech them in their zeal for religion to act in unison with the bishops, and provide safe roads and inns for the pilgrims. They know well that these actions will benefit the peace of the realm and that God Himself will be appeased and favorable towards them in accordance with their own care to increase His glory among the people.

8. In order that this letter may more readily come to the knowledge of all the faithful in every place, We wish printed copies of it, signed by the public notary and with the seal of a person of ecclesiastical rank affixed, to be accepted exactly as if they were the original.

9. May no one be permitted to curtail this expression of Our proclamation, promulgation, concession, exhortation, request and desire or act against it in rash daring. But if anyone tries to do so he knows he will incur the wrath of Almighty God and of His blessed apostles, Peter and Paul.

Given at Rome in St. Mary Major's, April 30th, 1744 in the fifth year of Our pontificate.

†

LATIN TEXT: *Bull. Rom. Cont.*, 5:716-19.

ENGLISH TRANSLATION: Padraig M. O'Cleirigh.

POPE PIUS VI
1775-1799

Giovanni Angelo Braschi was born on Christmas Day, 1717 in Cesena (Emilia) of a noble but far from wealthy family. Educated by the Jesuits he received his *doctor utriusque iuris* and then went on to complete his studies in law at the University of Ferrara where his uncle was auditor to the cardinal legate. Appointed secretary to the cardinal he rapidly advanced to positions of greater importance and in 1758, at a mature age, was ordained priest. Under Clement XIII he was named finance minister of the States of the Church (1766); in 1773 partly on the recommendation of the Bourbon courts, the cardinalate was conferred on him. In 1775, after a conclave lasting 134 days, he was elected pope, receiving episcopal ordination six days after his election. Thus began one of the longest pontificates in history and probably the most spectacular in the eighteenth century.

For most of his reign Pius had to face the hostility of rulers and people against the Holy See and the influence of the Enlightenment in France and England. Although intent on fulfilling his duties as administrator and defender of the rights of the Church, he lacked the ability, firmness, and prudence for the task. Permitting himself to be concerned with secondary matters he authorized the expenditure of large sums of money on lavish projects in Rome and unsuccessful attempts to complete the draining of the Pontine marshes. His ostentacious manner, excessive nepotism, and concern for trivial matters contributed to the loss of prestige for the papal office.

With the death of King Joseph I of Portugal (1777) Pombal fell from power and Queen Maria I ordered an end to the anticlerical violence; Charles III of Spain, in his final years, was less demanding; Louis XVI in France seemed well disposed. Support from these areas, however, could only be depended on so long as the Holy See refrained from intervention and remained committed to the total suppression of the Society of Jesus. Pius, on the other hand, incurred the displeasure of Frederick II of Prussia and Catherine II of Russia by pressing them to apply the brief of suppression to the Jesuits under their jurisdiction.

In the years preceding the French Revolution the situation in Germany was of great concern. In 1783 "Febronius" (Johann von Hontheim, coadjutor to the archbishop of Trier) issued a statement with repercussions that verged on schism. Pius VI demanded and received a retraction from him but this did not check Febronianism in southern and western Germany. When Pius sought to establish a nunciature in Munich, the archbishops (also electors) issued the Punctuation of Ems affirming their stand of repudiating papal interference in all but purely spiritual matters.

In Austria Josephinism, which embodied the ideas of the Enlightenment and Febronianism to construct a new system of ecclesiastical government, was uncompromising in its demands. In 1782, concerned with Joseph II's rigorous application of this system, Pius VI made an extraordinary move by leaving Rome (the first pope to do so since 1533) for Vienna in order to make a personal appeal to the emperor. The latter received the pope courteously but they could come to no agreement. However, as a result of Joseph's ruthless and insensitive persistence in carrying out his reforms, insurrections broke out among the people. The pope was more successful in working against the influence of this movement in Italy, mainly by his apostolic constitution *Auctorem fidei* (1794) condemning the acts of the diocesan Synod of Pistoia.

The French Revolution opened up an entirely new trial for the Church. Pius VI at first hesitant to act, eventually, in order to stifle the movement, condemned without equivocation the principles embodied in the Declaration of the Rights of Man and of the Citizen and strove to build a holy league against the proponents of the Revolution. The pope, throughout this period, was extraordinarily generous in welcoming and caring for the numerous aristocrats and priests who sought refuge in the States of the Church. With the invasion of Italy by Napoleon (1796), however, the Revolution reached the Papal States. For two years Napoleon, who had refused to be the destroyer of the Holy See, exercised prudent patience in dealing with the pope, but while he was in Egypt General Berthier entered Rome (1798), proclaimed the Roman Republic, and relentlessly drove Pius VI and the Curia into exile. The aging and ailing, but serene and courageous, pontiff was finally taken prisoner and driven from city to city out of his own States until on August 29, 1799, a prisoner at Valence in the south of France, he died in the hands of his enemies.

INSCRUTABILE

ENCYCLICAL OF POPE PIUS VI ON THE PROBLEMS OF THE PONTIFICATE
DECEMBER 25, 1775
24

To the Patriarchs, Primates, Archbishops and Bishops of the Entire Catholic Church.

Venerable Brothers, We give you Greeting and Our Apostolic Blessing.

The mysterious design of divine wisdom, whose works are always marvellous, did not despise Our lowliness but willed instead to make Us the head of the bishops and to honor Us as the guide of His entire Church. Just as He chose the young David from among a thousand and raised him from herding sheep to rule His people on a glorious throne, and make them acceptable to God by means of the rod of guidance, so He chose Us. Others seemed more worthy of the papal tiara, especially since We had just been appointed to the college of cardinals and occupied the last place there.

As We gratefully reflect on His infinite kindness towards Us, We cannot refrain from tears at His beneficent mercy and omnipotence in conferring His graces so generously on one who was not recommended by his own merits. Despite Our lack of strength and merit, He established Us as leader of the peoples in order that, as representative on earth of the Eternal Shepherd, We should feed Israel, His inheritance, and lead it to the holy mountian of Sion, the heavenly Jerusalem.

Since it is most fitting for Us to show Our obedience and devotion as consecrated Pope by offering praise to the Lord, We cannot stifle Our exclamations of exultation as We praise Him and cry with the prophet: "Let Our mouth speak the praise of the Lord and Our soul, spirit, flesh and tongue bless His holy name."[1] "But if it is religious conduct to rejoice at a grace, it is also necessary to be anxious about deserving it. For what is so fearful as toil to the weak, height to the lowly and rank to one who does not deserve it?"[2]

Dangers Confronting the Church

2. Who would not be fearful at the present condition of the Christian people? The divine love by which we abide in God and God in us grows very cold as sins and wickedness increase every day. Who would not be shocked when considering that We have undertaken the task of guarding and protecting the Church at a time when many plots are laid against orthodox religion, when the safe guidance of the sacred canons is rashly despised, and when confusion is spread wide by men maddened by a monstrous desire of innovation, who attack the very bases of rational nature and attempt to overthrow them? Assuredly "with such reason for fear, we would have no hope of escaping slavery except that the Guardian of

Israel, who does not sleep, says to His disciples: 'Behold I am with you all days even to the consummation of the world.' He deigned to be not merely the guardian of the sheep, but the shepherd of the shepherds as well."[3]

Plea for Help from the Hierarchy of the Church

3. Now since divine graces descend on us most generously when Our prayer ascends to God, We make this special request of you, Our helpers and advisers, in this Our first address to you, for the love by which we are one in the Lord and for the faith by which we grow into one body. Beseech God every day to strengthen Us by His power and to pour out on Us the Spirit of counsel and of courage, in order that We may both decide what measures We should take in these difficult circumstances and that We may have the strength to carry through Our decisions. Therefore pray in the Spirit, and let your prayer be the surest proof of your love for Us and your brotherly union. Invoke the merits of the most holy Mary, mother of God, Our special patroness, and of all the heavenly court, that We may quickly obtain the help We need. Request for Us especially the protection and defense of St. Peter the Apostle. "We rejoice more to serve his See than to occupy it, in the hope that his prayers will make the God of mercies regard the time of Our ministry with kindness and deign to guard and feed the shepherd of his sheep."[4]

4. We urge you to show that you are faithful stewards of the mysteries of God. As the Lord is your portion, you know well what you should do and endure for the Church of God in the courageous fulfilment of your ministry. So We exhort you to rouse up the grace which is in you through the imposition of hands and to omit nothing which contributes to the growth of the body "which is built from Christ and joined together at every point of subministration"[5] in faith and in love.

Qualifications of Prospective Clergy

Therefore, since you know that the Church's chief good derives from admitting only those who are fully qualified into the clergy, We do not have to remind you to observe carefully the sanctions established in this matter by the canons. Prevent from entering the Church's service all who lack exceptional moral holiness, who are uninstructed in the law of the Lord, and who give little or no promise of becoming energetic members of the clergy. For instead of proving helpers to you in feeding and guiding your flock, they will increase your toil and troubles. They will hinder you from ensuring that the Lord receives from his workers the fruits of the vineyard which Christ in strictest justice will expect from you at the final judgment. A man who is going to be a priest should excel in holiness and learning. For God rejects as priests those who have rejected knowledge, and only the man who unites moral piety with the pursuit of knowledge can be a suitable worker in the Lord's harvest. Since this cannot occur without careful education, it has been decreed accordingly that each diocese should establish a college for clerics in accordance with its means; if such a college already exists, it should be carefully preserved. For how would young men, whose age impels them down the easy path, persevere in ecclesiastical training or make such progress in humane and sacred studies unless they were instructed in piety and religion from their early years and practiced in the interpretation of literature?

Such colleges have been established and carefully equipped with suitable regulations and even greatly expanded in individual dioceses as Benedict XIV recommended to each of you as an indispensable part of your office.[6] So just as We must praise the outstanding labor and concern shown in founding and expanding these colleges, We must also urge on strongly those in whose diocese a college has not been established or completed.

Beautify the Churches

5. For the same reason you should undoubtedly always give special attention to the beauty of the house of God and the splendor and dignity of objects dedicated to the divine service. Such beauty and splendor often greatly inspire the faithful, and draw them to the veneration of sacred realities. It would be very improper for the bishop's house to be cleaner and furnished more tastefully than the abode of holiness, the palace of the living God. It would make no sense to see holy vestments, adornments for the altar and all the furniture in the church worn out with age and torn or dirty, while the bishop's table is well laden, the priest's clothing very clean and finely coordinated. St. Peter Damian expressed this

well: "It is an accusation which brings great confusion on us that some men both offer and lay the Lord's Body on a dirty altar cloth and that they fearlessly place the Body of the Savior in a vessel which no lord, worm though he is, would put to his own lips!"[7] But We know that you are far from committting this sin of negligence of which the holy cardinal accuses those who spend the goods acquired by the Church "not in buying books or ornaments and utensils for their churches" but for their own use as "necessary expenses."

Heretical Sects

6. We thought it useful to speak to you lovingly on these matters in order to strengthen your excellent resolve. But a much more serious subject demands that We speak of it, or rather mourn over it. We refer to the pestilent disease which the wickedness of our times brings forth. We must unite our minds and strength in treating this plague before it grows rife and becomes incurable in the Church through Our oversight. For in recent days, the dangerous times foretold by the Apostle Paul have clearly arrived, when there will be "men who love themselves, who are lifted up, proud, blasphemous, traitors, lovers of pleasure instead of God, men who are always learning but never arriving at the knowledge of truth, possessing indeed the appearance of piety but denying its power, corrupt in mind, reprobate about the faith."[8] These men raise themselves up into "lying" teachers, as they are called by Peter the prince of the Apostles, and bring in sects of perdition. They deny the Lord who bought them and bring upon themselves swift destruction. They say they are wise and they have become fools, and their uncomprehending heart is darkened.

You yourselves, established as scouts in the house of Israel, see clearly the many victories claimed by a philosophy full of deceit. You see the ease with which it attracts to itself a great host of peoples, concealing its impiety with the honorable name of philosophy. Who could express in words or call to mind the wickedness of the tenets and evil madness which it imparts? While such men apparently intend to search out wisdom, "they fail because they do not search in the proper way. . . and they fall into errors which lead them astray from ordinary wisdom."[9] They have come to such a height of impiety that they make out that God does not exist, or if He does that He is idle and uncaring, making no revelation to men. Consequently it is not surprising that they assert that everything holy and divine is the product of the minds of inexperienced men smitten with empty fear of the future and seduced by a vain hope of immortality. But those deceitful sages soften and conceal the wickedness of their doctrine with seductive words and statements; in this way, they attract and wretchedly ensnare many of the weak into rejecting their faith or allowing it to be greatly shaken. While they pursue a remarkable knowledge, they open their eyes to behold a false light which is worse than the very darkness. Naturally our enemy, desirous of harming us and skilled in doing so, just as he made use of the serpent to deceive the first human beings, has armed the tongues of those men with the poison of his deceitfulness in order to lead astray the minds of the faithful. The prophet prays that his soul may be delivered from such deceitful tongues.[10] In this way these men by their speech "enter in lowliness, capture mildly, softly bind and kill in secret."[11] This results in great moral corruption, in license of thought and speech, in arrogance and rashness in every enterprise.

Inscrutabile
24

7. When they have spread this darkness abroad and torn religion out of men's hearts, these accursed philosophers proceed to destroy the bonds of union among men, both those which unite them to their rulers, and those which urge them to their duty. They keep proclaiming that man is born free and subject to no one, that society accordingly is a crowd of foolish men who stupidly yield to priests who deceive them and to kings who oppress them, so that the harmony of priest and ruler is only a monstrous conspiracy against the innate liberty of man.

Everyone must understand that such ravings and others like them, concealed in many deceitful guises, cause greater ruin to public calm the longer their impious originators are unrestrained. They cause a serious loss of souls redeemed by Christ's blood wherever their teaching spreads, like a cancer; it forces its way into public academies, into the houses of the great, into the palaces of kings, and even enters the sanctuary, shocking as it is to say so.

8. Consequently, you who are the salt of the earth, guardians and shepherds of the Lord's flock, whose business it is to fight the battles of the Lord, arise and gird on your sword, which is the word of God, and expel this foul contagion

from your lands. How long are we to ignore the common insult to faith and Church? Let the words of Bernard arouse us like a lament of the spouse of Christ: "Of old was it foretold and the time of fulfillment is now at hand: Behold, in peace is my sorrow most sorrowful. It was sorrowful first when the martyrs died; afterwards it was more sorrowful in the fight with the heretics and now it is most sorrowful in the conduct of the members of the household. . . . The Church is struck within and so in peace is my sorrow most sorrowful. But what peace? There is peace and there is no peace. There is peace from the pagans and peace from the heretics, but no peace from the children. At that time the voice will lament: Sons did I rear and exalt, but they despised me. They despised me and defiled me by a bad life, base gain, evil traffic, and business conducted in the dark."[12] Who can hear these tearful complaints of our most holy mother without feeling a strong urge to devote all his energy and effort to the Church, as he has promised? Therefore cast out the old leaven, remove the evil from your midst. Forcefully and carefully banish poisonous books from the eyes of your flock, and at once courageously set apart those who have been infected, to prevent them harming the rest. The holy Pope Leo used to say, "We can rule those entrusted to us only by pursuing with zeal for the Lord's faith those who destroy and those who are destroyed and by cutting them off from sound minds with the utmost severity to prevent the plague spreading."[13] In doing this We exhort and advise you to be all of one mind and in harmony as you strive for the same object, just as the Church has one faith, one baptism, and one spirit. As you are joined together in the hierarchy, so you should unite equally with virtue and desire.

The affair is of the greatest importance since it concerns the Catholic faith, the purity of the Church, the teaching of the saints, the peace of the empire, and the safety of nations. Since it concerns the entire body of the Church, it is a special concern of yours because you are called to share in Our pastoral concern, and the purity of the faith is particularly entrusted to your watchfulness. "Now therefore, Brothers, since you are overseers among God's people and their soul depends on you, raise their hearts to your utterance,"[14] that they may stand fast in faith and achieve the rest which is prepared for believers only. Beseech, accuse, correct, rebuke and fear not: for ill-judged silence leaves in their error those who could be taught, and this is most harmful both to them and to you who should have dispelled the error. The holy Church is powerfully refreshed in the truth as it struggles zealously for the truth. In this divine work you should not fear either the force or favor of your enemies. The bishop should not fear since the anointing of the Holy Spirit has strengthened him: the shepherd should not be afraid since the prince of pastors has taught him by his own example to despise life itself for the safety of his flock: the cowardice and depression of the hireling should not dwell in a bishop's heart. Our great predecessor Gregory, in instructing the heads of the churches, said with his usual excellence: "Often imprudent guides in their fear of losing human favor are afraid to speak the right freely. As the word of truth has it, they guard their flock not with a shepherd's zeal but as hirelings do, since they flee when the wolf approaches by hiding themselves in silence. . . . A shepherd fearing to speak the right is simply a man retreating by keeping silent."[15] But if the wicked enemy of the human race, the better to frustrate your efforts, ever brings it about that a plague of epidemic proportions is hidden from the religious powers of the world, please do not be terrified but walk in God's house in harmony, with prayer, and in truth, the three arms of our service. Remember that when the people of Juda were defiled, the best means of purification was the public reading to all, from the least to the greatest, of the book of the law lately found by the priest Helcias in the Lord's temple; at once the whole people agreed to destroy the abominations and seal a covenant in the Lord's presence to follow after the Lord and observe His precepts, testimonies and ceremonies with their whole heart and soul."[16] For the same reason Josaphat sent priests and Levites to bring the book of the law throughout the cities of Juda and to teach the people.[17] The proclamation of the divine word has been entrusted to your faith by divine, not human, authority. So assemble your people and preach to them the gospel of Jesus Christ. From that divine source and heavenly teaching draw draughts of true philosophy for your flock. Persuade them that subjects ought to keep faith and show obedience to those who by God's ordering lead and rule them. To those who are devoted to the ministry of the Church, give proofs of faith, continence, sobriety, knowledge, and liberality, that they may please Him to whom they have proved themselves and boast only of what is serious, moderate, and religious. But above all kindle in the minds of everyone that love for one another which Christ the Lord so often and so specifically praised. For this is the one sign of Christians and the bond of perfection.

9. These are the chief matters on which We wanted to address you in the Lord, Venerable Brothers. We urgently ask that We may personally experience the pleasure of us all harmoniously preserving faithfully the deposit entrusted to Our keeping. But Our sins prevent Us from obtaining this without the prior help of the Lord's mercies. May He favorably aid Us first with his blessings. So, may He forgive Us and strengthen Our weakness in order that Our common prayer may more speedily come into His presence. At the same time as We send you this letter, We are sending another letter granting a jubilee to all the faithful, hoping in God who is merciful and pities us, that as He gave Us the power of binding and loosing on earth for the building up of His Body, He may grant to you also and to your flocks for salvation that you may advance from virtue to virtue, strangers to every error. This is Our heartfelt prayer as We impart most lovingly to you, and to the peoples entrusted to your care, the Apostolic Blessing.

Given at Rome in St. Peter's, 25 December 1775 in the first year of Our Pontificate.

Inscrutabile
24

†

LATIN TEXT: *Bull. Rom. Cont.*, 6^1: 181-86; *Acta Pii VI*, 1: 1-12.

ENGLISH TRANSLATION: Padraig M. O'Cleirigh

REFERENCES:

1. Ps 144.21.
2. St. Leo the Great, serm. 1, chap. 2, and serm. 2, chap. 1 (ed. Ballerin, Venice).
3. Ibid., serm. 5 (4), chap. 2.
4. Ibid., chap. 5.
5. Eph 4.16.
6. Encyclical epistle of 1741.
7. Bk. 4, ep. 14 (Works, vol. 1, Rome, 1606)
8. 2 Tm 3.
9. Lactant, *divin. instit.*, bk. 3, chap. 28 (Paris 1748)
10. Ps 119.
11. St. Leo the Great, serm. 16 (15), chap. 3.
12. Serm. 33 on the Canticle, vol. 4, no. 16, Paris 1691)
13. Epistles 7-8, chap. 2, to the bishops throughout Italy.
14. Jdt 8.21.
15. Reg. Pastor. 11, *Operum*, vol. 2, chap. 4, Paris.
16. 4 Kgs 22-23.
17. 2 Paralip. 17.7f.

CHARITAS

ENCYCLICAL OF POPE PIUS VI
ON THE CIVIL OATH
IN FRANCE
APRIL 13, 1791

To Our Beloved Sons, the Cardinals of the Holy Roman Church, to Our Venerable Brothers the Archbishops and Bishops, and to Our Beloved Children the Capitulars, Clergy and People of the Kingdom of France.

Beloved Sons, Venerable Brothers and Beloved Children, We give you greeting and Our Apostolic Blessing.

Love, which is patient and kindly, as the Apostle Paul says, supports and endures all things as long as a hope remains that mildness will prevent the growth of incipient errors. But if errors increase daily and reach the point of creating schism, the laws of love itself, together with Our duty, demand that We reveal to the erring their horrible sin and the heavy canonical penalties which they have incurred. For this sternness will lead those who are wandering from the way of truth to recover their senses, reject their errors, and come back to the Church, which opens its arms like a kind mother and embraces them on their return. The rest of the faithful in this way will be quickly delivered from the deceits of false pastors who enter the fold by ways other than the door, and whose only aim is theft, slaughter, and destruction.

Civil Constitution of the Clergy

2. With these divine precepts in mind, We have just learned of the war against the Catholic religion which has been started by the revolutionary thinkers who as a group form a majority in the National Assembly of France. We have wept in God's presence, shared Our sorrow with the cardinals, and proclaimed public and private prayers. Then We wrote to King Louis, on July 9, 1790, and repeatedly encouraged him not to confirm the Civil Constitution of the Clergy which would lead his people into error and schism. For it was intolerable that a political assembly should change the universal practice of the Church, disregard the opinions of the holy Fathers and the decrees of the councils, overturn the order of the hierarchy and control the election of bishops, destroy episcopal sees, and introduce a worse form into the Church after removing the better.

To Further Impress the King

3. We sent two briefs on the following day to the archbishops of Bordeaux and Vienne who were with the King, urging them in fatherly fashion to advise the king that if he lent his authority to this Constitution, his kingdom

would be in schism; furthermore We would regard any bishops appointed in accordance with its decrees as schismatic and lacking all ecclesiastical jurisdiction. To remove all doubt that Our concern was solely with matters of religion and to silence the enemies of this Apostolic See, We gave orders that the collection of taxes from French revenues should be discontinued, although these taxes were due for Our services from unbroken custom and earlier agreements.

4. The king would certainly have refrained from approving the Constitution, but the National Assembly finally forced him to lend his authority to the Constitution as his letters to Us on July 28, September 6, and December 16 attest. He besought Us insistently to approve five, and later seven, articles at least provisionally. These articles were so similar in tenor that they formed a comprehensive summary of the new Constitution.

5. We saw at once, of course, that We could approve or tolerate none of the articles since they were at variance with canonical regulations. However, We did not want to give Our enemies an opportunity to deceive the nations by claiming that We were opposed to every sort of negotiations: therefore We told the King in Our letter of August 17 that We would consider the articles carefully and consult with the cardinals, who would meet to discuss every aspect of the proposal. After the cardinals had met on September 24 and December 16 to discuss the first two articles, they decided unanimously to request the opinions of the French bishops on these articles in case they could show some canonical reason for approval. Such a reason was not easily imaginable at this distance from France, as We had said earlier in other letters to the King.

French Clergy Support the Pope

6. In the meanwhile, We were greatly consoled when a majority of the French bishops firmly opposed the Constitution and attacked every point in it which referred to the government of the Church. Our consolation was increased when Cardinal Rochefoucauld, the archbishop of Aix, and thirty other archbishops and bishops appealed to Us for assistance in meeting such great dangers. On October 10 they sent an explanation of the main points contained in the Constitution of the Clergy and requested Our help and advice. We were further consoled because many other bishops joined the thirty in accepting this explanation. Only four out of one hundred and thirty-one bishops dissented. A great number of capitulars and most of the parish priests and lower clergy also joined the bishops. So this explanation, accepted with harmonious unanimity, should be regarded as the teaching of the entire French Church.

7. We Ourselves immediately engaged in the task of examining all the articles of the Constitution. The Assembly, although it heard the unanimous views of the French Church, did not abandon its design, but tried all the more to destroy the firmness of the bishops. But it knew well that none of the metropolitans or the senior bishops would agree to ordain new bishops who were elected in the municipal districts by laity, heretics, unbelievers, and Jews as the published decrees commanded. It also understood that this foolish form of Church government could nowhere survive, for without the bishops the entire appearance of the church would vanish. As a result the Assembly considered publishing other even more foolish decrees, and did so on November 15 and 27, 1790, and January 3, 4, and 26, 1791. These decrees, with the king's approval, provided that any bishop from a different district could consecrate the elected persons if the metropolitan or senior bishop refused to do so.

Civil Election of Bishops

Furthermore, to instantly disperse all faithful bishops and parish priests, the decrees provided that all pastors should swear unequivocally that they would observe the Constitution already published and the one which was to be published later. Those who refused were to be considered expelled from their office, and their sees and parishes were to lose their pastor. When the lawful pastors and ministers were driven out, by force if necessary, the municipal districts could set about electing new bishops and parish priests. Upon election these men were to disregard the metropolitans and senior bishops who had refused the oath, and to go to the Assembly Executive which would appoint some bishops to ordain them.

8. These later decrees have immeasurably renewed Our sorrow. Moreover they made it more difficult for Us to send the bishops the answer which We were then preparing, since We then had to take account of these developments.

They caused Us to proclaim public prayers to beseech God for help. New pastoral letters to their flocks were published by the French bishops who had already begun the attack on the Constitution of the Clergy with remarkable astuteness. Now they devoted all their efforts to oppose the provision on the deposition of bishops, the vacating of episcopal sees, and the election and ordination of new bishops. They agreed that these civil oaths should be regarded as perjury and sacrilege, unbefitting not merely the clergy but any Catholic; all actions which are based on these oaths should be seen as schismatic, null, void, and liable to servere censures.

Dissenting Bishops

9. These praiseworthy statements of the French clergy have been put into effect. Almost all the bishops and most of the parish priests have refused the oath with unconquerable firmness. The enemies of religion then realized correctly that their vicious plans would come to nothing unless they persuaded some bishop, either by appealing to his ambition or his stupidity, to take the oath to observe the Constitution and to undertake sacrilegious consecrations and so, to initiate a schism. Among those who have been overcome by this wicked deceit the first was Charles bishop of Autun, the greatest enthusiast for the Constitution; second was Jean-Joseph bishop of Lidda; third was Louis bishop of Orléans; fourth, Charles bishop of Viviers; fifth, Cardinal de Lomenie, Archbishop of Sens; and a few wretched pastors of lower rank.

10. As regards Cardinal de Lomenie, he tried to excuse himself for taking the oath in a letter to Us last November 25. He stated that it was not to be regarded as mental assent and claimed that he was quite undecided on the question of ordaining bishops who had been elected. (He had not yet done so.) Since it was most important that none of the bishops should consecrate those elected and so broaden the road to schism, We decided to postpone a little Our answer to the bishops, which was near completion; instead We wrote to the cardinal without delay on February 23. We pointed out to him the error of his opinion in taking the oath, and the canonical penalties which with sadness We would be obliged to apply, stripping him of the rank of Cardinal unless he removed the public scandal by a timely and appropriate retraction.

As to his indecision about ordaining those elected, in answer We commanded him not to ordain new bishops for any reason whatsoever, and so join new rebels to the church. For the right of ordaining bishops belongs only to the Apostolic See, as the Council of Trent declares; it cannot be assumed by any bishop or metropolitan without obliging Us to declare schismatic both those who ordain and those who are ordained, thus invalidating their future actions.

Threatened Excommunication for Schismatics

11. When We had completed this business, We resumed the task of replying to the bishops. This task had become more troublesome and time-consuming because of the many new developments which subsequently affected it. After examining all the articles in order to make clear to everyone that in the judgment of this Holy See, which has been sought by the French bishops and is eagerly awaited by French Catholics, We declared that the new Constitution of the Clergy is composed of principles derived from heresy. It is consequently heretical in many of its decrees and at variance with Catholic teaching. In other decrees it is sacrilegious and schismatic. It overturns the rights and primacy of the Church, is opposed to ancient and modern practice, and is devised and published with the sole design of utterly destroying the Catholic religion. For it is only this religion which cannot be freely professed, whose lawful pastors are removed, and whose property is taken over. Men of other sects are left at liberty and in possession of their property. We pointed all this out clearly, but We stated mildly that We had hitherto refrained from excommunicating the authors of the ill-omened Civil Constitution of the Clergy. It was Our duty, however, to emphasize that We would be obliged against Our will to declare schismatic all who did not reject the errors We had revealed (the customary procedure of this Holy See in these cases). This threat applied to the authors of the Constitution as well as to those who swore to observe it, whether they supervised the election of new bishops, consecrated those who were elected, or accepted this consecration. For none of these would have either a lawful appointment or be in communion with the Church.

12. We are ready to show as much favor to the French people as We can without prejudicing the teaching and universal practice of the Church. Thus We have followed the advice of the Cardinals whom We consulted on this matter, repeating the message which We sent by letter to the King. We have urged the bishops who are living in the midst of these developments to inform Us of any other possible method of action which is not in opposition to Catholic teaching and universal practice, and to submit it for Our consideration. We have mentioned Our intentions to the King and have sent him a copy of Our answer to the bishops. We have also urged him to take the wiser bishops into his counsel in order to apply an appropriate remedy to the disease which derives in part from the royal authorization. Finally We have informed him that out of pastoral duty, We will take the same measures against those who remain obstinate in their error as Our predecessors took when faced with a similar necessity.

13. Our March 10 letters to the King and to the bishops were both entrusted to an express messenger who left early the next day. On the 15th a regular messenger arrived from France, and We learned from many sources that the schism had been completed in Paris on February 24th. For on that day the bishop of Autun, already stained with perjury and guilty of desertion for relinquishing his church into the hands of laymen on his own authority, defied his chapter, by joining with the bishops of Babylon and Lidda. The bishop of Babylon had received the honor of the *pallium* from Us and temporal aid as well, but he showed that he was a worthy successor of another bishop of Babylon, Dominicus Varlet, notorious for the schism of Utrecht. The bishop of Lidda was also guilty of perjury, and had incurred the hatred and abhorrence of good men for his dissent from the correct teaching of the bishop and chapter of the church at Basel of which he is a suffragan.

Sacrileges

So on that day the bishop of Autun, with the assistance of these two bishops, rashly and sacrilegiously consecrated Alois Alexandre Expilly and Claude Eustache Francois Marolles, in a church of the priests of the Oratory without permission of the Ordinary. They had received no commission to do so from the Apostolic See; they omitted the oath of obedience to the Pope; they neglected the examination and confession of faith which are prescribed in the Roman pontifical which should be observed universally; and they broke and despised all laws. They did this even though they must have known that the former candidate had been wrongly elected bishop of Quimper against the serious and repeated objections of the chapter, and that the latter was far more wrongly given as bishop to the church of Soissons since this church has a lawful pastor alive and well, Our venerable brother Henry Joseph Claude de Bourdeilles. He consequently considered that it was his duty to attack violently this great act of profanation and to provide ready help for his diocese. His letter published on the following day, the 25th, attests that he did so.

14. At the same time We learned that the bishop of Lidda had piled sin on top of sin. For on February 27, with the assistance of the new spurious bishops Expilly and Marolles, he rashly and sacrilegiously in the same church consecrated the parish priest Saurine as bishop of Aix, although this flourishing church rejoices in its own bishop, Our venerable brother Charles Auguste Lequien. Perhaps in appreciation of these actions, the bishop of Lidda, Jean Joseph Gobel, was elected archbishop of Paris, while the archbishop there was still living. He is following the example of Ischyras, who was proclaimed bishop of Alexandria at the Council of Tyre as payment for his sinful service in accusing St. Athanasius and ejecting him from his See.

15. This sad and burdensome news overwhelmed Us with sorrow. But uplifted by hope in God, We again sommoned the assembly of the Cardinals on March 17 to learn their views on this important development. While We were engaged in consultation with the cardinals on the 21st, another messenger from France brought Us word that the bishop of Laye had grown even more evil. With the assistance of the spurious bishops Expilly and Saurine, he had on the 6th in the same church and with the same sacrilege consecrated as bishop of Beauvais the parish priest Massieu, a deputy of the French Assembly; as bishop of Evreux another deputy, the parish priest Lindet; as bishop of Moulins the parish priest Laurent, also a deputy; and the parish priest Heraudin as bishop of Chateauroux.

They dared to do this, even though the first two of these churches have their own lawful pastors and the other two have not yet been created episcopal sees by Apostolic Authority. The proper view regarding men who allow themselves to be elected and consecrated for churches whose bishops are still governing and administering, was well expressed by St. Leo many years ago. In a letter to Julian, bishop of Cos, (chap. 4), he attacked a certain Theodosius who had occupied the see of Bishop Juvenal while he was still alive. "The nature of the deed leaves no doubt about the character of a man who usurps the place of a bishop in his lifetime. It is perfectly clear that he is wicked, since he is loved by the enemies of the faith."

16. The Church has at all times rightly rejected men elected by a low mob of the laity, men who share the same wrong opinions as their electors. This is abundantly proved by the pastoral letter of "Bishop" Expilly brought by the same messenger. It was published on February 25 to deceive the simple-minded, and obviously aimed at rending the seamless garment of Christ.

This man first mentions the oath (that is, the perjury) he has sworn, and introduces all the principal assertions of the French Constitution which he copies almost word-for-word. In accord with the statements of the Assembly, he attempts to prove that Christian dogma is not affected by this Constitution, while a better form of Church order is introduced which is closer to the purity of early centuries. He states that this is particularly true of the section which restores ecclesiastical elections to the people and consecrations to the metropolitans; but he established his claim only by former decrees of the French Assembly. The better to impress the simple-minded, he mentions his letter to Us of November 18, 1790, as if he enjoyed communion with this Apostolic See. He then addresses the different groups in the diocese and admonishes them all to receive him as their lawful pastor and to embrace the Constitution unreservedly.

17. Woe to the wretch! We purposely pass by matters relating to the civil government, but how rash he was to try to defend a Constitution concerning the affairs of the Church which nearly all the bishops of the French Church and many others of the clergy condemned and rejected as opposed to Church teaching and completely at variance with common practice, especially in regard to the election and consecration of bishops! Not even he could have concealed the evident truth, if he had not carefully avoided any mention of the most recent foolish decrees to come from the Assembly. For alongside other wickedness, these decrees go so far as to give the right of consecrating to any bishop at the discretion of the Assembly Executive.

18. Let this unfortunate man, who has advanced so far along the road to perdition, read Our answer to the French bishops; he will see the truth which he hates shining clear in every article, for at the start We have refuted the amazing errors contained in his letter. Meanwhile let him be aware that he has pronounced sentence on himself. He claims that the one elected must be consecrated by his metropolitan to obtain his lawful title in accordance with the ancient practice deriving from a canon of Nicaea; this right of the metropolitans derives from the right of the Apostolic See. If this is true, then how can Expilly think that he is lawfully and canonically installed since he owes his consecration not to the archbishop of Tours to whom the church of Quimper is suffragan, but to other bishops? For even if these men by their rash sacrilege could confer the rank of bishop on him, they certainly could not give him a jurisdiction which they themselves do not possess in accordance with the practice of every century, since they belong to different provinces. Moreover, this power of giving jurisdiction as a consequence of a new practice established now for several centuries and confirmed by general councils and even by concordats, has returned to its point of origin and does not belong in any way to metropolitans, but resides solely in the Apostolic See. So today the Pope as a duty of his office appoints bishops for each of the churches, and no lawful consecration may take place in the entire Catholic Church without the order of the Apostolic See (Trent, session 24, chap. 1, de Reformat.).

19. His letter to Us, far from relieving his plight, worsens it, and must be called schismatic. For that letter makes a mere pretense of establishing communion with Us, since it does not even mention the confirmation which We must give; it simply informs Us of the unlawful election as provided for in the French decrees. Hence, following the precedent of Our predecessors, We did not consider answering his letter; rather We gave orders that he should be warned to proceed no further, since We expected that he would attempt to do so. The bishop of Rennes indeed, of his own accord, had given him similar warning when he refused him the confirmation which he was insistently asking for.

Therefore, instead of accepting him as their pastor, the people should reject him with abhorrence as an intruder. For he has failed to profess the truth which he must acknowledge; he has begun to put his so-called pastoral duty to bad uses; and lastly he has become so presumptuous as to relax the Lenten observance commanded by the Church, at the end of his pastoral letter. So "he is an imitator of the devil and does not stand firm in the truth, but makes bad use of the appearance and name of the office he has attained," as St. Leo the Great wrote to some Egyptian bishops concerning a similar intruder.

20. From this series of sins schism is being introduced and spread in the kingdom of France, which is so dear to Us and has served religion so well; for the same reason pastors of first and second rank are being everywhere elected as the days go by, legitimate ministers are ejected from their positions, and ravening wolves are put in their place. We are certainly saddened by this sorrowful situation. Therefore to hinder the spread of schism from the start, to recall to their duty those who have strayed, to fortify the good in their purpose, and to preserve religion in that prosperous kingdom, We follow the advice of the Cardinals and answer the prayers of the entire group of bishops of the French church. Imitating the example of Our predecessors, We proclaim that each and every cardinal, archbishop, bishop, abbot, vicar, canon, parish priest, curate and member of the clergy, whether secular or regular, who has purely and simply taken the Civil Oath as ordered by the National Assembly is suspended from the exercise of his office and will act irregularly if he exercises his office unless he abjures his oath within forty days from this date. For the oath is the poisoned source and origin of all errors and the chief cause of the sorrow of the French Catholic church.

Elections Nullified

21. Furthermore, We declare specifically that the elections of the said Expilly, Marolles, Saurine, Massieu, Lindet, Laurent, Heraudin, and Gobel as Bishops of Quimper, Soissons, Aix, Beauvais, Evreux, Moulins, Chateauroux, and Paris are unlawful, sacrilegious, and utterly void. We rescind, efface, and abrogate them, as well as the recent creation of the so-called dioceses of Moulins, Chateauroux, and others.

22. We similarly declare and decree that their consecrations were sinful, and are illicit, unlawful, sacrilegious, and at variance with the regulations of the sacred canons; since they were rashly and wrongfully elected, they lack all ecclesiastical and spiritual jurisdiction for the guidance of souls, and have been suspended from all exercise of the episcopal office.

23. We declare likewise that Charles, bishop of Autun; Jean-Baptiste, bishop of Babylon; and Jean-Joseph, bishop of Lidda have been suspended from all exercise of their episcopal office as sacrilegious consecrators or assistants; all who gave them help, consent, or counsel at those accursed consecrations have been suspended from the exercise of their priestly, or other, office.

24. We therefore severely forbid the said Expilly and the other wickedly elected and illicitly consecrated men, under this punishment of suspension, to assume episcopal jurisdiction or any other authority for the guidance of souls since they have never received it. They must not grant dimissorial letters for ordinations. Nor must they appoint, depute, or confirm pastors, vicars, missionaries, helpers, functionaries, ministers, or others, whatever their title, for the care of souls and the administration of the Sacraments under any pretext of necessity whatsoever. Nor may they otherwise act, decree, or decide, whether separately or united as a council, on matters which relate to ecclesiastical jurisdiction. For We declare and proclaim publicly that all their dimissorial letters and deputations or confirmations, past and future, as well as all their rash proceedings and their consequences, are utterly void and without force.

25. We also command and prohibit under the same punishment of suspension both the men consecrated and their consecrators from illicitly conferring the sacrament of confirmation or of orders, or exercising in any way the episcopal office from which they have been suspended. Consequently anyone ordained by them should realize that he is suspended and will be guilty of irregularity if he exercises the orders he has received.

26. However to prevent greater evils, We decree and declare by this letter and Our authority that all other elections by the electors of municipal districts to French cathedral and parochial churches, whether vacant or occupied, whether old-established or recently and unlawfully created in accordance with the said Constitution of the Clergy, have been, are, and will be void, unlawful, sacrilegious, and utterly null, and We hereby rescind, efface, and revoke them. We therefore declare that men who have been or will be elected wickedly and wrongfully, whether to cathedral or parochial churches, lack all ecclesiastical and spiritual jurisdiction for the guidance of souls and that bishops who have been or will be illicitly consecrated are suspended from all exercise of their episcopal office; parish priests who have been or are to be invalidly appointed are suspended from their priestly ministry.

Accordingly We prohibit severely both those who have been or are to be elected as bishops from rashly accepting episcopal consecration from any metropolitan or bishop as well as the spurious bishops and their sacrilegious consecrators and all other archbishops and bishops from daring to consecrate on any pretext those who have been or are to be wrongfully elected. Furthermore, We command those who have been or are to be elected, to behave in no way as archbishops, bishops, parish priests, or vicars nor to call themselves by the name of any catherdral or parochial church, nor to assume any jurisdiction, authority, or faculty for the care of souls under the penalty of suspension and invalidity. None of those who have been named can ever be freed from the punishment of suspension, except by Us or by delegates of the Apostolic See.

27. With the greatest possible kindness, We have declared the canonical penalties imposed until the present in order that the evil deeds already accomplished may be corrected and prevented from spreading abroad. We hope in the Lord that the consecrators, the intruders in cathedral and parochial churches, and all the authors and supporters of the published Constitution will recognize their error and return repentant to the fold from which they were seduced by treacherous deceit.

For this reason, We insistently urge them to retire from their ministry, to draw back from the way to perdition on which they are travelling at full speed, and never to allow strange doctrines which are opposed to the teaching of Christ, the tradition of the Fathers, and the law of the Church to be spread among the people by men inspired by the philosophy of the present age. However, if Our mild manner of action and paternal warnings come to nothing—may God prevent this!—they should be aware that We do not intend to spare them those heavier penalties to which they are liable under the canons. They may be quite certain that We will anathematize them and proclaim them as such to the whole Church, since they are schismatic and cut off from communion with the Church and with Us.

For it is very fitting "that as each one chooses to lie in the mud of his own foolishness, so the laws should stay firm, and he should have the same lot as those whose error he has followed," as Leo the Great says in his letter to Julian, bishop of Coensum.

28. We now address you, who with few exceptions know your duty to your flocks, and publicly professed it, disregarding human calculations. You judged that the greatest care and labor should be given to counter the greatest dangers. We apply to you the lavish praise given by Leo the Great to the Egyptian Catholic bishops in Constantinople: "Although I heartily share your loving labors for the observance of the Catholic faith, and I regard the attacks of the heretics on you as attacks on my person, I realize that your invincible constancy by the strength of the Lord Jesus Christ in the evangelical and apostolic teaching is reason for joy rather than for sorrow. And when the enemies of the Christian faith removed you from the sees of the churches, you preferred to endure the evil of travel than to be defiled by any contact with their impiety." Indeed as We consider you, We are consoled and strongly urge you to stand fast in your purpose. To this end, We remind you of the bond of spiritual marriage which unites you to your churches and which only death or Our Apostolic authority can dissolve, according to the provision of the canons. Stay with your churches, then, and never leave them at the bidding of ravening wolves whose plots you have condemned in holy zeal as you unhesitatingly performed the tasks of lawful authority.

29. Next We address you, beloved sons, canons of excellent chapters. Subject to your archbishops and bishops, as is right, you form one clerical body as limbs which are united with their head, which the civil power is unable to destroy or overthrow. You have won great praise in following the remarkable example of your prelates: never turn aside from the right road, on which you are set, and never allow anyone in false bishop's garments with a company of subordinates to take possession of your churches. For if the churches are deprived of their bishops, they will be your concern alone, despite all new plots hatched against you. Therefore, united in mind and counsel, keep as far from you as possible all intrusion and schism.

30. We also address you, beloved sons, parish priests and curates, who in great numbers and firm virtue have performed your duty far differently from your colleagues who, overcome by weakness or swept away by the tide of ambition, have gone over to the service of error. We hope that these men will soon return to their duty on receiving Our admonition. Press on bravely with the work you have begun, and bear in mind that the appointment you received from your lawful bishops can be taken from you only by them. Consequently, even if you are removed from your place by the civil power, you will still always be the lawful pastors, in duty bound as far as you are able to keep off the thieves who try to sneak into your place with the sole aim of destroying the souls entrusted to your care, whose salvation you will have to account for.

31. We address you too, beloved sons, priests, and other clergy and ministers of France. Since you have been called to the Lord's work, you ought to stay close to your lawful pastors and be firm in faith and doctrine. Above all, avoid and condemn the sacrilegious intruders.

32. At length We beseech you all, beloved Catholic children, in the kingdom of France; as you recall the religion and faith of your fathers, We urge you lovingly not to abandon it. For it is the one true religion which both confers eternal life and makes safe and thriving civil societies. Carefully beware of lending your ears to the treacherous speech of the philosophy of this age which leads to death. Keep away from all intruders, whether called archbishops, bishops, or parish priests; do not hold communion with them especially in divine worship. Listen carefully to the message of your lawful pastors who are still living, and who will be put in charge of you later, according to the canons. Finally, in one word, stay close to Us. For no one can be in the Church of Christ without being in unity with its visible head and founded on the See of Peter.

To inspire all to fulfil their duties more ardently, We implore the heavenly Father to send you the Spirit of counsel, truth, and constancy. As a pledge of Our paternal love, beloved sons, venerable brothers and beloved children, We impart to you the Apostolic blessing.

Given at Rome in St. Peter's under the Ring of the Fisherman on April 13, 1791, in the 17th year of Our pontificate.

†

LATIN TEXT: *Bull. Rom. Cont.*, 6^3: 2324-33.

ENGLISH TRANSLATION: Padraig M. O'Cleirigh.

COMMENTARY:

Brugière, Pierre. *Instruction pastorale sur le bref du pape* [13 avril 1791]. Paris, 1791.

PAX

POPE PIUS VII
1800-1823

The island monastery of S. Giorgio Maggiore in Venice was the site selected for the beginning of a new era in papal history. Here on December 1, 1799 the Benedictines welcomed twenty-four of the thirty-six living cardinals to elect the successor of Pius VI. On March 1, 1800 Cardinal Barnaba Chiaramonti, bishop of Imola, was elected pope and chose the name of Pius VII.

Barnaba Chiaramonti was born at Cesena (Emilia) on August 14, 1740 of an old aristocratic family that numbered among its ancestors a famous astronomer and some well-known jurists and physicians. His mother, whose family was closely connected with that of Pius VI, was widowed in 1750 and, after rearing her five children, entered a Carmelite convent (1762). At the age of sixteen Barnaba entered the Benedictines taking Gregorio as his religious name. He studied at St. Justina's in Padua and later at St. Anselm's in Rome where one of his professors was Andrea Bina, the inventor of the seismograph. Barnaba was appointed professor at the Abbey of St. John in Parma (1766-1775), abbot of San Callisto in Rome (1775), and professor at St. Anselm's (1775-1781). Named titular abbot of St. Paul's in Rome and bishop of Tivoli (1783) he was transferred to the See of Imola in 1785 and simultaneously raised to the cardinalate.

As bishop he showed pastoral care for his people, was concerned with spiritual interests, energetic in repressing abuses, and successful in defending his episcopal rights against the Holy Office. During the first invasion of the French (1796) he prevented an uprising in Lugo, but made it clear that while he recognized the existing government he would resist strongly whenever spiritual values were at stake. On matters of principle he was inflexible but through diplomatic skill and a willingness to conciliate seemed able to conserve the essentials.

Upon assuming office as pope Pius VII appointed Cardinal Ercole Consalvi as his secretary of state and began a pontificate that was to have as its main concern relations between Church and State in France. When Napoleon, after his arrival in Rome, made overtures for a concordat with France, Pius responded in the spirit that was to characterize his entire pontificate. He was interested in the overtures for a religious peace but was displeased with the implication that the safety of the States of the Church depended upon accommodation in religious matters; he made it clear that he would not tolerate a confusion of temporal and spiritual values. He did not hesitate, however, to take the risk of negotiating through Cardinal Consalvi, and the Concordat of 1801 was signed. This concordat was to continue to regulate the ecclesiastical affairs in France until the arbitrary abrogation by the third Republic in 1905. The Italian concordat followed in 1803 but was disappointing in its conditions.

In 1805 Napoleon occupied Ancona despite the protests of the pope, was crowned in Milan as king of Italy, and encircled Rome. In 1808 General Miollis invaded Rome, Pius was taken prisoner, carried off (July 10, 1809), and deported to Savona (near Genoa). The States of the Church were incorporated into the French Empire. In 1812 the pope was transferred to Fontainebleau where exhausted and ill he signed a project of concordat. Napoleon published the so-called concordat of Fontainebleau in 1813 as if it were a final agreement; the pope drew up a testament in which he abrogated all the concessions given in the project he had signed. After the military reverses in Russia and the consequent fall of Napoleon, Pius was released, reentered Rome (May 24, 1814), and in the same year issued his motu proprio (August 7) revoking the brief of suppression of July 21, 1773 and ordering the complete restoration of the Society of Jesus.

Pius VII's pontificate marks a transition between the troublesome times of the French Revolution and the quiet pontificates that were to follow. The Congress of Vienna in 1815 restored the States of the Church which were reorganized by Consalvi, one of the ablest diplomats of the age. New concordats were concluded with Bavaria and Sardinia in 1817, followed by a series of concordats with other states. The pope had won the admiration of the world by his heroic resistance to Napoleon and by his magnanimous charity to the emperor in his defeat and exile. With the sword conquered by the spirit Pius VII died on August 20, 1823.

DIU SATIS

ENCYCLICAL OF POPE PIUS VII
ON A RETURN TO GOSPEL
PRINCIPLES
MAY 15, 1800
26

To His Venerable Brothers, All Patriarchs, Primates, Archbishops and Bishops in Union and Favor with the Apostolic See.

Venerable Brothers, We Give you Greeting and Our Apostolic Blessing.

Long enough have We been silent. Two months have already passed, months of anxiety and toil, since God conferred on Us, despite Our weakness, the burden of this high office of guiding the entire Church. It is not so much custom as Our great love for you which impels Us to address you by at least this letter. We could have no sweeter nor so pleasant a task.

2. The particular part of Our duty which is expressed in the words, "strengthen your brethren," also urges Us to do so. For at the present turbulent time, as much as ever, Satan "has sought after us all in order to sift us as wheat." Still who is so sluggish, so different-minded to Us not to understand fully that Christ does what He said He would do: "to pray for Peter that his faith should not fail"[1] even in the present grim circumstances. Later ages will be amazed at the wisdom, magnanimity, and firmness of Our predecessor Pius VI. We could wish that We had also inherited his courage which withstood unshaken the blows of every storm and misfortune.

Pope Martin I

3. Indeed, the famous Martin who long ago won great praise for this See, commends faithfulness and fortitude to Us by his strengthening and defense of the truth and by the endurance of labors and pains. He was driven from his See and from the City, stripped of his rule, his rank, and his entire fortune. As soon as he arrived in any peaceful place, he was forced to move. Despite his advanced age and an illness which prevented his walking, he was banished to a remote land and repeatedly threatened with an even more painful exile. Without the assistance offered by the pious generosity of individuals, he would not have had food for himself and his few attendants. Although he was tempted daily in his weakened and lonely state, he never surrendered his integrity. No deceit could trick, no fear perturb, no promises conquer, no difficulties or dangers break him. His enemies could extract from him no sign which would not prove to all that Peter "until this time and forever lives in his successors and exercises judgment as is particularly clear in every age"[2] as an excellent writer at the Council of Ephesus says.

Expulsion of Cardinals

4. It is a fact of very great importance, and it

should be recalled gratefully, that God conferred death on Pius VI (this expression is better than that He took life from him) at a time when there was no obstacle to duly deciding on his successor. Remember Our fear and suspense when the Cardinals were personally expelled from their sees. Several of them were imprisoned, some hunted for their lives, and many forced to cross the sea in depths of winter, deprived of their possessions—all of them in want and separated from one another by great distances. Since the enemy occupied the roads, they could not correspond with one another nor were they allowed to go anywhere. It was clear that they could never assemble to assist the Church if any misfortune struck down Pius VI who was daily said to be between life and death.

5. Who would have dared at that time, with our affairs assailed and almost destroyed, to hope on the basis of human plans and help for what has actually happened by the special kindness of God? Before he died, Pius VI established the mode of holding the elections of his successors and most of Italy was restored to peace. All arrangements were made for the cardinals to meet in Venice to vote under the protection of Francis, Apostolic King of Hungary, illustrious King of Bohemia, and Emperor-elect of the Romans.

6. From these events men should realize that all attempts to overthrow the "House of God" are in vain. For this is the Church founded on Peter, "Rock," not merely in name but in truth. Against this "the gates of hell will not prevail"[3] "for it is founded on a rock."[4] There has never been an enemy of the Christian religion who was not simultaneously at wicked war with the See of Peter, since while this See remained strong the survival of the Christian religion was assured. As St. Irenaeus proclaims openly to all, "by the order and succession of the Roman pontiffs the tradition from the Apostles in the Church and the proclamation of the truth has come down to us. And this is the fullest demonstration that it is the one and the same life-giving faith which has been preserved in the Church until now since the time of the Apostles and has been handed on in truth."[5]

Attacks Upon Church

7. This is the direction of attack chosen by those men of today who replace with the defiling plague of false philosophy, the philosophy (as the Greek Fathers in particular rightly name Christian teaching) which the Son of God, who is eternal wisdom, brought down from heaven and imparted to men. But "it has been written"—and these words of Paul are aimed directly at such men—"'I will destroy the wisdom of the wise, and the sense of the sensible I will reject.' Where is a wise man, where a scribe, where the examiner of this world? Has not God made foolish the wisdom of this world?"[6]

Uphold the Church

8. We are led to recall those words, venerable brothers, especially since they marvellously refresh Us. They inspire Us to shun no toil on behalf of Christ's Church which He has entrusted to Us to rule, protect, adorn, and extend, despite Our fear of this unexpected burden. Assuredly "He will make us fitting ministers of the new testament as exaltation derives from the power of God and not from Ourselves." Therefore I now urge you to join me and devote your eager effort to this objective. May Christ's prayer to His Father never leave our minds: "Holy Father, keep them in your name that they may be one as We. . . .not for these only (i.e. the Apostles) do I pray, but also for those who through their word will believe in me that they all may be one as you, Father, in me and I in you, that they also may be one in Us."[7]

9. "It is Our particular duty," as Cyprian says (in *On the Unity of the Church*), "to uphold and defend this unity" so that the world may see, wonder and believe "that you have sent me," as Christ's prayer continues. Christ is with Us and never leaves Our side; he strengthens Us with the words: "Let not your heart be troubled, nor let it fear. You believe in God, believe also in me."[8] Relying on His help, let us work for the common safety with combined zeal.

10. Consolation and cure is called for by cities, towns, countryside, states, provinces, kingdoms, and nations, which for many years have been attacked, defeated, destroyed, and made wretched. But this can be sought and hoped for only from the teaching of Christ. We can now, with greater confidence, rebuke those who think otherwise with the words of St. Augustine: "Let them give us an army composed of soldiers such as Christ's teaching demands, such provincials, such veterans, such spouses, such parents, such children, such masters, such servants, such

kings, such judges, and finally such men as repay debts to the public treasury and such tax-officials as the Christian teaching prescribes." Since they are not able to do so, "let them admit at once that obedience to this teaching would be of great assistance to the state."[9]

Help Those in Distress

11. Therefore it is Our duty to help men and nations who are in distress, and to eliminate all present and threatening evils. For "Christ has given pastors and teachers for the perfecting of the saints, for the work of the ministry, for the building up of Christ's Body, until we all come together to the unity of faith and knowledge of God's son."[10] If ever anything deters, prevents, or delays any one of us from performing this task, what a disgraceful sin he will commit! Therefore, omit no watchfulness, diligence, care, and effort, in order to "guard the deposit" of Christ's teaching whose destruction has been planned, as you know, by a great conspiracy.

12. Do not admit anyone to the clergy, entrust to no one the ministry of the mysteries of God, allow no one to hear confessions or preach sermons, do not transfer any administration or office to anyone, before you carefully weigh, examine and "test their spirit to see if they are of God."

Guard Against False Apostles Who Corrupt the Young

13. Would that We had not learned by experience how many "false apostles" the present age has spawned! These are "deceitful workmen who transform themselves into apostles of Christ." Unless we are on our guard "they will destroy the understanding of the faithful as the serpent seduced Eve by his cleverness, and they will fall away from their simplicity which is in Christ."[11] While you must care for the whole flock over which the Holy Spirit has placed you as bishop, the watchfulness, eagerness, and effort of your fatherly love and benevolence is demanded in particular by boys and young men. Christ by example and statement has particularly entrusted these to us[12] and the enemies of private property and states who are striving to confound all laws, divine and human, hope to effect their wicked plans chiefly by corrupting their young minds. For they are aware that the young are like soft wax and can easily be drawn in any direction, bent and moulded and that they firmly retain a form once they have received it and it has been hardened by advancing years; then they will reject a different form. Hence the well-worn proverb from scripture: "A young man will not depart from his way even when he has grown old."[13]

14. Do not allow "that the children of this world be wiser in their generation than the children of light." Carefully investigate the directors given charge of boys and young men in seminaries and colleges, and the courses they are to follow, the teachers chosen for secondary schools, and the schools which are to be run. Keep out the ravening wolves who do not spare the flock of innocent lambs, and expel them if necessary by the way they entered. Eliminate them at once "according to the power which the Lord gave you for edification."[14] We must use to the full this power to eradicate this very serious threat to our children. This course is required for the safety of Church, state, leaders, and all human beings; their safety should be dearer and more important to Us than Our own life. Clement XIII treated this subject in his Brief to you on 25th November 1766.

Dangerous Books

15. Books which openly oppose the teaching of Christ are to be burned. Even more importantly, the eyes and minds of all must be kept from books, which do so more stealthily and deceitfully. To recognize such books, as St. Cyprian says in *On the Unity of the Church*, "there is not need of a long treatise and arguments: The sum of truth is a proof easy for faith: the Lord says to Peter, 'feed my sheep.' " So the sheep of Christ should consider safe and eat cheerfully the food to which Peter's voice and authority directs them; but despite any beauty and charm, they should shun as harmful and plague-ridden, what this voice forbids them. Those who do not comply are certainly not to be counted among the sheep of Christ.

16. In this case We cannot overlook, keep silent or act sluggishly. For unless this great license of thinking, speaking, writing, and reading is repressed, it will appear that the strategy and armies of wise kings and generals have relieved us for but a short time from this evil which has crushed us for so long. But so long as its stock and seed is not removed and destroyed (I shudder to say it but it must be said), it will spread abroad and be strengthened to reach over the whole world. To destroy it later or to rout it, legions, guards, watches, the armories of cities, and the defenses of empires will not be enough.

17. Is any one of Us not aroused by the words God speaks to Us through the prophet Ezechiel: "Son of man, I have given you as a guide to the house of Israel: and you shall hear a word from my mouth, and you shall proclaim to them from me. If when I say to the wicked, you shall die the death, you do not proclaim it to him. . . .the wicked man shall die in his iniquity but I shall look for his blood from your hand."[15] I confess this statement startles me and prevents me from being slothful and fearful in executing the demands of my office. I promise and swear that I will always be not only your helper and supporter, but your chief and leader.

Protect the Laws of the Church

18. Still another deposit which We must firmly protect is that of the Church's holy laws by which it establishes its own practice, and over which it alone has power. Under these laws, virtue and piety thrive; the spouse of Christ terrifies her enemies as an army set in battle array. Many of these laws are like foundations laid down to bear the weight of the faith, as Our predecessor St. Zosimus says.[16] There is no greater benefit or boast for kings and political leaders, as another wise and brave predecessor, St. Felix, wrote to Emperor Zeno, than "to allow the Catholic Church to enjoy its own laws and not to let anyone interfere with its liberty. . . .For it is certain that it is beneficial for their own affairs, as God has laid down, for kings to submit their will to the priests of Christ when God's business is in question, rather than imposing it."

Wealth of the Church

19. Regarding the Church's property, wealth which has been vowed, holy money, the substance of the saints—the business of God, as Fathers, councils and scripture state—shall We give you any instructions about this now that the Church has been wretchedly stripped of them? Only this: to devote your efforts so that everyone will realize the truth of the short statement of the synod of Aachen long ago. "Whoever takes away or intends to take away what other faithful have given from the heritage of their possessions for the care of their souls, the honor of God, the beauty of His Church and the use of its ministers, assuredly turns the gifts of others into danger for his own soul."[17] "Not from an eagerness to hold what we have or for the sake of worldly benefit, but from reflection on the divine judgment, are we moved to reiterate the command to be faithful and wise stewards."[18] (Indeed, We can rightly affirm this to all, no less strongly than Our predecessor St. Agapitus.) Christian kings and princes who rightly hold and boast that they are "guardians"[19] of the Church as Isaiah said, will withdraw from no place at Our prayers, exhortations, warnings, or actions. But certainly their faith, piety, justice, wisdom, and religion have given Us great hope that they will ensure immediately that God receives His own and that they will not let their ears resound with God's complaints. "You have taken my silver and gold and my lovely desirable things."[20] Constantine the Great and Charlemagne were like these kings, and their noble generosity and justice were chiefly directed to the Church. The former asserted that he had known many kingdoms whose kings had perished because they had despoiled the Church. Because of this he commanded and urged his children and their successors at the head of the state: "We forbid them to the extent of Our power by God and all the merits of his saints to do such acts or agree with those who desire to do them. But let them be helpers and defenders of the churches and of the service of God insofar as they can."[21]

20. I cannot conceal from you at the end of this letter, venerable brothers, "Since my sorrow is great and the pain of my heart unceasing," my feelings for my children, the peoples of France, and other peoples still seething with the same madness. Nothing would be more desirable to me than to give my life for them if their safety could be achieved by my death. We do not deny—rather, We proclaim—that the bitterness of Our grief is much diminished by the invincible purpose which several of you have displayed. We remember this daily. Men of all kinds, age, and rank have followed this example. They do so, preferring to suffer any insults, dangers, losses, and penalties, and to face death itself. They consider this nobler than to be defiled by the stain of an illicit and wicked sacrament thereby committing sin and disobeying the decrees of the Apostolic See. Indeed, the courage of ancient times has been renewed no less than the cruelty.

21. But every people is embraced by my fatherly love, thoughts, and concern. We grieve and suffer greatly if any are separated from the truth, and We desire to assist them. Join us, then, in Our prayers that after this long-lasting disturbance, "the Church may have peace to be built up as it walks in the fear of the Lord and in the consolation of the Holy Spirit." May nothing hinder all peoples from becoming one fold with one shepherd.

22. Meanwhile We most willingly impart the Apostolic Blessing to you in your courage and preparedness, and to the flock you govern.

Given at Venice in the monastery of San Giorgio Maggiore on the 15th of May 1800 in the first year of Our pontificate.

†

LATIN TEXT: *Bull. Rom. Cont.*, 7^1: 24-29.

ENGLISH TRANSLATION: Padraig M. O'Cleirigh.

REFERENCES:

1. Lk 22.
2. *Actio* 1, no. 11.
3. Mt 16.
4. Mt 7.
5. *Adversus haereses*, bk. 3, chap. 3.
6. I Cor 1.19-20.
7. Jn 17.
8. Jn 14.
9. Bk. 83, Question.
10. Eph 4.12.
11. II Cor 11.
12. Mt 19, Mk 10, Lk 18.
13. Prv 22.
14. II Cor 13.
15. Ez 3.17-18.
16. Epistle 7.
17. Chap. 37, Harduin, *Conc.*, vol. 4, col. 1423.
18. Epistle 4 to Caesarius, Bishop of Arles.
19. Is 49.23.
20. Jl 3.
21. Ad. Balut., bk. 1, chap. 3.

POPE LEO XII
1823-1829

Annibale Sermattei della Genga was born at the Castello della Genga in the territory of Spoleta on August 22, 1760. At the age of thirteen he entered the Collegio of Osimo, transferred to the Collegio Piceno in Rome (1778), and from there went to the Accademia dei Nobili Ecclesiastici. A dispensation, because he was only twenty-three, was necessary for his ordination in 1783. Handsome, with an engaging manner, he soon attracted the notice of Pope Pius VI who raised him to the prelature as secret chamberlain.

In 1790 he was selected to deliver an oration in the Sistine Chapel on the death of the Emperor Joseph II. He became a canon of St. Peter's Basilica (1792), the following year was consecrated titular archbishop of Tyre, sent as nuncio to Lucerne, and then transferred to the nunciature of Cologne (1794-1805), a post which he occupied for eleven years in spite of the domination of the ambitious Napoleon I. In 1805 he was accredited as nuncio extraordinary to the Diet of Ratisbon so that he might arbitrate the differences between the Church in Germany and the Prussian rulers. Returning to Rome he learned that Napoleon had asked for the substitution of another nuncio who would be more amenable to his plans. Pius VI, however, stood firm and Della Genga returned to Munich.

In 1808 when Della Genga went to Paris with Cardinal Caprara to arrange an agreement between the Holy See and Napoleon I he was received coldly and the negotiations were fruitless. When he returned to Rome it was to witness the humiliation and indignities Pius VII was suffering at the hands of his French captors. Returning to Monticelli, he spent his time teaching the peasants of the area. Expecting to spend the rest of his life there he erected a tomb for his mother and for himself in the abbey church.

In 1814 with the fall of Napoleon Pius VII returned to Rome and sent Della Genga to Paris as envoy extraordingary to convey the pope's congratulations to Louis XVIII. Cardinal Consalvi, whose policies the envoy opposed, resented his mission. Della Genga returned to Rome and again went to Monticelli. Two years later (1816) he was created a cardinal and named bishop of Senigallia but because of illness he resigned after two years the see in which he had never been installed. With health improved, he was appointed vicar general of Rome (1820), archpriest of the Liberian Basilica, and prefect of several congregations. On the death of Pius VII in 1823 the conclave opened at the Quirinal, and after the Austrian veto of Cardinal Severoli, elected Della Genga pope (September 23, 1823). He took the name of Leo XII.

Leo's pontificate aimed at the restoration of religion, struggled against errors that undermined the faith, condemned Freemasonry and the Carbonari, provoked press censorship, condemned indifferentism in religious matters, and proscribed biblical societies. As ruler of the Church he showed intelligence and energy but was unequal to the difficulties that confronted him, and his inefficiency as the administrator of the States of the Church left much to be desired. In the face of the new social and political order he defended the *ancien regime* and evidenced little insight into the hopes and visions of the pioneers of the new freedom. It had been expected that he would reverse the conciliatory policy of Pius VII but meeting with determined opposition from the powers his foreign policy, in spite of his own inclinations to severe measures, began to follow the moderate lines laid down by Cardinal Consalvi.

In the papal states he pursued a regressive policy although the people were asking for greater self-determination and lay administration. In his relations with the European powers he was more conciliatory than with his own subjects but on the whole his efforts in dealing with them were unsuccessful. He restored the Gregorian University to the Jesuits (1824), reestablished the Vatican printing press, enriched the Vatican Library, and revived the practice of holding jubilees (1825).

During the summer of 1828 with the appointment of Cardinal Tomaso Bernitti, a disciple of Consalvi, as secretary of state a new orientation for the papacy seemed imminent. Bernetti had no opportunity of implementing the change of policy, however, because Leo XII died on February 10, 1829.

UBI PRIMUM

ENCYCLICAL OF POPE LEO XII ON
HIS ASSUMING THE PONTIFICATE
MAY 5, 1824

To All Patriarchs, Primates, Archbishops, and Bishops.

Venerable Brothers, We Give You Greeting and Our Apostolic Blessing.

As soon as We were raised to the supreme pontificate, We began to exclaim immediately with St. Leo the Great: "O Lord I have heard your utterance and been afraid: I have reflected on your works and been terrified. For what is so unaccustomed and so much to be feared as toil to the weak, height to the lowly, rank to the undeserving? Yet We do not despair or faint since it is not on Ourselves that We depend but on Him who works in Us."[1] That praiseworthy pope spoke thus to humble himself, but We can say and confess this in very truth.

2. We desired to address you as soon as possible, venerable brothers, and to reveal Our feelings to you. For you are Our crown and joy, as your flocks, We feel sure, are crown and joy to you. But partly because We were preoccupied with the serious concerns of Our Apostolic office and partly, indeed principally, because We were afflicted by a long illness, until now We have been unable to do so. This has caused Us great sorrow. But Our merciful God now grants the fulfillment of Our desire. The silence, however, which until now We were constrained to observe possessed its own consolation. For God who consoles the humble consoled Us too by the love and enthusiasm of your religious devotion for Us. This was a signal instance of the piety of Christian unity, causing Us to rejoice greatly and to give thanks to God. And so as a proof of Our love We are sending you this letter to give you additional encouragement to observe the divine commandments and to fight bravely the Lord's battles.

Be An Example to Your Flock

3. You know that the Apostle Peter instructed bishops in these words: "Feed God's flock which is given to you, caring for them not under constraint but freely for God's sake, not for the sake of base gain but willingly, nor as lording it over the clergy but being examples to your flock from the heart."[2] From this you understand rightly the method of action which is proposed for you. You also understand the virtues of the mind which you should increasingly practice, the richer knowledge with which you should adorn it, and the fruit of piety and love which you should not only produce but also share with your flock. In this way you will certainly attain the object of your ministry and be examples to your flock from the heart. To some you will give milk, to others

meat. You will train your flock not only by teaching, but by work and example as well, to lead a quiet life on earth in Christ Jesus. You will lead them to obtain eternal happiness with you. For the chief of the Apostles says: "And when the prince of shepherds appears you will receive an imperishable crown of glory."

4. We had hoped to bring many matters to your attention but We shall simply touch on some of them, and then deal at greater length with the more serious questions as the need of Our sad times demands.

5. You already understand the teaching of the Apostle on the great caution required in promoting candidates to minor and especially to major orders. He writes to Timothy: "Lay hands on no one quickly."[3] You understand also the decrees of the Council of Trent on the appointment of pastors and on the seminaries for clerics[4] and the clarification of these decrees by Our predecessors.

Precept of Residence

6. You know too the importance of residing personally in your diocese, a duty to which your office strictly obliges you. This is evident from the decrees and apostolic constitutions of many councils, and was confirmed by the holy Council of Trent in the following words: "The divine commandment orders everyone entrusted with the care of souls to know their sheep and to offer sacrifice for them. They must also feed them by preaching the divine word, by administering the sacrament, and by setting a good example. Furthermore, they must take fatherly care of the poor and other wretched persons and perform their other pastoral duties. Since none of these can be accomplished by men who do not attend their flock but abandon it as hirelings do, the holy council warns and exhorts them to remember the divine commandments by being an example to their flock, feeding and guiding them in justice and in truth."[5] Bound as We are by the obligation of this great office and zealous as We are for the glory of God, We heartily praise those who observe this command strictly. But We warn and exhort those who disobey these ecclesiastical sanctions—for it is sad but not surprising that there are some such men among the great number of bishops—to reflect seriously that the supreme judge will demand the blood of their sheep from their hands and judge with great strictness those who are their leaders.

Precept of Visitation

7. This fearful sentence, as you know well, does not strike only those who do not reside in person in their diocese or seek to leave it on every empty pretext; it includes also those who refuse without reason to perform the task of visitation according to the prescriptions of the canons. For they will never satisfy the requirements of the decree of Trent unless they take care to approach their charges in person and like a good shepherd cherish the good while they seek the strays and lead them at last to the fold, by calling and driving some of them strongly and others gently.

8. Bishops who do not with due concern try to obey the precepts of residence or visitation will not avoid the fearful judgment of Our Savior the supreme shepherd by pleading that they fulfilled their duties through delegated ministers.

9. For care of the flock has been entrusted to themselves not to their ministers; it was to themselves that the gifts of the Spirit were promised. Consequently the sheep listen more gladly to the voice of their own shepherd than to that of a representative. They seek salutary food with more confidence from the shepherd's hand than from his representative's, and rejoice more to obtain it. For His hand is as the hand of the Lord, whose person is reverenced in His bishops. All this is also amply borne out by experience, the world's instructor.

10. It would be enough to write to you on the previous topics since you are not thankless in keeping silence about your gifts nor proud in presuming on your merits.[6] Certainly men who desire ardently to progress from virtue to virtue ought to be such as We have described. Inspired by the example of holy bishops, ancient and recent, they boast in the Lord of smiting the Church's enemies and reforming evil morals. But always keep in mind the golden saying of Leo the Great. "In this struggle no victory is definitive enough to prevent the recurrence of conflict."[7]

Religious Tolerance and Indifferentism

11. Who can reflect without weeping on the fierce and mighty conflicts which have raged in Our times and continue to rage almost daily against the Catholic religion? Listen to St. Jerome: "It is no small spark, no small spark, I say, which is scarcely seen in being observed; it is not a little leaven which is obviously a small thing. It is rather a flame which attempts to devastate almost the entire world and to burn up walls, cities, broad pastures and districts; and a leaven which mixes with the flour and tries to destroy its whole substance."[8] With this reason for fear, We would lose all heart for Our apostolic service were it not that the Guardian of Israel does not slumber or sleep, and says to His disciples: "Behold I am with you all days even to the end of the world," and condescends to be shepherd of shepherds as well as guardian of the sheep.[9]

12. But at what are these remarks aimed? A certain sect, which you surely know, has unjustly arrogated to itself the name of philosophy, and has aroused from the ashes the disorderly ranks of practically every error. Under the gentle appearance of piety and liberality this sect professes what they call tolerance or indifferentism. It preaches that not only in civil affairs, which is not Our concern here, but also in religion, God has given every individual a wide freedom to embrace and adopt without danger to his salvation whatever sect or opinion appeals to him on the basis of his private judgment. The apostle Paul warns us against the impiety of these madmen. "I beseech you, brethren, to behold those who create dissensions and scandals beyond the teaching which you have learned. Keep away from such men. They do not serve Christ Our Lord but their own belly, and by sweet speeches and blessings they seduce the hearts of the innocent."[10]

13. Of course this error is not new, but in Our days it rages with a new rashness against the constancy and integrity of the Catholic faith. Eusebius cites Rhodo as his source for saying that the heretic Apelles in the second century had already produced the mad theory that faith should not be investigated, but that each man should persevere in the faith he was raised in.[11] Even those who put faith in a crucified man were to be saved, according to Apelles, provided that they engaged in good works. Rhetorius too, as We learn from St. Augustine, used to claim that all the heretics walked on the right road and spoke truth. But Augustine adds that this is such nonsense that he cannot believe it.[12] The current indifferentism has developed to the point of arguing that everyone is on the right road. This includes not only all those sects which though outside the Catholic Church verbally accept revelation as a foundation, but those groups too which spurn the idea of divine revelation and profess a pure deism or even a pure naturalism. The indifferentism of Rhetorius seemed absurd to St. Augustine, and rightly so, but it did acknowledge certain limits. But a tolerance which extends to Deism and Naturalism, which even the ancient heretics rejected, can never be approved by anyone who uses his reason. Nevertheless—alas for the times; alas for this lying philosophy!—such a tolerance is approved, defended, and praised by these pseudo-philosophers.

14. Certainly many remarkable authors, adherents of the true philosophy, have taken pains to attack and crush this strange view. But the matter is so self-evident that it is superfluous to give additional arguments. It is impossible for the most true God, who is Truth Itself, the best, the wisest Provider, and the Rewarder of good men, to approve all sects who profess false teachings which are often inconsistent with one another and contradictory, and to confer eternal rewards on their members. For we have a surer word of the prophet, and in writing to you We speak wisdom among the perfect; not the wisdom of this world but the wisdom of God in a mystery. By it we are taught, and by divine faith we hold one Lord, one faith, one baptism, and that no other name under heaven is given to men except the name of Jesus Christ of Nazareth in which we must be saved. This is why we profess that there is no salvation outside the Church.

15. But Oh! the depth of the riches of the wisdom and knowledge of God! How incomprehensible His judgments![13] God, who destroys the wisdom of the wise, has clearly given the enemies of His Church, who despise supernatural revelation, a perverted mind[14] corresponding to the symbol of iniquity which was written on the forehead of the wicked woman in the Apocalypse.[15] For what greater iniquity is there than for those proud men not only to abandon true religion, but also to seek to ensnare the imprudent by criticisms of every sort, in speech and writings filled with all deceit! Let God arise and restrain, make futile and destroy this unbridled license in all its manifestations.

16. Furthermore, quite apart from the flood of evil books which are intrinsically hostile to religion, the wickedness of our enemies has gone so far as to try to turn against religion the sacred writings divinely given to us for the building up of religion.

The Bible Society

17. You have noticed a society, commonly called the Bible society, boldly spreading throughout the whole world. Rejecting the traditions of the holy Fathers and infringing the well-known decree of the Council of Trent,[16] it works by every means to have the holy Bible translated, or rather mistranslated, into the ordinary languages of every nation. There are good reasons for fear that (as has already happened in some of their commentaries and in other respects by a distorted interpretation of Christ's gospel) they will produce a gospel of men, or what is worse, a gospel of the devil![17]

18. To prevent this evil, Our predecessors published many constitutions. Most recently Pius VII wrote two briefs, one to Ignatius, Archbishop of Gniezno, the other to Stanislaus, Archbishop of Mohileu, quoting carefully and wisely many passages from the sacred writings and from the tradition to show how harmful to faith and morals this wretched undertaking is.

19. In virtue of Our apostolic office, We too exhort you to try every means of keeping your flock from those deadly pastures. Do everything possible to see that the faithful observe strictly the rules of our Congregation of the Index. Convince them that to allow holy Bibles in the ordinary language, wholesale and without distinction, would on account of human rashness cause more harm than good.

20. Experience also shows that this is true, and aside from other Fathers, St. Augustine states it in the following words: "Heresies and other wicked teachings which ensnare souls and cast them into the deep, arise only when the good scriptures are badly understood and when what is not well understood in them is affirmed with daring rashness."[18]

21. Such is the object of this society and it leaves no means untried to achieve its objective. For it delights in printing its own translations, as well as in dashing through every city to distribute them itself to the common people. Indeed, to seduce the minds of the simple, it is careful to sell them in one place, while elsewhere it wants to give them as a gift with calculating generosity.

22. But if one wishes to search out the true source of all the evils which We have already lamented, as well as those which We pass over for the sake of brevity, he will surely find that from the start it has ever been a dogged contempt for the Church's authority. The Church, as St. Leo the Great teaches,[19] in well-ordered love accepts Peter in the See of Peter, and sees and honors Peter in the person of his successor the Roman pontiff. Peter still maintains the concern of all pastors in guarding their flocks, and his high rank does not fail even in an unworthy heir.[20] In Peter then, as is aptly remarked by the same holy Doctor, the courage of all is strengthened and the help of divine grace is so ordered that the constancy conferred on Peter through Christ is conferred on the apostles through Peter. It is clear that contempt of the Church's authority is opposed to the command of Christ and consequently opposes the apostles and their successors, the Church's ministers who speak as their representatives.[21] He who hears you, hears me; and he who despises you, despises me; and the Church is the pillar and firmament of truth, as the apostle Paul teaches.[22] In reference to these words St. Augustine says: "Whoever is without the Church will not be reckoned among the sons, and whoever does not want to have the Church as mother will not have God as father."[23]

23. Therefore, venerable brothers, keep all these words in mind and often reflect on them. Teach your people great reverence for the Church's authority which has been directly established by God. Do not lose heart. With St. Augustine We say that "all around us the waters of the flood are roaring, that is, the multiplicity of conflicting teaching. We are not in the flood but it surrounds us. We are hardpressed but not overwhelmed, buffeted but not submerged."[24]

24. So We urge you again not to lose heart. We are confident that you will have the powerful support of secular princes since the question of the Church's authority has a bearing on their own authority, as both reason and experience prove. For Caesar can receive what is his only if God is given what is His. As St. Leo said, "Our duty to serve you all will give you additional support. In difficulties, in doubts and in every need, have recourse to this Apostolic See. For God has placed the teaching of truth in the see of unity, as St. Augustine says."[25]

25. Finally, We beseech you, by the Lord's mercy. Assist Us by your prayers to God that the Spirit of grace may abide in Us and that your decisions may not falter. May He who has given you the desire for agreement grant the blessing of peace to us all in general, that We may be able all the days of Our life to serve Almighty God and hold you in reverence and pray to the Lord with confidence: "Holy Father, preserve them whom you have given me in your holy name."[26]

In this confidence We impart wholeheartedly both to you and to your flock the Apostolic blessing, pledge of Our love.

Given at Rome in St. Mary Major's on the 5th day of May 1824, in the first year of Our Pontificate.

†

LATIN TEXT: *Bull. Rom. Cont.*, 8:53-57.

ENGLISH TRANSLATION: Padraig M. O'Cleirigh.

REFERENCES:

1. Serm. 3, on his birthday, delivered on the anniversary of his elevation to the pontificate.
2. 1 Pt 5.2-3.
3. 1 Tm 5.22.
4. Session 23, chap. 18.
5. Session 23 on reform, chap. 1.
6. St. Leo, serm. 5 on his birthday.
7. Ibid.
8. Comm. on Gal 3.8.
9. St. Leo, serm. 5.
10. Rom 16.
11. *Hist. eccl.*, 5.
12. *De haeresibus*, no. 72.
13. I Cor 1.
14. Rom 1.28.
15. Apoc 17.5.
16. Session 4 on the publication and use of sacred books.
17. St. Jerome on Gal 1.
18. Treatise 18 on Jn 5.
19. St. Leo, serm. 2, on his birthday.
20. Ibid., serm. 3, on his birthday.
21. Lk 10.
22. I Tm 3.
23. Bk. 4, de Symb. ad catech., chap. 13.
24. Enarrat. 2 in Ps 31.
25. Ep 103 (166) to the Donatists.
26. St. Leo, serm. 1, and Jn 17.

COMMENTARY:

The encyclical letter of Pope Leo XII. . . .to which are annexed pastoral instructions by the R.C. archbishops and bishops to the clergy and laity of their communion throughout Ireland. Dublin, 1824.

QUOD HOC INEUNTE

ENCYCLICAL OF POPE LEO XII PROCLAIMING
A UNIVERSAL JUBILEE
MAY 24, 1824
28

To all the Christian Faithful, Who will see this Present Letter; Greetings and Apostolic Benediction.

That which at the beginning of this century was grievously omitted because of the evil condition of the times now at last is at hand through the merciful intervention of God. We may now announce to you with joy that it will proceed in accord with the happy custom and institution of our ancestors. For that most auspicious year during which pilgrims from all over the world come to Our city, the seat of Saint Peter, is upon us. All the faithful are now summoned to pious duties, and perfect aids to reconciliation and grace are offered for the salvation of souls. We are happy to announce that an admirable occasion has now been given us, after a lamentable series of evils, to strive to renew all things in Christ by a salutary purification of the entire Christian people. We have therefore decided to throw open that heavenly treasure of the merits, sufferings, and virtues of Christ the Lord, of his Virgin Mother and of all the saints, the treasure which the Author of human salvation has entrusted to Us for distribution. Indeed in this matter it is fitting that We esteem the infinite efficacy of merit which Christ poured out over all the parts of His mystical body. They in turn may be helped by mutual works and by the salutary benefits of faith, which operates through charity. Thus by the invaluable blood of the Lord and by the meritorious prayers of the saints, the faithful may obtain the remission of that temporal punishment which, as the fathers of Trent taught, is not always entirely removed in the sacrament of penance (as it is by baptism).

Announcement of the Holy Year

2. Therefore let the earth hear the words of Our mouth and the music of the sacerdotal trumpet sounding the sacred jubilee to the people of God, and may the whole world listen with joy. We announce that the year of expiation and forgiveness, of redemption and grace, or remission and indulgence has come, the year of renewal in Christ. The old law, a harbinger of the future, had already set aside every fiftieth year among the Jewish people. If indeed sold fields and the goods which had fallen into the hands of others were then restored, we now receive back through the infinite liberality of God the virtues, merits, and gifts lost by sin. If the human law of servitude then ceased, now, with the yoke of diabolical domination cast off, we are recalled into the freedom of the sons of God, namely into that

liberty which Christ himself gave us. If, finally, by provision of that law debts were cancelled, we are likewise absolved from the more serious debts of sin and the punishments for them.

Requirements for the Indulgence

3. Eager therefore for these great blessings, in accordance with the tradition of Our predecessors and with the consent of our Venerable Brothers, the Cardinals of the Roman Church, We publish and promulgate a great and universal jubilee in this sacred city. It shall begin with the first vespers of the coming vigil of the Nativity and last through the whole year 1825, to further the glory of God, the exaltation of the Catholic Church and the sanctification of all Christian peoples. Now during the year of the jubilee, to fulfill the requirements for a plenary indulgence, the Christian faithful must repent, confess their sins, and receive holy communion. They must then visit the basilicas of the blessed Peter and Paul, and also those of St. John Lateran and of St. Mary Major, at least once a day for thirty continuous or interpolated days, either natural or ecclesiastical, counted from the first vespers of one day to the evening twilight of the following day, if they live in Rome. If they are pilgrims from outside the city, at least fifteen such days are required. If they have poured out pious prayers to God for the exaltation of the Church and the extirpation of heresies, for concord among Catholic princes and the salvation of the Christian peoples, We impart a complete indulgence, remission, and pardon of all their sins.

Those Unable to Complete the Requirements

4. Some of those who begin the journey may be prevented by some legitimate cause, such as illness or even death itself, from executing the prescriptions and visiting the basilicas. If they are truly penitent, have confessed, and have received holy communion, We desire that they share in the indulgence and remission just as though they had actually visited the basilicas on the days prescribed.

Exhortation to Expend the Necessary Effort

5. These things We announce to you with paternal affection, so that you who labor and are burdened may hurry there where you know for certain that you will be refreshed. It is hardly proper to be negligent in seeking the salutary riches from the eternal treasury of divine grace, which now stands open, when such great zeal is spent to acquire earthly riches, which worms consume and rust destroys. A vast and continuous multitude of people of every class, even in past times, have streamed to Rome, the center of the arts, from all over the world, despite the dangers of the journey. It would be shameful and counter to the zeal for eternal beauty if the uncertain fortunes of the journey or any other similar reason were used as a pretext for not making the Roman pilgrimage. The pilgrimage will compensate you many times over, even for serious inconveniences. Indeed any sufferings you may incur will be insignificant compared with the blessings of God which you will reap. For you will reap the rich fruits of penitence, by which you may offer to God the punishment of the body from unpleasant acts. By performing the words prescribed by the law of indulgences, you may excel in holiness, and by the accepted and constant will to overcome and drive off sins, you will add this new aggregate of good works.

6. Come therefore to this holy Jerusalem, a priestly and royal city which the sacred seat of Peter has made the capitol of the world. Truly it rules more widely by divine religion than by earthly domination. As St. Charles was wont to say to his fellow citizens in exhorting them to go to Rome during the holy year: "This is a city whose ground and walls, altars and churches, martyrs' tombs and whatever the eyes can see, impress on the soul something sacred. Those who, rightly prepared, visit her hallowed places, know this." Just think how much visiting these hallowed places enkindles faith and charity in the souls of the spectators. What profit is gained from visualizing the thousands of martyrs who sanctified this earth with their blood, from going to their basilicas, from reading their inscriptions and venerating their relics! Indeed, since the sky is so resplendent when illumined by the sun, what then of the city of Rome whose two lights, Peter and Paul, illumine the whole world? As St. John Chrysostom often said: "Who except one on fire with the most intense devotion would dare to approach their reliquaries and kneel at their graves, or to kiss the chains more precious than gold or gems? Who, finally, could restrain his tears when he sees the birthplace of Christ and

Quod hoc ineunte
28

recalls the infant Jesus crying in the manger, or when he venerates the holy instruments of the passion of the Lord and meditates on the crucifixion?

7. By a special divine favor these memorials of Our religion have been assembled in this holy city alone. Surely they are a certain and pleasing pledge of how God loves the gates of Sion above all other tabernacles of Jacob. They invite all of you, Beloved Sons, to cast off your hesitation and to ascend the mountain where it has pleased God to dwell.

The Citizens of Rome Should Set an Example

8. At this point we must remind all the citizens of Our city that the eyes of the faithful from all over the world are upon them. Therefore they should be restrained and moderate, as befits a Christian, so that others may find in their conduct an example of modesty, innocence, and virtue. May the visitors learn from this elect people to reverence the Catholic Church and her authority, to obey her precepts, and to honor ecclesiastical men and things. May due reverence for churches flourish among the people of Rome, so that the pilgrims may find nothing which suggests that worship and the place itself are despised, nothing which offends good and chaste souls. May the visitors learn that the people of Rome are present for divine services not only in body but also with devoted affection of mind and heart. This We also urge for the feastdays, lest these times instituted for performing sacred rites and honoring God and the saints appear in this holy city to be devoted to banquets and games, to disorderly activities, and lascivious license. Finally whatever is true, whatever pure, whatever is just, whatever holy, whatever is amiable, whatever of good repute, may these shine forth in the Roman people, just as they received from their ancestors the glory of faith and piety commended even by the apostle Paul as the best of all possible inheritances. We rejoice that it is unstained and illumined with the zeal and distinguished habits of the heirs.

9. We indeed are refreshed with this good hope, that everyone will emulate the better gifts and that the sheep of the Lord will come running as in battle array under the standard of charity to the embrace of the pastor. Look about you, Jerusalem, and behold: your sons come from afar, and your heart will wonder and rejoice. . . .Would that their sons would come prostrate to you, those who have humbled themselves, and may all who take away your honor worship the footprints of your feet! . . . We address all of you who are still removed from the true Church and the road to salvation. In this universal rejoicing, one thing is lacking: that having been called by the inspiration of the Heavenly Spirit and having broken every devisive snare, you might sincerely agree with the mother Church, outside of whose teachings there is no salvation. We shall receive you happily with Our paternal embrace and praise the God of all consolation, who will enrich us with His mercies in the greatest triumph of Catholic truth.

Teach the Faithful

10. Venerable Brothers, Patriarchs, Primates, Archbishops, and Bishops: share in these cares and labors of Ours. Call an assembly, gather the people so that your sons may be eager to receive those gifts which God has entrusted to you for distribution to the chosen. Let them recall that the days of our sojourn here are brief, and We do not know at what hour the Father may come. We must therefore watch, carrying lighted lamps filled with the oil of charity, so that when He does come, We may run with eager love to meet him. You must also discuss carefully how much efficacy there is in indulgences; how great is the fruit of remission, not only of the canonical but also of the temporal punishment due for sins; and finally, how much aid from the treasure of merits from Christ and the saints may be applied to those who died truly penitent before they had made adequate satisfaction for their sins. Their souls must be purified in the fires of purgatory so that entry into the eternal fatherland may open to them. Be alert here, venerable brothers, for there are those who have followed a wisdom which is not from God. Clothed in sheep's clothing, and pretending for the most part a semblance of piety, they have spread falsehood among the people. Now teach the flock what they have to do, what works of piety and charity they must exercise, with what sorrow they are to weigh themselves and their lives. Teach them to eliminate and correct whatever may be defective in their habits, so that they may truly benefit from this holy indulgence.

11. Furthermore, you must see that those of

your flock who have decided to make the pilgrimage may do so religiously, avoiding all the things on their journey which could disturb their pious determination and lead them to abandon their holy resolve. Rather may they follow eagerly and constantly those things which kindle and inspire religion. If you are free to come to this citadel of religion, you will add much splendor to this celebration. You will obtain the greatest blessings of divine mercies and, bringing them back as a rich reward, you will share them to the pleasure and profit of the rest of your people.

Help from the Princes

12. We have no doubt that the Christian princes will aid Us in this matter with all their authority, so that these plans for the salvation of souls may attain their desired effect. We therefore exhort them to second the efforts of their bishops and aid them in their labors. We also ask them to prepare throughout their territories safe roads and hostels for the pilgrims, lest any harm come to them in this pious undertaking. The princes know what conspiracies have everywhere arisen to weaken both the sacred and civil law in this holy matter. They also know what wonders God has wrought, the God who has humiliated the arrogance of the mighty with his right arm. May they continue to give thanks to the victorious Lord of lords and with humble and frequent prayer seek His aid. Let them pray that, although the iniquity of the wicked and impious may still creep like a cancer, He may conclude the work that He began. We thought of this when We first considered the celebration of a jubilee. We know well what kind of sacrifice of praise is offered to God by this unanimity of striving for celestial gifts. To this same end therefore may the Christian princes also strain. Since they are of a generous and exalted character, may they zealously safeguard this most sacred undertaking. Furthermore, they will recognize that they will really have done for their own authority whatever they may have done for the safety of the sacred cause and for the promotion of piety, so that when every seed of vice has been killed, a happy harvest of virtues may grow strong.

13. So that all these things may happen, We ask your prayers to God. We trust indeed that with common desires and entreaties you may ask for the good of the Catholic faith, for the return to truth of those in error, and for the happiness of the princes. Thus you will support Our infirmity in bearing up under the duties of Our onerous office.

14. In order that this present letter may be more widely disseminated among the faithful, We desire that even printed copies, signed by a public notary and fortified with the seal of someone who has attained ecclesiastical dignity, should be given the same full confidence which this letter would itself arouse.

15. It is in no manner permitted anyone to infringe upon this page of our indiction, promulgation, concession, exhortation, rogation, and desire, or to go rashly against it. If anyone may have presumed to do so, let him know that he will incur the indignation of the omnipotent God and of the blessed apostles Peter and Paul.

Given at Rome, at St. Peter's, in the year of the Incarnation 1824, on May 24th, in the first year of Our Pontificate.

†

LATIN TEXT: *Bull. Rom. Cont.*, 8:64-68.

ENGLISH TRANSLATION: Bernard A. Hausmann, S.J.

CHARITATE CHRISTI

ENCYCLICAL OF POPE LEO XII EXTENDING
JUBILEE TO THE ENTIRE CHURCH
DECEMBER 25, 1825

29

To the Whole Catholic Flock.

Venerable Brothers, Greetings and Apostolic Benediction.

The love of Christ urges Us to make the fruits of His passion available to all, in so far as We are able. During the universal jubilee, both the inhabitants of this city and the many pilgrims who have come here have shown faith, piety and every other virtue. We therefore conceived the great hope that the same zeal for the profit of their souls, for the glory of God, and for His Church might be kindled in the faithful everywhere. We also wish to grant your request, venerable brothers, and that of the Catholic princes, who have at heart the real happiness of the people subject to them. We have thus thought of opening the treasures of the Church to all the regions of the world, as was done in Rome this past year of the jubilee, and as Benedict XIV and Pius VI did.

Extension of Jubilee

Therefore We have published a Constitution addressed to all the Christian faithful by which We extend the jubilee and its indulgences; it also designates which good works, and within what space of time, they must be performed to obtain the indulgence, though We are leaving to your discretion the authority to change the enjoined works for the convenience of those who are legitimately impeded. So that all may learn of Our decree, We send you this letter. You know how necessary your labor is and how much effort you must expend so that the happy outcome may correspond to Our intentions. Indeed, the people will receive as much profit from this jubilee year as they will have employed diligence and zeal to prepare themselves for it. That they prepare diligently depends on the care which you exercise in your pastoral office. Let your people know therefore the nature and value of what is offered them. Show them the price of the treasures which We open for them, and how easily all may share in the riches unlocked, both because of the sweeping authority over the remission of sins that We grant to confessors, and also because of the nature of the works themselves which are imposed for the expiation of sins.

Severe Requirements of Old

You know the severity of Church discipline in this matter prior to the fourteenth century. "Whoever for the sake only of devotion," says Urban II in the Council of Claremont, "not for honor or money, set out for the liberation of the Church of God in Jerusalem, that journey was counted a complete penance." Certainly no other plenary indulgence was customarily given at the time, as We know from the blessed cardinal Joseph Mary Thomas. He says: "This plenary indulgence, in which the work enjoined was most arduous because of the expense, the discomfort, the labor of the journey, and the imminent danger to life, so that it appeared to be rather a change of penance than a relaxation... this plenary indulgence, I say, other pontiffs later always confirmed for the Holy Land."

Easier Requirements

Let the faithful consider how the Church pities the weakness of her children and now imposes labors so much lighter and easier for invaluable goods. Surely no one is so weak and negligent as not to desire those goods at so small a price. But we must diligently take care lest "on this account," to use the words of the Council of Trent, "they look upon the sins themselves as less serious, less offensive and insulting to the Holy Spirit, and so fall into more grievous sins, laying up for themselves treasures of wrath for the day of wrath." Thus let the liberality of the Church be shown, but let nothing at all be relaxed with regard to the diligence and industry by which men recall their sins, grieve over them, detest them, and confess them sincerely and fully. They may thus be led to wonder at and love the liberality of a God who offers himself so easily to those whose impiety is never sufficiently punished, "who once were delivered from the servitude of sin and the devil by baptism and received the gift of the Holy Spirit, yet have not feared to violate knowingly the temple of God and to sadden the Holy Spirit."

2. For this reason, following the example of our predecessors, We have published a solemn jubilee and commanded that God's assistance be publicly requested, for without such help human weakness cannot accomplish anything of this kind. We also order the Eucharistic Sacrament for the people both in the churches and on the roads, where with the aid of zealous ministers the Catholic doctrine concerning indulgences and jubilees should be diligently taught. Finally, the people should be admonished about every duty of the Christian way of life and with serious sermons be summoned to sincere repentance.

3. May each one of you consider as addressed to himself those words of the prophet: "Cry out and cease not: like a trumpet raise your voice and tell my people their crimes, and the house of Jacob their sins." You yourselves and your duly chosen preachers should impress on the ears of all what Christ threatened: "Unless you shall have done penance, you shall all likewise perish." Let them teach that for us to repent we must ask with humble prayer what the prophet implored: "Convert us to you, Lord, and we shall be converted." Show what a great offense against God sin is. Implant in the minds of the people a salutary fear; dwell on the severity of the impending divine judgment and the agony of the punishments prepared for those who die in sin. But rouse hope in all of obtaining mercy from the infinite goodness of God, who affirms that He hopes to be merciful, for His are these sweet words: "Be converted and do penance for all your iniquities, and iniquity will not be ruin for you. Cast off your prevarications and make for yourselves a new spirit. . . . Because I do not desire the death of the dying," says the Lord God, "turn back and live." From this we easily see how worthy of love a Father so good and merciful is. From this let us consider how unworthy of such great goodness is the intent of offending Him. Then let inner grief spring up, along with detestation of sins and the certain and deliberate resolve to correct life and morals.

4. After showing the necessity of inner penance and preparing the souls of the faithful for its acquisition, teach them penance as a sacrament. Let the ministers admonish them that it is as necessary for those who have fallen after baptism as baptism is for those who have not yet received it, and therefore it is appropriately called "a plank after shipwreck" with which alone it is possible to reach the port of eternal salvation. Let them show with what sentiments of grief and humility, with what faith, with what integrity they ought to confess their sins. Let them mention that a general confession is often useful, and in certain cases entirely necessary. Even when sins have been washed away by absolution and eternal punishment relaxed, temporal punishment often remains. Thus divine justice strictly demands that men at least receive punishments of definite duration when eternal punishment would still be inadequate. Thus instructed, the faithful will be able to acquire the fruits of the holy jubilee.

Recipients of Indulgences

For their sakes you must make sure that they

Charitate Christi 29

understand and believe that Christ left the inexhaustible treasury of his merits to the Church, that this treasure was enriched with the merits of the Blessed Virgin and all the saints, and that the distribution of these riches to men is in the hands of Him whom Christ make the visible head for Himself of the invisible Church. Accordingly it is left to the Pope to apply these merits now more amply, now less amply, to the living in the form of absolution, to the departed after the manner of suffrage. In the former case, He may apply the merits if they have purged their sins in the sacrament of penance and have been absolved of the eternal punishment, and in the latter if they have departed this life joined to God by love. The indulgence obviates the temporal punishments owed to God for our sins to a greater or less degree, according to the manner of application set up by the Pope and the preparation of the faithful. Finally the indulgence of the jubilee is plenary and distinct from other similar indulgences, because in the jubilee year of solemn remission ministers are given more authority to absolve from sins and to relax bonds and impediments. While the prayers of the entire Christian people rise in chorus, the Lord is placated by penitence and His mercy descends more certainly on all.

5. And these indeed are what the people are to be taught, but the apt and timely work of the priest to whom they confess their sins is necessary for them to act on what they have learned. For this reason you must take diligent care that those who hear confessions exemplify what our predecessor Innocent III prescribes for the minister of penance, namely that he be discreet and cautious. According to the manner of the wise physician, he should pour wine and oil on the wounds of the injured and diligently inquire into the circumstances of the sinner and of the sin, so as to learn what kind of advice he ought to give and what kind of remedy must be applied. Let him keep before his eyes the documents of the Roman ritual and weigh diligently when and to whom absolution is to be given or denied or deferred, lest he absolve those who are incapable of receiving such a blessing (that is those who show no signs of grief, those who do not wish to give up hatreds and enmities, to make restitution when they can, to avoid the proximate occasions of sin, or to use other means of amending their lives, and those who have given public scandal and refuse to repent through public satisfaction). Anyone can see how far removed these things are from those priests who, hearing some serious crime or finding someone infected with many kinds of sin, at once say that they are not able to give absolution. To be sure, they refuse to attend those very ones whose needs they have been established to watch over, for Christ said, "Those who are well have no need of a physician, but those who are sick." This is also far removed from those priests in whom any little diligent examining of conscience or sign of grief and intention seems sufficient that they think they are able to absolve. And finally, they think they have taken a safe plan if they dismiss the people to another time for absolution. Indeed, they think that they have given safe counsel by sending the people away to be absolved at another time. It is necessary to observe the mean in this matter because excessive ease in granting absolution may encourage facility in sinning, and excessive rigor may alienate souls from confession and tempt them to despair over salvation.

Indeed many imagine themselves entirely unprepared, but can usually ready themselves by understanding how to deal zealously, patiently, and gently with their people. For priests are clothed in the mercy of Jesus Christ, who did not come to call the just but to call sinners. Indeed, those who have been guilty of grievous crimes or have been away from the confessional for many years are not for this reason only unworthy of confession, for the mercy of the Lord is not limited but is rather an infinite treasure. Those who are uneducated or retarded and so have not examined themselves sufficiently—they will need assistance from their priest for this—are likewise eligible for confession. Unworthy however are those for whom the priest has done what is necessary, not burdening them beyond measure in questioning but diligently endeavoring to elicit detestation of sin, not failing to pray to God for them but exhausting the diligence of love. He may then judge them to lack the spirit of grief and penitence by which they may attain the grace of the sacrament. But whatever the penitents' disposition of soul, the confessor must never dismiss anyone with mistrust of God's goodness or hostility to the sacrament of reconciliation. If for a just reason absolution must be postponed, it is necessary to persuade the penitents with kindness that the duty and obligation of the confessor's office and their heavenly salvation demand this. The priest should encourage them most tenderly to return as soon as possible; having done faithfully the things which were prescribed for their salvation, they may break the bonds of sin and be refreshed by the sweetness of heavenly grace. An apt model of this charity is St. Raymond of Penafort, whom the Church calls a renowned minister of the sacrament of penance. He writes: Knowing the sins of his people, let the confessor be benevolent and prepared to raise up and carry the burden himself. Let him show affection, compassion, and discretion. The confessor should aid the penitent with prayer, giving of alms, and other good works; he should assist with mildness, consolation, and a promise of hope and, when the occasion demands, also with rebuke.

6. If you receive them with patient love like this, sinners will also accept their penances with greater equanimity. The sinners must understand that a jubilee indulgence does not remit the penance enjoined by the priest. The integrity of the sacrament demands penance, even when an indulgence has been granted. Remind the ministers of penance of those words of the Council of Trent: priests ought to enjoin salutary satisfaction appropriate to the nature of the crime and the ability of the penitent. Remind them also of what the catechism of the same holy council teaches concerning the penalty, that nothing should be assigned by whimsy, but everything should be directed through justice, prudence, and piety. In this way sins may be measured as by a ruler so the penitents may recognize the gravity of their crimes. It will also be worthwhile to explain to them at times what penalties had been set for certain crimes according to the penitential prescription of the ancient canons; you should also explain that the nature of satisfaction is to be adjusted to the intention of sin.

Appropriateness of Penance

7. Particularly at this time of mercy and remission, the priests should remember what the angelic Doctor says: "It is better that the priest explains to the penitent how great a penance he deserves and then enjoins something quite tolerable." Chrysostom likewise had taught: "If in no way you desire to spare the penitent, use a fitting procedure. It will often happen that, despondent even to the point of rejecting everything, both the medicine and the chains, he may cast himself headlong, the yoke broken, the snare loosed. For my part I am able to list many great sinners who were only saved because a worthy penance, one on a par with the crime, was exacted."

8. The authority to dispense the merits of Christ the Lord and his saints after penance has been attended to allows the faithful to complete whatever punishments are still owed for their sins. See to it that they understand why, in what order, and with what piety the works enjoined for this purpose are to be executed. They should learn that the supplications which are prescribed for certain sacred places are like those stations where in the very early days the faithful customarily assembled on fixed days for fasting, prayer, and self-examination.

9. But if the Church today asks so much less for a plenary indulgence, this certainly does not mean that she now thinks that we owe God less compensation for our sins. Rather, as she takes away from the difficulty of external expiation, so she desires that by more intense contrition and zeal, an interior advance of souls may proceed.

10. Among the works enjoined, the reception of the holy eucharist is listed. Since in it Christ the Lord, the font of all celestial grace and gifts, is contained, surely there is no more efficacious means to enkindle perfect love. Therefore you must expend great care that the faithful are taught the efficacy and nature of so great a sacrament and approach it with affection and spiritual preparation.

11. Thus, We especially desire that the faithful be admonished about these things. Relying on your zeal for the salvation of the souls committed to you, We have confidence that through Our instructions all will obtain the plenary indulgence which We offer from the inestimable treasure of the Church. We are likewise confident that the faithful will gain this indulgence so that its fruits remain in the future. As We extend such a benefit to all the Catholics of the world, We wish that every corruption of morals among the Christian people be removed forever, if possible. You know well that vices are especially dominant in your flocks. Your pastoral zeal should never waver as you strive to eradicate sin and vice. That monstrous crime of blasphemy, for instance—who would ever have believed that it could be heard among Christians? And yet there is almost no region now where oaths are not taken rashly, and the holy and terrible name of

God is used irreverently in every land. Some even dare to blaspheme Him whom the angels glorify. With fiery zeal, search out and attack this impiety which so greatly injures God.

Sanctity of the Church

12. You especially should love the beauty of the house of the Lord, and you must take care lest any inappropriate appearance and dress or any irreligious conduct violate it. Do not let the faithful ever forget these words of the Lord: "My house is a house of prayer" and "The zeal for your house consumes me."

Observe the Sabbath

13. Admonished by you, may the people remember the precept which the Lord himself announced: remember to keep holy the sabbath. Let them also remember the frightful judgment pronounced against the violators: My sabbaths they have greatly violated. I said therefore I will pour out my wrath over them and consume them. In this however, the perversity of many is so great that either they do not hesitate to do servile work, or they themselves abuse the exemption from such work prescribed to worship God in order to worship the devil. So on feastdays they give themselves up to banquets, to insobriety, to wantonness, and to all the works of the devil. Abolish this wickedness forever, as best you are able, and replace it with zeal for prayer and for hearing the word of God. Replace it with assistance at mass and with the Eucharist itself, a salutary participation in Christ's sacrifice.

14. But what shall We say about the precepts of the Church, what in particular about abstinence, about keeping the fasts? How many are there who do not care about this precept as they should, or even despise it entirely? In this matter too you understand how necessary it is that the faithful understand to what extent the precepts pertain to the Church and with how much veneration they are to obey the authority of so great a parent, of whom the bridegroom himself, Jesus Christ said: Whoever does not hear the Church, let him be to you like a gentile and publican.

Threats to Church and Society

15. You must care for the faithful of all ages, but especially for those on which the future state of the Church and human society depends. Indeed impiety, sworn to achieve the destruction of both, attempts with all her might to bring the young under her banner. Either negligence or perversity in the education and discipline of the young must account for that disregard for the sanctity and duties of matrimony which now seems to have overtaken men. Often a civil contract, as they call it, is used in many regions, so that the holy laws of that sacrament so esteemed by Paul the Apostle and writer are violated. The iniquitous convention between Catholics and heretics has grown to such an extent that either all the children follow the religion of the father, or the boys that of the father and the girls that of the mother. You see therefore how solicitous you must be that the faithful adhere to Catholic doctrine about that sacrament and obey the laws of the Church. Strive to cleanse the faithful from the evil destruction that has overtaken Christian education. Strive with all your ability to saturate youth with Catholic customs and rules of life, demanding this of them, of their parents, and of their teachers. Especially however, see that they are on their guard against seduction, so that they may shudder at the evil opinions propagated by these miserable times and at the books inimical to religion, morals, and public peace, from which this foul crop of wickedness has grown. May it be kept as a pest, far from the faithful people. Remind them again and again how popes and princes of the past attacked such books; in this matter do not consider your care and vigilance too great. If the faithful are nourished with the word of God, if the frequent reception of the sacraments is stressed, if pious societies are promoted wherever they are, or established where they do not yet exist—if these things are done, the needs of every age, sex, and human condition will be met.

16. But to do these things you will need helpers, whom the Lord has called as laborers into his vineyard. Admonish them diligently not to be idle and to labor to keep the morals of the people within bounds. Seriously investigate their lives, their conversations, their lifestyles, and their habits, for "a dirty hand (as Gregory the martyr says) does not wash another, and an eye full of dust does not see the blemish; so one who desires to correct others must himself be clean." Attend diligently to gravity and modesty in their external appearance. In order that they may be suited to teach the faithful and perform the ecclesiastical ministries correctly, do not be content with the proof they may have given before ordination; take care that the initiated may never cease to exercise themselves actively in sacred studies. The Roman council held under Benedict XIII in the jubilee year 1725 decreed that meetings of clerics should be held once each week, in which cases of ceremony and conscience are discussed and resolved. We wish to commend this to you even more earnestly.

17. It is proper for the other ecclesiastics to excel in all things as they excel in dignity. For this reason you must observe them diligently so that the people may notice nothing reprehensible in those they look up to. Let them cooperate with you by counsel and labor in the work of the ministry, in the building up of the body of Christ, that they may be deservedly called a senate of the Church according to the Council of Trent. Sharpen especially the care and industry of parish priests, that, according to the prescriptions of the same holy synod, they may constantly and in person instruct the people. They should refresh them with the sacraments and pour out petitions and prayers daily to God. Finally by a laudable example of life and conduct and by their virtues and character, they should illumine all and point out before them the way of salvation as they perform the other prescribed offices.

Supervision of Clerics

18. Guard the seminary as the pupil of the eye, and may the education of clerics, who grow up as the hope of the Church, be your first care. Watch sharply lest anyone who does not give evidence by talent, virtue, and knowledge that he is truly called to the lot of the Lord is ordained. With no less care look into the practices of religious communities, using the authority which is given you by the sacred Council of Trent, either as ordinaries or as delegates of the Apostolic See. Inspect the schools and colleges frequently, to keep out the poison of the present corrupt age and to direct all things according to the norms of sacred discipline. Insist that nuns who have taken religious vows excel in their duties. See that the girls (as the Roman council admonishes) they have taken as boarders are piously instructed by them in the Catholic tradition, and see to it that their dress may not be inappropriate for girls living amidst the spouses of Christ. Take seriously the holding of synods and the visitation of the diocese as ordained by the Council of Trent. We exhort you repeatedly to discharge your obligations at the times prescribed by that council and in a religious manner. In so doing you will learn to know your sheep, understanding for which of their ills a remedy is required and what opportunities are considered suitable.

Care for the Poor

The care of all classes is committed to you, but especially that of the poor, for whom Christ confessed that he was sent by the Father and in whose favor he gave such renowned and singular arguments of good will. However you understand how easy it is for the destitute to lose every benefit of God's presence. Therefore use the resources of the Church to fulfull the precepts of the Lord in an exemplary manner; what is left over, give in alms, and always do faithfully what the Church prescribes for bishops in the use of these goods. May the groans of the needy have easy access to you. Seek the aid of the wealthy for them in almsgiving, and defend them from all oppression and harm to the best of your ability. Move zealously against the injustice of money lenders, who, as the Roman catechism says, plunder the people and kill them with usury, for this evil has grown strong in present times. A defense against that evil theft was devised by pious men in the bank of commodities and of money lending, approved by popes and spread all over the world. We grieve that in many places they have been closed by the rapacity of those who had boasted to be liberators of the popular happiness. Strive to restore them, and inform the faithful of the indulgences which our predecessors granted to those who contribute to promote so pious a work.

Orphans and the Ill

19. Among the poor We commend especially to your loving care those for whom either orphanhood or illness is a burden added to their poverty. Diligently prepare homes to care for and educate young people of both sexes and to receive the sick and infirm, both for the needs of health and family and for the needs of the soul.

20. But enough. You are pastors and teachers of the people. For this reason, venerable brothers, it is not enough for you to watch lest the flocks entrusted to you suffer attacks from spiritual beasts. You must also nourish them with the warnings and salutary laws of heavenly doctrine, and especially with good example. In this regard the words of our Lord apply also to you when he said: "You are the light of the world. . . so let your light shine before men, that they may see your good works and glorify your Father, who is in heaven." This alone is sufficient to influence souls and to stop those who speak ill, according to these words of the Apostle: "In all things show yourself an example of good works, in doctrine, in integrity, in gravity, with sound and irreprehensible speech, so that he who is opposed, fears, having nothing evil to say of you." Then it will come about not only that the people see what must be done, but that they themselves act, and so, like the Apostles, you too may be the salt of the earth. This means that when the odor of sin has been taken away and men have been instructed by you, the integrity of life and morality will be preserved for a long time. These are our desires, and We trust that, relying on your virtuous zeal and God's assistance, We shall obtain them. With error and vice banished and with piety strengthened, the chosen faithful may thus put on, as the Apostle exhorts, mercy, benignity, humility, and modesty; supporting one another patiently, they may give to each each other, even as the Lord has given to us. Above all, however, may they have love, the bond of perfection, which brings with it all the Christian virtues joined together. It preserves them and joins man with God—and the whole perfection of man consists in this. May you obtain this fruit of the sacred jubilee through the merits of Jesus Christ and all the saints. May the Father of mercies and the God of all consolation grant us Our desires through the same Son of God, our Redeemer, who had the same prayer: I ask you Father, that all may be one, as we are one. Begging this with all Our energy of soul, We most lovingly impart the Apostolic Blessing to you, and to the flocks committed to your care. Given at Rome, at St. Peter's, December 25, 1825, in the third year of our pontificate.

†

LATIN TEXT: *Bull. Rom. Cont.*, 8:351-57; *Acta Sanctae Sedis*, 8:237-56; *Acta Pii IX*, 6:361-80.

ENGLISH TRANSLATION: Bernard A. Hausmann, S.J.

POPE PIUS VIII
1829-1830

The conclave that followed the death of Leo XII found the cardinals assembled there fully aware of the problems the Church faced and of the hostility toward the late pope and his policies. The situation called for the election of a successor who would show wisdom and moderation in the government of the States of the Church, more sympathy for the political hopes of the Italian people, and less intransigence in dealing with the liberal Catholics. On March 31, 1829 after five weeks of deliberations, they chose Cardinal Castiglioni who took the name of Pius VIII.

Francesco Saverio Castiglioni was born in Cingoli (Ancona) on November 20, 1761 of a noble family. Educated at the Jesuit school at Osimo he later studied law at Bologna and Rome, received a laureate in theology in 1785 and was ordained in the same year. While in Rome he collaborated with his professor, Msgr. Devoti, in compiling *Institutiones iuris canonici* (1792) and was secretary of the commission that examined the decrees of the Synod of Pistoia. He served as vicar general at Anagni (under Devoti), Fano, Ascoli, Piceno, and Cingoli, but was finally appointed bishop of Montalto in 1800. In 1808 he refused to take the oath of allegiance to Napoleon I and was arrested and imprisoned. After Pius VII had returned to Rome, Castiglioni was raised to the cardinalate and named bishop of Cesena (1816). Called to Rome in 1821 he became grand penitentiary and bishop of Frascati and was a leading candidate in the conclave that elected Leo XII. At the time of his election in 1829 he was in a precarious state of health.

Because of his poor health most looked on the pontificate of Pius VIII as a transitional one; it did, indeed, last but twenty months. Moderately liberal and prepared to cooperate with legitimate governments, the pope's poor health did not hinder him from pursuing a vigorous policy that ran counter to the conservative path of his predecessor. His encyclical, *Traditi humilitati* (May 24, 1829), indicated that he would work against religious indifferentism, maintain the marriage laws, promote Christian education, and oppose secret societies. His brief of March 25, 1830 declared that a marriage could be blessed only when the proper promises were made regarding the Catholic education of children. In the government of the States of the Church, Pius VIII was less rigorous than Leo XII, seeking to improve conditions economically as well as socially.

During his pontificate the Catholic Emancipation Act was passed in England (1829), permitting Catholics to sit in Parliament and to hold office and opening the way for the Oxford Movement. In Germany the Church was involved in serious conflict with the civil authorities over mixed marriages. In the United States after the bishops had held their first formal meeting, the First Provincial Council of Baltimore (1829), Pius VIII approved their decrees. These decrees were effective in strengthening the ties with Rome and in promoting greater uniformity of practice among the various dioceses of the United States. In Latin America the main problems were those caused by the movement toward independence from Spain.

Relations with Prussia were also concerned with legislation regarding mixed marriages. In France, the pope did not approve but neither did he condemn the program of Catholic liberalism advocated by Lamennais and his followers. The July Revolution (1830), which ended Bourbon rule and brought the bourgeois monarchy to France, took on a decidedly anticlerical tone because of the close union of Church and State during the preceding years (1815-1830). In spite of protests the pope was determined to maintain good relations with the new government and asked clergy and Catholics of France to give their support to the new regime contrary to the action urged by *L'Avenir* under the direction of Lamennais and his associates. In the Netherlands the conflict over the confirmation of episcopal appointments was referred to Rome but the matter was still unsettled when in August (1830) the Belgian Catholics joined the liberals and won independence for Belgium.

The twenty months of this short pontificate fell in troublesome times; aside from the activities noted, the gentle pope could do little more than remain passive and hope for the best. Chronic ill health soon brought his reign to a close. His death on November 30, 1830 delayed but could not prevent the inevitable conflict between the papacy and the liberal Catholics, the forerunners of the Modernists.

TRADITI HUMILITATI

ENCYCLICAL OF POPE PIUS VIII ON HIS PROGRAM FOR THE PONTIFICATE

MAY 24, 1829

30

To Our Venerable Brothers, Patriarchs, Primates, Archbishops, and Bishops.

Venerable Brothers, Greetings and Apostolic Benediction.

According to the custom of Our ancestors, We are about to assume Our pontificate in the church of the Lateran. This office has been granted to Us, even though We are humble and unworthy. We open Our heart with joy to you, venerable brothers, whom God has given to Us as helpers in the conduct of so great an administration. We are pleased to let you know the intimate sentiments of Our will. We also think it helpful to communicate those things from which the Christian cause may benefit. For the duty of Our office is not only to feed, rule, and direct the lambs, namely the Christian people, but also the sheep, that is the clergy.

Praise for Clergy

2. We rejoice and praise Christ, who raised up shepherds for the safekeeping of His flock. These shepherds vigilantly lead their flocks so as not to lose even one of those they have received from the Father. For We know well, venerable brothers, your unshakeable faith, your zeal for religion, your sanctity of life, and your singular prudence. Co-workers such as you make Us happy and confident. This pleasant situation encourages Us when We fear because of the great responsibility of Our office, and it refreshes and strengthens Us when We feel overwhelmed by so many serious concerns. We shall not detain you with a long sermon to remind you what things are required to perform sacred duties well, what the canons prescribe lest anyone depart from vigilance over his flock, and what attention ought to be given in preparing and accepting ministers. Rather We call upon God the Savior that He may protect you with His omnipresent divinity and bless your activities and endeavors with happy success.

Heresies

3. Although God may console Us with you, We are nonetheless sad. This is due to the numberless errors and the teachings of perverse doctrines which, no longer secretly and clandestinely but openly and vigorously, attack the Catholic faith. You know how evil men have raised the standard of revolt against religion through philosophy (of which they proclaim themselves doctors) and through empty fallacies devised according to natural reason. In the first place, the Roman See is assailed and the bonds of

unity are, every day, being severed. The authority of the Church is weakened and the protectors of things sacred are snatched away and held in contempt. The holy precepts are despised, the celebration of divine offices is ridiculed, and the worship of God is cursed by the sinner.[1] All things which concern religion are relegated to the fables of old women and the superstitions of priests. Truly lions have roared in Israel.[2] With tears We say: "Truly they have conspired against the Lord and against His Christ." Truly the impious have said: "Raze it, raze it down to its foundations."[3]

On True Religion

4. Among these heresies belongs that foul contrivance of the sophists of this age who do not admit any difference among the different professions of faith and who think that the portal of eternal salvation opens for all from any religion. They, therefore, label with the stigma of levity and stupidity those who, having abandoned the religion which they learned, embrace another of any kind, even Catholicism. This is certainly a monstrous impiety which assigns the same praise and the mark of the just and upright man to truth and to error, to virtue and to vice, to goodness and to turpitude. Indeed this deadly idea concerning the lack of difference among religions is refuted even by the light of natural reason. We are assured of this because the various religions do not often agree among themselves. If one is true, the other must be false; there can be no society of darkness with light. Against these experienced sophists the people must be taught that the profession of the Catholic faith is uniquely true, as the apostle proclaims: one Lord, one faith, one baptism.[4] Jerome used to say it this way: he who eats the lamb outside this house will perish as did those during the flood who were not with Noah in the ark.[5] Indeed, no other name than the name of Jesus is given to men, by which they may be saved.[6] He who believes shall be saved; he who does not believe shall be condemned.[7]

No Private Interpretation of Scripture

5. We must also be wary of those who publish the Bible with new interpretations contrary to the Church's laws. They skillfully distort the meaning by their own interpretation. They print the Bibles in the vernacular and, absorbing an incredible expense, offer them free even to the uneducated. Furthermore, the Bibles are rarely without perverse little inserts to insure that the reader imbibes their lethal poison instead of the saving water of salvation. Long ago the Apostolic See warned about this serious hazard to the faith and drew up a list of the authors of these pernicious notions. The rules of this Index were published by the Council of Trent;[8] the ordinance required that translations of the Bible into the vernacular not be permitted without the approval of the Apostolic See and further required that they be published with commentaries from the Fathers. The sacred Synod of Trent had decreed[9] in order to restrain impudent characters, that no one, relying on his own prudence in matters of faith and of conduct which concerns Christian doctrine, might twist the sacred Scriptures to his own opinion, or to an opinion contrary to that of the Church or the popes. Though such machinations against the Catholic faith had been assailed long ago by these canonical proscriptions, Our recent predecessors made a special effort to check these spreading evils.[10] With these arms may you too strive to fight the battles of the Lord which endanger the sacred teachings, lest this deadly virus spread in your flock.

Secret Societies

6. When this corruption has been abolished, then eradicate those secret societies of factious men who, completely opposed to God and to princes, are wholly dedicated to bringing about the fall of the Church, the destruction of kingdoms, and disorder in the whole world. Having cast off the restraints of true religion, they prepare the way for shameful crimes. Indeed, because they concealed their societies, they aroused suspicion of their evil intent. Afterwards this evil intention broke forth, about to assail the sacred and the civil orders. Hence the supreme pontiffs, Our predecessors, Clement XII, Benedict XIV, Pius VII, Leo XII,[11] repeatedly condemned with anathema that kind of secret society. Our predecessors condemned them in apostolic letters; We confirm those commands and order that they be observed exactly. In this matter We shall be diligent lest the Church and the state suffer harm from the machinations of such sects. With your help We strenuously take up the mission of destroying the strongholds which the putrid impiety of evil men sets up.

Corruption of Youth

7. We want you to know of another secret society organized not so long ago for the corruption of young people who are taught in the gymnasia and the lycea. Its cunning purpose is to engage evil teachers to lead the students along the paths of Baal by teaching them un-Christian doctrines. The perpetrators know well that the students' minds and morals are molded by the precepts of the teachers. Its influence is already so persuasive that all fear of religion has been lost, all discipline of morals has been abandoned, the sanctity of pure doctrine has been contested, and the rights of the sacred and of the civil powers have been trampled upon. Nor are they ashamed of any disgraceful crime or error. We can truly say with Leo the Great that for them "Law is prevarication; religion, the devil; sacrifice, disgrace."[12] Drive these evils from your dioceses. Strive to assign not only learned, but also good men to train our youth.

Careful Selection of Seminarians

8. Also watch the seminaries more diligently. The fathers of Trent made you responsible for their administration.[13] From them must come forth men well instructed both in Christian and ecclesiastical discipline and in the principles of sound doctrine. Such men may then distinguish themselves for their piety and their teaching. Thus, their ministry will be a witness, even to those outside the Church and they will be able to refute those who have strayed from the path of justice. Be very careful in choosing the seminarians since the salvation of the people principally depends on good pastors. Nothing contributes more to the ruin of souls than impious, weak, or uninformed clerics.

The Spread of Heretical Books

9. The heretics have disseminated pestilential books everywhere, by which the teachings of the impious spread, much as a cancer.[14] To counteract this most deadly pest, spare no labor. Be admonished by the words of Pius VII: "May they consider only that kind of food to be healthy to which the voice and authority of Peter has sent them. May they choose such food and nourish themselves with it. May they judge that food from which Peter's voice calls them away to be entirely harmful and pestiferous. May they quickly shrink away from it, and never permit themselves to be caught by its appearance and perverted by its allurements."[15]

Sanctity of Marriage

10. We also want you to imbue your flock with reverence for the sanctity of marriage so that they may never do anything to detract from the dignity of this sacrament. They should do nothing that might be unbecoming to this spotless union nor anything that might cause doubt about the perpetuity of the bond of matrimony. This goal will be accomplished if the Christian people are accurately taught that the sacrament of matrimony ought to be governed not so much by human law as by divine law and that it ought to be counted among sacred, not earthly, concerns. Thus, it is wholly subject to the Church. Formerly marriage had no other purpose than that of bringing children into the world. But now it has been raised to the dignity of a sacrament by Christ the Lord and enriched with heavenly gifts. Now its purpose is not so much to generate offspring as to educate children for God and for religion. This increases the number of worshippers of the true divinity. It is agreed that the union of marriage signifies the perpetual and sublime union of Christ with His Church; as a result, the close union of husband and wife is a sacrament, that is, a sacred sign of the immortal love of Christ for His spouse. Therefore, teach the people what is sanctioned and what is condemned by the rules of the Church and the decrees of the Councils.[16] Also explain those things which pertain to the essence of the sacrament. Then they will be able to accomplish those things and will not dare to attempt what the Church detests. We ask this earnestly of you because of your love of religion.

Other Concerns

11. You know now what causes Our present grief. There are also other things, no less serious, which it would take too long to recount here, but which you know well. Shall We hold back Our voice when the Christian cause is in such great need? Shall We be restrained by human arguments? Shall We suffer in silence the rending of the seamless robe of Christ the Savior, which even the soldiers who crucified Him did not dare to rend? Let it never happen that We be found lacking in zealous pastoral care for Our flock,

beset as it is by serious dangers. We know you will do even more than We ask, and that you will cherish, augment, and defend the faith by means of teachings, counsel, work, and zeal.

12. With many ardent prayers We ask that, with God restoring the penitence of Israel, holy religion may flourish everywhere. We also ask that the true happiness of the people may continue undisturbed, and that God may always protect the pastor of His earthly flock and nourish him. May the powerful princes of the nations, with their generous spirits, favor Our cares and endeavors. With God's help, may they continue vigorously to promote the prosperity and safety of the Church, which is afflicted by so many evils.

13. Let us ask these things humbly of Mary, the holy Mother of God. We confess that she alone has overcome all heresies and We salute her with gratitude on this day, the anniversary of Our predecessor, Pius VII's, restoration to the city of Rome after he had suffered many adversities. Let us ask these things of Peter, the Prince of the Apostles, and of his co-apostle Paul. With Christ's consent, may these two apostles grant that We, firmly established on the rock of the Church's confession, suffer no disturbing circumstances. From Christ Himself We humbly ask the gifts of grace, peace, and joy for you and for the flock entrusted to you. As a pledge of Our affection We lovingly impart the apostolic benediction.

Given in Rome, at St. Peter's, May 24, 1829, the first year of Our pontificate.

†

LATIN TEXT: *Bull. Rom. Cont.*, 9:23-27.

ENGLISH TRANSLATION: Bernard A. Hausmann, S.J.

REFERENCES:

1. Wis 1.32.
2. Jer 2.25.
3. Ps 136.7.
4. Eph 4.5.
5. Epistle to Damasus, the 37th pope.
6. Acts 4.12.
7. Mk 16.16.
8. Rule 4 of the Index, and the addition to same from the decree of the Index of 13 June 1737.
9. Session 4 on the decree concerning holy books.
10. Read, among other things, the apostolic letters of Pius VII to the archbishops of Gnesen (1 June 1816) and Mohilev (3 September 1816).
11. Clement XII, constitution *In eminenti*; Benedict XIV, constitution *Providas*; Pius VII, constitution *Ecclesiam a Jesu Christo*; Leo XII, constitution *Quo graviora.*
12. In sermon 5 on fasting of the tenth month, chap. 4.
13. Session 25, chap. 18, on reform.
14. 2 Tm 2.17.
15. In the encyclical letter to all bishops published in Venice.
16. Read the Roman catechism for parish priests on matrimony.

POPE GREGORY XVI
1831-1846

Bartolomeo Alberto Cappellari was born of a noble family at Belluno (Lombardy) on September 18, 1765. At the age of eighteen he joined the Camaldolese order (1783) entering the Monastery of San Michele in Murano and taking the name of Mauro. Ordained in 1787, professor of science and philosophy for five years, he was sent in 1795 to Rome to assist the order's procurator general. In 1799 he published a work of merit that went through three editions in Venice. Elected abbot of the Monastery of San Gregorio on the Caelian Hill (1805), he was expelled from Rome because of his opposition to the French during the occupation of Napoleon. He fled to Murano and from there to Padua. In 1814 he returned to Rome where he spent the remainder of his life. Abbot, professor of theology, consultor to several Roman congregations, and prefect of the Congregation for the Propagation of the Faith were but a few of the positions he held. In March of 1830 he helped draft the address of Pius VIII to the German bishops on mixed marriages. On February 2, 1831 he was elected pope in a conclave in which Spain exercised its veto to exclude Cardinal Giustiniani.

Not a warm personality, he retained his austere monastic life-style throughout his pontificate, and was obviously more prepared to fulfill the spiritual duties of his office than the temporal ones. Although he had no affection for the pomp of sovereignty, he did believe strongly, as a result of his training, in hierarchy, order, and the virtue of obedience. In his opposition to naturalistic liberalism Gregory failed to dissociate it sufficiently from political liberalism and therefore was in the position of trying to block an inevitable development. Throughout his term of office he upheld the unalterable supremacy of the supernatural.

He disapproved of the separation of Church and State, suppressed all revolutionary movements, and urged support for monarchical regimes. His *Mirari vos*, forerunner of the Syllabus of Errors of Pius IX (1864), was provoked by the political situation in Italy, the increasing influence of Lamennais among the Catholic liberals, and the continued conservative presence of Metternich.

The concordats concluded during Gregory's pontificate did make concessions to the secularizing tendencies of the states, but the pontiff struggled for guarantees to control espicopal nominations allowing, however, for some local customs at variance with this objective. In France, Spain, Portugal, and Austria nominations continued to be made by governments; in

Ireland, from lists submitted by the local clergy; and in the United States, from lists drawn up by the resident bishops. Greatly through Gregory's efforts the Church was firmly established in the Americas.

Diplomatic relations with Portugal were severed in 1833 and not reopened until 1844. The concordat with Spain was not concluded until the time of Pius IX. In France, the concordat of 1801 still regulated Church/State relations, and religious orders were restored. The Articles of Baden in Switzerland (1835), eliminating papal authority over Swiss Catholics, were condemned in an effort to reiterate the independence of the Church. Legislation in Prussia regarding mixed marriages continued to be a problem.

Gregory, personally interested in rebuilding the missions, increased missionary personnel, eliminated the *patronato* and *padroado* privilege of Spain and Portugal, set up guidelines for missionaries, encouraged the development of native clergy, called on religious orders to staff the missions, and condemned slavery. He assured financial support for the missions by encouraging the Society for the Propagation of the Faith and the Pontifical Association for the Holy Childhood to help relieve the material needs previously cared for by the Catholic governments of Europe. He named residential bishops for Latin America and despite Spanish opposition favored national emancipation of the Latin American republics.

He was strongly opposed to the construction of railways in the papal states but was a great patron of art and letters, taking pleasure in the company of writers and artists and aiding them in their work. He opened the Museum of Etruscan Antiquities and the Egyptian Museum in the Vatican and continued the reconstruction of the Basilica of St. Peter. His private secretary, Gaetano Moroni, began at this time his still useful *Dizionario di erudizione storico-ecclesiastica* (1840-61, 103 v. in 53) which is especially good for its coverage of this period.

Gregory died suddenly on June 1, 1846, leaving the consequences of his policies as a heavy burden for his successor.

SUMMO IUGITER STUDIO

ENCYCLICAL OF POPE GREGORY XVI
ON MIXED MARRIAGES
MAY 27, 1832
31

Venerable Brothers, Greetings and Apostolic Benediction.

The Apostolic See has always ensured that the canons forbidding the marriages of Catholics with heretics have been observed religiously. Occasionally such marriages have been tolerated in order to avoid more serious scandals. But, even then, the Roman Pontiffs saw to it that the faithful were taught how deformed these marriages are and what spiritual dangers they present. A Catholic man or woman would be guilty of a great crime if he presumed to violate the canonical sanctions in this matter. And if the Roman Pontiffs themselves very reluctantly relaxed this same canonical prohibition in some serious cases, they always added to their dispensation a formal condition: that the Catholic party must not be perverted, but rather must make every effort to withdraw the non-Catholic party from error and that the offspring of both sexes must be educated entirely in the Catholic religion.

Mixed Marriages

2. Therefore, guided by the example of Our predecessors, We are grieved to hear reports from your dioceses which indicate that some of the people committed to your care freely encourage mixed marriages. Furthermore, they are promoting opinions contrary to the Catholic faith: namely, they dare to affirm that a Catholic may freely and legally contract marriage with a heterodox party, not only without asking for a dispensation (which must be obtained from the Apostolic See in each individual case), but also without agreeing to the necessary obligations, especially the duty to educate all the offspring in the Catholic religion. Indeed it has even come to the point that these same persons insist that mixed marriages ought to be approved when the heretical partner is a divorced person whose former spouse is still alive. To this end they issue serious threats of punishments in order to induce priests to announce mixed marriages in the churches and, afterwards, to defend the act by which these marriages were contracted or, at least, to grant the contracting parties what they call dimissory letters. Finally some of these misguided people attempt to persuade themselves and others that men are not saved only in the Catholic religion, but that even heretics may attain eternal life.

Praiseworthy Situations

3. Some circumstances, however, lighten

Our grief which arises from this matter: namely, the constancy of most of the Bavarian people in holding fast to the Catholic faith, their sincere obedience to ecclesiastical authority, and the steadfastness of nearly all of their clergy in carrying out their ministry according to the canons. We know that, although you may not all hold the same opinion in this business of mixed marriages, all of you are resolved to hearken to the Apostolic See and, with its guidance, to protect the flocks entrusted to you, not even fearing to encounter dangers in order to safeguard the sheep.

Help from King Louis

4. Through these letters We hope to strengthen your fraternity so that in the matter under consideration you may continue to preach the unchangeable Catholic teachings and to safeguard the observance of the canons. Since Our opinion has been made known to you, We hope it will result in a more perfect agreement between all of you and the Holy See. We hope that Our dear son in Christ, Louis, the illustrious king of Bavaria, when he understands the present problem, may assist Us and you with his patronage because of his grandfather's zeal for the Catholic religion which Louis has inherited. If he does, the evils which threaten the Catholic cause from this source may be prevented and our most holy religion may be restored and protected throughout Bavaria. Then Catholic clergy may enjoy complete liberty in carrying out their ministry, just as was provided for in the agreement entered into with the Apostolic See in 1817.

History of Dictum Against Mixed Marriages

5. Next let Us start with the things which concern the faith which, as We mentioned above, some are endangering in order to introduce greater freedom for mixed marriages. You know how zealously Our predecessors taught that very article of faith which these dare to deny, namely the necessity of the Catholic faith and of unity for salvation. The words of that celebrated disciple of the apostles, martyred St. Ignatius, in his letter to the Philadelphians are relevent to this matter: "Be not deceived, my brother; if anyone follows a schismatic, he will not attain the inheritance of the kingdom of God." Moreover, St. Augustine and the other African bishops who met in the Council of Cirta in the year 412 explained the same thing at greater length: "Whoever has separated himself from the Catholic Church, no matter how laudably he lives, will not have eternal life, but has earned the anger of God because of this one crime: that he abandoned his union with Christ." Omitting other appropriate passages which are almost numberless in the writings of the Fathers, We shall praise St. Gregory the Great who expressly testifies that this indeed is the teaching of the Catholic Church. He says: "The holy universal Church teaches that it is not possible to worship God truly except in her and asserts that all who are outside of her will not be saved." Official acts of the Church proclaim the same dogma. Thus, in the decree on faith which Innocent III published with the synod of Lateran IV, these things are written: "There is one universal Church of all the faithful outside of which no one is saved." Finally the same dogma is also expressly mentioned in the profession of faith proposed by the Apostolic See, not only that which all Latin churches use, but also that which the Greek Orthodox Church uses and that which other Eastern Catholics use. We did not mention these selected testimonies because We thought you were ignorant of that article of faith and in need of Our instruction. Far be it from Us to have such an absurd and insulting suspicion about you. But We are so concerned about this serious and well known dogma, which has been attacked with such remarkable audacity, that We could not restrain Our pen from reinforcing this truth with many testimonies.

Help the Bavarian People Avoid Mixed Marriages

6. Strive to eradicate these slithering errors with all your strength. Inspire the populace of Bavaria to keep the Catholic faith and unity as the only way of salvation with an ever more ardent zeal, and, thus, to avoid every danger of forsaking it. Once the Bavarian faithful understands this necessity of maintaining Catholic unity, admonitions and warnings to them against joining in marriage with heretics will certainly not be in vain. If on occasion some grave cause should suggest such a mixed marriage, they will then apply for a dispensation from the Church and observe the conditions We mentioned above. You and their parents and others who have care of them are responsible for

teaching them what the judgment of the canons is in this matter. They must be warned lest they should dare to break these canons and, thus, jeopardize their souls. Hence if the circumstances suggest it, it may be necessary to remind them of that well-known precept of the natural and divine law, which commands us to avoid not only sins but the next occasion of sin as well. Remind them also of the other precept of the same law which enjoins parents to rear their children in the discipline and admonitions of the Lord (Eph 6.4). Therefore, they must instruct them in the true worship of God, which is unique to the Catholic religion. Hence, exhort your faithful to weigh seriously how great an offense they commit against the supreme Deity and how cruelly they act toward themselves and their future children when, by rashly contracting a mixed marriage, they may expose themselves and their children to the danger of perversion. So that the gravity of such danger may appear more clearly, recall for them those salutary admonitions of the Apostles, of the Fathers, and of the canons, which warn that familiar association with heretics is to be shunned.

Responsibility of Clergy

7. But it may happen that these warnings and admonitions go unheeded and that some Catholic man or woman is unwilling to give up his perverse intention of entering upon a mixed marriage. If a dispensation is not requested or not obtained from the Church or if the necessary conditions or a certain one of them is not fulfilled, then it wil be the duty of the priest to abstain not only from honoring the marriage itself with his presence, but also from announcing the marriage and from granting dimissory letters. You must admonish the priests and demand that they abstain from every such act. For one who has the care of souls and who acts differently, especially in the circumstances prevalent in Bavaria, would seem in some way to approve these illicit marriages by his actions. His works would encourage the liberty of those souls, a liberty which is pernicious to their salvation and even to the cause of faith.

Cases Involving Divorce

8. After these things it is hardly necessary to add statements concerning those other, far more serious, cases of marriages contracted between Catholics and heretics in which the heretical party may have a previous partner still living from whom he separated by divorce. You know how strong by divine law the bond of marriage is. This bond cannot be broken by human authority. Therefore, a mixed marriage in such cases is not only illicit, but entirely invalid and adulterous. The only exception is when the former marriage, which the heretical party considers dissolved by divorce, was entirely invalid because of some canonical impediment. In this last case, not only must all the things which were said above be observed, but the new marriage must not be permitted until after the first marriage has been declared invalid by an ecclesiastical judgment made according to canonical standards.

9. These are the things, venerable brothers, which We thought should be called to your attention in this matter. Meanwhile We do not cease to ask our omnipotent and merciful God with fervent prayers to clothe you and all the clergy of Bavaria with virtue from on high and to cover you with His right hand and defend you with His holy arm. May the Apostolic Benediction be a pledge of the great love with which We regard your fraternity in the Lord. We most lovingly bestow this benediction on you. Distribute it to the clergy and faithful laity of your dioceses.

Given in Rome, at St. Peter's under the ring of the Fisherman, May 27, 1832, the second year of Our Pontificate.

†

LATIN TEXT: *Acta Greg. XVI*, 1:140-42.

ENGLISH TRANSLATION: Bernard A. Hausmann, S.J.

CUM PRIMUM

ENCYCLICAL OF POPE GREGORY XVI
ON CIVIL OBEDIENCE
JUNE 9, 1832
32

To All Archbishops and Bishops Dwelling in the Kingdom of Poland.

Venerable Brothers, Greetings and Apostolic Benediction.

When the first report of the calamities, which so seriously devastated your flourishing kingdom reached our ears, We learned simultaneously that they had been caused by some fabricators of deceit and lies. Under the pretext of religion, and revolting against the legitimate authority of the princes, they filled their fatherland, which they loosed from due obedience to authority, with mourning. We shed abundant tears at the feet of God, grieving over the harsh evil with which some of our flock was afflicted. Afterward We humbly prayed that God would enable your provinces, agitated by so many and so serious dissensions, to be restored to peace and to the rule of legitimate authority.

Encyclical Letters

2. We were immediately eager to send an encyclical letter to you that you might understand that We too were oppressed by the weight of your troubles. We hoped to add some solace and strength to your pastoral solicitude by which you might apply yourselves with new and more ardent zeal to propagating sounder doctrines and to persuading your precious followers, both in the clergy and among the laity. That letter never reached you because of the troubles of the times; therefore, now that God has restored quiet and tranquility, We again open our heart to you. We hope to kindle your zeal and solicitude as much as We can with the help of God, so that you may diligently protect your flock from the true causes of your past troubles. Watch earnestly lest deceitful men and the promoters of novelties continue to spread erroneous doctrines and false dogmas in your flock. Using the pretext of the common good, as is their custom, they take advantage of the credulity of those who are naive and rash, so that they may have them as blind servants and supporters in disturbing the peace of the kingdom and in overturning the order of society.

Refuting the Deceivers

3. Surely the fraud of these would-be teachers must be uncovered in clear words for the good and the instruction of the faithful. The fallacy of their thought must be refuted courageously everywhere with the words of divine scripture and the testimony of Church tradition. From these most pure fountains (from which the Catholic clergy ought to draw the plan of their lives and

the material for their sermons to the people) We are taught most clearly that the obedience which men are obliged to render to the authorities established by God is an absolute precept which no one can violate, except if by chance something is commanded which runs counter to the laws of God or of the Church. "Let everyone" says the Apostle, "be subject to higher authorities, for there exists no authority except from God, and those who exist have been appointed by God. Therefore he who resists the authority resists the ordination of God . . . wherefore you must needs be subject not only because of the wrath, but also for conscience sake" (Rom 13.1,2,5). Similarly St. Peter (1 Pt 2.13) teaches all the faithful: "Be subject to every human creature for God's sake, whether to the king as supreme, or to the governors sent through him . . . " for (he says) such is the will of God, that by doing good you would silence the ignorance of foolish men." By observing these admonitions the first Christians, even during the persecutions, deserved well of the Roman emperors themselves and of the security of the state. "Christian soldiers," says St. Augustine, "served an infidel emperor: when it came to the subject of Christ, they recognized no one except Him who is in heaven. They distinguished between the eternal Lord and the temporal lord, but also were subject to the temporal lord because of the eternal Lord" (St. Aug. on Ps 124).

Advice for Clergy

4. The holy Fathers have always taught this doctrine. The Catholic Church has taught it and continues to teach it. Having been taught it, the first Christians lived and acted in such a manner that, although the crime of cowardice and desertion had contaminated the pagan army, it never contaminated the Christians. On this point Tertullian reports: "Concerning the majesty of the emperor, we Christians are brought into ill repute. Nevertheless, no Christians will be found among men like Albinus or Niger or Cassius. But among these very peoples, who recently had sworn by their gods, who had offered sacrifices for the safety of emperor and state, and who frequently condemned the Christians, enemies of the state have been found. No Christian is an enemy, certainly not of the emperor. Since we know that the emperor is appointed by God, it is necessary that he be loved and reverenced, and that we wish him well." We understand that you know these things. We do not intend to say them as if we might be afraid that you would not propagate and disseminate sounder doctrine concerning the obedience which subjects must have for their legitimate prince. Nonetheless We have said them so that you may easily understand that We desire all clerics of your kingdom to shine forth in purity of doctrine, in splendor of knowledge, and in sanctity of life, that they may appear in the eyes and the judgment of all without blemish. In this manner, We hope everything will proceed more happily. Your emperor will act kindly toward you; at no time will he deny his patronage for the good of the Catholic religion and he will always listen patiently to your requests. Those who are wise will follow you with richly deserved praise, and those who are opposed will fear you, but will have nothing evil to say of Us. Meanwhile raising our hands to heaven, We pray God for you that he may enrich and fill each one of you more and more every day with an abundance of heavenly virtues. Having you always in our heart, We exhort you to complete our joy. Sharing the same love, may you also think alike, unanimously perceiving the same things. May all of you proclaim, as is fitting, sound doctrine and sound words; preserve that which was entrusted to you and stand as one, united in the spirit, working together for the faith. Finally pray to God for us without ceasing. We impart most lovingly the Apostolic Benediction to you and to the flock committed to you as a pledge of paternal charity.

Given in Rome, at St. Peter's, June 9, 1832, the second year of Our Pontificate.

†

LATIN TEXT: *Acta Greg. XVI*, 1:143-44.

ENGLISH TRANSLATION: Bernard A. Hausmann, S.J.

MIRARI VOS

ENCYCLICAL OF POPE GREGORY XVI
ON LIBERALISM AND RELI-
GIOUS INDIFFERENTISM
AUGUST 15, 1832

33

To All Patriarchs, Primates, Archbishops, and Bishops of the Catholic World.

Venerable Brothers, Greetings and Apostolic Benediction.

We think that you wonder why, from the time of Our assuming the pontificate, We have not yet sent a letter to you as is customary and as Our benevolence for you demanded. We wanted very much to address you by that voice by which We have been commanded, in the person of blessed Peter, to strengthen the brethren.[1] You know what storms of evil and toil, at the beginning of Our pontificate, drove Us suddenly into the depths of the sea. If the right hand of God had not given Us strength, We would have drowned as the result of the terrible conspiracy of impious men. The mind recoils from renewing this grief by enumerating so many dangers; instead We bless the Father of consolation Who, having overthrown all enemies, snatched Us from the present danger. When He had calmed this violent storm, He gave Us relief from fear. At once We decided to advise you on healing the wounds of Israel; but the mountain of concerns We needed to address in order to restore public order delayed Us.

2. In the meantime We were again delayed because of the insolent and factious men who endeavored to raise the standard of treason. Eventually, We had to use Our God-given authority to restrain the great obstinacy of these men with the rod.[2] Before We did, their unbridled rage seemed to grow from continued impunity and Our considerable indulgence. For these reasons Our duties have been heavy.

3. But when We had assumed Our pontificate according to the custom and institution of Our predecessors and when all delays had been laid aside, We hastened to you. So We now present the letter and testimony of Our good will toward you on this happy day, the feast of the Assumption of the Virgin. Since she has been Our patron and savior amid so many great calamities, We ask her assistance in writing to you and her counsels for the flock of Christ.

4. We come to you grieving and sorrowful because We know that you are concerned for the faith in these difficult times. Now is truly the time in which the powers of darkness winnow the elect like wheat.[3] "The earth mourns and fades away. . . .And the earth is infected by the inhabitants thereof, because they have transgressed the laws, they have changed the ordinances, they have broken the everlasting covenant."[4]

Difficult Times

5. We speak of the things which you see with

your own eyes, which We both bemoan. Depravity exults; science is impudent; liberty, dissolute. The holiness of the sacred is despised; the majesty of divine worship is not only disapproved by evil men, but defiled and held up to ridicule. Hence sound doctrine is perverted and errors of all kinds spread boldly. The laws of the sacred, the rights, institutions, and discipline—none are safe from the audacity of those speaking evil. Our Roman See is harassed violently and the bonds of unity are daily loosened and severed. The divine authority of the Church is opposed and her rights shorn off. She is subjected to human reason and with the greatest injustice exposed to the hatred of the people and reduced to vile servitude. The obedience due bishops is denied and their rights are trampled underfoot. Furthermore, academies and schools resound with new, monstrous opinions, which openly attack the Catholic faith; this horrible and nefarious war is openly and even publicly waged. Thus, by institutions and by the example of teachers, the minds of the youth are corrupted and a tremendous blow is dealt to religion and the perversion of morals is spread. So the restraints of religion are thrown off, by which alone kingdoms stand. We see the destruction of public order, the fall of principalities, and the overturning of all legitimate power approaching. Indeed this great mass of calamities had its inception in the heretical societies and sects in which all that is sacrilegious, infamous, and blasphemous has gathered as bilge water in a ship's hold, a congealed mass of all filth.

Evils Must be Deplored

6. These and many other serious things, which at present would take too long to list, but which you know well, cause Our intense grief. It is not enough for Us to deplore these innumerable evils unless We strive to uproot them. We take refuge in your faith and call upon your concern for the salvation of the Catholic flock. Your singular prudence and diligent spirit give Us courage and console Us, afflicted as We are with so many trials. We must raise Our voice and attempt all things lest a wild boar from the woods should destroy the vineyard or wolves kill the flock. It is Our duty to lead the flock only to the food which is healthful. In these evil and dangerous times, the shepherds must never neglect their duty; they must never be so overcome by fear that they abandon the sheep. Let them never neglect the flock and become sluggish from idleness and apathy. Therefore, united in spirit, let us promote our common cause, or more truly the cause of God; let our vigilance be one and our effort united against the common enemies.

Fulfill Your Duty

7. Indeed you will accomplish this perfectly if, as the duty of your office demands, you attend to yourselves and to doctrine and meditate on these words: "the universal Church is affected by any and every novelty"[5] and the admonition of Pope Agatho: "nothing of the things appointed ought to be diminished; nothing changed; nothing added; but they must be preserved both as regards expression and meaning."[6] Therefore may the unity which is built upon the See of Peter as on a sure foundation stand firm. May it be for all a wall and a security, a safe port, and a treasury of countless blessings.[7] To check the audacity of those who attempt to infringe upon the rights of this Holy See or to sever the union of the churches with the See of Peter, instill in your people a zealous confidence in the papacy and sincere veneration for it. As St. Cyprian wrote: "He who abandons the See of Peter on which the Church was founded, falsely believes himself to be a part of the Church."[8]

Everyone's Duties

8. In this you must labor and diligently take care that the faith may be preserved amidst this great conspiracy of impious men who attempt to tear it down and destroy it. May all remember the judgment concerning sound doctrine with which the people are to be instructed. Remember also that the government and administration of the whole Church rests with the Roman Pontiff to whom, in the words of the Fathers of the Council of Florence, "the full power of nourishing, ruling, and governing the universal Church was given by Christ the Lord."[9] It is the duty of individual bishops to cling to the See of Peter faithfully, to guard the faith piously and religiously, and to feed their flock. It behooves priests to be subject to the bishops, whom "they are to look upon as the parents of their souls," as Jerome admonishes.[10] Nor may the priests ever forget that they are forbidden by ancient canons to undertake ministry and to assume the tasks of teaching and preaching "without the permission of their bishop

to whom the people have been entrusted; an accounting for the souls of the people will be demanded from the bishop."[11] Finally let them understand that all those who struggle against this established order disturb the position of the Church.

Discipline of the Church Must Not Be Questioned

9. Furthermore, the discipline sanctioned by the Church must never be rejected or be branded as contrary to certain principles of natural law. It must never be called crippled, or imperfect or subject to civil authority. In this discipline the administration of sacred rites, standards of morality, and the reckoning of the rights of the Church and her ministers are embraced.

Papal Authority

10. To use the words of the fathers of Trent, it is certain that the Church "was instructed by Jesus Christ and His Apostles and that all truth was daily taught it by the inspiration of the Holy Spirit."[12] Therefore, it is obviously absurd and injurious to propose a certain "restoration and regeneration" for her as though necessary for her safety and growth, as if she could be considered subject to defect or obscuration or other misfortune. Indeed these authors of novelties consider that a "foundation may be laid of a new human institution," and what Cyprian detested may come to pass, that what was a divine thing "may become a human church."[13] Let those who devise such plans be aware that, according to the testimony of St. Leo, "the right to grant dispensation from the canons is given" only to the Roman Pontiff. He alone, and no private person, can decide anything "about the rules of the Church Fathers." As St. Gelasius writes: "It is the papal responsibility to keep the canonical decrees in their place and to evaluate the precepts of previous popes so that when the times demand relaxation in order to rejuvenate the churches, they may be adjusted after diligent consideration."[14]

Celibacy

11. Now, however, We want you to rally to combat the abominable conspiracy against clerical celibacy. This conspiracy spreads daily and is promoted by profligate philosophers, some even from the clerical order. They have forgotten their person and office, and have been carried away by the enticements of pleasure. They have even dared to make repeated public demands to the princes for the abolition of that most holy discipline. But it is disgusting to dwell on these evil attempts at length. Rather, We ask that you strive with all your might to justify and to defend the law of clerical celibacy as prescribed by the sacred canons, against which the arrows of the lascivious are directed from every side.

Mirari vos 33

Indissolubility of Marriage

12. Now the honorable marriage of Christians, which Paul calls "a great sacrament in Christ and the Church,"[15] demands our shared concern lest anything contrary to its sanctity and indissolubility is proposed. Our predecessor Pius VIII would recommend to you his own letters on the subject. However, troublesome efforts against this sacrament still continue to be made. The people therefore must be zealously taught that a marriage rightly entered upon cannot be dissolved; for those joined in matrimony God has ordained a perpetual companionship for life and a knot of necessity which cannot be loosed except by death. Recalling that matrimony is a sacrament and therefore subject to the Church, let them consider and observe the laws of the Church concerning it. Let them take care lest for any reason they permit that which is an obstruction to the teachings of the canons and the decrees of the councils. They should be aware that those marriages will have an unhappy end which are entered upon contrary to the discipline of the Church or without God's favor or because of concupiscence alone, with no thought of the sacrament and of the mysteries signified by it.

Indifferentism

13. Now We consider another abundant source of the evils with which the Church is afflicted at present: *indifferentism*. This perverse opinion is spread on all sides by the fraud of the wicked who claim that it is possible to obtain the eternal salvation of the soul by the profession of any kind of religion, as long as morality is maintained. Surely, in so clear a matter, you will drive this deadly error far from the people committed to your care. With the admonition of the apostle that "there is one God, one faith, one baptism"[16] may those fear who contrive the notion that the safe harbor of salvation is open to persons of any

religion whatever. They should consider the testimony of Christ Himself that "those who are not with Christ are against Him,"[17] and that they disperse unhappily who do not gather with Him. Therefore "without a doubt, they will perish forever, unless they hold the Catholic faith whole and inviolate."[18] Let them hear Jerome who, while the Church was torn into three parts by schism, tells us that whenever someone tried to persuade him to join his group he always exclaimed: "He who is for the See of Peter is for me."[19] A schismatic flatters himself falsely if he asserts that he, too, has been washed in the waters of regeneration. Indeed Augustine would reply to such a man: "The branch has the same form when it has been cut off from the vine; but of what profit for it is the form, if it does not live from the root?"[20]

Liberty of Conscience

14. This shameful font of indifferentism gives rise to that absurd and erroneous proposition which claims that *liberty of conscience* must be maintained for everyone. It spreads ruin in sacred and civil affairs, though some repeat over and over again with the greatest impudence that some advantage accrues to religion from it. "But the death of the soul is worse than freedom of error," as Augustine was wont to say.[21] When all restraints are removed by which men are kept on the narrow path of truth, their nature, which is already inclined to evil, propels them to ruin. Then truly "the bottomless pit"[22] is open from which John saw smoke ascending which obscured the sun, and out of which locusts flew forth to devastate the earth. Thence comes transformation of minds, corruption of youths, contempt of sacred things and holy laws—in other words, a pestilence more deadly to the state than any other. Experience shows, even from earliest times, that cities renowned for wealth, dominion, and glory perished as a result of this single evil, namely immoderate freedom of opinion, license of free speech, and desire for novelty.

Freedom of Publication

15. Here We must include that harmful and never sufficiently denounced freedom to publish any writings whatever and disseminate them to the people, which some dare to demand and promote with so great a clamor. We are horrified to see what monstrous doctrines and prodigious errors are disseminated far and wide in countless books, pamphlets, and other writings which, though small in weight, are very great in malice. We are in tears at the abuse which proceeds from them over the face of the earth. Some are so carried away that they contentiously assert that the flock of errors arising from them is sufficiently compensated by the publication of some book which defends religion and truth. Every law condemns deliberately doing evil simply because there is some hope that good may result. Is there any sane man who would say poison ought to be distributed, sold publicly, stored, and even drunk because some antidote is available and those who use it may be snatched from death again and again?

Remedies for this Evil

16. The Church has always taken action to destroy the plague of bad books. This was true even in apostolic times for we read that the apostles themselves burned a large number of books.[23] It may be enough to consult the laws of the fifth Council of the Lateran on this matter and the Constitution which Leo X published afterwards lest "that which has been discovered advantageous for the increase of the faith and the spread of useful arts be converted to the contrary use and work harm for the salvation of the faithful."[24] This also was of great concern to the fathers of Trent, who applied a remedy against this great evil by publishing that wholesome decree concerning the Index of books which contain false doctrine.[25] "We must fight valiantly," Clement XIII says in an encyclical letter about the banning of bad books, "as much as the matter itself demands and must exterminate the deadly poison of so many books; for never will the material for error be withdrawn, unless the criminal sources of depravity perish in flames."[26] Thus it is evident that this Holy See has always striven, throughout the ages, to condemn and to remove suspect and harmful books. The teaching of those who reject the censure of books as too heavy and onerous a burden causes immense harm to the Catholic people and to this See. They are even so depraved as to affirm that it is contrary to the principles of law, and they deny the Church the right to decree and to maintain it.

All Authority Comes from God

17. We have learned that certain teachings are being spread among the common people in writings which attack the trust and submission due to princes; the torches of treason are being lit everywhere. Care must be taken lest the people, being deceived, are led away from the straight path. May all recall, according to the admonition of the apostle that "there is no authority except from God: what authority there is has been appointed by God. Therefore he who resists authority resists the ordinances of God; and those who resist bring on themselves condemnation."[27] Therefore both divine and human laws cry out against those who strive by treason and sedition to drive the people from confidence in their princes and force them from their government.

18. And it is for this reason that the early Christians, lest they should be stained by such great infamy deserved well of the emperors and of the safety of the state even while persecution raged. This they proved splendidly by their fidelity in performing perfectly and promptly whatever they were commanded which was not opposed to their religion, and even more by their constancy and the shedding of their blood in battle. "Christian soldiers," says St. Augustine, "served an infidel emperor. When the issue of Christ was raised, they acknowledged no one but the One who is in heaven. They distinguished the eternal Lord from the temporal lord, but were also subject to the temporal lord for the sake of the eternal Lord."[28] St. Mauritius, the unconquered martyr and leader of the Theban legion had this in mind when, as St. Eucharius reports, he answered the emperor in these words: "We are your soldiers, Emperor, but also servants of God, and this we confess freely . . . and now this final necessity of life has not driven us into rebellion: see, we are armed and we do not resist, because we wish rather to die than to be killed."[29] Indeed the faith of the early Christians shines more brightly, if with Tertullian we consider that since the Christians were not lacking in numbers and in troops, they could have acted as foreign enemies. "We are but of yesterday," he says, "yet we have filled all your cities, islands, fortresses, municipalities, assembly places, the camps themselves, the tribes, the divisions, the palace, the senate, the forum. . . .For what war should we not have been fit and ready even if unequal in forces—we who are so glad to be cut to pieces—were it not, of course, that in our doctrine we would have been permitted more to be killed rather than to kill? . . .If so great a multitude of people should have deserted to some remote spot on earth, it would surely have covered your domination with shame because of the loss of so many citizens, and it would even have punished you by this very desertion. Without a doubt you would have been terrified at your solitude. . . . You would have sought whom you might rule; more enemies than citizens would have remained for you. Now however you have fewer enemies because of the multitude of Christians."[30]

19. These beautiful examples of the unchanging subjection to the princes necessarily proceeded from the most holy precepts of the Christian religion. They condemn the detestable insolence and improbity of those who, consumed with the unbridled lust for freedom, are entirely devoted to impairing and destroying all rights of dominion while bringing servitude to the people under the slogan of liberty. Here surely belong the infamous and wild plans of the Waldensians, the Beghards, the Wycliffites, and other such sons of Belial, who were the sores and disgrace of the human race; they often received a richly deserved anathema from the Holy See. For no other reason do experienced deceivers devote their efforts, except so that they, along with Luther, might joyfully deem themselves "free of all." To attain this end more easily and quickly, they undertake with audacity any infamous plan whatever.

20. Nor can We predict happier times for religion and government from the plans of those who desire vehemently to separate the Church from the state, and to break the mutual concord between temporal authority and the priesthood. It is certain that that concord which always was favorable and beneficial for the sacred and the civil order is feared by the shameless lovers of liberty.

21. But for the other painful causes We are concerned about, you should recall that certain societies and assemblages seem to draw up a battle line together with the followers of every false religion and cult. They feign piety for religion; but they are driven by a passion for promoting novelties and sedition everywhere. They preach liberty of every sort; they stir up disturbances in sacred and civil affairs, and pluck authority to pieces.

Exhortation for Help

22. We write these things to you with grieving mind but trusting in Him who commands the winds and makes them still. Take up the shield of faith and fight the battles of the Lord vigorously.

You especially must stand as a wall against every height which raises itself against the knowledge of God. Unsheath the sword of the spirit, which is the word of God, and may those who hunger after justice receive bread from you. Having been called so that you might be diligent cultivators in the vineyard of the Lord, do this one thing, and labor in it together, so that every root of bitterness may be removed from your field, all seeds of vice destroyed, and a happy crop of virtues may take root and grow. The first to be embraced with paternal affection are those who apply themselves to the sacred sciences and to philosophical studies. For them may you be exhorter and supporter, lest trusting only in their own talents and strength, they may imprudently wander away from the path of truth onto the road of the impious. Let them remember that God is the guide to wisdom and the director of the wise.[31] It is impossible to know God without God who teaches men to know Himself by His word.[32] It is the proud, or rather foolish, men who examine the mysteries of faith which surpass all understanding with the faculties of the human mind, and rely on human reason which by the condition of man's nature, is weak and infirm.

23. May Our dear sons in Christ, the princes, support these Our desires for the welfare of Church and State with their resources and authority. May they understand that they received their authority not only for the government of the world, but especially for the defense of the Church. They should diligently consider that whatever work they do for the welfare of the Church accrues to their rule and peace. Indeed let them persuade themselves that they owe more to the cause of the faith than to their kingdom. Let them consider it something very great for themselves as We say with Pope St. Leo, "if in addition to their royal diadem the crown of faith may be added." Placed as if they were parents and teachers of the people, they will bring them true peace and tranquility, if they take special care that religion and piety remain safe. God, after all, calls Himself "King of kings and Lord of lords."

24. That all of this may come to pass prosperously and happily, let Us raise Our eyes and hands to the most holy Virgin Mary, who alone crushes all heresies, and is Our greatest reliance and the whole reason for Our hope.[33] May she implore by her patronage a successful outcome for Our plans and actions. Let Us humbly ask of the Prince of the Apostles, Peter and his co-apostle Paul that all of you may stand as a wall lest a foundation be laid other than that which has already been laid. Relying on this happy hope, We trust that the Author and Crown of Our faith Jesus Christ will console Us in all these Our tribulations. We lovingly impart the apostolic benediction to you, venerable brothers, and to the sheep committed to your care as a sign of heavenly aid.

Given in Rome at St. Mary Major, on August 15, the feast of the Assumption of the Virgin, in the year of Our Lord 1832, the second year of Our Pontificate.

†

LATIN TEXT: *Acta Greg. XVI*, 1:169-74.

ENGLISH TRANSLATION: Bernard A. Hausmann, S.J.

REFERENCES:

1. Lk 22.32.
2. 1 Cor 4.21.
3. Lk 22.53.
4. Is 24.5.
5. St. Celestine, Pope, epistle 21 to Bishop Galliar.
6. St. Agatho, Pope, epistle to the emperor, apud Labb., ed. Mansi, vol. 2, p. 235.
7. St. Innocent, epistle 11 apud Constat.
8. St. Cyprian, *de unitate eccles.*
9. Council of Florence, session 25, in definit. apud Labb., ed. Venet., vol. 18, col. 527.
10. St. Jerome, epistle 2 to Nepot. a. 1, 24.
11. From canon ap. 38 apud Labb., ed Mansi, vol. 1, p. 38.
12. Council of Trent, session 13 on the Eucharist, prooemium.
13. St. Cyprian, epistle 52, ed. Baluz.
14. St. Gelasius, Pope, in epistle to the bishop of Lucaniae.
15. Heb 13.4.
16. Eph 4.5.
17. Lk 11.23.
18. Symbol .s. Athanasius.
19. St. Jerome, epistle 57.
20. St. Augustine, in psalm. contra part. Donat.
21. St. Augustine, epistle 166.
22. Ap 9.3.
23. Acts 19.
24. Acts of the Lateran Council 5, session 10, where the constitution of Leo X is mentioned; the earlier constitution of Alexander VI, *Inter multiplices*, ought to be read, in which there are many things on this point.
25. Council of Trent, sessions 18 and 25.
26. Letter of Clement XIII, *Christianae*, 25 November 1766.
27. Rom 13.2.
28. St. Augustine in psalt. 124, n. 7.
29. St. Euchenius apud Ruinart. Acts of the Holy Martyrs concerning Saint Maurius and his companions, n. 4.
30. Tertullian, in apologet., chap. 37.
31. Wis 7.15.

32. St. Irenaeus, bk. 14, chap. 10.
33. St. Bernard, *serm. de nat b.M.v.*, sect. 7.

COMMENTARIES:

Rupert, Louis, *La liberté moderne jugée par l'Église; encyclique Mirari Vos de Gregoire XVI contre L'Avenir; allocution Jamdudum de Pie IX contre le libéralisme.* Paris, Chaumont, 1862.

Ryan, John A. "Condemnation of L'Avenir." *Catholic Historical Review,* 23 (April, 1937), 31-39.

QUO GRAVIORA

ENCYCLICAL OF POPE GREGORY XVI ON
THE "PRAGMATIC CONSTITUTION"
OCTOBER 4, 1833

34

To the Bishops of the Province of Upper Rhineland.

Venerable Brothers, Greetings and Apostolic Blessing.

Troubles in the Rhineland

As more serious ills threaten the Catholic Church from the heinous contrivances of its enemies, the popes who have been placed in the See of St. Peter should be so much the quicker in taking action to repel them. The popes have been delegated the supreme power of nourishing and directing the Church. Our predecessor Pius VIII clearly understood this. Many daring things were attempted—and not in vain—against the teaching of the Church and its divine authority in the ecclesiastical province of the Rhineland. As soon as he knew this, Pius VIII sent you a letter at the end of June, 1830, to arouse your pastoral concern, if it was indeed necessary. This letter urged you to protect the rights of the Church with every zeal, to watch over sound doctrine, and to show those who must act how to oppose with reason and justice those ideas harmful to the Church, ideas which you should zealously strive to have revoked. He was extremely concerned with the situation of those churches because of the immense scandal caused by the reforms. He requested an answer from you as soon as possible, either confirming his desires and soothing his grief or—a possibility not to be entertained—contrary to his will, so that he might take the counsel required by the duty of his apostolic office.

2. These exhortations and encouragements of so great a pope in such a serious matter should arouse you. This is appropriate for those who were called to share in the administration and defense of the Church. Moreover, what Our predecessor never thought of, and what would have certainly disturbed him very much if he were still alive, was reserved for Us to mourn. This is in spite of the fact that We have been appointed in his place with vastly inferior merits and have no desire to hold this position. We cannot say that a matter so opposed to the wishes of this Holy See had ceased. This See is thus generally unaware of whatever efforts you have made among those leaders for the welfare of the Catholic religion and whatever result you have obtained. We still await more accurate reports, which Pius VIII so greatly commended to you, though three years have elapsed. Nor in truth can We assume from this that you did not neglect your duty, that some salutary remedy had been brought at that time to the wounds inflicted on the Catholic Church. On

the contrary, an occasion of sharper sorrow is in store for Us. Those matters are already ratified and in full force, to the detriment of the Church and against the agreements entered into between this Holy See and the united leaders. The Church is thus subjected to an unworthy slavery, having been violently deprived of the liberty which Christ gave it. What is more, its condition in those regions worsened because of new causes coming from everywhere, a condition which We (and you) may not contemplate. From that company of priests some men arose who say evil things. They shamelessly condemn that deluded (as they call it) regeneration and restoration of the reformers, thereby rashly enkindling this Apostolic See. They do this in order to draw followers and to deceive the unwary. Therefore, in whatever club they gather and hold meetings or discussions, they never hesitate to treat the Catholic Church, as they say, to reform it.

The Offenburg Reformers

3. Many of the priests of the city of Offenburg openly showed this kind of blindness not long ago, according to F. L. Mersy, their dean, adviser, and leader. They no longer proposed, for the approval of the archbishop of Freiburg, various points of reform contrived in their meetings. In the individual rural chapters, they spread the same ideas and aroused a wicked conspiracy. Moreover, now and again, they produced a pamphlet with many additions and dared to print it under the bold title: "Are reforms necessary in the Catholic Church?" We wish that the priests of Offenburg gather together and publicly and openly demonstrate their devotion, and that others, both from the diocese of Freiburg and from the rest of the ecclesiastical provinces, might not trouble themselves over this! We wish that this very evil sedition of the reformers contain itself within the boundaries of that city! But We heard long ago and We very sorrowfully recall that this discontent has extended into almost all those regions, especially in the diocese of Rothenburg, and that it extended even outside the ecclesiastical province of the Rhineland.

The Christian Religion Cannot Become Perfect

4. You know, venerable brothers, on what erroneous principles the above-mentioned men and their followers depend and where that desire which moves them to begin effecting a revolution in the Church has its origin. We do not think it superfluous to clarify many of those things and to explain them here. A false idea has for a long time grown stronger and spread widely through these regions. This idea is spread by an impious and absurd system of indifference toward religious matters which claims that the Christian religion can become perfect in time. While the patrons of such a false idea are afraid to adapt the shaky possibility of perfection to the truths of faith, they establish it in the external administration and discipline of the Church. Moreover, in order to bring about faith in their error, they wrongfully and deceitfully usurp the authority of Catholic theologians. These theologians propound here and there a distinction between the teaching and the discipline of the Church which underlies this change, that it will always stand firm and never be harmed by any alteration. Once this is established, they state categorically that there are many things in the discipline of the Church in the present day, in its government, and in the form of its external worship which are not suited to the character of our time. These things, they say, should be changed, as they are harmful for the growth and prosperity of the Catholic religion, before the teaching of faith and morals suffers any harm from it. Therefore, showing a zeal for religion and showing themselves as an example of piety, they force reforms, conceive of changes, and pretend to renew the Church.

Dangers of Reform

5. Truly such reformers use these principles. In addition, they disclose and propose them in many pamphlets, which they distribute especially in Germany. This is now very clear from the booklet printed in Offenburg. It is especially clear from those things which the aforementioned F. L. Mersy, head of the seditious meeting held there, imprudently compiled in his republication of the same book. While these men were shamefully straying in their thoughts, they proposed to fall upon the errors condemned by the Church in proposition 78 of the constitution *Auctorem fidei* (published by Our predecessor, Pius VI on August 28, 1794). They also attacked the pure doctrine which they say they want to keep safe and sound; either they do not understand the situation or craftily pretend not to understand it. While they contend that the entire exterior form

of the Church can be changed indiscriminately, do they not subject to change even those items of discipline which have their basis in divine law and which are linked with the doctrine of faith in a close bond? Does not the law of the believer thus produce the law of the doer? Moreover, do they not try to make the Church human by taking away from the infallible and divine authority, by which divine will it is governed? And does it not produce the same effect to think that the present discipline of the Church rests on failures, obscurities, and other inconveniences of this kind? And to feign that this discipline contains many things which are not useless but which are against the safety of the Catholic religion? Why is it that private individuals appropriate for themselves the right which is proper only for the pope?

6. We will now discuss those sections of discipline which are in effect for the whole Church. Because they are free from ecclesiastical instruction, they can undergo change, but only by the pope, whom Christ placed over the entire Church to judge concerning the necessity of change for various reasons of circumstance. Thus, as St. Gelasius wrote: "Balance the decrees of the canons and consider the precepts of your predecessors, so that those things which the demands of the times require to be relaxed for the rebuilding of the churches may be moderated through careful consideration." It is tedious to detain you with a long speech, venerable brothers, about the false principles which the reformers depend on. They add rashness to error with the usual verbal license of such men, since they attack this Holy See as if it were too persistent in outdated customs and did not look deeply inside the character of our time. They accuse this See of becoming blind amid the light of new knowledge, and of hardly distinguishing those things which deal with the substance of religion from those which regard only the external form. They say that it feeds superstition, fosters abuses, and finally behaves as if it never looks after the interests of the Catholic Church in changing times. Where does all this lead? Actually, so that the most Holy See of Peter in which Jesus Christ placed the foundation of His Church is hastened toward envy. Its divine authority is subjected to the hatred of the people, and the union of other churches with it is broken. The dissidents give up hope then that they would obtain what they want at this Apostolic See. They assert that the Church—one nation, as they call it—should be ruled by its own laws. From here they continue so as to grant free authority to revoke or abrogate the laws of the whole Church to each individual pastor, if the expediency of his diocese demands it. What then? Since they do not perceive any advantage among you, they try to free those same priests from the submission due to the bishops. They are not afraid to concede to the priests the right of administrating the dioceses. It is quite clear that these men, acting against the truth of faith, have overthrown the ecclesiastical hierarchy which was established by divine will and defined by the fathers of the Council of Trent. It is also clear that they want to return to the very errors in the propositions 6, 7, 8, and 9 proscribed by the aforesaid dogmatic constitution *Auctorem fidei.*

Quo graviora 34

Celibacy

7. This appears to clearly concern those priests of Offenburg. The condemned doctrines are especially contained in the additions inserted in the re-edited pamphlet so that there is no room for doubt. It now seems a good idea to review individually some of the many other errors with which that pamphlet everywhere abounds. Here occur for the first time the objections of the promoters of the vile plot against clerical celibacy. They do not dare to openly criticize the law of celibacy, as others do; nonetheless, they chatter with daring equal only to their error! They want the priests who are not up to keeping the law of celibacy and whose mores are already so hopelessly corrupted to be moved to lay status, so that they might thus contract valid marriages within the Church. This is hardly in keeping with the intention of the fathers of the Council of Trent, which was explained in session 7, can. 9 concerning the sacraments in general as well as in session 23, chapter 4 and canon 4. It does not escape Us with what means they might try to distort the teaching of the Council of Trent.

8. They contend that according to the opinion of the Council of Trent, he who was once a priest cannot again become a layman by his own authority. He can do this only by the authority of the Church, and they understand by the word "Church" each bishop to whom they give the power to reduce priests to the lay state. Then they affirm that the character which is imprinted in

the sacrament of Orders, which the Council said was indelible makes the sacrament of Orders unable to be repeated. It does not in the least, they say, forbid a priest to become a layman in the aforementioned manner. Finally, they hardly shrink from numbering that same character among the things recently agreed upon by the scholastics. Moreover, as they contrive such things, what else can they really do unless to wickedly scoff at and oppose the true meaning of the previously mentioned decrees of the Council of Trent and the whole Church concerning them, thereby piling error upon error?

Indulgences

9. They shrink no less from sound doctrine in the things which they boldly propose concerning the power and use of indulgences. They propose either openly or through equivocations the idea that indulgences can hardly be referred to the temporal pains of sin which remain and which must be expiated, either in this life or in the next. Up to the eleventh century, they explain there were no penalties other than the canonical ones which were to be removed by the Church. For the first time, at the time of the holy wars, the punishments which God imposed on the sinner were subjected to the power of the keys. Then, they continue, a great distortion of the Church's discipline emerged. The treasure established by the merits of Jesus Christ and the satisfactions of the saints, unknown to earlier centuries, was discovered by Pope Clement V. Finally, to make matters brief, the indulgences were used to that end only, in order to recall to mind the present penalties by the Church and the ancient canonical ones, and so to lead sinners to penance. Where can they go from there, unless to arouse the proscribed propositions 17 and 19 of Luther, 6 of Peter of Osma, 60 of Baius, and finally 40, 41, and 42 of the cited constitution *Auctorem fidei* and to restore shamelessly the hostile errors in them?

10. These men want to utterly reform the holy institution of sacramental penance. They insolently slander the Church and falsely accuse it of error, and their shamelessness should be deplored even more. They claim that the Church, by ordering annual confession, allowing indulgences as an added condition of fulfilling confession, and permitting private Eucharist and daily works of piety, has weakened that salutary tradition and subtracted from its power and efficacy. The Church is the pillar and foundation of truth—all of which truth is taught by the Holy Spirit. Should the church be able to order, yield to, or permit those things which tend toward the destruction of souls and the disgrace and detriment of the sacrament instituted by Christ? Those proponents of new ideas who are eager to foster true piety in the people should consider that, with the frequency of the sacraments diminished or entirely eliminated, religion slowly languishes and finally perishes.

Other Erroneous Ideas

11. Venerable brothers, it would be too long to pursue the many erroneous ideas of the reformers concerning the stipend for Masses, which they conclude should be abolished. They object to the practice of offering several Masses for the same deceased, which they translate as being contrary to the Church's teaching on the infinite value of that same sacrifice of the new law. Nor do We want to discuss their errors concerning the new ritual written in the vernacular, which they want to have adapted more to the character of our times. We shall also pass over their ideas on holy societies, public prayers, and holy pilgrimages, which they disapprove in various ways. It should be enough to indicate that these ideas do not flow from any other corrupt source nor come from any other principles than those which were already solemnly condemned by the Church in the constitution *Auctorem fidei* cited several times, especially in propositions 30, 33, 66, and 78.

12. Venerable brothers, We are following a little more broadly the examples of Our predecessors in similar situations, as the cause of the apostolic duty seems to require. We resolved to discuss these things so that, with the errors of those men revealed, it might become known where the wicked passion for introducing novelties into the Church might lead. As for the rest, it is enough to suggest that the bitterness of the times in which Catholicism now finds itself oppresses Us with many sorrows. We mourn the pure spouse of the immaculate lamb, Jesus Christ, for it is pillaged by the attack of internal and external enemies and by the evils which oppress it and reduce it to this disgraceful captivity. We deplore with unending tears what is done by children shamefully straying from the bosom of a loving mother and uttering lies about her.

Call to Religious Purity

13. May We not fail in spirit! May We not stifle Our apostolic voice in so serious a Catholic necessity! May We not allow the Lord's flock to be plundered and the sheep of Christ to be devoured by all the beasts of the field, while We put aside the strength, judgment, and virtue of the spirit of the Lord like dumb dogs unable to bark. Know therefore, venerable brothers, that We are prepared to endure anything which threatens Us. We shall not retreat until the Catholic Church is restored to the original freedom which totally belongs to its divine constitution and until the mouth of the slanderers is blocked up. We cannot do anything more than to arouse your constancy and virtue and to strongly exhort you to take up the cause of the Spirit of God and of the Church. You share in a part of the concern whose fulness is given to Us. It is your duty to protect the holy deposit of faith and sacred doctrine. It is your duty to drive every profane reform far away from the Church and to exert yourselves with your whole heart against those who try to infringe on the rights of this Holy See. Therefore, draw the sword of the spirit, which is the word of God. Preach as the apostle Paul impresses upon you in the person of Timothy his disciple. Stand firm in good times and in bad. Denounce, beseech, rebuke in all patience and teaching. Nothing should deter you from throwing yourselves into every conflict for the glory of God, for the protection of the Church, and for the salvation of the souls entrusted to your care. Meditate on Him who endured a smiliar opposition from sinners. If you fear the daring of the wicked, remember that the decision is made concerning the strength of the episcopacy and the divine power of governing the Church. So it only remains for you to remember the serious duties of your office and the difficult judgment which hangs over everyone in authority. The overseers of the house of Israel should especially meditate for a while at the feet of the Lord. We trust then that you will be aroused with zeal to help the Catholic religion and to protect it from the impious snares of its enemies. In this zeal you may show even greater results than these of which We wrote. Fully resolute and refreshed in that faith, We lovingly impart the apostolic blessing to you and to the people entrusted to your faith, as a sign of every good thing.

Quo graviora 34

Given at Rome, at St. Mary Major, under the ring of the fisherman, October 4, 1833, in the third year of Our Pontificate.

†

LATIN TEXT: *Acta Greg. XVI*, 1:307-10.

ENGLISH TRANSLATION: Norman Desmarais.

SINGULARI NOS

ENCYCLICAL OF POPE GREGORY XVI ON
THE ERRORS OF LAMMENAIS
JUNE 25, 1834

To All the Patriarchs, Primates, Archbishops, and Bishops.

Venerable Brothers, Greetings and Apostolic Blessing.

The illustrious examples of faith, obedience, and devotion conveyed by the enthusiastic reception given everywhere to Our encyclical letter of August 15, 1832, gave Us great joy. We declared in it the only sound doctrine to be followed concerning the main points in the fulfillment of the duties of Our office for the whole Catholic flock. The statements made by many who had approved those counsels and opinions which so grieved Us have increased Our joy, for they have acted as prompt defenders and supporters of Our decrees. We recognized that that evil which is still inflamed against both sacred and civil matters is not yet removed. Widely disseminated but very shameless pamphlets and certain gloomy machinations openly denoted those things which We condemned in a letter sent to Our venerable brother, the bishop of Rennes, in the month of October. Moreover, his response to those things which cause Us so much concern and anxiety has been gratefully received. His statement sent to Us on December 11 of last year distinctly confirmed that he would follow solely and absolutely the teaching transmitted in Our encyclical letter and that he would not write or approve anything which differs from it. In that matter We opened Our heart in paternal love to the son who was moved by Our warnings. We should also have trusted that he would produce more brilliant writings in time to confirm his compliance in word and deed with Our decision.

Heretical Pamphlet

2. It hardly seemed believable that he whom We welcomed with such good will and affection would so quickly forget Our kindness and desert Our resolution. We can hardly believe that the good hope which occupied Us with the fruit of Our teaching has died. However, We have learned of the pamphlet written in French under the title *Paroles d'un croyant*, for it has been printed by this man and disseminated everywhere. It was written under a pseudonym, but matters of public record make clear the author's identity. Though small in size, it is enormous in wickedness.

3. We were very much amazed, venerable brothers, when at first We understood the blindness of this wretched author, for in him knowledge does not come from God, but from the elements of the world; this "knowledge" bursts

forth. Against the oath solemnly given in his declaration, he cloaked Catholic teaching in enticing verbal artifice, in order ultimately to oppose it and overthrow it. We expressed this in Our letter mentioned above concerning both the dutiful submission toward authorities and the prevention of the fatal contamination of the people by indifferentism. It also concerned measures to use against the spreading license of ideas and speeches. Finally, it concerned that freedom of conscience which should be thoroughly condemned and the repulsive conspiracy of societies enkindling destruction of sacred and state affairs, even from the followers of false religions, as We have made clear by the authority handed down to Us.

4. The mind shrinks from reading through those things in which the author tries to break the bond of loyalty and submission toward leaders. Once the torch of treason is ignited everywhere, it ruins public order, fosters contempt of government, and stimulates lawlessness. It overthrows every element of sacred and civil power. From this, the writer transposes the power of princes, through a new and wicked idea, to the power of Satan and an omen of subterfuge, as if it were dangerous to divine law, even a work of sin. He brands the same marks of wickedness on the priests and rulers because of the conspiracy of crimes and labors in which he dreams they are joined against the rights of the people. Not content with such temerity, he thrusts forth every kind of opinion, speech, and freedom of conscience. He prays that everything will be favorable and happy for the soldiers who will fight to free liberty from tyranny, and he encourages groups and associations in the furious combat which engulfs everything. He stands so firm in such heinous thoughts that We feel him trample right from the beginning Our advice and orders.

5. It is annoying to recount here everything which throws all human and divine affairs into confusion with the wicked fruit of impiety and daring. But these things especially arouse Our indignation and should clearly not be tolerated by religion. Especially dangerous is the fact that holy Scriptures that have been tainted with the errors of this author are disseminated to the unwary. Acting as if he were sent and inspired by God, he speaks in the name of the Trinity and then uses Scripture as a pretext for releasing the people from the law of obedience. He twists the words of holy Scripture in a bold and cunning manner in order to firmly establish his depraved ravings. He does this in order that, as St. Bernard used to say, "He might spread clouds for light or give poison for honey, or rather in the honey, creating a new Gospel for the people and laying a different foundation from the one which is already laid."

Condemnation of Pamphlet

6. He who placed Us as scouts in Israel forbids Us to hide in silence the great harm brought to sound doctrine. So We must warn about the error those whom Jesus, the author and perfector of the faith, entrusted to Our care. Therefore, We consulted many of Our venerable brothers, the cardinals of the Holy Roman Church. We have studied the book entitled *Paroles d'un croyant*. By Our apostolic power, We condemn the book: furthermore, We decree that it be perpetually condemned. It corrupts the people by a wicked abuse of the word of God, to dissolve the bonds of all public order and to weaken all authority. It arouses, fosters, and strengthens seditions, riots, and rebellions in the empires. We condemn the book because it contains false, calumnious, and rash propositions which lead to anarchy; which are contrary to the word of God; which are impious, scandalous, and erroneous; and which the Church already condemned, especially in regard to the Waldensians, Wycliffites, Hussites, and other heretics of this kind.

7. Venerable brothers, it will now be your duty to strongly support Our orders which We urgently demand as necessary for the safety and welfare of both sacred and civil affairs. Let us see that no writing of this kind comes out of hiding into the light, since it would be that much more harmful if it were to set sail through the passion of insane reform and creep far and wide like a crab among the people. It should be your duty to encourage sound doctrine through this whole affair and to make known the craftiness of the innovators. Watch more keenly over the care of the Christian flock, so that zeal for religion, piety of actions, and public peace might happily flourish and increase. We wait for this, trusting in your faith and commitment to the common good so that, with the help of God who is the Father of lights, We might give thanks (with St. Cyprian) that the error has been understood and weakened and

then laid low, because it was recognized and discovered.

8. As for the rest, We greatly deplore the fact that, where the ravings of human reason extend, there is somebody who studies new things and strives to know more than is necessary, against the advice of the apostle. There you will find someone who is overconfident in seeking the truth outside the Catholic Church, in which it can be found without even a light tarnish of error. Therefore, the Church is called, and is indeed, a pillar and foundation of truth. You correctly understand, venerable brothers, that We speak here also of that erroneous philosophical system which was recently brought in and is clearly to be condemned. This system, which comes from the contemptible and unrestrained desire for innovation, does not seek truth where it stands in the received and holy apostolic inheritance. Rather, other empty doctrines, futile and uncertain doctrines not approved by the Church, are adopted. Only the most conceited men wrongly think that these teachings can sustain and support that truth.

9. While We write these things to understand and preserve the sound doctrine divinely delegated to Us, We sign over the harsh wound inflicted to Our heart by the error of Our son. In the great sadness We suffer, there is no hope of consolation, unless We can recall him to the way of righteousness. Therefore, at the same time, let Us raise Our eyes and hands to Him who is the leader of wisdom and the corrector of the wise. Let Us beseech Him with repeated prayer to give this man a docile heart and a great spirit to hear the voice of the most loving and most sorrowful Father. May he hasten the joy of the Church, the joy of your order, the joy of this Holy See, and the joy of Our unworthiness. Certainly We shall provide an auspicious and happy occasion to take hold of him and embrace him as a son returning to the bosom of his Father. We are and We shall be very optimistic from his example that others will come to their senses, others who might have been led into error by the same author. May there be an agreement of teaching, one course of thinking, one harmony of action and study, among all for the good of sacred and public matters. We need you and We expect you to beseech the Lord with Us in your pastoral concern for this great gift. We pray for divine assistance in this work and We lovingly impart Our apostolic blessing on you and on your flock as a sign of this.

Given in Rome, at St. Peter's, on June 25, 1834, in the fourth year of Our pontificate.

†

LATIN TEXT: *Acta Greg. XVI*, 1:433-34.

ENGLISH TRANSLATION: Norman Desmarais.

COMMENTARY:

"Un ejemplo de definición *ex cathedra* en una encíclica y de la obligación del asentimiento absoluto que impone, puede ser la *Singulari Nos* de Gregorio XVI." *Miscelanea Comillas*, 17 (1952), 162.

Singulari nos
35

COMMISSUM DIVINITUS

ENCYCLICAL OF POPE GREGORY XVI ON
CHURCH AND STATE
MAY 17, 1835
36

To the Clergy of Switzerland.

Venerable Brothers and Dearly Beloved Sons, Greetings and Apostolic Benediction.

The duty of the apostolic office which God entrusted to Us demands that We continually watch over the Lord's flock. We especially direct all Our zeal and thoughts to provide as much assistance as We can whenever the eternal salvation of the sheep and the Catholic religion seem to be in danger. We are aware of and deplore the fact that Our enemies cunningly try many things, and not without success. Their works are an open blow against the Christian flock and an injury to the Catholic cause. This sorrow is aggravated because those who want to deceive the unwary claim that they do not intend to subtract anything from the integrity of the faith. They pretend to have as their only purpose the protection of the rights of the laity. They attempt, by a false pretense of public interest, to introduce, widely disseminate, establish, and somehow sanction the erroneous and wicked teachings which they follow.

Articles of Baden

2. Hence they dared to call together an assembly to deliberate, and to fabricate a rule whereby aspects of the temporal power in ecclesiastical affairs were revealed and defined. You already know that We are speaking about those things which were nefariously accomplished during January of last year in Baden in the canton of Aargau. Because of them you experienced sharp sorrow and even now they make you anxious and concerned. We cannot keep secret the fact that in the beginning We were influenced to do nothing. We believed that the laymen gathered in the appointed place with no other intention than to study those matters which concern religion. We further believed they wanted to proceed so that they might not only discuss the many aspects of the ecclesiastical power, but also so that they might offer plans to those who wield high civil authority; those persons might then confirm and sanction the plans by force of law.

3. The acts of that meeting were recently published by Gynopedius at Frauenfeld. These acts contain the names of the men who were present at the meeting, the speeches given by some of them in the sessions, and the articles passed there. We were horrified in reading those speeches and articles and the principles contained in them. We knew then that novelties were being introduced in the Catholic Church which are contrary to its

teaching and discipline and which lead to the destruction of souls. We cannot allow this in any way.

Errors of the Articles

4. He who made everything and who governs by a prudent arrangement wanted order to flourish in His Church. He wanted some people to be in charge and govern and others to be subject and obey. Therefore, the Church has, by its divine institution, the power of the magisterium to teach and define matters of faith and morals and to interpret the Holy Scriptures without danger of error. It also has the power of governance to preserve and strengthen in the true doctrine those whom it welcomes as children and to make laws concerning all things which pertain to the salvation of souls, the exercise of the sacred ministry, and divine worship. Whoever opposes these laws makes himself guilty of a very serious crime.

5. This power of teaching and governing in matters of religion, given by Christ to His Spouse, belongs to the priests and bishops. Christ established this system not only so that the Church would in no way belong to the civil government of the state, but also so that it could be totally free and not subject in the least to any earthly domination. Jesus Christ did not commit the sacred trust of the revealed doctrine to the worldly leaders, but to the apostles and their successors. He said to them only: "Whoever hears you, hears Me; whoever rejects you, rejects Me." These same apostles preached the Gospel, spread the Church, and established its discipline not in accordance with the pleasure of lay authority, but even in spite of it. Moreover, when the leaders of the synagogue dared command them to silence, Peter and John, who had used the evangelical freedom, responded: "You be the judge of whether it is right in the eyes of God to listen to you rather than to God." Thus, if any secular power dominates the Church, controls its doctrine, or interferes so that it cannot promulgate laws concerning the holy ministry, divine worship, and the spiritual welfare of the faithful, it does so to the injury of the faith and the overturning of the divine ordinance of the Church and the nature of government.

6. These principles are firm, unchangeable, and supported by the authority and tradition of the ancient Fathers. Bishop Ossius of Córdoba wrote to Emperor Constantius: "Do not become involved in ecclesiastical matters nor give us orders concerning these affairs. But rather learn this from us: God gives you the empire; He entrusts ecclesiastical power to us. Whoever secretly tries to snatch the empire away from you opposes God. By the same token, take care that you do not draw ecclesiastical power to yourself and become guilty of a great crime." The Christian leaders were aware of this and they considered it a glorious thing to acknowledge publicly. Among them was the great leader Basil who said in the eighth synod: "What more can I say about you lay people? I have nothing else to say except that it is not permitted for you to speak concerning ecclesiastical matters. It is the duty of patriarchs, popes, and priests, to whom the duty of governing has been entrusted, to investigate and study these matters. They have the power of binding and loosing and of sanctifying. They are the ones who have the ecclesiastical and heavenly keys, not those who must be fed, sanctified, bound, and loosed."

7. However, in the Baden meeting the matter was discussed differently. The articles which came forth from it attack the sound doctrine of ecclesiastical power and lead the Church itself into a scandalous and unjust slavery. It is even subject to the judgment of lay authority in the promulgation of decrees concerning dogma, and its disciplinary laws are declared to lack force and effect unless they are promulgated by the agreement of secular authority with an added proposition concerning the penalties against those who disobey. What then? Power is given to that same civil authority either to approve or to oppose the celebration of the diocesan synods, to inspect the synods, to oversee seminaries, and to confirm the system of their internal governance established by bishops, to remove clerics from ecclesiastical duties, to govern the religious and moral instruction of the people, and finally to regulate everything which, they claim, pertains to the external discipline of the Church, although these things may be of a spiritual nature or character and may concern the worship of God and the salvation of souls.

Sacraments

8. There is nothing which belongs more to

the Church and there is nothing Jesus Christ wanted more closely reserved for its shepherds than the dispensation of the sacraments He instituted. The power to judge concerning their dispensation belongs only to those whom He established as ministers of His work on earth. It is wicked if the civil authority appropriates for itself anything in this holy office! It is wicked if the civil authority prescribes anything at all concerning it or gives orders to the ministers of the sacraments! It is wicked if it tries with its laws to oppose the rules handed down to Us in writing or by oral tradition from the early Church concerning the distribution of the sacraments to the Christian people. Our predecessor St. Gelasius said in his letter to Emperor Anastasius: "You know, most merciful son, that you are allowed to rule over the human race. Nevertheless, submit yourself to the bishops and seek from them the means of your salvation. In receiving the heavenly sacraments and in distributing them appropriately, you know that you should be subject rather than govern. You know therefore that in these things you depend on their judgment and that they do not want to be subjected to your power." What seems to be incredible and portentous is that the meeting at Baden progressed to the point that even the right and office of dispensing the sacraments was attributed to secular authority. The articles which were rashly written concerning the sacrament of marriage in Christ and the Church certainly incline in this direction as does the support given for contracting mixed marriages. The requirement that Catholic priests bless these marriages while ignoring the religious differences between the spouses and the threats of punishment for those who refuse to do this illustrate this tendency.

9. These things ought to be condemned because the civil authority makes laws concerning the celebration of a divinely established sacrament and dares to order the priests in such a serious matter. But they ought to be reproached even more so because they foster an absurd and impious idea which they call "indifferentism;" indeed they depend on it as necessary. Moreover, they oppose Catholic truth and Church doctrine which forbids mixed marriages as disgraceful because of the communion in holy things and because of the serious danger of the perversion of the Catholic spouse and the perverted education of the future children. Nor did the Church ever grant the free power to contract such a marriage unless conditions were added which prevented the causes of danger and deformity.

Primacy of the Papacy

Commissum divinitus 36

10. Jesus Christ conferred on His Church the supreme power of administering religion and governing Christian society. This is not subject to the civil authority. In his letter to the Ephesians the apostle teaches that Christ established this ecclesiastical power for the benefit of unity. And what is this unity unless one person is placed in charge of the whole Church who protects it and joins all its members in the one profession of faith and unites them in the one bond of love and communion? The wisdom of the Divine Lawgiver ordered that a visible head be placed over a visible body so that "once so established, the opportunity for division might be removed." Wherefore, although for all the bishops whom the Holy Spirit placed as governors of the Church of God there is a common dignity and in matters of rank there is nevertheless equal power, there is not the same rank in the hierarchy for all and they do not all have the same extent of jurisdiction.

Using the words of St. Leo the Great; "Among the holy apostles there was a similarity of honor but a distinction of power: while the election of all was equal, it was given only to one to have preeminence among the others . . . because the Lord wanted the sacrament of evangelical duty to belong to the office of the apostles; thus He placed it principally in St. Peter, the head of all the apostles." He granted this to Peter alone out of all the apostles when He promised him the keys of the kingdom of heaven and entrusted to him the obligation of feeding the Lord's sheep and lambs and the duty of strengthening his brothers. He wanted this to extend to Peter's successors whom He placed over the Church with equal right. This has always been the firm and united opinion of all Catholics. It is Church dogma that the pope, the successor of St. Peter, possesses not only primacy of honor but also primacy of authority and jurisdiction over the whole Church. Accordingly the bishops are subject to him.

11. In the words of St. Leo, who continues speaking about the Holy See of Peter: "It is necessary that the Church throughout the world be united and cleave to the center of Catholic unity and ecclesiastical communion, so that whoever dares to depart from the unity of Peter might understand that he no longer shares in the divine mystery." St. Jerome adds: "Whoever eats the lamb outside of this house is unholy. Those who were not in the ark of Noah perished in the flood." Just as he who does not gather with Christ, so he who does not gather with Christ's Vicar on earth, clearly scatters. How can someone who destroys the holy authority of the Vicar of Christ and who infringes on his rights gather with him? It is through these rights that the pope is the center of unity, that he has the primacy of order and jurisdiction, and that he has the full power of nurturing, ruling, and governing the universal Church.

12. We tearfully admit that this was attempted at the meeting in Baden. The pope alone and no bishop has the right to transfer the days fixed by the Church for celebrating feasts and observing fasts and to annul the precept of attending Mass. This was clearly established in the constitution *Auctorem fidei* published by Our predecessor Pius VI on August 28, 1794, against the Pistoians.

Pontifical Religious Congregations

13. The items contained in the Baden articles are contrary to this and are much more harmful because on the issue of discipline they reserve the right for the civil authority. The special privilege of removing religious congregations which live under a rule from the jurisdiction of the bishops and subjecting these congregations directly to himself belongs to the pope—a right popes have used from the earliest times. The articles of the Baden convention abridge this right. They make no mention of the necessity of asking and obtaining the permission of the Holy See. Thus plans may be undertaken by a secular authority through which, after the exemption of the monastic orders is abolished in Switzerland, regular congregations can be made subject to the authority of the ordinary bishops.

Rights of Bishops

14. To these, We should add those things which they indicate have been authorized concerning the rights of bishops. If these things are examined more deeply and referred back to the principles from which the articles made in the Baden conference proceed, they seem to confirm that the jurisdiction of the bishops neither can nor should be swayed by the supreme authority of the pope. Nor should they be circumscribed by any limitations. Neither should We omit those things which were proposed concerning either the erection of a metropolitan see or the unification of some of those dioceses to another cathedral church located beyond the boundaries of Switzerland. The rights of the Holy See in this matter were ignored. Thus civil authority acted as if it were totally free in these serious issues to establish by its own right those things which it considered to be advantageous for the spiritual needs of the people. We pass over many other things which would be too tiresome to enumerate individually. However, they inflict great harm on this Holy See of Peter and threaten, violate, and despise its dignity and authority.

Reasons for Pope's Delay in Criticizing Assembly

15. Since this is the situation and the Church is confronted by so great and open a disturbance of sound doctrine and ecclesiastical rights and by so great and serious a danger to the Catholic cause in these regions, it behooved Us to raise Our voice from this holy mountain soon after the meeting of Baden was held and to openly criticize, reprove, and condemn those articles to everyone who participated in the conference. We delayed Our decision on their wickedness up until now because We hoped that those who administer civil affairs would totally reject and disapprove of them. The matter did not, for the most part, come to pass according to Our expectation. On the contrary, We, greatly sorrowing, learned that laws were enacted which confirmed those articles and protected them by public decree.

Condemnation of Articles

16. We, in Our role as teacher and universal doctor, ought diligently to beware lest anyone be led into error by Our action and conclude that the articles of the Baden meeting are not inconsistent with the teaching and discipline of the Church. We know that We cannot hesitate or be silent any longer. As this is a matter of very serious importance, We subjected these articles to a careful examination. We have heard the advice and received the opinions of the cardinals of the Holy Roman Church and have considered the entire matter carefully by Our own will and with sure knowledge. With the fullness of the apostolic power, We reprove and condemn the aforementioned articles of the meeting of Baden as containing false, rash, and erroneous assertions; as detracting from the rights of the Holy See, overthrowing the government of the Church and its divine constitution, and subjecting the ecclesiastical ministry to secular domination; and as proceeding from condemned premises. We decree that they should forever be considered condemned.

Source of Comfort

17. While We intend to point these things out openly because of Our apostolic duty, it remains for Us to speak with paternal affection to you who have taken on a part of His governance, the fullness of which the Prince of Shepherds entrusted to Us. Among so many evils which besiege the Catholic Church in these evil times, what great trials press upon Our heart! We have experienced great sadness, especially from those things which were daringly attempted recently. It should be enough to direct your attention to it, and it should not be necessary to explain the details.

18. In Our sorrow We must not neglect to mention that what you did in guarding the Catholic cause and caring for the salvation of the flock entrusted to your care brought Us great solace. Therefore, We give thanks to the Father of mercies and the God of all consolation who comforted Us with you while We were oppressed by such tribulation. We must arouse your devotion. We exhort you to fight for the cause of God and the Church with greater zeal as the attacks of the enemy become more severe. It is your duty to stand as a wall so that no other foundation can be placed other than the one which has already been laid. It is also your duty to keep the faith undefiled. There is another sacred trust which you should firmly defend, namely, the holy laws by which the Church establishes its discipline, and the rights of this Apostolic See. Therefore, act according to the position which you hold, according to the dignity with which you are vested, according to the authority which you received, according to the sacrament by which you bound yourselves in solemn consecration. Unsheathe the sword of the spirit which is the word of God. Denounce, beseech, rebuke in all patience and teaching. Labor and struggle for the Catholic religion, for the divine authority and laws of the Church, for the See of Peter and its dignity and rights "so that not only those who are upright may remain safe but also so that those who were deceived by seduction may be called back from error."

19. Moreover, so that the desired outcome may result from these cares and labors undertaken by Our venerable brothers, We also address those of you who are ministers of the sacraments, shepherds of souls, and preachers of the divine word. It is your duty to be totally united with them in will, to be inflamed with the same zeal, and to be in harmony with them in this work so that the people might be protected from all danger of error and contamination. Exert yourselves so that everyone thinks the same thing and no one allows himself to be led astray by strange teachings. Let everyone avoid profane novelties, cling to the Catholic faith, and submit himself to the power and authority of the Church. Each person should bind himself ever more firmly to this See which the strong Redeemer of Jacob placed as an iron pillar and as a bronze wall against the enemies of religion. You should receive these enemies as people who ought to be educated in the law of Christ and of the Church.

20. It should be obvious that the secular power and those laws enacted by it concerning the welfare of civil society ought to be obeyed, not only because of the fear of wrath but also because of conscience. It is never permitted, however, to shamefully abandon the faith because of it. Since the spirits of the people are trained in this way, consider your labors to be both for the tranquility of the citizens and the welfare of the Church; these two things cannot be separated from one another.

21. May the most merciful God, from whom comes every perfect gift, accomplish these Our wishes. May Our apostolic blessing which We lovingly impart to you, venerable brothers, to Our brothers in the Lord, and to the faithful be a sign of good things which We ardently desire for this part of the Catholic flock.

Given in Rome, at St. Peter's, on the 17th day of May in the year 1835, the fifth year of Our Pontificate.

†

LATIN TEXT: *Acta Greg. XVI*, 2:32-36.

ENGLISH TRANSLATION: Norman Desmarais.

PROBE NOSTIS

ENCYCLICAL OF POPE GREGORY XVI ON
THE PROPAGATION OF THE FAITH
SEPTEMBER 18, 1840
37

Venerable Brothers, We Give You Greeting and Our Apostolic Blessing.

You are well aware, venerable brothers, of the many misfortunes which now afflict the Catholic Church. You know, too, that holy religion is being attacked by the pollution of errors of every kind and by the unbridled rashness of renegades. At the same time heretics and unbelievers attempt by cleverness and deceit to pervert the hearts and minds of the faithful. You are aware, in short, that practically no effort has been left untried in the attempt to overthrow the unshakeable building of the holy city. In particular, We are obliged, alas! to see the wicked enemies of truth spread everywhere unpunished. They harass religion with ridicule, the Church with insults, and Catholics with arrogance and calumny. They even enter cities and towns, establish schools of error and impiety, and publish their poisonous teachings which are adapted to secret deceit by misusing the natural sciences and recent discoveries. Furthermore they enter the hovels of the poor, traverse the countryside, and seek the acquaintance of the farmers and the lowest classes. They try every method of attracting the uneducated, especially the youth, to their sects, and of making them desert the Catholic faith, whether by means of Bibles inaccurately translated into the vernacular, pestilential newspapers and pamphlets of little weight, or by seductive speeches, pretended charity, and gifts of money.

Activities of Heretics

2. We mention events which you yourselves witness. For despite your sorrow and your pastoral denunciations, you are obliged to tolerate in your dioceses these men spreading heresy and unbelief, these assertive preachers who ceaselessly waylay and ravage your flock by going around in sheep's clothing while inwardly they are ravening wolves. What more can We add? There is hardly any uncivilized district left in the entire world to which headquarters of the main societies of heretics and unbelievers have not sent scouts and emissaries without counting the cost. These men, by waging secret or open war on the Catholic religion and its pastors and ministers, tear the faithful from the bosom of the Church and prevent unbelievers from entering it.

3. You can easily imagine the straits in which We live, since We are laden with the care of Christ's flock and the churches, and must therefore render a detailed account to the divine Prince of Shepherds. For this reason We decided

to recall in this letter the causes of the troubles which beset both Us and you. You can then reflect how important it is for all the bishops to redouble their efforts so as to break the assault of the enemies, to beat back their attacks, and to forewarn and protect the faithful from their clever appeals. We have been doing this, and We shall not stop. We know that you have likewise done so, and We are confident that you will continue.

Christ's Promises of Help

4. However, in order not to lose heart, "we should all be sure not to fear them as if We had to overcome them by our own strength, since Christ is both our counsel and our courage. As we can do nothing without Him, with Him we can do all things. To give strength to the preachers of the Gospel and ministers of the sacraments, He says, 'Behold I am with you all days even to the end of the world' and also, 'I have spoken these things to you that you may have peace in me; in the world you shall have affliction but take heart, I have overcome the world.' So clear and indisputable are these promises that no scandals should make us weak lest we seem unthankful for God's choice of us even though His help is as effective as His promises are true."[1]

5. Even in our time all can see those clear results of the divine promise which never have failed and never shall fail in the Church. They are plainly seen in the unconquerable constancy of the Church amid so many enemy attacks, in the spread of religion amid such disturbance and dangers, and in the consolation which "the Father of mercies and the God of all consolation gives us in every trial." On the one hand We have to lament the loss which the Catholic religion has suffered and continues to suffer in certain districts. But the many victories which the unconquerable constancy of Catholics and their priests has won and continues to win even in those districts gives us ground for joy. We rejoice greatly also at its marvellously abundant gains despite so many hindrances. This proves even to our enemies that oppression of the Church frequently contributes to its glory and strengthens the faithful.

Apostolic Missions

6. We are thankful for the success of apostolic missions in America, the Indies, and other faithless lands. The indefatigable zeal of many apostolic men has led them abroad into those places. Relying not on wealth nor on any army, they are protected by the shield of faith alone. They fearlessly fight the Lord's battles against heresy and unbelief by private and public speech and writings. They are inspired with a burning love and undeterred by rough roads and heavy toil. They search out those who sit in darkness and the shadow of death to summon them to the light and life of the Catholic religion. So, fearless in the face of every danger, they bravely enter the woods and caves of savages, gradually pacify them by Christian kindness, and prepare them for true faith and real virtue. At length they snatch them from the devil's rule, by the bath of regeneration and promote them to the freedom of God's adopted sons.

Martyrs in the Far East

7. However, We are reduced to tears both of sorrow in Our detestation of cruel persecutors and executioners, and of consolation in beholding the heroic constancy of the confessors of the faith, as We recall here the glorious deeds of the new martyrs in the Far East. We have already praised them at length in an address to the consistory. Tonkin and Cochin are still wet with the blood of many bishops, priests, and faithful. They have repeated the achievement of the early Christian martyrs in facing a cruel death for Christ undismayed by torture. This is a major victory for the Church and for religion. It casts the persecutors into confusion when they see that even today the divine promises of unending protection and help are really fulfilled. This is the reason why, in the words of St. Leo: "the religion established by the sacrament of the Cross of Christ cannot be destroyed by any kind of cruelty."[2]

New Societies Working for Catholicism

8. These events bring consolation and glory to the Catholic religion. But there are other grounds of consolation for the Church. Pious organizations are developing for the good of religion and Christian society. Some of these assist the work of the holy apostolic missions. God, who ceaselessly protects His Church, raises up within it new societies as times, places, and circumstances require. Under the Church's authority each society in its own ways devotes its full energy to works of charity, the instruction of the faithful, and the spread of the faith.

9. Likewise a source of joy to the Catholic

world, and a wonder to non-Catholics, are the many widespread sodalities of pious women. Under the rule of St. Vincent de Paul or in association with other approved Institutes, they are remarkable in their practice of the Christian virtues. They devote themselves entirely either to saving women from the way of perdition, or to training girls in religion, solid piety and the tasks suited to their state in life, or to relieving the dire want of their neighbors with every assistance. No natural weakness of their sex or fear of any danger holds them back.

10. A similar cause of joy for Us and for all good men are those groups of the faithful who recently have begun to meet regularly in many cities, especially the larger ones. Their purpose is to combat bad books with good ones written by themselves or others, displaying purity of doctrine instead of foul forms of error and Christian gentleness and charity instead of insults and attacks.

Society for the Propagation of the Faith

11. Finally We must praise most highly the well-known society which is constantly expanding, not alone in Catholic territories but even in the countries of non-Catholics and unbelievers. This society enables the faithful of every class to help the apostolic missions and to have a share themselves in the spiritual graces of these missions. We are referring, as you realize, to the famous Society for the Propagation of the Faith.

12. Now you know both the sorrows which afflict Us for Our losses and of the consolations which sustain Us in the victories of the Catholic religion. We are concerned though that these societies should continue to grow. We earnestly urge you, then, to cherish, protect, and augment them in your own dioceses.

13. The principal society which We recommend to you is the Society for the Propagation of the Faith. First organized in Lyons in 1822, it spread with marvellous speed and success. But certainly We recommend equally other societies of this type founded at Vienna and elsewhere. Their names are different, but they work at the same task of the propagation of the faith, a task which enjoys the religious support and favor of Catholic princes.

14. This task is sustained and strengthened by the moderate offerings and daily prayers to God said by each of the members. It is directed to supporting the apostolic workers, to practicing the works of Christian charity towards neophytes, and to delivering the faithful from the attack of persecution. Consequently, We consider it deserving of the admiration and love of all good men. A work so beneficial to the Church can have begun so recently only by the special design of divine providence. For when every kind of plot of the infernal enemy besets the beloved spouse of Christ, the Church could have no more timely good fortune than this ardent desire of the faithful to spread Catholic truth.

15. For this reason, established as We are despite Our unworthiness in the Papacy, We Ourselves affirm with Our predecessors Our complete support for this great work. Sharing Our concern, you should see to it that this important work flourishes among your flock. "Sing with the trumpet in Sion" and by your fatherly advice see to it that those not already members of the pious society are eager to become members, and that those who are members persevere in their purpose. This is surely the time "when the Christian battle line should smash the devil as he rages all over the world;"[3] it is indeed the time for the faithful to join in this holy union with the priests. We have the strongest hope that God, who ceaselessly supports His Church in its long hard fight with its enemies and also gives it joy in the firmness, love and devotion of the faithful, will grant it the peace it desires when He is placated by Our combined prayers and pious works.

In the meantime We lovingly impart the apostolic blessing to yourselves, venerable brothers, and to all the clergy and lay faithful entrusted to your charge.

Given in Rome at St. Mary Major with the seal of the fisherman on the 18th day of September 1840, in the tenth year of Our Pontificate.

†

LATIN TEXT: *Acta Greg. XVI*, 3:83-86; *ASS* 12:545-50.

ENGLISH TRANSLATION: Padraig M. O'Cleirigh.

REFERENCES:

1. Cf. St. Leo the Great, epistle to Rusticus of Narbonne.
2. Sermon 82 (80) on the feast day of the Apostles Peter and Paul.
3. Cf. St. Leo the Great, epistle to Rusticus of Narbonne.

QUAS VESTRO

ENCYCLICAL OF POPE GREGORY XVI
ON MIXED MARRIAGES
APRIL 30, 1841
38

To the Prelates of Hungary.

Venerable Brothers, Greetings and Apostolic Blessing.

The letter from you and the bishops of your country which Joseph, the bishop of Csamád delivered has caused Us both sorrow and joy. Since We must diligently safeguard the integrity of sound doctrine and practice, We cannot help but be displeased with whatever might imperil them. And yet what the church has always thought about marriages between Catholics and non-Catholics is more than abundantly clear. Indeed she has always considered such marriages to be illicit and destructive both because of the disgraceful sharing in sacramental matters involved and because of the ever present danger of the Catholic spouse and improper upbringing of offspring. And this is the tenor of most ancient canons severely prohibiting such marriages and more recent sanctions of supreme pontiffs. What Benedict XIV says about such marriages in his encyclical to the bishops of Poland and in his well-known work, *de Synodo dioecesana*, is more than sufficient. If, indeed, in certain places, because of difficulties of place and conditions, such marriages are tolerated, the reason is surely a sort of moderation. It is in no way to be considered approbation or approval, but merely a toleration, brought about not willingly but by necessity to avoid greater evils. The letter of Pius VII to the archbishop of Mainz, on 9 October 1803, in response to the bishops of Wrocław, Rožnava, and Spiš, wisely states this. Moreover, if this Apostolic See, mitigating to some extent the full letter of the canons, has, on occasion, allowed such mixed marriages, it has done so only in serious cases and reluctantly. Moreover, it has done so only when precautions are taken to prevent the perversion of the Catholic spouse by the non-Catholic party. Also the Catholic party realized an obligation to work for the conversion of the other party; the Catholic party also realized that all offspring from such marriages be educated only in the sanctity of the Catholic religion. Such precautions are surely founded on divine law, against which, without any doubt, one seriously sins who rashly exposes himself or herself and future offspring to the danger of perversion.

Spread of Mixed Marriages

2. Thus, from your letter We learn that in your dioceses an abuse has become common: namely, that marriages between Catholics and non-Catholics, without any previous dispensation from the Church and without necessary

precautions, are dignified with priestly blessing and sacramental rites. It must be clear to you how deeply We are affected by this, especially since We perceive that once this license with regard to mixed marriages was introduced, it became widely disseminated. This in turn resulted in a rapidly spreading deadly indifference toward religion in your great kingdom, once so preeminent in the glory of the Catholic faith. Let us not be mistaken: We would scarcely have overlooked this practice if it had been known to Us earlier. This was the reason for Our silence. In the past the Apostolic See granted no dispensation whatsoever for entering such mixed marriages without the necessary preliminary conditions and without the customary regulations.

Efforts to Eradicate the Evil

3. Nevertheless, it is no small consolation that at the same time as We were informed of this growing evil, We have likewise learned of your efforts and those of your colleagues to remedy it opportunely. We are joyful to learn with what zeal you are jointly inflamed to preserve intact the purity of the Catholic faith and with what reverence and devotion you support the Apostolic See, the leader and teacher of truth, which entrusted the exercise of the pastoral office to you. For when you realized that this practice, which had grown strong, was totally adverse to the laws and principles of the Church and therefore could no longer be tolerated without grave danger, you did not hesitate to insist on its removal and were fully prepared, if necessary, to endure danger for the sake of your eternal salvation and that of your flock. And completing Our joy are the abundant fruits which have emanated from your concern. Nor are we ignorant of how your pastors and other clergy have faithfully complied with your orders so that this illegitimate custom has been suppressed in many places out of regard for the ancient discipline of the sacred canons. And so we congratulate you all the more, venerable brothers, and render thanks to God who has endowed you with courage for the protection of the faith and its sacred teaching. We do not desist from exhorting you to continue to espouse the cause of the Church lest this evil usage ever revive, and that if any traces of it remain, it be totally eradicated.

Pastor's Presence at a Mixed Marriage

4. Meanwhile We have not failed to pay careful attention to your letter in which you point out that sometimes a Catholic, despite his pastor's persuasion and exhortation to the contrary, persists in the intention of undertaking such a mixed marriage without the necessary precautions. You suggest that if the matter cannot be prevented without greater danger to the Catholic religion, the pastor be present at the marriage in a passive fashion only, abstaining completely from all religious rites and any other sign of approval. By way of precaution, you decided that such a serious matter should be brought to Our attention at once, in order to secure Our assent. And, indeed, We, who otherwise are intent on properly preserving intact the most holy doctrines and practices of the Catholic Church, will aid you in view of the calamitous circumstances of your region and the difficulties for you arising from them, by approving of the arrangement undertaken by your counsel and by agreeing that your petition should be conceded.

5. We do this in keeping with what We permitted some time ago, following the example of Our predecessors, with regard to regions of other countries and with regard to what Pius VI declared on several occasions for one of the dioceses of Hungary itself. In a reply from Vienna to the bishop of Spiŝ in 1782, which was repeated the following year after his return to Rome and in 1795 to that bishop's successor, he, in accord with the circumstances of the time, explained as follows: "Whatever be the laws regarding the matter, the bishop and pastors ought to see that marriages of this nature not take place. But if they do, all offspring should be educated in the Catholic faith. If these marriages do take place, they must always abstain from granting the nuptial blessing. Their presence, if necessity urges it, must be merely physical and not be joined with words or actions which would encourage or approve of the offspring being allowed to be raised other than in the Catholic religion."

6. Sometimes because of conditions of time, person, or place, the marriage of a non-Catholic to a Catholic without the precautions prescribed by the Church cannot be prevented without danger of greater evil or scandal to the detriment of religion. Pius VII in the above-mentioned letter to the archbishop of Mainz judged that it can tend to the benefit of the Church and the common good if marriages of this nature, although forbidden and illicit, be celebrated before a Catholic pastor rather than before a heretical

minister to whom the parties could easily have recourse. On such occasions the Catholic pastor, or any other priest with his delegation, can be present at these marriages in a merely physical manner, without benefit of any sort of ecclesiastical rite. He could act merely as a qualified, as they say, or authorizing, witness; having heard the consent of both spouses, he may afterwards in accord with his office enter the act as valid in the matrimonial records.

7. Nevertheless, in these circumstances, as Our same predecessor aptly commends, bishops and pastors must zealously take precautions that the danger of perversion on the part of the Catholic party, as far as possible, be removed; that care be taken for the education of offspring of both sexes in the Catholic religion; and that the Catholic spouse be seriously admonished of the obligation by which he is bound to procure, as best as he can, the conversion of the non-Catholic spouse, which will be the best means for more easily obtaining pardon from God for the sins he has committed.

8. We grieve that this type of toleration is necessary in a kingdom so outstanding in the profession of the Catholic faith. We are compelled to this expedient to prevent more serious damage to the Catholic Church. Therefore, We beseech you and all your colleagues that in such a serious matter, having first implored that inspiration of the Holy Spirit, you strive to carry out what you truly judge to correspond to this end. Also see that such toleration towards mixed marriages does not extinguish the memory of the canons execrating such marriages as well as of the constant care of the Church to prevent her children from entering into such marriages to the loss of their souls. It will be your task and that of your fellow bishops and pastors in educating these faithful either privately or publicly to zealously recount the teaching and laws pertaining to such marriages and to enjoin their strict observance. In the assurance that you will carry out all these instructions because of your proven observation, faith, and reverence for this chair of blessed Peter, We lovingly impart as a guarantee of heavenly aid and witness of Our paternal affection the apostolic blessing to you and all your colleagues to be communicated to the proper flocks of each.

Given in Rome at St. Peter's under the fisherman's ring on 30 April 1841, in the eleventh year of Our Pontificate.

†

LATIN TEXT: *Acta Gre. XVI*, 3:123-24, cf. also Benedict XIV's *Nimiam licentiam* (May 18, 1743), no. 3.

ENGLISH TRANSLATION: Robert F. Healey, S.J.

INTER PRAECIPUAS

ENCYCLICAL OF POPE GREGORY XVI ON
BIBLICAL SOCIETIES
MAY 8, 1844
39

To the Venerable Brothers, Patriarchs, Primates, Archbishops and Bishops.

Venerable Brothers, Greetings and Apostolic Benediction.

Among the special schemes with which non-Catholics plot against the adherents of Catholic truth to turn their minds away from the faith, the biblical societies are prominent. They were first established in England and have spread far and wide so that We now see them as an army on the march, conspiring to publish in great numbers copies of the books of divine Scripture. These are translated into all kinds of vernacular languages for dissemination without discrimination among both Christians and infidels. Then the biblical societies invite everyone to read them unguided. Therefore it is just as Jerome complained in his day:[1] they make the art of understanding the Scriptures without a teacher "common to babbling old women and crazy old men and verbose sophists," and to anyone who can read, no matter what his status. Indeed, what is even more absurd and almost unheard of, they do not exclude the common people of the infidels from sharing this kind of a knowledge.

Aims of the Biblical Societies

2. But you know the aim of these societies. In his sacred writings, Peter, after praising the letters of Paul, warns that in these epistles "certain things are difficult to understand, which the unlearned and the unstable distort just as they do the rest of the Scriptures, which also leads to their destruction." He adds at once, "Since you know this beforehand, be on your guard lest, carried away by the error of the foolish, you fall away from your own steadfastness."[2] Hence it is clear to you that even from the first ages of Christianity this was a skill appropriate for heretics. Having repudiated the given word of God and rejected the authority of the Catholic Church, they either interpolate "by artifice" into the Scriptures or pervert "its meaning through interpretation."[3] Nor finally are you ignorant of the diligence and knowledge required to faithfully translate into another language the words of the Lord. In the many translations from the biblical societies, serious errors are easily inserted by the great number of translators, either through ignorance or deception. These errors, because of the very number and variety of translations, are long hidden and hence lead the faithful astray. It is of little concern to these societies if men reading their vernacular Bibles fall into error. They are concerned primarily that the reader becomes accustomed to judging for himself the meaning of the books of Scripture, to scorning divine tradition preserved

by the Catholic Church in the teaching of the Fathers, and to repudiating the very authority of the Church.

The Church Instructs the Faithful

3. For this end the same biblical societies never cease to slander the Church and this Chair of Peter as if We have tried to keep the knowledge of sacred Scripture from the faithful. However, We have documents clearly detailing the singular zeal which the Supreme Pontiffs and bishops in recent times have used to instruct the Catholic people more thoroughly in the word of God, both as it exists in writing and in tradition. The decrees of the Council of Trent even commanded the bishops to see to it that "the sacred Scriptures and the divine law" are preached more frequently in the dioceses.[4] In expanding the provisions of the Lateran Council,[5] they order that in each church, either cathedral or collegiate in the cities and better known towns, individuals able to explain and interpret sacred Scripture must be obtained.[6] Later action was taken in many provincial synods[7] concerning the establishment of an ecclesiastical benefice according to the norms of articles sanctioned by the Council of Trent, and about readings to be given publicly to the clergy and also to the people by a canonical theologian. Also, in the Roman Council of 1725, Benedict XIII assembled not only the sacred bishops of the Roman province but also many of the archbishops, bishops and other ordinaries of places in no way subject to this Holy See to deal with this same matter.[9] In addition, for the same purpose he proposed several measures in apostolic letters which he wrote expressly for Italy and the adjacent islands.[10] You customarily report on the condition of diocesan affairs at stated times to the Apostolic See.[11] It is clear from the answers of our Congregation of the Council, sent repeatedly to your predecessors or to you yourselves, how this same Holy See congratulates bishops if they have beneficed theologians who give public readings of the sacred Scriptures. The Holy See never fails to admonish and aid the pastoral care of those bishops, if anywhere this matter has not succeeded according to plan.

Reading of Vernacular Translations Restricted

4. Moreover, regarding the translation of the Bible into the vernacular, even many centuries ago bishops in various places have at times had to exercise greater vigilance when they became aware that such translations were being read in secret gatherings or were being distributed by heretics. Innocent III issued warnings concerning the secret gatherings of laymen and women, under the pretext of piety, for the reading of Scripture in the diocese of Metz.[12] There was also a special prohibition of Scripture translations promulgated either in Gaul a little later[13] or in Spain before the sixteenth century.[14] But later even more care was required when the Lutherans and Calvinists dared to oppose the changeless doctrine of the faith with an almost incredible variety of errors. They left no means untried to deceive the faithful with perverse explanations of the sacred books, which were published by their adherents with new interpretations in the vernacular. They were aided in multiplying copies and quickly spreading them by the newly-invented art of printing. Therefore in the rules written by the fathers chosen by the Council of Trent, approved by Pius IV,[15] and placed in the Index of forbidden books, we read the statute declaring that vernacular Bibles are forbidden except to those for whom it is judged that the reading will contribute "to the increase of faith and piety."[16] Because of the continued deceptions of heretics, this rule was further restricted and supplemented by a declaration of Benedict XIV: for the future the only vernacular translations which may be read are those which "are approved by the Apostolic See" or at least were published "with annotations taken from the holy Fathers of the Church, or from learned and Catholic authors."[17]

Jansenists

5. Meanwhile there was no dearth of new sect members in the school of Jansenius. Borrowing the tactics of the Lutherans and Calvinists, they rebuked the Apostolic See on the grounds that because the reading of the Scriptures for all the faithful, at all times and places, was useful and necessary, it therefore could not be forbidden anyone by any authority. But this audacity of the Jansenists we find reprehended by the grave censures of two recent supreme pontiffs, namely Clement XI in the Constitution *Unigenitus* in 1713[18] and Pius VI in the Constitution *Auctorem Fidei* in 1794.[19]

Papal Efforts to Deter the Societies

6. So before the biblical societies were

founded, the faithful had already been alerted by the aforementioned decrees against the deception of the heretics, which works in their specious zeal to spread the divine writings for the common use. However Pius VII, who understood that these societies founded in his time were flourishing, opposed their efforts by means of his apostolic nuncio, by his letters, by published decrees,[20] by various Congregations of Cardinals of the Holy Roman Church, and by two of his pontifical letters which he addressed to the archbishops of Gniezno[21] and Mohilev.[22] Immediately thereafter Leo XII continued the battle against the biblical societies with an encyclical letter addressed to all the bishops of the Catholic world, published on May 5, 1824, and Pius VIII did the same in an encyclical letter published May 24, 1829. And lastly, We who, though unworthy, have succeeded to his place have taken great pains to remind the faithful of the ancient laws concerning vernacular translations of the Scriptures.[23]

7. However We have reason to congratulate you, since, moved by piety and prudence and strengthened by these letters of Our predecessors, you warned Catholics to be on their guard against the snares which the biblical societies were spreading for them. Thus, by the efforts of God and His Church, it has come to pass that some incautious Catholic men who imprudently favored the biblical societies have understood how they were deceived. They have left the societies, and the remaining faithful have continued almost immune from the contagion which threatened them from this source.

8. In the meantime, the biblical societies did not doubt that they would obtain high praise for leading infidels in some manner or other to the profession of the Christian name by the reading of the sacred books published in their own language. They strove to distribute these in immense numbers by their missionaries and scouts, who even forced them upon the unwilling. But for the men striving to propagate the Christian name outside of the rules established by Christ himself, almost nothing happened according to plan. They were able at times to create new impediments for Catholic priests who set out to these peoples with a commission from this Holy See. These priests spared no labor to bring forth new sons of the Church by preaching the word of God and administering the Sacraments; they even prepared to shed their blood under all kinds of intense tortures for their salvation and for the defense of the faith.

Christian League

9. Now, however, these sect members are deprived of their expectations and regret the immense outlay of money spent in publishing their Bibles and spreading them without success. Some have now been found who have directed their efforts toward Italians, especially the citizens of Rome herself, after the manner of a new first assault. Actually We learned from reports and documents just received that a number of men of various sects met in the city of New York last year on June 12 and founded a new society called *Christian League*. Their common purpose is to spread religious liberty, or rather an insane desire for indifference concerning religion, among Romans and Italians. They assert that the institutions of the Roman and Italian peoples have been so influential that anything of any consequence that has happened in the world had its origin in Rome. They arrive at this conclusion not because the Supreme See of Peter is here according to the plan of the Lord, but because there has been a certain residue of ancient Roman domination, usurped by Our predecessors, as they often repeat, but still active. Therefore they are determined to give everyone the gift of liberty of conscience, or rather of error; they liken it to a fountain from which political liberty and increased public prosperity may spring forth. But they feel that they can accomplish nothing unless they make some progress with Roman and Italian citizens, thereafter using their authority and efforts to influence other nations. And they are confident that they will achieve this easily, since there are so many Italians everywhere on earth, many of whom will return to their fatherland. Of these, some are attracted to new things, some have corrupt morals, and some are oppressed with poverty and may thus be lured to join the society voluntarily or to join for a price. Therefore the societies have concentrated on these people so that they will bring corrupt, vernacular Bibles here and secretly spread them among the faithful. They will also distribute other evil books and pamphlets composed with the aid of some Italians or translated into Italian in order to alienate the minds of the readers from the Holy Church and from obedience to it. Among these they designate particularly the *Histoire de la réformation* by Merle d'Aubignè and *Fostes de la Reforme en Italie* by John Cric. The nature of these

books and of their future publications can be understood from the fact that no two members on the committee selecting books may ever be of the same religious sect.

Concern for the Assault on Rome

10. When these things were first brought to Our attention, We were greatly saddened by the dangers to religion not only in places far from Rome, but in the very center of Catholic unity. We need fear little that the See of Peter may ever fall because the impregnable foundation of his Church was laid by Christ the Lord; however We must not cease to defend its authority. Besides the divine Leader of pastors will demand of Us a severe reckoning for the growth of weeds in the field of the Lord if they have been sown by an enemy while We were asleep, and for the blood of the sheep who have perished here through Our fault.

Condemnation of Biblical Societies

11. Therefore, taking counsel with a number of Cardinals, and weighing the whole matter seriously and in good time, We have decided to send this letter to all of you. We again condemn all the above-mentioned biblical societies of which our predecessors disapproved. We specifically condemn the new one called *Christian League* founded last year in New York and other societies of the same kind, if they have already joined with it or do so in the future. Therefore let it be known to all that anyone who joins one of these societies, or aids it, or favors it in any way will be guilty of a grievous crime. Besides We confirm and renew by Our apostolic authority the prescriptions listed and published long ago concerning the publication, dissemination, reading, and possession of vernacular translations of sacred Scriptures. Concerning other works of any writer We repeat that all must abide by the general rules and decrees of Our predecessors which are found in the Index of forbidden books, and indeed not only for those books specifically listed, but also for others to which the aforementioned prohibitions apply.

Warn the Faithful

12. Thus, We emphatically exhort you to announce these Our commands to the people accredited to your pastoral care; explain them in the proper place and time, and strive mightily to keep the faithful sheep away from the *Christian League* and other biblical societies, as well as away from their followers. Also take from the faithful both the vernacular Bibles which have been published contrary to the sanctions of the Roman Pontiffs and all other books which are proscribed and condemned. In this way see that the faithful themselves by your warnings and authority "are taught that they ought to consider what kind of food is healthful for them, and what is noxious and deadly."[24] Meanwhile be more zealous each day to preach the word of God, both through yourselves and through the individual pastors in each diocese, and through other ecclesiastical men fit for the task. In particular, watch more carefully over those who are assigned to give public readings of holy scripture, so that they function diligently in their office within the comprehension of the audience; under no pretext whatsoever should they dare to explain and interpret the divine writings contrary to the tradition of the Fathers or the interpretation of the Catholic Church. Finally it is proper for a good pastor not only to safeguard and nourish his sheep, but also to seek and recall to the sheepfold those who have gone to a distant place. So it will also be your duty and Ours to direct Our fullest zeal to this end, that all who have been seduced by such sect members and the distributers of evil books recognize the gravity of their sin and strive to expiate it with penance. Nor indeed are the seducers to be deprived of the same priestly solicitude, especially the teachers of impiety themselves; although their sin is greater, We should not shrink from their salvation, which We may be able to procure by some means.

13. We ask those of you who rule churches in Italy, or in other places where Italians live in great numbers, or where there are trading centers and ports from which passage into Italy is frequent, that special and intense vigilance be exercised against the deceits and labors of the members of the *Christian League*. Since it is there that the sect members have determined to bring their plans to fruition, it follows that the bishops in those places especially must collaborate with Us in ready and constant zeal to dissipate their machinations. We earnestly desire the help of the Lord in this task.

14. We have no doubt that these cares of Ours and yours will be seconded with the aid of the civil powers, especially by the more influential princes of Italy. This is because of their exceptional zeal for preserving the Catholic religion and because they realize that the state would benefit if the efforts of the above-mentioned sect members should fail. Experience shows that there is no more direct way of alienating the populace from fidelity and obedience to their leaders than through that indifference to religion propagated by the sect members under the name of religious liberty. And this not even the members of the *Christian League* conceal: although they profess themselves strangers to inciting sedition, they advocate allowing every man of the masses to interpret the Bible as he likes. As complete liberty of conscience, as they call it, spreads among the Italian people, political liberty will result of its own accord.

15. But what is truly first and foremost, let Us raise Our hands together to God and let Us commend to him, with the humility of prayer as fervent as We can make it, Our cause and that of the whole flock and of the Church; let Us also invoke with pious petitions Peter the prince of the apostles, the other saints, and especially the Blessed Virgin Mary, who has the power to end all the heresies in the whole world.

16. Finally, as a pledge of Our ardent love, We grant the Apostolic Benediction with an outpouring of affection to all of you, venerable brothers, and to the clergy and faithful laity committed to your care.

Given at Rome at St. Peter's, May 8, 1844, in the fourteenth year of Our Pontificate.

†

LATIN TEXT: *Acta Greg. XVI*, 3:332-36.

ENGLISH TRANSLATION: Bernard A. Hausmann, S.J.

REFERENCES:

1. Epistle to Paulinus, 7, which is epistle 53, vol. 1, of Vallarsius edition of the *Operum* of St. Jerome.
2. 2 Pt 3.16, 17.
3. Tertullian, *de Praescriptionibus*, chaps. 37, 38.
4. Council of Trent, session 24, chap. 4 on reform.
5. Lateran Council (1215) under Innocent III, chap. 11 (chap. 4, *de Magistris*).
6. Council of Trent, session 5, chap. 1 on reform.
7. Council of Milan 1 (1565), *de Praeb. Theol.* par. 1, tit. 5; Council of Milan 5 (1579), quae ad Beneficior collat. attin. par. 3, tit. 5; Council of Aix (1585), *de Canonicis*, et al.
8. Tit 1, chap. 6ff.
9. In the letter of indiction of the Council, 24 December 1724.
10. Constitution *Pastoralis officii*, 19 May 1725.
11. From the constitution of Sixtus V, *Romanus Pontifex*, 20 December 1585, and the constitution of Benedict XIV, *Quod Sancta Sardicensis Synodus*, 23 November 1740, vol. 1 of the *Bullarium*, vol. 1, and from the instruction that is found in the Appendix to vol. 1.
12. In three letters given to the people of Metz, and to their bishop abbots of Morimond and LaCrest, and the capitulars, and to the Cistercian, letters 141; 142, bk. 2, and 235, bk. 3, in the edition of Balutius.
13. Council of Toulouse (1229), can. 14.
14. From the statement of Cardinal Pacecco at the Council of Trent (in Pallavicinus, *Storia del Concil. di Trento*, bk. 6, chap. 12).
15. Constitution *Dominici gregis*, 24 March 1564.
16. Rules 3 and 4 of the Index.
17. In addition to the previous Rule 4 from the Congregation of the Index, 17 June 1757.
18. The proscription of propositions 79 to 85 of Quesnel.
19. Condemnation of proposition 67 of the Pseudo-Synod of Pistoia.
20. Especially through the letter (3 August 1816) of the Congregation for the Propagation of the Faith to the apostolic vicars of Persia, Armenia, and other Eastern regions, and through the decree (23 June 1817) concerning all such versions published by the Congregation of the Index.
21. 1 June 1816.
22. 4 September 1816.
23. In the monitum added to the decree (7 January 1836) of the Congregation of the Index.
24. From the mandate of Leo XII.

POPE PIUS IX
1846-1878

The conclave of 1846 opened on June 14 and forty-eight hours later announced the unexpected selection of Cardinal Mastai-Ferretti as the successor of Pope Gregory XVI. History would prove him to be a controversial figure: revered by some as a saint; by others as an autocrat manipulated by reactionaries.

Giovanni Maria Mastai-Ferretti was born in Senigallia (Ancona) on May 13, 1792. His family, which belonged to the lower nobility of Lombardy, was noted for their moderate reform tendencies. The future pope studied at the Piarist College of Volterra until he had what was probably an epileptic attack. This saved him from conscription under Napoleon but also prevented his joining the Noble Guard as his father wished. After completing his studies at the Roman College his ill health seemed to be an obstacle to his entering the priesthood, but eventually after the intervention of Pius VII he was ordained (1819) at the age of twenty-seven.

His first years as a priest were spent at Ricovero di Tata Giovanni, an orphanage in Rome. In 1823, Pius VII sent him with the apostolic delegation to Chile, and while there he visited Peru and Colombia. In 1825 he was back in Rome in charge of the hospice of San Michele. In 1827 he was named archbishop of Spoleto, transferred to the see of Imola (1832), and created a cardinal in 1840. His mild but firm handling of the revolutionary disturbances and his episcopal administration at Imola showed him capable of handling the liberal advocates of the area. His prayerfulness and pastoral zeal drew great response from his people. He sympathized with those who found it difficult to accept the reactionary policies of Gregory XVI and the rigorous measures that were used to rule the States of the Church. He remained at Imola until his election as pope on June 16, 1846. He took the name of Pius in honor of Pius VII, his benefactor and predecessor in the see of Imola.

Approval of his election came from the most unlikely places. An enlightened conservative rather than a liberal by conviction, he began his pontificate by granting a general amnesty to all political prisoners and exiles, visiting jails, schools, and hospitals and introducing liberal reforms. Unfortunately after two years of this feverish activity, the Italian war on the Austrians (without papal support) and the spread of revolutions throughout Italy effected an inevitable reaction in Rome. The pope's lack of political ability precipitated a crisis. Besieged in the Quirinal after the assassination of the papal minister, Count Pellegrino Rossi, the pope fled in disguise to Gaeta

(1848) and Mazzini took over the rule of Rome.

When Pius returned to Rome on April 12, 1850, his attitude had changed completely; he no longer made any attempts to introduce liberal reforms. In 1861 he delivered a violent allocution denouncing the principles of progress and liberalism. He rapidly became more firmly convinced of the connection between the principles of the French Revolution and the destruction of traditional values. By 1864 the progressive liberal of 1847 had become the symbol of European reaction.

Cavour capitalized on this opportunity to hasten Italian unification, but French military aid made it possible for the pope to retain Rome and its environs for another decade. When the French troops were recalled because of the Franco-Prussian War, the Italian troops moved in and occupied Rome (September 20, 1870) ending the temporal power of the pope. When Pius subsequently rejected the Law of Guarantees (May 13, 1871), he became a voluntary prisoner of the Vatican.

The conflicts of those years, when he was surrounded by counselors whose zeal did not compensate for their isolation from the social and political changes of the times, did not prevent him from the internal guidance of the Church. He restored the hierarchy in England (1850) and in the Netherlands (1853), erected more than two hundred bishoprics and apostolic delegations, established a Latin patriarch for Jerusalem, approved at least one hundred and twenty-five religious congregations of women in the United States, and expanded missionary work throughout the world.

The publication of the encyclical *Quanta cura* (December 8, 1864), a general condemnation of modern errors, followed by the compilation of the Syllabus of Errors, a list of inadmissible propositions, denounced the delusion of socialism and the conception of religion and society held by the liberals. The solemn definition of the dogma of the Immaculate Conception (1854) and the convoking of the first Vatican Council (1869-70) which defined papal primacy and infallibility aroused widespread antagonism. The Kulturkampf in Germany, the religious situation in Austria, difficulties in Latin America, and the expulsion of the papal nuncio from Switzerland testified to the reaction toward the increased centralization of authority in the Church.

In spite of his limitations and failures Pius IX emerges as the "creator of the modern papacy," a man of prayer who endures innumerable defeats, betrayals, and humiliations, while maintaining an inexplicable charity for his enemies that nothing ever corrupted.[1] Soon after his death on February 7, 1878 his cause for beatification was introduced; it was renewed in 1956 under Pope Pius XII.

†

REFERENCE:

1. Philip Hughes, "Portrait of Pio Nono," *Tablet*, 203 (March 6, 1954), 225.

QUI PLURIBUS

ENCYCLICAL OF POPE PIUS IX ON
FAITH AND RELIGION
NOVEMBER 9, 1846
40

To All Patriarchs, Primates, Archbishops, and Bishops.

Venerable Brothers, We Greet You and Give You Our Apostolic Blessing.

For many years past We strove with you, venerable brothers, to devote Our best powers to Our episcopal office—an office full of labor and worry. We strove to feed those committed to Our care on the mountains of Israel, at its streams and in its richest pastures. Our illustrious Predecessor, Gregory XVI, whose famous actions are recorded in the annals of the Church in letters of gold, will surely be remembered and admired by future generations. Now though, upon his death, by the mysterious plan of divine providence, We have been raised to the supreme Pontificate. We did not purpose this nor expect it; indeed Our reaction is great disquietude and anxiety. For if the burden of the Apostolic ministry is rightly considered to be at all times exceedingly heavy and beset with dangers, it is to be dreaded most particularly in these times which are so critical for the Christian commonwealth.

2. We are well aware of Our weakness. So when We reflect on the most serious duties of the supreme apostolate especially in a period of great instability, We would simply have fallen into great sadness, did We not place all Our hope in God who is Our Saviour. For He never abandons those who hope in Him. Time and again, so as to demonstrate what His power can accomplish, He employs weak instruments to rule His Church; in this way, all men may increasingly realize that it is God Himself who governs and protects the Church with his wonderful providence. We are also greatly supported by the comforting consideration that We have you, venerable brothers, as Our helpers and companions in the work of saving souls. For since you have been called to share a portion of Our care, you strive to fulfill your ministry with attentiveness and zeal, and to fight the good fight.

Admonitions to the Hierarchy

3. For this reason, as soon as We were placed, despite Our unworthiness, on this high See of the prince of the apostles as the representative of the blessed Peter, and received from the eternal Prince of Pastors Himself the most serious divinely given office of feeding and ruling not only the lambs, that is, the whole Christian people, but also the sheep, that is, the bishops, We surely had no greater wish than to address you all with a deep feeling of love. Therefore, since We have now assumed the supreme pontificate in Our

Lateran Basilica, We are sending this letter to you without delay, in accordance with the established practice of Our predecessors. Its purpose is to urge that you keep the night-watches over the flock entrusted to your care with the greatest possible eagerness, wakefulness and effort, and that you raise a protecting wall before the House of Israel; do these as you battle with episcopal strength and steadfastness like good soldiers of Christ Jesus against the hateful enemy of the human race.

Fight Against Heresy

4. Each of you has noticed, venerable brothers, that a very bitter and fearsome war against the whole Catholic commonwealth is being stirred up by men bound together in a lawless alliance. These men do not preserve sound doctrine, but turn their hearing from the truth. They eagerly attempt to produce from their darkness all sorts of prodigious beliefs, and then to magnify them with all their strength, and to publish them and spread them among ordinary people. We shudder indeed and suffer bitter pain when We reflect on all their outlandish errors and their many harmful methods, plots and contrivances. These men use these means to spread their hatred for truth and light. They are experienced and skillful in deceit, which they use to set in motion their plans to quench peoples' zeal for piety, justice and virtue, to corrupt morals, to cast all divine and human laws into confusion, and to weaken and even possibly overthrow the Catholic religion and civil society. For you know, venerable brothers, that these bitter enemies of the Christian name, are carried wretchedly along by some blind momentum of their mad impiety; they go so far in their rash imagining as to teach without blushing, openly and publicly, daring and unheard-of doctrines, thereby uttering blasphemies against God.[1] They teach that the most holy mysteries of our religion are fictions of human invention, and that the teaching of the Catholic Church is opposed to the good and the prerogatives of human society. They are not even afraid to deny Christ Himself and God.

5. In order to easily mislead the people into making errors, deceiving particularly the imprudent and the inexperienced, they pretend that they alone know the ways to prosperity. They claim for themselves without hesitation the name of "philosophers." They feel as if philosophy, which is wholly concerned with the search for truth in nature, ought to reject those truths which God Himself, the supreme and merciful creator of nature, has deigned to make plain to men as a special gift. With these truths, mankind can gain true happiness and salvation. So, by means of an obviously ridiculous and extremely specious kind of argumentation, these enemies never stop invoking the power and excellence of human reason; they raise it up against the most holy faith of Christ, and they blather with great foolhardiness that this faith is opposed to human reason.

Faith and Reason are Reciprocal

6. Without doubt, nothing more insane than such a doctrine, nothing more impious or more opposed to reason itself could be devised. For although faith is above reason, no real disagreement or opposition can ever be found between them; this is because both of them come from the same greatest source of unchanging and eternal truth, God. They give such reciprocal help to each other that true reason shows, maintains and protects the truth of the faith, while faith frees reason from all errors and wondrously enlightens, strengthens and perfects reason with the knowledge of divine matters.

Doctrine of Human Progress

7. It is with no less deceit, venerable brothers, that other enemies of divine revelation, with reckless and sacrilegious effrontery, want to import the doctrine of human progress into the Catholic religion. They extol it with the highest praise, as if religion itself were not of God but the work of men, or a philosophical discovery which can be perfected by human means. The charge which Tertullian justly made against the philosophers of his own time "who brought forward a Stoic and a Platonic and a Dialectical Christianity"[2] can very aptly apply to those men who rave so pitiably. Our holy religion was not invented by human reason, but was most mercifully revealed by God; therefore, one can quite easily understand that religion itself acquires all its power from the authority of God who made the revelation, and that it can never be arrived at or perfected by human reason. In order not to be deceived and go astray in a matter of such great importance, human reason should indeed carefully investigate the fact of divine revelation. Having done this, one would be definitely convinced

that God has spoken and therefore would show Him rational obedience, as the Apostle very wisely teaches.[3] For who can possibly not know that all faith should be given to the words of God and that it is in the fullest agreement with reason itself to accept and strongly support doctrines which it has determined to have been revealed by God, who can neither deceive nor be deceived?

8. But how many wonderful and shining proofs are ready at hand to convince the human reason in the clearest way that the religion of Christ is divine and that "the whole principle of our doctrines has taken root from the Lord of the heavens above";[4] therefore nothing exists more definite, more settled or more holy than our faith, which rests on the strongest foundations. This faith, which teaches for life and points towards salvation, which casts out all vices and is the fruitful mother and nurse of the virtues, has been established by the birth, life, death, resurrection, wisdom, wonders and prophecies of Christ Jesus, its divine author and perfector! Shining forth in all directions with the light of teaching from on high and enriched with the treasures of heavenly wealth, this faith grew famed and notable by the foretellings of so many prophets, the lustre of so many miracles, the steadfastness of so many martyrs, and the glory of so many saints! It made known the saving laws of Christ and, gaining in strength daily even when it was most cruelly persecuted, it made its way over the whole world by land and sea, from the sun's rising to its setting, under the single standard of the Cross! The deceit of idols was cast down and the mist of errors was scattered. By the defeat of all kinds of enemies, this faith enlightened with divine knowledge all peoples, races and nations, no matter how barbarous and savage, or how different in character, morals, laws and ways of life. It brought them under the sweet yoke of Christ Himself by proclaiming peace and good tidings to all men!

Faith Comes from God

9. Now, surely all these events shine with such divine wisdom and power that anyone who considers them will easily understand that the Christian faith is the work of God. Human reason knows clearly from these striking and certain proofs that God is the author of this faith; therefore it is unable to advance further but should offer all obedience to this faith, casting aside completely every problem and hesitation. Human reason is convinced that it is God who has given everything the faith proposes to men for belief and behavior.

Qui pluribus
40

10. This consideration too clarifies the great error of those others as well who boldly venture to explain and interpret the words of God by their own judgment, misusing their reason and holding the opinion that these words are like a human work. God Himself has set up a living authority to establish and teach the true and legitimate meaning of His heavenly revelation. This authority judges *infallibly* all disputes which concern matters of faith and morals, lest the faithful be swirled around by every wind of doctrine which springs from the evilness of men in encompassing error. And this living *infallible* authority is active only in that Church which was built by Christ the Lord upon Peter, the head of the entire Church, leader and shepherd, whose faith He promised would never fail. This Church has had an unbroken line of succession from Peter himself; these legitimate pontiffs are the heirs and defenders of the same teaching, rank, office and power. And the Church is where Peter is,[5] and Peter speaks in the Roman Pontiff,[6] living at all times in his successors and making judgment,[7] providing the truth of the faith to those who seek it.[8] The divine words therefore mean what this Roman See of the most blessed Peter holds and has held.

11. For this mother and teacher[9] of all the churches has always preserved entire and unharmed the faith entrusted to it by Christ the Lord. Furthermore, it has taught it to the faithful, showing all men truth and the path of salvation. Since all priesthood originates in this church,[10] the entire substance of the Christian religion resides there also.[11] The leadership of the Apostolic See has always been active,[12] and therefore because of its preeminent authority, the whole Church must agree with it. The faithful who live in every place constitute the whole Church.[13] Whoever does not gather with this Church scatters.[14]

Warn the Faithful

12. We, therefore, placed inscrutably by God upon this Chair of truth, eagerly call forth in the Lord your outstanding piety, venerable brothers. We urge you to strive carefully and zealously to continually warn and exhort the faithful entrusted to your care to hold to these first principles. Urge them never to allow themselves to be deceived and led into error by men who have become abominable in their pursuits. These men attempt to destroy faith on the pretext of human progress, subjecting it in an impious manner to reason and changing the meaning of the words of God. Such men do not shrink from the greatest insults to God Himself, who cares for the good and the salvation of men by means of His heavenly religion.

Goals of Heretics

13. You already know well, venerable brothers, the other portentous errors and deceits by which the sons of this world try most bitterly to attack the Catholic religion and the divine authority of the Church and its laws. They would even trample underfoot the rights both of the sacred and of the civil power. For this is the goal of the lawless activities against this Roman See in which Christ placed the impregnable foundation of His Church. This is the goal of those secret sects who have come forth from the darkness to destroy and desolate both the sacred and the civil commonwealth. These have been condemned with repeated anathema in the Apostolic letters of the Roman Pontiffs who preceded Us.[15] We now confirm these with the fullness of Our Apostolic power and command that they be most carefully observed.

14. This is the goal too of the crafty Bible Societies which renew the old skill of the heretics and ceaselessly force on people of all kinds, even the uneducated, gifts of the Bible. They issue these in large numbers and at great cost, in vernacular translations, which infringe the holy rules of the Church. The commentaries which are included often contain perverse explanations; so, having rejected divine tradition, the doctrine of the Fathers and the authority of the Catholic Church, they all interpret the words of the Lord by their own private judgment, thereby perverting their meaning. As a result, they fall into the greatest errors. Gregory XVI of happy memory, Our superior predecessor, followed the lead of his own predecessors in rejecting these societies in his apostolic letters.[16] It is Our will to condemn them likewise.

No Choice of Religion

15. Also perverse is the shocking theory that it makes no difference to which religion one belongs, a theory which is greatly at variance even with reason. By means of this theory, those crafty men remove all distinction between virtue and vice, truth and error, honorable and vile action. They pretend that men can gain eternal salvation by the practice of any religion, as if there could ever be any sharing between justice and iniquity, any collaboration between light and darkness, or any agreement between Christ and Belial.

Celibacy

16. The sacred celibacy of clerics has also been the victim of conspiracy. Indeed, some churchmen have wretchedly forgotten their own rank and let themselves be converted by the charms and snares of pleasure. This is the aim too of the prevalent but wrong method of teaching, especially in the philosophical disciplines, a method which deceives and corrupts incautious youth in a wretched manner and gives it as drink the poison of the serpent in the goblet of Babylon. To this goal also tends the unspeakable doctrine of *Communism*, as it is called, a doctrine most opposed to the very natural law. For if this doctrine were accepted, the complete destruction of everyone's laws, government, property, and even of human society itself would follow.

17. To this end also tend the most dark designs of men in the clothing of sheep, while inwardly ravening wolves. They humbly recommend themselves by means of a feigned and deceitful appearance of a purer piety, a stricter virtue and discipline; after taking their captives gently, they mildly bind them, and then kill them in secret. They make men fly in terror from all practice of religion, and they cut down and dismember the sheep of the Lord. To this end, finally—to omit other dangers which are too well known to you—tends the widespread disgusting infection from books and pamphlets which teach the lessons of sinning. These works, well-written and filled with deceit and cunning, are scattered at immense cost through every region for the destruction of the Christian people. They spread pestilential doctrines everywhere and deprave the minds especially of the imprudent, occasioning great losses for religion.

Results of Heresy

18. As a result of this filthy medley of errors

which creeps in from every side, and as the result of the unbridled license to think, speak and write, We see the following: morals deteriorated, Christ's most holy religion despised, the majesty of divine worship rejected, the power of this Apostolic See plundered, the authority of the Church attacked and reduced to base slavery, the rights of bishops trampled on, the sanctity of marriage infringed, the rule of every government violently shaken and many other losses for both the Christian and the civil commonwealth. Venerable brothers, We are compelled to weep and share in your lament that this is the case.

Defend the Church

19. Therefore, in this great crisis for religion, because We are greatly concerned for the salvation of all the Lord's flock and in fulfillment of the duty of Our Apostolic ministry, We shall certainly leave no measure untried in Our vigorous effort to secure the good of the whole Christian family. Indeed, We especially call forth in the Lord your own illustrious piety, virtue and prudence, venerable brothers. With these and relying on heavenly aid, you may fearlessly defend the cause of God and His holy Church as befits your station and the office for which you are marked. You must fight energetically, since you know very well what great wounds the undefiled Spouse of Christ Jesus has suffered, and how vigorous is the destructive attack of Her enemies. You must also care for and defend the Catholic faith with episcopal strength and see that the flock entrusted to you stands to the end firm and unmoved in the faith. For unless one preserves the faith entire and uninjured, he will without doubt perish forever.[17]

Protect the Faith

20. So, in accordance with your pastoral care, work assiduously to protect and preserve this faith. Never cease to instruct all men in it, to encourage the wavering, to convince dissenters, to strengthen the weak in faith by never tolerating and letting pass anything which could in the slightest degree defile the purity of this faith. With the same great strength of mind, foster in all men their unity with the Catholic Church, outside of which there is no salvation; also foster their obedience towards this See of Peter on which rests the entire structure of our most holy religion. See to it with similar firmness that the most holy laws of the Church are observed, for it is by these laws that virtue, religion and piety particularly thrive and flourish.

21. "It is an act of great piety to expose the concealments of the impious and to defeat there the devil himself, whose slaves they are."[18] Therefore We entreat you to use every means of revealing to your faithful people the many kinds of plot, pretense, error, deceit and contrivance which our enemies use. This will turn them carefully away from infectious books. Also exhort them unceasingly to flee from the sects and societies of the impious as from the presence of a serpent, earnestly avoiding everything which is at variance with the wholeness of faith, religion and morality. Therefore, never stop preaching the Gospel, so that the Christian people may grow in the knowledge of God by being daily better versed in the most holy precepts of the Christian law; as a result, they may turn from evil, do good, and walk in the ways of the Lord. You know that you are acting as deputies for Christ, who is meek and humble, and who came not to call the just but sinners. This is the example that we should follow. When you find someone disregarding the commandments and wandering from the path of truth and justice, rebuke them in the spirit of mildness and meekness with paternal warnings; accuse, entreat and reprove them with all kindness, patience and doctrine. "Often benevolence towards those who are to be corrected achieves more than severity, exhortation more than threats, and love more than power."[19]

22. Strive to instruct the faithful to follow after love and search for peace, diligently pursuing the works of love and peace so that they may love one another with reciprocal charity. They should abolish all disagreements, enmities, rivalries and animosities, thus achieving compatibility. Take pains to impress on the Christian people a due obedience and subjection to rulers and governments. Do this by teaching, in accordance with the warning of the Apostle,[20] that all authority comes from God. Whoever resists authority resists the ordering made by God Himself, consequently achieving his own condemnation; disobeying authority is always sinful except when an order is given which is opposed to the laws of God and the Church.

Clergy Should be Example

23. However, priests are the best examples of

piety and God's worship,"[21] and people tend generally to be of the same quality as their priests. Therefore devote the greatest care and zeal to making the clergy resplendent for the earnestness of their morals, the integrity, holiness and wisdom of their lives. Let the ecclesiastical training be zealously preserved in compliance with the sacred canons, and whenever it has been neglected, let it be restored to its former splendor. Therefore, as you are well aware, you must take the utmost care, as the Apostle commands, not to impose hands on anyone in haste. Consecrate with holy orders and promote to the performance of the sacred mysteries only those who have been carefully examined and who are virtuous and wise. They can consequently benefit and ornament your dioceses.

24. These are men who avoid everything which is forbidden to clerics, devoting their time instead to reading, exhorting and teaching, "an example to the faithful in word, manner of life, in charity, in faith, in chastity."[22] They win the highest respect from all men, and fashion, summon forth and inspire the people with the Christian way of life. "For it would certainly be better," as Benedict XIV, Our Predecessor of undying memory very wisely advises, "to have fewer ministers if they be upright, suitable and useful, than many who are likely to accomplish nothing at all for the building up of the body of Christ, which is the Church."[23] You must examine with greater diligence the morals and the knowledge of men who are entrusted with the care and guidance of souls, that they may be eager to continuously feed and assist the people entrusted to them by the administration of the sacraments, the preaching of God's word and the example of good works. They should be zealous in molding them to the whole plan and pattern of a religious way of life, and in leading them on to the path of salvation.

25. When ministers are ignorant or neglectful of their duty, then the morals of the people also immediately decline, Christian discipline grows slack, the practice of religion is dislodged and cast aside, and every vice and corruption is easily introduced into the Church. The word of God, which was uttered for the salvation of souls, is living, efficacious and more piercing than a two-edged sword.[24] So that it may not prove to be unfruitful through the fault of its ministers, never cease, venerable brothers, from encouraging the preachers of this divine word to carry out most religiously the ministry of the Gospel. This should not be carried out by the persuasive words of human wisdom, nor by the profane seductive guise of empty and ambitious eloquence, but rather as a demonstration of the spirit and power.

Objectives of Clerical Duties

26. Consequently, by presenting the word of truth properly and by preaching not themselves but Christ crucified, they should clearly proclaim in their preaching the tenets and precepts of our most holy religion in accordance with the teaching of the Catholic Church and the Fathers. They should explain precisely the particular duties of individuals, frighten them from vice, and inspire them with a love of piety. In this way the faithful will avoid all vices and pursue virtues, and so, will be able to escape eternal punishment and gain heavenly glory.

27. In your pastoral care, continuously urge all ecclesiastics to think seriously of their holy ministry. Urge them to carefully fulfill their duties, to greatly love the beauty of God's house, to urgently pray and entreat with deep piety, and to say the canonical hours of the breviary as the Church commands. By these means they will be able both to pray efficaciously for God's help in fulfilling the heavy demands of their duty, and to graciously reconcile God and the Christian people.

Education of Clerics

28. You know that suitable ministers can only come from clergy who are very well trained, and that the proper training greatly influences the whole future life of clerics. Therefore, continually strive to ensure that young clerics are properly molded even from their earliest years. They should be molded not only in piety and real virtue, but also in literature and the stricter disciplines, especially the sacred ones. So your greatest desire should be, in obedience to the prescript of the fathers at Trent,[25] to set up skillfully and energetically, seminaries if they do not yet exist. If necessary expand those already established, supplying them with the best directors and teachers. Watch continuously and zealously that the young clerics in them are educated in a holy and religious manner, in the fear of the Lord and in ecclesiastical discipline. See that they are carefully and thoroughly improved, especially by the sacred sciences, according to Catholic doctrine, far from all danger of any error. They should also be improved by the traditions of the Church and the writings of the holy Fathers, as well as by sacred ceremonies and rites. Thus you will have energetic, industrious workers endowed with an ecclesiastical spirit, properly prepared by their studies, who in time will be able to tend the Lord's field carefully and fight strenuously in the Lord's battles.

29. Furthermore, you realize that spiritual exercises contribute greatly to the preservation of the dignity and holiness of ecclesiastical orders. Therefore do not neglect to promote this work of salvation and to advise and exhort all clergy to often retreat to a suitable place for making these exercises. Laying aside external cares and being free to meditate zealously on eternal divine matters, they will be able to wipe away stains caused by the dust of the world and renew their ecclesiastical spirit. And stripping off the old man and his deeds, they will put on the new man who was created in justice and holiness.

30. Do not regret that We have spoken at length on the education and training of the clergy. For you are very well aware many men are weary of the difference, instability and changing nature of their errors, and therefore want to profess our most holy religion. These men, with God's good help, will more easily embrace and practice the teaching, precepts and way of life of this religion if they see that the clergy surpass all others in their piety, integrity and wisdom, and in the noble example they give of all the virtues.

Praise for the Clergy

31. We recognize your many worthy attributes: your burning charity towards God and men, your exalted love of the Church, your almost angelic virtues, your episcopal bravery, and your prudence. Being inspired to do His holy will, you are all followers in the footsteps of the Apostles. As bishops, you are the deputies, and thus the imitators of Christ. In your harmonious pursuits you have become a sincere model for your flock, and you enlighten your clergy and faithful people with the splendor of your sanctity. In your compassionate mercy you seek out and overtake with your love the straying and perishing sheep, as the shepherd in the Gospel did. You place them paternally on your shoulders and lead them back to the fold. At no time do you spare either cares or plans or toils in religiously fulfilling your pastoral duties and defending all Our beloved sheep who, redeemed by Christ, have been entrusted to your care from the rage, assault and snares of ravening wolves. You keep them away from poisonous pasture land and drive them on to safe ground, and in all possible ways you lead them by deed, word and example to the harbor of eternal salvation.

32. Therefore, to assure the greater glory of God and the Church, venerable brothers, join together with all eagerness, care and wakefulness to repulse error and to root out vice. When this is accomplished, faith, religion, piety and virtue will increase daily. Then all the faithful, as sons of light, casting aside the works of darkness, may walk worthily, pleasing God in all things and being fruitful in every good work. And in the very great straits, difficulties and dangers which must beset your serious ministry as bishops, especially in these times, do not ever be terrified; rather, be comforted by the strength of the Lord "who looks down on us who carry out his work, approves those who are willing, aids those who do battle, and crowns those who conquer."[26]

33. Nothing is more pleasing to Us than to assist you, whom We love, with affection, advice, and exertion. We devote Ourselves wholeheartedly together with you to protect and spread the glory of God and the Catholic faith; We also endeavor to save souls for whom We are ready to sacrifice life itself, should it be necessary. Come to Us as often as you feel the need of the aid, help and protection of Our authority and that of this See.

34. We hope that Our political leaders will keep in mind, in accordance with their piety and religion, that "the kingly power has been conferred on them not only for ruling the world but especially for the protection of the Church."[27] Sometimes We "act both for the sake of their rule and safety that they may possess their provinces by peaceful right."[28] We hope that with their aid and authority they will support the objects, plans and pursuits which we have in common, and that they will also defend the liberty and safety of the Church, so that "the right hand of Christ may also defend their rule."[29]

35. We hope that all these matters may turn out well and happily. Let us together entreat God in urgent and unceasing prayers, to make up for Our weakness by an abundance of every heavenly grace, to overwhelm with His all-powerful strength those who attack us, and to increase everywhere faith, piety, devotion and peace.

Then when all enemies and errors have been overcome, His holy Church may enjoy the tranquillity it so greatly desires. Then too there may be one fold and one shepherd.

36. That the Lord may more readily respond to Us, let us call as intercessor Her who is always with Him, the most holy Virgin Mary, Immaculate Mother of God. She is the most sweet mother of us all; she is our mediatrix, advocate, firmest hope, and greatest source of confidence. Furthermore, her patronage with God is strongest and most efficacious. Let us invoke too the prince of the Apostles to whom Christ Himself gave the keys of the kingdom of heaven, and whom He made the rock of His Church, against which the gates of hell will never prevail; let us also invoke his fellow-apostle Paul, and all the heavenly saints who are already crowned and hold the palm of victory. We ask that they implore for all Christians the abundance of divine favor which they desire.

37. Finally, as an augury of all the heavenly gifts and as witness of Our great charity towards you, receive the Apostolic Blessing which from deep in Our heart We most lovingly impart to yourselves, venerable brothers, and to all clerics and the faithful laity who are entrusted to your care.

Given in Rome at St. Mary Major's on the 9th of November 1846 in the first year of Our Pontificate.

†

LATIN TEXT: *Acta Pii IX*, I, 1:4-24.

ENGLISH TRANSLATION: Padraig M. O'Cleirigh.

REFERENCES:

1. Ap 13.6.
2. Tertullian, *de Praescript.*, chap. 8.
3. Rom 13.1
4. St. John Chrysostom, hom. 1 in Isaiah.
5. St. Ambrose on Ps 40.
6. Council of Chalcedon, Act. 2.
7. Synod of Ephes., Act. 3.
8. St. Peter Chrysologus, epistle to Eutyches.
9. Council of Trent, session 7 on baptism.
10. St. Cyprian, epistle 55 to Pope Cornelius.
11. Synod. Letter of John of Constantinople to Pope Hormisdas and Sozomen, *Hist.*, III. 8.
12. St. Augustine, epistle 162.
13. St. Irenaeus, *Adv. Haer.* III, 3.
14. St. Jerome, epistle to Pope Damasus.
15. Clement XII, constitution *Providas*; Pius VII, constitution *Ecclesiam a Jesu Christo*; Leo XII, constitution *Ubi graviora*.
16. Gregory XVI, encyclical letter *Inter praecipuas machinationes*.
17. *Ex Symbolo Quicumque*.
18. St. Leo. sermon 8.4.
19. Council of Trent, session 13, chap. on reform.
20. Rom 12.1-2.
21. Council of Trent, session 22. chap. 1 on reform.
22. Tm 4.12.
23. Benedict XIV, encyclical letter *Ubi primum*.
24. Heb 4.12.
25. Council of Trent, session 23, chap. 18, on reform.
26. St. Cyprian, epistle 77 to Nemesianus and other martyrs.
27. St. Leo, epistle 156 (123) to Emperor Leo.
28. St. Leo, epistle 43 (34) to Emperor Theodosius.
29. Ibid.

COMMENTARY:

"Encyclical letter of Pope Pius IX." *Tablet*, 7, (December 12, 1846), 789.

PRAEDECESSORES NOSTROS

ENCYCLICAL OF POPE PIUS IX
ON AID FOR IRELAND
MARCH 25, 1847
41

To all Patriarchs, Primates, Archbishops and Bishops.

Venerable Brothers, We give you Greetings and Our Apostolic Blessing.

You know from your study of the Church's history, that Our predecessors in the Roman Pontificate assiduously assisted Christian nations. You know too that this zeal included not only spiritual benefits conferred on the Christian people, but also disaster relief whenever calamity struck. This fact is confirmed by documents of ancient[1] and more recent times, as well as by Our own recollection of recent events. Who indeed could, or should, more fittingly display this fatherly concern of spirit than those whom the Catholic faith teaches "are the Fathers and Teachers of all Christians"?[2] And to whom should afflicted peoples have recourse but to those who have proved by actual deeds over a long period of time that they are sympathetic benefactors?

Famine and Disease in Ireland

2. Inspired by this notable example of Our predecessors, and at the behest of Our own will, We immediately made every effort, as far as in Us lay, to bring help to the Irish nation in their time of peril. Therefore as soon as We learned that the kingdom of Ireland was suffering a great dearth of food, both grain and other provisions, and that the nation was hard pressed by a series of awful diseases caused by this lack of food, We immediately came to their aid. We proclaimed that public prayers should be made by God in this city of Ours; We exhorted the Roman clergy and people, as well as the rest of Rome's residents, to come to the aid of Ireland and to pray for them. By contributing Ourselves and by collecting money in Rome, We were able to send a contribution to Our venerable brothers, the Archbishops of Ireland. They distributed it among the needy.

Situation Worsening

3. But letters reach Us daily from Ireland, bringing news of the calamity worsening. We are distressed and again want to help that nation. Ireland deserves our aid for so many reasons. The clergy and people of Ireland have always revered the Apostolic See. Indeed that nation has persevered in professing the Catholic religion in all distressful times, and the Irish clergy has worked industriously to spread the Catholic religion in the farthest parts of the globe. Finally

the Irish nation zealously honors and understands divine Peter whose humble representative We are, and whose dignity, to quote the words of Leo the Great, "does not fail in the person of an unworthy heir."[3]

4. So, after carefully weighing this serious matter and ascertaining also the view of several cardinals on the implementation of Our plan, We have decided to write this letter to you, venerable brothers, so that we may provide for the needs of the Irish people.

Pray for Ireland

5. In this matter We advise you all in the dioceses and districts subject to your jurisdiction to proclaim three days of public prayers in churches and other holy places, as has previously been done in Rome. Do this in order to beseech God, the Father of mercies, to set the Irish people free from this great disaster, and to prevent such a misfortune befalling the other kingdoms and lands of Europe as well. To encourage these prayers, We grant an indulgence of seven years to those who are present at these prayers on any occasion; and, in addition, on those who attend the prayers for the entire three days and who also within a week receive the sacraments of penance and of the most holy Eucharist, We bestow by Our Apostolic authority a plenary indulgence.

Take Up Contributions

6. In addition, We urge you to exhort the people under your jurisdiction to give alms for the relief of the Irish nation. You know the power of almsgiving and the rich fruits which proceed from it. You know the noteworthy praises showered on almsgiving by the holy Church Fathers and especially by St. Leo the Great in many of his sermons.[4] And you readily recall the well-known letter of St. Cyprian, martyr and Bishop of Carthage, to the Bishops of Numidia,[5] which contains clear evidence of his people's zeal in generous almsgiving for those Christians who needed help. You can, furthermore, remember the words of St. Ambrose, Bishop of Milan,[6] that "the beauty of wealth lies not in the manner of life of the rich but in food given to the poor; wealth is more resplendent among those who are weak and in want; Christians should learn to use money in looking not for their own goods but for Christ's, so that Christ in turn may look after them." When you recall these and other praise, We hope that you will vigorously assist the poor whom We are discussing.

7. We could indeed end Our letter here. But since you are about to proclaim public prayers, We must add, venerable brothers, what "Our daily urgency, the care of all the Churches"[7] warns Us of, day and night: that is, the furious, savage storm that We have seen for a long time raised up against the whole Church. Our spirit shrinks to recall "how greatly His enemy hates the holy one"[8] and what evil scheming now goes on "against the Lord and His Christ."[9] Therefore We strongly recommend that when you proclaim public prayers for Ireland, you ask your people to beseech God at the same time for the whole Church.

Meanwhile, venerable brothers, We most lovingly impart to you Our Apostolic Blessing.

Given in Rome at St. Mary Major's on the 25th of March, 1847, in the first year of Our Pontificate.

†

LATIN TEXT: *Acta Pii X*, I, 1:32-37.

ENGLISH TRANSLATION: Padraig M. O'Cleirigh

REFERENCES:

1. Euseb., *Eccles. Hist.*, vol. 4, p. 23 (Cambridge edition) for the letter of Dionysius, bishop of the Corinthians, to Pope Soter at Rome where he says that from the very start of the religion, the Roman Church used to send to Christians the help necessary for living, and that this custom was expanded by the blessed Bishop Soter. Likewise Euseb., *Eccles Hist.*, vol. 7, p. 5, recalls the letter of Dionysius, Bishop of Alexandria to Pope Stephen I, who had sent necessary aid to the province of Syria and Arabia. There is also a letter of St. Basil to Pope Damasus which speaks of aid sent by Pope St. Dionysius, to the church at Caesarea.
2. Council of Florence on the definition of the Faith.
3. Serm. 2 on the anniversary of his elevation.
4. On the fast of the tenth month and on almsgiving.
5. Epistle 60 (Balut. edit.) in dealing with the money collected at Carthage and sent to the bishops of Numidia for the purpose of redeeming Christians, states that "we have sent a hundred thousand sesterces, which were collected here in the church of which by God's kindness we are the leader, by contribution from the clergy and people who stand firm with us. In your diligence you will distribute this money in your district."
6. Epistle 2 to Bishop Constantius (vol. 2, Maurist edit., Paris, 1690).
7. 2 Cor 2. 28.
8. Ps 73. 3.
9. Ps 3. 2.

UBI PRIMUM

ENCYCLICAL OF POPE PIUS IX ON
DISCIPLINE FOR RELIGIOUS
JUNE 17, 1847
42

To All Supreme Moderators, Abbots, Provincials and Other Superiors of the Regular Orders.

Beloved Sons in Religion, We give you Greetings and Our Apostolic Blessing.

Among the chief goals of Our Apostolic ministry is to embrace your religious families with fatherly love, giving them Our most zealous attention, support and protection, and planning and providing for their greater good and dignity. For your Orders were founded by extremely holy men under the inspiration of the Holy Spirit for the greater glory of Almighty God and for the salvation of souls. In this, the founders were encouraged by this holy See. By their many different forms, they adorn the Church with variety. As the select auxiliary troops among the soldiers of Christ, they have always been of very great benefit, adornment and protection to both the Christian and the civil commonwealth. Their members, called by God despise all earthly things with their sublime unconquerable spirit. In regarding only heavenly things, they devote themselves to and accomplish with noble toil those important works which are an excellent service to the Catholic Church and civil society.

Qualities of the Religious Families

2. From their beginnings, the religious families have been noted for their talented members who excel in every sort of teaching and learning. These are virtuous and distinguished men of high offices, aflame with burning love for God and men, and superb examples to the world, to angels and to men. They wished nothing more than to meditate on divine things day and night and to endure suffering in imitation of Jesus. They wished also to spread the Catholic faith and teaching and to fight bravely for it, eagerly enduring bitterness, torture, and punishment. They were even willing to sacrifice their very life to bring primitive savage peoples out of the darkness of error, ferocious customs, and the mud of vices to the light of Gospel truth, the practice of virtue, and the pursuits of civil society. They also developed and supported letters, studies, and arts, thus protecting them from perishing. They formed the tender minds and malleable hearts of the young by instilling in them sound teaching. In addition, they recalled the wandering to the path of salvation. Furthermore, since they are merciful, they have practiced every sort of heroic charity at the risk of their lives. This enables them to lovingly provide aid for those who are captive in jail,

those who are sick or dying and all who are wretched in want or struck by disaster; they hope to lessen their pain, wipe away their tears, and look after their needs with their entire resources and efforts.

Some Evils Have Crept In

3. For this reason the Fathers and Doctors of the Church were right in lavishly praising these searchers for evangelical perfection; they were also right to take strong exception to those who rashly attacked them on the grounds that these holy organizations were useless and destructive of society. Our predecessors always kindly regarded and showed respect to the Regular Orders; furthermore, they protected them their patronage and accorded them with greater privileges and duties in their awarenes that great good and benefit for the whole Christian commonwealth always resulted from these Orders. Our predecessors learned that an enemy was secretly sowing cockle among the wheat and that little foxes were destroying the blossoming vine shoots; they at once gave their attention to rooting out and destroying whatever could prevent the seed which had been sown from producing the richest and most abundant harvest. For this reason then Our predecessors, especially Clement VIII of happy memory, and likewise Urban VIII, Innocent X, Alexander VII, Clement IX, Innocent XI, as also Innocent XII, Clement XI, Pius VII and Leo XII elaborated beneficial plans and published wise Decrees and Constitutions. In doing this, they devoted their Pontifical watchfulness and foresight to completely removing the evils which at critical periods had crept into religious families, and also to protecting or re-establishing their regular discipline.

4. Therefore, in Our great love and care for these Orders, in imitation of Our Predecessors, and abiding by the wise sanctions of the Fathers of Trent in particular (session 25 on Regular and Monastic Clergy) with regard to Our duty, We have decided to turn Our thoughts to your religious families. If there is anything weak in them We may strengthen it, if anything ill We may heal it, if anything broken We may bind it up, if anything lost We may lead it back, if anything cast down, We may raise it up. We do this in order that integrity of morals, holiness of life, observance of regular discipline, letters, sciences—the sacred sciences especially—and the particular laws of each Order may everywhere be revitalized to thrive and flourish more day by day.

5. We rejoice that many members of these sacred families remember their holy vocation, conduct themselves virtuously, excel in their teaching, follow in the footsteps of their famous founders, and toil in the ministry of salvation, spreading abroad the good news of Christ. Yet We grieve that some forget their profession and rank, and stray far from the purpose they embraced. This causes great harm to their orders because to the faithful they present merely the appearance and habit of piety, but they actually contradict the holiness, good name and state of their professed purpose by their life and morals.

Plans to Improve the Religious Orders

6. Therefore We are sending these letters to you, the Moderators of these Orders, to tell you what plans We have for the renewal of regular discipline. Our plan is devoted to achieving and preserving the safety and prosperity of each religious family, to providing benefits for the nations, to improving divine worship and to promoting the glory of God. For in renewing the discipline of your Orders, We hope to produce diligent and industrious workers, accomplished men of God ready for every good work. These men would cultivate the Lord's vineyard, spread the Catholic faith among pagan races in particular, and work on the serious business of the Church and this Apostolic See. But in order that an affair of such importance for religion and for the regular orders themselves may succeed, We have established a special Congregation of cardinals which We have named the *Congregation on the State of Regulars*. With their remarkable wisdom, prudence, advice and practical experience, these brothers may give us a helping hand in this great work.

7. But We call you too, beloved sons, to be partners in this work, and We ask that you collaborate eagerly with Us in accomplishing Our object, so that your order may shine again with its former honor and brightness. Therefore, in accordance with your position and your office, leave nothing unattempted, so that the religious men under your authority meditate earnestly upon the vocation to which they have been called, walk worthily in it, and endeavor religiously to fulfill their vows. Guard their holy discipline and oppose the attractions, sports, and business

of the world which they have renounced; instead let them press on with unceasing prayer and the recollection, teaching and reading of heavenly things. Let them labor for the salvation of souls presenting themselves as modest, humble, sober, kindly, patient, and just men, irreproachable in integrity and chastity, burning with charity, and reputed for wisdom. Let them not offend anyone, but offer to all an example of good works so that the Adversary must fear when he cannot speak any evil of them.

8. These men have renounced entirely the charms, pleasures, deceitfulness and vanity of all things human; they have instead promised and professed that they are devoted to the worship of God. Because of this, they must live a holy and virtuous life so that other Christians may be inspired to emulate them. Since the well-being of every sacred family clearly depends first upon careful selection of novices, and secondly, upon the excellence of their training, We exhort you to examine carefully beforehand the character, spirit and morals of those who wish to join you. Also investigate closely their prudence, spirit and reason for entering the religious life. If their only aim in embracing the religious life is the glory of God, the benefit of the Church, and the salvation of themselves and of others, then admit them to your order. Teach them piously and holily using excellent teachers during their novitiate so that they receive the best possible formation in all virtue and in the way of the religious life which they have entered.

9. The regular orders have always been noted for their promotion of an enthusiasm for writing and for the illumination of our knowledge of human and divine affairs by their many learned and painstaking works. Therefore promote a correct method of study in accordance with the rules of your Order, and to make every effort to see to it that your members ceaselessly apply themselves to learning humane letters and the stricter disciplines, especially the sacred ones. Then, they themselves, once they have been trained in the best and soundest teaching, may fulfill religiously and wisely the demands of their position and the sacred ministries.

10. Now We earnestly hope that all who are soldiers in the camp of the Lord honor God with one mind and one tongue and strive to maintain the unity of the Spirit in the bond of peace. Hence, We repeatedly demand of you that in intimate concord, charity, and great unanimity with the bishops and with the secular clergy, you unite your aims, and strive might and main at the work of the ministry in order to build up the body of Christ. Moreover be zealous always for the better graces. For "there is one universal Church outside of which no one at all is saved; it contains regular and secular prelates along with those under their jurisdiction, who all profess one Lord, one faith and one baptism. Therefore, it is fitting that all who are of this one body be also of one mind, and be bound to each other like brothers in the bond of charity." (Clement I on the excesses of prelates).

11. Beloved sons, what We wished to convey to you in this letter of Ours was to let you know Our great good will towards you and your religious families, and Our eagerness to provide for the affairs, benefits, dignity and splendor of these families. We do not doubt that you will be proud to act in accordance with Our desires and careful advice. In this confident hope then, as an indication of Our dedicated will and charity towards you and all your companions in religion, and as an augury of all heavenly gifts, We lovingly and from Our heart impart to you all, beloved sons in religion, Our Apostolic Blessing.

Given in Rome at St. Mary Major's on the 17th of June, 1847 in the first year of Our Pontificate.

†

LATIN TEXT: *Acta Pii IX*, I 1:46-54.

ENGLISH TRANSLATION: Padraig M. O'Cleirigh.

UBI PRIMUM

ENCYCLICAL OF POPE PIUS IX ON
THE IMMACULATE CONCEPTION
FEBRUARY 2, 1849

43

To Our Venerable Brothers, Patriarchs, Primates, Archbishops and Bishops of the Entire Catholic World.

We Give You Greetings, Venerable Brothers, and Our Apostolic Blessing.

No sooner had We been elevated to the sublime Chair of the Prince of the Apostles and undertook the government of the universal Church (not, indeed, because of Our own worthiness but by the hidden designs of Divine Providence) than We had the great consolation, Venerable Brethren, in recalling that, during the pontificate of Gregory XVI, Our Predecessor of happy memory, there was in the entire Catholic world a most ardent and wondrous revival of the desire that the most holy Mother of God—the beloved Mother of us all, the immaculate Virgin Mary—be finally declared by a solemn definition of the Church to have been conceived without the stain of original sin.

Liturgical Use of the Term "Immaculate"

2. Both to Our Predecessor and to Us this most devout desire was clearly and unmistakably made manifest by the petitions of illustrious bishops, esteemed canonical chapters, and religious congregations, among whom was the renowned Order of Preachers. These appeals vied with one another in the insistent request that official permission be granted for the word *Immaculate* to be publicly used and be added to the sacred liturgy, particularly in the Preface of the Mass of the Conception of the Blessed Virgin. With the greatest delight, both Our Predecessor and We acceded to these requests.

Requests for Definition

3. Moreover, Venerable Brethren, many of you have sent letters to Our Predecessor and to Us begging, with repeated insistence and redoubled enthusiasm, that We define as a dogma of the Catholic Church that the most blessed Virgin Mary was conceived immaculate and free in every way of all taint of original sin.

Nor do we lack today eminent theologians—men of intellectual brilliance, of virtue, of holiness and sound doctrine—who have so effectively explained this doctrine and so impressively expounded this proposition that many persons are now wondering why this honor has not already been accorded to the Blessed Virgin by the Church and the Apostolic See—an honor which the widespread piety of the Christian people so fervently desires to have accorded to the Most Holy Virgin by a solemn decree and by the authority of the Church and the Holy See.

The Devotion of the Holy Father

4. Welcome indeed have such requests been to Us. They have filled Us with joy. From our earliest years nothing has ever been closer to Our heart than devotion—filial, profound, and wholehearted—to the most blessed Virgin Mary. Always have We endeavored to do everything that would redound to the greater glory of the Blessed Virgin, promote her honor, and encourage devotion to her. Accordingly, from the very beginning of Our supreme pontificate We have most fervently directed Our energies and Our thoughts to this matter of such great importance. Nor have We failed, through humble and fervent prayers, to beg almighty God to enlighten Our mind with the light of His grace in order that We might know what We should do in this matter.

Great indeed is Our trust in Mary. The resplendent glory of her merits, far exceeding all the choirs of angels, elevates her to the very steps of the throne of God.[1] Her foot has crushed the head of Satan. Set up between Christ and His Church,[2] Mary, ever lovable and full of grace, always has delivered the Christian people from their greatest calamities and from the snares and assaults of all their enemies, ever rescuing them from ruin.

Mary's Solicitude for Her Children

5. And likewise in our own day, Mary, with the ever merciful affection so characteristic of her maternal heart, wishes, through her efficacious intercession with God, to deliver her children from the sad and grief-laden troubles, from the tribulations, the anxiety, the difficulties, and the punishments of God's anger which afflict the world because of the sins of men. Wishing to restrain and to dispel the violent hurricane of evils which, as We lament from the bottom of Our heart, are everywhere afflicting the Church, Mary desires to transform Our sadness into joy. The foundation of all Our confidence, as you know well, Venerable Brethren, is found in the Blessed Virgin Mary. For, God has committed to Mary the treasury of all good things, in order that everyone may know that through her are obtained every hope, every grace, and all salvation. For this is His will, that we obtain everything through Mary.[3]

Accordingly, We have appointed certain priests of recognized piety and theological learning, as well as several cardinals of the Holy Roman Church who are renowned because of their ability, piety, wisdom, prudence, and knowledge of the things of God; and We have directed them to make, carefully and thoroughly, a most diligent examination into this most important matter and then provide Us with a complete report. Through such a procedure, We feel that We are following in the clearly marked footsteps of Our Predecessors and that We are emulating their example.

Appeal to the Bishops

6. Wherefore, Venerable Brethren, We sent you this communication that We may effectively encourage your admirable devotion and your pastoral zeal and thus bring it about that each of you, in such manner as you will see fit, will arrange to have public prayers offered in your diocese for this intention: that the most merciful Father of all knowledge will deign to enlighten Us with the heavenly light of His Holy Spirit, so that in a matter of such moment We may proceed to do what will redound to the greater glory of His Holy Name, to the honor of the most Blessed Virgin, and to the profit of the Church Militant.

We eagerly desire, furthermore, that, as soon as possible, you apprise Us concerning the devotion which animates your clergy and your people regarding the Immaculate Conception of the Blessed Virgin and how ardently glows the desire that this doctrine be defined by the Apostolic See. And especially, Venerable Brethren, We wish to know what you yourselves, in your wise judgment, think and desire on this matter.

Liturgical Privilege Granted

7. And inasmuch as We have already granted to the clergy of Rome permission that, instead of what is contained in the common breviary, they may recite the special canonical hours, in honor of the Conception of the Blessed Virgin, which were recently arranged and published, We likewise, by this present Letter, grant to you, Venerable Brethren, the faculty, if you wish to use it, of permitting the clergy of your own diocese to recite, licitly and validly, the same

canonical hours of the Conception of the Blessed Virgin now in use with the clergy of Rome. This may be done without obtaining further authorization from Us or from the Sacred Congregation of Rites.

Knowing well, Venerable Brethren, your tender devotion toward the Blessed Virgin Mary, We are sure that it will be your pleasure to cooperate, zealously and diligently, with Our wishes and that you will hasten to supply Us with the replies which We have requested.

8. Meanwhile, receive as a pledge of all celestial favors, and above all as a witness of Our good will towards you, the Apostolic Benediction which We give from the bottom of Our heart to you, Venerable Brethren, as well as to all the clergy and the faithful entrusted to your guidance.

Given at Gaeta, on the 2nd day of February, in the year 1849, in the third year of Our Pontificate.

†

LATIN TEXT: *Acta Pii IX*, I, 1:162-66.

ENGLISH TRANSLATION: *Papal Documents on Mary*, comp. by William J. Doheny and Joseph P. Kelly (Bruce, 1954), p. 1-5.

REFERENCES:

1. St. Gregory, Pope, *de Exposit.* in libros *Regum*.
2. St. Bernard, *Serm.* in cap. *XII Apocalyps.*
3. St. Bernard, *In Nativit.* S. Mariae de Aquaeductu.

COMMENTARY:

"State of Rome—the Immaculate Conception." *Tablet*, 10 (December 22, 1849), 808.

Ubi primum
43

NOSTIS ET NOBISCUM

ENCYCLICAL OF POPE PIUS IX ON THE CHURCH
IN THE PONTIFICAL STATES
DECEMBER 8, 1849
44

To the Archbishops and Bishops of Italy.

Venerable Brothers, We Give You Greetings and Our Apostolic Blessing.

You know as We do, venerable brothers, the recent wrongdoing which has strengthened some wretched enemies of all truth, justice and honor, who strive both openly and deceitfully with plots of every sort to spread their disorders everywhere among the faithful people of Italy. These disorders include the unbridled license of thinking, speaking and hearing every impious matter. They spread these like the foaming waves of a savage sea, and they exert themselves not only to shake the Catholic religion in Italy itself, but if possible to utterly destroy it. The method of their diabolical design has been made very clear both elsewhere and particularly here in this fair city, the seat of Our pontificate, where upon Our forced withdrawal, they gave free rein to their rage, although only for a few months. Here, in their wicked recklessness, as they cast divine and human affairs into confusion, they finally grew enraged enough to interfere with the work of the respected clergy of the city, disregarding the authority of their superiors, who, on Our orders, were attending fearlessly to religious matters. Consequently, when some of their own number fell sick and struggled with death, they were deprived of all the helps of religion and compelled to breathe their last in the arms of a wanton prostitute.

2. Subsequently, the city of Rome and the other provinces of the Papal State were restored to Our civil authority by God's mercy and the arms of Catholic nations. The disturbance of wars ended in the other parts of Italy as well. Nonetheless, those wicked enemies of God and men still continue their lawless work, if not by open force, at least in other deceitful ways which are not always concealed. We find it formidable to be responsible for the supreme care of the whole of the Lord's flock in these difficult times, and We are greatly pained by the particular dangers which beset the churches of Italy. However, We are powerfully consoled in Our sufferings by your pastoral zeal, venerable brothers, which you not only proved to Us in the full blast of the recent storm, but which you continue to demonstrate. However, the very gravity of this affair compels Us to exhort you further, since you must steadfastly fight the battles of the Lord with Us. We must make all prudent provision for offsetting the losses already incurred by most holy religion throughout Italy and for guarding against dangers which threaten in the future.

3. These enemies of the Church usually employ a variety of deceits for turning the spirits of the Italian people away from the Catholic faith. For instance, they shamelessly affirm and cry it abroad that the Catholic religion is opposed to the glory, greatness and prosperity of the Italian nation. So they say that Protestantism should be brought in, set up and increased to replace Catholicism. Then Italy could once more acquire its former splendor of ancient, that is, pagan, times. It is hard to decide which is the more hateful aspect of this fiction of theirs—the malice of their raving impiety or the effrontery of their lying wickedness.

Advantages of Catholicism

4. In fact, there is great spiritual advantage in being transferred from the power of darkness to the light of God, thereby being justified by grace and becoming heirs of Christ in our hope of eternal life. This advantage for souls is, of course, so worthwhile that all the glory and blessedness of this world must be reckoned as nothing in comparison with it. "For what does it profit a man if he gains the whole world but suffers the loss of his soul? Or what exchange will a man make for his soul?"[1] But it is untrue that the temporal losses of the Italian race occurred because they professed the true faith. This race should indeed reckon among the benefits it received from the Catholic religion the fact that at the collapse of the Roman Empire, it did not decline as much as the peoples of Assyria, Chaldaea, Media, Persia and Macedonia did when an alteration of the times ended their dominion. In fact, every wise man knows that Catholicism not only rescued Italy from the darkness of the many errors which were overwhelming it, but that amid the ruins of the ancient empire and the invasion of the barbarians, it raised Italy nonetheless to a glory and a greatness beyond all the other nations of the world. Thus, because Christ placed the holy See of Peter there, Italy exercises a more widespread and more real leadership by its divine religion than it once exercised by its earthly empire.

5. From this exceptional privilege of possessing the Apostolic See and the consequent deep roots which the Catholic religion has put down among the people of Italy, very many other remarkable benefits have accrued. Christianity is the teacher of true wisdom, the defender of mankind, and the fertile mother of all virtues. Thus, it rejects the splendor of the unhappy glory of the Italian people. Their ancestors established that unhappy glory by an unending tumult of wars, by conquering foreigners, and by very harshly imprisoning a great number of men; they could do this since their empire flourished by the law of war. But the religion of Christ enlightened the Italians in truth, justice, and mercy; and consequently they became zealous in outstanding works of piety towards God and in beneficent works towards men. So, in the chief Italian cities, many holy temples and other reminders of Christian times have been erected not by the bloody toil of men groaning in captivity, but sincere and life-giving charity. Pious institutions exist for religious exercises and for the education of the young and the proper study of literature, arts and disciplines. They also exist for relieving the illness and want of the wretched. This then is the divine religion on which, quite simply, the safety, prosperity and glory of Italy depends. Is this the religion which those men call on the Italian people to reject? We cannot restrain Our tears, when We see that some Italians now are so wicked and so wretchedly deceived that they admire the vile teachings of impious men. In fact, they are not afraid to plot with them for this great destruction of Italy.

Socialism and Communism

6. You are aware indeed, that the goal of this most iniquitous plot is to drive people to overthrow the entire order of human affairs and to draw them over to the wicked theories of this *Socialism* and *Communism*, by confusing them with perverted teachings. But these enemies realize that they cannot hope for any agreement with the Catholic Church, which allows neither tampering with truths proposed by faith, nor adding any new human fictions to them. This is why they try to draw the Italian people over to Protestantism, which in their deceit they repeatedly declare to be only another form of the same true religion of Christ, thereby just as pleasing to God. Meanwhile they know full well that the chief principle of the Protestant tenets, i.e., that the holy scriptures are to be understood by the personal judgment of the individual, will greatly assist their impious cause. They are confident that they can first misuse the holy scriptures by wrong interpretation to spread their errors and claim God's authority while doing it. Then they

can cause men to call into doubt the common principles of justice and honor.

7. But do not let Italy, which other peoples have used as a paradigm ever since the Holy See was established in Rome, be to them a stone of offense and a rock of scandal in the coming time. Do not let this portion of the Lord's vineyard be given as prey to all the beasts of the field: do not let the Italian people, maddened by draughts from the poisoned goblet of Babylon, take up deadly arms against their mother the Church.

8. By the secret judgment of God, We and you have been detailed to fight this critical danger. We must beware of dreading the deceit and attacks of the men who plot against the faith of Italy, as if they had to be vanquished by our own strength. For our counsel and our bravery is Christ, without Whom we can do nothing but through Whom we can do all things.[2] So, watch zealously over the flock entrusted to you and protect it energetically from the plots and attacks of ravening wolves. Share your counsels with one another; continue to meet with one another so that by sharing the inquiry, you may detect the main causes for the start of these dangerous evils in different districts. Thus you will be able to provide more timely remedies for them under the authority and guidance of this Holy See. In this way, in union with Us, you should attempt to nullify every attack, artifice, plot and endeavor of the enemies of the Church.

Instruct the Laity and the Clergy

9. So that all their efforts may be fruitless, sufficiently instruct the laity in Christian doctrine and the law of the Lord. Hopefully, they are not too weakened by long license in manifold and increasing vices to be able to recognize the snares laid for them and also the vileness of the errors proposed to them. So We earnestly require you, in your pastoral care, to ceaselessly ensure that the faithful entrusted to you are carefully taught the holy doctrines and precepts of our religion in accordance with their individual capacity; exhort and inspire them in every way to conform their lives and morals to these norms. For this purpose, inflame the zeal of the Churchmen, who care for these souls. Instruct them to reflect seriously on their ministry, to keep in view the prescripts of the Council of Trent,[3] and to devote great energy to instructing the Christian people, as the state of the times demands. Let them be eager to sow in all hearts the words of God and the precepts of salvation. This they can accomplish by declaring in concise and comprehensible sermons the vices Christians should avoid and the virtues they should practice in order to escape eternal punishment and gain eternal glory.

10. In particular, ensure that the faithful are deeply and thoroughly convinced of the truth of the doctrine that the Catholic faith is necessary for attaining salvation.[4] The Catholic laity and clergy should repeatedly offer special thanks to God in public prayers for the priceless gift of the Catholic religion. They should also beseech God to protect the profession of this faith in our country and to keep it unharmed.

11. Meanwhile, ensure that all the faithful receive from you at the proper time the sacrament of Confirmation; this confers the strength of special grace for the steadfast profession of the Catholic faith in times of trouble. It would also be helpful if the faithful, cleansed of their sins by the sacrament of Penance, devoutly receive more frequently the most holy sacrament of the Eucharist. The Eucharist contains spiritual food and the antidote to free us from daily faults and keep us from mortal sin. Furthermore, it is the symbol of Christ's Church which He hopes will unite us by faith, hope and charity; as the result of this unity, we should all say the same thing and there should be no divisions among us.[5]

12. Indeed, We do not doubt that parish priests and their helpers, and other priests who are usually appointed to the ministry of preaching on particular days, especially in periods of fasting, will earnestly aid your labor in all these affairs. Still their efforts should be supplemented from time to time by the extraordinary measures of spiritual exercises and holy missions. These will nourish the piety of good people and stir sinners to saving penitence, even those who have been depraved for a long time. As a result, the faithful people will grow in the knowledge of God, bear fruit in every good work, and steadfastly abhor the perverted teachings of the Church's enemies.

Scandals

13. But in all these affairs, one of your aims should be to instill in the faithful a greater aversion for sins which scandalize others; your priests should share this aim. You are aware of the increase in the number of those who sin in a scandalous manner: those who blaspheme the heavenly saints and the holy name of God as well; those who live in concubinage and sometimes in incest; those who openly do servile work on holy days; those who despise in the presence of many the precepts of the Church on fasting and the selection of food; and those who shamelessly commit various other sins in the same way. So, make the faithful consider the seriousness of sins of this kind and the heavy penalties for them, both for the guilt of the sin itself and for the spiritual danger in which they place their brothers by the infection of their bad example. For it is written: "Woe to the world because of scandals . . . Woe to that man by whom the scandal comes!"[6]

Misuse of Publications

14. The crafty enemies of the Church and human society attempt to seduce the people in many ways. One of their chief methods is the misuse of the new technique of book-production. They are wholly absorbed in the ceaseless daily publication and proliferation of impious pamphlets, newspapers and leaflets which are full of lies, calumnies and seduction. Furthermore, under the protection of the Bible Societies which have long since been condemned by this Holy See,[7] they distribute to the faithful under the pretext of religion, the holy bible in vernacular translations. Since these infringe the Church's rules,[8] they are consequently subverted and most daringly twisted to yield a vile meaning. So you realize very well what vigilant and careful efforts you must make to inspire in your faithful people an utter horror of reading these pestilential books. Remind them explicitly with regard to divine scripture that no man, relying on his own wisdom, is able to claim the privilege of rashly twisting the scriptures to his own meaning in opposition to the meaning which holy mother Church holds and has held. It was the Church alone that Christ commissioned to guard the deposit of the faith and to decide the true meaning and interpretation of the divine pronouncements.[9]

15. In order to check the contagion of bad books, it would be useful if your clerics who are renowned for sound doctrine likewise publish short works, to build up the faith to instruct the people. You would, of course, have to approve these before publication. Distribute these works and other useful and doctrinally sound authors among the faithful.

The Importance of the Holy See

16. All who defend the faith should aim to implant deeply in your faithful people the virtues of piety, veneration, and respect for this supreme See of Peter. Let the faithful recall the fact that Peter, Prince of Apostles is alive here and rules in his successors,[10] and that his office does not fail even in an unworthy heir.[11] Let them recall that Christ the Lord placed the impregnable foundation of his Church on this See of Peter[12] and gave to Peter himself the keys of the kingdom of Heaven.[13] Christ then prayed that his faith would not fail, and commanded Peter to strengthen his brothers in the faith.[14] Consequently the successor of Peter, the Roman Pontiff, holds a primacy over the whole world and is the true Vicar of Christ, head of the whole Church and father and teacher of all Christians.[15]

17. Indeed one simple way to keep men professing Catholic truth is to maintain their communion with and obedience to the Roman Pontiff. For it is impossible for a man ever to reject any portion of the Catholic faith without abandoning the authority of the Roman Church. In this authority, the unalterable teaching office of this faith lives on. It was set up by the divine Redeemer and, consequently, the tradition from the Apostles has always been preserved. So it has been a common characteristic both of the ancient heretics and of the more recent Protestants—whose disunity in all their other tenets is so great—to attack the authority of the Apostolic See. But never at any time were they able by any artifice or exertion to make this See tolerate even a single one of their errors. For this reason the enemies of God and human society at the present time are making every attempt to tear the Italian people from their allegiance to Us and to this Holy See. They think, no doubt, that then at last, they could have the good fortune of contaminating Italy itself with their impious teaching and the plague of their novel theories.

Communism and Socialism

18. As regards this teaching and these theories, it is now generally known that the special goal of their proponents is to introduce to the people the pernicious fictions of *Socialism* and

Communism by misapplying the terms "liberty" and "equality." The final goal shared by these teachings, whether of *Communism* or *Socialism*, even if approached differently, is to excite by continuous disturbances workers and others, especially those of the lower class, whom they have deceived by their lies and deluded by the promise of a happier condition. They are preparing them for plundering, stealing, and usurping first the Church's and then everyone's property. After this they will profane all law, human and divine, to destroy divine worship and to subvert the entire ordering of civil societies. In this critical period for Italy, it is your duty, venerable brothers, to help the faithful realize that if they let themselves be deceived by such perverted doctrines and theories, these theories will cause their temporal and their eternal destruction.

Allegiance to Authority

19. Therefore, warn your faithful that the very nature of human society obligates its members to obey its lawfully established authority; nothing in the precepts of the Lord on this subject, which are proclaimed in holy scripture, can be altered. For it is written: "Be subject to every human institution for God's sake, to the king as supreme or to governors as sent by him to punish wrongdoers and to praise those who do right. For it is God's will that by doing right, you should put to silence the ignorance of foolish men. Be as free men, yet without using freedom as a pretext for evil, but be as servants of God."[16] And again: "Let every soul be subject to the higher authorities. For there is no authority except from God, and those that exist have been instituted by God. Therefore, he who resists authority resists what God has appointed, and those who resist will incur their own condemnation."[17]

20. Let them furthermore know that it is likewise a mark of the natural, and so of the immutable, condition of human affairs that even among those who are not in higher authority, some surpass others in different endowments of mind or body or in riches and such external goods; therefore it can never be lawful under any pretext of liberty or equality to usurp or injure in any way the good or rights of other men. Divine precepts on this subject are clear and can be found throughout the holy scriptures. They forbid us strictly even to desire the goods of other men, much less seize them.[18]

Aid for the Poor

21. In addition, let the poor and all the wretched recall their great debt to the Catholic religion which keeps the teaching of Christ unspoiled and preaches it publicly. For He proclaimed that whatever benefits are conferred on the poor and wretched are likewise conferred on Himself.[19] Furthermore, He wishes that all be informed of the special account He will take of these works of mercy on the Day of Judgment; that is, He will give the gift of eternal life to the faithful who engaged in works of mercy, and He will punish with eternal fire those who neglected them.[20]

22. This proclamation of Christ and His other stern warnings on the use of wealth and its dangers[21] have meant that the condition of the poor and wretched in Catholic nations is much less harsh than in any other nations. The poor would receive even greater aid if the many institutions which our pious ancestors established for their relief had not been closed down or plundered in the recent recurrent public demonstrations. Let Our poor recall the teaching of Christ Himself that they should not be sad at their condition, since their very poverty makes lighter their journey to salvation, provided that they bear their need with patience and are poor not alone in possessions, but in spirit too. For He says: "Blessed are the poor in spirit, for theirs is the kingdom of heaven."[22]

Misuse of Power

23. All the faithful should know too that the old kings of the pagan nations and other chiefs of state misused their power in more serious ways and more often. The faithful should reckon it to the credit of our most holy religion that princes in Christian times feared "the stern judgment in store for governors," and the eternal punishment prepared for sinners, in which "the strong will suffer strong torments."[23] Because of this fear, they have ruled the peoples subject to them more justly and clemently.

Judgment Day

24. Finally, let the faithful recognize that

Christian law protects true liberty and equality. God Almighty, who has made "the small and the great" and who "takes equal care of everyone,"[24] "will not withdraw from anyone nor fear anyone's greatness."[25] He has established a day "on which He will judge the world in justice"[26] in His Only-Begotten Son Christ Jesus, "who will come in the glory of His Father with His angels and will then make return to each man according to his works."[27]

25. But if the faithful scorn both the fatherly warnings of their pastors and the commandments of the Christian Law recalled here, and if they let themselves be deceived by the present-day promoters of plots, deciding to work with them in their perverted theories of *Socialism* and *Communism*, let them know and earnestly consider what they are laying up for themselves. The Divine Judge will seek vengeance on the day of wrath. Until then no temporal benefit for the people will result from their conspiracy, but rather new increases of misery and disaster. For man is not empowered to establish new societies and unions which are opposed to the nature of mankind. If these conspiracies spread throughout Italy there can only be one result: if the present political arrangement is shaken violently and totally ruined by reciprocal attacks of citizens against citizens by their wrongful appropriations and slaughter, in the end some few, enriched by the plunder of many, will seize supreme control to the ruin of all.

Advice for Clergy

26. Now the life and example of the clergy help keep the faithful safe from the snares of the impious in their profession of the Catholic religion and help stir them to the works of true virtue. But, alas! there have been in Italy some men of the Church, although they were few, who by deserting to the Church's enemies, helped them greatly in deceiving the faithful. The lapse of these men doubtless incited you afresh, venerable brothers, to watch daily with keener zeal over the discipline of the clergy. And now since We desire to provide, as We should, for the future, We recommend what We emphasized in Our first encyclical letter to the bishops of the whole world:[28] that you should lay hands on no one in haste,[29] but show the greatest possible care in selecting soldiers for the Church's army. Candidates for holy orders especially must be examined at thorough length to determine whether their learning, serious morals and zeal for divine worship indicate that they will by their life and work edify and bring spiritual benefit to your flock, like lanterns burning in the house of the Lord.

27. Properly organized monasteries convey great honor and benefit for the Church of God, and the regular clergy also work to save souls. Therefore, first of all, inform the religious families in your dioceses that We lament the particular troubles which many of them suffered in the recent disasters. But We were inwardly consoled to observe their patient spirits and their steadfast pursuit of virtue and religion; some though forgot their profession and vilely played a double role, scandalizing good men and sorrowing Us and their brothers. Secondly, exhort the leaders and superior moderators of these families to ensure that where regular discipline is preserved, it continues to thrive and flourish, and that where it has faltered, it is completely revived and restored. Let those superiors insistently advise, convince and spur on the members of their families to seriously consider their vows so that they are eager to observe them and the rules of their organization carefully and fully. They should carry around in their body the mortification of Jesus and keep away from everything which is at variance with their particular vocation. They should be actively engaged in works which evince a love of God and neighbor in the pursuit of perfect virtue. Let these moderators of the Orders admit no one to a religious institution before they consider very carefully their former life, morals and character; then they should admit to religious profession only those who indicate that they are embracing the religious life for no reason except to live only for God and to obtain the salvation of themselves and others. But in addition, they should observe all the statutes and prescripts for the good of religious families which are contained in the Decrees of Our Congregation on the State of Regular Clergy published on January 25th last year and sanctioned by our Apostolic authority.

Catholic Education

28. To turn now to the selection of the secular clergy, We wish chiefly to recommend that you instruct and educate young clerics, since most suitable ministers of the Church are those who

from their earliest years have been duly molded for these sacred duties. Continue then your energetic efforts to recruit very young men for God's holy army. Then nurture them in religion, modesty, innocence of life, and ecclesiastical spirit. At the same time teach them literature and the major and minor fields of study, especially the sacred ones. Their teachers should be carefully selected and should follow doctrine which is free from all danger of error.

29. It is unlikely that you will succeed in educating all young clerics in seminaries. The other young men in the lay state certainly pertain to your pastoral care also. Therefore be vigilant, with regard to all other schools, both public and private. Strive to ensure that their studies conform to the standard of Catholic teaching. Furthermore, see to it that the students are educated by suitable teachers. The students also must be taught to recognize the snares laid for them by the impious, to avoid their pernicious errors, and so to adorn and benefit themselves and the Christian and civil commonwealth.

30. In these matters, you have authority over professors of the sacred disciplines and all other matters which belong to religion or closely pertain to it. See to it that in the entire program of the schools and especially in the matters which belong to religion, books are provided which are free from the suspicion of every error. Advise those who care for souls to be your continuous helpers in matters concerning schools for the very young. Appoint respectable male and female teachers and provide only books approved by this Holy See. Ministers should themselves set an example by daily instructing boys in the rudiments of Christian doctrine. Furthermore, they should take this instruction seriously.[30] Advise these men, that when they are instructing, to keep in view the Roman Catechism, which was published by a decree of the Council of Trent and the order of St. Pius V Our Predecessor of immortal memory. Other supreme pontiffs, to name one, Clement XIII of happy memory, recommended this book as "a most suitable aid for removing the deceits of bad opinions and for spreading and establishing true and sound doctrine."[31]

31. You will hardly be surprised, venerable brothers, that We have written on these subjects with a slightly too fluent pen. For you know that in these dangerous days, We must strive together with every effort and resolve, and must be vigilant in every matter which pertains to schools and the education of the young, both male and female. For you know that our enemies diabolically try to pervert young minds and hearts from their earliest years. And for this reason they try to remove schools completely from the authority of the Church and the watchfulness of its holy pastors.

Political Leaders

32. In addition, We strongly hope that the political leaders of Italy will support you with their powerful protection in performing your duty more fruitfully in all these matters, and that they will also protect the Church and all its rights, both spiritual and temporal. This indeed would befit their religion and the piety of their ancestors, which obviously inspires them in an exemplary way. Furthermore, they realize that the evils that afflict us so grievously originate in the losses, which for a long time now, but especially since the rise of Protestantism, have been inflicted on religion and the Catholic Church. They see clearly that when the authority of bishops is oppressed and when increasing numbers of men infringe divine and ecclesiastical commandments without penalty, then the respect of the people for civil authority is likewise diminished. Similarly, the present enemies of public calm instigate revolts against the government more easily. They observe too that the frequent seizure, robbery and open sale of temporal goods which belong to the Church shows a decrease in the people's respect for property consecrated to the use of religion. Consequently the men who rashly proclaim *Socialism* and *Communism* find many prepared to listen to them when they falsely claim that in other similar cases, the property of others can be taken and divided or in some other way turned to the use of everyone. They furthermore observe that the long-standing impediments preventing the pastors of the Church from exercising their sacred authority freely are now gradually affecting civil authority. Finally, they observe that there is no readier or more effective remedy for the disasters which harry us than to make religion and the Catholic Church flourish again throughout Italy; in the Church, there is no doubt that men will get immediate and appropriate aid in accordance with their condition and need.

33. For, to use the words of St. Augustine, "the Catholic Church attaches itself not only to God Himself but also to love and charity of one's neighbor, so that it excels in healing all the diseases which men suffer for their sins. It trains and teaches boys in a boyish manner, young men strongly, old men calmly, in accordance with the individual's bodily and spiritual age. It subjects wives to their husbands in chaste and faithful obedience, not for the gratification of lust but for the begetting of progeny and the society of the family; and it places husbands over their wives not in scorn of the weaker sex but under the law of pure love. It subordinates sons to their parents in a sort of free slavery and puts parents in charge of sons with a loving control. It binds brother to brother with the bond of religion, which is stronger and tighter than the bond of blood. It strengthens in reciprocal love all relationships of birth and marriage by preserving the ties of nature and of oaths. It teaches slaves to remain true to their masters, not as much from the compulsion of their state as from delight in duty, and makes masters kind to their slaves by the thought that the supreme God is their common Lord and more apt to advise than to compel them. By recalling our first parents, it unites citizen with citizen, nation to nation, and all humanity in society and brotherhood. It teaches kings to take care of their people, and people to submit to their kings. It teaches carefully who should have honor, who love, who reverence, who fear, who consolation, who warning, who exhortation, who discipline, who reprimand, who punishment, while showing how all things are not due to all men, but charity is due to all and harm to none."[32]

34. Therefore, it is our mutual duty to spare no effort and to shrink from no problem in protecting the practice of the Catholic religion among the Italian people. It is also our duty to eagerly resist the attempts of the impious who are engaged in separating Italy from the bosom of the Church, as well as to vigorously recall to the way of salvation those degenerate sons of Italy who have already let themselves be won over by the artifices of their enemies.

35. But since every good gift and every perfect gift comes down from above, let us ceaselessly supplicate and entreat the heavenly Father of lights and mercies, in public and private prayers, to turn His face from our sins and graciously illuminate the minds and hearts of all with the strength of His grace. May He gather to Himself the wills of rebels and enlarge His holy Church with new victories and triumphs, so that in all Italy and everywhere in the whole world, the people who serve Him may increase in merit as in number. Let us also call on the most blessed Mother of God, the Virgin Mary Immaculate, who by her powerful patronage with God obtains what she asks for and who cannot be denied. In addition let us call on Peter, the Prince of Apostles, on Paul, his fellow-apostle, and on all the heavenly saints to pray that the most clement Lord may take away the scourges of His anger from His faithful people and graciously give His grace to all who are accounted Christians; then they could reject all that is at variance with the Christian name and pursue what is in accord with it.

Finally, venerable brothers, receive Our Apostolic Blessing as an indication of Our eager benevolence towards you. With deep feeling We impart it lovingly to yourselves and to the clergy and faithful laity who are entrusted to your watchfulness.

Given at Naples in the Suburban Portico on the 8th day of December in the year 1849 in the fourth year of Our Pontificate.

†

LATIN TEXT: *Acta Pii IX*, I, 1:198-223.

ENGLISH TRANSLATION: Padraig M. O'Cleirigh.

REFERENCES:

1. Mt 16.26.
2. St. Leo the Great, epistle to Rusticus, Bishop of Narbonne.
3. Sess. 5, chap. 2—session 24, chaps. 4 and 7 on Reformation.
4. This doctrine, received from Christ and emphasized by the Fathers and Councils, is also contained in the formulae of the profession of faith used by Latin, Greek, and Oriental Catholics.
5. Council of Trent, session 13, decree on the Sacrament of the most holy Eucharist, chap. 2.
6. Mt 18.
7. On this matter, apart from earlier decrees there is the encyclical letter of Gregory XVI *Inter praecipuas machinationes* (8 May 1844) whose sanctions We upheld in Our encyclical letter (9 November 1846).

8. See Rule 4 of the Rules drawn up by a committee of Council Fathers at Trent and approved by Pius IV in the constitution *Dominici gregis* (24 March 1564) and the addition made to it (17 June 1757) by the Congregation of the Index by authority of Benedict XIV. (This addition is usually placed in the front of the Index of Forbidden Books.)
9. Council of Trent, session 4, decree on the publication and use of the sacred books.
10. Council of Ephesus Acts 3 and St. Peter Chrysologus' epistle to Eutyches.
11. Leo the Great, Sermon on anniversary of his elevation.
12. Mt 16.18.
13. Mt 16.19.
14. Lk 22.31-32.
15. Council of Florence, definition or decree on union.
16. 1 Pt 2.13f.
17. Rom 13.1f.
18. Ex 20.45, 17. Dt 5.19, 21.
19. Mt 18.15; 25.40-45.
20. Mt 25.34f.
21. Mt 19.23f—Lk 6.4; 18.22f—Jas 5.1f.
22. Mt 5.3.
23. Wis 6.6, 7.
24. Wis 6.8.
25. Ibid.
26. Acts 17.31.
27. Mt 16.27.
28. 9 November 1846.
29. 1 Tm 5.22.
30. Council of Trent, session 24, 4—Benedict XIV, constitution *Etsi minime*, 7 February 1742.
31. In his encyclical epistle 14 June 1761.
32. St. Augustine, *de Moribus Cathol. Ecclesiae*, bk. 1.

COMMENTARIES:

Sarzano, Giuseppe. "Apologia storica della enciclica degli 8 decembre 1849." *L'Osservatore Romano*, 2 (18 febbraio-29 marzo 1850), 81, 85-86, 89, 93-94, 97-98, 101-02, 105-06, 117, 133-34, 137, 141, 145, 149.

______ "Risposta alle obiezioni sull'enciclica degli 8 decembre 1849." *L'Osservatore Romano*, 2 (24-29 aprile 1850), 193, 197, 201.

EXULTAVIT COR NOSTRUM

ENCYCLICAL OF POPE PIUS IX ON
THE EFFECTS OF THE JUBILEE
NOVEMBER 21, 1851

To All Patriarchs, Primates, Archbishops, Bishops and other Ordinaries of Places in Favor and Communion with the Apostolic See.

Venerable Brothers, Greetings and Apostolic Benediction.

Our soul rejoices in the Lord, venerable brothers, and We have humbly given thanks to God when, in the midst of the continuous and grave anxieties which oppress Us in these wicked times, We learned of the rich and happy fruits which overflowed among your people on the occasion of the sacred Jubilee. For you notified Us that on this occasion the faithful people of your dioceses with humble spirit and contrite heart eagerly thronged the churches to hear the preaching of God's word. With their stains washed away in the sacrament of reconciliation, they approached the divine table; at the same time they offered fervent prayers to God according to Our desires. And so it happened that, aided by heavenly grace, many left filth and vice, for the paths of truth and a salutary way of life. All of this gave Us the greatest consolation and joy, since We are most anxious and solicitous for the salvation of all men divinely committed to Our care. We strongly desire that all peoples walk in the paths of faith, loving God and following His laws on the road to salvation.

Current Evils

2. On the one hand, venerable brothers, We ought to rejoice greatly because the people of your dioceses received great spiritual blessings from the holy Jubilee; on the other hand, though, We have to grieve when We see the afflicted and lamentable appearance of our religion and civil society in these miserable times. You know with what crafty arts, with what monstrous opinions and evil contrivances the enemies of God and the human race strive to pervert the minds of all and corrupt their morals. Their goal is nothing less than to eliminate religion and to pull apart the bonds of civil society and overturn it from the ground up. Therefore we must deplore all the following: the blindness covering the minds of many; the fierce war against everything Catholic and this Apostolic See; the hideous hatred of virtue and rectitude; the profligate vice dignified with the deceitful label of virtue; the unbridled liberty of thinking, living, and daring everything at will; the unrestrained intolerance of all rule, power, and authority; the mockery and contempt for sacred things, for holy laws, for even the finest

institutions; the lamentable corruption of improvident youth; the annoying aggregate of bad books, pamphlets, and posters flying about everywhere and teaching sin; the deadly virus of *Indifferentism* and incredulity; the tendency to impious conspiracies, and the fact that both human and divine rights are despised and ridiculed. Nor is it hidden from you what anxieties, what doubts, and what hesitation and fear arise from these things to distress all upright minds. Serious evils indeed are to be feared in private and public affairs when men, miserably deserting the norms of truth, justice, and religion, enslave themselves to their own evil and unbridled desires in resolute labor for all that is sinful.

Ask God for Help

3. In such a great crisis, everyone can see that all our hopes must be placed in God alone. We must offer Him continual and fervent prayers, so that He may pour out the riches of His mercy on all peoples. We must implore Him to illumine all minds with the light of His heavenly grace, to bring back the erring to the path of justice, to turn back to Himself the rebellious wills of His enemies, to bestow on all a love and fear of His holy name, and to give them the spirit of always thinking and doing whatever is right, whatever is true, whatever is modest, whatever is just, whatever is holy. The Lord is sweet, mild, merciful, and rich for all who call on Him. He receives the prayers of the humble and shows His power in pardon and mercy. Let us approach, venerable brothers, with confidence to the throne of grace, so that we may receive mercy and find favor in His timely aid. Everyone who asks receives, everyone who seeks finds, and everyone who knocks enters.[1] But first let us give perpetual thanks to the Lord of mercies and let us praise His holy name since He deigns to work the wonders of His mercy throughout the Catholic world. Therefore with one mind and animated with the same sincerity of faith, strength of hope, and ardor of love, let us humbly and strenuously beseech God to deliver His holy Church from all calamities, to expand and exalt it more and more every day among all nations and everywhere on earth, to purge the world of all errors, to lead all men in mercy to the recognition of truth and the way of salvation, to propitiously avert the scourge of His anger which we deserve for our sins, to rule the sea and wind and bring tranquility, to grant peace, to save His people and bless His inheritance and bring it to heaven. That God may more easily incline His ear to our prayers and grant our desires, let us raise our eyes and minds to the most holy Mother of God, whose patronage with God is more prompt and efficacious than any other, for she is our most loving Mother and our greatest source of confidence. Then too let us seek the intercession of the Prince of the Apostles, to whom Christ Himself gave the keys of the Kingdom of Heaven and whom He made the rock of His Church against which the gates of hell can never prevail. Let us also seek the intercession of his Co-apostle Paul, and the particular patrons of each city and region, and all the heavenly company, that by them our gracious Lord may pour out the rich gifts of His goodness.

4. Therefore, venerable brothers, while We in Our gracious City order public prayers to be made, We call upon you and the people committed to your care to join Us in Our desires. With all zeal We enkindle your renowned religious devotion and piety so that in your dioceses also you take care to order public prayers for mercy. And in order that the faithful may more fervently perform these prayers which you order, We have decided to offer again the heavenly treasures of the Church in the form of a Jubilee, as you will clearly understand from Our other letters that accompany this one.

5. We are surely consoled by the hope, venerable brothers, that angels of peace with golden cruets and a golden censer in hand will offer Our humble prayers and those of the whole Church on a golden altar to the Lord. Surely He will receive them with a friendly countenance and assent to the common desires of Us, you, and all the faithful. May He dispel all the darkness of error, dissipate the storms of all evils, and give His right arm in aid to both Christian and civil affairs. May He grant one and the same faith of mind to all, one and the same piety of action, one and the same love of religion, virtue, truth and justice, one and the same zeal for peace, and one and the same bond of love, so that the kingdom of His only begotten Son, Our Lord Jesus Christ, may be extended more from day to day and strengthened and exalted in the whole world.

6. Finally as a sign of all heavenly gifts and as a testimony of Our burning love, receive the Apostolic Benediction which We most lovingly impart with heartfelt affection to you, venerable

brothers, and to all clerics and lay faithful committed to your care.

Given in Rome at St. Peter's, November 21, 1851, in the sixth year of Our Pontificate.

†

LATIN TEXT: *Acta Pii IX*, I, 1:342, 47.

ENGLISH TRANSLATION: Bernard A. Hausmann, S.J.

REFERENCE:

1. Mt 7.8.

Exultavit cor Nostrum
45

NEMO CERTE IGNORAT

ENCYCLICAL OF POPE PIUS IX ON
DISCIPLINE FOR CLERGY
MARCH 25, 1852
46

To the Venerable Brothers, Archbishops, and Bishops of Ireland.

Venerable Brothers, Greetings and Apostolic Benediction.

Certainly no one is ignorant, venerable brothers, with what outstanding and constant trust and respect for this Chair of Peter, the Mother and Teacher[1] of all the faithful Christians, and with what singular concord and constancy the bishops of Ireland always strove to excel in protecting Catholic interests and fulfilling their episcopal duties. Even during grievous storms, to their great credit and to Our consolation, they strenuously fulfilled their ministry together and earned the Church's deep gratitude. They considered nothing more precious than with one accord to prevent the people of Ireland entrusted to their care from being contaminated by the contagion of error. The bishops have diligently protected, defended, and safeguarded the legacy of faith and Catholic truth in their flock.

Unite to Resist Current Evils

2. We rejoice when We think of your accomplishments; they give Us pleasure and they merit honor for you. Nonetheless We are anxiously concerned to learn by what strategies the ancient enemy strives to damage and weaken your union of minds, since at present he is inciting dissensions. We have such an opinion of your devotion that We do not doubt at all that you will bravely resist the snares of the enemy and fight constantly and prudently, with ever greater zeal, for God and Church. Yet because of Our office of Apostolic ministry and because of the great love We entertain for you and for your faithful people, We cannot but impress upon you again and again the need of mutual concord. "For indeed We know and it is certain (to use the very words of St. Gregory the Great, Our predecessor) that the battle line of a camp appears terrible to an enemy when it is continuous and crowded together, with no open spaces. For if there is a vacant place by which the enemy could enter, then it no longer arouses fear in him. And therefore, since we make a spiritual line of battle against the evil spirits, we must of necessity always be found united, drawn together by love and never severed by discord. Whatever good works may be found in us, if love is lacking, a place is opened by evil discord in our line of battle by which the enemy is able to enter and to strike us."[2] You are daily bound together by a most stringent covenant of love, and you are obligated to spread the glory of God, to safeguard the doctrine of the Catholic Church, to fight for

its rights, to protect the safety of the flocks entrusted to you, to overthrow the plots and errors of the enemies, and to satisfy the other serious episcopal duties. Therefore, from the depths of our hearts, We exhort, even beg you to be more of one mind each day, unifed in the same perceptions and in the same judgments, and concerned with preserving the unity of spirit in the bond of peace.

United with Bishops of England and Scotland

3. In your wisdom you know well how much this sacerdotal and trusting agreement of minds, wills, and judgment is necessary and advantageous to the good of the Church and the profit of the faithful. Therefore We are convinced by your exceptional piety and virtue that you will consider nothing more important than to continually cultivate such concord, not only among yourselves, but also with other venerable brothers, especially with the bishops of England and Scotland. For you know well that both you and they must work very much with one and the same zeal and with the support of your mutual love. You must stand watch for the perfection of the saints in the words of the ministry and build up the body of Christ. With united forces, you must under the leadership of this Apostolic See do all you can to promote the glory of God and the eternal salvation of men. We trust that you will always be eager for such concord, since We joyfully recall with what unanimity you signed the Acts of the Synod of Tullamore in 1850, called to protect the affairs of the Catholic Church in Ireland.

The Decree of the Apostolic See

4. And here is something related to that Synod. You will recall the letter that twelve of your number sent to Us following the Synod on September 11, 1850. It was also signed by the Venerable Brother Daniel, Archbishop of Dublin, over whose death We grieve. There was particular question in the letter about Queens Colleges, as they called them. Nor are you unaware of the Decree, prepared by Our Congregation for the Propagation of the Faith, which We published after due consideration of the matter. Since We wanted you to know how, in this important matter, We had written to the same Archbishop of Dublin in a personal letter dated November 17 of the preceding year, We decided to use the same words in this letter. They are as follows: "Concerning the Queens Colleges you spoke of in your letter, We are pleased to learn that after the Decree of the Apostolic See concerning this important matter was published, you promptly agreed to obey it. We are convinced that you will carefully execute the Decree and do so with every zealous effort. We know that you will see to it that the bishops who signed the September 11 letter along with you, will respect and obey this Decree, complying with it promptly and zealously. This Decree was always dear to Us. We greatly desire that it be earnestly and religiously observed by all, since in it there is question of safe-guarding Catholic doctrine, and nothing can be or should be more important for us." From this you can easily understand how that venerable brother, admonished and encouraged by Us, applied all his energies to seeing that the Decree would be diligently observed both by himself and by others. Because he died, he perhaps was unable to complete the task that We had intended; therefore We again commend and urge all of you that for the sake of your religion, the Decree under consideration be observed with diligence and accuracy by all. Now it is concealed from no one that We approved the Ordinances and Statutes of the same Synod you held at Tullamore. This We did after a careful examination and with some emendations, as early as May 23 of the preceding year, by a Decree issued by Our Congregation for the Propagation of the Faith, supported by Our Supreme Authority. We decided to approve, confirm, and sanction again in a more solemn manner the same ordinances and statutes in accordance with all the changes. Our Apostolic Letters, sealed with the ring of the Fisherman and issued on the twenty-third day of this month did this. Now your episcopal solicitude must carefully and zealously watch that these statutes may be scrutinized freely as documents in good condition.

Catholic University of Ireland

5. We praise you because in the assembly at Tullamore mentioned above, solicitous for the salutary, Catholic education of youth, you wisely agreed to erect a Catholic University of Ireland as quickly as possible. There, young men, without danger to their Catholic faith, will be taught literature and the more austere disciplines. We encourage you to spare no zealous attention so

that this most salutary work may rapidly achieve its desired success. We gladly approve the foundation of this same Catholic University with the promised Apostolic Letters. We rejoiced greatly when We learned that the faithful of Ireland seconded your splendid plans with ready good will and liberality, so that substantial subsidies have already been received to bring your plans to fruition. Therefore while We greatly congratulate you and the faithful, We certainly entertain the hope that this Catholic University with God's help will rise in prosperity and happiness as soon as possible, according to Our and your desires.

Proper Mien and Duties of Clerics

6. Now, however, as you know, nothing instructs others more in piety and the service of God than the lives and example of those who have dedicated themselves to the divine ministry. Therefore labor so that all who are called to the vineyard of the Lord, mindful of their proper vocation and office, abstain entirely from things forbidden to clerics and from things that are not proper for them. Then they may be an example for the faithful in word, in their dealings with others, in love, in faith, and in chastity. They must wear a clerical habit appropriate to their order and dignity, and they must perform their ministry piously and reverently. Further they must administer to the faithful, with fitting piety and reverence, the holy sacrament of the Eucharist. With it all true justice begins; or if already begun, is increased; or if already lost, is recovered. They should be devoted to prayer and study, especially sacred studies, and under your guidance let them zealously serve the salvation of souls. Each one of you knows very well how eager the Church is, especially in these hard times, to have suitable servants, who come only from well-trained clerics. Therefore devote all your care, thoughts, and diligent study to this, that the young clergy, even from their earliest years, are trained in all piety, virtue, and ecclesiastical spirit, and that they are carefully taught literature and the more serious disciplines, especially the sacred ones, free entirely from every danger of profane innovations and error. Then resplendent with the raiment of all the virtues and armed with salutary and solid doctrine, they may in time be able to teach the Christian people by word and example and to refute those who contradict them.

Nemo certe ignorat
46

You have in these letters, venerable brothers, what We in Our great love for you and for the faithful have thought worthy to emphasize, and We have no doubt at all that you will be happy to agree as one man with Our desires. Your religious sense, your piety, your reverence for Us and for this Apostolic See, and your episcopal virtue and solicitude are commendable. Because of these attributes, We trust that you will concur with Us, never leaving anything untried. Furthermore, aided by divine grace, We trust that you will proceed with every constancy, zeal, and prudence to set up a wall for the house of Israel, to keep the flock entrusted to your care away from poisoned pastures, and to lead them to good ones. We expect to see you bringing the miserably lost back to the paths of truth and justice and attempting everything by which all may grow in the knowledge of God and of our Lord Jesus Christ. Meanwhile in all Our humble prayers We shall beseech the most clement and merciful Father to pour out the richest gifts of his goodness over you and the sheep entrusted to you. As a sign of this heavenly aid, and as a pledge of Our burning love for you, accept the Apostolic Blessing, proceeding from the depths of Our heart and joined with a prayer for all true happiness We most lovingly give Our blessing to you, venerable brothers, to all the clergy, and to the faithful laity entrusted to your care.

Given at Rome, at St. Peter's, March 25, 1852, in the sixth year of Our Pontificate.

†

LATIN TEXT: *Acta Pii IX*, I, 1:353-60.

ENGLISH TRANSLATION: Bernard A. Hausmann, S.J.

REFERENCES:

1. Lateran Council 4, ch. 5.
2. St. Gregor M. on Ez, bk. 1, homil. 8.6.

PROBE NOSCITIS VENERABILES

ENCYCLICAL OF POPE PIUS IX ON THE DISCIPLINE FOR CLERGY

MAY 17, 1852

47

To the Venerable Brothers, Archbishops, and Bishops of the Spanish Kingdom.

Venerable Brothers, Greetings and Apostolic Benediction.

You know well, venerable brothers, how concerned We have been even from the beginning of Our Pontificate to review and arrange the affairs of the Catholic Church in Spain. You also recall the Agreement which was entered upon after long and laborious negotiations with Our Daughter in Christ, Maria Isabel, the Catholic Queen of the Spaniards. Nor are you unaware of how zealously We desired to make safe and inviolable certain items in the Agreement itself; namely, that the Church might fully enjoy all the rights which she exercises by divine institution and by the prescriptions of Canon Law, and that all of you should have full and entire liberty to perform your episcopal ministry. We do not doubt, because of your admirable trust in the Church and your paternal solicitude, that you will devote full labor, industry, and diligence to safeguard the liberty of the Church itself and to preserve your episcopal rights; nevertheless, that you may accomplish this, We have thought it well to add to your determination. For this reason We address you with deepest affection, venerable brothers, and We repeatedly call forth your outstanding piety, episcopal virtue, and vigilance. Because of the position you occupy and the dignity with which you are marked, We exhort you to zealously execute and defend all the things which are in the Agreement itself, especially for the safety of the Church and for the liberty to exercise your episcopal ministry. In your wisdom, you know very well how such priestly and faithful unity of mind, will, and opinion is of advantage to the Church. Therefore We earnestly exhort you all to be of one mind and intention: to fight with concord of spirit for the cause and rights of the Church herself, and to exercise freely all aspects of your episcopal duties and sacred ministry in accord with what has been prescribed and sanctioned by the Agreement. But in order that this vital concord of minds and conformity of action may flourish more readily each day, you should confer among yourselves by letter, particularly in important matters like this. Those of you who have received the rank of Archbishop should first communicate the matter among yourselves; after you have diligently weighed everything, you should inform your suffragans of the conclusions reached. In that way, under the stimulus of your religious zeal, all of you may reach unity. With joined forces and shared zeal, you may then be able to promote the greater glory of God, to preserve whole and inviolable the venerable rights of the Church, to labor for the salvation of souls, and to protect a full-preserved freedom to exercise your episcopal ministry. You know what rich and salutary fruits the Christian people have gathered from episcopal councils, especially from the Council of Trent; therefore, after you have corresponded concerning the more serious matters, begin again with all zeal to hold provincial synods. These have been neglected because of the difficulties of the times. Synods will ensure that the needs of each province are accurately perceived and that one norm of action is undertaken. You will thus be able, with God's aid for your singular virtue, prudence, pastoral care, and solicitude, to find again what has been lost by the people entrusted to your vigilance, to restore what has been abandoned, to bind what has been broken, to strengthen what is weak, and to devote all your energy so that our divine religion and its salutary doctrine may flourish in your regions. And do not neglect to reestablish diocesan synods, according to the prescriptions of the same Council of Trent.

Training of Clergy

2. Devote your constant thoughts and efforts to those who have dedicated themselves to the sacred ministry. See that they remain mindful of their vocation and direct their manner of life according to the standards of the sacred canons and ecclesiastical discipline. They should glow in the gravity of their character, the sanctity of their life, and the praise of their wholesome doctrine. They should also give an example of all the virtues to the Christian people; perform the duties of their ministry fully, skillfully, and religiously; and labor zealously for the salvation of souls. The young clergy, even from their earliest years, should be guided opportunely toward piety, virtue, and an ecclesiastical spirit. See that they are diligently taught literature, especially the sacred disciplines, untouched by the danger of any error. The faithful entrusted to you should be nourished daily with the words of faith and strengthened by the spiritual gifts of grace so that they can grow in the knowledge of God and walk in the ways of the Lord; they must never permit themselves to be deceived and led into error by the manufacturers of lies and the followers of perverse dogmas. Since, however, as each one of you well understands, nothing contributes more to the preservation of sacred and public affairs than the proper education of youth. Therefore, watch carefully that in all the public and private schools a doctrine entirely Catholic is taught and that the young people are trained scrupulously according to the precepts of our holy religion.

3. We know the great anxieties and difficulties, especially in these evil times, that the episcopal ministry is exposed to; We also know how you must constantly labor and keep watch to fulfill the duties of your vital ministry. But no labor or difficulty must ever keep you from the duty of your proper office. Relying on divine help, act manfully for the glory of God, for the cause of His most holy Church, and for the eternal salvation of men; keep before your eyes the incorruptible crown of glory promised by the eternal Prince of Pastors to those who persevere. We are completely convinced that you will comply fully with these Our desires; We also have confidence that Our dear and pious daughter in Christ, Maria Isabel, and her ministers will realize how greatly Our holy religion and its doctrines add to the happiness and tranquility of their people. Thus you will have their powerful patronage by which you will be able to exercise all the duties of your episcopal ministry in prosperity and happiness.

4. Meanwhile, We will pour out fervent prayers to the most clement Father of mercies and the God of all consolation, that in the abundance of His divine grace He may always look with favor on you and bless your pastoral labors and cares. It is after all by your efforts that the faithful entrusted to your care walk worthily, pleasing God in all things and bearing fruit in all good works. As an auspice of this heavenly aid and a proof of Our most ardent love for you, We most lovingly impart the Apostolic Blessing from the depths of Our heart, to you, venerable brothers, and to all the clergy and faithful laity entrusted to your care.

Given at Rome at St. Peter's, May 17, 1852, in the sixth year of Our Pontificate.

†

LATIN TEXT: *Acta Pii IX*, I, 1:361-65.

ENGLISH TRANSLATION: Bernard A. Hausmann, S.J.

INTER MULTIPLICES

ENCYCLICAL OF POPE PIUS IX PLEADING
FOR UNITY OF SPIRIT
MARCH 21, 1853
48

To Our Beloved Sons Cardinals of the Holy Roman Church, and Venerable Brothers Archbishops and Bishops of France.

Beloved Sons of Ours and Venerable Brothers, Greetings and Apostolic Benediction.

Among the many anxieties arising from Our concern for all the churches given to Us, though unworthy, by the hidden deliberation of divine Providence, far too many are the people about whom the Apostle foretold, "There will come a time when they will not endure sound doctrine; having itching ears, they will heap up to themselves teachers to suit their own likings. But the wicked and imposters will go from bad to worse, erring and leading into error."[1] We are thus overjoyed when We turn to that renowed nation of France, a nation of many famous men and worthy of merit from Us. In that nation We are consoled to see how with God's help the Catholic religion and its salutary doctrines flourish, flower, and prevail more every day. We are consoled by the care and zeal with which you fulfill your ministry and care for the safety and salvation of your beloved flock. And Our consolation increases as We learn more and more from the letters you write to Us: more, that is, about the filial piety, love, and reverence with which you glory to follow Us and this Chair of Peter. This chair is the center of Catholic truth and unity, that is, the head, mother, and teacher of all the Churches[2] to which all honor and obedience must be offered.[3] Every church must agree with it because of its greater pre-eminence—that is, those people who are in all respects faithful.[4]

2. We are also joyful because We know that you, aware of the seriousness of your episcopal duties, labor to increase the glory of God and to defend the cause of His Holy Church. You also use all your pastoral care and vigilance to see that the ecclesiastics of your dioceses set forth each day more worthy of the vocation to which they are called and that they give example of all the virtues to the Christian people, performing the offices of their ministry diligently. We rejoice in your concern that the faithful entrusted to you are daily nourished with the words of faith, confirmed by the gifts of grace, grow in the knowledge of God, and walk the road that leads to life. Finally, we rejoice in your concern for those who stray from the truth, that they may return to the paths of salvation. Hence We joyfully recognize how eagerly you strive to obey Our desires and admonitions to celebrate provincial synods. This means that in your dioceses the inheritance of faith is maintained whole and inviolate; pure doctrine is

taught; the honor of divine worship increased; the training and discipline of the clergy strengthened; and good character, virtue, religion, and piety are aroused and everywhere confirmed with auspicious and happy progress. And We rejoice very much when We see that by your special zeal the liturgy of the Roman Church has been restored according to Our desires in many of your dioceses, where thus far particular circumstances least resisted. And We are so much the more pleased since We know that in many dioceses of France, because of the condition of the times, even those things were hardly observed which Our predecessor St. Pius V wisely and providently ordained in his Apostolic Letter of July 9, 1568 *(Quod a nobis postulat).*

Eliminate Dissensions

3. We rejoice to recall all these things with praise for your distinguished order, beloved sons and venerable brothers; nevertheless We cannot hide the grave sadness and grief which afflicts Us now, when We learn what dissensions the ancient enemy strives to excite among you in order to weaken your concord of minds. Therefore, because of Our Apostolic duty and the great love which We cherish for you and those faithful people, We write this letter in which We address you with the intimate affection of Our heart. At the same time We admonish and beseech you that, daily bound by a covenant of love and mutually perceiving the same things with one mind, you strive in virtue to drive off and eliminate all dissensions which the ancient enemy labors to sow. Strive with all humility and mildness to preserve an all-embracing unity of spirit in the bond of peace. For you are wise enough to know how necessary that sacerdotal and faithful unity of mind, will, and judgment is, and how it contributes to the prosperity of the Church and the procurement of eternal salvation. This concord of minds and wills must be cultivated among you with all zeal, especially now, because by the admirable will of Napoleon, Emperor of the French, and because of the work of his government, the Catholic Church there enjoys all peace, tranquility, and good will. And this fortunate combination of affairs and times in that empire ought to be a greater stimulant for you to strive to do all things with one and the same purpose, so that the divine religion of Christ, His doctrine, and the probity of morals and piety may take the deepest roots in France. Then the finest, uncontaminated education of youth may prevail more from day to day. By these means, hostile attacks may then be more easily restrained and overcome, attacks which arise from the efforts of those who were and are the constant enemies of the Church and Jesus Christ.

Education of the Clergy

4. Thus We ask you again and again with the greatest zeal We can muster that, in matters concerning the safeguarding of the Church and its salutary teaching and liberty, and in fulfilling all the other episcopal duties of your ministry, your greatest aim should be unity among yourselves. We want you to confidently consult Us and this Apostolic See to remove controversy in all matters of whatever kind. First of all, since you know how much a good education, especially for the clergy, contributes to both sacred and public prosperity, do not neglect with concord of judgment to apply your thoughts and cares to this important matter. Never leave anything untried so that the clerics in your seminaries are formed early in all virtue, piety, and an ecclesiastical spirit; then they can grow in humility, without which we can never please God. At the same time, they should be diligently taught the humanities and the more austere disciplines, especially the sacred ones, free from the danger of any error. Thus they may acquire not only elegance in speaking and writing (this eloquence being both from the wisest works of the Holy Fathers and from the most renowned pagan authors expurgated of all flaws), but also an especially full and solid knowledge of the history of theological doctrines, ecclesiastical history, and the sacred canons, acquired from a source approved by this Apostolic See.

Results of Good Education and Training

5. Then that illustrious clergy of France, which is resplendent with so much talent, piety, knowledge, ecclesiastical spirit, and singular service to this Apostolic See, will abound more each day with knowledgeable and zealous workers. These workers, distinguished in virtue and armed with salutary knowledge, may be able in time to help in cultivating the vineyard of the Lord and in refuting those who contradict them. They will be able not only to confirm the faithful of France in our holy religion, but also to propagate it by sacred missions among distant and pagan

nations. To the great credit of their name, the clergy up to the present have done this, for the good of religion and the salvation of souls. Along with Us, you detest the great number of pestilential books, pamphlets, magazines, and posters which the virulent enemy of God and man incessantly spews forth to corrupt morals, attack the foundations of faith, and weaken the most sacred dogmas of our religion. Therefore, never cease to lead the flock entrusted to your care away from these posion pastures. Never cease to instruct, defend, and confirm them against the deluge of so many errors; use salutary and opportune admonitions and publications to do this.

Encourage Catholic Writers

6. And here We cannot help but remind you of the admonitions and counsels with which, four years ago, We strongly summoned all the bishops of the Catholic world to exhort men outstanding for talent and sound doctrine to publish appropriate writings with which they might enlighten the minds of people and dissipate the darkness of creeping errors. Strive to remove this deadly pestilence of books and magazines from the faithful given into your care. At the same time encourage with all benevolence and favor those men who, animated by a Catholic spirit and educated in literature and learning, will endeavor to write books and publish magazines. Do this so that the Catholic doctrine is defended and spread, that the venerable rights and documents of this Holy See remain sound, that opinions and doctrines opposed to the same See and its authority may be suppressed, and that the darkness of error is banished and the minds of men illumined with the sweet light of truth. And it will be for your episcopal solicitude and love to arouse such inspired Catholic writers, so that they continue with ever greater zeal and knowledge to defend the cause of Catholic truth. You must also admonish them like a prudent father if their writings should offend Catholic teaching.

Adherence to the Apostolic See

7. Now you know well that the most deadly foes of the Catholic religion have always waged a fierce war, but without success, against this Chair; they are by no means ignorant of the fact that religion itself can never totter and fall while this Chair remains intact, the Chair which rests on the rock which the proud gates of hell cannot overthrow[5] and in which there is the whole and perfect solidity of the Christian religion.[6] Therefore, because of your special faith in the Church and special piety toward the same Chair of Peter, We exhort you to direct your constant efforts so that the faithful people of France may avoid the crafty deceptions and errors of these plotters and develop a more filial affection and obedience to this Apostolic See. Be vigilant in act and word, so that the faithful may grow in love for this Holy See, venerate it, and accept it with complete obedience; they should execute whatever the See itself teaches, determines, and decrees. Here, however, We are hardly able to restrain Ourselves from telling you of the grief We experienced when, among other things, a recently published book reached Us; it was written in French with the title *Sur la situation présente de l'Eglise Gallicane relativement au droit coutumier*. Its author is totally opposed to all We so fervently commend, and so We have sent the book to Our Congregation of the Index to be disapproved and condemned.

8. But before We conclude, We remind you again of what We most desire: that is, that you reject all questioning and controversy which, as you know, disturb the peace and injure love and which afford arms to the enemies of the Church, arms with which to oppose and destroy her. Therefore let it be nearest to your heart to have peace among yourselves and to pursue peace with all, seriously reflecting that you are legates for Him who is not a God of dissension but of peace. He never ceased to prescribe peace to His disciples; indeed Christ, as each one of you knows, "promised all of his gifts and rewards in the preservation of peace. If we are the heirs of Christ, let us remain in the peace of Christ. If we are the sons of God, we must be peacemakers .... It is necessary that the sons of God be peaceful, meek of heart, simple in speech, united in affection, and joined faithfully among themselves with the ties of concord."[7] We certainly have confidence in your virtue, religion, and piety; We do not doubt that by obeying most willingly Our paternal admonitions and desires, you will root out the seeds of all dissensions. By supporting each other patiently in love and collaborating in the Evangelical faith, you will continue with ever more active zeal to keep watch by night over the flocks entrusted to your care and execute

PIUS IX

assiduously every part of your duties, even to the consummation of the saints in the building up of the body of Christ. Be convinced of this, however, that nothing will be more pleasing to Us, nothing more desirable, than that you do all those things which We know contribute to your greater profit and that of your faithful. Meanwhile in the humility of Our heart We pray and beseech God always to pour out the abundance of His heavenly grace upon you. We ask His blessing upon your pastoral concerns and labors by which the faithful entrusted to your care may continue to progress toward their heavenly goal, pleasing God in all things and bearing fruit in every good work. As an auspice of this divine help and as a proof of the burning love with which We embrace you, We eagerly bestow the Apostolic Blessing on you, beloved sons of Ours and venerable brothers, on all the clerics of those churches, and on the faithful laity.

Given at Rome at St. Peter's, March 21, 1853, in the seventh year of Our Pontificate.

†

LATIN TEXT: *Acta Pii IX*, I, 1:439-48.

ENGLISH TRANSLATION: Bernard A. Hausmann, S.J.

REFERENCES:

1. 2 Tm 4.3,4; 3.13.
2. St. Cyprian, epistle 45; St. Augustine, epistle 162; and others.
3. *Acts of the Ephesian Council*, 4.
4. St. Irenaeus, *adversus haereses*, chap. 3.
5. St. Augustine, *in Psal. contr. part. Donat.*
6. Synodical letter of John of Contantinople, *ad Hormisd. Pont.*
7. St. Cyprian, *de int. Eccles.*

NEMINEM VESTRUM

ENCYCLICAL OF POPE PIUS IX ON THE PERSECUTION OF ARMENIANS
FEBRUARY 2, 1854

49

To the Venerable Brothers the Archbishop Primate and the Bishops and to the Beloved Sons, Priests and Religious, and to all the Faithful of the Catholic Nation of Armenia in the Province of Constantinople.

Venerable Brothers and Dearly Beloved Sons, Greetings and Apostolic Blessing.

You know, venerable brothers and beloved sons, the paternal affection which the popes of old showed you in honoring your illustrious nation of Armenia with so many titles. You also know how eager they were to recall that same nation to Catholic unity. Nor are you ignorant of the fruits which Our predecessors in the papacy reaped from this zeal toward your country. They were filled with great joy when they could effect the return of many Armenians to the profession of Catholic unity, people who have persevered strong and unmoved in their faith. It is also clear to you that the Armenian Catholics have suffered many hardships, to their supreme glory and honor. They did this in grievous times when their very lives hung in the balance, yet they preserved and professed the Catholic faith and unity in whose love and devotion they suffered so much. This Apostolic See never ceased to offer vigorous assistance to the Armenians, so that it could deliberate and assist their spiritual needs in every way, according to their own rite. And because the episcopal hierarchy of the Armenian bishops, already restored in those regions which were removed from the heat of persecution, can be preserved, this Holy See is inclined to spare itself no deliberations in its great anxiety and concern for the spiritual welfare of the Armenians living in Constantinople and in the outlying provinces where the bishops could hardly take a stand; in this way We shall provide for the salvation of those same people. For this reason, this Holy See took care to ordain priests for your nation through the work of Our Urban College and to add souls to those students of religious congregations who are charged to diligently procure the spiritual welfare of the Armenians.

2. You know very well, venerable brothers and beloved sons, that, when circumstances first permitted, this Apostolic See established the bishop of the Armenians with episcopal dignity in the city of Constantinople. After the Armenian Catholics were given a certain freedom in religious matters through the clemency of the Turkish emperor, religious affairs could thus thrive and flourish in a greater way along with the mutual harmony of souls. The archiepiscopal primatial see was established at this point in that

same city for the Armenian Catholics. They were given their own archbishop, as the apostolic letters of Our predecessor Pius VIII, show clearly.[1] Everyone knows the special and untiring cares Our predecessor Gregory XVI used to establish the order of that large diocese and to bring about and foster daily the welfare and the prosperity of the Armenian Catholics. When We became Pope, We immediately strove to improve the situation of the Armenian Catholic nation, embracing all the while the whole Christian world in Our mind and thoughts. Through the efforts of Innocent, Archbishop of Sidon, whom We sent as Our extraordinary representative to the supreme ruler of the Turks to express Our friendship and Our respects to that ruler, We have hardly forgotten to repeatedly commend to that powerful Ottoman emperor the Armenians and the other eastern Catholic nations living under his authority. As it is Our supreme desire to bring about the greater welfare of your Armenian nation, We entrusted to Our venerable brother a careful investigation of the condition in which the Armenian nation dwells. We also instructed him to refer everything to Us so that, having weighed matters carefully, We might know what is the best advice for Us to give to provide for your increasing spiritual welfare. Therefore, after Our venerable brother accomplished the task delegated to him, he gave Us an accurate report. We have studied various decrees edited by the cardinals of the Holy Roman Church, the cardinals of Our Congregation for the Propagation of the Faith. Among others, one condemned the so-called Connational Society, by which many future harms were foreseen. Therefore, what We write in this just apostolic letter will conclude the matters which Pius VIII intended to accomplish. We have also established five other bishops of the Armenian rite, among whose dioceses a great part of the ancient and great city of Constantinople has been divided.

Harmful Dissensions in Armenia

3. While We relied on expressed faith that Our paternal concern could make the new ecclesiastical province of Armenia prosper, with great sorrow We have learned that harmful dissensions of souls in your country have already been introduced by the enemy and grow stronger every day. There are many who foster dissensions of this kind or who disguise those counsels by which this Apostolic See wished to greatly help your country. We can never adequately deplore that blazing discord of souls in which both disputing parties began to discuss and dispute openly in writings published for everyone concerning the country's religious matters. The enemy in turn cultivated these writings, especially in harsh words and pronouncements which are totally inconsistent with Christian love. They clearly oppose those things which are sought to protect mutual harmony, and bring to light those things which are unknown and unwanted by this Apostolic See. We thus wanted these matters to be made clear through the repeated letters of that Congregation for the Propagation of the Faith. Each one of you knows what scandals resulted from this, with discernible harm to your country. You also know with what zeal We hastened to remove all contentions and dissensions from you and to totally eradicate their seeds. We were certainly blessed with great happiness because Our first cares produced the desired result. Anthony, your archbishop of Constantinople, and Julian, archbishop of Petra in pagan lands, as well as Our apostolic delegate there for the faithful of the Latin rite, came to Us. After they explained everything, they came to an agreement among themselves and published what they had determined with Our approval. Moreover, We wish that all the orders of your nation would have obeyed Our wishes with the same swiftness according to the prescriptions of Our Congregation for the Propagation of the Faith. We wish they would have trusted Our advice and arrangements, which seek the common good of each and every one of you. Would that We were not compelled to mourn such losses which have abounded among you—especially, to Our great sadness, from the dissension of souls.

4. Therefore as these fatal contentions and disagreements did not cease, We ordered Our Congregation for the Propagation of the Faith to prepare as quickly as possible an accurate account of both the older and the more recent concerns of the Armenian nation. We also ordered the cardinals of the same congregation to diligently examine them in various meetings for the wisdom particular to each one of them. We Ourselves presided at one of these meetings, since We were greatly troubled over an issue of this sort. After hearing the opinions of the cardinals, We indicated what We thought about the principal issues. We have continually asked God, who is

rich in mercies, to help and favor Our humble work for the good of your souls with the all-powerful assistance of His divine grace. As nothing is more important to Us than to advance your peace and prosperity, We took care to accomplish those things which would lead to such a happy ending. Therefore, knowing that the harm to your nation would be greatly increased because of the aforementioned published writings, We ordered that the principal ones be prohibited and condemned in a special examination. We have also strongly disapproved of all similar things, either before or after the condemned writings came to light, whether they were written in Armenian, Armenian dialect, Italian, French, or some other language, since they proposed especially a common hatred totally against Christian love. We have turned all Our attention to promoting a more correct and accurate education of the clergy in the seminary of Constantinople.

Religious Communities

5. In order that the religious communities might enjoy better order, We instructed Our Congregation for the Propagation of the Faith to issue an appropriate decree, which We order all parties to observe diligently. In order to remove entirely every controversy and suspicion concerning the doctrine of the Mechitharist monks of Venice, We want you to know that those same monks sent Us a splendid profession of Catholic faith and doctrine, using all the necessary signatures. This declaration brought Us great consolation and totally satisfied Our wishes. They eloquently acknowledged and freely received the regulations and decrees which the popes and the sacred congregations published or would publish—especially those which prohibit *communicatio in divinis* (communion in holy matters) with schismatics. They declare clearly and openly: "Part of their nation whose good and welfare the institute looks after principally and solely is unfortunately found apart from communion with the Roman Catholic Apostolic Church. For that reason, they declare that they recognize and embrace as their brothers those whom the Holy Roman Apostolic Church recognizes as its sons. They acknowledge that they condemn the error of the schismatic Armenians and recognize that they are outside of the Church of Jesus Christ. They profess that they will never cease to pray, to preach, and to care either in words or deeds or writings that those who stray might return to the one and only fold of Jesus Christ, who is alone the highest shepherd and head and whose center is the pope, the successor of Peter, prince of the apostles." We also indicate to you that they have accepted other suitable advice from Us so that every fear might be plainly put aside concerning the colleges in which these same monks educate the Armenian youth. We ordered that the Congregation for the Propagation of the Faith issue appropriate instructions so that the principal task begun by Our predecessors and by Us might progress prosperously, the ordinary hierarchy of the bishops might be led to the desired conclusion, and the election of both the archbishop primate and the other holy bishops (his suffragans) might be held. We also ordered these instructions to be conveyed to the archbishop and the other bishops.

6. All these things show how concerned We are for your spiritual welfare and with what paternal Christian charity We consider your Armenian nation. We now exhort you above all to clothe yourselves as the chosen ones of God with kindness, humility, modesty, and patience. Bound by a tight mutual bond of harmony and love, put off all rivalries, contentions, envy, anger, and dissensions. Follow peace and holiness in everything; be of the same mind and the same opinion. Carefully preserve the unity of spirit in the bond of peace which the Lord Jesus recommended and prescribed so often. We trust that you will follow these loving counsels of Ours because of your filial devotion toward Us and this Holy See. Taught by sad experience, you know how many catastrophes your illustrious nation endured because of spiritual discord. Matters would have progressed favorably and successfully if everyone had been bound in a mutual harmony of wills and if, loving one another, they would have walked in the love of God. Therefore, remember the misfortunes you suffered because of discord and seriously consider that "every city or house divided among itself will not stand."[2] Keep in mind the warning of the apostle, "that if you go on biting and tearing one another to pieces, take care! You will end up in mutual destruction."[3] Let nothing be of greater concern to you in the future than, with singular care and zeal, to cherish Christian concord of spirit and to keep the peace. You all remember with what

paternal care Our predecessor Pius VIII pressed this harmony upon you. He concluded his apostolic letter establishing the archiepiscopal primatial see of Constantinople with these words of St. Leo the Great: "The unity of the whole body makes one health and one beauty; and this unity of one body requires unanimity, but principally demands the harmony of the priests." Gregory XVI repeated this salutary advice in order to encourage all of you to preserve this mutual harmony of spirit.

7. Now We address Ourselves principally to you, venerable brothers, the bishops of this ecclesiastical province of Constantinople. Continually exhort and enkindle the faithful entrusted to your care to mutual harmony, peace, and love, using unity of spirit and repeated efforts of word or deed or example. Break and suppress any dissension. Meet diligently all parts of your episcopal duty in the supreme harmony of spirit, will, and opinion. "Take care of the flock of God which is in your midst. Watch over it willingly as God would have you do, not under constraint . . . nor lording it over the clergy; but be examples to your flock."[4] First of all, do not spare anything, neither cares, nor advice, nor efforts, to preserve safe and sound the deposit of our divine faith in your dioceses. Take care to educate the clergy piously, forming them accurately to every virtue and ecclesiastical spirit. Educate them especially in the sacred disciplines, keeping them free from every foreign danger. Let the faithful be instructed more each day in the salutary teaching of the Catholic faith and in its holy precepts, and let them be strengthened by the gifts of grace so that, avoiding evil and doing good, they may grow in the wisdom of God. They will thus progress more quickly on the paths of the Lord and enter the way which leads to life. Thus moral decency, integrity of life and virtue, religion, and piety will grow each day, flourishing and dominating in the souls of all. Keep before your eyes the example of the Prince of shepherds who showed himself "meek and humble of heart and left us an example to follow in His footsteps. Venerable brothers, strive zealously on a spirit of forgiveness and kindness to bring back to the straight path of truth and justice those unfortunate people who stray. Explain, beseech, and reprove with all goodness, patience, and teaching, according to the apostle's directive. "Kindness in correction often prevails more than harshness, exhortation more than threats, love more than power."[5] Meanwhile if you take the side of harshness and severity when the seriousness of the disease prescribes sharp remedies and milder ones have already been tried in vain, consider the guilty person according to the prescription of the holy canons. Temper your judgment with mercy, your zeal with kindness, and your harshness with leniency. This especially befits the pastors of the Church, who should show themselves to their subjects as a mother in piety and a father in discipline.

8. We also address all of you, beloved sons, both secular and religious priests. You have given yourselves to the Lord in ministry, as a part of your inheritance. Be subject to each of your bishops, as is fitting. Mindful of your vocation and dignity, strive to maintain them and protect them in seriousness of character and holiness of life, so that you might lead the people to a greater love and veneration of your order and bring about each day an increased growth for the Church. Therefore, you should carefully avoid everything which is prohibited to the clergy, everything which does not befit them. Never allow anything which could present a scandal to others. Take care to show yourselves more and more as a good example in word and unfeigned love, in learning, faith, and chastity. When you are busy in the homes of the people, either from necessity or the compulsion of your sacred ministry, strive to sustain the dignity and greatness of churchmen in all your deeds, so that you might be the good fragrance of Christ, shining with every virtue.

9. Also keep in mind the decree of Our congregation of August 20 of last year and published by Our order; take care to obey it religiously. All clergymen, both secular and religious, should pray unceasingly. Pray to God without fail that he might always more favorably bestow the abundant gifts of his heavenly grace upon you and the Christian people. Do not cease to refine the study of the religious literature and sacred disciplines with which you might respond to those who seek the law from you and with which you can teach the commandments of God to those who are ignorant and in error.

10. Beloved sons, seek with a special effort and diligence not what is yours but what is Jesus Christ's. Fulfill piously all the duties of your sacred ministry. Never cease to work together with your bishops in everything in order to obtain the eternal salvation of the faithful. In this way you will promote our holy religion and its teaching, and you will also remove the seeds of discord and bring about a love of Christian harmony and peace for everyone. As all wisdom comes from God, those among you who are wise should never exalt themselves, but rather give humble thanks to the most gracious God, the giver of all good things. They should use learning for their own edification and that of others, for they should seriously consider that God resists the proud but gives His grace to the humble. He will judge more severely whoever has received more than others, for, as St. Gregory the Great wisely warns: "As the gifts increase, the account of those gifts increases. Therefore, everybody should be more humble and quick to serve God as he sees himself more obliged to give account."[6] None of you should ever covet those gifts of others in your ecclesiastical order, gifts from which the spiritual welfare of your neighbor might flow.

11. We are ready to address all of you, dearly beloved sons in Christ, Catholics of the Armenian nation who live in the ecclesiastical province of Constantinople, of every order, age, sex, and condition. We advise and encourage you repeatedly in Our paternal love to put off all hypocrisy, dissension, envy, and disagreement. Maintain harmony and peace among yourselves, supporting one another in love. You should willingly persevere in the profession of the Catholic religion and adhere firmly and consistently to Us and to this See of the blessed Prince of the apostles. Show the love of God and neighbor in deeds. Keep each of God's commandments in those of the Church, doing everything in the name of our Lord Jesus Christ. Be subject to your bishops and obey them whom the Holy Spirit has established to rule the Church of God. Your salvation is entrusted to them and they will some day have to give account to the eternal Prince of shepherds. Therefore, it is their duty to watch over you and work so that they lead you to the path of salvation. They should strengthen the weak in truth and in suitable teaching. They should also put together the things torn apart, convert the wicked, and distribute the word of life in the food of eternity. Therefore, listen attentively to the voice of those bishops and to their authority. None of you should ever resist his bishop or want to impose any law on him, especially in all of those things which pertain to the episcopal ministry and authority.

12. We address Ourselves to all of you who are preeminent in nobility of birth, splendor of gifts, authority, and wealth in this Catholic country of Armenia. There could certainly be nothing more useful or notable for your illustrious nation than if all of you use your honor and dignity in such a way that you shine forth in virtue. The Christian people seek from you examples to imitate. We beseech you over and over again in the love of religion and in the pursuit of mutual harmony to follow Our advice. Exert yourselves more ardently each day so that you do not ever wish to do anything either against the Church or against your bishops, as those who are separated from Catholic unity are accustomed to doing. You should also devote yourselves to deliberation and studies, so that the Catholic Church may receive increased growth through them. In this way everybody will follow with due reverence, compliance, and obedience that full and supreme authority which our Lord Jesus Christ gave to Peter and to his successors, the popes: namely to feed, rule, and govern the universal Church and the sacred and venerable authority which the bishops exercise over their flocks, an authority which can never be subject to civil powers. You see how much glory you can accumulate and how rich a reward you can receive from God, the giver of all good things, if you strive to bring about the advantage and prosperity of our most holy religion and if you obey these warnings, wishes, and requests of Ours.

13. Before We conclude this letter in order to remove all ambiguities and doubts, We wish to proclaim openly and clearly Our opinion concerning a matter in which great confusion has arisen and which has stimulated dissensions among you. All of you who have longed to return to Catholic unity that part of your Armenian nation which is still miserably turned toward schism certainly deserve the highest praise. Moreover, this desire clearly corresponds to the most ardent wishes of Our Holy Mother Church, which never ceases to pray and beseech God that all dissident children return to her bosom, and to the untiring efforts of this Holy See, which has worked much for this and never ceases to so labor. As you well know, from the very beginning of Our pontificate We used Our legate to the illustrious emperor of the Turks to send a letter to Our Eastern peoples.[7] In this letter, We lovingly and zealously aroused these people to return to the profession of Catholic unity.

14. May your whole nation respond to heavenly grace. May it reject error and return to the one fold of Christ in a spirit of docility and unity, a spirit clearly absent from all who are not joined with this Holy See of Peter. From this Holy See, rights of holy communion flow to all men[8] and to it every obedience and honor must be given.[9] Every church (that is the faithful everywhere) should come together to the See of Peter for greater authority.[10] Indeed, We would be greatly consoled and the whole church would exult greatly, if your whole nation would return to Catholic unity. You should understand from this, venerable brothers and dearly beloved sons, that We cannot approve the course of those who habitually deal harshly with the schismatics of your nation. In fact We completely and vigorously disapprove of those who pursue with harshness and severity, not with love and good will, those who have turned from fatal schism to Catholic unity.

15. At the same time We cannot tolerate the fact that certain people under the pretext of promoting Catholic unity, wish that there be no distinction in regard to the errors of the schismatics. They abuse the zeal by which this Holy See took care to protect the ancient and holy rites of the eastern Church. They think—and We cannot tolerate this—that what is at present being done by the schismatics is to be wholly maintained. They also want to eliminate many practices which were justly introduced into your Catholic nation in order to show how strongly you abhor heresy and schism and adhere to Catholic unity. Moreover these men also want to remove certain works and ecclesiastical rules which the experience of the ancient canons clearly showed were to be added to discipline. At the same time the Catholic Church, totally unlike the heresies and schisms which are now dead, enjoys eternal life and is endowed with the treasures of heavenly riches. It is the teacher of truth and the guide to salvation, the fruitful parent and nourisher of so many holy works and beautiful institutions by which it fosters religion, piety, humanity, and every virtue. It never ceases to deliberate for the common good, the order, prosperity, and harmony of everybody. You are certainly aware that Our predecessor Gregory XVI published an apostolic letter against the ideas of those men on February 3, 1832, beginning, "Inter gravissimas." It seems truly unique and worthy of admiration that these people who study the rites so much do not hesitate in other articles to turn from the canons of that same eastern Church.

16. Moreover, venerable brothers and dearly beloved sons, We have discussed all these thing in this letter because of Our zealous love for your catholic nation of Armenia, and to dispel every doubt and ambiguity. We hope that with the help of God, according to Our fondest wishes, this harmony and peace will bring your nation every true prosperity, reviving and dominating in all of your souls. In order for you to more easily obtain that salutary and desired peace, We impose, with this letter, perpetual and absolute silence on past questions and controversies, and We totally forbid every disapproval and any speech which can disturb the peace among the Armenian faithful. We also expressly and severely prohibit the heretics or schismatics from consuming those in grace and communion with this Apostolic See. If some people who act incorrectly or arouse suspicions suddenly appear—and We trust that would never happen—it will be provided for with due cause. The matter will first of all be clarified by this Apostolic See with the appropriate canonical documents; therefore, after Our declaration and warnings, every disturber regardless of class and order will be guilty of serious fault in the future. They will not in any way be able to excuse themselves and avoid due severity. But the repeated and splendid testimonies of filial piety, love, and obedience toward Us and this Holy See, testimonies which We receive from every order of your Catholic nation of Armenia, arouse in Us great hope that your nation will fill Us with consolation, joy, and happiness. Therefore, relying on this trust, We humbly and strenuously beseech the Father of mercies in every prayer and supplication with thanksgiving that He might always bestow on all of you every beneficial and desired gift. "May the peace of God which surpasses all knowledge keep your heart and minds, and may the grace of Jesus Christ and the communion of the Holy Spirit be with all of you." As a pledge of those things and as a sign of Our very ardent love for you, We lovingly bestow on you the apostolic blessing from the bottom of Our heart, venerable brothers and dearly beloved sons.

Given in Rome, at St. Peter's, on February 2, 1854, in the eighth year of Our Pontificate.

†

LATIN TEXT: *Acta Pii IX*, I, 1:561-79.

ENGLISH TRANSLATION: Norman Desmarais.

REFERENCES:

1. Apostolic Letters of Pius VIII, *Quod jamdiu* and *Apostolatus officium*, 6 July 1830.
2. Mt 12.25.
3. Gal 5.15.
4. 1 Pt 5.2-3.
5. Council of Trent, session 13, chap. 1 on Reform.
6. St. Gregory, homily 9 on the Gospels.
7. Letter *In Suprema Petri*, 6 January 1848.
8. St. Ambrose, epistle 12 to Damasus, nos. 2 and 4.
9. Council of Ephesus, act. 4.
10. St. Irenaeus, *adversus haeres.*, Chap. 3.

OPTIME NOSCITIS

ENCYCLICAL OF POPE PIUS IX ON THE PROPOSED CATHOLIC UNIVERSITY OF IRELAND

MARCH 20, 1854

50

To the Venerable Brothers, the Archbishops and Bishops of Ireland.

Venerable Brothers, Greetings and Apostolic Benediction.

You know very well how great Our joy and consolation was when We first learned that in your devotion, you willingly followed Our advice and that of the Holy See. In the Synod of Thurles, held in 1850, you decided, among other things, to establish a Catholic university as soon as possible. There the youth of your illustrious nation could be shaped in piety and every virtue and educated in letters and in the more difficult disciplines free from any danger to their faith. You also remember clearly how We approved both the acts of that synod and the establishment of this university in Our apostolic letter published on March 23, 1852. Then in Our encyclical letter of March 25, 1852, which We sent to you, We gave thanks regarding this plan for the advancement of religion and knowledge. We also gave well-deserved praise to those faithful people who had already contributed substantial aid in support of that Catholic university in Ireland.

Establishment of Catholic University

2. As We greatly desired to see this Catholic lyceum or university founded quickly in Ireland, We recommended in Our apostolic letter to Paul, who was then Archbishop of Armagh, that the office of Apostolic Delegate be prolonged. By this office he could see to it that the decrees of the Synod of Thurles were diligently observed and especially that the establishment of the Catholic university which that synod approved and which We confirmed was brought quickly to the desired result. Therefore, when that venerable brother was transferred to govern the archiepiscopal church of Dublin, it seemed appropriate to Us that he should continue in the office of Apostolic Delegate in the same manner as We set forth in Our apostolic letter of May 3, 1852. We thought for certain, that you would put your hand to the task without delay and that you would apply all of your understanding and enthusiasm toward the speedy founding of this university. We trust that great benefits will flow from it to the faithful.

3. Thus, it was with great annoyance that We learned that this Catholic university, which We and all good people desire, has not yet been founded, although you already have all the necessary materials to build it. Therefore, we write this letter to you and implore you to put aside all hesitation and to direct all your thoughts and attention with redoubled efforts toward its

construction. With the goal of accomplishing this pious and salutary work more quickly, We command all of you to hold a meeting within a period of three months after you receive this letter with Paul, the Archbishop of Dublin. We name him as Apostolic Delegate; he will preside over this meeting. You will meet there and convene according to the rule of the sacred canons. After your plans have been discussed again without public celebration and you are all of one mind, may you arrange everything which pertains to the quick building and opening of the university.

4. It will be your episcopal concern in this meeting to adopt appropriate plans so that this university may live up to the sanctity and dignity of the Catholic name with which it is adorned. Therefore, see to it that divine religion is regarded as the soul of the entire institution of learning. For that purpose encourage the fear of God and His worship so that the sacred trust of faith may be preserved and all studies may proceed, joined in a close bond with religion. Thus may the shimmering rays of Catholic doctrine illuminate all kinds of intellectual pursuits. Decorous language should be firmly maintained so that whatever is Catholic, whatever proceeds from this See of Saint Peter, the safe harbor of the whole Catholic communion[1] and the mother and teacher[2] of all churches, may be welcomed and believed. May whatever is against it be rejected, so that every error and profane novelty may be repelled and eliminated. The professors of this university should show themselves to be models of good works in doctrine, in purity, and in seriousness. Their primary concern should be shaping the minds of the youth to piety, decency, and every virtue; instructing them in the finest matters; and educating them carefully in letters and studies according to the teachings of the Catholic Church, which is the pillar and chief support of truth.

Newman—Head of University

5. As We know that you have already chosen Our beloved son, Father John Henry Newman, to govern that university, We want to approve your choice that this priest, blessed with such wonderful gifts of mind and soul and endowed with piety, sound doctrine, and zeal for the Catholic religion, assume the care and governance of this university and preside over it as Rector.

6. We certainly do not doubt that in this same meeting, you will take care to establish by consensus other things which might increase the glory of God in your dioceses, promote the discipline and sanctity of the clergy, and foster the piety and devotion of the people. In addition, you know very well that it is entirely necessary, especially in these harsh times, for the shepherds of the Church to apply untiring care, attention, diligence, and effort toward fulfilling every aspect of the episcopal duty. Therefore do not neglect in that same meeting to make plans by which you, fulfilling your ministry, may preserve the purity of our holy faith in those areas, promote worship, and encourage the proper education and sanctity of the clergy. May these plans enable you to educate the faithful entrusted to you in the commandments of holy religion, to strengthen them through the gifts of heavenly graces, to keep them away from poisoned pastures, and to guide them to good ones. Lead back to the one fold of Christ the unfortunates who stray from it. Destroy the snares, the deceptions, and the errors of our enemies and break their force.

7. Because you are aware of what bountiful fruits holy Missions bring to the Christian people with the help of heavenly grace, you should not neglect to form a company of priests, both secular and regular. This will ensure that you have a ready supply of energetic and industrious workers who, adorned with every virtue and handling the word of truth rightly, can exercise the salutary ministry of the holy Missions beneficially in your dioceses.

8. Now We must stress again with great fervor that you should commit all your efforts and authority to seeing that everyone devoutly obeys the decrees of the Synod of Thurles which We approved and confirmed. They should zealously accomplish all that was ratified in those decrees. In order to more easily accomplish this, promulgate the decrees of the Synod of Thurles more solemnly. Command their observance in both provincial and diocesan synods which, as you know, you should convene according to the rules of the Council of Trent.

9. Moreover, considering on this serious occasion the circumstances and affairs in each diocese and province, do not cease to extend your episcopal fervor so that you may strengthen what is weak, heal what is sick, bind up what is broken, bring back what is discarded, and seek what is lost. Thus by the strength which God supplies,

may He be glorified in everything through Jesus Christ Our Lord.[3] Your supreme desire should be to visit the tombs of the apostles Peter and Paul at times specified according to the Apostolic Constitutions and to explain to Us the cares, the condition, and the affairs of your dioceses so that you might receive help to perform your office with eagerness and zeal.

10. We are convinced that because of your eminent devotion and singular piety, love, and obedience toward Us and this Apostolic See, you will accomplish these desires, warnings, requests, and orders of Ours. These requests clearly show how concerned We are for the spiritual well-being and prosperity of your country. Meanwhile, We humbly ask God who is rich in mercy to be with you at all times in the abundance of His divine grace. May He bless you and your pastoral cares and works so that the faithful entrusted to you might daily walk more worthily before God, pleasing Him in everything and bearing fruit in every good work. As a pledge of these things and as a sign of Our paternal affection for you, We lovingly impart Our apostolic blessing to you and to all the clergy and faithful of your churches.

Given in Rome at St. Peter's on the 20th day of March in the year 1854, the eighth year of Our pontificate.

†

LATIN TEXT: *Acta Pii IX*, I, 1:580-86.

ENGLISH TRANSLATION: Norman Desmarais

REFERENCES:

1. St. Jerome, epistle 16.
2. Council of Trent, session 7 on Baptism, canon 3.
3. 1 Pt 4.11.

APOSTOLICAE NOSTRAE CARITATIS

ENCYCLICAL OF POPE PIUS IX URGING PRAYERS FOR PEACE

AUGUST 1, 1854

51

To the Venerable Brothers, the Patriarchs, Primates, Archbishops, Bishops, and other Local Ordinaries Who Share Grace and Communion with the Apostolic See.

Venerable Brothers, Greetings and Apostolic Benediction.

Trials Besetting the Church

When We contemplate the whole Catholic world with the care and affection of Our apostolic love, We can hardly put into words how deeply saddened We are at seeing Christian and civil society disturbed and thoroughly confused, opressed and torn apart by all kinds of disasters. Moreover you know very well how the Christian people are afflicted and harassed by ferocious wars, internal discords, plagues, earthquakes, and other serious troubles. In addition, it is lamentable that among so many injuries and evils perpetrated by the sons of darkness, who are more artful than the sons of light, they try energetically to wage a bitter war against the Catholic Church and its doctrines. In this they use diabolic deceits, arts, and labors. They attempt to overthrow the authority of the Church's legitimate power and to currupt the minds and souls of everyone. They want to spread everywhere the deadly virus of *indifferentism* and *unbelief*; to mix together all human and divine rights; to promote dissension, discord, and movements of impious rebellion; and to commit vicious deeds and cruel crimes. They leave nothing untried so that if it were possible, Our religion would be uprooted and human society itself might be destroyed.

2. Well aware of these dangerous circumstances, We have not failed to raise Our eyes to the holy mountain whence We trust every future help will come. We asked to obtain all the good things which We lack and to avoid the evils We dread. We do not cease to beseech Our merciful God with fervent prayers so that, banishing war to the ends of the earth and removing all disagreements from the Christian princes, He might grant peace and tranquillity to their people. May God especially grant to those princes a pious zeal for preserving and spreading the Catholic faith and doctrine. The happiness of the people depends upon this. May He also save those leaders and people from all the evils which afflict them and make them rejoice in true prosperity. May He bestow the gift of His grace on those who stray so that they may return from the path of perdition to the way of truth and justice and may be turned toward God with a sincere heart.

Moreover We have ordered that prayer imploring the divine mercy be offered in this Our beloved city. Following in the footsteps of Our predecessors, We decided to have recourse to your prayers and to those of the whole Church.

Exhortation

3. Therefore, We are writing this letter to you. We implore you to arouse the faithful entrusted to your care concerning the matters mentioned above so that they might strive to appease the wrath of God provoked by the shameful deeds of men. They should do this by true penance with prayers, fasting, almsgiving, and other good works. Also explain to the faithful how God is merciful to all who call upon Him and how powerful prayer is if We go to the Lord without permitting any enemy of our salvation to have access to us. To use the words of Chrysostom, prayer is "the source, the root, and the mother of innumerable good things. The power of prayer extinguishes the strength of fire, restrains the raging of lions, settles wars and fights, endures storms, escapes devils, opens the doors of heaven, breaks the bonds of death, casts out diseases, repels injuries, and strengthens shattered cities. Prayer endures the blows inflicted from heaven, all the snares of men, and every evil."[1]

4. We strongly desire that when you pray to the Father of Mercies about these matters you do not forget to pray to Him humbly, ardently, and zealously, following the guidelines of Our encyclical letter dated February 2, 1849. Pray that He will desire to enlighten Our mind with the light of His Holy Spirit by which We might issue a decree as soon as possible concerning the conception of the Most Holy Mother of God, the Immaculate Virgin Mary. This would result in the greater glory of God and the praise of that Virgin, the loving mother of us all.

Plenary Indulgence

5. Indeed We have decided to offer the treasures of divine gifts, whose dispensation the Most High entrusted to Our care, so that your faithful may pray with more fervent love and more abundant fruit. For this reason, by the mercy of almighty God and trusting in the authority of His blessed apostles Peter and Paul, We confer, by the power of binding and loosing which the Lord gave to Us, a plenary indulgence of all sins as in a jubilee. This indulgence will be granted to all the faithful of your dioceses who accomplish the following acts within a three month span to be determined by each one of you and computed from the day which you decide upon. They must have humbly confessed their sins with sincere regret for them, and after being purified with sacramental absolution, they must have reverently received the sacrament of the Eucharist. They must also visit three churches designated by you or one of the churches three times and must say prayers there for the exaltation and prosperity of Holy Mother Church and the Apostolic See, for the elimination of heresies, for the peace and harmony of the Christian princes, and for the tranquillity and unity of the whole Christian people. Moreover they should fast once within the same period and give some alms to the poor. This indulgence can also be applied to the souls in purgatory. Since We desire even cloistered nuns and other people permanently in cloister to participate in this indulgence, as well as people in prisons, invalids, and other people prevented by any handicap from carrying out some of the aforementioned works, We grant the confessors the ability to exchange one work of piety for another or to defer it to another time. In addition, the confessors will have the power to give communion to children who have not yet had their first communion. Therefore, We authorize you on this occasion and during this three month period to bestow on the confessors of your dioceses all those same powers which We gave in the other jubilee announced through Our encyclical letter of November 21, 1851. We published that letter which begins with "Ex aliis nostris" and sent it to you. All those things which We excepted in that letter must be observed. In addition, We also grant you the favor of giving the faithful—both laymen and clerics—the ability on this occasion to choose their own confessors, either secular or regular, from those approved. We also grant this same power to the cloistered nuns exempt from the jurisdiction of the Ordinary and to other women living in cloister.

6. Set to work then, venerable brothers, since you have been called to share in Our cares and have been placed as guardians over the walls of Jerusalem. Do not cease night and day to cry to the Lord Our God with Us. Implore His divine mercy so that He may turn away the scourge of

His wrath, which we deserve for our sins and may mercifully bestow the riches of His goodness on everyone. We do not doubt that you will be totally content with these wishes and requests. And We know for certain that everyone, especially the clergy, the men and women in religious orders, and the faithful laity who worthily walk in the vocation to which they were called, will send prayers and supplications unceasingly to God. Nor would We neglect to ask the help of those who have obtained the palm of victory so that God might more easily bend His ear to Our prayers. Above all, We constantly call upon the Virgin Mary, the Immaculate Mother of God, who is the most suitable and most powerful intercessor with God and who is the mother of graces and mercies. Then We invoke the patronage of the blessed apostles Peter and Paul and of all the saints who reign with Christ in heaven. Nothing should be more important, nothing more preferable to you than to exhort the faithful entrusted to your care so that they, daily more firm and immovable, may persist in the profession of the Catholic faith; avoid the snares, lies, and deceptions of their enemies; advance more quickly in the ways of God's commandments; and carefully abstain from sin. From sin comes all the evils of the human race. For this reason never cease to inflame the zeal of the parish priests so that in discharging their office diligently, they may never stop instructing the Christian people entrusted to them in the principles and teachings of our faith, nourishing them through the administration of the sacraments, and exhorting them in sound doctrine.

7. Finally, as a sign of all heavenly gifts and as a witness of Our ardent love for you, receive the apostolic benediction which We affectionately impart to you and to all the clergy and laity entrusted to your care.

Given in Rome at St. Peter's on the first day of August in the year 1854, the nineth year of Our Pontificate.

†

LATIN TEXT: *Acta Pii IX*, I, 1:587-93.

ENGLISH TRANSLATION: Norman Desmarais.

REFERENCE:

1. St. John Chrysostom, homily 15 on the incomprehensible nature of God against the Anomaei.

OPTIME NOSCITIS

ENCYCLICAL OF POPE PIUS IX
ON EPISCOPAL MEETINGS
NOVEMBER 5, 1855
52

To Our Dearly Beloved Sons, the Cardinals of the Holy Roman Church, and Our Venerable Brothers, the Archbishops and Bishops of the Whole Austrian Empire.

Dearly Beloved Sons and Venerable Brothers, Greetings and Apostolic Benediction.

Faithfulness of Franz Josef

Beloved sons and venerable brothers, you know that Franz Josef Emperor of Austria has earned titles of respect from Us and from this Holy See for his ancient faith and piety and his extraordinary zeal for the Catholic cause. He obeyed Our wishes from the very beginning of his reign. He applied his concern and his thoughts to protecting the freedom of the Catholic Church in his jurisdiction. When he published his decree of April 18, 1850, he took positive action in this regard to the glory of his name and the rejoicing of all good men. Hence this exceptionally religious emperor and king complied with Our demands with an ever increasing filial piety. He realized how much the Catholic Church and its salutary doctrine leads to the true happiness and tranquillity of the people. He urgently asked Us if We wanted to enter an agreement with him. We would thus be able by Our apostolic authority to meet and to consult on the ecclesiastical affairs of his entire empire and of all areas in which his authority is established.

Agreement with Franz Josef

2. Therefore, with great joy, We freely consented to the pious wishes of this prince, and We decided to enter into an agreement with him. We derived great solace from this, since through that agreement, with the help of God, We can better protect the freedom of the Catholic Church and her rights (which ought to be upheld), and We can arrange even the most serious ecclesiastical affairs in his vast empire.

3. For this reason, while We greatly rejoice with Our beloved son in Christ and give him great and richly deserved praises because he glories in honoring Our religion and in following Us and the See of Peter with respect, We write this letter to you. By this letter We stir up your faith and pastoral solicitude. Thus perceiving all the advantages deriving from this greater freedom which the Catholic Church ought to enjoy in the Austrian Empire through this agreement, may you fulfill every aspect of your ministry with the greatest care, diligence, and zeal for the growth,

the glory, and the prosperity of the Church and for the salvation of souls.

Duties of Austrian Clergy

4. It will be your duty to zealously watch over the councils held among you so that the sacred trust of Our Catholic faith may be kept whole and inviolate in your dioceses. Be zealous and vigilant in supervising the proper education of priests, protect clerical discipline in good order, and restore it where it has deteriorated. Confer the office of parish priest and other ecclesiastical benefices only on worthy, suitable, and proven churchmen. Consider the salutary education of the youth and feed and nourish the flock entrusted to your care with the proclamation of the divine word and with useful advice and suitable writings. You should also hold both provincial and diocesan synods so that you might better provide for the good of your faithful. We think that some things ought to be mentioned to you which principally concern certain articles of that agreement and which We desire you to accomplish. Thus, the harmony from which the greatest benefits accrue to both Christian and civil society might be promoted more and more among that Catholic empire and the Church and the Apostolic See.

5. First of all, We advise you that when you publish your pastoral letters and other proceedings, send a copy of them to his Imperial and Apostolic Majesty and indicate to the government when you will hold synods. For that same reason, be careful to send the government a copy of the synodal acts since these things are matters of public interest. As for what pertains to the diocesan synods, know that many of your bishops strongly desire to provide themselves with that faculty which We granted to the bishop of Liège in the rescript published on May 4, 1851. We desire to comply with the wishes of those who requested this of Us and who explained at the same time the peculiar circumstances of each of their dioceses so that We might make the decisions which We deem most suitable for each diocese. We know for certain that nothing will ever be a better thing to stir up and promote in this Catholic government than religion and piety. Consequently, if the government indicates that it has some preference as to the form and method by which the religion textbooks used in the schools are written, you ought to consider the reason behind their wishes. However, your judgment and your right concerning the teachings which these books contain will always be preserved. Take care that those books are used for catechetical instruction in the primary or elementary schools through which the youth may learn the one and same immutable doctrine of the Catholic Church. See to it also that no change is ever made concerning those books unless there is a serious reason and after councils have been held among you. It is clear to you how important it is for both the sacred and civil orders that the youth, especially those destined for the clergy, be conformed to piety, to every virtue, and to an ecclesiastical spirit from an early age. They should be instructed in the humanities and especially in sacred studies, free from any danger of error. Therefore, as you are gathered in council take care that the foundation of ecclesiastical education is sure in your seminaries and that the system of the best course of studies thrives there. This system is able to prepare and to effect the greater welfare of the Church, so that the clergy shines forth in knowledge and teaching. Take special care and vigilance in choosing professors and teachers. Entrust the serious responsibility of teaching only to those men who are outstanding in religion, piety, purity, seriousness of conduct, and praise of sound doctrine.

6. However, through the sad and well-known vicissitudes of affairs, it may come about that one of the churchmen is found to be unacceptable to his Imperial and Apostolic Majesty. In order to entirely remove every difficulty, it will be your concern in granting parish ministries and other ecclesiastical benefices that churchmen who are not acceptable to his Imperial and Apostolic Majesty are not chosen for these duties. You will be able to determine this either by the character and condition of the clerics, by the precedents set by the government, or by other suitable means. In addition, it is necessary that you diligently inquire whether his Imperial and Apostolic Majesty has something against the candidates in political matters before you choose professors and teachers for the seminary. Finally, it should be your duty to carefully and constantly watch that in ecclesiastical functions and especially in the holy sacrifice of the Mass and in the administration of the sacraments, the formulae of the

Church should be adopted in the language of every rite which has been approved by the Holy See.

7. You should not cease to take care that prelates subject to the bishops do not celebrate sacraments in the future by the pontifical rite unless they have already obtained a special privilege from the Holy See and only on condition that those who obtain that privilege should carefully observe all those things outlined in Pope Alexander VII's decree published on September 27, 1659, and in Pius VII's apostolic letter of July 4, 1823.

8. You now have heard what We wanted to tell you. We do not doubt that you will welcome Our counsels with eager ears and will take care to diligently receive and execute everything We spoke of because of your piety and your singular obedience toward Us and this Holy See. Meanwhile, We do not cease to humbly beseech Almighty God to bestow upon you His abundant gifts of goodness. May He bless your pastoral concerns, plans, and labors to the end that Our holy religion and its doctrines may grow daily in your dioceses and may thrive and flourish everywhere. As a sign of all heavenly gifts and as a testimony of Our love for you, We affectionately grant Our apostolic blessing to each one of you and to all the priests and the faithful entrusted to your care.

Given in Rome, at St. Peter's, on the fifth day of November in the year 1855, the tenth year of Our Pontificate.

†

LATIN TEXT: *Acta Pii IX*, I, 2:485-91.

ENGLISH TRANSLATION: Norman Desmarais.

SINGULARI QUIDEM

ENCYCLICAL OF POPE PIUS IX ON
THE CHURCH IN AUSTRIA
MARCH 17, 1856
53

To Our Beloved Sons the Cardinals of the Holy Roman Church and to Our Venerable Brothers the Archbishops and Bishops of the Austrian Empire.

Beloved Sons and Venerable Brothers, Greetings and Apostolic Blessing.

Implementation of the Concordat

It is with a special joy that We learn of your willing response to Our wishes and those of Our dear son in Jesus Christ, Franz-Josef, emperor of Austria and apostolic king. These wishes were communicated to each of you at almost the same time. In your eminent devotion and pastoral concern, you met in the imperial city of Vienna to discuss the most suitable means of executing the provisions of the concordat which We agreed upon with the Emperor. This illustrious and religious prince wished to conclude the concordat with Us to protect the Church in its rights—to Our great consolation, to the immortal glory of his name, and to the joy of all good people. That is why We cannot now refrain from showing you Our intimate and affectionate feelings. At the same time, We thank you for showing such remarkable love for the Church by gathering in these conferences. You will thus better understand the goodwill We feel for you and for all the faithful of this empire who are entrusted to your care. First of all, let us consider the execution of that concordat which contains, as you know, many articles whose implementation depends especially on you. We ardently desire that you all agree and follow the same method of putting them into practice, while keeping in mind the diverse demands of the various provinces in that vast empire of Austria. If any doubt or difficulty arises concerning the meaning of some article—which We do not believe will happen—you should submit these difficulties to Us. After having come to an understanding with his Imperial Majesty (as stipulated in article 35 of the concordat), We shall offer an appropriate solution.

2. We embrace the Lord's entire flock, which was entrusted to Us by Jesus Christ, with ardent love. Furthermore Our apostolic ministry imposes on Us the duty of using all Our powers to obtain the eternal salvation of all peoples and all nations. Our love and Our ministry urge Us to arouse more and more your eminent piety, strength, and pastoral concern. We do this so that you might continue to fulfill all the duties of your episcopal office with an ever greater ardor and so that you spare no care, no counsel, and no effort to keep the deposit of our holy faith pure

and intact in your dioceses. You should assure the safety of your flock and defend it against all the snares and deceptions of the enemies. You are familiar with the perverse schemes and monstrous errors of opinion which the astute partisans of impious doctrines use to lead people—especially the imprudent and the uneducated—from the path of truth and justice into error and perdition.

Indifferentism

3. Among the many deplorable evils which disturb and afflict both ecclesiastical and civil society, two stand out in our day and are justly considered to be the cause of the others. In effect, you are aware of the innumerable and fatal damages which the hideous error of *indifferentism* causes to Christian and civil society. It causes us to forget out duties to God in whom we live and act and have our being. It causes us to slacken our concern for holy religion and shakes almost to destruction the very basis of all law, justice, and virtue. There is little difference between this hideous form of indifference and the devilish system of *indifference between the different religions*. This belief embraces people who have strayed from the truth, who are enemies of the true faith and forget their own salvation, and who teach contradictory beliefs without firm doctrine. They make no distinction between the different creeds, agree with everybody, and maintain that the haven of eternal salvation is open to sectarians of any religion. The diversity of their teachings does not concern them as long as they agree to combat that which alone is the truth.[1]

4. You see, dearly beloved sons and venerable brothers, how much vigilance is needed to keep the disease of this terrible evil from infecting and killing your flocks. Do not cease to diligently defend your people against these pernicious errors. Saturate them with the doctrine of Catholic truth more accurately each day. Teach them that just as there is only one God, one Christ, one Holy Spirit, so there is also only one truth which is divinely revealed. There is only one divine faith which is the beginning of salvation for mankind and the basis of all justification, the faith by which the just person lives and without which it is impossible to please God and to come to the community of His children.[2] There is only one true, holy, Catholic church, which is the Apostolic Roman Church. There is only one See founded in Peter by the word of the Lord,[3] outside of which we cannot find either true faith or eternal salvation. He who does not have the Church for a mother cannot have God for a father, and whoever abandons the See of Peter on which the Church is established trusts falsely that he is in the Church.[4] Thus, there can be no greater crime, no more hideous stain than to stand up against Christ, than to divide the Church engendered and purchased by His blood, than to forget evangelical love and to combat with the furor of hostile discord the harmony of the people of God.[5]

Worship

5. Divine worship consists in these two things: pious doctrines and good works, in such a way that doctrines without good works cannot please God, nor does God accept works divorced from religious doctrines. The narrow and difficult path which leads to life can be found not in the practice of the virtues alone or in the observance of precepts, but on the way of faith.[6] Constantly arouse your faithful people so that they will persevere ever more firmly and constantly in the profession of the Catholic religion. Let them likewise endeavor to assure their calling and their election by means of good works. While you work at the salvation of your flock, strive also, in all goodness, patience, and teaching, to recall the unfortunate strays to the one fold of Christ and to Catholic unity. Address to them especially these words of St. Augustine: "Come, brothers, if you wish, so that you may be grafted to the vine. We are saddened to see you thus cut off and lying so. Count the bishops who have occupied the See of Peter; see this uninterrupted succession of popes. See the rock against which the powers of hell will not be able to prevail."[7] "Whoever eats the lamb outside of this house is an impious person. Whoever is not in Noah's ark will perish in the flood."[8]

Rationalism

6. Another disease just as dangerous is spreading, a disease to which the name of rationalism has been given, because of the pride and a certain vanity of reason associated with it. Certainly the Church does not condemn[9] the efforts of those who want to know the truth, since it is God who made it the nature of man to be most

eager to grasp truth. Nor does she condemn the efforts of healthy and right reason, for it is through this reason that we cultivate the spirit, study nature, and bring to light its most hidden secrets. This tender mother recognizes and justly maintains that reason is the most notable of the heavenly gifts,[10] since it is through reason that we raise ourselves above the senses and display a certain image of God in ourselves. She knows that we must search until we find and that we must believe what we have believed. But we must also believe, in addition, that there is nothing else to believe and to seek once we have found and believed what was taught by Christ, who does not command us to seek anything other than what He taught.[11] What is it that the Church does not tolerate? What is it that she censures and absolutely condemns in virtue of her mission to preserve what has been entrusted to her? The Church has always condemned and continues to condemn the conduct of those who abuse their reason; those who do not fear to foolishly and criminally prefer reason to the authority of what God Himself says; those who boldly exalt themselves; those who, blinded by their pride and their vanity, lose the light of truth and proudly spurn the faith of which it is written: "Whoever does not believe will be condemned."[12] Full of confidence in themselves,[13] they deny that we must believe in God for Himself and accept what He taught us about Himself. The Church does not cease to oppose these people,[14] since whenever something deals with the very knowledge of God, it is God whom we should believe. It is from Him that all we believe about Him comes, because man could not know God if He Himself did not communicate this salutary knowledge.

7. These are the people whom the Church seeks to bring back to sound reasoning with these words: "What is there more contrary to reason than to seek to exalt oneself above reason by means of reason itself? And what is more contrary to faith than to not want to believe that which we cannot attain by reason?"[15] She never ceases to repeat to them that faith bases itself not on reason but on authority[16] because it is not suitable that God, in speaking to mankind, should use arguments, as if we could refuse to believe. Rather, He spoke as was appropriate, as the supreme judge of everything, who does not have to argue but who rather issues His pronouncements.[17] The Church clearly declares that the only hope of salvation for mankind is placed in the Christian faith, which teaches the truth, scatters the darkness of ignorance by the splendor of its light, and works through love. This hope of salvation is placed in the Catholic Church which, in preserving the true worship, is the solid home of this faith and the temple of God. Outside of the Church, nobody can hope for life or salvation unless he is excused through ignorance beyond his control. The Church teaches and proclaims that if sometimes we can use human wisdom to study the divine word, our wisdom should not for that reason proudly usurp to itself the right of master. Rather, it should act as an obedient and submissive servant, afraid of erring if it goes first and afraid of losing the light of interior virtue and the straight path of truth by following the consequences of exterior words.[18]

Singulari quidem 53

Progress in the Church

8. We should not conclude that religion does not progress in the Church of Christ. There is great progress! But it is truly the progress of faith, which is not change. The intelligence, wisdom, and knowledge of everybody should grow and progress, like that of the whole Church of the ages. In this way we might understand more clearly what we used to believe obscurely; in this way posterity might have joy of understanding what used to be revered without understanding. In this way the precious stones of divine dogma might be worked, adapted exactly and wisely decorated, so that they increase in grace, splendor, and beauty—but always in the same fashion and doctrine, in the same meaning and judgment, so that we can speak of a new manner rather than new substance.[19]

9. We do not think that any one of you will be surprised if We speak again about these sorrowful matters so destructive to religious and civil society. In this way we fulfill the office of Our primacy and sovereignty in the faith.[20] Nor will you be surprised if We presume to arouse your episcopal vigilance. Since the enemy does not cease to sow weeds among the wheat, We have been placed in charge of the cultivation of the Lord's field. We have been placed by divine Providence at the head of God's family as faithful and prudent servants,[21] so We should not neglect for

an instant to fulfill these duties which are inseparable from Our apostolic ministry.

Church Councils

10. Now We entreat you by your singular piety and prudence to take with wisdom and foresight the means which you believe at this meeting to be especially suitable for obtaining the greater glory of God and the eternal salvation of mankind in this vast empire. We sincerely rejoice to see the numerous faithful, both clergy and laity, animated by the spirit of faith and Christian love and spreading the good name of Jesus Christ. We are nonetheless deeply afflicted to know that in certain places some members of the clergy forget their dignity and their duty, choosing not to walk in the way of the vocation to which they were called. The Christian people, too little instructed in the holy precepts of our divine religion and exposed to serious dangers, unfortunately abstain from works of piety and from frequenting the sacraments. They stray from good moral practices and from the discipline of a Christian life and hurry to their ruin. Knowing your pastoral concern, We are persuaded that you will use all your cares and all your thoughts to bring about the complete cessation of the evil which We have just described. You know that the canonical decrees wisely prescribed provincial councils and Our holy bishops always celebrated them to the great advantage of the Church. These councils contribute very much to the renewal of ecclesiastical discipline, to correcting the habits of the people, and to the removal of whatever might be harmful to them. We ardently desire that you celebrate provincial councils in conformity with the holy canons, so that suitable and salutary remedies might be applied to the evils which commonly afflict the ecclesiastical provinces of the empire.

11. Many serious matters need to be treated in these provincial councils. We desire that, at your meeting in Vienna, you take united measures by which you are able to agree on the principal points which need to be treated and established in the provincial synods. Furthermore you should with one and the same zeal take action so that in all the provinces of this empire, Our divine religion and its salutary doctrine might thrive, flourish, and rule. Then the faithful will walk as sons of light in all goodness, justice, and truth, leaving the bad and doing the good. There is nothing more effective in leading others to virtue, piety, and divine worship than the life and example of those who have consecrated themselves to the holy ministry. Do not neglect to establish as soon as possible whatever can restore ecclesiastical discipline where it has fallen and foster its accurate establishment wherever necessary.

Exhortation to the Clergy

12. Beloved sons and venerable brothers, see to this matter with a common accord. Unite your efforts and your cares so that the clergy never forget their dignity and their duty, avoiding everything which is forbidden to them. Shining with every virtue, they should be an example for the faithful in their words, in love, in faith, and in chastity. They should pray the breviary each day with suitable attention and devotion and should exercise themselves in holy prayer. They should apply themselves to the meditation of heavenly matters and should love the beauty of God's house. Let them exercise the sacred duties and ceremonies according to the Pontifical and the Roman Ritual, and let them fulfill the offices of their ministry with diligence, wisdom, and holiness. They should work continually to obtain the eternal salvation of mankind, never ceasing in their zealous discharge of sacred discipline.

13. Watch with equal care that the canons and the other beneficiaries of the metropolitan, cathedral, and collegiate churches who are bound to chair duty excel in seriousness of conduct, integrity of life, and zeal for piety. They should shine like brilliant lights placed on the lampstand in the Lord's temple, carefully fulfilling all the duties of their charge and observing the law of residence. They should concern themselves with the distinction of divine worship. Full of ardor in the Lord's vigils, let them celebrate the divine lauds with attention, exactness, piety, and religion, and not with a distracted mind, wandering eyes, and unsuitable conduct. They should always remember that they gather in choir not only to render to God the honor and worship which are due Him, but also to implore Him for every good thing for themselves and for others.

14. Each of you knows very well how spiritual exercises contribute to preserving and fostering an ecclesiastical spirit and to retaining a salutary constancy. For that reason the popes of the past enriched them with countless indulgences, and you should constantly recommend them to the priests placed under your authority. They should retire frequently for a certain number of days to a suitable place where, far from human cares, they can purify themselves from the stains accumulated with the dust of the world. They should also occupy themselves with reviving the grace which the imposition of hands conferred on them, and with putting off the old man and his works and putting on the new man created in justice and holiness. They should do this through the careful consideration before God of their thoughts, words, and deeds. They should also meditate with care on eternity and remember the immense gifts they have received from God.

Education of Clerics

15. The lips of the priests must protect the wisdom which allows them to respond to those who consult them on the law and to convince those who combat it. It is thus necessary that you apply yourselves with the greatest care to the correct and precise instruction of the clergy. Especially in your seminaries, see that an excellent and entirely Catholic course of studies flourishes, a course by which the young clerics, under the direction of approved teachers, might be formed right from their most tender years to piety, virtue, and a Christian spirit. They should be instructed in the knowledge of Latin, in the humanities, and in philosophy, free from every danger of error. Then apply yourselves to teaching them carefully, for a sufficiently long period, dogmatic and moral theology based on the Holy Scriptures, on the tradition of the holy Fathers, and on the infallible authority of the Church. Give them a solid knowledge of the Holy Scriptures, of the sacred canons, of church history, and of the liturgy. Exercise the greatest precaution in choosing books, lest in the deluge of errors which prevails everywhere the young seminarians might be imprudently led off the path of sound doctrine. You know that there are learned men who dissent from this Holy See in religious matters and who are cut off from the Church. They are publishing the Holy Scriptures and the works of the holy Fathers, undoubtedly with a pleasing elegance but often—We cannot deplore this enough—in an altered condition, turned away from their true meaning by perverted commentaries.

16. Each of you knows how much the Church needs capable ministers, especially in these times. It needs ministers who valiantly watch over the cause of God and His holy Church. It needs ministers who stand out in holiness of living and reputation for salutary teaching, who are powerful in word and deed and who build a faithful house for the Lord. Do not neglect anything in educating the young clerics in holiness and wisdom even from their tender years, for they will not be able to become useful ministers of the Church unless they are properly taught. Also, to more easily effect that clerical education on which the good of the Church and the salvation of its people greatly depends, seek money from the leading churchmen of your dioceses and the wealthy laymen who are especially zealous for Catholic interests. At your example, they might offer the money for you to establish new seminaries and endow them suitably, so that the young seminarians might receive a good education right from their early years.

Singulari quidem
53

Education of Catholic Youth

17. Be equally zealous that, regardless of sex or status, the youth of your dioceses might be educated in an ever more Catholic manner. Let this youth be full of the spirit of the fear of God and nourished with the milk of piety. Let Catholic youth be carefully instructed in the elements of the faith and brought to a fuller understanding of our holy religion. They should be formed in virtue, moral uprightness, and a Christian way of life. Let them be kept from all the flatteries and dangers of perversion and corruption. Constantly arouse the faithful people entrusted to you to greater religion and piety. Do everything possible so that, ever more nourished by the salutary food of truth and Catholic doctrine, these faithful people might love God with all their heart and zealously observe His commandment. Let them enter His temple frequently and religiously and keep holy the Sabbath, for they should piously attend the celebration of the divine sacrifice and the holy sacraments of Penance and Eucharist. May they honor the holy Mother of God, the Immaculate Virgin Mary, with a special devotion. They should maintain a mutual love among themselves and, persevering in prayer, they should approach God worthily, pleasing Him in everything and bearing fruit in every good deed. Furthermore, the holy missions given by suitable workers arouse the spirit of faith and religion among the people and recall them to the path of virtue and salvation. Thus We ardently desire that you support them as much as possible in your dioceses. We also bestow great and well-deserved praise on those among you who have already introduced such a salutary work in your dioceses. We are happy to see that, with the help of God's grace, they have produced abundant fruit.

Diocesan Synods and Visitation

18. Keep these points in mind so that your common action might bring suitable remedies to your common ills. Furthermore, nothing is more effective in repairing serious damage and in obtaining prosperity than the frequent visitation of your dioceses and the convocation of diocesan synods. You know that these are two things which the Council of Trent especially recommended. In your concern and your love for the flock entrusted to you, do not neglect the zealous visitation of your dioceses, in conformity with the canonical prescriptions. Do everything necessary to make this visitation produce happy fruits. Above all, eradicate entirely the errors, abuses, and vices which have penetrated into your diocese. Use vigilance, paternal punishments, useful discussions, and whatever means you find suitable to remove them. Spread salutary teaching and preserve intact the clerical discipline. Help and strengthen the faithful with all sorts of assistance, especially with spiritual aids; win everyone to Jesus Christ. Convene the diocesan synods, according to the prescriptions of the holy canons, with equal zeal. Take the measures which you think are the most beneficial to your dioceses. We ardently desire that you hasten to establish conferences in all the regions of your dioceses with suitable regulations. In this way the priests who must apply themselves to reading and study, to teaching the people everything they must know for eternal salvation, and to administering the sacraments,[22] will not see their taste for the sacred disciplines diminish or their zeal languish. These conferences should bear especially on questions of moral theology and liturgy. Each and every priest should be bound to attend and to bring a written treatise on the topic you propose. You should set aside a time in these conferences to discuss moral theology or liturgical discipline after one of these priests has presented his speech on the duties of the priesthood.

Supervision of Priests

19. The priests are your assistants in the government of your flock, and they are called to share your cares and to be your collaborators in the exercise of very important matters. Do not forget to enkindle their zeal so that they will fulfill their own duties with suitable diligence and piety. Encourage them to preach the divine word to the people entrusted to their care. They should administer the sacraments and bestow on the people the grace of God in all its aspects. Let them lovingly and patiently instruct the ignorant—especially the children—in the mysteries of the Christian faith and in the teachings of our religion. Exhort them to bring back to the path of salvation those who have strayed, for they should use all their strength to destroy hatreds, rivalries, enmities, discords, and scandals. They should strengthen the weak and visit the infirm, helping them with all kinds of aids, especially spiritual ones. Encourage them to console the afflicted, and the unfortunate. They should exhort everyone in sound doctrine and warn all people to render conscientiously to Caesar what is Caesar's and to God what is God's. They should teach everybody to be subject to the princes and to the authorities in everything that is not contrary to the laws of God and of the Church, not only because of the threat of punishment but also for the sake of conscience itself. Continue, as you are doing to your great praise, to send reports concerning the situation of your dioceses to Our Congregation for the Council. Carefully inform Us of everything which concerns them, so that We might always take the necessary measures for your greater good and the greater good of your diocese. We have learned that in a few dioceses of Germany some customs have arisen concerning the union of parishes—customs which some of you wish to preserve. We are disposed to look with favor on this; but first of all We wish to carefully examine each one of these customs, in order to allow them only within the limits of necessity and of particular circumstances. It is a duty of Our apostolic ministry to watch with the greatest care that in general, the canonical prescriptions are strictly observed.

Concern for the Eastern Rite

20. Before terminating this letter, We address Ourselves particularly to those Austrian archbishops and bishops who are united to us in the true faith and in Catholic unity, adhere to the See of Peter, and follow the rites and praiseworthy customs of the Eastern Church, customs approved or permitted by the Holy See. You know how this Apostolic See has always esteemed your rites. It has tried to bring about their observance in many ways, as shown by the decrees and constitutions of the popes who have preceded Us. Among these, let it suffice to recall the letter of Benedict XIV which begins *Allatae* and is dated July 26, 1755, and Our own letter of January 6, 1848, which begins with the words, *In Suprema Petri Aposotli Sede.* We exhort you then to fulfill your ministry in conformity with your devotion and pastoral concern. Keep in mind everything about which We have spoken. Use your cares, efforts, and vigilance so that your clergy might be adorned with every virtue and educated in the best teachings, especially in the ecclesiastical disciplines. May they apply themselves diligently to obtaining the eternal salvation of the faithful in such a way that these people persevere in the way which leads to life, so that the holy unity of the Catholic religion may increase and spread. May the sacraments be administered and the divine office celebrated according to your own teachings, using the books approved by this Holy See. As We ardently desire to meet your needs and those of your people promptly, do not hesitate to turn to Us and report on the situation in your dioceses by sending a report every four years on this matter to Our Congregation for the Propagation of the Faith.

Closing Remarks

21. Finally, We solemnly entreat you to preserve, strengthen, and increase peace and harmony among the clergy of each diocese, both of the Latin rite and of the Greek Catholic rite. Thus, all who fight in the army of the Lord should overtake each other in mutual affection and fraternal charity, serving in unanimity and zeal the glory of God and the salvation of souls.

22. Dearly beloved sons and venerable brothers, these are the things which We especially wanted to communicate to you, in Our ardent love for you and for the faithful people of this vast Empire. In considering your excellent virtue, your religious piety, and your proven fidelity to Us and to the See of Peter, We are confident that you will willingly support these wishes and paternal counsels. We do not doubt that you will contemplate unceasingly your model, Jesus Christ the Chief Shepherd. We expect you to follow in the footsteps of Him who showed Himself meek and humble of heart and who gave His life for His sheep in order to leave us His example to follow. Put all your efforts into following His examples and practicing His teachings. Watch over your flock and fulfill your ministry; seek not that which comes from you but that which comes from Jesus Christ. Consider yourselves not as exercising a power of domination over the clergy but as shepherds—rather as loving fathers who desire to become models for the flock. May nothing ever seem to you to be too burdensome, too difficult, too trying. Always be ready to suffer everything in all patience, gentleness, meekness, and prudence to try everything for the salvation of your sheep. As for Us, in the humility of Our heart, We do not cease to raise continuous and fervent prayers to the all-loving father of lights and mercies, the God of all consolation. We pray that He will see fit to bestow on you the most abundant gifts of his goodness and to bestow them with the same abundance on the dear sheep entrusted to you. As a pledge of this divine help and as a sign of Our affection for you, We lovingly impart the apostolic blessing to you, dearly beloved and venerable brothers, and to all the faithful of your dioceses, both clergy and laity.

Given in Rome, at St. Peter's, on the 17th day of March in the year 1856, in the tenth year of Our pontificate.

†

LATIN TEXT: *Acta Pii IX*, I, 2:510-30.

ENGLISH TRANSLATION: Norman Desmarais

REFERENCES:

1. Tertullian, *de praescript.*, chap. 41.
2. Rom 1; Heb 11; Council of Trent, session 6, chap. 8.
3. St. Cyprian, epistle 43.
4. Ibid., *de unitat. Eccl.*
5. Ibid., *epistle* 72.
6. St.Cyril of Jerusalem, Cath. 4. Illumind., no. 2; St. Leo, sermon 5, *de Nativit. Dom.*
7. *In psal. contr. part. Donat.*
8. St. Jerome, epistle 14(57) to Damasus.

9. Lactantius, *divin. institut.*, bk. 3, chap. 1.
10. Clemens Alex, *Stromat*, bk. 1, chap. 3 and bk. 2, chap. 2; Gregory, *thaumaturg*, panegyrical speech, 7. 13.
11. Tertullian, *de praescript.*, chap. 9.
12. Mk 16.16.
13. St. Hilar., *de Trin.*, bk. 4.
14. Cassian, *de Incarnat.*, bk. 4, chap. 2.
15. St. Bernard, epistle 190.
16. Ibid, *de Considerat*, bk. 5, chap. 3.
17. Lactantius, *divin. institut.*, bk. 3, chap. 1.
18. St. Peter Damian, opuscul. 36, chap. 5.
19. Vinc. Lirin. Commonitor.
20. St. Ambrose, *de Incarnat.*, chap. 4, no. 32; Cassian, *de Incarnat.*, bk. 3, chap. 12.
21. Ibid., *de fide ad Gratian*, bk. 5, prologue.
22. Council of Trent, session 23, chap. 14 on reform.

CUM NUPER

ENCYCLICAL OF POPE PIUS IX
ON CARE FOR CLERICS
JANUARY 20, 1858
54

To Our Venerable Brothers, the Archbishops, Bishops and other Ordinaries of the Kingdom of the Two Sicilies.

Greetings and Apostolic Blessing.

Last Christmas We received your kind letter, in which once more professing your singular piety, love, and observance toward Us and this See of Peter, you indicate that you are constantly praying that God may aid Our humble person as We labor with the greatest solicitude for all the Churches throughout the world. These extraordinary expressions moved Us to write this encyclical letter to all of you who discharge your pastoral office in the Kingdom of the Two Sicilies, so that you may understand the love and concern We feel toward you and the faithful committed to your care.

2. Indeed We can scarcely express Our deep sorrow upon learning last December that a great many of your towns were so profoundly shaken by terrible earthquakes that a countless multitude of your peoples were killed by collapsing walls. King Ferdinand II, greatly grieved, has continuously offered support and financial help for the afflicted and prostrate inhabitants of these towns. As soon as the sad news of this great calamity reached Us, We implored God's mercy for these unhappy people and begged Him to heal the tribulations of the earth, whose foundations were so dreadfully shaken.

3. Holy Scripture clearly teaches that these scourges of God are provoked by the sins of men; therefore we exhort that, in fulfilling your ministry, your primary concern may be to turn the faithful committed to your care aside from sin and wrong-doing and to lead them in the paths of virtue, justice, and religion.

Excesses of the Clergy

4. To Our mutual grief some clergy in your Kingdom, having forgotten their vocation, arouse the indigation of God by their reprehensible manner of life which, of course sets a bad example for the Christian people. For this reason you should strive to obliterate the corruption and abuses which have made their inroads into the conduct of the Clergy; support instead a sound way of life for them in keeping with the discipline of the holy canons. Properly train the younger clergy from their earliest years in piety, holiness, and religious spirit; see that they have a strong foundation in liberal arts, solid learning, and knowledge of the sacred canons.

Who Should be Ordained

5. First and foremost, keeping always in mind the precepts of the Apostle, be most careful

not to lay hands prematurely on anyone and be extremely cautious in conferring sacred orders. Never, from a misplaced sense of obligation, partisanship, or favor, join to the clergy and promote to ecclesiastical grades and orders those who, not having even minimally the gifts required by the sacred canons, should be totally rejected from sacred ministry. He who does not fear to initiate into sacred orders those who are unworthy inflicts great harm on the Church. Therefore, your first concern is to strictly follow the prescriptions of the sacred canons. Carefully examine and scrutinize each candidate's origin, training, talents, character, and teaching. Ordain only those outstanding individuals who can truly benefit your dioceses. If they earnestly reject all things which are forbidden to clerics and which never become them, they may be an example to the faithful in "word, speech, charity, faith, and chastity."

Clerical Responsibilities

6. Moreover, examine most intently the conduct, honesty, piety, knowledge, and prudence of those to whom the care and direction of souls is to be committed. Be ever vigilant that pastors fulfill their office zealously, wisely and holily. They should never fail to feed the Christian people entrusted to them by means of preaching the divine word, of administering the sacraments, and of dispensing of the multiple grace of God. They should diligently imbue young people especially and the uneducated with the mysteries and teachings of our divine religion and form them in all piety and virtue. If pastors do not fulfill their duty, religion and public life are damaged, morals are perverted, Christian discipline weakens, the exercise of religious worship declines, and all sorts of vices overwhelm people.

7. Moreover, you must be especially watchful that young people of both sexes be educated in fear of the Lord and His law and that they be trained in moral integrity. Accordingly, diligently inspect both private and public schools; see that your young people are free from all danger and that they receive a sound and completely Catholic education. Stretch, therefore, every fiber of your pastoral zeal to obtain this goal, since you know that the prosperity of the spiritual and civil communities depends greatly on the proper education of the youth. You know also the manifold evils by which, in these iniquitous times, the enemies of God and man attempt to pervert and corrupt the innocence of youth.

8. With similar diligence instruct the faithful in the doctrines of Catholic religion by word and by writing. Defend the people from the contagion of so many diabolic errors. Warn them to stand firm and unmoveable in the profession of our most holy faith and to observe most diligently the laws of God and His holy Church, never allowing themselves to be deceived and led into error by the followers of perverse doctrine. However, unwholesome books emerge everywhere; in them the most skillful fabricators of lies attempt to mislead everyone by corrupt and evil opinions of all sorts and to confuse things human and divine in order to cause the foundations of Christian and civil society to collapse. Strive to avert and repel this deadly pestilence of books from your flock. And, that you may the more easily and readily protect sound doctrine and good morals and close even avenues of approach to error and corruption, do not fail to inspect accurately all books, especially those which treat of philosophy, theology, and sacred matters and also those which deal with canon and civil law.

9. You know that it is also part of your episcopal duty to protect and vindicate at all times the venerable rights of the Church. You must preserve its goods and be concerned for their careful administration. Take the utmost care that pious legacies, especially those with regard to Masses, and other obligations be scrupulously observed and religiously carried out with all fraud and base gain far removed. With skill and prudence, you must provide that all business in your individual episcopal Curias be handled with all fairness, equity, and honesty. Therefore, venerable brothers, take great care that in your episcopal Curias, those men alone be engaged who, approved because of their integrity of life and skill in managing things, can carry out wisely and honestly the tasks delegated by you. And We most strongly ask that you try to judge ecclesiastical cases which belong to your tribunals according to the prescripts of the sacred canons and the force of convention with great care and inquiry. Likewise strive to see that your sentences are properly carried out, and, if there is need, seek the help and assistance of the civil power to this end.

10. Moreover, since Religious men are supplied to bishops to be helpers in the cultivation of the Lord's vineyard, as Benedict XIV, advises,[1]

continually exhort them, emulating their founders, to return in a thoroughly religious fashion that which they vowed and to lead their lives according to the prescribed laws and to perform useful work in word, example, and prayer for you and your dioceses.

11. Also, with special concern and charity look after virgins sacred to God. They are the choice part of your flocks, the flower of the ecclesiastical plant, the ornament of spiritual grace. Afford them assistance, so that mindful of their holy vocation by which they have dedicated themselves to God, they may avert their eyes from human things and raise them always to heavenly ones. Then daily advancing from virtue to virtue, they may strive to diffuse the spirit of Christ everywhere. And We especially request that you attempt to carry out exactly what Benedict XIV wisely advised in His Constitution concerning the designation of extraordinary confessors for nuns.[2]

12. Finally, venerable brothers, We greatly desire that you be careful to hold Provincial Councils according to the precepts of the holy canons. For surely, you know that in this way, having consulted among yourselves and weighed everything properly, you may more wisely provide opportune remedies for ills and promote the prosperity of your dioceses; thereafter you will hold diocesan synods, which are mandatory under canonical sanction. In your Kingdom some archbishops lack suffragans, and some bishops do not have their metropolitan present; therefore they cannot hold a provincial council. It will be up to the prudence of these same holy bishops, having duly weighed all circumstances of place, time and situation, to convene with bishops with whom they think it more expedient in the Lord to hold councils of this sort without however any detriment to the rights and privileges enjoyed by any absent bishops and without the slightest change regarding the status of their Churches.

13. We have indicated to you those things which We thought should be indicated to you above all else. We know that you will wish to satisfy Our wishes and admonitions because Ferdinand II, illustrious King of the Two Sicilies, stretches out to you now his helping hand. We are confident that under his leadership, the Church in his kingdom will enjoy all liberty and exercise all its rights, as God and the sanctions of the sacred canons ordain.

14. Meanwhile, We humbly but earnestly pray and beseech Our merciful God to continue to pour more propitiously His richest gifts of goodness upon you. May He bless your pastoral cares, counsels, and labors, so that the faithful entrusted to you may daily and with greater fortitude turn aside from evil and do good. Growing in the knowledge of God and the love of Our Lord Jesus Christ may they walk worthily before God, pleasing Him in all things, and may they be fruitful in all good works. As a guarantee thereof and a clear sign of Our special benevolence to you, receive the apostolic blessing, venerable brothers, which from the bottom of Our heart We lovingly impart to you yourselves and all the clergy of your churches, and to the faithful laity.

Given in Rome at St. Peter's, 20 January 1858, in the 12th year of Our Pontificate.

†

LATIN TEXT: *Acta Pii IX*, I, 3:8-16.

ENGLISH TRANSLATION: Robert F. Healey, S.J.

REFERENCES:

1. Apostolic constitution *Impositi Nobis*, 27 February 1746.
2. Apostolic constitution *Pastoralis curae*, 5 August 1748.

AMANTISSIMI REDEMPTORIS

ENCYCLICAL OF POPE PIUS IX ON PRIESTS
AND THE CARE OF SOULS
MAY 3, 1858
55

To Our Venerable Brothers, the Patriarchs, Primates, Archbishops, Bishops, other Ordinaries who have Friendship and Communion with the Apostolic See.

Greetings and Apostolic Blessing.

Christ's love towards men was so great that not only was He willing to endure most cruel sufferings for our salvation and an atrocious death on the cross, but also He wished to nourish us eternally in the sacrament of His body and blood. In this way, He might strengthen us by the presence of His divinity and be the safest bulwark of our spiritual life. And not content to have loved us with such an outstanding and truly divine love, He heaped benefits on benefits, poured out the riches of His love upon us, and, as you know so well, having loved His own He loved them to the end. For, declaring Himself to be an eternal Priest according to the order of Melchisedech, He instituted permanently His priesthood in the Catholic Church. He decreed that that same sacrifice which He performed is to redeem the whole human race from the yoke of sin to reconcile all things in heaven and earth, and to remain until the consummation of the world. He decreed that it be renewed and take place daily by the ministry of the priesthood. Only the reason for the offering is diverse, namely, that the salvific and most abundant fruits of His passion might forever be dispersed upon mankind.

2. In the unbloody sacrifice of the Mass, celebrated by priests, the same life-giving victim is offered up. This entreaty reconciles us to God the Father. It "renews in a mysterious way the death of Christ, who having risen from the dead dies no longer. Death no longer has domination over Him. Still, He is sacrificed for us in the mystery of this sacred oblation."[1]

Benefits of the Mass

3. No unworthiness or wickedness on the part of those offering it can ever defile this oblation. The Lord predicted through Malachy that it would be great and would be cleanly offered from sunrise to sunset in all places to His name.[2] This oblation abounding with an unspeakable richness of fruit embraces the present and future life. For by this oblation God is pleased and, granting the grace and gift of repentance, remits even great crimes and sins. Although grievously offended by our sins, He is moved from anger to mercy, from the severity of just chastisement to clemency; by it the title and obligation of temporal punishment is dissolved; by it the souls of the departed in Christ

who have not yet been fully purged are aided; by it temporal goods also are obtained, if they do not stand in the way of greater benefits; by it singular honor and cult are procured for the saints and especially for the Immaculate and most holy Mother of God, the Virgin Mary. Wherefore, from the apostolic tradition, we offer the divine sacrifice of the Mass "for the universal peace of the Churches; for the right disposition of the world; for rulers, soldiers, allies; those laboring with infirmity; those oppressed by afflictions; for all who are in need; for those detained in purgatory; with the belief that it will be a help to those souls for whom prayer is offered before the holy and most awesome victim lying before us."[3]

Specifications for the Mass

4. Nothing is greater or holier than the unbloody sacrifice of the Mass, in which the body and blood of Christ are offered to God for the salvation of all. Holy Mother the Church has always been careful and diligent in order that the Mass be celebrated by priests with clean and pure hearts. It should be celebrated with the proper splendor of sacred ceremonies and rites so that the greatness of this mystery will shine forth all the more even from external appearances. This will also arouse the faithful to the contemplation of divine things hidden in such an admirable and venerable sacrifice. And with like solicitude and devotion, the same most holy Mother has never ceased to urge, exhort, and influence her faithful sons to frequently attend this divine sacrifice with due piety, veneration and devotion. She teaches that they must at all cost be present at it on all holy days of obligation, with their minds and eyes religiously intent on that from which the divine mercy and an abundance of all good things might be acquired.

Obligation of Offering and Attending Mass

5. The sacrifice of the Mass must be offered by pastors of souls for the people committed to their care; this obligation comes from a divine precept according to the teachings of the Council of Trent, since the same Council teaches in most express and grave words: "it is by divine mandate that all those to whom the care of souls is committed are to know their sheep and offer sacrifice for them."[4] The encyclical letter of Benedict XIV of 19 August 1744[5] speaks most wisely about this obligation, explaining and confirming more fully the mind of the Fathers of Trent. In order to remove all controversies, questions, and uncertainties, he clearly declares that pastors and all others actually having the care of souls ought to offer the sacrifice of the Mass for the people committed to them on all Sundays, and holy days of obligation, as well as on those days on which he, lessening the number of holy days of obligation in some dioceses, allowed people to engage in servile work, with the provision that the faithful fulfill the obligation of hearing holy Mass.

6. We are joyful when We learn from you in your communications that those in charge of souls diligently fulfill the obligation of their office on Sundays and other holy days of obligation, on which they rarely omit to offer the sacrifice of the Mass for the people entrusted to them. But we are not ignorant of the fact that in many places the Mass is now customarily omitted by pastors on those other days which were formerly kept as holy days of obligation according to the constitution of Our Predecessor Urban VIII.[6] Agreeing to petitions of various holy bishops and having before his eyes their causes and reasons, He lessened the holy days of obligation and not only permitted people to perform servile work, but granted also that they be exempt from the obligation of attending holy Mass. But where this generous indult of the Holy See was promulgated, straight-away the pastors of many regions, considering that they were free from the obligation of celebrating Mass for their people on these reduced holy days, neglected the obligation altogether. Hence the custom evolved that pastors in these regions stopped offering holy Mass for their people on the said days, and some did not even hesitate to defend and justify this custom.

7. We are greatly grieved by this situation; therefore, We have decided to remedy this matter especially since We are aware that this Apostolic See has taught that pastors are obliged to celebrate Mass for their people even on the reduced holy days. Our Predecessors were moved by the vigorous pleas of holy bishops; and many and varied needs of the faithful; and the grave concerns of circumstances, times, and places. As a result, they decided to lessen the number of holy days of obligation, and allowed people to undertake servile work on these days and to miss Mass. Nevertheless these same Predecessors, in granting these indults, wished that the law remain intact

and inviolate. They wished that on the aforesaid days no innovation ever be made in the churches as to the customary order and rite of the divine offices. They meant for all things to be carried out the exact way they were before, while the constitution of Urban VIII was in force. This prescribed the holy days of obligation. On those days pastors are not free from the obligation of offering Mass for their people; they will realize this, especially when they recall that the pontifical rescripts are to be strictly interpreted. Moreover, We have frequently decreed, that pastors are bound by the obligation of saying Mass for their people even on those days which were removed from the number of holy days of obligation.

New Ruling

8. Wherefore, having weighed this matter carefully and having consulted certain Cardinals of Our Congregation for the Preservation and Interpretation of the Decrees of the Council of Trent, We have decided to write this encyclical letter to establish norm and law to be observed carefully and diligently by all pastors. Accordingly in this letter We declare that pastors and all those actually having care of souls should celebrate holy Mass for their people on all Sundays and on days of obligation. Mass must also be offered on those days, which by indult of this Holy See were removed or transferred from the number of holy days of obligation, just as the clergy were obliged to do when the constitution of Urban VIII was in full force before holy days of obligation were lessened or transferred. As for feasts which have been transferred we make one exception, namely when the divine office of a solemnity has been moved to a Sunday, only one Sunday Mass need be offered by pastors for their people, since the Mass, being the principal part of the divine office, is considered as transferred along with the same office.

9. Concerned with the peace of soul of those pastors who, on account of the asserted custom, have omitted to offer Mass for their people on the days previously mentioned, We, by Our Apostolic authority, fully absolve them from each and every past omission. And, because some claim that they have received from this Apostolic See a special indult of reduction, We grant that they can continue to enjoy the benefit of this indult, according, however, to the conditions expressed in the indult and as long as they exercise the office of pastor in the parishes which they presently govern and administer.

10. While, however, We make these provisions and grant these indults, We hope that pastors will glory in satisfying most diligently and religiously this obligation of offering Mass for their people. They should seriously consider the rich abundance of heavenly favors and earthly goods which redound on the Christian people committed to their care from the offering of this unbloody and divine sacrifice. Since, however, we know that peculiar circumstances can arise in which a remission of the obligation for a particular reason and time should be granted to pastors, We wish to inform you that all must apply uniquely to Our Congregation of the Council to obtain this sort of indult. Only those who depend on the Congregation for the Propagation of the Faith are exempted since We have given the proper faculties for this purpose to both congregations. We have no doubt that you will inform every pastor of your dioceses concerning their obligation of offering the holy sacrifice of the Mass for the people committed to them. And We are convinced also that you will apply the greatest vigilance that those in charge of souls fulfill diligently this part of their task also, and carefully observe what We have decreed and sanctioned by this encyclical. We hope that a copy of this letter will be permanently kept in the records of each of your episcopal curias.

11. Since, venerable brothers, you yourselves know full well the holy sacrifice of the Mass contains a great source of instruction for the faithful, never cease to exhort pastors especially and other preachers of the divine word and those to whom the task of educating the Christian people is delegated to explain to the faithful the necessity, excellence, greatness, purpose and fruits of so holy and admirable a sacrifice. Likewise inflame the faithful themselves to frequently attend this sacrifice with the faith, religion, and piety it deserves, that they may be able to obtain the divine mercy and all kinds of benefits they need. Nor should you cease encouraging the priests of your dioceses to be outstanding in moral integrity, dignity, innocence of life, and sanctity. Those who alone are given the privilege of consecrating the divine host and accomplishing so holy and awesome a sacrifice should display these qualities. Therefore, frequently exhort all who are initiated into the most holy priesthood to give serious consideration to the ministry which they have received in the Lord. They should fulfill their ministry, being always mindful of the dignity and heavenly power with which they are endowed; they should shine forth with the splendor of all kinds of virtue; they should occupy themselves with divine worship, divine things, and the salvation of souls. Then, offering themselves as a living and holy host to the Lord, and always carrying about in their bodies the mortification of Jesus, they may duly offer with pure minds and clean heart to God the propitiatory host for their own salvation and that of all the world.

12. Finally, We are pleased to use this occasion also, to testify again to the special benevolence We have for you. We hope you will quickly proceed to carefully fulfill all aspects of your pastoral ministry and that you will concern yourselves with the salvation and well-being of your beloved flock.

13. Be assured that We are most ready to carry out lovingly all those things which We know can greater benefit your own and your dioceses' well-being. Meanwhile receive as a guarantee of all heavenly gifts and a witness of our deepest benevolence for you, the apostolic blessing, which we lovingly impart from the deepest sentiments of Our heart to you yourselves, venerable brothers, and all the clergy, and faithful laity committed to the vigilance of each of you.

Given in Rome at St. Peter's, 3 May 1858, in the 12th year of Our Pontificate.

†

LATIN TEXT: *Acta Pii IX*, I, 3:17-27.

ENGLISH TRANSLATION: Robert F. Healey, S.J.

REFERENCES:

1. St. Gregory the Great, *Diolog.*, bk. 44, chap. 58.
2. Malachy, chap. 1.
3. St. Cyril of Jerusalem, *Catechesis* 23, *Mystagogia 5 de sacra Liturgia.*
4. Council of Trent, session 23, chap. 1, *De Reformat.*
5. Benedict XIV, encyclical *Cum semper oblatas*, 19 August 1744.
6. Urban VIII, apostolic constitution *Universa per orbem*, 13 September 1642.

CUM SANCTA MATER ECCLESIA

ENCYCLICAL OF POPE PIUS IX PLEADING FOR PUBLIC PRAYER

APRIL 27, 1859

56

To Our Venerable Brothers, the Patriarchs, Primates, Archbishops, Bishops and other Ordinaries in Friendship and Communion with the Apostolic See.

Venerable Brethren: Greetings and the Apostolic Blessing.

Now when holy Mother Church is joyously celebrating the annual solemnity of the Paschal Sacrament, she reminds her faithful of the joyful message of peace, which the risen Jesus Christ, having conquered death and overthrown the tyranny of the evil one, frequently and lovingly announced to His apostles and disciples; by contrast, the most dire sound of war among Catholic nations arises and is heard by all. Christ at His birth announced His peace to men of good will through angels, and later, left His peace to His disciples. Because of our love and care for Catholic peoples, we cannot refrain from crying out again and again for peace.

2. And so We exhort you, to stir the faithful committed to your vigilance in view of your outstanding piety, to turn to God in prayer, so that He might grant His deeply desired peace to all. For the same reason We have ordered that public prayers be offered by all within the Papal Territories to the most kind Father of Mercies. Following the illustrious example of Our predecessors, We have decided to have recourse to your prayers and those of the whole Church. And so We ask that you order public prayers in your dioceses as soon as possible. Having implored the patronage of Mary, may your faithful strenuously beseech our merciful God to turn his wrath from us and banish war to the very ends of the earth. By doing this, he may illuminate all minds by His divine grace and inflame all hearts with the love of Christian peace. He may insure that all may be rooted in faith and love. These then would diligently keep His holy Commandments and humbly beseech His forgiveness for their sins. Turning aside from evil and doing good, they would walk in the ways of justice, exercise mutual charity among themselves and obtain salutary peace with God, with themselves, and with all men.

3. We do not doubt that in view of your proven respect toward Us and this Holy See, that you will be desirous to fulfill with all diligence these Our desires and prayers. But to encourage the faithful in the prayers you decree, We have resolved to proffer and draw from the treasury of heavenly graces, whose dispensation the Most High has granted to Us. Wherefore We grant to these faithful, as often as they have been devoutly

present at and completed the prayers We have mentioned, three hundred days indulgence in the customary form granted by the Church. Moreover, during the time of these prayers, We grant to these faithful a plenary indulgence once a month; it is to be received on the same day on which they have been duly absolved of their sins in Confession, have received Holy Communion, and have piously visited a place of worship where they have recited prayers for this purpose.

4. In conclusion, We are indeed happy to use this occasion also to attest again and confirm the special benevolence which We have for you all, venerable brothers. May the Apostolic Blessing which from the depths of Our heart We most lovingly grant especially to you, venerable brothers, and to all the clergy and laity entrusted to each of you, be a guarantee of Our most zealous good will toward you.

Given in Rome at St. Peter's, 27 April, 1859, in the 13th year of Our Pontificate.

†

LATIN TEXT: *Acta Pii IX*, I, 3:64-66.

ENGLISH TRANSLATION: Robert F. Healey, S.J.

QUI NUPER

ENCYCLICAL OF POPE PIUS IX
ON PONTIFICAL STATES
JUNE 18, 1859
57

To Our Venerable Brothers, the Patriarchs, Primates, Archbishops, Bishops, and other Ordinaries in Friendship and Communion with the Apostolic See.

Venerable Brethren: Greetings and the Apostolic Blessing.

The revolutionary movement throughout Italy against legitimate princes has broken out even in regions close to those of the papal territory. The flames of this conflagration, as it were, have invaded some of Our own Provinces; moved by this pernicious example and driven by incitement from outside, certain of them have withdrawn from Our paternal rule. They seek, although with few supporters, to become subject to that Italian Government which for these last years has acted as an adversary to the Church and its legitimate rights and sacred ministry. We reprove and grieve over the actions of this rebellion by which only a certain part of the people in these troubled provinces unjustly respond to Our paternal cares and concerns. We declare openly that temporal power is necessary to this Holy See, so that for the good of religion it can exercise spiritual power without any hindrance. These most cunning enemies of the Church seek to wrest away its temporal sovereignty.

2. In the midst of such turmoil We sent you the present letter in order to seek some consolation in Our sorrow. Moreover, on this occasion We also exhort you to make it your concern to do what we read that Moses prescribed once to Aaron, the high priest of the Hebrews (Nm 16): "Take the censor, fill it with fire from the altar, put incense in it and hurry to the people to perform the rite of atonement over them. For wrath has come down from the Lord and the plague has begun." Likewise we exhort you to pour forth prayers as those holy brothers, Moses and Aaron, who "threw themselves face downward on the ground, and cried out, 'O God of the spirits that gives life to every living thing, will you be angry with all the people for the sins of a few?' " (Nm 16).

3. This is why we send you the present letter, from which we take no small consolation because we are confident that you will respond abundantly to Our desires and concerns. Moreover We openly affirm that endowed with virtue from God as the result of the prayers of the faithful, We will suffer any danger and any bitterness before We forsake in any way the apostolic office. Nor will We permit anything against the sanctity of

the oath by which We were bound when, however undeservingly, We ascended the supreme seat of the prince of the apostles, the citadel and bulwark of the Catholic faith. As you carry out your pastoral offices, We pray that everything may turn out happy and successful for you, venerable brothers, and We lovingly grant as a sign of heavenly blessing the apostolic blessing to you and your flocks.

Given in Rome at St. Peter's, 18 June 1859, in the 14th year of Our Pontificate.

†

LATIN TEXT: *Acta Pii IX*, I, 3:82-83; *Acta Sanctae Sedis*, 6:157-58

ENGLISH TRANSLATION: Robert F. Healey, S.J.

NULLIS CERTE VERBIS

ENCYCLICAL OF POPE PIUS IX ON THE
NEED FOR CIVIL SOVEREIGNTY
JANUARY 19, 1860
58

To the Venerable Brothers, the Patriarchs, Primates, Archbishops, Bishops and other Ordinaries Keeping Favor and Communion with the Apostolic See.

Greetings and the Apostolic Blessing.

We cannot express in words what a consolation and what a joy to Us, in the midst of the greatest unpleasantness, are your admirable loyalty and respect, and that of your faithful, for Us and this Apostolic See, We are referring to your truly outstanding unanimity, willingness, zeal, and constancy in defending the rights of this same See and the claims of justice. From Our encyclical of last June 18 and then from Our two allocutions in Consistory, you learned of the evils oppressing civil and sacred affairs in Italy and the attempts against the legitimate Princes of Italy and the holy and legitimate dominion which belongs to Us and this Holy See. In compliance with Our wishes, you immediately ordered public prayers in your dioceses.

Civil Power of the Holy See

2. Afterwards, in kind letters sent to Us and by pastoral letters of other religious and learned writings, you vehemently denounced the sacrilegious attacks made on the civil power of the Roman Church. And defending constantly this dominion, you proclaimed and taught that God gave the civil power to the Roman Pontiff, so that he, never subject to any power, might exercise in full liberty and without any impediment the supreme task of the apostolic ministry divinely committed to him by Christ our Lord.

Worldwide Support

3. Moreover, Our beloved sons of the Catholic Church, imbued with your teaching and aroused by your example, have striven valiantly and still strive to make the same sentiments known to Us. For from every region of the whole Catholic world, We have received practically innumerable letters from ecclesiastics and laity alike of every dignity, rank, grade, and condition. These are signed by hundreds of thousands of Catholics, in which they declare their filial devotion toward Us and this Chair of Peter. They vehemently oppose the revolution and the attacks made in some of Our provinces. They maintain that the patrimony of blessed Peter ought to be preserved completely intact and inviolate and should be defended from all injury. Some of them have, in addition, asserted this wisely in suitable printed works.

Appreciation of Support

4. These outstanding expressions have so

moved Us that We could not forbear to gladly proclaim, "Blessed be God, the Father of Our Lord Jesus Christ, the Father of mercy and the God of all consolation, who consoles Us in all our tribulation." For nothing in the midst of the gravest straits in which We are oppressed, could be more welcome and more pleasing than to behold your zeal and that of the faithful for the protection of the rights of this Holy See. And you yourselves can easily understand how strongly Our paternal benevolence towards you and these Catholics grows deservingly by the day.

Problems with Napoleon III

5. Now, however, a new cause of sorrow has arisen from a different source. And so We write to you to make Our sentiments well known. Recently, as many of you know, in a Paris newspaper called *Le Moniteur*, a letter of the Emperor of the French was published replying to Our letter. In it, We asked that he, by his most powerful patronage in the Congress at Paris, defend the integral and inviolate nature of the temporal power belonging to us and the Holy See, and that he be willing to safeguard it from evil rebellion. In his letter the great Emperor, recalling his somewhat earlier proposal to Us concerning rebellious provinces of Our papal states, advises that We should of Our own accord surrender the possession of these same provinces, since it seems to him to be the only way to amend the present disorder.

Response to Napoleon

6. You all know that We could not keep silence at the receipt of such a letter. Therefore, without delay, We responded to the same Emperor, declaring freely and openly that We could in no way assent to his counsel. We said that "it offers insuperable difficulties, in consideration of Our dignity and that of the Holy See and Our sacred character and the rights of the same Holy See, which pertain not to the succession of any royal family but to all Catholics." Likewise We professed "what is not Ours cannot be given up by Us, and We plainly understand that the victory he wishes to be conceded to the traitors of Emilia, would be a stimulus for future internal and external disturbers of other provinces to perpetrate the same things, when they saw the prosperous fortune of the rebels."

7. And, among other things, We informed the same Emperor, that "We could not abdicate the provinces in Emilia without violating solemn oaths by which We are bound, without exciting quarrels and disturbances in the rest of Our provinces, without committing injustice to all Catholics, and without, finally, weakening the rights not only of the Princes of Italy but of all Princes of the whole Christian world who could not watch with indifference the introduction of most destructive principles." Nor did We omit to point out that "his majesty could scarcely ignore by what men and by what money and resources the recent attempts at rebellion in Bologna, Ravenna, and elsewhere were inflamed and carried out, while the far greater part of the population showed itself in no way induced to support these movements, something it little expected. It was, in fact, amazed."

8. And since the Emperor felt that We ought to give up these provinces because of the rebellions stirred up in them, We replied appropriately that an argument of this kind, inasmuch as it proved excessive, has no validity. Similar rebellions have often occurred in Europe and other areas, yet anyone can see that a legitimate argument cannot be deduced from that fact to diminish civil sovereignty. We reminded the Emperor that his first letter, sent to Us before the Italian war, which offered Us consolation, not affliction, differed from his most recent ones.

9. From certain words in his newspaper letter, We gathered that there were grounds for fear that the above cited provinces of Ours in Emilia were already considered as if they had been taken away from Our dominion. We, accordingly, begged him in the name of the Church, that for his own Majesty's good and utility as well, to vanquish this fear. We reminded him that all must give an exact account at some time before the tribunal of Christ and undergo a most severe judgment; therefore each one must take care that he experience the effect of mercy rather than justice.

10. These are the chief matters, among others, that We replied to the Emperor of France. We judged they should be made known to you that you and the universal Catholic world recognize that We will without fear leave nothing untried in fighting bravely for the cause of religion and for preserving the civil dominion of the Roman Church and its temporal possessions

and rights. Intact and inviolate these pertain to the entire Catholic world, and We look to the just cause of other Princes.

11. And supported by the divine aid of Him who said "you will have tribulation in the world, but be confident, I have overcome the world" (Jn 16.33) and "blessed are they who suffer persecution for justice sake" (Mt 5.10), We are prepared to follow the illustrious footsteps of Our Predecessors, to emulate their example and to suffer harsh hard things and even lay down Our life, before deserting the cause of God, the Church, and justice in any way. But you can easily conjecture with what bitter sorrow We are affected, seeing the dreadful war which harasses our religion to the greatest detriment of souls and seeing the great whirlwinds which toss about the Church and this Holy See. And you can also easily understand our disquietude at the great danger for souls in these disturbed provinces, where piety, religion, faith, integrity, and morals are weakened daily especially from the pernicious writings published there.

12. Do you, therefore, defend this cause and inflame more and more daily the faithful entrusted to your care so that under your leadership they do not cease either defending the Catholic Church and this Holy See or protecting the civil dominion of the same See and the patrimony of St. Peter. Together with your faithful pray that God may command the winds and the water and come to the benefit of Us and His Church. Pray also that He may enlighten enemies to bring them back to the paths of truth, justice, and salvation.

13. And so that God may incline His ear to Our prayers and yours and those of all the faithful, We ask first the recommendation of the Virgin Mary, who is our most beloved mother and most trustworthy hope and ever present guardian of the Church. Nothing is more powerful with God than her patronage. We also implore the support of Peter, then of his co-apostle Paul, and of all the heavenly citizens who reign with Christ in heaven. We do not doubt that in the light of your outstanding religion and priestly zeal, you will obey these Our prayers and petitions. Meanwhile as a pledge of Our burning charity toward you, from Our deepest heart and with a wish for all every true happiness, We lovingly impart Our Apostolic Blessing to you yourselves and all the clergy, and faithful laity committed to each of your vigilance.

Given in Rome at St. Peter's, 19 January 1860, in the 14th year of Our pontificate.

†

LATIN TEXT: *Acta Pii IX*, I, 3:129-36; *Acta Sanctae Sedis*, 6:161-65.

ENGLISH TRANSLATION: Robert F. Healey, S.J.

AMANTISSIMUS

ENCYCLICAL OF POPE PIUS IX ON THE
CARE OF THE CHURCHES
APRIL 8, 1862

59

To the Bishops of the Eastern Churches.

Venerable Brothers, Greetings and Apostolic Benediction.

Our most beloved Redeemer, Christ the Lord, willed as you well know, venerable brothers, to deliver all men from the captivity of the devil, free them from the yoke of sin, call them from darkness into his wonderful light and be their salvation. When he had blotted out the handwriting of the decree against us, fastening it to the cross, he formed and established the Catholic Church, won by his blood, as the one "Church of the living God,"[1] the one "kingdom of heaven,"[2] "the city set on a hill,"[3] "one flock,"[4] and "one body" steadfast and alive with "one Spirit,"[5] one faith, one hope, one love joined and firmly held together by the same bonds of sacraments, religion and doctrine. He further provided his Church with leaders whom he chose and called. In addition, he decreed that the Church will endure as long as the world, embrace all peoples and nations of the whole world, and that whoever accepts his divine religion and grace and perseveres to the end will attain the glory of eternal salvation.

2. To preserve forever in his Church the unity and doctrine of this faith, Christ chose one of his apostles, Peter, whom he appointed the Prince of his Apostles, his Vicar on earth, and impregnable foundation and head of his Church. Surpassing all others with every dignity of extraordinary authority, power and jurisdiction, he was to feed the Lord's flock, strengthen his brothers, rule and govern the universal Church. Christ not only desired that his Church remain as one and immaculate to the end of the world, and that its unity in faith, doctrine and form of government remain inviolate. He also willed that the fullness of dignity, power and jurisdiction, integrity and stability of faith given to Peter be handed down in its entirety to the Roman Pontiffs, the successors of this same Peter, who have been placed on this Chair of Peter in Rome, and to whom has been divinely committed the supreme care of the Lord's entire flock and the supreme rule of the Universal Church.

3. You above all, venerable brothers, have known how this dogma of our religion has been unanimously and unceasingly declared, defended and insisted upon in synods by the Fathers of the Church. Indeed, they have never stopped teaching that "God is one, Christ is one, the Church established upon Peter by the voice of the Lord is one;"[6] "the massive foundation of the great Christian state has been divinely built upon, as it were,

PIUS IX

this rock, this very firm stone;"[7] "this Chair, which is unique and the first of gifts, has always been designated and considered as the Chair of Peter;"[8] "shining forth throughout the world it maintains its primacy;"[9] "it is also the root and matrix whence sacerdotal unity has sprung;"[10]it is not only the head but also the mother and teacher of all the Churches;"[11] "it is the mother city of piety in which is the complete and perfect stability of the Christian religion"[12] "and in which the pre-eminence of the Apostolic Chair has always been unimpaired;"[13] "it rests upon that rock which the haughty gates of hell shall never overcome;"[14] "for it the Apostles poured out their entire teaching with blood;"[15] "from it the rights of the venerable communion are extended to all;"[16] "all obedience and honor must be given to it."[17] "He who deserts the Church will vainly believe that he is in the Church;"[18] "whoever eats of the lamb and is not a member of the Church, has profaned;"[19] "Peter, who lives and presides in his own Chair, proffers the truth of faith to those seeking it;"[20] "Peter, who lives up to this time and always lives, exercises jurisdiction in his successors;"[21] "he himself has spoken through Leo;"[22] "the Roman Pontiff, who holds Primacy in the entire world, is the Successor of Blessed Peter the Prince of the Apostles and the true Vicar of Christ, the head of the whole Church, and is the visible Father and Teacher of all Christians."[23] There are other, almost countless, proofs drawn from the most trustworthy witnesses which clearly and openly testify with great faith, exactitude, respect and obedience that all who want to belong to the true and only Church of Christ must honor and obey this Apostolic See and Roman Pontiff.

4. Now, truly, a multiplicity of holy things, a variety of legitimate rites, obviously in no way oppose the unity of the Catholic Church; rather, indeed, such diversity greatly enhances the dignity of the Church itself. Not one, moreover, of you, venerable brothers, is unaware that there are some who are striving to deceive and lead into error the unguarded, especially, and the inexperienced by maligning this Holy See as if the Holy See itself upon receiving the separated Orientals into the Catholic faith required them to abandon their own rite and embrace that of the Latin Church. That this is false and far from truth is clearly shown by the many constitutions and apostolic letters of our Predecessors. They not only consistently declared to the Orientals that such a condition was never intended, but also professed that it was wholly their desire that the rites of the Eastern Churches, into which no error against the Catholic Church or against moral integrity had crept, would be completely preserved.

5. Not only past, but recent acts of our departed Predecessors clearly agree with such repeated and definite declarations of our Predecessors. It can never be said that this Apostolic See has ever enjoined upon the bishops, ecclesiastics, or the Oriental peoples, who have returned to the Catholic faith, to change their legitimate rites. In fact, the universal City of Constantinople recently saw how our venerable brother Miletus, archbishop of Dramea, to our deepest comfort and the joy of all good men, returned to the bosom of the Catholic Church with his own rite and solemn ceremonies, and how a great throng of people solemnly processed after the event. Hence, venerable brothers, with solicitude incessantly impress upon your dioesan clergy the need to be zealous at every opportunity and by every means to expose and refute the calumny by which evil men lead the inexperienced into error and attempt to incite envy and hatred against this Holy See.

6. Ever since we have been placed on this Chair of Peter by the hidden plan of divine providence and have thus been elevated to the supreme rule of the universal Church, we have striven to fulfill the duties of our apostolic ministry as the daily direction and solicitude for the Churches demand of us. Because we depend utterly on divine help, we do not fear the many nefarious and sacrilegious destructions, attempts and attacks by which in these disturbed times the enemies of the Catholic religion endeavor to undermine its foundations, if that were ever possible. No, indeed, the spiritual good and salvation of all people are our constant concern.

7. For indeed the charity of Christ compels us, and nothing could be more pleasing than to undertake most willingly all the cares, labors, deliberations necessary to hasten all people into the unity of faith, the growth in the knowledge of God and the recognition of our Lord, Jesus Christ "who is the way and the truth and the life: the way certainly of a holy life, the truth of divine doctrine, and the life of everlasting happiness."[24]

8. Nor are you unknowing, venerable

brothers, with what singular love and assiduous zeal from the very beginning of our supreme Pontificate, we have devoted our paternal care to that chosen portion of the Lord's flock committed to your vigilance. From our most recent letter, published on the 7th of last January, you are able more and more to understand how strongly we feel about the good and prosperity of the Oriental Churches.

9. With this same letter, we have set up a special Congregation as part of the Propagation of the Faith and of great assistance to it—almost overwhelmed as it is with constant and very serious services. This new department so excellently administers work from the Congregation for the Propagation of the Faith as it takes care to manage expeditiously the affairs of the Oriental Churches. We are sustained by the hope that our solicitude and counsel will spiritually profit the Oriental peoples. We are in complete confidence, furthermore, that the new special department so recently established by us will never in any way swerve from the purpose intended: that in handling your affairs, there will be a steady progress in every way possible toward Catholic unity; an increase in the success of your Churches; the protection of the integrity of your legitimate rites; greater spiritual happiness for all the faithful.

10. That this Congregation may conscientiously carry out the duty we entrusted to it and direct its zeal and efforts toward the greater prosperity of your Churches, it is extremely necessary that it thoroughly understand the spiritual needs of the Oriental peoples. Since, venerable brothers, you fully know the condition and state of the flock entrusted to you, in your wisdom you will properly understand how important it is that you inform us as soon as possible of all that concerns your Churches and your flocks. It is, likewise, essential that you send us an accurate report on the status of your dioceses in which you carefully explain whatever pertains to the dioceses themselves that we may attentively provide for the necessities of the faithful residing in them.

11. It will comfort us greatly if each of you, venerable brothers, in assiduously reporting all the affairs of your respective diocese, will indicate the number of the faithful in the diocese; the number of ecclesiastics who minister to the faithful; the procedure for attending to the same faithful not only in regard to faith but also to discipline of morals; the doctrine with which the clergy is instructed; the education of the clergy; the means and method of instructing the people in our most holy religion and in moral integrity; the plan whereby the same people are inspired and daily educated into greater piety and moral integrity. We also desire to know exactly the condition of your schools and how many youth customarily attend them. Since, venerable brothers, you well know that all hope of both sacred and public affairs depends on the right, salutary and religious education of children, it is of particular concern that from their tender years they attend Catholic schools where, diligently learning the truth of our religion and commandments, they will escape the danger of having their sensitive minds tainted with evil principles.

12. If you need books, do not hesitate to make it known and at the same time inform us of the books you consider most appropriate to provide dogma for the clergy, promote the education of the people, refute the teachings of those who are not Catholic, and foster the piety of the faithful. Most importantly, when we hear from you that in some places liturgical and ritual books are being used into which either some error has crept or a change has been arbitrarily introduced, it will be your duty to mention which books these are and if at any time they have been approved by the Holy See. Specify, too, if in your judgment they contain errors to be corrected or abuses to be abolished. We especially desire to learn from you, moreover, what progress holy catholic unity has made in your dioceses, what obstacles have hindered it, and what propitious means will remove such impediments so that unity itself may daily advance and increase.

13. Truly, venerable brothers, you see with how much love and earnestness we have been mindful of your Eastern Churches and how ardently we hope that among the Eastern people our most blessed faith, religion and piety will take hold, thrive and flourish. We are certain that you will devote all your energy and thought to protecting and propagating our religion and to caring for the salvation of your flock.

14. Hostile men in these lamentable times never stop planting thorns in the Lord's field, first with destructive and ephemeral books and then with monstrous and depraved suppositions plainly opposed to Catholic faith and dogma.

Consequently, you rightly understand how you must labor and ever be on your guard to keep the faithful from those poisonous pastures, to urge them on to eternal salvation, and to imbue them in greater measure with the teachings of the Catholic Church.

15. In order that you may more readily attain this goal, constantly inspire the zeal of guardians of souls that in the conscientious performance of their duty, they may untiringly announce the good news of the Gospel to the wise and the foolish. Urge them to help the Christian people by every good and holy work. Exhort them to give instruction, especially to boys and those inexperienced in the proofs of the Catholic Faith so that they may be guided in moral discipline. Always admonish your diocesan priests that, seriously reflecting upon the ministry they received in the Lord, they take care to fulfill it fervently. In such a way they give Christian people an example of all virtues, are attentive to prayer, perfectly cultivate sacred studies, and exert all their power to win the everlasting salvation of the faithful.

16. Then, too, that you may always have at hand diligent and industrious workers in cultivating the vineyard of the Lord, spare no effort, venerable brothers, that the most excellent teachers train young clerics in piety from the very beginning. May these be formed in a true ecclesiastical spirit and very carefully instructed, primarily in Sacred Scripture and the sacred sciences, against any danger of error. To be sure, we are by no means ignorant, venerable brothers, of the many difficulties you have been exposed to in the exercise of your episcopal ministry. Take comfort in the Lord, however, and recalling the powerful memory of his virtue, be ambassadors for Christ, who gave up his life for his sheep and left us an example that we may follow in his footsteps.

17. Everyone knows how much service and honor the families of monks have been to the Catholic Church in the East. By the integrity of their lives, the gravity of their conduct, and the fame of their religious discipline, they were striving to present models of good works to the faithful, to teach youth, to perfect themselves in Scripture and studies, and to work zealously for their bishops in beneficial service. In the distressing instability of conditions and times, these holy families, valuable to the Christian and civil state alike, have been deviating, in some places, from the discipline of their own Order or have become completely extinct. Since it would certainly be a great benefit to our religion if these holy families, especially where they have died out, might be restored and shine again among the Eastern nations in their pristine glory, we earnestly ask that you express to us your feelings on this matter and how the renewal of these holy families might be achieved.

18. We are thoroughly convinced that you, venerable brothers, will not only most happily and willingly satisfy these our desires and requests, but also that you will promptly reveal any other concerns that you think should be mentioned for the greater welfare in these regions of our most holy religion—and not only of the clergy, but also of the faithful.

19. From the Encyclical Letter of the Cardinal Prefect of the Council of Our Congregation, you will know how pleasing it will be to us to enjoy your presence next Pentecost when We, God willing, will celebrate the solemn canonization of many saints. On that occasion, if the circumstances of your dioceses permit, we shall be able to see you, greet you lovingly, and receive from you the reports of your dioceses.

20. Meanwhile, venerable brothers, continue to fulfill your ministry with ever greater ardor and effort. In all earnestness, provide for the salvation of your faithful, both admonishing and exhorting them to persevere more firmly in the profession of the Catholic Religion; to observe religiously all the commandments of God and of his holy Church; to walk worthily, pleasing to God and fruitful in every good work.

21. In accordance with your customary kindness, receive with paternal affection those who, to our very great joy, return to the bosom of the Church: expend all your care that they be nourished more fervently with the words of faith. Strengthened thus through the spiritual gift of grace, may they rein steadfast in their holy calling and ardently walk with constancy in the path of the Lord, following closely the way that leads to life. On behalf of your admirable religion, never forsake all goodness, patience, learning, gentleness and mildness as you try to gain for Christ the pitiful errant: lead them back into his one sheepfold and restore them to the hope of their eternal inheritance.

22. In the critical difficulties that beset your episcopal office in these worst of times, trust in the grace of our Lord, Jesus Christ, keeping ever before you that those who teach many unto justice will shine as the stars for all eternity. Finally, venerable brothers, we want you to be sure of the special benevolence with which we wait upon you in the Lord. In the meantime, by no means do we omit in every prayer to beg humbly and earnestly that God propitiously pour forth upon you the richest gifts of his goodness: that they may also descend abundantly upon the chosen flock committed to your vigilance.

23. As a witness of all that we have said and as a pledge of our most disposed will toward you, we affectionately bestow upon you our Apostolic Blessing from the depth of our heart, venerable brothers, and upon all the clergy and the faithful laity committed to your care.

Given at Rome at St. Peter's, 8 April, 1862. In the sixteenth year of our Pontificate.

†

LATIN TEXT: *Acta Pii IX*, I, 3:424-36.

ENGLISH TRANSLATION: Marie Liguori Ewald, I.H.M.

REFERENCES:

1. 1 Tm 3.15.
2. Mt. 13.45 *passim.*
3. Mt. 5.14.
4. Jn 10.16.
5. Eph 4.4 *passim.*
6. St. Cyprian, epistle 40.
7. St. Cyril of Alexandria, in Ioan., Lib. II, c. 42.
8. St. Optatus of Milevis, 2 cont. Parmen., bk. 2, chap. 2.
9. Council of Nicea II, Act. 2.
10. St. Cyprian, epistles 15 and 55.
11. Pelagius II, epistle 1 to the Oriental bishops, and the Council of Trent, session 7 on baptism, can. 3.
12. Synodal letter from John of Constantinople to Pope Hormisdas; also Sozomen, *Ecclesiastical History*, book 3, chapter 8.
13. St. Augustine, epistle 62.
14. St. Augustine, in psalm *contra part. Donat.*
15. Tertullian, *de praescript.*, 36.8.
16. St. Ambrose, epistle 12 to Damasus.
17. Council of Ephesus, *Act. 4.*
18. St. Cyprian, *de unit, Ecclesiae.*
19. St. Jerome, epistle 15 to Damasus.
20. St. Peter Chrysologus, epistle to Eutyches.
21. Council of Ephesus.
22. Council of Chalcedon, *Act. 2.*
23. Council of Florence in its decree *union. Graecorum.*
24. St. Leo, sermon 2 on the resurrection of the Lord.

QUANTO CONFICIAMUR MOERORE

ENCYCLICAL OF POPE PIUS IX ON PROMOTION OF FALSE DOCTRINES

AUGUST 10, 1863

60

To Our Beloved Sons, S. R. E. Cardinals and to Our Venerable Brothers, the Archbishops and Bishops of Italy.

Our Beloved Sons and Venerable Brothers, Greetings and Apostolic Benediction.

How much cause we have to grieve over the most cruel and sacrilegious war brought upon the Catholic Church in almost all regions of the world during these turbulent times, and especially declared upon unhappy Italy before our very eyes many years ago by the Piedmontese Government and stirred up more violently day by day, each of you, our beloved sons and venerable brothers, easily understands. In the midst of our great distress, however, as long as you keep watch with us, we are deeply comforted and consoled. Although you are, indeed, most deplorably harassed by every grave injustice possible, torn away from your own flock, exiled and even cast into prison, nevertheless, with your profound virtue you have never neglected to speak and to write in ardent defense of the teachings of God, his Church, and this Apostolic See.

2. Consequently, we give thanks because you fervently rejoice to suffer insult in the name of Jesus. We extend to you merited praise in the words of our most saintly predecessor, Leo: "May you endure with all your heart the trials of your love, which you have undergone in reverence for the Catholic faith; may I accept the sufferings inflicted upon you as if I were bearing them myself. I know, however, that it is a cause of joy rather than of sorrow that with the strength of our Lord, Jesus Christ, you have persevered invincible in your evangelical and apostolic teaching. . . And when the enemies of the Christian faith were tearing you away from your respective churches, rather than being contaminated by their impiety, you preferred to endure the injustice of undergoing exile."[1]

3. Would that we could announce the end of such terrible calamities besetting the Church! Never will there be grief enough over the corruption of morals so extensively increasing and promoted by irreligious and obscene writings, theatrical spectacles and meretricious houses established almost everywhere; by other depraved arts and monstrous portents of every error disseminated in all directions; by the abominable impurities of all vices and crimes growing constantly and the deadly virus of *unbelief* and *indifferentism* spread far and wide; by contempt for ecclesiastical authority, sacred things, and laws and by the outrageous plundering of Church possessions; by the bitter and constant abuse of

consecrated Church officials, of the students of religious communities, of virgins dedicated to God; by the diabolical hatred of Christ, his Church, teaching, and of this Apostolic See. These and almost innumerable other evils perpetrated by the embittered enemies of the Catholic Church and faith, we are daily compelled to lament.

4. All these agonies seem to prolong and delay that most yearned for time when we shall see the full triumph of our most holy religion, of justice, and of truth. This triumph cannot fail us, however, even if it is not given us to know the time destined for it by almighty God. Even though our heavenly Father permits his holy Church to be afflicted and plagued by various tribulations and distresses while serving during this most miserable and earthly pilgrimage, nevertheless, because it has been founded by Christ, the Lord, upon an immovable and most firm rock, it cannot be shaken or overthrown by any force or violence. Rather, "it is strengthened, not weakened by persecutions. The Lord's vineyard is always clothed with a richer harvest, for while each grain dies singly, it is born again manyfold."[2]

5. That is what we see happening, beloved sons and venerable brothers, even in these most sorrowful times as a special blessing from God. For although the immaculate Spouse of Christ may be vehemently troubled at the present time by the work of the wicked, yet she is triumphing over her enemies. Yes, indeed, she is conquering her enemies and shines wonderfully bright with your unparalleled faithfulness, love, and respect towards us and this Chair of Peter, and with your outstanding constancy and that of the other venerable brothers, the bishops of the whole Catholic world. She shines with many pious works of Christian charity multiplying rapidly each day; with the light of blessed faith illuminating many regions evermore each day; with the exceptional love and devotion shown by Catholics towards the Church itself, towards us, and this Holy See; with the eminent and immortal glory of martyrdom. You know, in fact, how in Tonkin and especially in the regions of Cochin China, bishops, priests, laymen and even peaceful women themselves, and young boys and girls, emulating the martyrs with their unconquerable spirit and heroic virtue, disdained the most inhuman torture, and greatly rejoiced to pour out their lives for Christ. All these joys should be no slight consolation to us and to you in the midst of the overwhelming anguish that torments us.

6. Now, since our Apostolic Office demands we carefully and zealously defend the cause of the Church committed to us by Christ, we condemn those who attack and despise the Church itself, its sacred laws, ministers, and this Apostolic See. Hence, with this letter, once more we confirm, proclaim and condemn totally and singly that which in many consistorial allocutions and in our other Letters we have been forced to deplore, declare and condemn.[3]

7. Here, too, our beloved sons and venerable brothers, it is again necessary to mention and censure a very grave error entrapping some Catholics who believe that it is possible to arrive at eternal salvation although living in error and alienated from the true faith and Catholic unity. Such belief is certainly opposed to Catholic teaching. There are, of course, those who are struggling with invincible ignorance about our most holy religion. Sincerely observing the natural law and its precepts inscribed by God on all hearts and ready to obey God, they live honest lives and are able to attain eternal life by the efficacious virtue of divine light and grace. Because God knows, searches and clearly understands the minds, hearts, thoughts, and nature of all, his supreme kindness and clemency do not permit anyone at all who is not guilty of deliberate sin to suffer eternal punishments.

8. Also well known is the Catholic teaching that no one can be saved outside the Catholic Church. Eternal salvation cannot be obtained by those who oppose the authority and statements of the same Church and are stubbornly separated from the unity of the Church and also from the successor of Peter, the Roman Pontiff, to whom "the custody of the vineyard has been committed by the Savior."[4] The words of Christ are clear enough: "If he refuses to listen even to the Church, let him be to you a Gentile and a tax collector;"[5] "He who hears you hears me, and he who rejects you, rejects me, and he who rejects me, rejects him who sent me;"[6] "He who does not believe will be condemned;"[7] "He who does not believe is already condemned;"[8] "He who is not with me is against me, and he who does not gather with me scatters."[9] The Apostle Paul says that such persons are "perverted and self-condemned;"[10] the Prince of the Apostles calls

them "false teachers . . . who will secretly bring in destructive heresies, even denying the Master . . . bringing upon themselves swift destruction."[11]

9. God forbid that the children of the Catholic Church should even in any way be unfriendly to those who are not at all united to us by the same bonds of faith and love. On the contrary, let them be eager always to attend to their needs with all the kind services of Christian charity, whether they are poor or sick or suffering any other kind of visitation. First of all, let them rescue them from the darkness of the errors into which they have unhappily fallen and strive to guide them back to Catholic truth and to their most loving Mother who is ever holding out her maternal arms to receive them lovingly back into her fold. Thus, firmly founded in faith, hope, and charity and fruitful in every good work, they will gain eternal salvation.

10. Furthermore, beloved sons and venerable brothers, we cannot be silent about another most pernicious error, an evil that is pitifully tearing apart and deeply disturbing minds, hearts, and souls. We are referring to that unbridled and damnable self-love and self-interest that drive many to seek their own advantage and profit with clearly no regard for their neighbor. We mean that thoroughly insatiable passion for power and possessions that overrides all the rules of justice and honesty and never ceases by every means possible to amass and greedily heap up wealth. Completely absorbed in the things of earth, forgetful of God, religion and their souls, they wrongly place all their happiness in procuring riches and money. Let such people recollect and meditate seriously upon the very sobering words of Christ, the Lord: "What will it profit a man, if he gains the whole world and forfeits his life?"[12] Let them also reflect upon the teaching of Paul: "Those who desire to be rich fall into temptation, into a snare, into many senseless and hurtful desires that drag men down to ruin and destruction. For the love of money is the root of all evil; it is through this craving that some have wandered away and pierced their hearts with many pangs."[13]

11. Now, truly, we cannot conceal the fact that we are in great anguish since there are some clergy in Italy who, forgetful of their vocation, do not blush in the least to spread abroad false doctrine, even in subversive writings. They arouse the people against us and this Apostolic See; they oppose our civil rule and that of the Chair itself; they shamelessly and zealously support the wicked enemies of the Catholic Church and this same See. Deserting their bishops and us, emboldened by the approval of the Piedmontese government and its Parliament, these ecclesiastics in open contempt of ecclesiastical censure and penalty have become impudently fearless in organizing certain condemnable societies commonly known as Liberal Clerical, of Mutual Assistance, For the Emancipation of the Italian Clergy, and other associations animated by the same depraved spirit. Although deservedly forbidden to perform their holy ministry, nevertheless, like brazen intruders, they sinfully and illicitly exercise it in many churches. We, therefore, disapprove and condemn the behavior of the same ecclesiastics. At the same time, we admonish and exhort, again and again, these unfortunate men to return to their right mind and heart and take thought for their own salvation, seriously considering "that God tolerates no example of conduct more from others than from priests when He sees those, whom He ordains for the improvement of others, give example of their own depravity."[14] Let them fervently reflect that their confused state must be repaired before the tribunal of Christ. May these pitiful churchmen heed our paternal advice and willingly render us the consolation of a repentant clergy. May they seek refuge in us day by day, begging pardon for their defection with suppliant prayer and humbly imploring absolution from ecclesiastical censure.

12. You are certainly aware, our beloved sons and venerable brothers, that every kind of impious and deceitful writing, lies, calumny, and blasphemy has been let loose from hell. No pain has been spared to transfer schools to non-Catholic teachers and to appropriate churches for non-Catholic worship. With a multiple of other, surely diabolical treacheries, arts, and undertakings, the enemies of God employ every effort to destroy completely—if that were possible—the Catholic Church, seduce and corrupt the people, especially guileless youth, and uproot our holy faith and religion from the souls of all.

13. We are fully confident that you, our beloved sons and venerable brothers, strengthened by the grace of our Lord, Jesus Christ, will continue steadfast in your outstanding episcopal zeal. With one mind and heart and with redoubled dedication, may you persist in defending the

House of Israel, may you fight the good fight for the faith and defend from the snares of the enemy the faithful entrusted to your care. Admonish and exhort them to be strong in our sacred faith, without which it is impossible to please God. Urge them to persevere firmly established in our divine religion, which alone is true and eternal and prepares for salvation and even, to a very great extent, preserves and prospers civil society.

14. Through the parish priests chiefly and other ecclesiastics known for integrity of life, gravity of morals, and constant adherence to sound doctrine, may you teach unremittingly and accurately: at one time preaching the divine word, at another instructing the people in the mysteries of our august religion, its doctrine, precepts, and discipline. You, above all, know that many evils generally arise from ignorance of divine matters essential for salvation. Hence, you will understand that it behooves you to use every care and diligence that so detrimental a condition be prevented.

15. Before we bring our letter to its close, however, we cannot restrain from bestowing due praise upon the Italian clergy, who with the highest degree of devotion to us and this Chair of Peter and to their bishops, have certainly not strayed. Following the noble example of their bishops and bearing all hardships with utmost patience, they fulfill their duty most laudably. We put our trust in the hope, moreover, that this same clergy, with the help of divine grace and walking worthily in their vocation, will always strive to be shining examples of piety and virtue.

16. We continue, too, with fitting and public praise for the many consecrated virgins who violently driven from their monastaries, despoiled of their recompense, and reduced to beggary, have not broken faith with their Spouse. Enduring the most deplorable conditions, they pray day and night in the holy house of God where they patiently await His mercy and beseech Him for the salvation of all, even that of their enemies.

17. We rejoice, also, in praising the people of Italy who, with deep Catholic sensibilities, abhor the many impious and destructive efforts taken against the Church. With filial piety, respect and obedience, they take great pride in honoring us, this Holy See, and their bishops. Amid very serious difficulties and impeded by dangers, each day and in many ways they faithfully offer us tokens of their love and devotion, alleviating the wants of this Apostolic See, at times with money, at other times with other gifts.

18. In the midst of so many calamities and confronted with such fury against the Church, we are not despondent for "Christ is our counsel and our strength; without him we can do nothing, through him we can do all things. While confirming the preachers of the Gospel and the ministers of the sacraments, he said: 'Lo, I am with you always, to the end of time.' "[15] We know for certain, moreover, that the gates of hell will never prevail against the Church which stands and will stand immovable with Christ Jesus, our Lord, as guardian and protector, who has built the Church and who has been "yesterday and today and forever."[16]

19. With ever more ardent zeal and humility of heart, let us, our beloved sons and venerable brothers, never stop offering our prayers and petitions to God through Jesus Christ that His Church, driven by this most turbulent tempest, may recover from such great disasters, enjoy the most blessed peace and freedom throughout the world, and gain new and more splendid triumphs over her enemies. Let us pray that the errant be flooded with the light of his divine grace, may turn back from the path of error into the way of truth and justice and, experiencing the worthy fruit of repentance, may possess perpetual love and fear of his holy name.

20. That the merciful God may more readily grant our most fervent prayers, let us invoke patronage of the immaculate and most holy Virgin Mary, Mother of God. Let us seek likewise the intercession of the most holy Apostles, Peter and Paul, and of all the blessed in heaven, that with their efficacious prayers before God, they may implore mercy and graces for all and powerfully avert all adversities and dangers afflicting the Church everywhere and especially in Italy.

21. Finally, as a most certain pledge of our singular benevolence toward you, we lovingly impart our heartfelt Apostolic Blessing upon you, beloved sons and venerable brothers, and upon the flock committed to your care.

Given at Rome, at St. Peter's, 10 August, 1863, in the eighteenth year of Our Pontificate.

†

LATIN TEXT: *Acta Pii IX*, I, 3:609-21.

ENGLISH TRANSLATION: Marie Liguori Ewald, I.H.M.

REFERENCES:

1. St. Leo, epistle 154 to the bishops of Egypt, ed. Baller.
2. St. Leo, sermon 82 on the feast of the apostles Peter and Paul.
3. Addresses on 20 June 1859; 26 September 1859; 13 July 1860; 28 September 1860; 17 December 1860; 18 March 1861; 30 September 1861; and 9 June 1862. Encyclical letters on 18 June 1859 and 19 January 1860. Apostolic letter on 26 March 1860.
4. Ecumenical Council of Chalcedon in its letter to Pope Leo.
5. Mt 15.17.
6. Lk 10.16.
7. Mk 16.16.
8. Jn 3.18.
9. Lk 11.23.
10. Ti 3.11.
11. 2 Pt 2.1.
12. Mt 16.26.
13. 1 Tm 6.9-10.
14. St. Gregory the Great, homily 17 *in Evangel.*
15. St. Leo, epistle 167 to Rusticus, bishop of Narbonne.
16. Heb 13.8.

INCREDIBILI

ENCYCLICAL OF POPE PIUS IX
ON PERSECUTION IN
NEW GRANADA
SEPTEMBER 17, 1863
61

To the Venerable Brothers Anthony, Archbishop of Santa Fe de Bogotá, and his Suffragan Bishops in the Republic of New Granada.

Venerable Brothers, Greetings and Apostolic Benediction.

We are afflicted with incredible grief and groan together with you, venerable brothers, to learn of the nefarious and horrible ways in which the government of the republic of New Granada impedes, disturbs, and tears asunder the Catholic Church. Indeed words can scarcely express the many sacrileges with which the same government inflicts grievous injuries on Us and this Apostolic See; it strives to trample and destroy our most holy religion along with respect for its rights, doctrine, worship, and ministers. In particular, two years ago this same government passed abominable laws and decrees which greatly oppose the Catholic Church, her doctrines, her authority, and her rights. These iniquitous laws and decrees prohibit, among other things, sacred ministers from exercising their ecclesiastical ministry without the consent of the government. All properties of the Church have been confiscated and sold. Thus, with their own property having been yielded up, parishes religious communities of both men and women, the clergy, hospitals, houses of refuge, religious brotherhoods, benefices, and chaplaincies are despoiled, even of the right of patronage. These same unjust laws and decrees attack the legitimate right of the Church to acquire and possess property. They also declare liberty for non-Catholic sects. Furthermore, all the religious communities of both men and women have been banished from the territory of New Granada and their very existence interdicted. Forbidden also is the promulgation of all letters and every papal rescript. If any refuse to obey these ordinances, the penalty for all clergy is exile, for the laity, imprisonment without trial. Moreover it has been ordained by these detestable laws and decrees that both higher and lower clergy suffer exile if they refuse to obey the law concerning the confiscation of the goods of the Church. Furthermore, ecclesiastics may not go about the duties of their sacred ministry unless they have first sworn that they will abide by the constitution of the republic of New Granada and all its laws which are so adverse to the Church. All who refuse to take such an impious and illicit oath suffer the punishment of exile. These and many other unjust acts, which it is wearisome to mention individually, are promulgated against the Church by the government of New Granada and stand opposed to all divine and human laws.

Attacks on the Church by the Government of New Granada

2. Because of your renowned religious spirit and virtue, you have, both in word and in writing, consistently resisted many iniquitous and sacrilegious attempts and decrees of this government; you have fearlessly defended the cause of the Church and its rights. Because of your resistance, the fury of this government has not ceased to rage against you, against all of your clerics who are mindful of their proper office and vocation, and against all things which pertain to the Church. For this reason almost all of you have been most miserably treated, arrested by the military, forcibly separated from your flocks, thrown into prison, driven into exile, and sent away to regions with a pestilential climate. Priests and monks, rightly resisting the wicked decrees of the government, have either been put in jail, driven into exile where they died, or forced to live in the jungle. All nuns were furiously and cruelly driven from their convents by the governments and reduced to indigence; but they were taken into the homes of the faithful, who were moved by their sad condition, much to the displeasure of the government which threatened to expel them from these homes and disperse them. Hence with holy churches and monasteries stripped, plundered, polluted, and transformed into military barracks, and with their sacred furniture and ornaments stolen, the worship of sacred things is taken away and the Christian people are orphaned of their legitimate pastors and miserably deprived of all the divine aids of our religion. They are in great peril of losing eternal salvation, to Our and your great grief. Would not anyone, animated by Catholic and human sensibilities, grieve when he sees with what cruel persecution the government of New Granada attacks the Catholic Church, its doctrine, its authority, and its clergy, and how it inflicts great wrongs and outrages on Our supreme authority and that of the Apostolic See?

Some Clerics Sided with the Government

3. And what is most deplorable is that some ecclesiastics did not hesitate to obey and support the perverse laws and counsels of the government and to take the illicit oath of obedience. This caused Us and you great sorrow and scandalized and grieved all good people.

Condemnation of the Government of New Granada

4. In this great Catholic calamity and this tremendous ruin of souls, mindful of Our Apostolic office and solicitous of the welfare of the whole Church, We consider the words of the prophet of old as addressed to Us: "Cry, cease not, lift up thy voice like a trumpet and show My people their wicked doings and the house of Jacob their sins."[1] With this apostolic letter, We raise Our voice and lament without ceasing while reproaching the government of New Granada for the great damage and injustices it has inflicted on the Church, her sacred ministers, her property, and this Holy See. And by Our Apostolic authority We condemn everything which has been decreed, accomplished, or attempted in any way by the government of New Granada or by any of its lower magistrates, either in this matter or in others concerning the Church and her rights. Furthermore, by this same authority We abrogate the laws and decrees themselves with all their consequences and declare them entirely invalid, never to have had any force nor to have any in the future.

Retractions

And We also implore their leaders, that they may at length open their eyes and see the most grievous wounds suffered by the Church. At the same time, may they recall and seriously consider the censures and punishments which the Apostolic Constitutions and the Decrees of General Councils inflict on all invaders of the rights of the Church. Therefore pitying their own souls may they consider the words "For the strictest judgment awaits those who are leaders. And with all zeal, We also warn and exhort those ecclesiastics who, by supporting the government, have failed miserably in their proper office, to consider their holy vocation. We exhort them further to return quickly to the paths of justice and truth, and to emulate the example of those clerics who, though they also unhappily fell and took the oath demanded by the government, nevertheless, to Our great consolation and that of their bishops, gloried to retract and condemn their oath.

Defenders of the Church

5. Meanwhile We give you full and well-deserved praise, venerable brothers, who have labored like good soldiers of Christ Jesus, and strenuously fought with remarkable constancy and fortitude, both in word and in writing. You defended the cause of the Church, its doctrine, its rights, and its liberty. You have carefully kept in mind the salvation of your flock and fortified it against the impious machinations of the enemies of man and the dangers besetting the faith. You have borne the gravest wrongs, annoyances, and many trials with episcopal fortitude. Therefore We cannot doubt but that you will continue to defend the cause of our divine religion and to care for the salvation of the faithful with the same zeal and effort, just as you have done up to the present time. This has brought great glory to your name.

6. We also bring due praise to the devoted clergy of the republic of New Granada who, most observant of their vocation, were greatly disturbed for the sake of the Church, truth, and justice, and who suffered most patiently monstrous persecutions of all kinds.

7. We cannot help but admire and praise so many nuns who, though they have been violently driven from their convents and reduced to sad indigence, nevertheless firmly cling to their heavenly Spouse. They bear with Christian virtue the most miserable conditions in which they live. Never ceasing day or night to pour out their hearts before God, they humbly and zealously pray for the salvation of all, including their persecutors. We also praise the Catholic people of the republic of New Granada of which most in their ancient faith, in obedience, and in reverence for the Catholic Church, for Us, and this Apostolic See, and for their bishops.

Seek God's Intervention

8. We, moreover, venerable brothers, do not cease to approach the throne of grace with confidence, to implore the most merciful Father and the God of all consolation with humble and fervent prayers. We ceaselessly ask that He rise and judge His cause, and snatch His holy Church from the great calamities by which she is oppressed here and almost everywhere on earth. We ask that He console her with timely aid and mercifully bestow on her the desired serenity and peace in the midst of so many and such great adversities. We ask further that He pity all according to His great mercy and that by His omnipotence He bring it to pass that all peoples, races, and nations come to know, adore, and fear Him and His only-begotten Son our Lord Jesus Christ, together with the Holy Spirit. May they love Him with their whole heart, soul, and mind and, religiously observing all divine commands and precepts, may they walk as sons of light in all goodness, justice, and truth.

9. Finally, as an auspice of all heavenly gifts and as a pledge of Our special benevolence for you, We lovingly impart the apostolic benediction to you, venerable brothers, and to the flock entrusted to you.

Given in Rome at St. Peter's, on September 17, 1863, the 18th year of Our Pontificate.

†

LATIN TEXT: *Acta Pii IX*, I, 3:622-28.

ENGLISH TRANSLATION: Bernard A. Hausmann, S.J.

REFERENCES:

1. Is 58.1.
2. Wis 8.

MAXIMAE QUIDEM

ENCYCLICAL OF POPE PIUS IX ON
THE CHURCH IN BAVARIA
AUGUST 18, 1864
62

To the Venerable Brothers Gregory Archbishop of Munich and Freising and Michael Archbishop of Bamberg and their Suffragan Bishops in Bavaria.

Venerable Brothers, Greetings and Apostolic Benediction.

Your very welcome letter of July 20, was a source of great consolation to Us, venerable brothers, amid the grave cares and concerns which press upon Us. It was sent from the synod which you convened at Bamberg where you took counsel together so that you might decree those things which are of use, especially in these difficult times, in safeguarding the Catholic cause and its doctrines and rights, and in providing for the salvation of its faithful. This same letter clearly shows on every page your renowned and proven faith, love, and obedience toward Us and toward this See of Peter; it also manifests the admirable zeal which animates you to do everything so that the faithful committed especially to your vigilance may reverently and obediently follow Us and the See of Peter. This center of Catholic unity is not only the head of all the churches, but also their mother and teacher; it dispels the darkness of error and is the safest port for all who are tossed about. Therefore We rejoice greatly because of your extraordinary episcopal virtue and solicitude. We warmly congratulate you that by your deeds and your pastoral letters sent to the faithful entrusted to your care, you have made known that most close and admirable union of all the bishops of the Catholic world; that union with the Vicar of Christ here on earth and this Apostolic See flourishes even in these most lamentable times by a singular blessing of God and shines forth daily in many splendid deeds.

2. And We rejoice at the synod which you celebrated in Bamberg, in which all of you with great harmony and mindful of the duties of your episcopal ministry, approved plans to safeguard the cause of the Church, to care for its affairs, and to repress the efforts of the nefarious enemies of men. These must be overcome by the united and persistent vigilance of the bishops. If at any time whatsoever, then surely now in this most sad age, it is the duty of bishops to battle most strenuously against the enemies of the faith. Hence the bishops, relying on divine aid, must raise their episcopal voice and must preach the gospel to all. They must announce, teach, explain, and impress upon both the wise and the foolish, the eternal truths of our divine faith along with its doctrines and precepts. The bishops are also bound to explain and to show to both the highest princes

and the government the deplorable evils and damage which affect the people and the princes themselves. This is the result of the present-day contempt of religion and of the spirit of unbelief rising from the darkness under the fallacious appearance of social progress; this, of course, harms the Christian and the civil government. Everywhere it daily grows stronger; it perverts and corrupts the minds and souls of men. Therefore We were glad to hear that you have sent a letter to the illustrious king of Bavaria concerning the defense of our religion and its rights. We hope that because of his piety, his justice, and his equity, he will earnestly and most willingly endeavor to grant your requests.

Defend the Rights of the Church

3. There is also something else that holy priests ought to do. They must defend the liberty of the Catholic Church and manfully fight in defense of the rights with which His Church has been divinely endowed. Bishops are also required to continually remind all people that this Church has always been not only the mother and teacher of all virtues, but also the founder and governor of civilization and its benefits, of peace, of progress, and of prosperity. She alone is able to preserve the public order which is so gravely disturbed by impiety and rebellion.

Public Schools

4. Moreover We praise you for in the letter you sent to the government concerning the administration of the public schools, you, concerned about the affairs of the Church, strenuously and knowledgeably defended her authority, doctrine, and rights. In the same sense We, in Our July 14 letter to Herman, Archbishop of Freiburg im Briesgau, were compelled to safeguard and vindicate these rights of the Church. The enemies of the Church in the Grand Duchy of Baden had already proposed laws which destroy and entirely eliminate the Christian nature of the schools. We understand why you were concerned with defending the rights of the Church with regard to public schools. We want you also to labor diligently so that these same rights of the Church are recognized and observed in schools of higher education and more serious studies. For you know well that if these schools stray from the doctrine, authority, and vigilance of the Church, serious harm and evil will result. Those honorable men who are destined for the duties of public government and who can contribute so much to the formation of the common spirit of civil society will be infected with errors and false doctrines. And here We ask you to not forget what We wrote last December 21 to Gregory, Archbishop of Munich concerning the teaching of the disciplines of theology and philosophy. We exhort you to promote daily the correct education of the clergy. Leave nothing untried in order that your clergy may have that solid instruction, drawn from uncontaminated sources and based on the common teaching system of the Catholic Church. This system removes all those dangers inherent in the new modern style of teaching, which is based on the freedom—or rather license—of knowledge. Wherefore We desire that you support everything which at other times We have commended concerning erecting and governing the seminaries according to the prescriptions of the Council of Trent. Because of your proven religious and episcopal zeal, We are convinced that you will assiduously defend other rights of the Church which up to now have not been fully recognized in Bavaria. The bishops of Bavaria, particularly in the Synod of Freising, registered their protest against such abridgement of the Church's rights. Therefore We entirely approve your proposal to have annual meetings among yourselves. This should in no way interfere, however, with your making every effort to hold provincial synods according to the prescriptions of the sacred canons, as do the other bishops in Germany. Nothing certainly can be more pleasing to Us than to offer you Our resources and help in this matter. Finally We desire that you consider as certain Our special benevolence for you. And as proof of it receive the apostolic benediction which proceeds from the bottom of Our heart, and which We lovingly impart to you, venerable brothers, to all the clergy and the faithful laity committed to your care.

Given at the Castel Gandolfo, August 18, 1864, the nineteenth year of Our Pontificate.

†

LATIN TEXT: *Acta Pii IX*, I, 3:674-79.

ENGLISH TRANSLATION: Bernard A. Hausmann, S.J.

QUANTA CURA

ENCYCLICAL OF POPE PIUS IX CONDEMNING CURRENT ERRORS

DECEMBER 8, 1864

63

To *Our Venerable Brethren, all Patriarchs, Primates, Archbishops, and Bishops having favor and Communion of the Holy See.*

Venerable Brethren, Health and Apostolic Benediction.

With how great care and pastoral vigilance the Roman Pontiffs, our predecessors, fulfilling the duty and office committed to them by the Lord Christ Himself in the person of most Blessed Peter, Prince of the Apostles, of feeding the lambs and the sheep, have never ceased sedulously to nourish the Lord's whole flock with words of faith and with salutary doctrine, and to guard it from poisoned pastures, is thoroughly known to all, and especially to you, Venerable Brethren. And truly the same, Our Predecessors, asserters of justice, being especially anxious for the salvation of souls, had nothing ever more at heart than by their most wise Letters and Constitutions to unveil and condemn all those heresies and errors which, being adverse to our Divine Fatih, to the doctrine of the Catholic Church, to purity of morals, and to the eternal salvation of men, have frequently excited violent tempests, and have miserably afflicted both Church and State. For which cause the same Our Predecessors, have, with Apostolic fortitude, constantly resisted the nefarious enterprises of wicked men, who, like raging waves of the sea foaming out their own confusion, and promising liberty whereas they are the slaves of corruption, have striven by their deceptive opinions and most pernicious writings to raze the foundations of the Catholic religion and of civil society, to remove from among men all virtue and justice, to deprave persons, and especially inexperienced youth, to lead it into the snares of error, and at length to tear it from the bosom of the Catholic Church.

2. But now, as is well known to you, Venerable Brethren, already, scarcely had we been elevated to this Chair of Peter (by the hidden counsel of Divine Providence, certainly by no merit of our own), when, seeing with the greatest grief of Our soul a truly awful storm excited by so many evil opinions, and (seeing also) the most grievous calamities never sufficiently to be deplored which overspread the Christian people from so many errors, according to the duty of Our Apostolic Ministry, and following the illustrious example of Our Predecessors, We raised Our voice, and in many published Encyclical Letters and Allocutions delivered in Consistory, and other Apostolic Letters, we condemned the chief errors of this most unhappy age, and we excited your admirable episcopal vigilance, and we again

and again admonished and exhorted all sons of the Catholic Church, to us most dear, that they should altogether abhor and flee from the contagion of so dire a pestilence. And especially in our first Encyclical Letter written to you on Nov. 9, 1846, and in two Allocutions delivered by us in Consistory, the one on Dec. 9, 1854, and the other on June 9, 1862, we condemned the monstrous portents of opinion which prevail especially in this age, bringing wtih them the greatest loss of souls and detriment of civil society itself; which are grievously opposed also, not only to the Catholic Church and her salutary doctrine and venerable rights, but also to the eternal natural law engraven by God in all men's hearts, and to right reason; and from which almost all other errors have their origin.

3. But, although we have not omitted often to proscribe and reprobate the chief errors of this kind, yet the cause of the Catholic Church, and the salvation of souls entrusted to us by God, and the welfare of human society itself, altogether demand that we again stir up your pastoral solicitude to exterminate other evil opinions, which spring forth from the said errors as from a fountain. Which false and perverse opinions are on that ground the more to be detested, because they chiefly tend to this, that that salutary influence be impeded and (even) removed, which the Catholic Church, according to the institution and command of her Divine Author, should freely exercise even to the end of the world—not only over private individuals, but over nations, peoples, and their sovereign princes; and (tend also) to take away that mutual fellowship and concord of counsels between Church and State which has ever proved itself propitious and salutary, both for religious and civil interests.[1] For you well know, venerable brethren, that at this time men are found not a few who, applying to civil society the impious and absurd principle of *naturalism,* as they call it, dare to teach that "the best constitution of public society and (also) civil progress altogether require that human society be conducted and governed without regard being had to religion any more than if it did not exist; or, at least, without any distinction being made between the true religion and false ones." And, against the doctrine of Scripture, of the Church, and of the Holy Fathers, they do not hesitate to assert that "that is the best condition of civil society, in which no duty is recognized, as attached to the civil power, of restraining by enacted penalties, offenders against the Catholic religion, except so far as public peace may require." From which totally false idea of social government they do not fear to foster that erroneous opinion, most fatal in its effects on the Catholic Church and the salvation of souls, called by Our Predecessor, Gregory XVI, *an insanity,*[2] viz., that "liberty of conscience and worship is each man's personal right, which ought to be legally proclaimed and asserted in every rightly constituted society; and that a right resides in the citizens to an absolute liberty, which should be restrained by no authority whether ecclesiastical or civil, whereby they may be able openly and publicly to manifest and declare any of their ideas whatever, either by word of mouth, by the press, or in any other way." But, while they rashly affirm this, they do not think and consider that they are preaching *liberty of perdition;*[3] and that "if human arguments are always allowed free room for discussion, there will never be wanting men who will dare to resist truth, and to trust in the flowing speech of human wisdom; whereas we know, from the very teaching of our Lord Jesus Christ, how carefully Christian faith and wisdom should avoid this most injurious babbling."[4]

4. And, since where religion has been removed from civil society, and the doctrine and authority of divine revelation repudiated, the genuine notion itself of justice and human right is darkened and lost, and the place of true justice and legitimate right is supplied by material force, thence it appears why it is that some, utterly neglecting and disregarding the surest principles of sound reason, dare to proclaim that "the people's will, manifested by what is called public opinion or in some other way, constitutes a supreme law, free from all divine and human control; and that in the political order accomplished facts, from the very circumstance that they are accomplished, have the force of right." But who does not see and clearly perceive that human society, when set loose from the bonds of religion and true justice, can have, in truth, no other end than the purpose of obtaining and amassing wealth, and that (society under such circumstances) follows no other law in its actions, except the unchastened desire of ministering to its own pleasure and interests? For this reason, men of the kind pursue with bitter hatred the Religious

Orders, although these have deserved extremely well of Christendom, civilization and literature, and cry out that the same have no legitimate reason for being permitted to exist; and thus (these evil men) applaud the calumnies of heretics. For, as Pius VI, Our Predecessor, taught most wisely, "the abolition of regulars is injurious to that state in which the Evangelical counsels are openly professed; it is injurious to a method of life praised in the Church as agreeable to Apostolic doctrine; it is injurious to the illustrious founders, themselves, whom we venerate on our altars, who did not establish these societies but by God's inspiration."[5] And (these wretches) also impiously declare that permission should be refused to citizens and to the Church, "whereby they may openly give alms for the sake of Christian charity"; and that the law should be abrogated "whereby on certain fixed days servile works are prohibited because of God's worship;" and on the most deceptive pretext that the said permission and law are opposed to the principles of the best public economy. Moreover, not content with removing religion from public society, they wish to banish it also from private families. For, teaching and professing the most fatal error of *Communism and Socialism,* they assert that "domestic society or the family derives the whole principle of its existence from the civil law alone; and, consequently, that on civil law alone depend all rights of parents over their children, and especially that of providing for education." By which impious opinions and machinations these most deceitful men chiefly aim at this result, viz., that the salutary teaching and influence of the Catholic Church may be entirely banished from the instruction and education of youth, and that the tender and flexible minds of young men may be infected and depraved by every most pernicious error and vice. For all who have endeavored to throw into confusion things both sacred and secular, and to subvert the right order of society, and to abolish all rights, human and divine, have always (as we above hinted) devoted all their nefarious schemes, devices and efforts, to deceiving and depraving incautious youth and have placed all their hope in its corruption. For which reason they never cease by every wicked method to assail the clergy, both secular and regular, from whom (as the surest monuments of history conspicuously attest), so many great advantages have abundantly flowed to Christianity, civilization and literature, and to proclaim that "the clergy, as being hostile to the true and beneficial advance of science and civilization, should be removed from the whole charge and duty of instructing and educating youth."

Quanta cura
63

5. Others meanwhile, reviving the wicked and so often condemned inventions of innovators, dare with signal impudence to subject to the will of the civil authority the supreme authority of the Church and of this Apostolic See given to her by Christ Himself, and to deny all those rights of the same Church and See which concern matters of the external order. For they are not ashamed of affirming "that the Church's laws do not bind in conscience unless when they are promulgated by the civil power; that acts and decrees of the Roman Pontiffs, referring to religion and the Church, need the civil power's sanction and approbation, or at least its consent; that the Apostolic Constitutions,[6] whereby secret societies are condemned (whether an oath of secrecy be or be not required in such societies), and whereby their frequenters and favourers are smitten with anathema—have no force in those regions of the world wherein associations of the kind are tolerated by the civil government; that the excommunication pronounced by the Council of Trent and by Roman Pontiffs against those who assail and usurp the Church's rights and possessions, rests on a confusion between the spiritual and temporal orders, and (is directed) to the pursuit of a purely secular good; that the Church can decree nothing which binds the conscience of the faithful in regard to their use of temporal things; that the Church has no right of restraining by temporal punishments those who violate her laws; that it is conformable to the principles of sacred theology and public law to assert and claim for the civil government a right of property in those goods which are possessed by the Church, by the Religious Orders, and by other pious establishments." Nor do they blush openly and publicly to profess the maxim and principle of heretics from which arise so many perverse opinions and errors. For they repeat that the "ecclesiastical power is not by divine right distinct from, and independent of, the civil power, and that such distinction and independence cannot be preserved without the civil power's essential rights being assailed and usurped by the Church." Nor can we pass over in silence the audacity of those who, not enduring sound doctrine, contend that

"without sin and without any sacrifice of the Catholic profession assent and obedience may be refused to those judgments and decrees of the Apostolic See, whose object is declared to concern the Church's general good and her rights and discipline, so only it does not touch the dogmata of faith and morals." But no one can be found not clearly and distinctly to see and understand how grievously this is opposed to the Catholic dogma of the full power given from God by Christ our Lord Himself to the Roman Pontiff of feeding, ruling and guiding the Universal Church.

6. Amidst, therefore, such great perversity of depraved opinions, we, well remembering our Apostolic Office, and very greatly solicitous for our most holy Religion, for sound doctrine and the salvation of souls which is intrusted to us by God, and (solicitous also) for the welfare of human society itself, have thought it right again to raise up our Apostolic voice. Therefore, by our Apostolic authority, we reprobate, proscribe, and condemn all the singular and evil opinions and doctrines severally mentioned in this letter, and will and command that they be thoroughly held by all children of the Catholic Church as reprobated, proscribed and condemned.

7. And besides these things, you know very well, Venerable Brethren, that in these times the haters of truth and justice and most bitter enemies of our religion, deceiving the people and maliciously lying, disseminate sundry and other impious doctrines by means of pestilential books, pamphlets and newspapers dispersed over the whole world. Nor are you ignorant also, that in this our age some men are found who, moved and excited by the spirit of Satan, have reached to that degree of impiety as not to shrink from denying our Ruler and Lord Jesus Christ, and from impugning His Divinity with wicked pertinacity. Here, however, we cannot but extol you, venerable brethren, with great and deserved praise, for not having failed to raise with all zeal your episcopal voice against impiety so great.

8. Therefore, in this our letter, we again most lovingly address you, who, having been called unto a part of our solicitude, are to us, among our grievous distresses, the greatest solace, joy and consolation, because of the admirable religion and piety wherein you excel, and because of that marvellous love, fidelity, and dutifulness, whereby, bound as you are to us, and to this Apostolic See in most harmonious affection, you strive strenuously and sedulously to fulfill your most weighty episcopal ministry. For from your signal pastoral zeal we expect that, taking up the sword of the spirit which is the word of God, and strengthened by the grace of our Lord Jesus Christ, you will, with redoubled care, each day more anxiously provide that the faithful entrusted to your charge "abstain from noxious verbiage, which Jesus Christ does not cultivate because it is not His Father's plantation."[7] Never cease also to inculcate on the said faithful that all true felicity flows abundantly upon man from our august religion and its doctrine and practice; and that happy is the people whose God is their Lord.[8] Teach that "kingdoms rest on the foundation of the Catholic Faith;[9] and that nothing is so deadly, so hastening to a fall, so exposed to all danger, (as that which exists) if, believing this alone to be sufficient for us that we receive free will at our birth, we seek nothing further from the Lord; that is, if forgetting our Creator we abjure his power that we may display our freedom."[10] And again do not fail to teach "that the royal power was given not only for the governance of the world, but most of all for the protection of the Church;"[11] and that there is nothing which can be of greater advantage and glory to Princes and Kings than if, as another most wise and courageous Predecessor of ours, St. Felix, instructed the Emperor Zeno, they "permit the Catholic Church to practise her laws, and allow no one to oppose her liberty. For it is certain that this mode of conduct is beneficial to their interests, viz., that where there is question concerning the causes of God, they study, according to His appointment, to subject the royal will to Christ's Priests, not to raise it above theirs."[12]

9. But if always, venerable brethren, now most of all amidst such great calamities both of the Church and of civil society, amidst so great a conspiracy against Catholic interests and this Apostolic See, and so great a mass of errors, it is altogether necessary to approach with confidence the throne of grace, that we may obtain mercy and find grace in timely aid. Wherefore, we have thought it well to excite the piety of all the faithful in order that, together with us and you, they may unceasingly pray and beseech the most merciful Father of light and pity with most fervent and humble prayers, and in the fullness of faith flee always to Our Lord Jesus Christ, who redeemed

us to God in his blood, and earnestly and constantly supplicate His most sweet Heart, the victim of most burning love toward us, that He would draw all things to Himself by the bonds of His love, and that all men inflamed by His most holy love may walk worthily according to His heart, pleasing God in all things, bearing fruit in every good work. But since without doubt men's prayers are more pleasing to God if they reach Him from minds free from all stain, therefore we have determined to open to Christ's faithful, with Apostolic liberality, the Church's heavenly treasures committed to our charge, in order that the said faithful, being more earnestly enkindled to true piety, and cleansed through the sacrament of Penance from the defilement of their sins, may with greater confidence pour forth their prayers to God, and obtain His mercy and grace.

10. By these Letters, therefore, in virtue of our Apostolic authority, we concede to all and singular the faithful of the Catholic world, a Plenary Indulgence in the form of Jubilee, during the space of one month only for the whole coming year 1865, and not beyond; to be fixed by you, venerable brethren, and other legitimate Ordinaries of places, in the very same manner and form in which we granted it at the beginning of our supreme Pontificate by our Apostolic Letters in the form of a Brief, dated November 20, 1846, and addressed to all your episcopal Order, beginning, "Arcano Divinae Providentiae consilio," and with all the same faculties which were given by us in those Letters. We will, however, that all things be observed which were prescribed in the aforesaid Letters, and those things be excepted which we there so declared. And we grant this, notwithstanding anything whatever to the contrary, even things which are worthy of individual mention and derogation. In order, however, that all doubt and difficulty be removed, we have commanded a copy of said Letters be sent you.

11. "Let us implore," Venerable Brethren, "God's mercy from our inmost heart and with our whole mind; because He has Himself added, 'I will not remove my mercy from them.' Let us ask and we shall receive; and if there be delay and slowness in our receiving because we have gravely offended, let us knock, because to him that knocketh it shall be opened, if only the door be knocked by our prayers, groans and tears, in which we must persist and persevere, and if the prayer be unanimous . . . let each man pray to God, not for himself alone, but for all his brethren, as the Lord hath taught us to pray."[13] But in order that God may the more readily assent to the prayers and desires of ourselves, of you and of all the faithful, let us with all confidence employ as or advocate with Him the Immaculate and most holy Virgin Mary, Mother of God, who has slain all heresies throughout the world, and who, the most loving Mother of us all, "is all sweet . . . and full of mercy . . . shows herself to all as easily entreated; shows herself to all as most merciful; pities the necessities of all with a most large affection;"[14] and standing as a Queen at the right hand of her only begotten Son, our Lord Jesus Christ, in gilded clothing, surrounded with variety, can obtain from Him whatever she will. Let us also seek the suffrages of the Most Blessed Peter, Prince of the Apostles, and of Paul, his Fellow-Apostle, and of all the Saints in Heaven, who having now become God's friends, have arrived at the heavenly kingdom, and being crowned bear their palms, and being secure of their own immortality are anxious for our salvation.

12. Lastly, imploring from our great heart for You from God the abundance of all heavenly gifts, we most lovingly impart the Apostolic Benediction from our inmost heart, a pledge of our signal love towards you, to yourselves, venerable brethren, and to all the clerics and lay faithful committed to your care.

Given at Rome, from St. Peter's, the 8th day of December, in the year 1864, the tenth from the Dogmatic Definition of the Immaculate Conception of the Virgin Mary, Mother of God.

In the nineteenth year of Our Pontificate.

†

LATIN TEXT: *Acta Pii IX*, I, 3:687-700; *Acta Sanctae Sedis*, 3:160-67 [omits announcement of the jubilee], published in conjunction with the Syllabus of Errors (*Acta Pii IX*, I, 3:701-09; *Acta Sanctae Sedis*, 3:168-76).

ENGLISH TRANSLATION: *Catholic Historical Review*, 13 (July, 1927), 247-53. The translation in the *Dublin Review* [n.s. 4 (April, 1965), 500-29] gives Latin and English on opposite pages and includes the text and translation of the Syllabus.

REFERENCES:

1. Gregory XVI, encyclical epistle *Mirari vos*, 15 August 1832.

2. Ibid.
3. St. Augustine, epistle 105 (166).
4. St. Leo, epistle 14 (133), sect. 2, edit. Ball.
5. Epistle to Cardinal De la Rochefoucault, 10 March 1791.
6. Clement XII, *In eminenti*; Benedict XIV, *Providas Romanorum*; Pius VII, *Ecclesiam*; Leo XII, *Quo graviora*.
7. St. Ignatius M. to the Philadelphians, 3.
8. Ps 143.
9. St. Celestine, epistle 22 to Synod. Ephes. apud Const., p. 1200.
10. St. Innocent. I, epistle 29 ad Episc. conc. Carthag. apud Coust., p. 891.
11. St. Leo, epistle 156 (125).
12. Pius VII, encyclical epistle *Diu satis*, 15 May 1800.
13. St. Cyprian, epist. 11.
14. St. Bernard, Serm. *de duodecim praerogativis B. M. V. ex verbis Apocalyp.*

COMMENTARIES:

Balan, Pietro. *I clericali, i liberali e l'enciclica dell'8 dic. 1864.* Padova, 1865.

Chanterel, J. *Les actes pontificaux cités dans l'encyclique et le Syllabus du 8 décembre 1864.* Paris, Librairie Poussiegle et Fils, 1865.

Ehler, Sidney Z. and J. B. Morrall. "Pope Pius IX: political sections of the *Syllabus errorum*, December 8, 1864." In *Church and State through the centuries* (Westminster, Md., The Newman Press, 1954), p. 281-85.

"The encyclical and the syllabus." *Dublin Review*, n.s. 4 (April, 1865), 441-99.

"The encyclical of December 8th, 1864." *Dublin Review*, n.s. 5 (July, 1865), 246-55.

L'encyclique et l'épiscopat français; recueil complet contenant l'encyclique et le Syllabus, les réponses, lettres, circulaires, instructions pastorales et mandements de NN. SS. les archevêques et evêques et autres documents authentiques pour servir à la l'histoire contemporaine de l'Eglise. Paris, Gauguet et Pougeois, 1865. 480 p.

Fenton, Joseph C. "*Humani generis* and its predecessors." *American Ecclesiastical Review*, 123 (December, 1950), 452-58.

"Foreign events of Catholic Interest." *Dublin Review*, n.s. 4 (April, 1865), 560-81.

Isaia, Antonino. *Storia ed esame della enciclica e del sillabo dell'8 dicembre 1864.* Torino, Unione Tipografico-Editrice, 1865. 158 p.

Ketteler, Wilhelm E. von., bp. *Hirtenbrief über die Encyklika vom 8 Dezember, 1864.* Mainz, 1865.

McElrath, D. "The *Quanta cura* and *Syllabus* of Pius IX; some reactions in England." [Summary of dissertation.] *Liber Annualis Pontif. Universitas Gregoriana*, (Rome, 1962), p. 288-89.

Martina, Giacomo. "Nuovi documenti sulla genesi del *Sillabo*." *Archivum Historiae Pontificiae*, 6 (1968), 319-70.

Newman, John Henry, cardinal. "The encyclical of 1864." In *Certain difficulties felt by Anglicans in Catholic teaching.*" (London, Longmans, 1914), p. 262-75.

______ "The Syllabus." *Ibid.*, p. 276-98.

Schneider, Burkhart. "Der Syllabus Pius' IX und die deutschen Jesuiten." *Archivum Historiae Pontificiae*, 6 (1968), 371-92.

Sokoni, B. "Reactions de la presse française à l'encyclique *Quanta cura* et au *Syllabus*." [Summar. diss.] *Liber Annualis Pont. Universitas Gregoriana*, (Rome, 1968) 304-05.

Woodlock, Thomas F. " 'Liberalism' and the Church; the *Syllabus errorum* justified." *Month*, 167 (June, 1936), 493-503.

______ " 'Liberals' and the *Syllabus*." *Catholic Mind*, 42 (January, 1944), 12-20.

MERIDIONALI AMERICAE

ENCYCLICAL OF POPE PIUS IX ON THE
SEMINARY FOR NATIVE CLERGY
SEPTEMBER 30, 1865

64

To the Venerable Brothers, Archbishops and Bishops of South America.

Venerable Brothers, Greeting and Apostolic Benediction.

For South America, oppressed on all sides by so many trials, We are consoled to see a happy hope rise from the indigenous young clergy whom We take care to imbue with enduring piety and sound doctrine here in Rome. You know how willingly We prepared the college to receive and educate them, and how promptly, despite our limited resources, We strove to provide the necessary means for so great an undertaking. Naturally there was the problem of preparing candidates suitable for the Church, of taking care of the salvation of souls in those regions through them, and also of establishing a new clergy through them on their return to their fatherland. But since our strength is limited, We found ourselves unable to bear the burden, and so We fear that this work, begun with so great an effort and with such a bright outlook, may perish on its own. To avert such a calamity, We thus entrust this work to your love. We know that you thoroughly understand and support the necessity of carefully training an indigenous clergy to care for your flock. But, because your attention is divided among so many distractions, anguish, and cares, We remind you of this grave concern. We certainly, if at all possible, shall not fail this youth, which We embrace with paternal charity. While We predict a generous growth for it, We ask of you, venerable brothers, constancy, heavenly strength, and every consolation. And We, desiring the Apostolic Benediction to be an auspice of this and a proof of our special benevolence, impart it most lovingly to you, to the clergy, and to the faithful entrusted to each one of you.

Given at Rome at St. Peter's, September 30, 1865, in the twentieth year of Our Pontificate.

†

LATIN TEXT: *Acta Pii IX*, I, 4:29-30.

ENGLISH TRANSLATION: Bernard A. Hausmann, S.J.

and authority of this Holy See and of the bishops, and on the liberty of the highest pastor of all the faithful. It therefore drives the faithful to a mournful schism and even tramples underfoot natural law in matters pertaining to faith and conscience.

7. Add to this that the Catholic Academy of Warsaw has been closed and that a sad ruin awaits the Ruthenian dioceses of Chelm and Belzium. And what is most grievous is that a certain priest Woicicki has been found whose faith is suspect and who has no regard for ecclesiastical penalties and censures, nor for the terrible judgment of God. He was not afraid to accept the rule and administration of this same diocese from that civil power, nor to issure ordinances contrary to ecclesiastical discipline and favoring schism.

8. In these calamitous difficulties, no one fights for Us except Our Lord and God. We earnestly beseech you, because of your love for things Catholic and your devotion to Us, that you join your most fervent prayers with Ours. Together with all your clergy and faithful people, beseech God unceasingly to snatch His Holy Church and Us from such great evils. The sons of this same Church, who are most dear to Us, are exposed to many plots and afflicted with many hardships almost everywhere, but especially in Italy, in the Russian Empire, and in the Kingdom of Poland. Pray that God may aid and defend them by His omnipotent power. Pray that He may preserve, confirm, and strengthen them more each day in the Catholic faith and the profession of its salutary doctrines. Pray that He thwart all the impious plans of hostile men, recalling them from the abyss of iniquity to the way of salvation and leading them in the path of His commandments.

Plenary Indulgences

9. Therefore We desire that within six months a three-day period of public prayer be proclaimed in your dioceses; for those beyond the sea, the proclamation should be made within one year. To encourage more ardent devotion at these prayers, We grant mercifully in the Lord a plenary indulgence and the remission of all their sins to each and all the faithful in Christ, both men and women, who are devoutly present at these prayers on these three days, who have prayed to God for the present necessities of the Church according to Our intention, who have expiated their sins by sacramental confession, and who have received holy communion. But to the faithful who with at least a contrite heart are present on any one of these days, and have performed the other works, We grant an indulgence of seven years, and We relax as many forty-day periods of the penance enjoined on them or otherwise owed by them, in accordance with the usual custom of the Church. We also grant that these indulgences, all and singly, the remission of sins, and the relaxation of penances are applicable by way of suffrage to the souls of the faithful who, joined to God by love, have left this life. We also declare that anything to the contrary has no power to resist Our decrees.

Levate 65

10. Finally, nothing is more pleasing to Us than that We may use this occasion to testify and confirm the great benevolence with which We embrace you in the Lord. Receive as a certain pledge of this the Apostolic Benediction which We impart most lovingly to you, venerable brothers, and to all the clergy and faithful laity entrusted to your vigilance.

Given at Rome at St. Peter's, October 27, 1867, in the twenty-second of Our pontificate.

†

LATIN TEXT: *Acta Pii IX*, I, 4:371-78; *Acta Sanctae Sedis*, 3:197-202.

ENGLISH TRANSLATION: Bernard A. Hausmann, S. J.

RESPICIENTES

ENCYCLICAL OF POPE PIUS IX PROTESTING THE TAKING OF THE PONTIFICAL STATES
NOVEMBER 1, 1870

66

To All Patriarchs, Primates, Archbishops, Bishops, and other Ordinaries having Favor and Communion with the Apostolic See.

Venerable Brothers, Greetings and Apostolic Benediction.

As We look back on all the things which for many years the government of Piedmont has undertaken in order to overthrow the civil rule which God granted Our Apostolic See, We are moved by profound sorrow. God's purpose in providing the successors of St. Peter with temporal jurisdiction was to enable them to perform their spiritual duties in complete freedom and security. This government, by force and contrary to all divine law, has finally executed the plan it has long considered: the sacrilegious invasion of Our dear City and the cities We continued to rule after the previous occupation. We, prostrate before God, cry out using the words of the prophet: "Therefore do I weep and my eyes run down with water, because the Comforter, the Relief of my soul, is far from me. My children are desolate because the enemy hath prevailed."[1]

History of the War

2. We have already narrated the history of this evil war to the Catholic world. We did this in addresses, in encyclicals, and in short letters. The short letters were issued at various times, namely November 1, 1850; January 22 and July 26, 1855; June 18 and 28 and September 26, 1859; and January 19, 1860. Our encyclical was released March 26, 1860, and the addresses took place September 28, 1860; March 18 and September 30, 1861; and September 20, October 17, and November 14, 1867. This series of documents reveals and confirms that serious injuries were perpetrated by the government of Piedmont even before the seizure of Our ecclesiastical sovereignty. Such injuries were inflicted by the enacting of laws contrary to the natural, divine, and ecclesiastical order. That government also subjected ministers, religious communities, and even bishops to degrading ill-treatment. It violated its solemn agreements with Us by resolutely denying the inviolable rights of the very agreements it had confirmed. At the same time the government indicated that it wanted to enter into new agreements with Us. These documents demonstrate by what arts and with what sly and disgraceful machinations this same government oppressed the rights of the Apostolic See; they also indicate the efforts We made to check its increasing audacity and to vindicate the cause of the Church.

3. In 1859 the cities of Emilia were stirred up to rebellion by the Piedmontese, who supplied propaganda, conspirators, arms, and money. Not much later, a plebiscite was feigned by announcing a popular election and stealing the votes. By that deceit Our provinces situated in that region were torn from Our paternal rule; the opposition of the faithful proved vain. The following year this same government used deceitful pretexts to launch an unexpected attack, in order to wrest Our provinces located in Picenum, Umbria, and Our patrimony from Our rule. The enemy surrounded Our soldiers and a band of volunteer Catholic youth. Such a sudden attack was not at all anticipated. Our army fought fearlessly for its faith, but was put down in a bloody battle. Everyone knows the extraordinary impudence and hypocrisy of this government. To minimize the odium of this sacrilegious usurpation, they boasted that they invaded these provinces to restore the principles of moral order there. But in fact they spread every kind of false doctrine; they gave free reign to cupidity and impiety; they inflicted undeserved penalties on the bishops and other clerics, even jailing them and permitting them to suffer public insults. Meanwhile, they let persecutors and those who did not even spare the dignity of the Supreme Pontiff go unpunished.

4. In the performance of Our duties, We have always refused the repeated offers and commands to betray Our office shamefully, either by surrendering the rights and possessions of the Church, or by entering a wicked compact with the usurpers. We also opposed these crimes against human and divine law with solemn protestations lodged before both God and man. We declared that the authors of these crimes and their partisans have incurred ecclesiastical censure, and whenever necessary We censured them again with the same sanctions. The previously mentioned government has nevertheless persisted in its contumacy and its schemes. It attempted to stir up rebellion in Our remaining provinces, especially in Rome, by sending in instigators and by all kinds of arts. But these attempts did not go according to plan because of the unshaken fidelity of Our soldiers and because of the love and zeal of Our people, who supported Us.

Enemy Defeated

5. Finally that turbulent storm erupted against Us in the autumn of 1897, when divisions of wicked men attacked Our borders and Our City. They received assistance from the Piedmontese and were inflamed with wrath and crime. A number of them had already secretly infiltrated the City. Because of their arms, along with their cruel and violent nature, We and Our subjects feared painful and bloody treatment. But Our merciful God by the strenuous resistance of Our troops and the assistance of the French legions, returned their ineffectual attacks.

Reputation of the City

6. The piety and zeal of you and your faithful people for Us, manifested by your charity, have consoled Us in the midst of so much grief. With strength from God We never relax Our concern in safeguarding the temporal welfare of Our subjects. People from all nations visit Our City. They note Our public tranquility and security, Our finest arts and sciences, and the confidence and good will of Our people for Us. These visitors stream into Our City at all times, but especially during the many masses and solemn feasts which We celebrate.

Another Attack

7. Just now when Our people were enjoying a state of peace, the King of Piedmont and his government seized the opportunity presented by a war between the two most powerful nations of Europe. They made an agreement with one of the warring nations that they would preserve the present state of ecclesiastical or spiritual authority of the Church and would not permit it to be violated by factious individuals. They decreed that they would, however, invade and subject to their own power the lands which remained under Our temporal authority and Our See itself. What was the purpose of this hostile invasion, and what causes were presented? Everyone knows what the king discussed in his September 8 letter, which was addressed to us and delivered by his own spokesman. With fallacious sophistries of word and thought he proferred the images of a loving son and of a loyal Catholic and pretended to have the cause of public order, of the pontificate itself, and of Our person at heart. Under these pretenses he asked that We not consider the loss of Our temporal power as a criminal act, but that We surrender that power willingly. He asked Us to trust in his empty promises by which the desires of the Italian people could be reconciled

with the freedom and the supreme spiritual authority of the Roman Pontiff.

Rejection of Proposals

8. For Our part We could not help but be astonished at his means of concealing the violence soon to be inflicted on Us. Nor could We help but pity the lot of this same king; driven by unjust counsels, he daily inflicts new wounds on the Church. Because of his reverence for man rather than God, he does not believe that the King of kings and Lord of lords reigns in heaven "who shows no partiality nor does He fear greatness, because He Himself made the great as well as the small . . . but for the powerful a rigorous scrutiny impends."[2] However concerning his proposals, We knew there was no time for delay. Obeying the laws of Our office and conscience, We followed the example of Our predecessors, particularly Pius VII whose problems were much like Our own. We borrow his words here:

> Let us recall with St. Ambrose "the saintly man Naboth who owned a vineyard and was petitioned by a royal demand to give up his vineyard, so that the king, after cutting down the vines, might sow lowly vegetables. Naboth answered him: 'Be it far from me to surrender the inheritance of my predecessors'."[3] We judged that there was far less right for Us to give up so ancient and sacred an inheritance (namely the temporal power of this Holy See, held by the Roman Pontiffs for many centuries). Nor could We tacitly consent that someone occupy Our City and destroy its holy form of government, bequeathed by Jesus Christ to His Church and ordered according to the sacred canons which were inspired by the Holy Spirit. It would be replaced by a system opposed not only to the sacred canons, but also to the precepts of the Gospel. Then, as is customary, a new order of things would be introduced which would tend to associate and confuse all sects and superstitions with the Catholic Church.
>
> "Naboth defended his vineyard with his own blood."[4] Similarly, could We restrain Ourselves—no matter what might happen to Us—from defending the rights and possessions of the Holy Roman Church when We had sworn to defend the same to the best of Our ability? Could We refuse to protect the freedom of the Apostolic See which is so closely joined with the freedom and welfare of the whole Church? In truth these events demonstrate how necessary this temporal rule is for protecting the safe and free exercise of the pope's spiritual power, which was divinely given to him.[5]

Occupation of the City

9. Therefore clinging to the observations which We had declared in Our addresses, We reproved the king's unjust demands in Our reply to him and We showed that Our bitter pain was joined with paternal charity, which cares even for those sons who imitate the rebellious Absalom. However before We sent this letter, his army occupied Our cities, which until then were untouched and peaceful; the soldiers on guard were easily dispersed when they attempted to resist. Shortly thereafter dawned that unlucky day, September 20, when this City, the Seat of the Prince of the Apostles, the Center of the Catholic religion, and the refuge of all nations, was occupied by many thousands of armed men. It is deplorable to Us that after the walls were breached and fear of the enemy's dreadful missiles spread on all sides, the City was taken at the king's command who, a little before, had professed his filial affection for Us and his fidelity to religion. What could be more lamentable for Us and for all good people than that dread day? After the troops entered the City, which was already filled with a multitude of foreign agitators, We saw public order immediately disturbed and overturned; We saw the dignity and sanctity of the pontificate impiously attacked; We saw Our faithful soldiers subjected to abuse of every kind; We saw unbridled license and wantonness reigning where a short time before the filial love of children who desire to comfort a common spiritual Parent in his grief had shone forth.

Resultant Evils

10. From that day forward We have seen with Our own eyes events which cannot be recalled without indignation by all good people: Wicked books filled with lies, infamy, and impiety; are offered for sale and disseminated widely; numerous magazines are published each day to corrupt minds and upright laws, to show contempt for religion, and to rouse public opinion against Us and this Apostolic See. In addition, filthy and shameful pictures and other things of this kind are published in which sacred things and persons are derided and exposed to public ridicule. Honors and memorials have been decreed for those convicted of grave crimes, while clerics have been repeatedly and wrongfully harassed, some even wounded by beatings from traitors. Some religious houses were subjected to unjust search and Our Quirinal houses were violated. A cardinal who had his See there was violently forced to flee, while other clerics of Our domestic staff were denied the use of the Quirinal houses and badgered. Laws and decrees were issued which obviously injure and destroy the freedom, immunity, properties, and rights of the Church of God. These evils will spread still more widely unless God intervenes. We, in the meantime, are prevented from bringing any cure because of Our condition. Every day We are violently reminded of Our captivity and of Our lost liberty. They declare with lying words that freedom has been left for Us in the exercise of Our apostolic ministry, and the usurping government boasts that it desires to strengthen this liberty with the necessary precautions, as they call them.

11. We must mention here the monstrous crime which you are certainly aware of. They made use of a ludicrous type of plebiscite in the provinces stolen from Us. As if the properities and rights of the apostolic See, long considered sacred and inviolable, might now be called into question, and as if the censures which are called down upon these violators might be loosened and the robbery which We have suffered might be made legitimate. Those who are accustomed to rejoice in evil events were not ashamed to carry rebellion and contempt for ecclesiastical censures through the cities of Italy on this occasion as in a triumphal procession. But the true feelings of the majority of the Italian people are impeded. Their religion, devotion, and confidence in Us and the Holy Church have been restrained in many ways so that these sentiments cannot flow forth freely.

Papal Protests against Usurpations

12. We have been placed by God to rule and govern the whole house of Israel and appointed as the protector of religion, justice, and the rights of the Church. If We remained silent, We could be accused before God and the Church of having consented to these perverse disturbances. We therefore renew and confirm what We have solemnly declared already in the addresses, encyclicals, and short letters cited above, and most recently a protest which Our cardinal in charge of public affairs made in Our name and at Our order on September 20. This protest was delivered to the ambassadors, ministers, and representatives of foreign nations who remained with Us and the Holy See. We now again solemnly declare to you that We are determined to retain all the dominions of this Holy See and its rights whole, entire, and unviolated, and to transmit them to Our successors. We declare all usurpations to be unjust, violent, null, and void. We announce now that any acts committed by Our enemies and invaders to confirm these usurpations—either at the present time or in the future—are condemned by Us and null and invalid. Furthermore, We protest before God and the whole Catholic world that while detained in such captivity, We are unable to exercise Our supreme pastoral authority safely, expediently, and freely. Finally, We obey the admonition of St. Paul: "For what has justice in common with iniquity? Or what fellowship has light with darkness? What harmony is there between Christ and Belial?"[6] We declare openly, mindful of Our office and of Our oath, that We will never assent to a conciliation or an agreement which in any way may destroy or diminish Our rights and therefore those of God and the Holy See. In like manner We confess that for the Church of Christ We are prepared, with the help of divine grace, to drink to the dregs that cup which the Lord first deigned to drink for her. We will never accept and obey unjust demands which are presented to Us. And indeed as Our predecessor Pius VII said: "To do violence to this highest power of the Apostolic See, to disjoin its temporal authority from its spiritual power, to disassociate, separate by force and cut off the duties of Pastor and Prince, is nothing less than to overturn and destroy the work of God. It is nothing less then to attempt to inflict the greatest damage on religion and to deprive it of its most effective defense. Then the highest Ruler of the Church would be unable to offer help to the Catholics spread all over the earth, who request his help and support because of his spiritual power."[7]

Excommunication for Usurpers

13. Our warnings, admonitions, and expostulations had no effect; therefore by Our own authority and that of God and of the Apostles Peter and Paul, We declare to you and to the whole Church that any who have invaded or usurped Our provinces or Our beloved City (as well as those commanding these things and their partisans, helpers, advisers, and followers) have incurred excommunication and the other censures and ecclesiastical penalties imposed by the sacred canons, Apostolic Constitutions, and decrees of Trent (Sess. 22, c. 11 de Reform.) following the form and duration expressed in Our apostolic letter of March 26, 1860.

Hope That Usurpers Will Reform

14. But mindful that We hold His place on earth who came to seek and save what was lost. We desire nothing more than that the wandering sons, returning to Us, may be embraced with paternal charity. We humbly beseech God, that He may be with Us and help Us. May He also be with His Church, reflecting on the eternal damnation which they pile up for themselves and fearing His justice, may strive to please Him before the Judgment Day. With their wicked schemes abandoned, may they alleviate the groans of Holy Mother Church and Our own grief.

15. But that We may obtain these blessings from the divine clemency, We earnestly request, venerable brothers, that you and your faithful flocks join your fervent prayers with Ours. Then all of us together shall approach the throne of grace and mercy, using as intercessors the Immaculate Virgin Mary, Mother of God, and the blessed Apostles Peter and Paul. "The Church of God from its beginning up to the present time was often in tribulation, and was often delivered. Her voice is: 'Often have they fought against me from my youth, but have not prevailed against me. On my back sinners have wrought havoc; they lengthened their iniquity.' Neither does the Lord now permit the rod of the wicked to rest over the lot of the just. The hand of the Lord has not been shortened, nor made incapable of salvation. Without a doubt He will now deliver His spouse whom He redeemed with His blood, endowed with His spirit, adorned with heavenly gifts, and enriched with terrestrial wealth."[8]

16. Meanwhile, We pray with all Our soul that you may be showered with the gifts of heavenly graces, venerable brothers, and that all the clergy and the lay faithful entrusted by God to your care may share in these gifts. As a pledge of Our special love, We affectionately impart the apostolic benediction to you and to Our beloved sons.

Given in Rome at St. Peter's, November 1, 1870, the 25th year of Our Pontificate.

†

LATIN TEXT: *Acta Pii IX*, I, 5:263-77; *Acta Sanctae Sedis*, 6:136-45.

ENGLISH TRANSLATION: Bernard A. Hausmann, S.J.

REFERENCES:

1. Lam 1.16.
2. Wis 6.8,9.
3. De Basil. trad. n. 17.
4. St. Ambrose, Ibid.
5. Apostolic letter, 10 June 1809.
6. 2 Cor 6.14,15.
7. Alloc., 16 March 1808.
8. St. Bernard, Epistle 244 to King Conrad.

UBI NOS

ENCYCLICAL OF POPE PIUS IX
ON PONTIFICAL STATES
MAY 15, 1871
67

To all the Patriarchs, Primates, Archbishops, Bishops, and other Local Ordinaries, who are in Loving Communion with the Apostolic See.

Venerable Brothers, We give you Our Greetings and Apostolic Blessing.

When We were defeated by Our enemies in accordance with the mysterious design of God, We observed the severely bitter fortunes of Our City and the downfall of the civil rule of the Apostolic See in the face of military invasion. Then We sent you Our letter of the 1st of November 1869 to tell you, and the whole Catholic world through you, the state of Our affairs and those of this City. We also told you of Our subjection to the excesses of impious and unbridled license. We testified before God and man that We desired the rights of the Apostolic See to be safe and unprejudiced, as the nature of Our supreme office demanded. We summoned you and all Our beloved children, the faithful entrusted to your care, to appease the divine majesty with fervent prayers. Since that time the ills and disasters of this City and Ourselves, foreshadowed by those first unhappy experiences, have really exceeded all bounds in assailing Our Apostolic rank and authority, the sanctity of religion and morals, and Our dearest subjects. What is more, venerable brothers, since conditions worsen daily, We are compelled to repeat the words of St. Bernard: "this is the beginning of the evils; we fear worse evil."[1] For wickedness advances on its path and promotes its designs. No longer does it take pains to conceal its worst deeds since they cannot remain hidden, but it is eager to carry off the last spoils from the overthrow of justice, honor, and religion. Our days are filled with bitterness, particularly when We consider the dangers and deceits to which the virtue of Our faithful people is subjected every day. When We recall the exceptional merits of yourselves, venerable brothers, and of the faithful embraced by your care, We are greatly pleased. For in every region of the earth, Christ's faithful have answered Our exhortations with wonderful enthusiasm, ever since the ill-starred day of the City's capture. Following your lead and example, they have prayed continually and fervently. They approach the throne of divine clemency with perseverance in repeated public supplication, in undertaking holy pilgrimages, in unceasingly thronging to the churches, in partaking of the sacraments, and in the other main works of Christian virtue.

Benefits of Prayer

2. This burning zeal for prayer cannot fail to produce the most abundant fruit in God's sight.

Many benefits indeed have already come from this source, and these give promise of further benefits which We confidently await. For We see the faith and charity growing and spreading daily, and We observe that the distressing attacks on this See and on the supreme Shepherd have aroused such concern in the spirits of Christ's faithful as only God could inspire. We perceive such great unity that never until now, since the first days of the Church, did the multitude of the faithful so clearly show that they are of one heart and one soul.[2] With this show of virtue before Us, We cannot be silent about Our dearest children, the citizens of this fair city, whose love and piety towards Us exceed all bounds. Their constancy too continues to be splendidly equal to the struggle, and their greatness of soul rivals that of their ancestors.

3. Consequently, We give unending glory and thanks to God for all of you and for Our beloved children, Christ's faithful. He continues to effect great deeds in you and in His Church, and has ensured that although malice abounds, the grace of faith, charity, and confession abound too. "What then is our hope and joy and crown of glory? Isn't it you in the presence of God? A wise son is the glory of his father. May God accordingly reward you and be mindful of the faithful service, pious compassion, consolation, and honor which you continue to give to the spouse of His Son in an evil time and in the days of her affliction."[3]

The Northern Government

4. Meanwhile indeed, the Piedmont government is on the one hand bent on making the city the talk of the world.[4] On the other hand, to deceive the Catholics and calm their anguish, it has promoted certain empty immunities and privileges, commonly called "guarantees." These "guarantees are compensation for stripping Us of Our civil rule; this they accomplished by a lengthy series of machinations and their unholy arms. We have already delivered Our judgment on these immunities and provisions, and stigmatized their absurdity, cunning and mockery in Our letter of last 2nd March to Constantine Patrizi, cardinal of the holy Roman Church, dean of the Sacred College, and Vicar of Our Authority in the City. This letter was immediately printed and published.

5. But it is characteristic of the Piedmont Government to unite continuous, base pretense with shameless contempt for Our papal rank and authority. It has also shown that it completely disregards Our protestations, complaints and censures. Accordingly it has not ceased in the least to press on with the serious discussion and examination of these "guarantees" before the highest bodies in the kingdom, despite Our expressed judgment on these provisions. In this disscussion, both the truth of Our judgment on the nature of these provisions and the vain attempt of Our enemies to conceal their malice and deceit have been clearly seen. Assuredly, these many errors and blasphemies are plainly at variance with the Catholic faith and with the very foundations of natural law. It is unbelievable that they could have been produced here in Italy, whose chief glory has always been in the practice of the Catholic religion and in the Apostolic See. And in fact, Italians join with Us in lamenting and deploring this novel and unheard-of sacrilege. Indeed, they have shown Us by ever-increasing notable proofs and deeds of piety that they are allied in one spirit and understanding with the rest of the world's faithful.

Warning Against Deceivers

6. Accordingly We address you again, venerable brothers. The faithful entrusted to you have clearly indicated both by letter and serious protestations how painful they find Our beleaguered state. They are far from being deceived by the measures which are disguised as "guarantees." Nevertheless We must solemnly declare through you to the whole world that not only these so-called guarantees, but all other titles, honors, immunities, and privileges—that is whatever else can be named a "guarantee"—cannot protect the due and free exercise of Our God-given power and cannot preserve the necessary liberty of the Church.

Necessity of Civil Rule

7. Therefore We can submit to no agreement which would in any way destroy or diminish Our rights, which are the rights of God and of the Apostolic See. If We did, We would be violating Our sworn trust, which We have often declared and professed. Similarly, We never can and never shall allow or accept those "guarantees" devised by the Piedmont Government, whatever their motive. Nor shall We ever accept other similar

ones. These are often offered under the guise of defending Our holy power and liberty in compensation for the civil rule they stripped Us of. But divine providence has willed this civil rule to be protection and strength for the Apostolic See; furthermore, legitimate and indisputable titles, as well as Our having possessed it for more than eleven centuries, confirm Our right to it. For if the Roman Pontiff were subject to the sway of another ruler, but no longer possessed civil power, neither his position nor the acts of the Apostolic ministry would be exempt from the authority of the other ruler. This ruler could be either a heretic or a persecutor of the Church or constantly at war with other rulers.

God-given Rights

8. Indeed, is not this concession of "guarantees" itself the clearest proof that laws are being imposed on Us? God has given Us the authority of making laws in regard to the religious and moral order. We have been established as interpreters of the natural and divine law for the entire world; these laws concern the government of the universal Church. Will their observance and execution be right only because they are commanded and established by the will of lay powers? We, as the representative of blessed Peter, have received directly from God Himself all the prerogatives and all rights of authority which are necessary for ruling the universal Church; those prerogatives and rights, as well as the liberty of the Church, were produced and acquired by the blood of Jesus Christ and must be valued in accordance with the infinite value of His divine blood. So We would not be valuing the divine blood of Our Redeemer if We borrowed Our rights for the rulers of the earth, especially in the curtailed and defiled condition in which they now want to present them.

Teaching of St. Anselm

9. For Christian rulers are sons, not lords, of the Church. St. Anselm, Archbishop of Canterbury, that great light of holiness and teaching, aptly used to say to rulers: "Do not think that the Church of God has been given to you to serve you as its master you are its advocate and defender. God loves nothing in this world more than the liberty of His holy Church."[5] To inspire rulers, he wrote elsewhere: "Never consider that your high rank is diminished if you love and defend the liberty of the Spouse of God and your Mother the Church; do not think you are humbled if you raise Her up: do not believe you are weakened if you strengthen Her. Look round and see: examples are ready: contemplate the rulers who fought against Her and trampled on Her. What was their reward? To what end did they come? It is clear enough and need not be stated. Assuredly those who glorify Her will be glorified with Her and in Her."[6]

10. Now from what We have just told you, as We have done on other occasions, it must be perfectly clear to all that injury suffered by this Holy See in these bitter times affects the entire Christian commonwealth. For, as St. Bernard used to say, an injury done to the Apostles, the glorious rulers of the earth, involves every Christian. And since the Roman Church works for all the churches, as St. Anselm says, whoever takes this church's goods away is regarded as guilty of sacrilege, not towards this church alone, but towards all churches.[7] No one can doubt that the preservation of the rights of this Apostolic See is most closely bound up with the most important advantages and benefits of the universal Church and the freedom of your episcopal ministry.

Civil Rule Given by God

11. Reflecting on all these matters, We are compelled to confirm again and profess without change what We have often declared to you and what you have all agreed with. Divine Providence gave the civil rule of the Holy See to the Roman Pontiff. This rule is necessary in order that the Roman Pontiff may never be subject to any ruler or civil power, but may be able to freely exercise his supreme power and authority of feeding and ruling the entire flock of the Lord, and of looking after the greater good of this Church, its well-being, and its needs.

Pray for the End of the Fighting

12. Since you and your faithful understand this well, you have all risen up for the sake of religion, justice, and tranquillity, which are the foundation of all good things. You make the Church of God glorious with the worthy show of your faith, charity, constancy, and virtue; by your faithful efforts in the Church's defense, you fashion a new and wonderful example in its history, which will be remembered by generations to come. But since the God of mercies is the

source of those good things, We raise Our eyes, Our hearts, and Our hope to Him. We continually beseech Him to strengthen and increase the illustrious understanding of you and of the faithful, the piety you share, your love, and your zeal. We strongly exhort you and your people likewise to cry to the Lord with Us more strongly day by day, as the fighting grows more stern, that He may Himself deign to hasten the days of His propitiation.

Unite the Rulers

13. The rulers of the earth do not want the usurpation which We are suffering to be established and to thrive to the ruin of all authority and order. May God unite all rulers in agreement of mind and will. By removing all discord, claiming the disturbance of rebellions, and rejecting the ruinous counsels of the sects, may these rulers join in a common effort to have the rights of the Holy See restored. Then tranquillity will once again be restored to civil society.

14. Then request the divine clemency to dispel the blindness of impious minds and convert their hearts to penitence before the great and awful day of the Lord arrives, or to check their lawless plans and show them how foolish those men are who attempt to overthrow the rock founded by Christ and infringe its divine privileges.[8] In these prayers may Our hope be set more strongly on God. "Do you think that God can turn His ear away from His dearest spouse when she cries while opposing those who straiten her? How shall He not acknowledge bone of His bones and flesh of His flesh and even in some manner spirit of His spirit? Now indeed is the hour of wickedness and the power of darkness. But it is the final hour and the power quickly passes away. Christ the strength of God and the wisdom of God is with us, and He is on our side. Have confidence: he has overcome the world."[9] Meanwhile let Us follow with great courage and assured faith the voice of eternal truth which says: fight for justice with your life, and struggle for justice even to death, then God will conquer your enemies for you.[10]

Finally, We heartily beseech from God the richest gifts of His heavenly grace for you, venerable brothers, and for all clerics and faithful laity entrusted to your individual care; and as a pledge of Our special and deep charity towards you and them, We lovingly impart to you and to these dear children Our Apostolic blessing.

Given at Rome in St. Peter's on the 15th of May in the year of the Lord 1871 in the twenty-fifth year of Our Pontificate.

†

LATIN TEXT: *Acta Pii IX*, I, 5:306-16; *Acta Sanctae Sedis*, 6:257-63.

ENGLISH TRANSLATIONS: Padraig M. O'Cleirigh

REFERENCES:

1. Epistle 243.
2. Acts 4.32.
3. St. Bernard, epistles 238 and 130.
4. St. Bernard, epistle 243.
5. Epistle 8.1.4.
6. Epistle 12.1.4.
7. Epistle 42.1.3.
8. St. Greg. VII, epistle 6.1.3.
9. St. Bernard, epistles 126,6, and 14.
10. Eccl 4.33.

BENEFICIA DEI

ENCYCLICAL OF POPE PIUS IX ON THE
TWENTY-FIFTH ANNIVERSARY
OF HIS PONTIFICATE
JUNE 4, 1871
68

To all Patriarchs, Primates, Archbishops, Bishops, and other Local Ordinaries in Loving Communion with the Apostolic See.

Venerable Brothers, We give you Greeting and Our Apostolic Blessing.

The favors of God summon Us to celebrate His kindness, especially since He continues to protect Us. For We are now in the 25th year of our papacy. You know well the painful crises We have endured. Truly it is clear, from the succession of so many events, that the Church militant in its many struggles and victories is prevailing; truly God governs change and rules over the world which is His footstool; truly He often makes use of weak and despicable instruments to accomplish the designs of His wisdom.

Accomplishments of the Papacy

2. Jesus Christ has strengthened and guided Our weakness and inadequacy through Our long papacy. So, relying on His divine aid and continually benefitting from the advice of the cardinals, and often from your advice also, venerable brothers, when many of you came to Rome adorning this See of truth with the brightness of your virtue and united piety. We have been able in the course of this Pontificate to declare and define as a dogma the Immaculate Conception of the Virgin Mother of God in fulfillment of the desires of the Catholic world and Ourselves. We have also decreed heavenly honors for the many courageous men and women of our religion. We do not doubt that they and the Mother of God will help the Catholic Church in these most unfavorable times. Because of God's help, We were able also, by sending evangelical laborers, to spread Catholicism to widely separated and even unfriendly districts, to establish the order of ecclesiastical hierarchy in many places, and to condemn the errors of our age opposed to human reason and good morals. Likewise with God's help, We made an alliance between the ecclesiastical and the civil power both in the regions of Europe and America. We also cared for the many needs of the eastern church, which from the start of Our Apostolic ministry We have always regarded with fatherly love. Not very long ago We undertook and promoted the work of the ecumenical Vatican Council. But because of the imfamous turn in events, We had to suspend it after some great results had been achieved, but while others were awaited by the Church.

Usurpation of the City

3. And, venerable brothers, We have never

neglected what the right and duty of Our civil rule demanded. The congratulations and applause which greeted the beginning of Our pontificate, quickly changed into insults and attacks so great that We were forced into exile from this Our beloved city. But when We returned to the See with the support of Catholic peoples and rulers, We immediatley toiled to achieve real prosperity, free from deceit for Our faithful subjects. We have always recognized this as the most serious duty of Our civil rule. But the greed of the neighboring ruler coveted the regions of Our temporal realm, and he obstinately preferred the advice of the sects of perdition to Our repeated warning and summonses. Most recently, he has far outdone the shamelessness even of the Prodigal Son. He has stormed Our city by force and now even controls it. We are, of course, greatly upset at this lawless usurpation of which We are the victim. We are utterly pained at the great wickedness of the plan to destroy Our civil rule, which at the same time would destroy Our spiritual power and the kingdom of Christ on earth. We are pained at the sight of so many serious evils, especially of those which jeopardize the eternal salvation of Our people. In this bitterness, nothing is more saddening for Us than to be prevented by the state of Our defeated liberty from applying the necessary remedies to so many evils.

Problems of the French

4. To these reasons for Our sorrow, We must add the long and pitiful succession of disasters and evils which have for so long smitten the illustrious French nation. These evils have recently increased enormously through the quite unheard-of excesses of beastly, God-forsaken scum. In particular, We are horrified and tormented by the murder of the Archbishop of Paris which has filled the whole world with fear and horror. Finally, another bitterness greater than the rest afflicts Us when We see so many sons in revolt, burdened by so many serious censures. They pay no heed to Our fatherly voice nor to their own salvation, but continue to despise the time which God still offers them for penitence; instead, they prefer to deride the anger of divine punishment rather then to experience the fruit of mercy in good season.

Praise for God

5. And now in the midst of such changes, We see that by the most kind protection of God, the anniversary of Our elevation has arrived. We succeeded to the See of blessed Peter, and now in length of years of Apostolic service We equal him, although We are far from equal to him in merit. This is truly a new, unique, and mighty gift of God's condescension, conferred only on Us in the whole line of Our holy predecessors throughout nineteen centuries. On this occasion, We recognize the even more wonderful kindness of God toward Us, when We see that He has deemed Us worthy to suffer persecution for the sake of justice, and when We see the marvelous feelings of devotion and love which strongly move the Christian people the world over, uniting them to this Holy See. Indeed, since He conferred these gifts on Us despite Our great unworthiness, We are unable to return thanks in a fitting manner.

6. Therefore, while We ask the Mother of God to teach Us to glorify God as she did with those sublime words, "He Who is Mighty has done great things for me," We urgently beseech you and your flocks to join with us in singing canticles and hymns of praise and thanks to God. Magnify the Lord with me, We say in the words of St. Leo the Great, and let us exalt His name to one another; then We may praise God who is the source of all the graces and mercies We have received. Let your people know, however, Our deep gratitude for their remarkable testimonies and services which they have given with such constancy for so long. As regards Ourselves, since We may claim with justice the words uttered by the Royal Prophet, "my habitation has been prolonged," We still need the help of your prayers to enable Us with strength and confidence to return Our soul to the Prince of Shepherds. In His bosom there is refreshment from the evils of this troubled and painful life and a blessed haven of eternal calm and peace.

7. However, in order that the gifts conferred on Our pontificate by God's generosity may be to His greater glory, on this occasion We empower each of you, by Our Apostolic authority, to give the Papal Blessing with the addition of a plenary indulgence in the usual form of the Church, on the 16th or 21st of this month or on another day of your choice. We desire to look after the spiritual benefit of the faithful. Consequently, We grant that all Christ's faithful who receive the sacraments of Penance and holy Communion and offer pious prayers for the harmony of Christian rulers, for the complete destruction of

heresies, and for the exaltation of Our Holy Mother the Church, can obtain a plenary indulgence for all their sins. The faithful can obtain the indulgence in any place in each of your dioceses on any day you choose. In dioceses where the cathedral see is vacant, the Vicars Capitular at the time can choose the day. We have no doubt that this opportunity will effectively arouse the Christian people to prayer, and that when prayers have been thus increased, We will receive the mercy which the present ills compel Us to pray for wholeheartedly.

8. Meanwhile, venerable brothers, We request for you from Almighty God constancy, heavenly hope, and all consolation. We wish the Apostolic blessing, which with the full abundance of Our love We impart to you, your faithful, and clergy to be an augury of those gifts and a witness of Our special benevolence.

Given at Rome in St. Peter's on the fourth of June, the feast of the Most Holy Trinity, in the year 1871 in the 25th year of Our Pontificate.

†

LATIN TEXT: *Acta Pii IX*, I, 5:324-30; *Acta Sanctae Sedis*, 6:269-73.

ENGLISH TRANSLATION: Padraig M. O'Cleirigh

SAEPE VENERABILES FRATRES

ENCYCLICAL OF POPE PIUS IX ON THANKSGIVING
FOR TWENTY-FIVE YEARS OF PONTIFICATE
AUGUST 5, 1871

69

To *Our Venerable Brothers the Patriarchs, Archbishops, Bishops and all Local Ordinaries of the Catholic World Who are in Loving Communion with the Apostolic See.*

Venerable Brothers, We give You Greeting and Our Apostolic Blessing.

Often, venerable brothers, in the course of Our long pontificate, We have addressed you and let you know how pleased We were to receive proofs of your devotion and love for Us and this Apostolic See which the God of mercies has inspired in you and in the faithful entrusted to your care. Certainly when the enemies of God began to invade His civil realm in order to defeat Jesus Christ and His Church, the Christian people and yourselves, never stopped beseeching God "Whom winds and seas obey" to calm the storm. You never stopped reiterating the testimonies of your love and performing every service which could console Us in Our affliction. But after Our city was taken and We were delivered into the hands of Our attackers, you and your people redoubled your prayers, and with frequent denunciations, you affirmed the sacred rights of religion and justice which are being trodden down with unbelievable effrontery.

Record Length of Papacy

2. We have reached the twenty-sixth year of Our papacy, an unusual event which has never before occurred in the succession of Roman pontiffs since the days of St. Peter. You have been so joyful for Us, and you have shown so clearly the vigorous life which everywhere inspires the Christian family, that We have been deeply touched. By joining Our prayers to yours, We have gained new strength to await with greater confidence the full and complete triumph of the Church.

Response of the Faithful

3. Thronging crowds everywhere filled the holy churches to pray for Us. All over the world the faithful attended in very great numbers to give thanks to God for the lengthy Papacy conferred on Us, and to request urgently from Him the victory of the Church. Our sorrow and anxieties were not only relieved but turned into joy, We felt, by the congratulation, obedience, and prayers manifested in your letters, and by the arrival of great numbers of people here from all parts of the world. Among these, many were remarkable for nobility of birth or their ecclesiastical or civil rank, but they were still more

remarkable for their faith. They all assembled here from widely scattered places and joined in loving action with many of the citizens of this city and the occupied provinces. They wanted to face the same dangers and insults to which We are subjected, in order to give personal witness to their own religious feelings for Us and to the feelings of their fellow-citizens. They also wanted to present Us with scrolls to which many hundreds of thousands of the faithful of every race had put their own names in sharp disapproval of the invasion of Our realm, demanding its restitution on compelling grounds of religion, justice, and even of politics.

Gifts for the Faithful

4. On this occasion too the poor as well as the rich made an unusually large contribution to offset Our recent lack of resources. We also received many kinds of remarkable gifts, a splendid tribute of Christian art and invention which was very well suited to aid Our twofold spiritual and royal power granted by God to Us. We received in addition an abundant and fine supply of sacred vestments and utensils so that We could everywhere remedy the poverty and need of so many churches. It was assuredly a wonderful spectacle of Catholic unity and plainly showed that although the universal Church is spread throughout the whole world and composed of peoples with different customs, talents, and pursuits, it is still inspired by the one spirit of God. The more madly impiety persecutes and oppresses it, and the more cunningly it attempts to deprive the Church of all human aid, the more wonderfully God strengthens the Church.

5. Great and ardent thanks be then to Him Who, while giving glory to His own name, lifts the hopes of the afflicted to certain triumph by the very effective demonstration of His power and might. But while We refer these gifts to the Giver of all good things, We feel the greatest gratitude at the same time towards those who showed themselves instruments of the divine Providence and gave Us lavishly the service of their aid, consolation, obedience, devotion, and love. Lifting Our eyes and hands to heaven, We offer to the Lord everything of this kind that Our sons sent Us in His Name. We urgently beseech Him soon to grant their united prayers for the liberty of this Holy See, the victory of the Church, and the peace of the world. In this way, He can return generous thanks, since We are unable to do so, to each one in heaven and on earth.

6. We would like to thank each person individually, but the very abundance of services offered from every side in goods, letters, and words obviously prevents Us. So We ask you to reveal and proclaim Our feelings to your clergy and people with eloquence. Exhort them all however to persevere firmly with you in confident prayer: for since Scripture assures us that the urgent prayer of the just man passes through the clouds and does not depart until the most High beholds, and since Christ has promised the He will be present where even two are joined in agreement in His name and that the heavenly father will do whatever they request then, all the more should the universal Church at last, by unceasing and united prayer, obtain the sight of the powers of hell crushed, the efforts of human wickedness scattered and destroyed, and peace and justice brought back to the earth.

7. Strive to achieve the closest unity among yourselves so as to advance in full phalanx against the enemies of God who are still attacking the Church with novel stratagems. Although the Church cannot be destroyed by any force, unite in order to withstand their onset and rout their ranks with greater ease and effect. This is what We greatly desire and strive to obtain; this is what We wholeheartedly pray for you and the entire Catholic family. In the meantime, as an augury of that desired event and of God's favor, and as a sure witness of Our particular benevolence and gratitude, We lovingly bestow from Our heart on each one of you, venerable brothers, and on the clergy and all the people committed to your separate care, Our Apostolic blessing.

Given at Rome in St. Peter's on the 5th day of August the feast of St. Mary on the Esquiline in the year of the Lord 1871 in the 26th year of Our Pontificate.

†

LATIN TEXT: *Acta Pii IX*, I, 5:343-47; *Acta Sanctae Sedis*, 6:337-40.

ENGLISH TRANSLATION: Padraig M. O'Cleirigh.

QUAE IN PATRIARCHATU

ENCYCLICAL OF POPE PIUS IX ON
THE CHURCH IN CHALDEA
NOVEMBER 16, 1872
70

To Our Venerable Brothers, the Archbishops, Bishops, and Beloved Sons, the Monks, and all the Faithful of the Patriarchate of Babylonia of the Chaldeans who have Grace and Communion with the Apostolic See.

Venerable Brothers and Beloved Sons, Greetings and Apostolic Benediction.

Although We do not believe you to be unaware of those things which were done many years ago and are even still done in the patriarchate of the Chaldean rite, it helps to recall them so that you know how these things came about, what We did, and what remains to be done in order to drive away these dangers threatening Catholic faith and unity. We are afraid that the truth will be obscured by deceptive stories. Our deeds would then either be calumniated or totally distorted. For this reason, We shall follow the example of Our predecessors who, in similar circumstances did not neglect to teach the bishops, clergy, and people about the true situation; We want to do the same in your regard so that We may not seem to neglect any part of our apostolic duty.

The Nestorian Heresy

2. The damage brought to your regions by the Nestorian heresy is so great that like a wild beast from the forest it will destroy the Lord's vineyard which once flourished there and devour it. Because the canonical discipline slowly disappeared, the authority of the popes, perished, the ambition of men who were not God-fearing leapt into ecclesiastical dignities, and the disgrace of the hereditary succession of patriarchs was introduced. Catholic doctrine was infected with both the old, nearly worn-out errors so that the Christian name seemed to be destroyed. The Roman Pontiffs did not neglect to direct careful attention to these evils. It was yet barely permitted for missionaries to be sent to the East, but through their labors and attentions some Nestorian bishops renounced the heresy and returned to the Catholic faith and unity. With what zeal and love these same people were welcomed when they gave letters to Our predecessors or when they came to Rome after enduring the labors and hardships of a long journey is apparent from the acts of the Apostolic See and the letters which We believe still exist in your archives.

Joseph Audo, Bishop of Amida

3. Nevertheless, the hoped for day dawned in which these obstacles were removed from your midst, especially the impediment of the hereditary

succession of the patriarchs and it could be hoped that the Church of the Chaldean rite, might revive and flourish. When the order of ecclesiastical discipline, which is the guardian of faith, had been restored, We hoped that this revival might come about through the work of Joseph Audo who was then the bishop of Amida. Moved by this hope, We named him as apostolic vicar of the patriarchate of Chaldea when it became vacant through the resignation of Isaide Yakob. We rejoiced when later We learned that this same man was requested for the patriarchal dignity by the votes of the bishops. We freely confirmed his selection in the consistory of September 11, 1848, and established him as patriarch of Babylonia of the Chaldeans. We strongly defended him from the many opponents already drawing near. Our hope was confirmed not only by the faith and obedience which he promised to us and to Our successors in a sacred oath, as is the custom of all Catholic patriarchs, but also by his respectful letters in which he showed the remarkable feelings of his will and spirit.

Discontent of the Malabars

4. It is true that not long after, he occasionally wrote to Our Congregation for the Propagation of the Faith that letters from the Malabars had been delivered to him. In these letters the Malabars requested the patriarch to give them a bishop of their own rite. They brought complaints and accusations against the Latin missionaries and the bishops carrying out their work in Our name. Even if their complaints were confirmed, that patriarch had no power of jurisdiction among the Malabars, whose complaints should be carefully considered so that We can minister effectively to their spiritual needs. For this reason We began a careful investigation so that We could safely determine what course of action would serve them best. When an explanatory response was delayed it became known (and was proven afterwards by his letter to a Malabar priest by the name of Emmanuel, signed and dated December 21, 1865) that that patriarch aroused the desires of the Malabars, fostered the hope, and suggested the manner by which they would finally be able to fulfill their wish. He advised them to vex the Apostolic See with complaints against the missionaries and with numerous requests. Meanwhile We desired to solve the matter gently. We took care to instruct Our pro-delegate in Mesopotamia to dissuade the patriarch from his undertakings. He was also advised that he should not dare to do anything in regard to the Malabars.

5. He was not obedient to our command and insisted that the region of the Malabars rightly came under his jurisdiction. While Henry Amanton, who was bishop of Arcadiopolis and Our delegate in Mesopotamia, vainly opposed him and forbade his actions under threat of censures, he chose Thomas Rocos from his household, raised him to the rank of bishop, and sent him to Malabar. He went there and stated falsely that he was sent from the patriarch by Our command. He usurped the ecclesiastical jurisdiction and promoted many unworthy people to holy orders. Moved by his audacious works and aroused by the complaints of the Malabar priests, We commanded Bernardino, Archbishop of Pharsalia, who at that time presided over the church with Our vicarial power, to warn Bishop Thomas to leave that place or to excommunicate him if he refused, which is what happened. Meanwhile the patriarch was called to Rome and seriously censured for his deeds. We ordered him to recall Bishop Rocos whom he had heedlessly sent into Malabar. We graciously granted the patriarch the pardon and absolution from censures which he requested.

6. We then ordered the whole matter to be considered by the cardinals of the Congregation for the Propagation of the Faith Concerning the Affairs of the Oriental Rite in a meeting held on March 6, 1865. In this meeting, after everything had been considered, a unanimous decision was reached. It was decided not to allow the jurisdiction of the patriarch of Babylonia of the Chaldeans to be extended to the Malabars. Many things were settled upon at the same time both in order to bring about the safety of the Malabars and to quiet the discords which were aroused among the Chaldeans because of those things which the patriarch had done heedlessly. The patriarch sadly agreed, or at least seemed to agree, to these apostolic orders. His later deeds confirmed this opinion. And even if We were grieved that he had not acted rightly, he showed himself to be obedient to Us and respectful of Our authority. He even showed himself as a model of obedience both in Our published decree in which we abrogated the censures heedlessly brought by him as well as in the refusal of episcopal consecration

to a certain Malabar which many proponents of new ideas in that region continually requested from him.

Restoration of Ecclesiastical Discipline

7. While these matters were occurring, which We Ourselves and the Apostolic See had desired for a long time, We led an examination of the Chaldean Church in order to restore the ecclesiastical discipline which was in a state of ruin. We maintained those rites which had been established by the holy fathers and had been approved by the Apostolic See. This project of Ours was made known to the patriarch by Our Congregation for the Propagation of the Faith on September 3, 1868; at the same time a copy of Our constitution published on July 12, 1867 was sent to him in which some chapters were devoted to discipline, especially in the selection of bishops. These principles ought to be maintained in the Armenian patriarchate. When he accepted these things, first through Bishop Elias Mellus who was then at Rome, then by his letter[1] to the aforementioned Congregation, he wanted it to be known to Us: that he fully agreed to what extent certain rules concerning the election of bishops should be followed; that he was optimistic about arranging episcopal elections (which had been omitted) if it seemed useful and appropriate to Us; and that he wanted that which is pleasing to Us to be accomplished at all times. When two churches of the Chaldean rites, Amida and Mardin, lost their shepherds, he proposed to us the names of several priests so that We could judge which ones were more worthy and could place them at the head of those dioceses by Our authority. We did this in Our apostolic letter dated March 22, 1869. We were moved by these manifestations of devotion and obedience; when he humbly explained that he preferred that the man We had chosen for Amida be placed instead over Mardin as bishop, we consented.

8. Not long after this We decided that the arrangement of discipline in the patriarchate of the Chaldean rite ought to be spread. The starting point should be the proper selection of bishops. Unless well-respected men who do everything according to the will of God, are selected, serious injuries and almost incurable losses befall the Church. The history of all times and places is witness to this, and experience confirms it. To this end and in the same spirit, We published the apostolic constitution which begins with the words *Cum ecclesiastica disciplina* on August 31, 1869. Concerning the election of bishops what the patriarch, as We mentioned above, did freely for the dioceses of Amida and Mardin was established: namely that when an episcopal see is vacant, three respected men should be proposed to Us by the synod of bishops so that We might decide which one is most worthy and place him over the vacant diocese. Moreover, if anything should be attempted contrary to these instructions, it should be declared null and void.

Quae in Patriarchatu 70

Infidelity of Chaldean Patriarch

9. The ecumenical Vatican Council had been announced and bishops of every nation and rite had been summoned to it. Among them was the Chaldean patriarch with almost all the bishops of his rite. However We quickly noticed that he who had shown Us many signs of reverence and obedience had changed very much. Lately he had refused to consecrate as bishops of the aforementioned churches, Amida and Mardin, Peter Attar and Gabriel Farso whom We chose from those he had proposed, although We had even assigned a church to each of them as he preferred. Then when he was about to leave the city, We ordered him to make a declaration of support and submission to the Constitution on the Church of Christ which was published in the fourth session of the ecumenical Vatican Council, which he had not attended. Indeed, We exhorted him and called to witness the example of the other bishops who were not at the fourth session and did not hesitate to make the declaration. He first devised delays and sought evasion and then declared stubbornly that he would be more useful after he had returned to his See. He promised at the same time that he would omit nothing which might satisfy Us. This deed brought Us great sorrow and anxiety which increased when he went to Constantinople surrounded by the flatteries and deceptions of the neo-schismatic Armenians and aroused by their example. He did not hesitate to occasionally share the sacraments with them. And while he professed his fidelity to the civil laws, he insinuated that Our apostolic constitutions were opposed to them. It happened at the same time that he neglected to show the necessary courtesies to Our extraordinary legate who was then living in Constantinople. He also totally ignored the letter of

warning sent by Our Congregation. Moreover, once he returned to Mesopotamia, he consorted with promoters of novelties and said many things rashly which, as it is reported, could be reconciled neither with the office of a Catholic bishop nor with the orthodox faith.

10. We were greatly saddened when We heard these things. The precept the Lord gave to Peter to strengthen his brothers came to mind together with the duty to watch over the Lord's flock and to obtain the salvation of souls. The condition to which Timothy, the Archbishop of the Chaldeans of Amida, was reduced by the hostility and the deceptions of certain people who claimed to be supporters of the patriarch seemed very serious to Us. He felt the patriarch's hostility toward him. Time and again he presented his sorrowful complaints to Us and his entreaties that We allow him to leave the episcopal office. We accepted Timothy's resignation and commanded Zachary Bishop of Maronea to meet Patriarch Mauxilius so that Mauxilius could establish him as Apostolic Delegate of the diocese of Amida. The patriarch preferred Zachary to Timothy. Zachary was told to persuade the patriarch to take the required oath of loyalty and to submit himself finally to the decrees of the fourth session of the Vatican Council. This was entirely necessary for the patriarch not only because the decrees are opposed to those things which the Neoschismatic Armenians babble and because the patriarch's behavior after his return was astonishing to the faithful, but also so that he might consider his eternal salvation and remove this scandal or at least forestall what was already rising from his silence.

11. Mindful of these warnings, the patriarch gave his agreement and signed the declaration of support adding a statement declaring that he wanted all his patriarchal rights and privileges to be preserved. We could suspect that this was done insincerely. Nevertheless, considering his long standing faith (which he recalled in his declaration) and the power which the wicked exercised against him, and bearing in mind His example of whom it is written, "He does not break the crushed reed, nor put out the smoldering wick,"[2] We preferred to see in that statement a legitimate desire of the patriarch, rather than an adverse situation or a restriction of his profession of faith. For this reason, We decided that his act of loyalty should be accepted, so that We might declare in what spirit We intended to receive it and thus might communicate Catholic teaching concerning the primacy of the pope and the rights of patriarchs. Therefore, We gave this apostolic letter to him on November 16, 1872.

†

LATIN TEXT: *Acta Sanctae Sedis*, 10:3-10.

ENGLISH TRANSLATION: Norman Desmarais

REFERENCES:

1. Letters dated 31 July 1868 and 24 May 1869.
2. Is 42.3; Mt 12.20.

QUARTUS SUPRA

ENCYCLICAL OF POPE PIUS IX ON
THE CHURCH IN ARMENIA
JANUARY 6, 1873
71

To Our Venerable Brothers Anthony Peter IX, Patriarch of Cilicia, and the Archbishops, Bishops, Clergy and Laity, Our Beloved Children of the Armenian Rite Who are in Loving Communion with the Apostolic See.

Venerable Brothers and Beloved Children, We give you Greetings and Our Apostolic Blessing.

Four and twenty years have now gone by since We addressed Our Apostolic letter to the men of the East (ad Orientales)[1] at this most holy season in which a new star shone forth in the East to enlighten the nations. We wrote that letter to strengthen Catholics in the faith and to call back to the one fold of Christ those who were unhappily outside the Catholic Church. We entertained a joyous and vivid hope that with the help of God and our Savior Jesus Christ, the purity of the Christian faith would be spread abroad and the zeal for ecclesiastical discipline flourish once again in the East. We promised to support with Our authority the establishment of this discipline in accordance with the sacred canons. Our great concern for the men of the East and the kindness and charity which We have shown them since that time are known to God. But all men too know what We took on Ourselves to achieve this purpose—if only all men correctly understood this as well! However by the mysterious judgment of God, these affairs have developed far differently from Our hopes and desires, and far from rejoicing, We must rather grieve and lament a new disaster which is afflicting some of the Eastern Churches.

Schism in Constantinople

2. Long ago Christ warned that many would come in His name, stating that they were the Christ, and as a result, seduce many;[2] this has proved true. For by means of the new schism which arose three years ago among the Armenians in Constantinople, the common enemy of the human race is wholly engaged in undermining faith, destroying truth and disrupting unity by worldly wisdom, heretical discussion, subtle, clever deceit, and even, where possible, by the use of force. While exposing the pretenses and plots of this enemy, St. Cyprian lamented that "he snatches human beings out of the very church and while they think they have already drawn near to the light and escaped from the night of the world, he brings darkness over them once more in ways of which they are unaware. Thus, although they do not observe Christ's gospel and His law, they call themselves Christians and judge that they possess the light while they walk in

darkness, attracted and deceived by the adversary. For he transfigures himself like an angel of light, as the Apostle says (2 Cor 11.14) and disguises his ministers as ministers of justice who present night as day, ruin as salvation, hopelessness in the guise of hope, faithlessness under the pretext of faith, the antichrist with the title of "Christ." Thus while telling lies which resemble truths, they make vain the truth by their subtlety."[3]

3. The beginnings of this new schism were, as is usually the case, complicated by many contributory factors. However, We observed its wickedness and its dangers beforehand, and resisted it at once in two Apostolic letters, one February 24, 1870, *Non sine gravissimo*, and the other on May 20 in the same year, *Quo impensiore*.[4] The affair has gone so far, however, that despite the urging, warnings and censures of this Apostolic See, the originators of this schism and their adherents have fearlessly chosen for themselves a false patriarch. We have declared in Our letter of 11 March 1871, *Ubi prima*,[5] that this election is wholly invalid and schismatic, and that the man elected and those who elected him have incurred canonical penalties. Furthermore, they have taken possession of Catholic churches by violent means: they have forced the lawful Patriarch, Our venerable brother Anthony Peter IX, to depart from the territories of the Ottoman Empire; they have even seized with military aid the patriarchal see of Cilicia which is in Lebanon; and having won the civil command of this province, they have assailed the Catholic people of Armenia, and are trying by every means to detach them from their communion with and obedience to the Apostolic See. John Kupelian, one of the neo-schismatic priests, is working vigorously to ensure that the affair proceeds according to their plan. By Our authority, this man has previously been publicly and specifically excommunicated and declared cut off from the Catholic Church by the Apostolic delegate for Mesopotamia and other districts, Our venerable brother Nicholas Archbishop of Mardin; the specific charge was encouraging disorder and fomenting schism in the state of Diarbekr or Amida. After being sacrilegiously consecrated as bishop by the pseudo-patriarch, and having gained power, he now attempts by argument and by open threats to bring the Catholics of the Armenian rite under his rule. If this should ever come about, the Catholics would be quite reduced to their wretched state of forty-two years ago when they were subjected to the power of the old schismatics of their rite.

Appeal to the Ottoman Emperor

4. We have indeed left no means untried in order to free you from this great evil. In this We follow the custom of Our predecessors whose authority, protection and help has usually been requested at such critical junctures by all the respected bishops and fathers of the Eastern Churches. To this end also We have sent an extraordinary legate to that region. We recently asked the supreme Ottoman emperor himself in a special letter that the losses suffered by Armenian Catholics be made good by process of law, and that their exiled shepherd be restored to his flock. But the fulfillment of Our wishes has been hindered by those men who call themselves Catholics, but are the enemies of the Cross of Christ.

Warning from the Holy See

5. We must now greatly fear that the originators of the new schism and their adherents may succeed in their plan of seducing both the weak in faith and the less prudent Catholics of the Armenian and other rites, leading them off on the path of perdition. Therefore We are compelled to address you again, and by dispelling that darkness and thick mist which, conceals the truth, to warn all men. It is Our duty to strengthen those who stand firm, to support the wavering, and also to recall to goodness, those men who have wretchedly abandoned the truth and Catholic unity, if only, they are willing to listen.

6. The chief deceit used to conceal the new schism is the name of "Catholic." The originators and adherents of the schism presumptuously lay claim to this name despite their condemnation by Our authority and judgment. It has always been the custom of heretics and schismatics to call themselves Catholics and to proclaim their many excellences in order to lead peoples and princes into error. St. Jerome, presbyter, referred to these men, among others, when he said: "The heretics are accustomed to say to their king or to Pharaoh, 'We are the sons of wise men who have handed down to us from the beginning the Apostolic teaching; we are the sons of ancient kings who are

called kings of the philosohers; and we possess the knowledge of the scriptures in addition to the wisdom of the world.' "[6]

7. But to prove that they are Catholics, the neo-schismatics appeal to what they call a declaration of faith, published by them on February 6, 1870, which they insist disagrees in no regard with the Catholic faith. However it has never been possible to prove oneself a Catholic by affirming those statements of the faith which one accepts and keeping silence on those doctrines which one decides not to profess. But without exception, all doctrines which the Church proposes must be accepted, as the history of the Church at all times bears witness.

8. That the statement of faith which they published was deceitful and sophistical is proved also by the fact that they rejected the declaration or profession of faith which was proposed to them on Our authority in accordance with custom. They were commanded to accept it by Our venerable brother Anthony Joseph Archbishop of Tyana, Apostolic Delegate at Constantinople, in a letter of warning sent to them on September 29 of the same year. For any man to be able to prove his Catholic faith and affirm that he is truly a Catholic, he must be able to convince the Apostolic See of this. For this See is predominant and with it the faithful of the whole Church should agree.[7] And the man who abandons the See of Peter can only be falsely confident that he is in the Church.[8] As a result, that man is already a schismatic and a sinner who establishes a see in opposition to the unique See of the blessed Peter[9] from which the rights of sacred communion derive for all men.[10]

Authority of the Papacy

9. This fact was well known to the illustrious bishops of the Eastern Churches. Hence at the Council of Constantinople held in the year 536, Mennas the bishop of that city affirmed openly with the approval of the fathers, "We follow and obey the Apostolic See, as Your Charity realizes and we consider those in communion with it to be in communion with us, and we too condemn the men condemned by it."[11] Even more clearly and emphatically St. Maximus, abbot of Chrysopolis, and a confessor of the faith, in referring to Pyrrhus the Monothelite, declared: "If he wants neither to be nor to be called a heretic, he does not need to satisfy random individuals of his orthodoxy, for this is excessive and unreasonable. But just as all men have been scandalized at him since the chief man was scandalized, so also when that one has been satisfied, all men will doubtless be satisfied. He should hasten to satisfy the Roman See before all others. For when this See has been satisfied, all men everywhere will join in declaring him pious and orthodox. For that man wastes his words who thinks that men like me must be persuaded and beguiled when he has not yet satisfied and beseeched the blessed Pope of the holy Roman Church. From the incarnate word of God Himself as well as from the conclusions and sacred canons of all holy councils, the Apostolic See has been granted the command, authority and power of binding and loosing for all God's holy churches in the entire world."[12] For this reason John, Bishop of Constantinople, solemnly declared—and the entire Eighth Ecumenical Council did so later—"that the names of those who were separated from communion with the Catholic Church, that is of those who did not agree in all matters with the Apostolic See, are not to be read out during the sacred mysteries."[13] This plainly meant that they did not recognize those men as true Catholics. All these traditions dictate that whoever the Roman Pontiff judges to be a schismatic for not expressly admitting and reverencing his power must stop calling himself Catholic.

10. Since this does not please the neo-schismatics, they follow the example of heretics of more recent times. They argue that the sentence of schism and excommunication pronounced against them by the Archbishop of Tyana, the Apostolic Delegate in Constantinople, was unjust, and consequently void of strength and influence. They have claimed also that they are unable to accept the sentence because the faithful might desert to the heretics if deprived of their ministration. These novel arguments were wholly unknown and unheard of by the ancient Fathers of the Church. For "the whole Church throughout the world knows that the See of the blessed Apostle Peter has the right of loosing again what any pontiffs have bound, since this See possesses the right of judging the whole Church, and no one may judge its judgment."[14] The Jansenist heretics dared to teach such doctrines as that an excommunication pronounced by a lawful prelate could be ignored on a pretext of injustice. Each person should perform, as they said, his own

particular duty despite an excommunication. Our predecessor of happy memory Clement XI in his constitution *Unigenitus* against the errors of Quesnell forbade and condemned statements of this kind.[15] These statements were scarcely in any way different from some of John Wyclif's which had previously been condemned by the Council of Constance and Martin V. Through human weakness a person could be unjustly punished with censure by his prelate. But it is still necessary, as Our predecessor St. Gregory the Great warned, "for a bishop's subordinates to fear even an unjust condemnation and not to blame the judgment of the bishop rashly in case the fault which did not exist, since the condemnation was unjust, develops out of the pride of heated reproof."[16] But if one should be afraid even of an unjust condemnation by one's bishop, what must be said of those men who have been condemned for rebelling against their bishop and this Apostolic See and tearing to pieces as they are now doing by a new schism the seamless garment of Christ, which is the Church?

11. The charity which obliges priests in particular to attend to the faithful should derive "from a pure heart and a good conscience and faith unfeigned"[17] as the Apostle warned. In reviewing the qualities which we ought to display as ministers of God, he also included "in charity unfeigned, in the word of truth."[18] But Christ Himself, however, the God who "is charity,"[19] openly declared that those who do not listen to the Church should be regarded as gentiles and publicans.[20] And Our predecessor St. Gelasius answered Euphemius, Bishop of Constantinople, when he stated that "the flock ought to follow the shepherd who calls them back to safe pastures, rather than the shepherd follow the flock as it wanders off the road."[21] For "the people must be taught, not followed: and if they do not know, we must impress on them what is permitted and not permitted, rather than give them our approval."[22]

Definition of a Schismatic

12. But the neo-schismatics say that it was not a case of doctrine but of discipline, so the name and prerogatives of Catholics cannot be denied to those who object. Our Constitution *Reversurus*, published on July 12, 1867,[23] answers this objection. We do not doubt that you know well how vain and worthless this evasion is. For the Catholic Church has always regarded as schismatic those who obstinately oppose the lawful prelates of the Church and in particular, the chief shepherd of all. Schismatics avoid carrying out their orders and even deny their very rank. Since the faction from Armenia is like this, they are schismatics even if they had not yet been condemned as such by Apostolic authority. For the Church consists of the people in union with the priest, and the flock following its shepherd.[24] Consequently the bishop is in the Church and the Church in the bishop, and whoever is not with the bishop is not in the Church. Furthermore, as Our predecessor Pius VI warned in his Apostolic letter condemning the civil constitution of the clergy in France,[25] discipline is often closely related to doctrine and has a great influence in preserving its purity. In fact, in many instances, the holy Councils have unhesitatingly cut off from the Church by their anathema those who have infringed its discipline.

Authority of the Holy See

13. But the neo-schismatics have gone further, since "every schism fabricates a heresy for itself to justify its withdrawal from the Church."[26] Indeed they have even accused this Apostolic See as well, as if We had exceeded the limits of Our power in commanding that certain points of discipline were to be observed in the Patriarchate of Armenia. Nor can the Eastern Churches preserve communion and unity of faith with Us without being subject to the Apostolic power in matters of discipline. Teaching of this kind is heretical, and not just since the definition of the power and nature of the papal primacy was determined by the ecumenical Vatican Council: the Catholic Church has always considered it such and abhorred it. Thus the bishops at the ecumenical Council of Chalcedon clearly declared the supreme authority of the Apostolic See in their proceedings; then they humbly requested from Our predecessor St. Leo confirmation and support for their decrees, even those which concerned discipline.

14. Indeed, "the successor of blessed Peter, by the very fact that he is such, has been assigned the whole flock of Christ, so that together with his bishopric he receives the power of universal rule. Then the other bishops must be assigned their portions of the flock so that they can rule over their flock."[27] If the supreme authority of this assignment to blessed Peter and his successors is rejected, the very foundations and prerogatives of the patriarchal churches in particular would be shaken. "Even if Christ willed that Peter and the other leaders have something in common, the other leaders have this only through Peter."[28] "And in fact Peter himself honored the See (of Alexandria) when he sent his disciple, the evangelist: he strengthened the See (of Antioch) which he occupied for seven years, even though he was going to leave it."[29] And both Anatolius,[30] Bishop of Constantinople, and Marcian,[31] the emperor, openly acknowledged that the approval and confirmation of the Apostolic See was altogether necessary to the decrees of the Council of Chalcedon concerning the see of Constantinople.

15. Accordingly, then, unless they abandon the unchanging and unbroken tradition of the Church which is so clearly confirmed by testimonies of the Fathers, the neo-schismatics can in no way convince themselves that they are Catholics even if they declare themselves such. If We did not thoroughly know the clever and subtle deceits of heretics, it would be incomprehensible that the Ottoman régime still regards as Catholics people it knows to be cut off from the Catholic Church by Our judgment and authority. For if the Catholic religion is to continue safe and free in the Ottoman dominion as the Emperor has decreed, then the essence of this religion should also be allowed, for instance the primacy of jurisdiction of the Roman Pontiff. Most men feel that the Church's supreme head and shepherd should decide who are Catholics and who are not.

False Accusations

16. But the neo-schismatics declare that they do not oppose the Catholic Church's principles in the least. Their sole aim is to protect the rights of their churches and their nation and even the rights of their supreme Emperor; they falsely allege that We have infringed these rights. By this means, they fearlessly make us responsible for the present disorder. Exactly in this way did the Acacian schismatics act towards Our predecessor St. Gelasius.[32] And previously the Arians falsely accused Liberius, also Our predecessor, to the Emperor Constantine, because Liberius refused to condemn St. Athanasius, Bishop of Alexandria, and refused to support their heresy.[33] For as the same holy Pontiff Gelasius wrote to the Emperor Anastasius on this matter, "a frequent characteristic of sick people is to reproach the doctors who recall them to health by appropriate measures rather than agree to desist from and condemn their own harmful desires." These appear to be the main grounds on which the neo-schismatics gain their support and solicit the patronage of powerful men for their cause, most wicked as it is. Lest the faithful be led into error, We must deal with these grounds more fully than if We merely had to refute unjust accusations.

Quartus supra 71

17. We do not wish to recall that after the schism succeeded, the fortunes of the Eastern Catholic Churches declined; then God overthrew the empire of the Greeks in punishment for the sundered unity of His Church. Neither do We desire to recall the energetic efforts of Our predecessors, as soon as it was possible, to call back the straying sheep to the one true flock of Christ the Lord. But even if the results did not fully match the efforts expended, still by God's mercy some churches of the different rites did return to the truth and Catholic unity of the Church. These the Apostolic See received in its arms like newborn infants and took particular care to strengthen them in the true Catholic faith and to keep them completely free from all stain of heresy.

Schism at the Time of Pius VII

18. When it was reported that the evil doctrines of a sect that Pope Pius VII had already condemned were being spread in the East, Pius VII became alarmed. Because they were trying to suppress the primacy of papal jurisdiction, the Pope decided on immediate measures to prevent their futile ambiguities and contentions from deceiving the faithful. Accordingly he ordered the ancient formula of St. Hormisdas, Our predecessor, to be sent to the patriarchs and eastern bishops.[34] In addition he commanded each within his jurisdiction to have every present or future clergyman subscribe to the profession of faith prescribed for men of the East by Urban VIII, unless they had already done so.

Continuation of Schisms

19. However soon afterwards, in the year 1806, the so-called Antioch Synod met at the monastery of Carcapha in the diocese of Beirut. The Pistoian Synod, which had already been condemned, quietly and deceitfully influenced the synod in many matters. This synod reproduced several statements, in part verbatim and in part ambiguously expressed, even though these had been condemned by the holy Roman See. Still other statements smacked of Baianism and Jansenism, and disturbed the position of the Church by their opposition to ecclesiastical power, sound doctrine and the approved discipline of the Church. This Synod of Carcapha published its decrees in Arabic in 1810 without reference to the Apostolic See; as a result, it occasioned complaints from many bishops and was finally censured and condemned in an Apostolic letter by Gregory XVI.[35] He bade the bishops derive the norm of their rule and teaching from the other ancient councils long approved by the Apostolic See. If only the errors in which it abounded had come to an end when the synod was condemned! But such wicked teachings did not cease to creep secretly throughout the East, waiting for the right moment to emerge into common view. Despite an unsuccessful attempt about twenty years ago, the new Armenian schismatics have now daringly brought this about.

Catholicism in Constantinople

20. But since discipline is the rampart of faith, the Apostolic See needed to restore discipline. It has certainly never abandoned this most serious duty even in adverse times when it could attend only to transitory needs while it awaited more the favorable times. The Ottoman emperor, at the insistence of Leo XII and Pius VIII, and relying on the support of the Catholic rulers of Austria and France, recognized the distinction which exists between Catholics and heretics; therefore, he removed Catholics from the civil power of the latter, decreeing that Catholics should have their own head or prefect. It was only then in Constantinople that bishops of the Armenian rite could safely exercise the authority of an ordinary, to raise Catholic churches of the same rite, and to profess and practice openly the Catholic religion. Accordingly Pius VIII set up at Constantinople the see of the primate and archbishop of the Armenians;[36] the Pope was eager that canonical discipline should thrive there in a suitable and timely manner.

21. After some years, as soon as it was clearly expedient, We set up episcopal sees subject to the primate at Constantinople and also prescribed the procedure to be observed for the election of bishops.[37] Finally in an imperial document issued on April 7, 1857, to Our venerable brother Anthony Hassoun, then the primate of that see, provision was made on the authority of the supreme Emperor of the Ottoman Empire to prevent the power of the civil Prefect, as he is called, from being exercised in religious affairs, which would be completely at variance with the laws of the Catholic Church. The Armenians themselves requested that We unite the primatial church at Constantinople to the patriarchal see of Cilicia; We did this and We abrogated the title of the former by Our Apostolic letter *Reversurus*. Then We decided that it was both timely and necessary to sanction certain chief points of discipline by the authority of the same Constitution. We commanded by Our Apostolic letter *Commissum* of July 12, 1867[38] that a patriarchal synod be held as soon as possible in order to carefully ensure that an exact order of discipline be correctly established in the whole Armenian patriarchate.

22. But an enemy proceeded to sow weeds in the Armenian church at Constantinople when shortly afterwards some men raised the question about the civil prefecture of the Armenian community, which they complained had been stolen by the new Patriarch. A serious disturbance soon followed this controversy: the same Patriarch was accused of betraying the rights of the state in accepting Our previously mentioned Constitution as a Catholic bishop was bound to do. In this way at last all the plans, artifices, and abuse of the dissidents have come to bear on this particular Constitution.

23. In this affair two points in particular have been called criminal: that is, the decrees concerning the election of holy bishops and the administration of the Church's property. For it has been falsely asserted that these are opposed to the national laws and the laws of the supreme Emperor. Although Our prescription on each of these headings ought to be very well known, it is well to repeat them at this point. For many speak as if they understand in spite of their ignorance of what is in Our prescriptions[39] and others, like soothsayers and interpreters of dreams, judge what they do not know.[40]

Selection of Hierarchy

24. We commanded that a synod composed exclusively of bishops elect the patriarch. However, We forbade the man elected to be enthroned until he received a letter of confirmation from the Apostolic See. We ordered bishops to be elected in the following way: all the bishops of the province were to gather in a synod and recommend three suitable churchmen to the Apostolic See. If it were not possible for all the bishops to come to the synod, the recommendation could be made by a synod of at least three diocesan bishops together with the patriarch, if those absent indicated their triple recommendation in writing. When this is done, the Roman pontiff will choose one of those recommended and put him in charge of the vacant see. We declared that We were certain that the bishops would recommend worthy and suitable men so that We would never have to select someone different from those recommended to be in charge of the vacant see.

25. If you consider these measures with a mind free from the passions of faction, you will find them all sanctioned by the universal sense of the canons. Concerning the exclusion of the laity from the election of bishops, a clear distinction must be made, lest a doctrine at variance with the Catholic faith result. This distinction is between the right to elect bishops and the ability to give testimony as to their life and morals. The former claim must be credited to the wrong notions of Luther and Calvin, who even asserted that it was a matter of divine law that the bishops should be elected by the people; as everybody realizes, such false teaching has been and is still rejected by the Catholic Church. For no power of electing bishops or other ministers of religion has ever been given to the people by either divine or ecclesiastical law.

26. Testimony of the people concerning the life and morals of those who are to be raised to the episcopate became important "when the Arians, to whom the emperor Constantius was partial, began to eject Catholic prelates from their sees and replace them with adherents of Arianism, as St. Athanasius laments (*History of the Arians*, ch. 4). The people felt that if they were present and if their testimony were heard at the election of bishops, then they would be more likely to support and help them."[41] That custom indeed lasted for some time in the Church, but when recurrent discord, disturbance, and other abuses resulted from it, it was necessary to remove the people from the process. For as St. Jerome observes, "sometimes the judgment of the ordinary people is wrong and in approving of priests each man is partial to his own ways and seeks a superior who resembles himself rather than one who is good."[42]

27. Nevertheless, in imposing a procedure of election, We left the synod of bishops freedom to examine the talents of the men to be elected in whatever way they preferred, even to the extent of summoning the testimony of the people if they so chose. And in fact, since the publication of Our Constitution, such an examination was conducted three years ago by the Armenian prelates *Quartus supra 71*
when a bishop was elected for the districts of Sebaste and Tokat. The proceedings sent to this Holy See testify to this. However We did not nor do We think it fitting to impose a similar procedure in the election of the patriarch for several reasons. In the first place, his rank is so high; secondly, he is in charge of all the bishops in his district; and lastly, it is clear to Us that only bishops have taken part in the election of the patriarch in each of the Eastern rites, except on particular and extraordinary occasions when circumstances demanded a different procedure. For instance, when the Catholics were protecting themselves against the strong power of the schismatics to whom they were subjected, they asked for a different patriarch for themselves. By this fact they ensured their separation from these schismatics and their true and sincere "conversion" to the Catholic faith as indeed happened when Abraham Peter I was elected.

28. However, some resent and bemoan both Our declaration that this Apostolic See has the right and power to elect a bishop either from the three names recommended or apart from them and Our prohibition against the enthronement of an elected Patriarch without Our prior confirmation. They call Our attention to the customs and canons of their churches as if We had abandoned the provisions of the sacred canons. We might respond to these men in the same way Our predecessor St. Gelasius did when the Acacian schismatics brought the same false accusation against him: "They cite the canons against Us without knowing what they are saying since they show that they are themselves in opposition to the canons by the very fact that they deny obedience to the first See although its advice is sound and correct."[43] For these are the very canons which recognize the full, divine authority of blessed Peter over the whole Church. Indeed, they proclaim that he lives and exercises judgment in his successors to the present time and forever, as the Council of Ephesus affirmed.[44] Rightly then did Stephan, Bishop of Larissa, give this firm answer to those who considered that the

privileges of the churches of Constantinople were somewhat diminished by the intervention of the Roman Pontiff: "the authority of the Apostolic See which was given by God and our Savior to the chief of the Apostles exceeds the privileges of all the holy churches. In acknowledging this, all the churches of the world should cease their opposition."[45]

29. Certainly, if you recall the history of your districts, you will find examples of Roman Pontiffs who used this power when they judged it necessary for the safety of the Eastern Churches. This was why the Roman Pontiff Agapetus used his authority to eject Anthimus from the See of Constantinople and replace him with Mennas without calling a synod. Our predecessor Martin I entrusted his power for the East to John, Bishop of Philadelphia, in regard to the regions of the East. He instructed him "by the Apostolic authority given to Us by the Lord through the most holy Peter, prince of the Apostles,"[46] to appoint bishops, priests and deacons in every city subject to the sees of Jerusalem and Antioch. In more recent times, you will recall that the bishop of Mardin of the Armenians was elected and consecrated by the authority of this Apostolic See even though Our predecessors granted the care of this see to the patriarchs of Cilicia. This was granted when the administration of the district of Mesopotamia was assigned to them by the Holy See. All these actions agree with the supreme power of the Roman See; the church of the Armenians has always recognized, proclaimed, and respected this except during unhappy times of schism. This is not surprising since even among your people still separated from the Catholic faith, the ancient tradition remains strong that the great bishop and martyr whom you regard as the Enlightener of your race, received his power from the Apostolic See. He came to the See in person, undeterred by the length and great hardship of the journey. This was Gregory whom Chrysostom described as a sun rising in the eastern regions whose shining rays reached as far as the Greek people.[47]

30. We decided on this arrangement by Ourselves after carefully studying both on ancient and recent events. Everyone knows that the eternal and at times the temporal happiness of people depends on the proper election of bishops; the circumstances of time and place must be considered referring all the authority for selecting the bishops to the Apostolic See. Still We decided to moderate the exercise of this power by allowing the synod of bishops to elect the patriarch and by having this synod recommend three suitable men to Us for vacant sees as was sanctioned in Our Constitution.

31. But on this matter too, to rouse the torpid and increasingly inspire those who are running well, We said that We hoped truly suitable men worthy of so important an office would be recommended to avoid the *necessity* of Our ever *having to* appoint to a vacant See someone apart from those recommended. This was provided for also in the procedure We established in 1853[48] for exactly the same purpose. We have heard that some have interpreted these otherwise mild words to mean that We would disregard and even deride the recommendations of the synod. Others have gone even further and developed a theory that a proposal to entrust the care of the Armenians to Latin bishops is veiled in these words. Such foolish accusations indeed deserve no answer: for only fearful and foolish men could utter such statements. But We considered that We should not keep silence on Our right to elect a bishop apart from the three recommended candidates, in case the Apostolic See should be compelled to exercise this right in the future. But even if We had remained silent, this right and duty of the See of blessed Peter would have remained unimpaired. For the rights and privileges given to the See by Christ Himself, while they may be attacked, cannot be destroyed; no man has the power to renounce a divine right which he might at some time be compelled to exercise by the will of God Himself.

32. Although it is now nineteen years since these pronouncements were made to the Armenians, and although bishops have been elected many times, We have never used that power, not even when recently, after the publication of the Constitution *Reversurus*, We received a triple recommendation from which We could not elect a bishop. In this case We told the synod of bishops to recommence the process of recommendation in acordance with the laws We prescribed rather than Our electing a bishop apart from their recommendations. This has been hindered so far by the new schism which has begun to tear apart the church of the Armenians. We are confident, furthermore, that such distressful times will never befall the Catholic churches of Armenia as to compel the Roman Pontiffs to impose bishops on them who have not been recommended by the synod of bishops.

33. We will add some remarks on Our prohibition of the enthronement of Patriarchs before they receive Apostolic confirmation from this Holy See. The writings of the ancients testify that the election of Patriarchs had never been considered definite and valid without the agreement and confirmation of the Roman Pontiff. Accordingly, it is learned, those elected to patriarchal sees always sought such confirmation, with the support of the emperors. Thus, to pass over other names in a well known affair, Anatolius Bishop of Constantinople (a man who certainly did not serve the Apostolic See very well), and even Photius himself (the first cause of the Greek schism), requested the Roman Pontiff to confirm their elections by his consent. To this end they employed the intervention of the emperors Theodosius, Michael and Basil. For this reason the Fathers of Chalcedon, even though they declared all the acts of the robber synod of Ephesus invalid, willed that Maximus Bishops of Antioch remain in the see. He had replaced Domnus by authority of that synod since "the holy and blessed Pope who confirmed the holy and venerable Maximus as bishop of the church of Antioch appeared to have approved his merit in a just judgment."[49]

34. But if you consider the patriarchs of those churches which in more recent times have renounced schism and returned to Catholic unity, you will find that all of them asked for confirmation from the Roman Pontiff; the Roman Pontiffs confirmed them all by letter in such a way that at the same time the Pontiffs appointed them and placed them over their churches. The Apostolic See has at times tolerated elected patriarchs using their power before being confirmed by the See. It has done so because their districts were so distant or because the journey was dangerous or because of the reverses threatening more and more frequently from the predominance of schismatics of the same rite. This dispensation has been granted even in the west to those who are very far away because of the needs and benefits of the churches.[50] But it is fair to remind you that such reasons are no longer valid since travel is much easier and since the Catholics have been delivered from the civil power of the schismatics by the kindness of the supreme Ottoman emperor. By following this procedure, safe provision is made for the preservation of the Catholic faith which could be disturbed at will by one who is unworthy of such high office occupying the patriarchal see before the Apostolic confirmation is received. Clearly, opportunities for disturbance which might arise when an elected Patriarch is rejected by the holy Apostolic See and has to relinquish his place will be forestalled.

35. Everything which is sanctioned in Our Constitution contributes to the preservation and development of the Catholic faith. It contributes as well to the protection of the real liberty of the Church and the authority of the bishops, whose rights and privileges find strength and repose in the stability of the Apostolic See. The Roman Pontiffs have always strongly defended these rights and privileges from heretics and ambitious men at the request of bishops of every rank, nation and rite.

Ecclesiastical Laws

36. We do not need to give a long answer to the question of the so-called national laws. For if it is a matter of civil laws only, the supreme ruler has the power to judge and decide whether he deems them useful and beneficial to his subjects. But if it is a matter of ecclesiastical laws, no one can be unaware that Catholics have never recognized any national or popular laws against the Church, its hierarchy and ordinations. For although peoples and nations have entered the Church from all places, still God has united them all under the supreme shepherd blessed Peter, the prince of the Apostles. Thus there might no longer be Gentile and Jew, barbarian and Scythian, slave and free, but that Christ may be all things in all men.[51] From Him the whole body, joined and knit together by every joint, increases bodily and builds itself up in love.[52] For God has not given any peoples or nations power over the Church, but has entrusted them to the Apostles for teaching and has commanded the duty of belief.[53] For this reason too, the blessed Peter openly declared at the meeting of Apostles and presbyters that God had decreed that the nations should hear the word of the Gospel through him and should believe.[54]

Calumnies against the Church

37. But it is also said that We have infringed upon the rights of the supreme emperor. This is a common calumny worn thin by the long use heretics have made of it. The Jews first invented it in opposition to Christ and God; then pagans very often used it not only before the Roman emperors and heretics, but even before Catholic princes. I could wish they had not brought it forward this time as well. To counter it, St. Jerome wrote that "heretics cringe before royal rank and often impute their own pride to kings; assuming the king did what they do, they accuse holy men and preachers of the faith in his presence and forbid teachers to preach in Israel lest they act contrary to the king's will arguing that Bethel, the 'house of God,' and the false church is the sanctuary of the king and the temple of the kingdom."[55] It would indeed be quite enough to trample in contemptuous silence on these shameless calumnies which are so far removed from the teachings, habits, and practices of the Catholic faith. But it is necessary to ensure that the simple and inexperienced do not suffer by wrongly judging Us and the Apostolic See as a result of the statement of ill-wishers "who in the course of attacking others attempt to increase their vices."[56]

Ecclesiastical Domain

38. Therefore, the teaching of the Catholic Church received from Christ Himself, and handed on by the holy Apostles, is that the things of Caesar must be given to Caesar, but to God must be given the things of God. For this reason, when it was necessary, Our predecessors never avoided impressing on princes their duty of faith and obedience. Hence the administration of civil affairs is proper to the ruler, but ecclesiastical affairs are entirely the concern of the priests. Among these affairs are to be reckoned everything which is necessary to establishing and maintaining the so-called exterior discipline of the Church. It would be heretical to affirm that the use of this power received from God is an abuse of the Church's authority; Pius VI already determined this.[57] The Apostolic See has often taken great pains to maintain this distinction of powers. St. Athanasius called the interference of secular rulers in Church affairs "a novel spectacle" and "an invention of the Arian heresy."[58] Other prelates openly condemned it, among them Basil of Caesarea, Gregory the Theologian, John Chrysostom and John Damascene. The last-named affirmed publicly that "no one would persuade him that the Church is governed by imperial edicts; it is ruled by the customs of the Fathers, both written and unwritten."[59] For the same reason the fathers of the ecumenical Council of Chalcedon declared publicly in the case of Photius, Bishop of Tyre, gaining the assent even of the servants of the Emperor, that "no pragmatic (that is, imperial decree) will be valid in opposition to the rules: let the canons of the Fathers be binding." And when the imperial servants inquired "whether the holy synod wanted this to be defined in regard to all pragmatics which were in conflict with the canons, all the bishops answered, 'All the pragmatics will come to an end: let the canons be binding, and let you see to this.' "[60]

39. However there are two points in which it is said that We have injured the rights of the Emperor: that is, by determining the procedure to be observed in electing and establishing holy bishops, and by forbidding the Patriarch to alienate Church property without informing the Apostolic See.

40. Now, what can be said to belong more to the area of ecclesiastical affairs than the election of bishops? We have read nowhere in the holy writings that these could be decided by princes or by peoples. Indeed, the Fathers of the Church, the ecumenical Councils, and the Apostolic constitutions have always both recognized and ordered that these elections constituted part of the Church's power. So if in the matter of establishing an ecclesiastical shepherd, the Apostolic See should define the procedure to be followed in conducting such elections, in what way could it be said that it has injured the rights of the supreme emperor? The rights it exercises are those of its own proper power, not those of another's power. The bishop has indeed a special and venerable authority over the people entrusted to him. The civil power need not fear it since the bishop will be no enemy to the civil power, but will affirm the legitimate rights of the ruler they share. But if it should turn out differently—since human beings are weak—the Apostolic See itself would attend to a bishop who was revolting against the faith and the subjection which is due his legitimate ruler. It need not be feared that anyone at enmity with the legitimate ruler will slink into the episcopal office. For according to the Church's laws, the qualities of the men being considered for promotion are carefully examined to determine that they are endowed with the virtues which the Apostle demands they have. The man outstanding in these virtues would heed the precept of blessed Peter: "Be subject to every human institution for God's sake: to the king as preeminent, to governors as sent by him to punish evildoers and to honor the good. For this is God's will, that by doing good, you may silence the ignorance of foolish men; as free men, do not use freedom as a pretext for wrongdoing, but use freedom for your work as servants of God."[61]

Combination of Civil Duties with Ecclesiastical

41. The first Ottoman emperor in Constantinople and his successors decided to confer civil duty and administration on bishops and other clerics. The full and unimpaired power of the Church in their election cannot be lessened for this reason. For it would be improper for heavenly and spiritual matters to be of smaller regard than earthly and civil affairs and to be their servant. But the supreme Emperor has the right to confer civil rank and power on another, if and when he judges this is expedient. He must, however, provide that the full and free exercise of ecclesiastical power remain with the Catholic bishops. However, a special document of the supreme Ottoman emperor in 1857 changed this.

False Accusations

42. We directed all these matters to the Ottoman court through the Archbishop of Thessalonica when he served as Our extraordinary legate at Constantinople. Now it is clearly time to put an end to the pain given by the repetition of these false and stale assertions, unless our opponents are envious men and prefer to be known as more eager for their faction than for the truth.

43. But We were astonished on learning that We were under attack for renewing and confirming the law on the alienation of ecclesiastical property. It was as if We wanted not only to infringe on the imperial rights, but even to claim for Ourselves the very property of the Armenian churches. Church property belongs to the churches and is under their power no less certainly than civilian property belongs to civilians. This fact is sanctioned not so much by the canons, but rather acknowledged by each man's natural reason. In the first centuries of the Church, the administration of this property was entrusted to the judgment and conscience of the bishops. Subsequent councils carefully regulated it by publishing laws to settle the method by which the administration should be carried out and the reasons for which alienation should be allowed. In this way, the ancient power of the bishops was limited and subservient to the prudent judgment of synods or sometimes to that of higher prelates. But since at this point adequate provision for the indemnity of Church property did not seem to have been made, either because synods did not meet often enough or for other reasons, the authority of the Apostolic See was bound to intervene. In this way care was taken that the property of the churches would not be alienated without the advice of the Roman Pontiffs.

Quartus supra 71

44. The matter indeed was considered very serious and necessary for the benefit of the churches; therefore, it was settled long ago that those who were elected to cathedral, metropolitan and even patriarchal churches should be obliged under solemn oath to observe this law. This oath was in fact taken also by the patriarchs of the Eastern rite in so far as their subsistence property was concerned ever since their churches returned to Catholic truth and unity. This is witnessed by the documents which are in Our Apostolic archives. Not even one of them declined to promise under oath that he would observe the aforesaid laws. The same oath is, and has been, taken daily by bishops of the Latin rite no matter what their nation, kingdom, or state, without the civil powers ever complaining that their rights were being injured by this action. And rightly so, for by these laws the Roman Pontiff does not claim or take anything for himself, but is concerned only with the benefit of the churches. This includes settling what a bishop should best do in particular cases by comparing counsels, or giving the bishop himself the power of determining what is best concerning a father's dealings with his sons. We had the most serious reasons, of which We will have to give an account to God, when We determined in Our Constitution that the law to which the Patriarchs were already subject, by which they were forbidden to alienate their subsistence property without the advice of the Apostolic See, should be extended to include other ecclesiastical property. Our Constitution ensures that safer and more effective measures have been taken for the indemnity of the churches and the preservation of church property, without prejudice to the legitimate rights of anyone.

45. But in what way the rights of the supreme emperor have been injured, as they allege, by these decrees of Ours We simply admit that We cannot at all understand, because We are so far from either wishing to do so or thinking that it could be accomplished. Patriarchs and bishops in the Ottoman empire possess the power of procuring church property; this is not at variance with the imperial rights. The Apostolic See duly and rightfully arranges the way in which bishops should use this property for building up rather than for destroying; this sometimes entails an authoritative intervention. But neither can this power be said to be at variance with the imperial rights. The way in which We protected the safety of this property is clear, and this affair will greatly benefit the Catholic churches established throughout the East. All will recognize this when the controversies have died down, and future generations will doubtless experience these benefits if they religiously observe these laws. But the supreme Ottoman emperor has affirmed the liberty of those churches in his decrees, and has indicated to Us that he will give them his humane protection. Thus We have no doubt that when the matter is examined fairly and the calumnies raised up by opponents are abandoned, rejoicing will replace sorrow over these events, bringing benefit to these churches in the future.

46. No less false is the fiction invented by some more recent men and avidly embraced by the eastern dissidents. They shamelessly represent the Roman Pontiff, the Vicar of Christ, as a foreign authority which insinuates itself into the domestic government of kingdoms and nations. They say this should be entirely forbidden to keep the rights of the supreme emperor unharmed and to forestall every encroachment to discourage other rulers from making similar attempts.

47. Now it is easy to see how false these allegations are, and how far they depart from right reason and the divine institution of the Catholic Church. It is particularly wrong to say that the Roman Pontiffs have exceeded the boundaries of their power or insinuated themselves into the civil administration of kingdoms and laid claim to the rights of the rulers. But if the Roman Pontiffs are stigmatized by such a calumny for determining any matter relating to the election or cases of bishops and the holy ministers of the Church, or any other point which concerns even exterior ecclesiastical discipline, it must be admitted either that their accusers do not know or that they reject the divine and accordingly unchanging institution of the Catholic Church. This Church indeed has always remained constant and will continue to do so. No one can demand that it should submit to changes, particularly in those regions where the imperial decrees of the supreme ruler have assured to the Catholic religion its proper freedom and safety. The Catholic faith teaches that there is one Church, with the Roman Pontiff as its head, the father and teacher of all Christians; therefore, he can surely be said to be foreign to no Christian, nor to any of the particular Christian churches, unless one should want to argue that the head is foreign to the limbs, the father to the children, the teacher to the pupils, and the shepherd to his flock.

48. But those who call the Apostolic See a "foreign authority," can rend the unity of the Church by this manner of speaking since by doing so, they deny to the successor of blessed Peter both the title and the rights of the universal shepherd. Consequently, they are lacking in the faith they owe the Catholic Church, if they are reckoned among its children; if they do not belong to the Church, they are assailing the freedom which is its due. For Christ revealed that sheep both hear and know the voice of the shepherd and follow him, but that they flee from a stranger "since they do not recognize the voice of strangers."[62] If then the supreme Pontiff is said to be foreign, that is a stranger, to any particular church, this church will in consequence be itself a stranger to the Apostolic See, that is to the Catholic Church, which is the only church established upon Peter by the voice of the Lord. Those who separate themselves from this foundation no longer preserve the divine and Catholic Church, but "try to make themselves a human church"[63] which is held together only by the human ties of so-called nationality. It is neither secured by the bond of priests who firmly adhere to the See of blessed Peter nor stabilized by its strength. It also does not accord with the unity of the Catholic Church whose members are everywhere intimately joined together.

Advice to the Faithful

49. Venerable brothers and beloved

children, We have decided in the present crisis to write all this to you to arouse your pure mind to the duty We have laid upon you. For you see that what the holy Apostles long ago foretold is still being fulfilled in your days, namely that in the last days, deceivers would come to deceive, walking according to their own passions. Be zealous then not to be won over from Him who called you in the grace of Christ to a different gospel. They do indeed wish to change the gospel of Christ by attempting to remove the foundation laid for His Church by Christ. Also, they either deny or reduce the universal task of feeding the sheep and the lambs which was entrusted to blessed Peter in the gospel. Indubitably, "these things are permitted and borne by the Lord, since the free decision of each individual will is assured, in order that while the testing of the truth exercises your hearts and minds, the unimpaired faith of the approved way may shine with clear light."[64] Still you should avoid those who grow daily worse, as the Apostle commanded. And you should continue to receive no one in your gathering under any pretext who holds communion with such men that you may preserve the Catholic faith unsullied in your hearts.

50. "But let no one try to trick you by saying that 'the controversy is not about religion but about customs,' as the ancient schismatics did, or that the Apostolic See is not dealing with the cause of Catholic communion and faith but is simply pained by the insult of being apparently despised by its critics since the dissidents do not rest from scattering such statements as these to deceive all the simpleminded."[65] For it is already clear from their declarations and published writings that they are openly assailing the primacy of jurisdiction given by Christ the Lord to this apostolic See in the person of blessed Peter; they do this when they attack the right of exercising this jurisdiction in the Churches of the Eastern rite. But Our Constitution could not be the cause of this error, although it has served as an opportunity and pretext for restless or inexperienced minds to bring it forth. "The Apostolic See, far from being grieved by insult, defends the faith and pure communion. It does this so that today, if all who have rebelled return in heartfelt sorrow to the fullness of faith and Catholic communion, it will receive them with love and full charity, following the regulations of the Fathers."[66] We have now long and fervently besought God in the humility of Our heart to deign to grant this favor. We desire and wish you also to do likewise.

51. For the rest, venerable brothers and beloved children, be strengthened in the Lord and the power of His might; receive the armor of God to enable you to stand fast in the evil day and take up the shield of faith in every affair; do not reckon your life more valuable than yourselves. Remember your ancestors who had no fear of suffering exile, imprisonment, and even death itself as they purposed to keep for themselves and you the unique gift of the true Catholic faith. For they rightly knew that not those who kill the body need be feared, but the one who is able to destroy body and soul in hell. Consequently cast all your concern on God: for He has care of you and will not allow you to be tempted beyond your ability. You will then rejoice that, at this time, you were somewhat saddened by different temptations so that your faith, more valuable than gold which is tested by fire, should on testing be found to merit praise, glory, and honor in the revelation of Jesus Christ. Finally We beseech you all to strive for perfect concord in your concern to preserve the unity of faith in the bond of peace. And may the peace of God which surpasses all understanding, maintain your hearts and minds in Christ Jesus Our Lord. In His name and by His authority We lovingly impart Our Apostolic Blessing to you, venerable brothers and beloved sons, as you continue in communion with the obedience to the Apostolic See.

Given at Rome in St. Peter's on the 6th of January 1873, the 27th year of Our Pontificate.

†

LATIN TEXT: *Acta Pii IX*, I, 6:97-137; *Acta Sanctae Sedis*, 7:244-74.

ENGLISH TRANSLATION: Padraig M. O'Cleirigh.

REFERENCES:

For the Acta of the Holy See in relation to the Armenian schism see the *Acta Sanctae Sedis*, vol. 5, pp. 444ff., 500ff., and 572; vol. 6, pp. 273ff. See also the *Acta* of the Sacred Consistory, vol. 3, pp. 337ff., and p. 386 for the famous bull *Reversurus*, and p. 394 for the apostolic letter *Commissum*. See also vol. 5, pp. 376, 380, and 615 for statutes of the Babylonian Patriarchate of the Chaldaeans passed after the bull *Reversurus*.

1. *In suprema*, 6 January 1848 (*Acta Pii IX*, vol. 1, p. 78).
2. Mt 24.5.
3. *Lib. de Unit*, no. 3.
4. *Acta Pii IX*, vol. 5, pp. 129 and 195.

5. Ibid., p. 290.
6. *Comment. in Isaiae* 19.12-13.
7. St. Irenaeus, *Contr. haeres.*, bk. 3, chap. 3.
8. St. Cyprian, *Lib. de Unitate*, no. 4.
9. St. Optatus of Milevis, *de schism. Donatist*, bk. 2.
10. Council of Aquileia and St. Ambrose, epistle 11 to the emperors.
11. Labbe, *Collect. Council.*, publ. Venice, vol. 7, cod. 1279.
12. Epistle *Ad Petrum illustrem*, *Coll. Counc.*, vol. 6, col. 1520.
13. Libell. of John, bishop of Constantinople to St. Hormisdas. Eighth Ecumenical Council, prop. I.
14. St. Gelasius, epistle 26, sect. 5, to the bishops of Dardania.
15. Const. *Unigenitus*, prop. 91, 92, 93.
16. Hom. 26 on the Gospels, sect. 6.
17. 1 Tm 1.5.
18. 2 Cor 6.6.
19. 1 Jn 4.8.
20. Mt 18.17.
21. Epistle 3, no. 15 to Euphemius.
22. St. Celestine, Pope, to the bishops of Apulia and Calabria, no. 3.
23. *Acta Pii IX*, vol. 4, p. 304.
24. St. Cyprian, epistle 66 to Florentius Pupianus, no. 8.
25. *Quod aliquantum*, 10 March 1791.
26. St. Jerome on the epistle to Titus 3.10-11.
27. Pius VI in his brev. *Super soliditate,* 28 November 1786.
28. St. Leo, serm. 3 on the anniversary of his elevation.
29. St. Gregory the Great, bk. 7, epistle 40 to Eulogius, bishop of Alexandria.
30. Anatolius to St. Leo, epistle 132, no. 4.
31. Marcian to St. Leo, epistle 100.
32. St. Gelasius epistle 12 to the emperor Anastasius, no. 1.
33. St. Athanas., *hist. Arianor ad Monach.*, no. 35.
34. Encyclical of the Sacred Congregation for the Propagation of the Faith, 6 July 1803.
35. Gregory XVI, apostolic letter *Melchitarum catholicorum*, 16 September 1835.
36. Apostolic letter *Quod iamdiu*, 6 July 1830.
37. Apostolic letter *Universis Dominici gregis*, 30 April 1850.
38. *Acta Pii IX*, vol. 4, p. 318.
39. Eph 4.17-18.
40. Prv 23.7.
41. Pius VI, apostolic letter *contr. civilem cleri constitutionem*, 10 March 1791.
42. *Advers. Iovinian*, bk. 1, no. 34.
43. *In Commonit. ad Faustum*, no. 5.
44. Ecumenical Council of Ephesus, Act. 3.
45. Stephen, Bishop of Larissa, in Libell. to Boniface II and the Roman Synod in 531.
46. Epistle to John of Philadelphia in Labbe, *Collect. Counc.*, tom. 7, col. 22.
47. Encomium of St. Gregory, Enlightener of the Armenians, from the Armenian homilies in the *Opera* of St. John Chrysostom, Paris, 1864, vol. 12, col. 943.
48. Instruction *Licet.* 20 August 1853.
49. Council of Chalcedon, *Act.* 10.
50. Lateran Council IV, canon 26.
51. Col 3.11.
52. Eph 4.16.
53. Mt 28.19.
54. Acts 15.7.
55. Comment. on Amos 7.10-11.
56. Gregory Nazianzen, oration 43 in praise of St. Basil, no. 68.
57. Const. *Auctorem fidei*, prop. 4.
58. Hist. Arianor. ad Monach., no. 52.
59. Oration 2 *de sacr. imaginib.*, no. 16.
60. Council of Chalcedon, prop. 4.
61. 1 Pt 2.13.
62. Jn 10.5.
63. St. Cyprian, epistle to Antonianus, no. 24.
64. St. Cyprian, *Lib. de Unit: Eccles.*, no. 10.
65. St. Gelasius, epistle 18 to the bishops of Dardania, no. 6.
66. Ibid.

ETSI MULTA

ENCYCLICAL OF POPE PIUS IX ON THE
CHURCH IN ITALY, GERMANY,
AND SWITZERLAND
NOVEMBER 21, 1873
72

To all Patriarchs, Primates, Archbishops, Bishops, and other Ordinaries in Favor and Communion with the Apostolic See.

Venerable Brothers Greetings and the Apostolic Blessing.

It has been Our lot from the very beginning of Our Pontificate to suffer many grievous and painful occurrences from various causes, which We have often explained to you in encyclical letters; in these last years the burden of distress has grown so that, if the divine goodness did not sustain Us, we would be all but overwhelmed. Indeed things have reached such a point that death itself would seem preferable to life tossed about by so many waves; with eyes lifted to heaven, we are compelled to cry out from time to time: "it is better for us to die, than to witness the ruin of our sanctuary."[1] Forsooth, from the time when this Our beloved city was forcibly captured and subjected to the rule of men who are disdainers of right and enemies of religion, men to whom all things human and divine are one and the same, scarcely no day has gone by without some new wound being inflicted on Our already wounded heart.

Evils Which Have Befallen Catholicism

2. We still hear lamentations of men and women of religious congregations, who driven from their houses and in need, are dispersed in a hostile manner; this usually happens when the dominating faction has as its aim the perversion of the social order. As the great St. Anthony, on the testimony of Athanasius, says, "The devil hates all Christians indeed, but cannot tolerate in any way upright monks and virgins of Christ." We have also seen recently something We never expected would happen, namely Our Gregorian University has been suppressed and abolished. It was instituted for this purpose: that to it would come (in the words of an ancient author writing for Anglo-Saxons about the Roman School) young clerics, even from distant regions, to be educated in Catholic doctrine and faith, so that nothing contrary to Catholic unity would be taught in their Churches. Thus strengthened in firm faith, they might return to their own people. Little by little all defenses and instruments by which We are able to rule and direct the universal Church are nefariously taken away from Us. It was affirmed that once the city was taken from Us, the Roman Pontiffs would still have complete freedom in the exercise of spiritual ministry and in carrying out religious matters. This is far from true. As we predicted, the purpose of the sacrilegious usurpation of Our rule is the destruction of the force and efficacy of the papal primacy

and eventually the Catholic religion itself.

3. However, it was not Our intention to write to you concerning these evils by which this Our city and all of Italy as well is infested; indeed, We would perhaps have suppressed these Our troubles in mournful silence, if it were permitted by divine clemency that We could lessen the bitter sorrows by which so many venerable brothers, bishops, and laity are tortured in other regions.

Problems in Switzerland

4. For you are well aware, that certain cantons of the Swiss Federation have perverted all order and have undermined the very foundation of the constitution of the Church of Christ. This was brought about not so much by heterdox men, some of whom even find fault with the crime, as by followers of sects who today have gained power far and wide. They not only subvert all of justice and reason, but they even go against their publicly declared trust as well. For it was solemnly pledged, with the approval and authority of the laws of the Federation as well, that religious liberty for Catholics would remain safe and sound. We deplored, indeed, in Our allocution of last 23 December the force applied to the religious situtation by the government of those cantons "whether in decisions about dogmas of the Catholic faith or by the favoring of apostates or by interfering with the exercise of episcopal power." We made these just complaints known when We sent Gestore to the Federal Council as Our negotiator, but they were wholly neglected. Nor were protests from Catholics of all ranks nor those repeatedly sent from the Swiss episcopacy treated any better; indeed the earlier injuries inflicted were greatly increased by worse ones.

New Laws Promulgated

5. The violent banishment of Our venerable brother Gaspar, bishop of Hebron and Vicar Apostolic of Geneva took place as decorously and gloriously for him who endured it as it was foul and indecorous for those who ordered and carried it out. After this banishment the government of Geneva on 12 March and 27 August of this year promulgated two laws fully in keeping with the edict proposed the previous October, the one with which We found fault in Our allocution mentioned previously. In effect the same government arrogated the right to itself of refashioning in that canton the constitution of the Catholic Church and of conforming it to the democratic form. This subjects the bishop, both in the exercise of his proper jurisdiction and administration and in the delegation of his power, to the civil authority. It forbids him to live in the canton and defines the number and limit of parishes. It also proposes the conditions for the election of pastors and vicars and the method of their recall or suspension from office. Furthermore it grants to laics the right of nominating them, entrusting to the same laity the temporal administration of cult and in general setting them in charge, as if inspectors, of ecclesiastical affairs.

Why the Laws Are Invalid

6. These same laws provide that without the government's favor, which is revocable, the pastors and vicars could not exercise any functions and could not accept any office more extensive than those which they received through popular election. Furthermore, they are compelled by the civil power to take an oath, the words of which denote apostasy. Everyone sees that laws of this nature are void and useless because lay legislators, who are for the most part heterodox men, do not have the power to make such laws. They are also invalid because in what they teach, they are opposed to dogmas of the Catholic faith and ecclesiastical discipline sanctioned by the Ecumenical Council of Trent and by pontifical constitutions. We must therefore condemn and disapprove them.

Condemnation of the New Laws

7. Therefore as is required by the duty of Our offices, with Our Apostolic authority We solemnly condemn them, declaring at the same time that the oath they impose is illicit and clearly sacrilegious; therefore all those who in Geneva or elsewhere are elected according to the decrees of these laws or in a similar way, by the vote of the people and with the confirmation of the civil power, and who subsequently dare to undertake the tasks of ecclesiastical ministry incur a major excommunication reserved specially to this Holy See and also incur other canonical penalties. Furthermore, they must all be avoided by the faithful according to the divine admonition, as aliens and thieves who come only to rob, kill, and destroy.[2]

Other Adversities

8. Sad and calamitous as these events are

which We have just recounted, more dreadful things have happened in five of the seven cantons which constitute the diocese of Basel, namely Solothurn, Bern, Basel-Landschaft, Aargau, and Zurich. Laws have also been passed there concerning parishes, the election of pastors, and vicars and their recall. These laws overturn the rule of the Church and its divine institution, subjugating ecclesiastical ministry to secular power. One of them, that passed by the Governor of Solothurn on 23 December 1872, is completely schismatical. We condemn it and decree that it be forever considered condemned. Indeed Our venerable brother, Eugene, Bishop of Basel, with just indignation and apostolic constancy, rejected certain articles drawn up and presented to him in his meeting. They call said meeting a diocesan conference, to which delegates of the five aforesaid cantons came. In rejecting the articles, he said that they were harmful to episcopal authority, subversive of hierarchical rule, and openly favorable to heresy. For this reason he was deprived of his bishopric, taken from his residence, and violently driven into exile. After this they omitted no type of fraud or vexation to lead the clergy and faithful in the previously mentioned cantons into schism. They forbade the clergy to have any communication with the exiled bishop. Additionally, they ordered the cathedral chapter of Basel to convene for the election of a vicar or administrator of the diocese, just as if the episcopal see were really vacant. The chapter strenuously rejected this proposal.

Difficulties in the Territory of Jura

9. Meanwhile by a decree and vote of the civil magistrates of Bern, sixty-nine pastors of the territory of Jura were first forbidden to carry out the functions of their ministry and then deprived of office. This was because they had openly attested that they recognized only Eugene as legitimate bishop and pastor, or were unwilling to separate themselves dishonorably from Catholic unity. This whole territory, has constantly held onto the Catholic faith and was earlier joined to the canton of Bern under the legal stipulation and agreement that it preserve the exercise of its religion free and inviolate. But now it is deprived of parish sermons, solemn baptisms, weddings, and funerals. The multitude of the faithful is protesting in vain that on account of consummate injury done to them, they are compelled either to accept schismatic and heretical pastors forced on them by the political authority or else be deprived of any priestly ministry and aid.

10. We, for Our part, give thanks to God who, with the same grace with which He formerly strengthened and confirmed martyrs, sustains and strengthens that select part of the Catholic flock which courageously supports their bishop as he builds a wall in defense of the house of Israel that it may stand in battle the day of the Lord.[3] Without fear they follow in the footsteps of the head of the martyrs of Jesus Christ; while offering the gentleness of the lamb to the ferocity of wolves, they constantly and readily fight for their faith.

11. This noble constancy of the faithful Swiss is emulated with no less commendation by the clergy and faithful in Germany, who themselves follow the illustrious example of their ecclesiastical leaders. The Germans, assuming the shield of Catholic truth and the helms of salvation, fight the battles of the Lord and are a wonder to the world, to the angels, and to men who look on them from every side. All the more is their fortitude of spirit and unbroken constancy admired and extolled with outstanding praise as the bitter persecution set in motion against them in the German Empire and especially in Prussia increases with each day.

Unwarranted Power Given to Laity

12. In addition to many grave injuries inflicted on the Catholic Church last year, the government of Prussia with harsh, iniquitous laws totally different from previous ones have subjected the whole institution and education of clerics to lay power. One can now legitimately ask how clerics are to be educated and formed for the priestly and pastoral life. Going further still, the government grants to the same lay power the right to bestow any office or ecclesiastical benefice and even the right to deprive sacred pastors of office and benefice.

13. Moreover so that the ecclesiastical government and the hierarchical order of subordination constituted by Christ Himself may be more quickly and fully subverted, these same laws impose many obstacles on bishops so that they cannot provide, through canonical censures and punishments, for the salvation of souls, the soundness of doctrine in Catholic schools, and the obedience due them from clerics. These same laws forbid bishops to do these things unless they are in accord with the wishes of the civil authority and the norms proposed by it. And so that nothing be lacking in the total oppression of the Catholic Church, a royal tribunal for ecclesiastical affairs has been instituted. Bishops and holy pastors can be summoned before it, both by private individuals and by public magistrates, so as to stand trial like criminals and be coerced in the exercise of their spiritual functions

Existence of Church Threatened

14. Thus the holy Church of Christ, whose necessary and full freedom of which religion had repeatedly been guaranteed by public pacts and the highest princes, has in these same places been deprived of all its rights and exposed to hostile men. Its final extinction now threatens. For the new laws, to be sure, have as their intent its destruction.

15. No wonder, then, that the former religious tranquility has been gravely disturbed in that Empire by this kind of law and other plans and actions of the Prussian government most hostile to the Church. But who would wish to falsely cast the blame of this disturbance on the Catholics of the German Empire! For if they are faulted for not acquiesing in such laws in which they could not acquiesce with good conscience, for the same reason the apostles of Jesus Christ and the martyrs, who preferred to undergo most dreadful tortures and death itself than to betray their duty and violate the rights of their most holy religion by obeying the commands of the princes who persecuted them, must also be faulted.

16. If no other laws than these of the civil authority existed and if they were of the highest order, it would be wrong to transgress them. If, moreover, these same civil laws constituted the norm of conscience, as some maintain both impiously and absurdly, the early martyrs and their followers would have been worthy of reprehension rather than honor and praise. Indeed it would have been against the laws and the wish of princes to hand down the Christian faith, propagate it, and found the Church. Nevertheless the faith teaches and human reason demonstrates that there is a twofold order of things. Two kinds of powers must be distinguished on earth—one natural that looks to the tranquility and secular business of human society; the other, whose origin is above nature, which is in charge of the Church of Christ, divinely instituted for the salvation and peace of souls. The offices of these two powers are wisely coordinated so that things which belong to God are returned to God and, because of God, those of Caesar to Caesar, who "for this reason is great because he is less than heaven for he belongs to Him whom heaven and all creatures belong."[4]

17. From this divine command, to be sure, the Church has never turned aside. It always and everywhere attempts to inculcate in the faithful an inviolable obedience towards their supreme rulers and their rights, insofar as they are secular, and it has taught, with the Apostle, that they are rulers not for fear of good works but of evil, teaching the faithful to be subject not only because of fear, because the prince bears the sword to carry out his ire against him who has done evil, but also because of conscience because in his office he is a minister of God.[5] However, this fear of princes the Church limits to evil acts, excluding the same totally from the observance of the divine law, being mindful of what blessed Peter taught the faithful; "May none of you suffer for being a murderer, a thief, a criminal or an informer, but if any of you should suffer for being a Christian, then he is not to be ashamed of it; let him glorify God in that name."[6]

18. Since these things are so, you understand how sad We must have been when We read in the recent letter from the German Emperor the unexpected accusation against certain of his Catholic subjects, especially against the Catholic clergy, and bishops. The reason for this accusation is that they, fearing neither bonds nor tribulations and not placing any great value on their lives,[7] refuse to obey the aforementioned laws. They protest with that same firmness shown before the passing of these laws. They pointed out their faults by serious, clear and most solid explanations which, with the approval of the whole Catholic world and even of some herterodox men, they delivered to the Prince, his administrators and the supreme council of the kingdom.

19. For the same reason now they are accused of treason, as if they were conspiring with those who strive to upset all orders of human society. No attention is paid to the excellent arguments in which they clearly attest their unbroken loyalty and obedience to the Prince and their lively devotion to their fatherland. Indeed We Ourselves are asked to exhort Catholics and holy pastors there to observe these laws; this would be equivalant to Our contributing to the oppression and dispersion of the flock of the Christ. However, supported by God, We are confident that the most serene Emperor, having more carefully weighed things, will reject the empty suspicion conceived against his most loyal subjects and will no longer allow their honor to be reviled with foul detraction. In addition, he will end the unmerited persecution against them. Moreover, We would have willingly passed over the imperial letter if it had not been published, against Our knowledge and in a most unusual fashion, by an official newspaper in Berlin. It was published together with other material written by Us, in which We appealed for justice from the Emperor for the Catholic Church in Prussia.

Harassing of the Church

20. What We have recounted so far is common knowledge. Monks and virgins devoted to God are deprived of the common liberty of ordinary citizens and ejected with enormous cruelty, Catholic schools are daily being taken away from the care of the Church, and sodalities for pious works and even seminaries are dissolved. Additionally, the liberty of evangelical preaching is interfered with, hindered, teaching religion in the native language is forbidden in certain parts of the kingdom. Curates are withdrawn from their parishes, and prelates themselves are deprived of revenues coerced in many ways, and frightened with threat of imprisonment. While Catholics are vexed with all kinds of harassment such as these, how can We possibly acquiesce to what is suggested and not invoke the religion of Jesus Christ and the truth?

Government Support for Heretics

21. Nor is this the limit of the injuries which are committed against the Catholic Church. In addition the Prussian and other governments of the German Empire openly support those recent heretics who call themselves Old Catholics. Their abuse of such a name would be plainly ridiculous if it were not for the fact that so many monstrous errors of this sect against the principal teachings of the Catholic faith, so many sacrileges in divine service and the administration of the sacraments, so many grave scandals, and so much ruin of souls redeemed by the blood of Christ did not force tears from Our eyes.

Further Heresies

22. And surely what these sons of perdition intend is quite clear from their other writings, especially that impious and most imprudent one which has only recently been published by the person whom they recently constituted as a pseudo-bishop. For these writings attack and pervert the true power of jurisdiction of the Roman Pontiff and the bishops, who are the successors of blessed Peter and the apostles; they transfer it instead to the people, or, as they say, to the community. They obstinately reject and oppose the infallible magisterium both of the Roman Pontiff and of the whole Church in teaching matters. Incredibly, they boldly affirm that the Roman Pontiff and all the bishops, the priests and the people conjoined with him in the unity of faith and communion fell into heresy when they approved and professed the definitions of the Ecumenical Vatican Council. Therefore they deny also the indefectibility of the Church and blasphemously declare that it has perished throughout the world and that its visible Head and the bishops have erred. They assert the necessity of restoring a legitimate episcopacy in the person of their pseudo-bishop, who has entered not by the gate but from elsewhere like a thief or robber and calls the damnation of Christ upon his head.

23. These unhappy men undermine the foundations of religion, overturn all its marks and properties, and invent so many foul errors, or rather, draw forth from the ancient store of heretics and gather them together and publish them. Yet they do not blush to call themselves Catholics and *Old Catholics*, while in their doctrine, novelty, and number they show themselves in no way to be either old or Catholic. Certainly the Church rises up with greater right against them than it once did through Augustine against the Donatists. Diffused among all people, the Church was built by Christ the Son of the living God upon the rock, against which the gates of Hell will not prevail, and with which He Himself, to Whom all power in heaven and on earth is given, said He would be with until the consummation of the world. "The Church cries to her Spouse: Why do certain men withdrawing from me murmur against me? Why do these lost men claim that I have perished? Announce to me the length of my days, how long I will be in this world? Tell me on account of those who say: it was and is no longer; on account of those who say: the scriptures have been fulfilled, all nations have believed, but the Church has apostatized and perished from all nations. And He announced and the voice was not vain. What did He announce? 'Behold I am with you all days even to the consummation of the world.' Moved by your voices and your false opinions, it asked of God that He announce to it the length of its days and it found that God said 'Behold I am with you all days even to the consummation of the world.' Here you will say: He spoke about us; we are as we will be until the end of the world. Christ Himself is asked; He says 'and this gospel will be preached in the whole world, in testimony to all nations, and then will come the end.' Therefore the Church will be among all nations until the end of the world. Let heretics perish as they are, and let them find that they become what they are not."[8]

Pseudo-bishop

24. But these men having progressed more boldly in the ways of wickedness and destruction, as happens to heretical sects from God's just judgment, have wished to create a hierarchy also for themselves, as we have intimated. They have chosen and set up a pseudo-bishop, a certain notorious apostate from the Catholic faith, Joseph Humbert Reinkens. So that nothing be lacking in their impudence, for his consecration they have had refuge to those very Jansenists of Utrecht, whom they themselves, before they separated from the Church, considered as heretics and schismatics, as do all other Catholics. However, this Joseph Humbert dares to say that he is a bishop, and, what passes belief, he is recognized and named in an explicit decree by the most serene Emperor of Germany and is proposed to all his subjects as a lawful bishop. But as even the rudiments of Catholic faith declare, no one can be considered a bishop who is not linked in communion of faith and love with Peter, upon whom is built the Church of Christ; who does not adhere to the supreme Pastor to whom the sheep of Christ are committed to be pastured; and who is not bound to the confirmer of fraternity which is in the world. And indeed "the Lord spoke to Peter; to one person therefore, so that He might found unity from one";[9] to Peter, "the divine dignity granted a great and wonderful consortium of his power, and if He wished anything to be common with him and the rest of the princes, He never gave, except through him, what He did not deny to the others."[10] Hence it is from this Apostolic See, where blessed Peter "lives and presides and grants the truth of faith to those seeking it,[11] that the rights of venerable communion flow to all";[12] and this same See "for the Churches spread throughout the whole world is certainly the head, as it were, of their members, from which if one cuts himself off, he becomes an exile from the Christian religion, as soon as he begins not to belong to its structure."[13]

25. Therefore the holy martyr Cyprian, writing about schism, denied to the pseudobishop Novatian even the title of Christian, on the grounds that he was cut off and separated from the Church of Christ. "Whoever he is," he says, "and whatever sort he is, he is not a Christian who is not in the Church of Christ. Let him boast and preach his philosophy and eloquence with a proud voice; he who does not have fraternal charity and does not retain ecclesiastical unity, loses also what he previously had. Since by Christ one Church was founded divided into many members throughout the world, so likewise one episcopate, diffused in the harmonious multiplicity of many bishops. Subsequent to the teaching of God and the conjoined unity of the Catholic Church, he attempts to build a human church. Therefore, he who does not retain unity of spirit nor communion of peace and thus separates himself from the bond of the Church and the college of the priesthood cannot have the power nor the honor of a bishop because he kept the unity or the peace of the episcopacy."[14]

Excommunication

26. We have been undeservingly placed on this supreme seat of Peter to preserve the Catholic faith and the unity of the universal Church. Therefore following the custom and example of Our Predecessors and of holy legislation, by the power granted to Us from heaven, We declare the election of the said Joseph Humbert Reinkens, performed against the sanctions of the holy canons to be illicit, null, and void. We furthermore declare his consecration sacrilegious. Therefore, by the authority of Almighty God, We excommunicate and hold as anathema Joseph Humbert himself and all those who attempted to

choose him, and who aided in his sacrilegious consecration. We additionallly excommunicate whoever has adhered to them and belonging to their party has furnished help, favor, aid, or consent. We declare, proclaim, and command that they are separated from the communion of the Church. They are to be considered among those with whom all faithful Christians are forbidden by the Apostle to associate and have social exchange to such an extent that, as he plainly states, they may not even be greeted.[15]

27. From these matters We have touched upon more by way of deploring than narrating them, venerable brothers, you understand how sad and full of danger is the condition of Catholics in those regions of Europe which We indicated. Nor, truly, are things much better or more peaceful in America, several of whose regions are so hostile to Catholics that their governments seem to deny in deeds their Catholic faith. For there, some years past, a most severe war was begun against the Church, its institutions, and the rights of this Apostolic See. If We were to pursue these matters, We would find much to say; since, however, because of the gravity of the situation, they cannot be touched on in passing, We will treat them more thoroughly at another time and place.

28. Some of you may perchance wonder that the war against the Catholic Church extends so widely. Indeed each of you knows well the nature, zeal, and intention of sects, whether called Masonic or some other name. When he compares them with the nature, purpose, and amplitude of the conflict waged nearly everywhere against the Church, he cannot doubt but that the present calamity must be attributed to their deceits and machinations for the most part. For from these the synagogue of Satan is formed which draws up its forces, advances its standards, and joins battle against the Church of Christ.

29. Our Predecessors, as watchers in Israel, denounced these forces from the very beginnings to rulers and nations. Against them they have struck out again and again with their condemnations. We Ourselves have not been deficient in Our duty. Would that the Pastors of the Church had more loyalty from those who could have averted such a pernicious plague! But, creeping through sinuous openings, never stinting in toil, deceiving many by clever fraud, it has reached such an outcome that it has burst forth from its hiding places and boasts itself lord and master. Grown immense by a multitude of followers, these nefarious bands think that they have been made masters of their desire and have all but achieved their goal. The have at last achieved what they have so long desired, that is, that in many places they obtained supreme power and won for themselves bulwarks of men and authority. Now they boldly turn to this, to hand over the Church of God to a most harsh servitude, to tear up the supports on which it rests, and to attempt to distort the marks by which it stands out gloriously. What more? They would, if possible, completely wipe it out from the world after they had shaken it with frequent blows, ruined it, and overturned it.

Efforts to Defeat Heresies

30. Since these things are so, venerable brothers, apply all your effort to protect the faithful committed to your care against the snares and contagion of these sects. Bring back those who have unhappily joined these sects. Expose especially the error of those who have been deceived or those who assert now that only social utility, progress, and the exercise of mutual benefits are the intention of these dark associations. Explain to them often and fix deeper in their minds the pontifical decrees on this matter. Teach them that these decrees refer not only to Masonic groups in Europe, but also those in America and in other regions of the world.

31. As for the rest since we have fallen on these evil times let us take care first and foremost, as good soldiers of Christ, not to lose heart. Indeed, in the very storms in which we are tossed, there is a certain hope of achieving future tranquility and greater serenity in the Church. So let us arouse ourselves and the toiling clergy and laity, propped up by divine help and inspired by that most noble statement of Chrysostom: "Many waves and dire storms, press on but we do not fear lest we be submerged, for we stand on a rock. Let the sea rage, it cannot dissolve the rock. Le the waves rise, they cannot sink the bark of Christ. Nothing is stronger than the Church. The Church is stronger than the heavens. *Heaven and earth shall pass away, but my words will not pass away*. What words? *Thou art Peter and upon this rock I will build my Church and the gates of Hell will not prevail against it.* If you do not trust the words, trust the deeds. How many tyrants have tried to

oppress the Church! How many cauldrons, furnaces, teeth of beasts, sharp swords! They have accomplished nothing. Where are those enemies? They are handed over to silence and forgetfulness. Where is the Church? It shines brighter than the sun. Their deeds are extinct, its deeds are immortal. If when they were few, the Christians were not conquered, how can you conquer them when the whole world is full of this holy religion? *Heaven and earth will pass, my words will not pass away.*[16] Therefore not moved by any danger and not hesitating at all, let us persevere in prayer. Let us all strive to placate the celestial anger provoked by the sins of mankind so that the Almighty will rise up and command the winds and bring about tranquility.

32. In the meantime, We lovingly grant the apostolic blessing as a testimony of the special benevolence We have to you all, venerable brothers, and the clergy and the entire people committed to the care of each of you.

Given in Rome at St. Peter's, 21 November 1873, in the 28th year of Our Pontificate.

†

LATIN TEXT: *Acta Pii IX*, I, 6:253-73; *Acta Sanctae Sedis*, 7:496-512.

ENGLISH TRANSLATION: Robert F. Healey, SJ

REFERENCES:

1. 1 Mc 3.59.
2. Jn 10.5, 10.
3. 3 Ez 13.5.
4. Tertullian, *apolog.*, chap. 30.
5. Rom 13.3f.
6. 1 Pt 4.14, 15.
7. Acts 20.24.
8. Augustine on Ps 101, enarratio 2, nos. 8, 9.
9. Pacian, epistle 3 to Sympronius, no. 11; Cyprian, *de unit. Eccl*; Optatus, *contra Parmen.*, bk. 7, no. 3; Siricius, epistle 5 to the Bishops of Africa; Innocent I, epistles to Victricius and the Councils of Carthage and Milevis.
10. St. Leo the Great, sermon 3 on his elevation; Optatus, bk. 2, no. 2.
11. Peter Chrysologus, epistle to Eutyches.
12. Council of Aquileia; Ambrose, epistle 11, no. 4; Jerome, epistles 14 and 16 to Damasus.
13. Boniface I, epistle 14 to the Bishops of Thessalonica.
14. Cyprian, *contra Novatian*, epistle 52 to Antonianus.
15. 2 Jn 1.10.
16. Homily, *ante exil.*, nos. 1 and 2.

VIX DUM A NOBIS

ENCYCLICAL OF POPE PIUS IX ON
THE CHURCH IN AUSTRIA
MARCH 7, 1874
73

To Our Beloved Sons, the Cardinals and Our Venerable Brothers the Archbishops and Bishops of the Austrian Empire.

Greetings and Apostolic Blessing.

Scarcely had We announced to the Catholic world in a letter dated last 24 November that a vast persecution had been stirred up against the Church, especially in Prussia and Switzerland, when a new concern was added to Our grief. News arrived concerning other injustices. The Church can now justly complain: "they have added above and beyond the pain of my wounds."[1] We are especially grieved by these injuries because they are inflicted by the Government of the Austrian nation, which in the great days of the Christian republic fought strenuously for the Catholic faith.

Hostile Laws

2. Indeed, some years ago that Empire had enacted certain laws and arrangements plainly hostile to the sacred rights of the Church and to our solemn pacts. In Our Allocution to the Cardinals on June 22, 1868, We condemned and nullified these laws.[2] Now, however, new laws are proposed and approved by the public assembly of the Empire; these intend that the Catholic Church be subjugated to the civil authority. This is, of course, against the ordination of Our Lord Jesus Christ.

Ecclesiastical Authority

3. God equipped the Church with the divine gifts of an infallible teaching authority for handing on sacred doctrine and of a most holy priesthood. He also equipped it with the power to pass laws, exercise judgments, and employ salutary coercion in all matters which pertain to the kingdom of God on earth.

4. This supernatural power of ecclesiastical rule is different from and independent from political authority. For this reason the kingdom of God on earth is a perfect society, which is held together and governed by its own laws and its own rights. Its own overseers keep watch in order to account for souls not to the rulers of civil society, but to the chief Pastor, Jesus Christ, from whom come pastors and teachers subject to no earthly authority in carrying out the task of salvation.[3] Wherefore, just as the duty to rule belongs to the holy bishops, so all the faithful, as the Apostle points out, are bound to obey and be subject to them; therefore, Catholic people have a

right not to be impeded in this divinely imposed duty of following the doctrine, discipline, and laws of the Church.

5. Indeed you yourselves know what a grave violation of this divine constitution of the Church and what an intolerable subversion of the rights of the Holy See, holy bishops, and Catholic people is promulgated in the proposal before the Austrian assembly.

Intent of the New Laws

6. For, according to these laws, the Church is held completely subject to the control of civil authority; and this is practically stated openly in that exposition of *Motivi*, which explains the force and meaning of those laws. Here also it is expressly stated that the civil government can pass laws for ecclesiastical matters because it must watch over and control the Church just as it does for any other private society within the boundaries of the Empire.

7. And so the civil government arrogates to itself the judgment, authority, and control over the constitution and rights of the Catholic Church. It can exercise this partly by itself through its laws and action, partly by ecclesiastics hired by itself. Hence it comes about that the judgment and power of earthly rule is substituted for the sacred power divinely instituted for the rule of the Church, the work of its ministry, and the building up of the body of Christ. Against such usurpations of sacred things, in defense of what is right and Catholic truth, Ambrose the Great replies "It is alleged: the emperor can do anything, everything is his. I respond: do not trouble yourself by thinking that you have an imperial right in those things which are divine. Do not extol yourself, but be subject to God. It is written: the things of God belong to God, those of Caesar to Caesar. The palace belongs to the emperor, the Church to the priest."[4]

8. As far as the laws themselves go, to which the exposition of *Motivi* mentioned before is affixed, although they may perhaps seem to present an appearance of moderation, if they are compared with the recent laws of Prussia, in reality they have the same intent: they prepare the way for the same destruction of the Catholic Church in Austria.

9. We do not intend to go through the individual headings of these laws, but We cannot in any way pass over the most grave injury which is done to all of us and the whole Catholic population of your Empire by their very proposal. The Convention We entered into with the most serene Emperor in the year 1855[5] was reinforced by a solemn promise by the same Catholic prince and promulgated in the form of public law to the whole empire. The imperial assembly now proposes to abrogate and nullify this Convention. They propose this without even having contacted Us, indeed with open contempt of Our just complaints.

10. What could not even be attempted in prior times when public faith was strong, is now attempted and carried out in these lamentable circumstances. Against this violation of a solemnly pledged Convention, We again protest before you or rather, with deep sorrow in Our hearts, We denounce and condemn this injury inflicted in the whole Church. The excuse for the abrogation of this concordat and other related laws is boldly given as the definition of revealed doctrine promulgated by the Ecumenical Vatican Council. These Catholic dogmas themselves are impiously labelled as innovations and changes in the doctrine with regard to faith and the constitution of the Church.[6] Indeed, even if some Austrians, because of these nefarious fictions, have abjured the Catholic faith, your august Prince, along with his glorious ancestors and with his whole imperial household, retains and professes it. And by far most of your people for whom these laws are passed also hold and profess it.

11. Now a new kind of law is proposed and a new power claimed for the civil government so that it can set up and decree, according to its arbitrary will, anything that pleases it concerning spiritual and ecclesiastical matters. These powerful laws would impede the inviolable liberty of the Church to care for souls, to rule the faithful, to carry out religious instruction of the people and the clergy as well, to exhort to evangelical perfection, and to administer and possess goods. They would also introduce the perversion of Catholic discipline, encourage defection from the Church, and strengthen the coalition and conspiracy of the sects against the true faith of Christ.

12. We could speak at great length on the nature and extent of the resultant evils if such laws are passed, but it cannot escape nor deceive your own prudence. To wit, all offices and ecclesiastical benefices, even the exercise of pastoral duties, would become subject to the civil power. If

holy bishops acquiesced to these new laws, they would no longer retain control over their dioceses, but would be compelled to regulate them according to the will and decision of those who preside over the state. For what could be expected of these proposals which are drawn up concerning the recognition of the religious orders? To be sure, their purpose and hostile intent is so clear that no one fails to recognize that they have been invented and conceived for the destruction of religious families. The threatened loss of temporal goods is so great that it is scarcely different from open confiscation and plundering. Indeed those goods would be brought under the control of the government. It would then claim the right to divide and to tax them so heavily that whatever remains could only be conceived as scornful and as a cover for injustice.

Role of the Clergy

13. Thus, you can clearly see how these laws threaten the flocks entrusted to your care. For the unity and peace of the Church is called into danger, and there is question of depriving it of its liberty, which St. Thomas of Canterbury calls "the soul of the Church without which it has no strength or force and cannot avail against those who seek to possess for their inheritance the sanctuary of God."[7] St. Anselm, the other intrepid defender of this liberty, earlier expressed the same opinion: "God loves nothing in this world more than the liberty of His Church; those who wish not to promote it so much as to dominate it are certainly known to be enemies of God: God wishes His bride to be free, not enslaved."[8] Wherefore We urge you all the more to strive to avert the danger which threatens. Greatly resolve to meet the test in a way worthy of your virtue. For We are certain that your spirit and virtue will be no less than that of those venerable brothers elsewhere who, publicly exposed to insults and violence amidst the most sharp vexations for the liberty of the Church, not only happily accepted being stripped of their belongings, but also underwent suffering in prison.[9]

14. Moreover all our hope is placed not in our strength but in the power of God; for at stake is the cause of God Who by an unfailing prophecy warned and aroused us thusly: In the world you will have distress, but have confidence, I have conquered the world.[10] And so We have become the leader in this atrocious war against the Church. We promise what the holy martyr of Canterbury once expressed. His words are appropriate to this age and danger: "The cause which the enemies of the Church exercise against us is between them and God, since we seek nothing from them except what God left to his Church in eternal testament. Therefore, join Us in defending the Church with the authority and prudence granted to you. Withstand those men to whom no amount of success suffices if the Church of God enjoys liberty. We are all the more confident in you since the cause is God's. As for us, be assured, that we are more willing to undergo temporal death than to continue enduring the straits of wretched servitude. For the outcome of this controversy will have consequences for future times, that is, whether the Church grieves with perpetual distress or enjoys perpetual liberty."[11]

15. Meanwhile you must strive to forestall with your authority, prudence, and zeal the dangers which threaten. Consult with each other to determine how to acquire more certainly and efficaciously the proposed goal. As long as the rights of the Church are attacked, you must rise up and place before its adversaries a wall for the house of Israel; your bulwark will be more solid and your defense more valid if your labors are united and your plans are foresighted. Wherefore We urge you to assemble together as soon as possible and with mutual counsel draw up a clear norm by which you may bravely defend the liberty of the Church and unanimously repel, in keeping with the nature of your office, the attacking evils. We must give you this admonition in order not to be deficient to Our office in such a serious matter. But We are persuaded that even without Our exhortation, you would have done this of your own accord. For the rest, We have not lost all hope that God will divert the impending calamities. We are moved to hope for the best by the piety and religious observance of Franz Joseph, Emperor and King. Today We have strenuously implored him in a new letter never to willingly permit the Church in his dominion to be handed over to a dishonorable servitude and never to permit the Catholic citizens of his Empire to be brought to such extreme straits.

16. Since many strive against the Church and any delay is always a danger, it ill befits you to be negligent and inactive. May God preside over your counsels and aid you with his powerful protection so that you may decide upon and

PIUS IX

bring about those things which pertain to the glory of His name and the salvation of souls. As a guarantee of this heavenly protection and a testimony of special benevolence, We lovingly impart the Apostolic blessing to each and all of you, beloved sons and venerable brothers, and to the clergy and faithful committed to your vigilance.

Given in Rome at St. Peter's, 7 March 1874, in the 28th year of Our Pontificate.

†

LATIN TEXT: *Acta Pii IX*, I, 6:297-306; *Acta Sanctae Sedis*, 7:565-73.

ENGLISH TRANSLATION: Robert F. Healey, S.J.

REFERENCES:

1. Ps 68.27.
2. *Actor*, vol. 4, p. 407.
3. Heb 13.17; Eph 4.11; I Pt 5.2.
4. Saint Ambrose, epistle 20, no. 19.
5. *Actor*, vol. 2, p. 459.
6. *Motivorum Expos.*, p. 25.
7. St. Thomas of Canterbury, epistle 75 to the bishops of England.
8. St. Anselm, epistle 9 to King Baldwin.
9. Heb 10.32 f.
10. Jn 16.33.
11. St. Thomas of Canterbury, epistle 33.

OMNEM SOLLICITUDINEM

ENCYCLICAL OF POPE PIUS IX ON THE
GREEK-RUTHENIAN RITE
MAY 13, 1874
74

To the Ruthenian Archbishops of Lwów, Halicz and Kamiensk and the other Bishops of the Same Rite in Friendship and Communion with the Apostolic See.

Venerable Brothers, Greetings and the Apostolic Blessing:

From the beginning years of Our lengthy Pontificate We have constantly striven to look after and foster the spiritual good of the Oriental Churches. We have solemnly declared, among other things, that their special Catholic liturgies, which Our Predecessors likewise held to be of the utmost importance, be scrupulously observed and kept in pristine condition.[1] In this regard, most clear indeed are the words of Clement VIII in His Constitution, *Magnus Dominus* (1595); Paul V in His Brief (10 December 1615); and especially, as well as others, Benedict XIV in His encyclical letters, *Demandatam* (1743) and *Allatae sunt* (1755).

2. Since, however, the closest possible link binds liturgical practice and dogmatic truths, the Apostolic See, as soon as it detected "any dangerous or unseemly rite creeping into the Oriental Church, has disapproved, condemned, and forbidden its use."[2]

3. On the other hand, this concern of preserving intact the ancient liturgies, has not prevented certain rites, borrowed from other Churches, from being admitted into the Oriental ritual. Gregory XVI of blessed memory wrote about these to the Armenian Catholics, "your ancestors, either admired them because they seemed more fitting and beautiful or, introduced them at various periods as a distinctive mark separating themselves from heretics and schismatics."[3] Therefore, as this same Supreme Pontiff declared, "that rule must be absolutely observed which states that, except for the most serious reasons and with the Apostolic See, no innovations are to be introduced into the holy rites of the liturgy, even under the pretext of restoring ceremonies which may seem to be more in conformity with liturgies approved by the same See."[4]

4. These principles were approved for the Churches of the Oriental rite as a whole. The liturgical practice of the Ruthenians, whom the Roman Pontiffs have always treated with singular signs of benevolence and special favors, is also governed by these principles, as has been frequently declared on appropriate occasions, especially in the earlier mentioned Brief of Paul V. Whenever their faith was endangered, the Apostolic See has immediately raised its voice to avert such an evil. Gregory XVI employed[5] solemn words when the Ruthenians became involved in the most painful situation in which 300,000 of them were lamentably torn from the bosom of the Church.

5. Likewise, the same Holy See helped the Ruthenians when long and grave controversies were stirred up in the ecclesiastical province of Lwów, not without detriment to Christian charity because of the diversity of discipline and rite and on account of the mutual relations existing between ecclesiastics of the Latin rite and those of the Greek, these controversies were happily settled and smoothed over by means of a convention or agreement proposed by the bishops of both rites and sanctioned by a decree of the Sacred Congregation of Propaganda for Oriental Affairs (October 6, 1863).

6. Truly, the present wretched conditions in Lwów and, to an even greater degree, in the neighboring diocese of Chelm, again demand Our vigilance and solicitude. Indeed, We have recently learned that a very bitter controversy has been raised over liturgical matters among Catholics of the Greco-Ruthenian rite, and that certain persons, even though invested with clerical orders, desirous of novelty, have attempted to change the rites to their own tastes. Some of these rites have been used from time immemorial, others solemnly confirmed by the sanction of the Synod of Zamósź, which had the approbation of the Apostolic See.[6]

7. But what pains Us even more is the wretched state of affairs now afflicting the diocese of Chelm. In effect, its bishop, whom We installed but a few years ago and who is still connected with that diocese by spiritual bonds, is gone and a certain pseudo-administrator, whom We long ago judged unworthy of episcopal dignity, has not feared to usurp ecclesiastical jurisdiction and overturn everything within that church. And beyond that he has even tampered with the canonically sanctioned liturgy on his own initiative.

8. To Our sorrow We have before Our eyes at this moment the circular letter published on 20 October 1873, in which the pseudo-administrator dares to make innovations in the exercise of divine worship and the sacred liturgy. No doubt his only purpose is to introduce the liturgy of the schismatics into the diocese of Chelm. In order to more easily deceive simple and uneducated people, he has unashamedly quoted certain constitutions of the Holy See and fraudulently interpreted them in his own way.

9. It is obvious to everyone that all the dispositions in the above-mentioned letter are null and void; We, by Our apostolic authority, expressly declare it null and void. To begin with, the previously mentioned pseudo-administrator totally lacks any ecclesiastical jurisdiction. Neither the legitimate bishop before his departure from the diocese nor subsequently the Apostolic See ever conferred any such authority on him. Thus he "has not entered the sheepfold by the door, but by some other way"[7] and should be considered an intruder, as is obvious to all.

10. Moreover the sacred canons of the Church prescribe that ancient Oriental rites legitimately introduced should be scrupulously retained. "Our Predecessors, the Roman Pontiffs, have frequently and purposefully agreed to approve or permit those rites insofar as they in no way oppose the Catholic faith nor cause danger to souls nor derogate from ecclesiastical dignity."[8] At the same time these canons have solemnly declared that no one whosoever, without consultation with this Holy See, may introduce even the slightest innovations into the liturgy. This is sufficiently and clearly indicated in the apostolic constitutions mentioned earlier.

11. Liturgical innovations of this nature proposed for the purpose of purifying the Oriental rites and restoring them to their pristine integrity are a pretext and therefore invalid. Indeed the liturgy of the Ruthenians can be no other than that which was either instituted by the holy fathers of the Church or ratified by the canons of synods or introduced by legitimate use, always with the express or tacit approval of the Apostolic See. If variations have occurred in this liturgy in the course of time, they have been instituted after consultation with the Roman Pontiffs and for the express purpose of freeing such rites from any taint of heresy or schism and expressing Catholic teaching more correctly and clearly for the preservation of the faith and the good of souls. Accordingly, nothing other is intended by the deceptive pretext of purifying rites and restoring them to their original condition than the preparation of pitfalls for the faith of the Ruthenians of Chelm, whom evil men are striving to tear from the bosom of the Church and to hand over to heresy and schism.

12. But among all our distressing difficulties,

We are refreshed by the truly heroic display of bravery and constancy of spirit which the Ruthenians of the diocese of Chelm have recently offered before God, angels and men. They rejected the iniquitous orders of the pseudo-administrator, preferring to endure every ill, even extreme danger to their own lives, rather than to reject their ancestral faith and to give up the Catholic rites which they desire to preserve forever incorrupt and intact.

13. We, for Our part, will not cease to ask God that rich in mercy as He is, He kindly pour the light of His grace into the heart of those who unjustly trouble the diocese of Chelm. We will also ask that He likewise grant to the unhappy faithful there, destitute of all help and spiritual direction, His aid, and that He hasten the longed for relief of tranquillity.

14. Moreover, venerable brothers, We exhort you, also, who with such labor and singular zeal have undertaken the care of the Ruthenians entrusted to you, to preserve scrupulously the liturgical practice approved by the Apostolic See or introduced with its knowledge and without its censure. Reject totally any innovation, and take care to instruct pastors and priests to observe most accurately, even under the strictest sanction of penalties, if need be, the sacred canons on these matters, especially those of the Synod of Zamósć. Indeed the question is a most grave one, that of the salvation of souls, since illegitimate innovations are causing the greatest peril to the Catholic Ruthenians in their faith and in their religious unity. Wherefore, no care is to be spared and nothing left untried so that all the disorder in liturgical matters excited there by evil men may be totally suppressed from its very beginning. We are confident, venerable brothers, that with God granting His grace, you will not fail to carry out these your duties both firmly and agreeably.

15. For this happy conclusion, venerable brothers, We lovingly in the Lord bestow the Apostolic Blessing on you and the flocks entrusted to your care.

Given in Rome at St. Peter's, 13 May 1874, in the 28th year of Our Pontificate.

†

LATIN TEXT: *Acta Pii IX*, I, 6:316-23.

ENGLISH TRANSLATION: Robert F. Healey, S.J.

REFERENCES:

1. Apostolic letter *In suprema*, 6 January 1848.
2. Benedict XIV, encyclical *Allatae sunt*, sect. 27, 26 July 1755.
3. Gregory XVI, letter *Studium paternae benevolentiae*, 2 May 1836.
4. Gregory XVI, letter *Inter gravissimas*, 3 February 1832.
5. An Allocation in Consistory, 22 November 1838.
6. Benedict XIII, brief *Apostolatus officium*, 19 July 1724.
7. Jn 10.1.
8. Benedict XIV, constitution *Etsi pastoralis*, 26 May 1742.

GRAVIBUS ECCLESIAE

ENCYCLICAL OF POPE PIUS IX PROCLAIMING A JUBILEE FOR 1875
DECEMBER 24, 1874
75

To All the Patriarchs, Primates, Archbishops, Bishops, other Ordinaries in Favor and Communion with the Apostolic See and to All the Faithful in Christ.

Greetings and Apostolic Benediction.

Moved by the grave calamities of the Church and this age and by the necessity of imploring divine aid, We have never ceased urging Christian people to please God by holy lives, works of penance, and pious supplication. For this purpose We have frequently granted indulgences to encourage true repentance; in this way, the faithful can become worthy of having their prayers graciously accepted by God. When the Ecumenical Vatican Council convened, We decided to do the same so that this grave undertaking might be aided by the prayers of the entire Church to God. Although the Council was suspended because of current calamities, nevertheless We proclaimed that said indulgence remained in effect.

Observance of Jubilee Year

2. The year 1875 signifies that sacred period of time which our ancestors and Our predecessors consecrated for the solemn celebration of a universal Jubilee. During tranquil times, the Jubilee year was observed with veneration and piety. It was always considered a year of redemption and grace, remission and indulgences, in which people from all over the world flock to Rome. It always resulted in the salvation of many souls.

Circumstances Affecting Jubilee Years

3. When Leo XII opened the Jubilee Year in 1825, it was accepted with such popular fervor that a constant stream of pilgrims arrived in this city throughout the whole year; the splendor of religion, piety, faith, charity, and all sorts of virtue shone in it. Because of the grievous conditions of the times, We had to omit the solemnity of the Jubilee in 1850. We wish that circumstances now were such that We could celebrate happily according to the custom of Our predecessors.

Current Evils

The difficulties which prohibited Us from opening the Jubilee have even increased. The many evils which afflict the Church include the following: attempts to separate souls from their faith in Christ, corruption of sound doctrine and the spreading of impiety, widespread scandals, the spreading corruption of morals, and the overturning of divine and human rights which could lead to the collapse of undistorted thinking. With such a collection of evils, We must see to the following: that faith, religion, and piety be defended and prosper; that the spirit of prayer be widely fostered; that those who have lapsed be aroused to repentance; that sins, which have deserved the wrath of God, be averted by holy works. Since the Jubilee is principally directed to these concerns, We thought that we should not allow the Christian people to be deprived of this salutary benefit, at least in that form which the condition of the times permits. Purified of their sins, they may more readily acquire divine favor and grace.

Announcement of 1875 Jubilee Year

4. Therefore We proclaim to the exaltation of the Church, to the sanctification of the Christian people, and to the glory of God, a universal Jubilee to last for the entire year of 1875 soon to begin. In view of this Jubilee We suspend the above mentioned indulgence conceded on the occasion of the Vatican Council; instead, We open that heavenly treasury of indulgences which is entrusted to Our dispensation.

Requirements for Indulgences

5. God has granted Us the power to grant indulgences to all the Christian faithful who are truly penitent and have confessed their sins and have been refreshed by holy Communion along with one of the following: either devoutly visiting the urban basilicas of Sts. Peter and Paul, St. John Lateran, and St. Mary Major at least once a day for fifteen continuous or interspersed days whether natural or ecclesiastical, that is, computing from first vespers of one day to the full evening twilight of the next day; or, devoutly visiting once a day for fifteen continuous or interspersed days their cathedral or principal church and three other churches of the same city or place or in its suburbs as designated by the Ordinaries, their vicars, or others delegated by them. There they should pray for the prosperity and exaltation of the Catholic Church and this Apostolic See, for the extirpation of heresies and the conversion of all in error, and for the peace and unity of the whole Christian people. All who fulfill these requirements may obtain once during 1875 the fullest indulgence, with remission and pardon for all their sins. These same indulgences may be applied to the departed souls.

Exemptions from Conditions for Indulgence

6. As for those at sea or journeying, they may obtain the same indulgence when they return home or elsewhere when they have fulfilled the above mentioned conditions and have visited the same number of times the cathedral or principal church or the parish church of their domicile or place of sojourn. Ordinaries may dispense with the prescribed visits in the case of nuns, oblates, and other girls or women living either in monastic cloister or in other religious or pious houses and communities; anchorites and hermits; others, whether laity or secular, in prison or captivity or prevented by some bodily infirmity or other impediment from carrying out the above mentioned visits. They may also dispense young people who have not yet made their first Communion from the condition of Communion. Instead, they may prescribe other works of piety, religion, or charity in place of the visits or the sacrament of Communion mentioned above. Priests, sodalities, confraternities, universities, or colleges and those visiting their churches in procession can validly reduce the number of these visits according to their prudent judgment.

Confessors

7. Moreover, in the case of cloistered nuns and their novices, We grant them permission to choose for themselves for this purpose any confessor approved by their Ordinary for hearing the confessions of nuns. The rest of the faithful may choose for this purpose any priest approved for hearing the confessions of the laity by the Ordinaries themselves. And by the same authority, We grant to these confessors the right to absolve, within the said year, all those who came to confession to them, who seriously desire to gain the present Jubilee indulgence, and who have fulfilled the other requirements for obtaining it. On this occasion and in the internal forum of conscience only, they may absolve from excommunication, suspension and other ecclesiastical sentences and censures *a iure* or *ab homine*, no matter for what reason they were passed or inflicted even by Ordinaries, Ourselves or the Apostolic See, and also in cases which are specially reserved to the above and which are not otherwise understood to be granted in any ample concession. They may also absolve from all sins and excesses, however grave

and enormous, even those reserved to the same Ordinaries, to Ourselves, and to the Apostolic See, as indicated above. However a salutary penance and whatever else is called for by law should be imposed. They may also commute to other pious and salutary works any vows, even those which are public and reserved to the Apostolic See. The only exceptions are vows of chastity, religion, and obligation which were received by a third party or which prejudice the rights of a third party, and also penalties which are labelled *praeservativa a peccato*, unless the commutation is judged to be of such a nature that it will prevent sin no less than the previous matter of the vow. They may also validly dispense penitents in sacred orders, and even religious men, from any hidden irregularity to the exercise of that order and the acquisition of higher orders, provided the irregularity has been contracted by the violation of censures.

8. We do not intend, however, by this letter to dispense from any other irregularity, whether public or hidden, nor from any defect, infamy, or any other inability or unfitness however contracted, nor to grant any faculty of dispensing beyond those mentioned, of making one suitable, or of returning one to a former state, even in the internal forum of conscience; nor to alter the apostolic constitution with its appropriate declarations of Benedict XIV, *Sacramentum poenitentiae*, 1 June 1741, in the first year of his pontificate. Nor do We intend in any way to reinstate by this letter those who have been excommunicated by name by Ourselves and the Apostolic See or any prelate or ecclesiastic judge, nor those who have been suspended, nor those who have fallen under interdict, nor those who have been declared to have incurred other sentences and censures, nor those who were publicly denounced, unless within the year, they have made satisfaction and, where necessary, have been reconciled with the persons concerned.

Other Unusual Circumstances

9. Moreover, if anyone sets out to obtain the indulgence but dies before completing the required number of visits, if he is truly penitent and has confessed and received holy communion, We grant him the indulgence anyway. If, moreover, after having obtained absolution from censures or commutation of vows or the aforesaid dispensations, anyone changes his intention of obtaining the indulgence, although he can scarcely be considered from this very fact to be free from the pain of sin, still We declare that the absolutions, communications, and dispensations which he has obtained with the above-mentioned disposition persist in force.

10. Moreover, We decree that this present encyclical is valid for all places. It applies to all Christians in favor and obedience with the Apostolic See dwelling in these places, even if they return to them afterwards from sea or land journeys. This encyclical is valid notwithstanding the following: decrees granting indulgences *ad instar* and other decrees of the Apostolic See or of universal, provincial, and synodal councils; general or special reservations of absolutions, relaxations, and dispensations; statutes, laws, usages, and customs of any mendicant or military order, congregation or institute even such as have been confirmed by vow, by apostolic approval, or by any other backing; privileges, indults, and apostolic letters granted to the above, especially those which expressly forbid a professed religious of any order, congregation or institute of this nature to confess their sins to a confessor who is not a member of their own religious family. For this time and for the purpose We mentioned, We fully abrogate all of the above even if for their proper modification they and their entire tenor must be specifically, expressly, and individually mentioned or if another special form must be employed for this purpose. Tenors of this kind are regarded as included in this abrogation. Such forms are considered as most exactly observed.

Inform the Faithful

11. On behalf of the Apostolic office which We administer and the solicitude with which We embrace the entire flock of Christ, We propose this salutary opportunity of obtaining forgiveness and grace. We earnestly beg and beseech all Patriarchs, Primates, Archbishops, Bishops, other Ordinaries, Prelates and those legitimately exercising ordinary jurisdiction where a bishop or prelate of this nature is lacking who have favor with the Apostolic See, in the name of Jesus Christ, to announce to your faithful this great good. Strive that all the faithful, reconciled to God by penance, direct the grace of the Jubilee towards the profit and advantage of their souls. Thus it will be your principal care that having first implored God to fill the minds and hearts of all with His light and grace, the Christian people be directed to receive the fruit of the Jubilee by opportune instructions and admonitions. They should understand that the nature of a Christian Jubilee is for the good of souls. In a spiritual way, those goods are most abundantly fulfilled every fiftieth year, according to the ancient Jewish law. They should also be taught the force of the indulgences and what is necessary for a fruitful confession of sins and for receiving piously the sacrament of the Eucharist.

12. Your labor as well as your example is required so that the faithful grow spiritually; therefore inspire your priests to work toward this also. They would set a good example if they first renewed the spirit of their holy vocation.

Current Evils

13. Today, there are many evils which must be corrected, and many good things which must be promoted. See that your people may come to detest the enormous crime of blasphemy which violates everything these days. Also, by observing the laws concerning keeping holy feast days and fast and abstinence, they may carry out their duties, thus avoiding the punishments which contempt of these things involves. Safeguard clerical discipline and care for the proper education of the clergy. In every way possible help beleaguered youth, which is exposed to so much danger. Christ hated this type of evil so much that He spoke the following words against its perpetrators: "whosoever scandalizes one of these little ones who believe in Me, it would be better for him to have a millstone placed around his neck and be put in the sea."[1]

Encourage Charity

14. Charitable works of all kinds should be exercised more fervently in a Jubilee year. Therefore, encourage almsgiving to assist the poor as sacred scripture recommends. Support especially those pious institutes which are most conducive to the well-being of souls and bodies. God will bestow heavenly gifts upon those who do so.

Advice to Clergy Personally

15. Finally We exhort each of you to utilize this occasion to acquire the grace of the Jubilee. If ever before, certainly now it is most necessary to cleanse your consciences from dead works, to offer sacrifices of justice, to produce worthy fruits of penance, and to sow in tears so that you may reap in joy. The divine Majesty has given abundant signs of what He asks of us, since for a long time now we labor because of our wickedness under his punishment, under the breath of the spirit of His anger. Truly "men are accustomed when they suffer any enormous difficulty to send ambassadors to neighboring peoples for help. We, as is better, send ambassadors to God;" therefore let us implore help from Him, let us turn to Him with hearts, prayers, fasts and almsgiving. "For the nearer we are to God, the further our adversaries are repelled from us."[2]

16. Listen carefully to those of you who labor and are heavily burdened and those who, wandering from the pathways of salvation, are burdened beneath the yoke of evil desires and enslavement to the devil. Do not disdain the riches of the goodness, patience and benignity of God; and, while such an easy means of obtaining pardon is offered to you, do not by your contumacy render yourselves inexcusable before the divine Judge, thereby piling up wrath for yourselves. Return from prevarication to wisdom, be reconciled with God. The world and its concupiscence is transitory; therefore, reject the works of darkness, put on the arms of light, and cease being enemies of your souls. Then you may win, at last, peace in this world and the eternal rewards of the just in the next.

17. These are Our dearest wishes; We do not cease asking them of our most clement Lord. If all Our sons in the Catholic Church join with Us in this prayer, We are confident that We will bountifully acquire these good things from the Father of Mercies.

18. As a guarantee, meanwhile, of all grace and heavenly blessings for the happy and salutary fruit of this holy work, We lovingly bestow from the depths of Our heart, the Apostolic Blessing on all of you, venerable brothers, and on you, beloved sons, who are enrolled in the Catholic Church.

Given in Rome at St. Peter's, 24 December 1874.

†

LATIN TEXT: *Acta Pii IX*, I, 6:347-60; *Acta Sanctae Sedis*, 8:181-92.

ENGLISH TRANSLATION: Robert F. Healey, S.J.

REFERENCES:

1. Mk 9.41.
2. St. Maximus of Turin, homily 91.

QUOD NUNQUAM

ENCYCLICAL OF POPE PIUS IX ON THE
CHURCH IN PRUSSIA
FEBRUARY 5, 1875
76

To *Our Venerable Brothers, the Archbishops and Bishops of Prussia.*

Venerable Brothers, Greetings and Apostolic Benediction.

What We never expected to happen has come about. Thus, We look back on those things which this Apostolic See established for the welfare of Catholics in agreement with the supreme ruler of Prussia in the twenty-first year of this century and We observe that it has turned out otherwise. A wild and unexpected storm now reigns in your land, where the Church of God once enjoyed peace and tranquillity. Other new laws have been added to those laws against the rights of the Church which were proposed recently and which struck down and removed from their positions many clerics and laymen. These new laws thoroughly overturn the divine establishment of the Church and totally destroy the holy rights of the bishops.

2. These laws gave power to lay judges to cast bishops and others in charge of caring for souls from their dignity and from the exercise of their duty. They placed many serious impediments before those who were appointed to exercise legitimate jurisdiction in the absence of the pastors. The cathedral chapters were told that they could elect vicars according to the canons when the episcopal see is not yet vacant. Finally, passing over many other things, they entrusted the prefects of the provinces with the power to appoint even non-Catholic men who, as substitutes for the bishops, preside over the administration of the temporal goods in the dioceses, even if those temporal goods were intended for holy people or the use of the Church. You know well, venerable brothers, what harm and abuses followed from these laws and from their harsh execution.

3. We shall pass over these matters in order not to increase our common sadness with recollections of them. However, we cannot keep silent concerning the damage to the dioceses of Gniezno and Poznań, as well as to the diocese of Paderborn. Miescyslaw, Archbishop of Gniezno and Poznań, and Konrad, Bishop of Paderborn, have been imprisoned and unjustly sentenced to be deposed from their episcopal see and divested of their authority. These dioceses are deprived of the assistance of their shepherds and are sorrowfully hurled into a mass of serious difficulties and sorrows.

4. However, We ought not to weep over Our brothers just mentioned. Rather We should esteem them and follow them with rejoicing. "Happy are you when people hate you, drive you out, abuse you, denounce your name as criminal

on account of the Son of Man."[2] Those who remember these divine words are not deterred by the punishment of the laws; instead they keep the laws and the commandments of the Church because of the seriousness of their ministry. These men have drawn honor and glory to themselves, just as other highly esteemed bishops from the same region. They suffer undeserved condemnation and the punishments of criminals for the sake of justice and show great virtue which overflows for the edification of the whole Church. They deserve praise rather than the tears of mourners.

5. However, the contempt of episcopal dignity, the violation of the Church's freedom and its rights, the abuses which oppress not only those dioceses mentioned above, but other Prussian dioceses as well, demand that We speak out. This is part of Our apostolic duty which God entrusted to Us, even though We did not deserve it. Thus We condemn those laws which produced so many evils and from which many more can be feared. We must vindicate the freedom of the Church which is depressed by unjust power. We intend to fulfill these aspects of Our duty through this letter announcing to everyone to whom the matter pertains and to the whole Catholic world that those laws are invalid insofar as they totally oppose the divine order of the Church. The Lord did not set the powerful of this world over the bishops in matters which pertain to the sacred ministry. Rather, He entrusted Saint Peter with the duty of feeding not only His lambs, but also His sheep.[2] Therefore, those "whom the Holy Spirit established as bishops to govern the Church of God"[3] cannot be deprived of the episcopal office by any lofty power of the world.

6. That thing happened which is unworthy of an illustrious nation and We believe that it will be seen so by the non-Catholics themselves—who hardly share Our partisan zeal. These laws were protected by severe sanctions, threatened harsh punishment to the disobedient, and had the support of the military power. These peaceful and unarmed citizens turned away from these laws because of the dictates of their consciences. The legislators should never ignore or despise the leadings of conscience, but they certainly have done so by enacting laws which place the people in a position in which they are miserable and afflicted. The power of the law is stronger than the people, and they cannot avert it. Therefore, those laws do not seem to be announced to free citizens in order to request reasonable obedience. On the contrary, they have been imposed, as if on slaves so that they may extort forced obedience by fear.

7. We do not, however, want you to think that We consider these people justified who prefer to obey men out of fear rather than God. The divine judge will condemn those unworthy men who, supported by the protection of civil authority alone, heedlessly occupy parish churches and have dared to seize the holy ministry in them. Moreover, We declare them to be lost. In the future, whoever intrudes into the government of the Church by a similar crime will incur excommunication according to the holy canons, and he will incur it *ipso facto*. We advise the pious faithful not to approach the holy rites of such people nor to receive the sacraments from them. They should prudently abstain from any business dealings and association with them so that the bad leaven does not corrupt the undefiled lump of dough.

8. Venerable brothers, your courage and faithfulness have helped to alleviate Our sorrow during these disasters. The rest of the clergy and the faithful emulated this courage and fidelity in encountering the bitter struggle. Their steadfast spirit in fulfilling Catholic duties and their glory were so great that they drew the eyes and admiration of everyone—even their staunchest opponents—upon themselves. This could not have happened differently for "as destructive as the fall of someone placed in authority is and as much as it contributes to the ruin of those who follow, it is salutary and useful to the same degree when the bishop offers himself to his brothers as an example worthy of imitation through the firmness of his faith."[4]

9. We wish that We could bring you some consolation in these difficulties! We shall not fail you meanwhile with Our firm protestation as far as all those matters which oppose the divine establishment of the Church and its laws, and We shall not fail you in sure counsel and warnings as far as that force which was unjustly brought against you.

10. Let those who are your enemies know that you who refuse to give to Caesar what belongs to God will bring no harm to the authority of the king and will subtract nothing from it. Scripture says, "it is better to obey God than to

obey men."[5] In addition, let them know that each one of you is prepared to give tribute and homage to Caesar in those matters which are subject to civil authority and power, not out of anger but on account of conscience.

11. Therefore, rightfully fulfill both duties. Obeying the ordination of God, be quick of mind and carry on with the task as firmly as you have begun it. You will gain much because you have patiently endured much in the name of Jesus and have not deserted Him.[6] Look up to Him who has preceded you in suffering and "encountered the penalty of a scandalous death so that His members might learn to flee the favors of the world, to be fearless, to love adversity for the sake of truth, and to shun riches."[7] He who put you in this battle line will give you strength equal to the fight. "In Him is our hope; we give ourselves to Him, and we implore His mercy."[8] See: what He foretold has already occurred. Therefore trust that He will accomplish what He promised. He says, "In the world you will have trouble, but be brave. I have conquered the world."[9]

12. Confident of that victory, We ask the Holy Spirit for peace and grace. Meanwhile, as a sign of Our special love, We lovingly impart Our apostolic blessing to you, to the entire clergy, and to the faithful entrusted to your vigilance.

Given in Rome, at St. Peter's, on the fifth day of February in the year 1875, the twenty-ninth year of Our Pontificate.

†

LATIN TEXT: *Acta Pii IX*, I, 7:6-12; *Acta Sanctae Sedis*, 8:251-55.

ENGLISH TRANSLATION: Norman Desmarais.

REFERENCES:

1. Lk 6.22.
2. Jn 21.16-17—St. Augustine, *De fund.*, chap. 4.
3. Acts 20.28.
4. St. Cyprian, Epistle 4.
5. Acts 5.29.
6. Ap 2.3.
7. St. Gregory the Great, *Reg. Past.*, pt. I chap. 3.
8. St. Augustine, Sermon 55.
9. Jn 16.33.

GRAVES AC DIUTURNAE

ENCYCLICAL OF POPE PIUS IX ON THE
CHURCH IN SWITZERLAND
MARCH 23, 1875
77

To Our Venerable Brothers the Bishops, to the Clergy, and to the Swiss People who enjoy Grace and Communion with the Apostolic See.

Venerable Brothers, Greetings and Apostolic Blessing.

The serious and long-lasting plots and efforts which the new heretics who call themselves Old Catholics use daily in your country to deceive the faithful and to tear them away from their ancient faith, urge Us, as a duty of Our supreme apostolate, to zealously devote Our paternal care and attention to protecting the spiritual welfare of our children. We are aware, and We sorrowfully deplore the fact, that these schismatics and heretics who enjoy the favor of the civil authority exercise the ministry of their wicked sect in the region of the diocese of Basel as in other regions of your country while the religious freedom of Catholics remains publicly oppressed by schismatic laws.

Deceit Characteristic of Schism

2. Having violently occupied parishes and churches with apostate priests, they have not neglected any deception or cunning to lead the children of the Catholic Church into wretched schism. Because it has always been especially characteristic of heretics and schismatics to use lies and deception, these sons of darkness are to be reckoned among those the prophet spoke of: "Woe to you deserting children who have faith in the shadow of Egypt. You have rejected the word and have hoped in trickery and rebellion." They love to deceive the unwary and the innocent and to draw them into error by deception and hypocrisy. They repeatedly state openly that they do not in the least reject the Catholic Church and its visible head but rather that they are zealous for the purity of Catholic doctrine declaring that they are the heirs of the ancient faith and the only true Catholics. But in fact they refuse to acknowledge all the divine prerogatives of the vicar of Christ on earth and do not submit to His supreme magisterium.

Condemnation of Errors

3. In order to spread their teachings more widely, We know that some of them have been appointed to teach sacred theology in the University of Bern, hoping to be able in this way to gain new followers from the Catholic youth for their wicked faction. However, We have already reproved and condemned this deplorable sect which has produced from the old store of the heretics so many errors opposed to the principal

tenets of the Catholic faith. This sect overthrows the foundations of the Catholic religion, shamelessly rejects the dogmatic definitions of the Ecumenical Vatican Council, and devotes itself to the ruin of souls in so many ways. We have decreed and declared in Our letter of 21 November 1873 that those unfortunate men who belong to, adhere to, and support that sect should be considered as schismatics and separated from communion with the Church.

4. We think it is Our duty to repeat this public declaration now and to request you to preserve the unity of faith among your faithful by every possible means in accordance with your eminent zeal and your renowned virtue. For you have given notable examples of this virtue in bearing tribulations for the cause of God. You should remind them to beware of these treacherous enemies of the flock of Christ and their poisoned foods. They should totally shun their religious celebrations, their buildings, and their chairs of pestilence which they have with impunity established to transmit the sacred teachings. They should shun their writings and all contact with them. They should not have any dealings or meetings with usurping priests and apostates from the faith who dare to exercise the duties of an ecclesiastical minister without possessing a legitimate mission or any jurisdiction. They should avoid them as strangers and thieves who come only to steal, slay, and destroy. For the Church's children should consider the proper action to preserve the most precious treasure of faith, without which it is impossible to please God, as well as action calculated to achieve the goal of faith, that is the salvation of their souls, by following the straight road of justice.

Anti-Catholic Marriage Laws

5. We recognize that apart from laws which injure the divine constitution and authority of the church, others have also been promulgated there by the civil authority which are totally opposed to the canonical prescriptions dealing with Christian marriage. These laws deeply oppose the authority and the jurisdiction of the Church. We are obliged to exhort you in the Lord to explain to your faithful by suitable instructions. Recall to their minds those truths which We have often stressed in Our apostolic letters or allocutions concerning this sacrament especially on 9 and 27 September 1852. We endeavored to give them a thorough appreciation of the sanctity and the power of marriage to enable them by pious conformity to the canonical laws in this matter, to avoid the evils which affect families and human society in consequence of contempt for the sanctity of marriage.

6. We are very confident in the Lord, beloved sons, pastors, and clerics, that you, who have been ordained not only for your own sanctification and salvation but also for that of others, in face of this huge conspiracy of the unholy and of so many dangerous allurements will prove yourselves a strong comfort and help to your bishops because of your demonstrated piety and zeal. Under their leadership, you will eagerly take up the task of diligently working for the cause of God, for the Church, and for the salvation of souls. You will strengthen the powers of the faithful who stand firm, assist the weakness of those who falter, and increase daily before God the merits which you have already attained by patience, constancy, and priestly fortitude. The labors which those who act as ambassadors of Christ must sustain are very heavy at this time. But our trust should be placed in Him who has conquered the world. He helps those who labor in His name and rewards them with a crown of unfading glory in heaven.

Obedience to Lawful Authority

7. Dearly beloved faithful children who live in Switzerland, We Speak to you with paternal affection in Our concern for your salvation. You know very well how precious is the gift of the Catholic faith which God has bestowed upon you. Never spare any care, any effort to faithfully preserve that gift. Preserve safe and sound the glory of the ancient religion which you received from your ancestors. Therefore, We urge you with the greatest enthusiasm to give support strongly and constantly to your legitimate shepherds who have received a legitimate mission from this Apostolic See. They watch over your souls since they will have to account to God for them. Listen obediently to their voices and keep in mind the words of eternal truth which Jesus spoke: "Whoever is not with me is against me; whoever does not gather with me scatters." Be odedient to His teaching. Love His easy yoke. Reject energetically those of whom Our Redeemer said: "Beware of the false prophets who come to you in sheep's clothing. On the inside however they are

ravening wolves." Therefore strong in the faith, resist the ancient enemy of the human face "until the right arm of Almighty God destroys all the weapons of the devil who is allowed a certain scope of action only in order to give Christ's faithful greater glory by his defeat . . . because where truth is the teacher, divine comfort is never lacking."[1]

Prayer for Quiet

8. We thought We should write these things to you because the duty of Our supreme ministry requires Us to deliver the universal flock of Christ from every danger of deception and to watch over its safety as well as the unity of the faith and of the Church. Therefore, since every good gift and every perfect gift comes down from above from the father of lights, We pray to Him from the bottom of Our heart that He strengthen your power in the struggle and defend you with His help and protection. May He look favorable on your country until when the errors and the counsels of the impious have been destroyed, it enjoys the tranquil peace of truth and justice. We do not neglect to implore the light from above for the wretched people who have gone astray. May they cease storing up wrath for themselves in the day of wrath and revelation of the just judgment of God. May they turn from the error of their ways while there is still time given to them for sincere repentance. Venerable brothers and dearly beloved children, join your fervent prayers of Ours to obtain mercy and find grace in suitable aid. Receive the apostolic blessing which We impart to you lovingly in the Lord from the bottom of Our heart. We grant it to each and every one of you as a pledge of our special love.

Given at Rome, at St. Peter's, on the 23rd day of March 1875, the twenty-ninth year of Our Pontificate.

†

LATIN TEXT: *Acta Pii IX*, I, 7:44-49.

ENGLISH TRANSLATION: Norman Desmarais.

REFERENCE:

1. St. Leo, epistle to Presbyter Martin.